Looking Toward the Future of Technology-Enhanced Education:
Ubiquitous Learning and the Digital Native

Martin Ebner
Graz University of Technology, Austria

Mandy Schiefner
University of Zurich, Switzerland

Information Science REFERENCE

INFORMATION SCIENCE REFERENCE
Hershey · New York

Director of Editorial Content:	Kristin Klinger
Senior Managing Editor:	Jamie Snavely
Assistant Managing Editor:	Michael Brehm
Publishing Assistant:	Sean Woznicki
Typesetter:	Kurt Smith, Sean Woznicki
Cover Design:	Lisa Tosheff
Printed at:	Yurchak Printing Inc.

Published in the United States of America by
Information Science Reference (an imprint of IGI Global)
701 E. Chocolate Avenue
Hershey PA 17033
Tel: 717-533-8845
Fax: 717-533-8661
E-mail: cust@igi-global.com
Web site: http://www.igi-global.com/reference

Library of Congress Cataloging-in-Publication Data

Looking toward the future of technology-enhanced education : ubiquitous learning and the digital native / Martin Ebner and Mandy Schiefner, editors.
p. cm.

Includes bibliographical references and index.
Summary: "This book evaluated the incorporation of technology into educational processes reviewing topics from primary and secondary school to higher education, from Second Life to wiki technology, from physical education to cultural learning"--Provided by publisher.

ISBN 978-1-61520-678-0 (hardcover) -- ISBN 978-1-61520-679-7 (ebook) 1. Educational technology. 2. Internet in education. 3. Education--Effect of technological innovations on. I. Ebner, Martin, 1975- II. Schiefner, Mandy, 1980-
LB1028.3.L66 2010
371.33'4--dc22

2009045238

British Cataloguing in Publication Data
A Cataloguing in Publication record for this book is available from the British Library.

List of Reviewers

Ralf Appelt, *University of Hamburg, Germany*
Andrea Back, *University of St. Gallen, Switzerland*
Oliver Bendel, *University of Applied Sciences FHNW, Switzerland*
Thomas Bernhardt, *University of Bremen, Germany*
Taiga Brahm, *University of St. Gallen, Switzerland*
Helena Bukvova, *Dresden University of Technology, Germany*
Martha Burkle, *SAIT Polytechnic, Canada*
Cristina Costa, *University of Salford, UK*
Bettina Dimai, *University of Innsbruck, Austria*
Johannes Dorfinger, *University of Teacher Education Graz, Austria*
Eric Duval, *Katholieke Universiteit Leuven, Belgium*
Urs Gröhbiel, *University of Applied Science FHNW, Switzerland*
Gabriela Grosseck, *West University of Timisoara, Romania*
Christian Gütl, *Graz University of Technology, Austria*
Nina Grabowski, *University of Augsburg, Germany*
Wolf Hilzensauer, *Salzburg Research, Austria*
Klaus Himpsl, *Danube University Krems, Austria*
Janet Holland, *Emporia State University, USA*
Andreas Holzinger, *Medical University Graz, Austria*
Mary Hricko, *Kent State University, USA*
Michael Kickmeier-Rust, *University of Graz, Austria*
Narayanan Kulathuramaiyer, *Universiti Malaysia Sarawak, Malaysia*
Patrick Kunz, *University of Teacher Education St. Gallen, Switzerland*
Anoush Margaryan, *Glasgow Caledonian University, Scotland*
Nadine Ojsterek, *University of Duisburg, Germany*
Jutta Pauschenwein, *University of Applied Science Graz, Austria*
Thomas Pfeffer, *University of Klagenfurt, Austria*
Annabelle Preussler, *University of Duisburg, Germany*
Wolfgang Reinhardt, *University of Paderborn, Germany*
Jochen Robes, *X-Pulse E-Learning GmbH, Germany*
Matthias Rohs, *University of Zurich, Switzerland*
Brigitte Römmer-Nossed, *University of Vienna, Austria*

Bernd Simon, *University of Economics and Business Vienna, Austria*
Sandra Schaffert, *Salzburg Research, Austria*
Christian Spannagel, *University of Teacher Education Ludwigsburg, Germany*
Kathryn Trinder, *Glasgow Caledonian University, Scotland*
Günther Wageneder, *University of Salzburg, Austria*
Anja C. Wagner, *University of Applied Sciences Berlin, Germany*
Edgar Weippl, *Vienna University of Technology, Austria*

Table of Contents

Section 5.3
Virtual Environments and Virtual Worlds

Detailed Table of Contents

An investigation into the students' use of internet services, media types and e-learning preferences tried to find out if students today are interested in the use of Web 2.0 methods for learning. More than 2.000 students participated in the survey conducted by the international architecture company DEGW and the author. The data of the survey are compared to the results of a parallel study by HIS GmbH that was answered by 4.400 students. The results of both studies throw a critical light on the popular discussion about the net generation or the so-called digital natives and may lend themselves to a more cautious or careful introduction of Web 2.0 methods in teaching and learning accompanied by instructional and tutorial assistance.

Students in schools should acquire media literacy and the development of new media can promote self-directed learning and so enhance the quality of the learning process. It has been assumed that teachers lack sufficient media literacy. Therefore, we developed a new chemistry teacher in-service training based on blended-learning. These courses should familiarize teachers with the application of new media and acquaint them with their students' world, the world of the so-called "digital natives". Three studies were performed to explore its acceptability, suitability and effectiveness. Participants' ratings on self-report measures of self-rated skills and perceived competence improved significantly after the training. Participants had more favorable attitudes towards the use of electronic media than subjects from a control group. Among participants the attitudinal measure "perceived competence" predicted the use of blended-learning at 6-month follow up. It is concluded that attitudes play an important role for promoting teachers' media literacy and their intention to apply new media in teaching. In addition to training programs focusing on skills and knowledge, future interventions should target on teachers attitudes.

Research into investigating how users navigate through Internet and multimedia resources in an educational context has revealed distinct preferences in how they approach the resource, their methods of interrogating it and both the quantity and quality of the information they obtain. Using highly sophisticated software even for digital natives involves learning a series of methods or techniques for easily manoeuvring through the vast quantities of data and developing schemas to do this efficiently and accurately. This chapter analyses methods that used for navigating through multimedia packages, explores users' preferences for navigation and visualisation, investigates design errors in multimedia that prevent good navigation and details newer visualisation methods and navigational tools. The chapter should give educational users a fresh perspective of issues of navigation and visualisation and allow them to develop these techniques in order to improve their use of Internet and web resources and teaching materials.

Section 3
Context of Learning

Traditional E-Learning programs mostly focus on disseminating knowledge. Motivation and the transfer to behavior in everyday situations are often neglected. Human Rights Education specifically encompasses attitudes and behavior, but the challenge is to bring this into a virtual setting. The Intercultural Courses on Human Rights Education were conducted with 80 learners from five different countries: USA, the Dominican Republic, Morocco, Germany, and Mongolia. The chapter first describes the practical background of these courses as well as theoretical considerations regarding computer-mediated communication and social constructivist learning approaches. The main focus lies on giving practical examples from the course, which include forum discussions, working with pseudonyms, internet research, and building a human rights conformant society in a simulation. A pre- and post-test enabled a thorough evaluation for all three learning areas: knowledge, attitudes and skills. The results of this evaluation, several lessons learned and a future learning scenario will be shared.

It seems like everyone is so busy today, it is easy to miss opportunities to reach out and make a positive difference. Though we are all experiencing the impact of tight economic times there is one lesson we are learning internationally. By putting our minds and actions towards mutual goals we all can benefit. What better way to live, learn, and work together than to share our knowledge and skills to improve our communities, both the one we live in immediately, and the one we thrive in globally. When we leave behind a legacy, will it be one of teaching service to our students to improve both academic learning and making valuable contributions to our communities for generations to follow? With the prevalence of computer-based technologies and the desire of youth to be digitally connected, it is an optimal time to share technology knowledge and skills for service learning opportunities.

The web 2.0 practices of user participation and experimentation have created models for social networking that influence the way people communicate and interact online. This chapter describes an initiative, OLnet, that is creating a technical environment based on web 2.0 principles to support the sharing of experiences around the design and use of Open Educational Resources (OER) in order to facilitate closer links between researchers and users. The aim is to combine online functionality, face-to-face events and research activities so that research outputs can inform users and users can help steer future areas for

Mobile learning extends the media dissemination of knowledge and learning in extremely varying educational contexts with mobility and independence of location. The chapter describes possibilities of mobile learning for situation-oriented, personalised and collaborative learning. It explains on the one hand existing conceptions and application scenarios with regard to learning theory backgrounds, and on the other thematises possibilities of Web 2.0 for mobile learning. In doing this, it presents in particular didactical scenarios for mobile learning situations in the context of learning on the job.

Mobile technology use is a major issue in higher education institutions, and one that is increasing daily. While the new generation of students (the "digital natives") move across programs and courses, their learning expectations have started to emerge. It is with these expectations and needs in mind that educators around the world are recognizing the advantages of using mobile technologies to engage with students and make learning a more collaborative, interactive activity that can be engaged in at anytime, anywhere. Using a case study approach, this chapter explores the challenges of transforming static curricula into a mobile experience, and the ways in which these challenges were overcome within a polytechnic institution where hands-on learning takes place inside the classroom or the lab. In addition to presenting a literature review on the use of mobile technologies for teaching and learning, and an analysis of the relevance of connectivism theory to analyze students learning in the digital age, this chapter also includes an analysis of student surveys and interviews, as well as further opportunities for research.

In subjects such as Civil Engineering, Architecture, Geology etc., education is mostly based on visual information. For example, in Civil Engineering every building can be seen as a unique object at a certain location. During the education of Civil Engineers many field based studies and excursions take place, however, not only the images but also geographical coordinates are essential. Wikis have been in use for collaborative learning for more than ten years. Mobile phones provide access to them from nearly everywhere. The availability of those technologies has led to rapid advances in the area of m-Learning and the possibility to apply challenging constructive educational concepts. Consequently, in this paper we describe the user centered design, development and evaluation of a combination of these technologies to support collaborative learning in the field: A Wiki-based mobile geospatial information system, the so-called TUGeoWiki. The primary objective of this geowiki is to provide a user-friendly tool for mobile collaborative learning for all areas where geo-tagged information could be useful. Moreover, TUGeoWiki was developed in order to provide the integration of external map material via map APIs including information such as that delivered by Google Maps. Subsequently, it is possible to provide both highly detailed maps and satellite images without having the need to license such material. Furthermore, the user interfaces used by such tools is well established, due to the increasing number of mapping related mashups. The evaluation during an extensive field test within a large civil engineering excursion to various large-scale construction sites in Austria demonstrated that collaborative learning can be successfully supported by the application of TUGeoWiki.

Section 5.2
Use of Collaboration Tools

Based on the implications of technological progress and socioconstructivist learning theory, trends are being developed for tools to promote learning in the information society of the 21st century. The future promises a massive increase in information and its ubiquitous availability, along with an increase in computer-mediated communication. It is particularly important to understand that the communication requests placed on the individual and the range of available communication channels will increase in coming years. Tools must therefore be conceptualized to manage the communication and information glut of the future in an "intelligent" way permitting a collaborative way of learning. Looking ahead, lifelong, rather informal and problem-based learning could become significantly more important than formal learning. The characteristics of wikis will be presented as a possible representative example and explored based on the above criteria. The chapter concludes with prognoses on the nature of ICT-supported learning in coming years.

Although Wikipedia has carved its way into the common vernacular, it faces resentments particularly in higher education institutions and many professors say students should think twice before turning to the free online encyclopedia for their academic work: "According to the criterion of scholarly standards, Wikipedia is citable on no account since authorship is not verifiable, and therefore an authentification of information is impossible." (Haber, 2007, p. 500). In spite of perceived quality deficits, Wikipedia is a popular information resource among students. Instructors increasingly take advantage of this student attitude through actively integrating Wikipedia as a learning tool into university courses in accordance with a constructivist teaching and learning paradigm. The chapter raises the question if Wikipedia is suited to make complex research, editing and bibliographic processes through which scholarship is produced transparent to students and to effectively improve their research and writing skills.

Section 5.3
Virtual Environments and Virtual Worlds

This paper gives an overview of the didactic elements relevant to learning opportunities in virtual worlds. Moreover, the specific requirements of virtual worlds are investigated in more detail using the C3-model of didactic components. Following this model, the specifications of virtual worlds are illustrated with regard to components content, communication and construction. The use of virtual worlds is often connected with the hope for stronger immersion, which is encouraged by the possibility of three-dimensionality and the representation of the learner by a virtual representative. However, learning-/teaching processes are not automatically improved by the use of virtual worlds. The possibilities offered by potential virtual worlds can only be honoured when a dedicated didactical concept is carried out. This means a complex composition process which has to take the specific features of virtual worlds into consideration.

New thinking on the design and purpose of learning solutions is needed where the focus is not only on what to learn, but also the strategies and tools that enhance students' capacity to learn and construct knowledge. The vision underpinning this chapter is to extend the notion of advanced learning environments that support learners' to construct and apply knowledge to include the capacity to understand how and why they learn as individuals. The purpose of this chapter is not to argue the need for 'virtual' learning environments – the literature abounds with positive endorsement for such applications. Instead, the strategies and factors that afford learners greater opportunities to engage in rewarding, productive learning experiences are examined with a view to laying down the groundwork and design principles to inform the development of a model for devising educationally effective, multi-modal (face-to-face and online) learning environments.

This chapter presents a survey methodology addressing learners' requirements, their expectations and experiences regarding challenges in the implementation process of new educational technology in educational institutions. The presented methodology was devised and applied during the pilot use of a web conferencing system (in its educational form as a virtual classroom) in distance education, and

Foreword

As its title suggests, '*Looking toward the future of technology-enhanced education*' is a book that sets itself a very important – but very difficult – brief. Commenting on the future of education and technology is a perilous pastime. Even the most informed commentators find technological forecasting to be a tricky business. Take, for instance, the assertion in 1943 that there only would ever be 'a world market for maybe five computers' (a quotation attributed to Thomas J Watson - then Chairman of IBM). Or fifty years later when the internet was dismissed by Bill Gates as 'a passing fad'. It seems that even those who are involved deeply in the development of new technology are reduced to guessing games when it comes to predicting the near future. In the same vein, the nature of educational change has proved to be just as difficult to forecast accurately – as is now evident in the many extravagant depictions of the 'classroom of 2000' offered throughout the second half of the twentieth century. All told, predicting the future forms and features of technology-enhanced education can be a thankless task.

This is not to say that efforts should not be made by education technologists to look forward toward the future. Indeed, all of the contributors to this book should be commended for engaging with the difficult questions that such forward thinking entails and providing a well-rounded and well-informed set of responses. The chapters in this collection manage to cover an impressive range of what could be considered to be 'state-of-the-art' education technologies – from virtual learning environments, wiki technologies and virtual conferencing, to open resources, mobile learning and serious games. Pleasingly, many of the chapters also pay attention to human aspects of education technology use. In this sense, the book offers a varied perspective on education, covering subjects such as civil engineering, physical education and cultural studies considering the learning that takes place in schools, colleges and universities, as well as episodes of 'informal' learning that occur outside the aegis of any education institution. This focus on the 'wetware' as well as the 'software' aspects of education technology is also apparent in chapters on user-centred design, new information competencies, media literacies, and using technology to engage with upcoming generations of young learners (or as one of the final chapters terms it, 'harnessing the drive to learn in members of 'Generation Me'').

This reference to Generation Me highlights an important theme that runs throughout the book – i.e. the notion that the education establishment is facing a growing disconnection from those that it seeks to work with. The potential distancing between institution and individual is perhaps the most important question that this book raises, and is certainly an issue that should be at the forefront of any reader's mind when reviewing these chapters. In particular, much of this book's content chimes with the general concerns within educational circles over new generations of learners who could be characterised as 'digital natives' – i.e. individuals who are seen to be natural technology users as a result of their early development and immersion in all things digital. These are learners, as Palfrey and Gasser (2008) put it, who many people consider to have been 'born digital.' As some of the contributors to this book imply, many educators feel that significant divisions that are arising between current generations of learners and their educational institutions. Some of the chapters in this book echo Marc Prensky's (2001, p.1) warning from the beginning of the century that "today's students are no longer the people our educational system was designed to teach". Thus one of the main questions that any reader of this book should bear in mind is how the described forms of technology-enhanced education may work to lessen this perceived gap. In other words, what is being suggested in these chapters that offers a break from the perennial cycles of hype, hope and disappointment which have blighted the institutional use of education technologies over the last thirty years? What is it about the technologies and practices described in this book that may help future education technologies buck the trend described so deftly in Larry Cuban's (1993) prognosis of 'computer meets classroom: classroom wins'? How will the use of these particular technologies in educational settings play out *in practice* as well as in potential?

In fact, once having read these chapters I would encourage any reader to move their attention away from the state-of-the-art and back towards what could be termed the 'state-of-the-actual'. As an academic 'tribe', education technologists certainly thrive on taking a forward-looking and fast-changing perspective – asking questions that are concerned primarily with what *should* happen, and what *could* happen once new technologies and digital media are placed into educational settings. Whilst these concerns are all well and good, the job for any reader of this book is to give some serious thought to how these artefacts and activities may be best integrated into the present-day realities of educational institutions and learners. In short, it seems appropriate that readers of this book are inspired to also ask questions concerning what is *actually* taking place when these education technologies meet education institutions – to look *beyond* the future of technology-enhanced education and back towards the present.

From this perspective there are many questions that need to be asked of the present state of technology-enhanced education. For instance, basic questions of equality and diversity remain concerning who is actually able to do what with these technologies, why and with what outcomes. Similarly, questions can be raised about the ends as well as the means of these forms of technology-enhanced learning. For example, what learning can actually be said to result from the use of these technologies and tools in education settings? What are the unintended and unexpected consequences of technology-enhanced education – its seductions and pleasures as well as its problems and anxieties? Above all, serious thought needs to be given to what really can be said to be 'new' about these emerging forms of technology-enhanced education – i.e. what are these artefacts and activities making possible that were not possible before; how are social relations being altered (if at all)? Can these forms of technology-enhanced education really be seen to constitute a new educational landscape, or do they more accurately represent a set of continuities from previous eras?

I expect that '*Looking toward the future of technology-enhanced education*' will provide much to inspire and interest any reader. Of course, no-one will agree with *everything* that is written in the book – there would surely be something wrong with either the reader or the book if this were the case! Yet agreeable or not, I am sure that these essays will provoke much thought and further discussion about technology-enhanced education.

Neil Selwyn
Institute of Education, University of London

REFERENCES

Cuban, L. (1993). Computer meets classroom: classroom wins. *Teachers College Record*, 95(2), 185-210.

Palfrey, J., & Gasser, U. (2008). *Born digital: understanding the first generation of digital natives*. New York: Basic.

Prenksy, M. (2001). Digital natives, digital immigrants. *On the Horizon*, 9(5), 1-6.

Neil Selwyn *is sociologist working at the London Knowledge Lab. His research and teaching focuses on the place of digital media in everyday life, and the sociology of technology (non)use in educational settings. He has written extensively on a number of issues, including digital exclusion, education technology policymaking and the student experience of technology-based learning. He has carried out funded research on information technology, society and education for the Economic and Social Research Council (ESRC), the BBC, Nuffield Foundation, the Spencer Foundation, Becta, Centre for Distance Education, the Welsh Office, National Assembly of Wales and various local authorities.*

Preface

Educational practice has been changing in recent years, with the integration of e-learning and now m-learning in teaching in schools and higher education. The use of Web 2.0 technologies for teaching and learning has been described by Stephen Downes as "e-Learning 2.0". Using the catchphrase, "The user is the content", he argues that a new approach to student participation in learning has developed around the incorporation of the Internet into education.

As a consequence of this social revolution, there is agreement among the experts that education has to be rethought. It is expected that learning as well as teaching will take place by using a range of devices in diverse environments. Traditional face-to-face teaching, otherwise known as "chalk and talk," is thought to be on the way out.

But to what extent do these expectations reflect reality, or predict developments that are likely come about in the near future? What will happen if technology is increasingly integrated into educational settings? What is our role/stance in this process, and what challenges do we face? These key questions need to be answered in order to establish what the education of tomorrow should be like.

However, predicting the future is always difficult, especially when anticipating change in the context of the educational system. Educational processes involve a high degree of complexity. It is therefore not the simplest of tasks to use digital media and technology to bring about a change in learning style, and it is even more difficult to make assumptions about the future.

With this in mind, the articles in this book reflect the breadth of the topic of the incorporation of technology into educational processes. They aim to trace the different discussions in different topics, from primary and secondary school to Higher Education, from Second Life to wiki technology, from physical education to cultural learning.

We have, as far as possible, organized the articles into the following main topic areas:

- Teacher and Learner
- Context of learning
- Learning Approaches
- Learning Technologies

Some articles cannot easily be allocated to a single topic, as they address different aspects, and cross the boundaries of each main topic. There are also articles that are closely linked to each other. This is shown in Figure 1 by means of intersecting circles to indicate that the article concepts overlap.

The main question implied in the book title is: "How can we predict the nature of future technologies and their implications for educational settings?"

There are different ways to go about this, such as using Gardner's Hype Cycle, or conducting a review of the literature.

Figure 1.

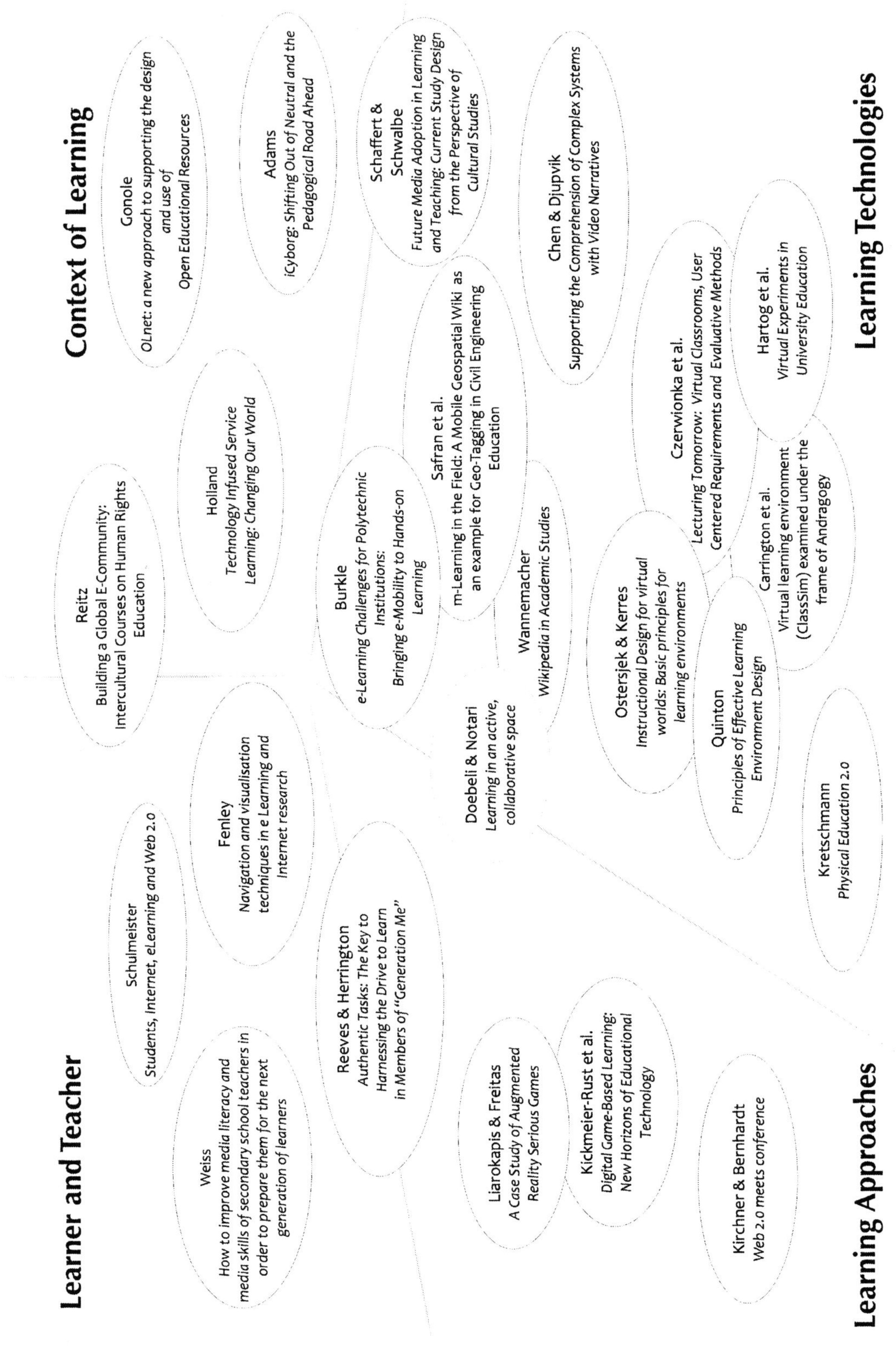
Context of Learning
Learner and Teacher
Learning Approaches
Learning Technologies
Gonole
OLnet: a new approach to supporting the design and use of Open Educational Resources
Adams
iCyborg: Shifting Out of Neutral and the Pedagogical Road Ahead
Schaffert & Schwalbe
Future Media Adoption in Learning and Teaching: Current Study Design from the Perspective of Cultural Studies
Chen & Djupvik
Supporting the Comprehension of Complex Systems with Video Narratives
Reitz
Building a Global E-Community: Intercultural Courses on Human Rights Education
Holland
Technology Infused Service Learning: Changing Our World
Safran et al.
m-Learning in the Field: A Mobile Geospatial Wiki as an example for Geo-Tagging in Civil Engineering Education
Czerwionka et al.
Lecturing Tomorrow: Virtual Classrooms, User Centered Requirements and Evaluative Methods
Hartog et al.
Virtual Experiments in University Education
Burkle
e-Learning Challenges for Polytechnic Institutions: Bringing e-Mobility to Hands-on Learning
Wannemacher
Wikipedia in Academic Studies
Carrington et al.
Virtual learning environment (ClassSim) examined under the frame of Andragogy
Ostersjek & Kerres
Instructional Design for virtual worlds: Basic principles for learning environments
Doebeli & Notari
Learning in an active, collaborative space
Quinton
Principles of Effective Learning Environment Design
Kretschmann
Physical Education 2.0
Schulmeister
Students, Internet, eLearning and Web 2.0
Fenley
Navigation and visualisation techniques in e Learning and Internet research
Reeves & Herrington
Authentic Tasks: The Key to Harnessing the Drive to Learn in Members of "Generation Me"
Weiss
How to improve media literacy and media skills of secondary school teachers in order to prepare them for the next generation of learners
Liarokapis & Freitas
A Case Study of Augmented Reality Serious Games
Kickmeier-Rust et al.
Digital Game-Based Learning: New Horizons of Educational Technology
Kirchner & Bernhardt
Web 2.0 meets conference

Sandra Schaffert and Christina Schwalbe take a meta-view of the book title and in their article they describe two different ways to obtain data about the future of media technology: the Delphi method and the scenario techniques. They focus strongly on a cultural studies perspective. What role does the adoption of new media play in educational systems like schools and universities? Besides the change in the way communication takes place and the way knowledge is managed, media adoption mostly depends on the changing roles of learners and teachers.

LEARNER AND TEACHERS

In different publications about the learner of the future, it is assumed that they will need more and different competencies than today's learners (Oblinger, 2005; Prensky).

In his article, *Rolf Schulmeister* analyses the connection between students, Internet, eLearning and Web 2.0. Based on a previous article about the myth of the "net generation" (Schulmeister, 2008), he examines the use of the Internet, E-Learning and Web 2.0 Tools of 2098 German-speaking students. How do they use the Internet and Web 2.0 Tools as well as the e-learning materials provided by their university? The results of this study are depressing to most of the "Net-Gen-Prayers": most students cannot be referred to as part of the net generation, as they do not use the internet, Web 2.0 or e-learning tools particularly often and are not sophisticated users. Care therefore has to be taken not to assume that all children, young people and students are members of the "net generation".

The need for today's children to be media literate is evident. As Bennett (2008) and Lorenzo and Dziuban (2006) found out, these children, who are often called the net generation, are very smart in their use of new technology, but they are not very sophisticated in terms of media literacy, and do not obtain high scores in judging and reasoning.

Teaching media literacy is therefore a task for teacher in schools all over the world. *Silke Weiss* focuses on this in her article. She asks how the media literacy and media skills of secondary school teachers can be improved in order to prepare them for the next generation of learners.

Sue Fenley analyses navigation and visualization techniques in e Learning material and Internet research. How do learners navigate through learning material and the Internet? The results of this analysis can help learners to learn more as they navigate through learning materials and can assist teachers in planning teaching materials.

CONTEXT OF LEARNING

The context of learning is an important subject of discussion. In which environment does learning take place? Two articles address the context and the framework of learning with digital media.

Learning in the 21st century, especially with technology, is often intercultural learning. Technology has facilitated the opportunity to learn in a virtual setting, with other people, often in other countries, who are members of a different culture. What does this mean for the learning process involving technology? *Sandra Reitz* describes a learning scenario in which learners from six different countries learned together about Human Rights Education. It is not the topic of the course that is important. It is the exposure to the differences in perspective of the other learners, especially when technology is used.

Jane Holland addresses service learning, a learning form which is becoming increasingly popular at universities. By integrating service learning at universities, academic learning and social responsibility are linked. Often a range of key competencies is acquired in such settings, from project management to media literacy. In the early days, service learning was mainly supported by e-mail technology. Today it is possible to integrate many technologies to support service learning: from Word to Photoshop to the point of web 2.0 Tools such as wikis and blogs, students' work can be better visualized inside and outside of universities.

Grainne Conole and Patrick McAndrew give us a brief overview of what a future technical environment can look like. How can emerging Web 2. 0 technologies and beyond be integrated to facilitate collaboration between researchers, teachers and students? Especially if one takes a closer look at open educational resources (OER), there seems to be huge potential for future learning behaviors. Grainne Conole and Patrick McAndrew provide us with an overview of the challenges and the backgrounds to their project as well as the tools used for visualizing and social networking. The authors point out further steps to be taken and how this initiative will help to enhance learning and teaching for tomorrow.

A further article written by *Catherine Adams* explores the importance of technology through learning and teaching. She discusses how technology influences the daily teaching process and how ubiquitous technology implicates? Complements? Replaces? Involves? old traditional educational settings. Vocative objects and mimetic interventions are carried out as well as new teaching and learning practices. Catherine concludes by pointing out that tomorrow's digital literacy is of great importance beyond the traditional domains of literacy such as language, arts, music, mathematics and sciences,. Children must be taught the basic vocabularies and languages of the machine; programming may become essential knowledge and will help them to understand the world of tomorrow.

LEARNING APPROACHES

New technologies often entail adopting new approaches and learning methods. Different learning methods are mentioned in connection with new technology: constructive learning, active, self-directed learning or game-based learning. Two articles address the last of these. *Michael D. Kickmeier-Rust, Elke Mattheiss, Christina Steiner, und Dietrich Albert* provide a brief overview of educational gaming and discuss the psycho-pedagogical foundations of "good" educational computer games.

Fotis Liarokapis and Sara de Freitas study game-based learning in more detail. They present a case study of Augmented Reality Serious Games.

With the dissemination of web 2.0 tools and the increasing use of these technologies there are new demands on learning processes, for example informal learning, at conferences. *Marcel Kirchner and Thomas Bernhardt* report on a new form of conferences, "EduCamp", as a special form of BarCamps for teaching and learning topics. Beside this characterization they describe the more general challenges involved in arranging an open "unconference" format. These "unconferences" are supported by strong member participation, and the employment of web 2.0 tools, such as wikis and blogs.

One characteristic of game-based learning is that the learner has to complete a task. Based on the "Generation me", *Thomas C. Reeves and Jan Herrington* describe different design principles that can be used for authentic tasks in learning processes. Their aim in working with authentic tasks is to engage learners more than would be usual when using traditional instruction methods.

EDUCATIONAL TECHNOLOGIES

When talking about learning methods, the question of educational technologies soon arises. Educational technologies can be classified into different categories of tools: First, we present all articles addressing mobile learning technology, followed by articles about wikis and virtual worlds.

Tools for Supporting Mobile Learning

Christian Safran, Martin Ebner, Frank Kappe and *Andras Holzinger* included a mobile geospatial wiki in educational processes. Pictures are of particular value in the field of civil engineering as they provide global coordinates. During learning and collaboration processes students can see the location on maps and can easily integrate and use theim in their learning behavior. Furthermore, with the help of mobile devices, pictures can be taken, geotagged and articles edited. The authors point out within this field study that mlearning has great potential for the future and predict that it will be the next step in technology integration.

Wiki

Using wikis in educational settings seems very promising (Cunningham, 2001). Several authors in this book refer to wikis. After Safran et al., who implemented a mobile wiki, *Beat Döbeli* and *Michele Notari* dealing to this technology and link the potentials and challenges of e-learning with the required key competencies of learners. They focus more on communication in informal learning settings, an approach that is becoming increasingly relevant to educational settings. They focus on problem based learning as a learning form that addresses the challenges of a world that is changing due to technology. One example they give is the integration of a wiki to support informal educational learning. This article therefore paves the way for articles on (future) learning methods.

After discussing wikis in informal learning settings, *Klaus Wannemacher* describes working with Wikipedia in formal learning settings in Higher Education. There are two ways to use Wikipedia: in the first way, it can be used as a tool of inquiry in scientific work. The second and more interesting way is to use Wikipedia as a learning tool in university seminars in accordance with a constructivist teaching and learning paradigm. Students can conduct complex research, editing and undertaking further bibliographic related processes using Wikipedia. After providing some background information on the use of Wikipedia among German students, he describes its use in different teaching projects and focuses on the advantages and disadvantages involved.

Virtual Worlds

A key topic in current and in future education settings is virtual worlds. Although not new, Second Life is still discussed in an educational context, in schools and higher education. The discussions of virtual worlds can have two components: technical and pedagogical.

Nadine Ostersjek and Michael Kerres both give an overview of didactic elements that are relevant to learning opportunities in virtual worlds. Learning does not automatically become more effective just because a new technology is adopted in the classroom. Usually, the first time technology is adopted, the learning process is hindered by technological questions and it takes time for the advantage of the new technology to become apparent. Ostersjek and Kerres strongly recommend paying attention to didactic considerations before adopting technology in educational settings. They describe the processes of interaction, construction and collaboration in new educational settings that have to be included in the instructional concept of the learning and teaching process.

Beside Kerres and Ostersjek, *Stephen R. Quinton* describes Principles of Effective Learning Environment Design more generally. He does not want to describe the advantages of 'virtual' learning environments in educational processes but rather describes the design principles for the construction of qualitative learning environments, both face to face and media-supported.

The benefit of educational technology is at first glance often not clear to learners. *Thomas Czerwionka, Michael Klebl and Claudia Schrader* describe a way to evaluate user requirements for technology in distance education. They use virtual classrooms for this evaluation. Beside the evaluation they take a meta-view of their evaluation method.

One concrete educational setting in which virtual worlds and simulations are often carried out is science education. The students have to get laboratory practice, but space is often limited at universities, and scientific experiment are very expensive. *Rob J.M. Hartog, Hylke van der Schaaf, Adrie J.M. Beulens and Johannes Tramper* present a project of virtual experiments in Higher Education. They discuss the benefits and also the limitation of this form of learning for students.

Simulations can also be implement in social sciences, but with different goals. Based on the theory of Andragogy, *Lisa Carrington, Lisa Kervin and Brian Ferry* describe the support of teacher education with a simulation program to reduce the theory-practice nexus. They describe their experiences in teacher education from Australia and come to the conclusion that simulations can be an appropriate way to learn with technology, particularly with adult learners.

With the diffusion of technology in more and more subjects, it is predicted that schools will not be able to get along without it. Technology will become an integral part of every school subject, even subjects where the use of technology is not immediately obvious. The integration of different tools to support learning in physical education is described by *Rolf Kretschmann*. When thinking about physical education one might think of action, perspiration and maybe of tools like the microchronometer. But this is changing very fast. In recent years the gap between technology and physical education has been narrowing, due to computer games, handhelds to record heart frequencies or walking routes, and game consoles like the WII. Kretschmann provides a brief overview of the potential of new media in this school subject and describes some examples of their use/integration.

CONCLUSION

It can be seen that new technologies will be an integral part of our live, both now and in future. The articles in this book range from physical education to Higher Education, from wikis to virtual learning environments, and from teacher education to chemistry.

We would like to thank all authors for their articles and their great and valuable work. We are very proud to have received such a huge amount of publications addressing how technology plays a role in different scenarios, at different levels and by different means. As we think about the future of learning and teaching it has become obvious that no one is able to predict what it will be like, but we all agree that future education of our children and students is based on the use of technology. A society where mobile phones, netbook and laptops are more or less integrated into daily life will require new strategies, methods and learning environments. We have to take care, research and help the growing generations to become 21st century citizens taking advantages of their access to the biggest information network in mankind to improve the environments in which they live.

Once again, the editors would like to thank all the authors and reviewers, all who contributed to making this book worthwhile, and all who will read it. The education of tomorrow is one of the most important topics today and we hope that this book will provide food for thought as well as suggestions as to how to integrate technology into education both appropriately and effectively.

Martin Ebner & Mandy Schiefner
Editors

REFERENCES

Bennett, S., Maton, K., & Kervin, L. (2008). The digital natives debate: A critical review of the evidence. *British Journal of Educational Technology*, *29*(5), 775-786.

Lorenzo, G., & Dziuban, C. (2006). Ensuring the Net generation is Net savvy. *ELI Paper 2*. Retrieved October 8, 2009, from http://net.educause.edu/ir/library/pdf/ELI3006.pdf

Oblinger, D. D., & Oblinger, J. L. (Eds.). (2005). *Educating the Net generation.* Retrieved October 8, 2009, from http://net.educause.edu/ir/library/pdf/pub7101.pdf

Prensky, M. (2001). Digital natives, digital immigrants. *On the Horizon*, *9*(5), 1-6.

Schulmeister, R. (2008). Is there a Net-gener in the house? Dispelling a mystification. *Online journal eLeed.* Retrieved October 8, 2009, from http://eleed.campussource.de/archive/5/1587/

Section 1
Introduction

Chapter 1
Future Media Adoption in Learning and Teaching:
Current Study Design from the Perspective of Cultural Studies

Sandra Schaffert
Salzburg Research, Austria

Christina Schwalbe
University of Hamburg, Germany

ABSTRACT

A lot of effort is put into studies to find more elaborated forecasts of future media adoption in learning and teaching. In this chapter, some methods of futurology, such as the Delphi method or the scenario technique, will be sketched. Afterwards, this current study design will be critically considered from the perspective of cultural studies. For this, the terms of media and culture will be introduced and Debray's approach of mediology and the adaptation on education will be discussed. Through this, we aim to illustrate that the current study designs could be enhanced by a bigger awareness of the insights of the cultural studies and their adaptations for education, the pedagogical media theory. The presented approach does not explicitly deal with the processes of adoption of new educational media systems on a practical level. But pedagogical media theories and studies on cultural and social changes and media provide a basic framework for various specific approaches dealing with the future of technology enhanced learning. Just as we can hardly understand how it feels to live in an oral culture, we are not able to imagine how we will think, act and communicate in the future of the evolving new "mediosphere".

INTRODUCTION

The invention of the World Wide Web in 1993 brought forth intensive discussions about the effect of (new) media on education. Indeed, the basic conditions for learning and teaching have changed a lot in the last decades, especially in the last years with the advent of Web 2.0. The Internet is a nearly ubiquitous medium providing fast access to information. Mobile devices especially allow for access to the Internet nearly independent from time and space. Although reality shows that not every student is naturally used to this new possibilities,

DOI: 10.4018/978-1-61520-678-0.ch001

these technologies reflect how the learning possibilities are changing.

Not surprisingly, a lot or discussion and also research is done to get more and better insights in future media adoption within learning and teaching. The dominant approach is currently to ask a group of experts in a more or less methodological sound way on what they think about future media adoption in education. From our point, this can be criticised for several reasons, but in this chapter we will concentrate on one point: Cultural studies in the field of media and education illustrate the problems of an estimation of future adoption. We will therefore describe theories and ideas of a pedagogical media theory. Afterwards, we will sum up our findings of this confrontation.

CURRENT STUDY DESIGN: USING THE WISDOM OF CROWDS OF EXPERTS

There are several methods available for use from the field. Futurology is derived from ideas about the future development of media within learning and teaching. In the following, we describe some methods of futurology, building on the idea of the "wisdom of crowds of experts" to illustrate each approach with some exemplary current studies. These approaches build on the idea that widespread information research and knowledge building should be the source for forecasts. The opinion of experts or crowds of experts are seen as superior to the knowledge of one person due to synergy effects and several perspectives on developments. In the following we describe the Delphi method, the scenario technique, and the method of road mapping as such approaches. All are already used in the field of educational technologies and media within learning and teaching. Additionally, we will sketch the methodology of the Horizon report with its own, newly derived format.

Delphi Method

The *Delphi method* involves experts from different related disciplines in two-step moderated group discussion to identify possible future developments. This strategy is described as helpful when new technological trends or innovations with a wide range of given possibilities should be discussed. There are several examples where these methods were used to get insights about future developments. For example, the Delphi method has been used for a prediction of future adoption of online assessment within higher education in Germany. Schaffert (2004) brings together the answers and ideas of 48 experts in a two-step process based on questionnaires. The experts came to the (not very surprising) conclusion that a moderate rise in of the adoption of online assessment is expected, especially in branches, where the usage of computers is a daily routine.

The Scenario Technique

According to Steinmüller (2002), the *scenario technique* is one of the most commonly used future analysis methods because it offers one of the widest approaches, including other well established prediction methods (Grunwald, 2002, p. 226). The scenario technique offers a method for deriving a set of predictions based on a present status and their most relevant influencing factors. The method is based on the strategic military developments of the 1950s, where scenarios were used to identify different outcomes of complex situations. Scenario technique tries to develop "orientation knowledge", which aims at a better understanding of what will happen in the near future. The scenario technique is typically applied in a set of three scenarios: "(1) a surprise free projection, describing the baseline and most likely scenario, (2) the worst case projection, offering the pessimistic scenario, and (3) the best case projection, referring to positive changes in the relevant area." (Boon et al. 2005, p. 207). Scenario construction aims to describe a plausible range of possibilities for the future, integrating qualitative and quantitative information from different sources into a coherent picture, it runs the risk of predicting an imaginary future (Boon et al., 2005). Concerning our topic of media adoption within learning and teaching, there are several studies which use the scenarios technique. For example, the Institute for Prospective Technological Studies used the scenario technique to get an impression about the future of learning. It "uses scenarios as a tool for calling into question current decisions without any expectation that the scenario used today will correspond to the scenario developed tomorrow" (Miller, Shapiro & Hilding-Hamann, 2008, p. 23). Hamburg, Busse & Marin (2005) propose e-learning scenarios as a base for decision making in organisations.

Road Mapping

Another approach to forecast future developments is the *road mapping method*. Road mapping serves as a framework for strategic decisions. Typically, road mapping is a systematic collection of central challenges and opportunities for action and an illustration of development goals and milestones on a time axis (Kosow & Gaßner, 2008, p. 65). Four main forms of road mapping can be distinguished (Kosow & Gaßner, 2008), road mapping enterprises, branches, research and development and problem oriented road mapping. Similar to the scenario technique, several alternative roadmaps can be developed. Additionally, road mapping can include back casting from (several variations of) future development and describe what factors and milestones are responsible. One example of road mapping in the field of media for learning is work done within a EU-project dealing with Open Educational Resources (OER). The OLCOS Roadmap 2012 on Open Educational Practises and Resources (Geser, 2007) explores possible pathways toward a higher level of production, sharing and usage of OER and provides recommendations on required measures to support decision making at the level of educational policy and institutions. The roadmap emphasises a knowledge based society demanding competencies and skills requiring innovative educational practices based on open sharing and evaluation of ideas, fostering of creativity, and teamwork among the learners.

Another Design: The Approach of the Horizon Report

Additionally, we describe the *methodology of the Horizon report* (Johnson, Levine & Smith, 2009), one of the most popular studies in the field of future developments of learning and teaching. Based on the ideas of the Delphi method, the Horizon report team used Wiki technology to collect nearly a "hundred technologies, as well as dozens of meaningful trends and challenges are examined for possible inclusion in the report" (p. 30), and then provide their experts with RSS-feeds and other materials with deeper discussion of learning trends or technologies. For the 2009 report, 45 international experts and practitioners were asked to find answers to the five Horizon report questions. For example, the first is: "What would you list among the established technologies that learning-focused institutions should all be using broadly today to support or enhance teaching, learning, research, or creative expression?" (ibid.). Each answer of the advisory board members is placed into a vote system that allows members to weight their selections. For the current issue, from "more than 80 technologies originally considered, the twelve that emerged at the top of the initial ranking process (...) were further researched" (ibid.).

In the latest report the first trend with a time-to-adoption horizon of one year or less are "mobiles": The authors describes the rapid pace of innovation of mobile applications, namely through concrete applications and numbers of users. The authors came to the tentative conclusions that mobile devices are "challenging our ideas of how they should be used and presenting additional options with each new generation of mobiles" (p. 9): It is "clear that mobiles are already well on the way to becoming a universal tool for communication of all kinds" (ibid.); concerning education that means: "The variety and quality of educational content is growing at a fantastic pace" (ibid.).

A Critical View on These Designs

When we did our research on current publications concerning e-learning trends and the future of technology enhanced learning, we got the impression a lot of current studies are still presented with a lack of description concerning their theoretical and methodological framework (e. g. Siozos & Palaigeorgiou, 2008; Sinclair, McClaren, & Griffin, 2006). Boon et al. analysed four studies from the years 2000 to 2002 and came to a similar conclusion, "It is remarkable that trend studies in the domain of e-learning are hardly based on sound methodological approaches" (p. 210). Besides this general remark on current studies, the study design of crowd wisdom itself produces additional problems:

As all these methods build on the idea of the crowd intelligence of experts in the field of media for learning and teaching, one effect is these methods build upon the (personal) histories of people: One's own experiences and (implicit) assumptions about learning and media or technologies are possible, perhaps even the most important, factors for people: Even if they are professionals in the field of media in education, prior knowledge and personal attitudes are key factors how to handle media in a general way; for example being optimistic, being critical, or being pessimistic. Theories that explain "technology acceptance" can be a source for further argumentation. For example, the technology acceptance model (Pituch & Lee, 2006) "appears to be the most widely accepted theory among information systems research for studying users' system acceptance behavior" (Rezaei et al., 2008, p. 86). According to this model the two key determinants of technology acceptance are the beliefs about the perceived usefulness of technology and the perceived ease of use. Both are influenced by external variables such as Internet experience, computer anxiety, computer self-efficacy (Rezaei et al., 2008, p. 86), and lead to a specific intention. Whereas this last variable is often seen as a factor in the use of e-learning of distance learners, similar effects should obviously be found in the forecasting of media adoption within education.

Even in a (at first glance) homogeneous group of educational scientists, the attitudes, beliefs, and opinions concerning (new) media vary a lot: Additionally, the cultural background seems to play a role. According to Klebl (2007) there are three metaphors or images in use to describe the role or affect of technologies or media on education. The German literature nearly always used the "potential" which derives from media usage; for example, new or better opportunities of media usage in education, which have to be developed and evaluated within learning and teaching experiences. A more common usage contributed from non-German literature seems to use more often the terms "catalyst" or "lever". Whereas the catalyst can be used to get similar or even faster results with smaller input and effort, the lever effect can only be used if the goals of the usage of technologies are already known (Klebl, 2007 refers to Venezky & Davis, 2002, p. 14). Additionally, the educational discipline or background influences and shapes the opinion and attitude about (new) media (see Sesink, 2008, p. 13f). New media are seen as endangering the "real" self-education from a critical perspective, where the main idea is to conserve an underlying educational concern (e. g. Hentig, 2002). In contrast, media educationalists gaze at new media as something new and challenging, which should be implemented in education. Last, but not least, media didactics and learning scientist look on new media as something that can make learning more effective and efficient. Following this finding, the background of the experts within studies should be explored and discussed carefully.

Additionally, the inclusion of several experts and their interactions (as in the Delphi method) and/or aggregation of data lead to general statements with adjusted and mean values. In other words, these values and conclusions can also be seen as mainstream. Even if all experts are well selected, this effect can also foil the idea of the generation of non-standard, non-usual or creative development of ideas on future developments. A related effect is that these methods tend to argue on the base of linear developments.

To sum up, the awareness that these approaches of study design are limited seems to be small. In the following, we want to introduce the relation of media, culture and education from a more general perspective. Through this, we aim to illustrate that the current study designs could be enhanced by a bigger awareness of the insights of the cultural studies and their adaptations for education, the pedagogical media theory.

THE CULTURAL PERSPECTIVE

The research methods described above are mainly focused on finding out about upcoming media didactical trends and innovations of teaching and learning on an application-orientated level. In different quantitative and qualitative studies the current and the potential future use of educational technologies is analysed. Next to this vast scientific discourse on future adoption of educational technologies a more theoretical discourse that is located in the field of cultural studies is more and more linked to the research area of media and education. Anthropologist, sociological and media-theoretical perspectives are taken to research fundamental correlations of media, culture and education (Meyer, 2002; Fromme & Sesink, 2008; Wesch, 2008; Baecker, 2007). These socio-cultural approaches form the basis to interpret and understand changes of media and their implications for processes of learning and teaching.

Medium and Culture

In the current discussions on the relation of media and education, the term *media* is very often reduced to electronic media technologies, only referring to technical devices such as computers, mobile phones or to a technical infrastructure such as the Internet. Yet, to have a closer look at the effects of the still so-called *new media* on educational processes and to anticipate the adoption of new media in an educational context the definition of medium needs to be widened.

Technical media are certain systems of encoding, storing, distributing and receiving information and knowledge – including writing and book print as well as electronic media. In several media theories the influence of technical media on the representation and construction of knowledge and reality, as well as on our perception and our thinking, and therefore also on cultural processes is discussed. Jack Goody (1986), Walter Ong (1987), Eric H. Havelock (1988) and others researched the impact of writing on socio-cultural processes, focusing on the contrast of orality and literacy. Following their argumentation that the technical medium influences socio-cultural structures Marshall McLuhan (1994) emphasises the importance of the technical structures and the form of a medium, resulting in the famous statement: "The medium is the message". He understands technical media as "extensions of men" (1994), which optimise or replace human actions. Friedrich Kittler (1986) goes beyond McLuhan, stating a technical apriority. According to Kittler the cultural development is a result of the development of media.

We do not have to take over such a strong technical deterministic perspective but these theories all focus on one common aspect: the correlation of the history of culture and the history of media. Changes of media have always brought forth

Table 1. Parts of the overview of the aspects of the three mediospheres by Régis Debray (1991, cited and translated in Reader, 1995, 58f.)

	Writing (Logosphere)	Printing (Graphosphere)	Audiovisual (Videosphere)
Spiritual Class Holding Sacred Power in Society	Church (prophets and clerics) Dogma is sacrosanct	Lay Intelligentsia (teachers and doctors) Knowledge is sacrosanct	Media (diffusers and producers) Information is sacrosanct
Statement of Personal Authority	God Told Me (Gospel truth)	I Read It In A Book (truth of the printed word)	I saw it on the TV (truth of the broadcast image)

changes of communication, a different handling and organisation of knowledge and information, and different processes of teaching and learning. These changes do not remain on an application-oriented level of cultural practices but also affect the underlying culture, such as symbolic forms, social organization, or distribution of power.

Mediology

For finding out about the interdependencies of media systems, social processes, symbolic forms and systems, the mediological approach according to Régis Debray provides a methodical basis. Debray's understanding of the term medium includes four characterizing elements: A process of symbolising (such as a word, writing, image), a social communication code, a material device for storing and storage, and a dispositive of records that is connected to a specific network of distribution, such as a handwritten manuscript, the book print or TV. Also educational institutions – and therefore also processes of learning and teaching – are part of a medium. To pass over, for example, the alphabetic writing a technical means such as paper or books, institutions such as editing houses and schools and teachers are necessary.

Not the media systems themselves are in the focus of research, instead the mediations are, the "informal in-between" (Debray, 2004, p. 68). Following Régis Debray's mediological considerations, cultural ages can be distinguished due to the technical media of transmission. Debray identifies four of these so called "mediospheres": the logosphere, the graphosphere, the videosphere and the currently evolving digital mediosphere or hypersphere: "From the 15th century up to yesterday the book print gave distinction to the graphosphere. Today we are surrounded by the videosphere in which due to a altered sense of time the moment crows over permanence, the direct over the indirect, the reactive over the discursive. The videosphere is about to fade to a kind of hypersphere, mainly characterised by digital signals." (Debray 2001/2002, p. 6, translated by the authors)

To understand the evolving digital mediosphere and, therefore, to be able to make predictions on media adoption processes in education on a cultural level, it is necessary to define alterations from the previous mediosphere that considerably coined our educational system, the graphosphere. According to Debray, the graphosphere starts with the invention of the book print. The graphic reproduction of books by copyists as an established media system is replaced by printing books. With the transition from an oral to a typographic culture, from the logosphere to the graphosphere, the human being as a learning individual came to the fore. In the logosphere the individual was a rather passive recipient of information ("God told me"). However, the growing transmission of printed information brought forward increasingly active studies of typographic media ("I read it in a book"). To learn meant to learn reading and writing in order to be able to conceptualise the world. The subjective grasp of the world was no longer primarily a result of orally transmitted interpretations of scripts, mostly imparted by the clerics. The ability to read and to write enabled the individual to delve into the transmitted messages independently (Schwalbe & Meyer, 2009). At the same time the development of printing presses and networks of distribution brought forward the massive reproduction of printed information. We reckon that only these technological, social and economic developments made the alphabetization of the populace necessary – and therefore led to the introduction of a general school system.

At this moment, with the development of the Internet and especially the World Wide Web, we are experiencing the emergence of a new technical medium of transmission, anticipated to have similar effects on cultural and educational processes as the introduction of the printed book (Debray, 2004; Castells, 2005; Baecker, 2007). It is not yet clear, how this coming digital mediosphere will be shaped. The sense of time and space is changing in comparison to the graphosphere; knowledge and information can be easily communicated over long distances, but the duration of the communicated information is very often getting shorter.

This corresponds with an increasing use of mobile devices, which are characterised by the convergence of different options for communication. It is one of the trends of the Horizon Report (Johnson, Levine & Smith, 2009, p. 8) mentioned above and is expected to provide an always available device for content delivery and data capture. Due to a permanent access to the Internet the instant communication independent from time and space using different codes (images, videos, writing, and speech) is always growing. It will be normal to be always online and connected.

Another characteristic of the digital mediasphere, next to the observation of a changing relation of time and space, is the evolvement of new forms of knowledge production. The possibilities of participation on the web bring to the fore collaborating processes in generating knowledge. The educated individual is confronted with the wisdom of the crowds.

Medium and Education

A mediological perspective on media and education is provided by Torsten Meyer (2008) with his *Pedagogical Media Theory*. His argumentation is based on a broader definition of the term medium in a cultural context. According to Meyer it is not possible to understand a medium as a system separate from us but more as a "milieu" we are living in. He claims the medium to be a realm of possibilities providing the basis for our actions and communications, or in other words: as culture, influencing our socialisation. This understanding of the term medium is closely connected to Michel Foucault's "archive" as a "historical a priori" (Foucault, 1969, cited in Meyer, 2008, p. 265) – or as Meyer calls it a "media-cultural-historical a priori": an age-specific set of conditions of cognitive, communicative, and social processing. The cultural techniques related to the medium affect our cognition, but we are hardly aware of the impact – the media-cultural-historical a priori can thus be described "as a kind of age-specific blind spot of thinking, knowing, gaining insight" (Meyer, 2008, p. 265). Blind spot means, we do not realise it is a spot we cannot see. It is the media educators' responsibility to make this blind spot visible – to raise awareness of the influence of the medial milieu on our thinking and our culture. The method Meyer uses to become aware of the current cultural changes related to the development of media, is to analyse former changes of the medium and the associated cultural effects.

Meyer describes one phenomenon that is in his opinion a crucial characteristic of an upcoming digital mediosphere: In reference to Jean-Francois Lyotard (1989) he states that the nature of knowledge in the "computerised society" is changing. Due to the ubiquitous computer technology it becomes to something that is more and more becomes some kind of external product. This of course is deeply affecting educational institutions and processes of teaching and learning (Meyer 2008, p. 91).

The trend towards mobile devices providing permanent access to the Internet (Johnson, Levine & Smith, 2009, p. 8) supports the theory of an increasing externalization of knowledge due to a different medium we are living in. The possibility of accessing knowledge bases such as Wikipedia, independent from time and space, supersedes the need for remembering factual knowledge.

How These Ideas Challenge Study Design

The presented approach does not explicitly deal with the processes of adoption of new educational media systems on a practical level. It does not solve the challenges of (i) a prognosis or forecast of new trends of technology enhanced learning or (ii) a revelation how these trends will influence the reality of learning. Pedagogical media theories and studies on cultural and social changes in relation to the development of media provide a basic framework for various specific approaches dealing with the future of technology enhanced learning: Just as we can hardly understand how it feels to live in an oral culture (cf. Markus, 2006), we are not able to imagine how we will think, act and communicate in the future of the evolving new mediosphere – our thinking is still affected by the graphosphere. Meyer (2008) comes to the point, in line with Sesink (2006) that we cannot just perceive the new media systems as new devices to support educational processes while at the same time sticking to a traditional system. We, rather, have to be aware of the process of cultural change, probably demanding re-thinking our concepts of learning, teaching and re-structuring the current educational system.

SUMMARY AND DISCUSSION

We described current study design from a critical perspective and introduce pedagogical media theories to illustrate the challenges of a change of media systems and the limited possibilities to handle with it on a methodological level. To illustrate the two different ways to look at and discuss (future) media adoption for learning and teaching, the following figure illustrates that the "frame" of symbolic forms, cultural organizations and social processes includes the perspective on applications and cultural practices (figure 1).

With our confrontation of current study design with ideas from the cultural studies in combination with pedagogical media theory we focused on two very different theoretical approaches, playing on two different levels of argumentations: Whereas the mediological approach is focusing on cultural studies provides an abstract and general perspective the study design concretely describe methodologies. Nevertheless, we think this confrontation is fruitful for further studies and reflections on future media adoption.

As we have shown within this chapter, current study design on future media adoption struggles from the perspective of pedagogical media theory with the following challenges:

- The current mediosphere strongly influences the thinking on media, and therefore the thinking of all, including experts in current study design without possibility to reflect this phenomenon.
- We are still settled and related to a typographic culture of the graphosphere; we

Figure 1. Frames of (future) media adoption

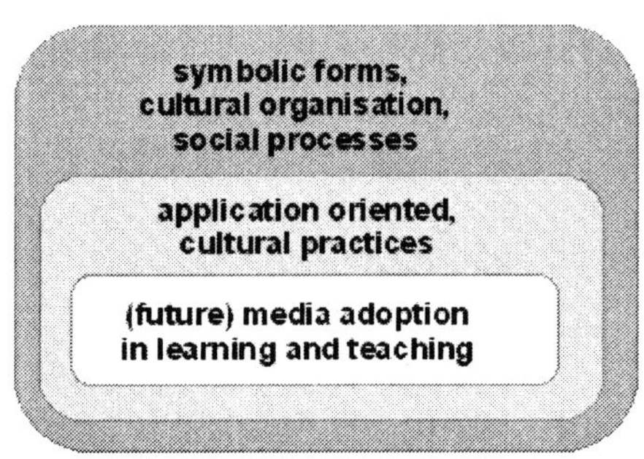

have no clear idea on how another (future) mediosphere can and will influence our thinking about media.

- Finally, we have to be aware of the process of cultural change, probably demanding re-thinking our concepts of "learning" and "teaching".

This chapter gives no overview about existing theories on future adoption of media. But in fact, there are some. They build for example on sociological ideas adapted for future media adoption in learning and teaching: From the perspective of social science, the theory of "Social Construction of Technology" or the "Actor Network Theory" (Latour 2007) describes and analyses the relationship and interdependences of education and technologies (Klebl, 2007). For instance, the "Social Construction of Technology" (SCOT) approach was developed by Pinch and Bijker (1987) and focuses on how human actions within different social groups shape technology and its usage. SCOT is also used as a methodology. For example, Klebl (2008) analysed the "One Laptop per Child" (OLPC) initiative and the Open Educational Resources movement, Gyambrah (2007) used it as a theoretical base for his descriptive comparison of e-learning technologies and their applications in higher education in Germany, the United Kingdom and the United States.

As far as we can see, our overview in this chapter emphasises an approach of cultural studies as one resource to get a clearer view on (possible) argumentations and could lead to more thoughtful handling of study design or of studies that builds on such designs.

POSSIBLE FUTURE RESEARCH DIRECTIONS

One question that is important for the described approach of mediology is how institutions of learning deal with the cultural and technological changes due to innovations of technology enhanced learning? Not only the adoption process of learners and educators needs to be taken into account but also the impact of technology on the roles of teachers within processes of teaching and learning. Due to new technologies and media systems, new forms of communication and collaboration are evolving; the handling of knowledge is changing. To be able to participate actively in this process of change and to take an active, formative role in re-structuring institutions of learning for a digital mediosphere, we need a profound understanding of the past, current and future influences of media and technology on learning and teaching, on the technical and social infrastructures within institutions of learning and on their function within society.

REFERENCES

Baecker, D. (2007). *Studien zur nächsten Gesellschaft*. Frankfurt, Germany: Suhrkamp.

Boon, M. J., Rusman, E., & van der Klink, M. R. (2005). Developing a critical view on e-learning reports: Trend watching or trend setting? [from http://www.qou.edu/homePage/arabic/researchProgram/eLearningResearchs/developingACritical.pdf]. *International Journal of Training and Development*, *9*(3), 1–27. Retrieved December 25, 2008. doi:10.1111/j.1468-2419.2005.00229.x

Castells, M. (1998). *The rise of the network society*. Cambridge, MA: Blackwell.

Debray, R. (2004). Für eine Mediologie. In *Kursbuch Medienkultur. Die maßgeblichen Theorien von Brecht bis Baudrillard* (pp. 76-75). Stuttgart, Germany: DVA.

Foucault, M. (1969). *Archäologie des Wissens*. Frankfurt, Germany: Suhrkamp.

Fromme, J., & Sesink, W. (2008). *Pädagogische Medientheorie*. Wiesbaden, Germany: VS Verlag für Sozialwissenschaften.

Geser, G. (2007). *Open educational practices and resources - OLCOS roadmap 2012*. Retrieved December 30, 2008, from http://edumedia.salzburgresearch.at/images/stories/EduMedia/Inhalte/Publications/olcos_roadma p.pdf

Grunwald, A. (2002). *Technikfolgenabschätzung: Eine Einführung*. Berlin, Germany: Edition Sigma.

Gyambrah, M. K. (2007). *E-learning technologies and its application in higher education: A descriptive comparison of Germany, United Kingdom and United States*. Dissertation, LMU München, Fakultät für Psychologie und Pädagogik. Retrieved December 30, 2008, from http://edoc.ub.uni-muenchen.de/7358

Hamburg, I., Busse, T., & Marin, M. (2005). Using e-learning scenarios for making decisions in organisations. In *6th European Conferene E-COMM-LINE 2005*, Bucharest. Retrieved December 26, 2008, from http://www.iatge.de/aktuell/veroeff/2005/hamburg01.pdf

Hentig, H. V. (2002). *Der technischen Zivilisation gewachsen bleiben*. Weinheim, Germany: Beltz.

Johnson, L., Levine, A., & Smith, R. (2009). *The 2009 horizon report*. Austin, TX: The New Media Consortium. Retrieved February 16, 2009, from http://wp.nmc.org/horizon2009

Kittler, F. A. (1986). *Grammophon, Film, Typewriter*. Berlin, Germany: Brinkmann & Bose.

Klebl, M. (2007). Die Verflechtung von Technik und Bildung -Technikforschung in der Bildungsforschung. *bildungsforschung,* 4(2). Retrieved December 30, 2008, from http://www.bildungsforschung.org/Archiv/2007-02/technik/

Klebl, M. (2008). Explicating the shaping of educational technology: Social construction of technology in the field of ICT and education. In *Reading in Education and Technology: Proceeding of ICICTE 2008*, 278-289.

Kosow, H., & Gaßner, R. (2008). Methoden der Zukunfts-und Szenarioanalyse Überblick, Bewertung und Auswahlkriterien. *WerkstattBericht Nr. 103. Berlin: Institute for Futures Studies and Technology Assessment*. Retrieved December 20, 2008, from http://www.izt.de/fileadmin/downloads/pdf/IZT_WB103.pdf

Latour, B. (2007). *Eine neue Soziologie für eine neue Gesellschaft.* Frankfurt, Germany: Suhrkamp.

Lyotard, J. (1989). *The postmodern condition: A report on knowledge*. Manchester, UK: University Press.

Markus, M. (2006): *Bild-Medien und Welt-Bild. Versuch einer geistesgeschichtlichen Kontextualisierung der Geschichtsmächtigkeit der Bild-Medien*. PhD thesis, University of Salzburg, Austria.

Mcluhan, M. (1994). *Understanding media: The extensions of man*. Cambridge, MA: MIT Press.

Meyer, T. (2008). Zwischen Kanal und Lebens-Mittel: pädagogisches Medium und mediologisches Milieu. In J. Fromme & W. Sesink (Eds.), *Pädagogische Medientheorie* (pp. 71-94). Wiesbaden, Germany: VS Verlag für Sozialwissenschaften.

Miller, R., Shapiro, H., & Hilding-Hamann, K. E. (2008). School's over: Learning spaces in Europe in 2020: An imagining exercise on the future of learning. *JRC Scientific and Technical Reports*. Retrieved December 26, 2008, from http://ftp.jrc.es/EURdoc/JRC47412.pdf

Pinch, J. T., & Bijker, W. E. (1987). The social construction of facts and artefacts: or how the sociology of science and the sociology of technology might benefit each other. In W. E. Bijker, T. P. Hughes & J. T. Pinch (Eds.), *The Social Construction of Technological Systems: New Directions in the Sociology and History of Technology* (pp. 17-50). Cambridge, MA: MIT Press.

Pituch, K. A., & Lee, Y. K. (2006). The influence of system characteristics on e-learning use. *Computers & Education*, *47*, 222–244. doi:10.1016/j.compedu.2004.10.007

Reader, K. (1995). *Régis Debray: a critical introduction*. London: Pluto Press.

Rezaei, M., Mohammadi, H. M., Asadi, A., & Kalantary, K. (2008). Predicting e-learning application in agricultural higher education using technology acceptance model. *Turkish Online Journal of Distance Education*, 9(1), 85-95. Retrieved February 2, 2009, from http://tojde.anadolu.edu.tr/tojde29/pdf/Volume9Number1.pdf

Schaffert, S. (2004). Einsatz von Online-Prüfungen in der beruflichen Weiterbildung: Gegenwart und Zukunft. *Deutsches Institut für Erwachsenenbildung*. Retrieved February 2, 2009, from http://www.die-bonn.de/esprid/dokumente/doc-2000/schaffert00_01.pdf

Schwalbe, C., & Meyer, T. (2009). Umbauten im und am Bildungsraum – Zum medieninduzierten Wandel der Kommunikationsstrukturen in der Hochschulbildung. In W. Marotzki & J. Fromme (Eds.), *Neue Kultur- und Bildungsräume*.

Sesink, W. (2008). Bildungstheorie und Medienpädagogik. Versuch eines Brückenschlags. n: J. Fromme & W. Sesink (eds.), *Pädagogische Medientheorie*. Wiesbaden: VS Verlag für Sozialwissenschaften, 13-35.

Sinclair, G., McClaren, M., & Griffin, M. (2006). *E-Learning and beyond: A discussion paper prepared as part of the Campus 2020 process for the British Columbia Ministry of Advanced Education*. Retrieved February 2, 2009, from http://www.aved.gov.bc.ca/campus2020/documents/e-learning.pdf

Siozos, D., & Palaigeorgiou, G. (2008). Educational technologies and the emergence of e-learning 2.0. In D. Politis (Ed.), *E-Learning Methodologies and Computer Applications in Archaeology* (pp. 1-17). Hershey, PA: IGI Global.

Steinmüller, K. (2002). *Workshop Zukunftsforschung. Teil 2 Szenarien: Grundlagen und Anwendungen*. Essen: Z_punkt GmbH.

Venezky, R., & Davis, C. (2002). Quo vademus? The transformation of schooling in a networked world. *OECD/CERI*. Retrieved February 2, 2009, from http://www.oecd.org/dataoecd/48/20/2073054.pdf

Wesch, M. (2008 June 17). *A portal to media literacy*. Presentation at University of Manitoba. Retrieved February 10, 2009, from http://mediatedcultures.net/ksudigg/?p=174

Section 2
Learner and Teacher

Chapter 2
Students, Internet, eLearning and Web 2.0

Rolf Schulmeister
University of Hamburg, Germany

ABSTRACT

An investigation into the students' use of internet services, media types and e-learning preferences tried to find out if students today are interested in the use of Web 2.0 methods for learning. More than 2.000 students participated in the survey conducted by the international architecture company DEGW and the author. The data of the survey are compared to the results of a parallel study by HIS GmbH that was answered by 4.400 students. The results of both studies throw a critical light on the popular discussion about the net generation or the so-called digital natives and may lend themselves to a more cautious or careful introduction of Web 2.0 methods in teaching and learning accompanied by instructional and tutorial assistance.

INTRODUCTION

The numbers are impressive: during the past 5 years since its commencement, 95% of all American students have become members of facebook, more than 150 million people use it worldwide and have uploaded over 10 billion photos. Since its initiation 3 years ago, 12 million German users have registered with StudiVz. YouTube's video Database has been in existence for a mere 3 years and already counts more than 100 million videos. Flickr contains more than 2 billion photos of its users. These numbers are truly impressive. Furthermore, primarily the younger members of our society have primarily been responsible for generating them. But can they be labelled the "net generation" based solely on these statistics?

Wolfgang Schweiger has found an explanation for the often-cited magnitude of internet use: "academics who intensively deal with online media and reiterate its massive prevalence increase its relevance and thus the legitimacy of their own research" (p. 97; italics in the original). Considering that Schweiger studied "The Myths of Internet Use"

DOI: 10.4018/978-1-61520-678-0.ch002

(2004), if his assertion is correct, my own research and this very article would loose their legitimacy. My analysis will not deal with enormous numbers, but rather with tiny statistics.

The Internet is full of fantasies about young people who have access to computers and internet since early childhood. Many proponents of Web 2.0 and eLearning 2.0 are presently fuelling such speculation (see Schulmeister, 2008). This theme has been indiscriminately adopted and disseminated by the OECD in its own Website for the "New Millennium Learner" (NML).[1] Francesc Pedró (2006) of OEDC-CERI asserted: "that NML seem to be a generation-wide phenomenon, growing steadily and already having a universal character in some OECD countries." He chooses the fact that more younger users than older users favour instant messaging as a criterion for his finding that: "instant messaging is considered to be a quite good indicator of the development of NML." The European Commission has also recently begun to study the topic by calling on the Director of its Institute for Prospective Technological Studies, Yves Punie, to edit and oversee a number of eLearning papers on the topic "New Learning Generation."[2] Despite various critical voices (Schulmeister, 2008; Evans, 2007; CIBER, 2007; Bennet, Maton & Kervin, 2008), the myth of a new net generation has increasingly found advocates in the cultural region of Europe.

The arguments are always identical: the universal access to new media and its extensive use by children and youth must be shaping this new Net Generation. I do not question the existence of many teenagers who are active in the internet as cited by Tapscott (1997), Opaschowski (1999), Howe & Strauss (2000), Prensky (2001a), Palloff & Pratt (2003), Oblinger & Oblinger 2005, and many others. It is not the appropriate place here to describe the claims of these authors here in detail. For an extensive criticism of these publications see Schulmeister (2008). The youth they describe communicate in virtual communities and volunteer for chats and interviews. However, generally speaking and from a scholarly viewpoint, those who write about such young people make certain unforgivable methodological mistakes (detailed data and argumentations are reported in Schulmeister, 2008):

- Media activities of youth are reviewed one-sidedly without regard for other aspects of their lives; empirical surveys show that youth are active in clubs, mostly sports clubs, that they spent much of their time in meeting friends outside; media use is just one of their ways to spend their leisure time;
- Seldom have both the actual content of youths' media use and an exact profile of their motives been studied; research into the actual use of media shows that youth still watch traditional television and hear music to an enormous extent and also read print media; with regard to the Internet the majority uses the communication methods and the social software;
- The publications make incorrect generalizations about to the whole generation based on the results of accidental samplings, while overlooking the biggest differences between youths, their activities, interests and preferences; all studies of large samples in the internet using differential statistical methods (factor and cluster analysis) demonstrate that young people as well as the older population break apart in different user groups with different interests, motivations, lifestyles, social orientations etc. (see for example Treumann, Meister & Sander, 2007);
- Most net generation authors assume the behaviour of youths is determined by the existence of digital media and assumed to influence the learning habits and preferences of an entire generation in high school and college, whereas thorough surveys involving students in higher education prove that

there is no transfer of Internet experience to study competences and learning preferences (e.g. Kvavik, 2005; Kvavik et al, 2004; Kvavik et al, 2005; Paechter, Fritz, Maier & Manhal et al., 2007).

In another study (Schulmeister, 2008), I extensively analysed the generational concept and proved, based on multivariable analyses of differential psychology, that collective groups always divide into subgroups of varying orientations. In that same study, referring to over 50 international large-scale empirical analyses of media use by children, youths and students, I was able to prove that media use and frequency of use are not suitable as sole variables in the interpretation of interests, attitudes, motives and preferences of youths. To the contrary, I was able to demonstrate that a closer look at all of their recreational activities is necessary, and that the types of internet and computer activities would need further and more detailed review. Having based that deconstruction of the Net Generation on empirical studies of other scholars, it seemed logical to conduct my own survey of media use, this time based on a random sampling of students. The opportunity arose when Martin Brübach of the consulting firm DEGW asked me to cooperate in a survey of university students. The intention of DEGW was to find out if future job applicants want different working environments. My aim with that study was to analyse if and for what purpose today's students use the Internet and if a transfer to learning in the university was possible.

BACKGROUND OF THE DEGW-STUDY "RECRUITING THE NEXT GENERATION" (RNG-STUDY)

The analyses in this article are partial evaluations of the study "The de-mystification of a phenomenon – Generation Y?! 'Recruiting the Next Generation'" (rng-study), that was conducted in cooperation with the consulting firm DEGW Germany from June 10 through July 28 2008 (7 weeks).

DEGW has been one of the leading consulting firms in the fields of design and architecture for more than 30 years. Its interests include analysing and optimising the interaction between people, buildings and their environments. The study's authors, Christine Kohlert, Sina Schlickum and Martin Brübach (2008), have explained their goal in this study:

We want to adjust the media perspective which links the classification of this young generation solely to its communications- and internet habits. One could also call it the de-mystification of a generation. Over the past six months, the DEGW-research project "Recruiting the Next Generation" was carried out in order to obtain a better-differentiated and more precise picture of this generation which is so important for the working world of tomorrow. (see http://www.recruitingthenextgeneration.de/index.php?article_id=62&clang=1)

The first part of the title of the rng-study "de-mystification of a phenomenon" was derived from my study "Does a Net Generation exist?" (Schulmeister, 2008), in which I referred to the assertion of the Medienpädagogischer Forschungsverbund Südwest: "The mystification of a 'generation @' does not stand up to the test of scholarly research." I chose this quote as a subtitle for a keynote at the DeLFI-Conference "Dispelling a Mystification" (Schulmeister, 2008b) as well as for the shortened English version of that presentation "Is There a Net Gener in the House? Dispelling a Mystification." (Schulmeister, 2008c)

The empirical internet survey was carried out over a seven-week period between June and July 2008. It was conducted solely online. A total of 2098 students from 23 cities and 20 universities, mostly from Germany, a few from Vienna, Austria, and St. Gallen, Switzerland, took part in the survey. The total survey included various items which are not relevant for this context, for example, questions about lifestyle-variables, career plans, perceptions of the working world, wishes for bosses, etc.

"STUDYING IN THE WEB 2.0": A STUDY OF HIS AND MULTIMEDIA KONTOR HAMBURG

Multimedia Kontor Hamburg and HIS GmbH Hannover conducted a joint study "Studying in the Web 2.0. Study-related web- and E-Learning-Services" at roughly the same time (summer 2008) and with similar goals (Kleimann, Özkilic & Göcks, 2008). The sample included 4400 students in the HISBUS student panel. The survey was also based on an online questionnaire. I will compare various data from the HIS-survey with the data of the rng-study wherever similar questions were asked of their respondents. Whereas both studies used similar questions and compiled consistent data, discrepancies in various cases provide possibilities for interesting interpretations and findings.

Questions and Question Categories in the RNG-study

The following questions were asked:

- How many hours do you spend in the internet per day?
- Which of the following devices do you own?
- How often do you use the following methods of communication, the internet or online media?
- Which of the following media do you use (actively – passively)?
- Which of the following internet-services do you use?
- What interests you the most about the internet?
- How often do the following statements concerning media use apply to your studies?
- Have you had experience with LMSs and/or virtual classrooms (web-conferencing, web-meeting) during your studies? (LMS = Learning Management System)?
- Have the following methods influenced your learning habits?

We used these questions to discover how often (in which intervals) and with which purposes (goals) students actively use the internet, which services they use for academic purposes and their views on the usefulness of individual functions and services. We also wanted to determine their perception of the relevance of eLearning and Web 2.0. To reach these goals, special question types were used to prevent the emergence of artefacts that arise from carelessly-given answers. And a differentiation in content was implemented to prevent superficial deductions which are often caused by interpreting screening questions incorrectly.

- Questions differentiate between activities (e.g. communication, research, weblog, book-marking etc), media (e.g. photos, film, podcast etc.), and membership in software communities (e.g. StudiVz, Facebook, Flickr, del.icio.us etc), since the use of software is not identical to the reason for its use, the use of a medium is not bound to particular software, and the participation in an environment does not require users to share the providers' motives;
- Furthermore we distinguished between active and passive use. We assumed that passive activities (reading, listening, watching) would be more prevalent than active activities (writing, discussion, producing) since productive use assumes different psychological factors, e.g. placing the need for self-determination after competence, social integration and autonomy according to Deci & Ryan (1985); extroversion, partialities, etc.;

- The usual question about the amount of use was replaced with a scale of the amount of use per day, week and month, since the mere indication of the amount provides less information than the distribution of use over time;
- Finally, nine questions were developed to ascertain the usefulness of media for educational purposes. Whereas the number of "missing values" was relatively low for all other categories of questions, a true "collapse" in responses could be measured here: fewer than 50% of the participants answered questions about the influence of media on their own studies.

Explanatory Notes about Methods Used

Categories of Answers

For most questions, whenever relevant, two categories of answers were offered so that participants who had little or no knowledge of a subject matter or did not use it did not have to provide responses about its content. The purpose of the two answer categories "I am not familiar with this" and "I do not use this" was to ensure the receipt of answers about frequency of use or subjective usability of methods from only such persons who actually used those methods. We were surprised to discover that the answer category "I am not familiar with this" was extremely important for the results since, to our surprise, a great number of students were not even acquainted with most internet services let alone used them. And that is actually a great overstatement! The vast majority of all students were not familiar with most Web 2.0 applications and did not use them.

Quality of Scales

Most categories can be viewed as nominal or ordinal scales, even when the order of the categories is arranged as a numerical scale (very often, often, sometimes, seldom, very seldom). This can even be observed with the scale "daily – weekly – monthly – every few months." For this reason, the mean and standard deviation were not useable measurements. Rather, frequency and percentage are the relevant statistical measurement. I preferred using mode or modal value[3] for precise representation, sometimes supplemented by information about the second most often chosen category.

Citation Problems

The difficulty of using so-called "screening questions," which are only answered by those persons who answered the previous question in the affirmative, arose when making comparisons with the HIS-study (example: screening question: "Have you ever used a podcast?" Following question: "For what have you used a podcast?") I avoided using such questions since, as mentioned above, the additional categories "I am not familiar with this" and "I do not use this" made such questions redundant. I would like to exemplify the problems in evaluating screening questions with the following example in the HIS-study. Question 3 states: "You use social communities to exchange information about matters concerning your studies." Question 5 sought information about the applications used by those individuals who answered question 3 in the affirmative.

The table in the HIS-study concerning Question 5 is properly introduced with the comment, "only those students who answered that they use social communities to exchange information about matters concerning their studies in question 3." One can easily assume that, during meetings, lectures or discussions, statements made out of context to the effect that "56% of all students use social communities for exam preparation" will be arise. The correct assertion would actually be: "56% of all users who use social communities in order exchange information about matters concerning their studies also use them for exam preparation." The

Table 1. Study-related activities (Kleimann, Özkelic &, Göcks, 2008)

	N	%
Exchange of documents and literature	1,597	48.7
Exam preparation	1,792	54.6
Preparation of homework, papers, etc.	970	29.6
Clarification of questions for self-study	1,917	58.5
For support with practical aspects of studying (apartment search, job or internship information)	1,496	45.6
Information about studying abroad	675	20.6
To make and maintain contacts with other students (meeting other students, etc)	2,166	66.0
Other:	129	3.9
Number of Participants who answered:	3,280	100.0

text of the HIS-study about question 5 does begin with a reference to the context of the questions. However, the second sentence, if quoted without the above-stated introduction, can already lead to misinterpretation: "66% of the students use communities very often to often in order to make contacts or maintain contacts with other students." Based on the entire random sampling, however, only 49% of all responding students gave that answer. Further aspects come to mind with the problematic methodology of this question.

Question 5: You use social communities to exchange information about matters concerning your studies. For which study-related activities do you use them?

Screening question: Only those students who answered that they use social communities to exchange information about matters concerning their studies in question 3.

It is helpful to see the number of people who answered the question. One can thus realise that 3280 students made a total of 10742 entries and gave on the average 3.3 responses to the 8 answer categories. Since, however, not all of the total number of 4400 students in the random sampling answered the question, the method of interpreting the percentages must be scrutinized. The 3280 students who answered comprised only 75% of the total sample. One can either put the values into the perspective of the total number of participants or put the percentages into the perspective of the basis of the total of 10742 responses, which would lead to implications about the ranking of the categories.

A second screening question in the HIS-study leads me to a further comment. The HIS-study asked students in Question 9 which applications exist at the student's own university. Furthermore, in Question 10, the questionnaire asked who uses which of these applications at the student's own university, and in Question 13, how often these applications are used. This is a multi-tiered screening question. The number of responses spirals downwards. In retrospect, even the study's authors view their procedure critically.

In their responses, more than half of the students indicated that, concerning nearly all of the applications mentioned, they thought their universities did not offer these opportunities for learning and studying. The previous responses to questions concerning the students' assessment of usefulness are thus likely to be based on speculations rather than experiences. Furthermore, the values for use are very low. (Kleimann, Özkelic & Göcks, 2008)

Question 14: Which are the main purposes for which you use the digital applications you named at your university? Screening question:

Table 2. Use of podcasts (Kleimann, Özkelic & Göcks, 2008)

Electronic audio-recordings/audio podcasts of events	**N**	**%**
For preparing / reviewing classes with other students	87	15.9
For individual preparation / review of classes	205	37.2
To prepare for examinations	180	32.6
As part of classroom-based courses	19	3.4
As individual method of study	42	7.6
Other	19	3.4
Total	551	100.0

Only those students whose answer in question 13 indicated that they use digital applications at their university.

In Question 14, only one answer could be chosen out of 6 available categories for each digital application (audio podcast, video podcast, blog, etc). This, however, is not evident in the table, but only when reviewing the questionnaire which offers 6 possible answers to questions in a pop-up menu.

4125 people answered Question 13: 2614 thought that there were no audio podcasts at their university, 922 said that they would not use audio podcasts. Thus, 589 people remained to answer Question 14, of whom 551 (552 according to my calculation) answered the question (12.5% of the surveyed individuals), i.e. a loss of 38 further participants.

One can expect statements in the short or in the long run to the effect that: "37.2% of all students use audio podcasts to prepare for classes, over 32% to prepare for exams" (for this example, I chose the two higher percentages!). These statements would be wrong. Since HIS considers this sampling of 4400 students to be representative, the study should state: 4.7% of all students use audio podcasts to prepare for classes, and 4.1% to prepare for exams. All other applications were used even less frequently.

The Treatment of Missing Values

These thoughts lead me to the next problem, namely the treatment of so-called missing values in statistics, i.e. missing answers in questionnaires. I do not refer to those cases in which a few people did not answer a few questions, so that a varying but small number of answers might be missing from a few individual questions. I refer to those cases in which a larger number of people did not respond to one or to various questions, whereby nothing is known about their motives. This is especially unexpected when a large number of "missing values" arise although the scale of answer categories included the answers, "I am not familiar with this" or "I do not use it." In these cases, one can distinguish between three groups of users who did not add input to the question. The reasons for not answering remain unclear for the first group, whereas they are known for the last two groups.

This problem arose in the last question of the rng-study, "Have the following methods influenced your learning habits?" Students were asked about the following applications, shown in Table 3.

1214 or 1216 participants in the survey (58%) consistently failed to answer these 9 questions. The reason for this reduction in participation could not be discerned. There was no other instance of a high quota of missing values in any other segment of the survey. I would like to illustrate the

Figure 1. Screening question 13 in Kleimann, Özkelic & Göcks, 2008

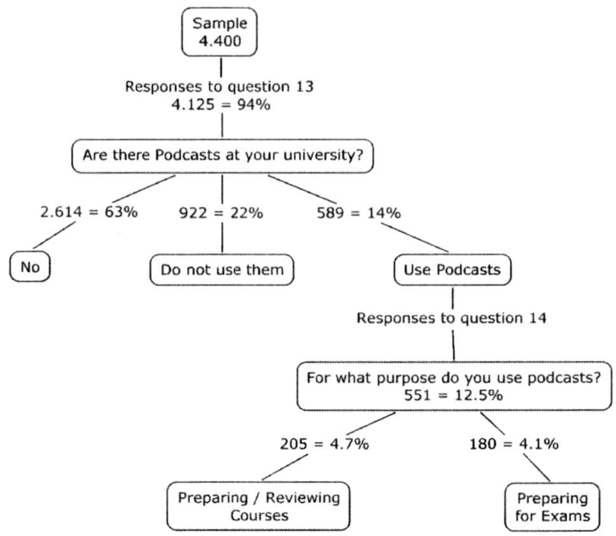

statistical problem using the example of online learning materials (see Table 4).

Considering the large number of missing values, one must decide whether the question should be evaluated at all, and if so, how to calculate the answers in percentages. The percentage of the total sampling are shown in the column "Percentage," while the column "Valid Percentage" contains the total percentage reduced by the missing values. I would like to illustrate this calculation, shown in Figure 2.

The uppermost graph demonstrates the conclusion that "32 = 1.6%" of the students found online learning materials useful. That would also be the value in the column "Percentage." The lower graph allows two variations to this conclusion. One possibility would be the claim that 32 = 3.7% out of the 42.1% of the participants who answered the question whether online learning materials are useful, answered the question in the affirmative. That would represent the answer in the column "Valid Percentage." Another possible answer would be: "32 = 42% of the 76 users of online learning materials, representing only 3.6% of the total survey, found online learning materials useful. This is not a question of which alternative is right, as they are all correct. It all depends on the complete linguistic presentation of the dependencies in the situation.

Figure 3 clarifies these calculations with a further example of the question whether audio podcasts were useful or not, whereby the values for "was useful" vary between 30.6% to 73% and even 88%.

The following report about the results of the rng-study attempts to come to terms with the above-mentioned methodological problems.

Table 3.

1 learning materials online	2 discussions in forums	3 tests online
4 contact per chat	5 group projects online	6 visualisations
7 interactive exercises	8 podcasts	9 simulations

Table 4. Learning materials online (rng-study)

Learning Materials Online						
		N	Percent	Valid Percent	Cumulated Percent
Valid	Was very helpful	5	.2	.6	.6
	Was helpful	27	1.3	3.1	3.6
	Was not helpful	44	2.1	5.0	8.6
	I did not use it	456	21.7	51.6	60.2
	does not exist/I do not know it	352	16.8	39.8	100.0
	Total	884	42.1	100.0	
Missing	System	1214	57.9		
Total		2098	100.0		

LIFESTYLE ANALYSIS IN THE RNG-STUDY

The rng-study ascertained lifestyle factors using a factor analysis.[4] A total of 111 variables were included in the study's factor analysis. These variables were made up of 6 groups, which were not all related to the internet: the choice of TV-stations (14 items), reading preferences (19 items), music preferences (17 items), hobbies (20 items), ownership of communication devices (9 items), and lastly, use of communication, internet and online media (32 items). I mention this because the relevant computer- and internet-based variables in this segment of the study emerge nearly entirely in one factor in the factor analysis. This means that in a survey which reviews variables other than lifestyle, culture and daily routine, there should be a clear contrast in the participants' perception of computer and internet-based variables.

The following four factors (shown in Table 5) were extracted that clearly show the diversity among the sample (for more details see the report by Kohlert, Schlickum & Brübach (2008) that may be purchased at http://www.recruitingthenextgeneration.de/index.php?article_id=62&clang=1).

Figure 2. Missing values, usefulness of online learning material (rng-study)

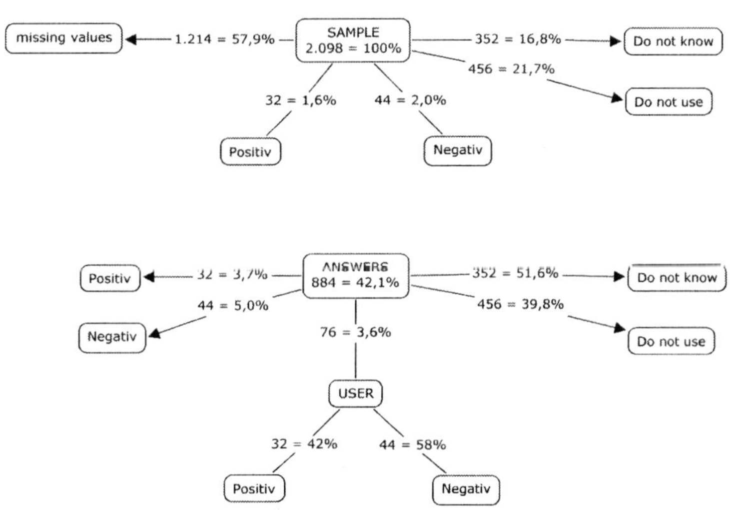

Figure 3. Missing values, usefulness of audio-podcasts (rng-study)

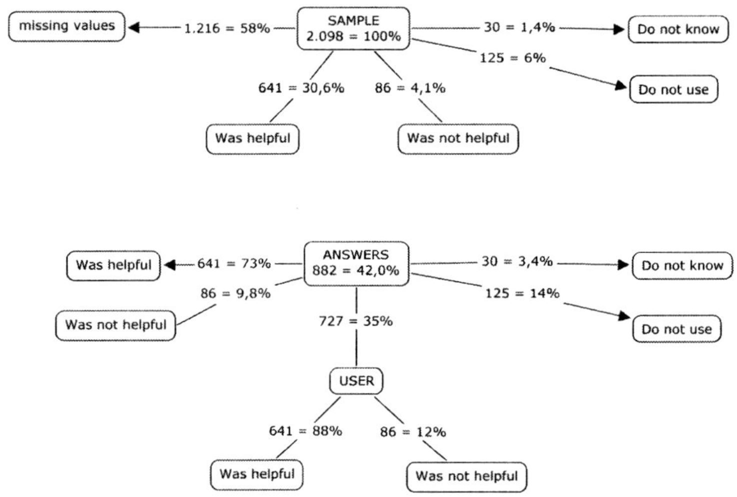

The first factor combines nearly all the variables which I included in the survey about internet use. The second factor comprises the variables which are related to cultural activities like museums, theatre, concerts, conventions, but also cooking, baking, reading cultural magazines, listening to music or playing music oneself. The third, which I would have called "acting in everyday life" included variables like functional activities in internet like online-tickets, -banking, -shopping, search engines, subject-related databases, but also reading economics-oriented magazines and conservative newspapers, and also a lot of communication (emails, text messaging). I would call the fourth factor the "lifestyle and entertainment factor," since it includes variables like TV (soap operas, music videos, comedies, movies), shopping, reading fashion magazines, visiting bars and discos, eating out, etc.

This diversity in the sample is especially notable since it prevents a one-sided focus on the computer and internet by using variables other than internet-variables. Furthermore, the role and meaning of internet-media vary according to the orientation. When differentiating between younger and older participants in the survey (under 28 and over 28), it even became clear that the younger participants were in the minority in the virtual-technical orientation category:

The principal conclusion can be observed that there is no stereotype in the group of under-28-year-olds, that bizarre generation labelled "Generation Y" by the media. Rather, there are various different parallel types which are stronger or weaker depending on sex, age and field of study. (rng-study, 47)

HOW DO STUDENTS USE THE INTERNET?

How Many Hours Per Day Do Students Spend in the Internet?

Means cannot be calculated because of unequally large intervals between the categories in the scale. Applying the ceilings (i.e. 1-2 equals 2, 4-6 equals 6 etc) would also be problematic in the written presentation of the results. 66.1% of the students surveyed spend less than 1-2 hours in the internet. Only a third is in the internet for longer than two hours. The data concerning length of time are not unambiguous since they do not necessarily mean

Table 5. Lifestyle factors (rng-study)

Factors	N	Characteristics	Under Age 28
Virtual/technical orientation	306	Predominantly male, high proportion of design, engineering, math and natural sciences; this factor does not constitute the highest proportion of any field of study.	14.7%
High cultural orientation	667	Predominantly female, high proportion of humanities, language, art and cultural studies, as well as education.	29.2%
Reality orientation	557	Predominantly male, high proportion of economics, law, engineering, natural science and mathematics.	27.5%
Sociable orientation	567	Predominantly female, higher proportion of economics and social sciences (not the highest proportion in any field of study.)	26.6%

that the users actively utilize the net for that period of time. That is especially clear with those users who maintain that they are in the net around the clock, since they probably mean that they leave their computers on 24 hours a day. The same is probably true for such students who leave their computers online 7-10 hours a day.

The data of the rng-study and the HIS-study do not vary greatly (see Table 7).

Which Devices Do Students Own?

Of all respondents, 92% own a cell phone, more than those owning a laptop, which, with 87.9% has far surpassed desktop computers, which only 50% of the participants own. MP3-players are represented with over 70%, other mobile devices such as PDAs or cell phones with PDA reach only 5.3% or 9.8%. The only interesting observation in this regard is that PDA-ownership increases with age (which could indicate it increases with income). See Table 8.

Which Functions and Services Do Students Use in the Internet?

Students have access to a wide range of functions, media and services in the internet. I tried to separate these diverse activities into three categories of questions:

- In Question 3C, students were asked which internet activities they use daily, weekly, monthly, or every few months. Examples

Table 6. Hours in the Internet (rng-study)

How many hours a day in the internet?					
		N	Percent	Valid Percent	Cumulated Percent
Valid	Never	2	,1	,1	,1
	less then 1 hour	230	11,0	11,0	11,1
	1 2 hours	1155	55,1	55,1	66,1
	4-6 hours	469	22,4	22,4	88,5
	7-10 hours	179	8,5	8,5	97,0
	24 hours	62	3,0	3,0	100,0
	Total	2097	100,0	100,0	
missing		1	,0		
Total		2098	100,0		

Table 7. Hours in the Internet (HIS-study)

less than one hour	11	0.3%
1 to 3 hours	3,190	72.6%
4 to 6 hours	988	22.5%
7 to 9 hours	139	3.2%
10 to 12 hours	56	1.3%
24 hours	10	0.2%
Total	4,395	100.0%

Table 8. Device ownership (rng-study)

Device Ownership	N	Percentage	Percentage of cases
PC	1046	15.2%	50.0%
Laptop	1838	26.8%	87.9%
MP3Player	1472	21.4%	70.4%
iPod	197	2.9%	9.4%
Cell phone	1924	28.0%	92.0%
PDA	111	1.6%	5.3%
Combined Handy/PDA	204	3.0%	9.8%
Wii	78	1.1%	3.7%
Total	6870	100.0%	328.4%

were Email, SMS, chat, search engine and research.

- In Question 3D, students were asked how often they use different types of media, e.g. films, photos, music, etc.
- In Question 3E, they were asked which software-community platforms such as YouTube, Flickr, del.icio.us, etc. they use daily, weekly, monthly, or every few months.

Question 3C: How Often Do You Use the Following Types of Communication, the Internet, or Online Media?

The scale contained the following values: Never — every few months — monthly — weekly — daily — I am not familiar with the method.

32 sub questions were posed. The survey asked about: emails, chatting/instant messaging/ sms/mms, internet-telephoning, telephone calls (land line or cell phone), real life meetings, social networks, virtual worlds, reading online-encyclopaedias, writing wikis, search engines, online-maps, researching in specialized databanks, researching in the online-catalogue of the university library, reading online magazines and professional journals, using the online-research assistant, searching for products/services, taking part in discussion forums, social bookmarking, web conferences, virtual classrooms, learning management platforms (LMS), podcast-lectures, file sharing community, use of data-exchange platforms, e-portfolios, online auctions, online shopping/reservations, administering own websites, using event platforms, reading e-books.

The intervals between the values "never—every few months—monthly—weekly—daily" are

Table 9. Usage of internet services (rng-study)

daily	%	weekly	%	monthly	%	Every few months	%
E-mail	93.8%	Online-encyclopaedias	54.2%	Online-Shopping	42.2%	Online-Auctions	35.4%
Telephoning	79.4%	Online-banking	48.8%				
Search engines	75.8%	Online-city maps	46.8%				
Real-life meetings	65.6%	Product searches	38.8%				
SMS / MMS	61.5%	Specialized databases	33.6%				
Social networks	38.9%	Online-catalogues	33.5%				
Chat / IM	36.4%	Online-magazines	28.7%				

not equal. I therefore undertook an analysis based on frequency and modal value (see note 3).

In general, for activities with a daily modus, the second most common value is weekly, and for activities with a weekly modus, the second most common value is monthly. That shows that the result does not become more positive by drawing on the second most common value.

Of the 32 functions which were sampled, 16, i.e. exactly half, had extremely high percentage of values in their modes of either "never used" or "I'm not familiar with the method." The values were so high that no appreciable values remained for other scale values. I added these two values together in the last column of the above table. It is surprising that LMSs[5], which, in the meantime are prevalent at many universities, and podcast-lectures, for which there has been so much publicity lately, belong to this category. Other functions which are quite easy to use such as social bookmarking[6] and ePortfolio are also found there. The fact that some of the interactive environments which require active participation (discussion forums, own websites, writing wikis[7]) are also found is this category is less unexpected.

The distribution clarifies that users clearly distinguish between daily, weekly and monthly use of applications, whereby their use of computers and the internet is markedly utilitarian in its approach: daily use for communication, weekly use for research, and monthly use for costly activities. A pragmatic and thoroughly plausible picture of the distribution of activities can be deduced from the time scale.

In the rng-study, the 32 items were subject to a factor analysis which led to the extraction of 5 factors: Web 2.0 services – Search for information – online services – communication in the web – communication outside the web. I mention this because the analysis of these factors according to the aforementioned lifestyles reveals marked differences between the lifestyles:

The first factor, characterised by Web 2.0 services, is a unique characteristic of the virtual/technical-oriented participants, who furthermore use the web for communication to a great extent. The cultural-oriented participants mainly use the web to search for information, whereas the sociably-oriented participants mainly communicate outside the internet. (rng-Study)

The factor analysis also clearly underscores differences between age groups:

Regarding generations or age groups, it is apparent that communication – whether via internet or not – decreases with age, certainly to a great extent because of professional or private constraints. However, the use of Web 2.0 services and internet-based information searches increases markedly with age, a phenomenon which would have rather

Table 10. Usage of internet services (rng-study)

never	%	I am not familiar with the method	%	Never plus I'm not familiar with the method	%
Virtual worlds	78.3%	Social Bookmarking	45.7%	Virtual worlds	93.2%
own Website	73.0%	Research assistant	43.6%	ePortfolio	92.2%
Web conferences	70.6%			Social Bookmarking	89.4%
Virtual classroom	70.6%			Virtual classroom	86.4%
Writing wikis	65.9%			Podcast-lecture	83.2%
Podcast lectures	64.8%			Data-exchange platforms	82.7%
Reading E-Books	59.3%			Web-conferencing	81.7%
e-Portfolio	52.9%			Event platforms	79.7%
Data exchange platforms	53.1%			Writing wikis	79.0%
Event platforms	51.8%			File Sharing Community	77.2%
File Sharing Comm.	51.5%			Own website	76.2%
LMS	50.1%			Research assistant	73.5%
Discussion forums	49.5%			Reading E-Books	64.9%
Internet telephoning	31.9%			LMS	63.5%
				Taking part in discussion forums	50.9%
				Internet-telephoning	34.0%

been anticipated with the younger age group. On reviewing the individual items, there is, roughly speaking, little difference between age-groups in the use of Web2.0 services.

Question 3D. Which of the Following Digital Types of Media Do You Use?

Based on a scale (never, seldom, sometimes, often, I'm not familiar with it), different types of media were inquired about twice in this question, once under the headline "active = self-produced, writing, uploading" and secondly under the headline "passive = viewing, reading, downloading." Ten media types were included: Audio podcasts, music, internet-radio, films, videos, video podcasts, internet-TV, weblogs, interactive games, photos.

The problem of missing answers, which was discussed in the introduction, arose with this question. The question regarding passive use had only few missing answers: here, the difference between total percentage and valid percentage was minimal. However, only 77% and 83.6% answered the question about active media use. One may, of course, assume that those who did not answer at all would have answered "never" or "not familiar", but we cannot be entirely sure.

Only music is used "often" passively, whereas internet-radio, films, videos and photos, which are used the next most frequently, are used "sometimes." Preferences are obvious: entertainment media are vastly preferred over participation media. Most media types are not even used passively: the most common value, the mode (see note 3 above), for more than a half of the media-types is "never."

Even though user numbers for audio podcasts[8] and video podcasts[9] are still very small, the trend, also found in the HIS-Study, clearly indicates that users prefer video podcasts. I would like to hypothesise that listeners do not bond with mere

Table 11. Media use (rng-study)

Media use	Passive					Active			
	often	sometimes	seldom	never	Not familiar	often	sometimes	seldom	never
Audio podcasts	5.7%	13.3%	20.2%	**44.2%**	14.8%	0.4%	1.1%	2.7%	**95.7%**
Music	**45.7%**	26.9%	14.3%	9.7%	0.5%	6.0%	5.5%	7.2%	**81.3%**
Internet-radio	17.3%	**29.7%**	24.6%	24.4%	1.4%	1.3%	2.0%	2.2%	**94.5%**
Films	21.2%	**28.7%**	21.3%	25.6%	0.9%	1.5%	2.6%	4.3%	**91.6%**
Videos	18.6%	**32.1%**	23.8%	21.7%	1.1%	1.7%	3.4%	7.9%	**87.0%**
Video podcasts	3.7%	11.9%	20.3%	**50.8%**	11.0%	0.4%	1.2%	2.4%	**96.0%**
Internet-TV	6.5%	17.5%	22.1%	**48.9%**	2.8%	0.8%	1.4%	1.8%	**96.0%**
Weblogs	6.1%	13.2%	23.5%	**45.6%**	8.9%	2.7%	5.7%	8.0%	**83.7%**
Interact. Games	3.6%	8.6%	16.9%	**63.4%**	5.2%	1.0%	1.5%	3.8%	**93.7%**
Photos	28.6%	**36.9%**	20.7%	8.8%	0.7%	16,7%	**31,0%**	22.7%	29.6%

audio presentations of lectures to the same extent as video viewers. This might be a question of concentration, since only the sense of hearing is used in the audio version, whereas the sense of vision remains unused and therefore seeks other activities. Podcast protagonists should further explore this point if they want to develop products for future markets.

Only photos are actively used to a noticeable extent. All other media have the mode (see note 3 above) "never", which lies between 81.6% and 96.0%. This is not unexpected for a number of media, since active or productive activities with, for example, films, TV or programming games would be difficult to achieve. However, the result is surprising for other media types: I would have expected higher involvement in music productions. And many readers would have surely wished for greater activities in writing weblogs[10].

Question 3E. Which of the Following Internet Services Do You Use?

Here the scale also varied between the values: "never, seldom, sometimes, often, I'm not familiar with it." The following 21 internet services, most of them Web 2.0 services which are currently popular, were included: StudiVz, facebook, Del.icio.us, LibraryThing, XING, LinkedIn, Lokalisten, MySpace, Amazon, eBay, ZOHO, Zotero, Wikipedia, Special Wikis, SecondLife, Flickr, Picasa, Ringo, Twitter, YouTube, Video.de.

Only Wikipedia[11] and StudiVz have a mode (see note 3 above) of "often." That is not surprising. Whereas StudiVZ is prevalent and often used, the same is not true of facebook, which is especially strong in the USA. Social communities generally have ties to countries, cultures, professions, or status, preventing more general use. Thus, facebook is used by 95% of American students, but not by German students, and XING is preferred by people looking for professional contacts.

The resources and services for everyday life and shopping (Amazon, Ebay) and the reference site Wikipedia are used "often" and "sometimes." Search engines were not part of the inquiry. The second-most common response for the three services in the category "sometimes" was "seldom" and not "often." All other services had the mode (see note 3 above) "not familiar" and "never." For 13 of the 21 services in the category "not familiar" and "never used," the second most common mode (see note 3 above) was the other of the two categories. If I combine these two categories, 15

Table 12. Use of Web 2.0 applications (rng-study)

Often	%	Sometimes	%	Never	%	Not familiar	%
Wikipedia	58.5%	Amazon	40.3%	Second Life	76.7%	Zoho	66.0%
StudiVZ	44.4%	YouTube	38.1%	MySpace	64.0%	Zotero	64.0%
		eBay	35.3%	Lokalisten	61.6%	Library Thing	63.1%
				Facebook	49.7%	Ringo	61.2%
				Video.de	48.2%	Twitter	62.6%
				Spec. Wikis	33.8%	Del.icio.us	58.8%
				XING	32.2%	LinkedIn	55.0%
						Picasa	45.0%
						Flickr	43.9%

communities and software services have shares between 96.6% and 58.7%, and 8 have values above 90%:

This list takes account of most of the Web 2.0 applications discussed in this study, including functions which have achieved excellent networking functions such as del.icio.us (by linking bookmarks) or LibraryThing (by linking book lists). It is surprising that our students are not aware of or do not take advantage of most of these Web 2.0 applications.

A factor analysis was also applied here. Four factors were extracted: Web 2.0 services, net-work/pictures, information/products, videos/friends. Age-related effects were also noted:

It is striking here that men, who use the internet more often per se, also use the various internet

Table 13. Not known or used Web 2.0 applications (rng-study)

"not familiar" and „never" together	Percentage
Zoho	96.6%
Second Life	96.2%
Twitter	96.0%
Library Thing	95.4%
Ringo	95.0%
Del.icio.us	94.5%
Zotero	93.6%
LinkedIn	91.0%
Lokalisten	86.3%
Video.de	82.1%
Flickr	81.0%
Picasa	80.3%
MySpace	72.6%
Facebook	67.1%
XING	58.7%

services more frequently. A small tendency was noted with women using entertainment platforms such as MySpace and Video.de, but also with Amazon (not significant), stronger with StudiVZ ($p<.001$) and Lokalisten ($p=.024$), which was reflected in the fourth factor. The interest in this area decreases with the age of the participants, whereas the use of Web 2.0 services increases. (rng-study)

Question 3F. What interests you most about the internet? Choose the three items which are most important to you from the list below.

This question requested respondents to tick off up to three categories out of a list of ten categories (the items can be seen in the table below).

Our students' two most important activities or purposes in the internet are:

- Finding sources comfortably and quickly and
- Shopping comfortably and cost-effectively

The two next most important applications, which were considerably less popular, are:

- Having access to thousands of photos and films and
- Keeping track of scholarly topics

All other purposes were considerably less accepted and had a share of under 10%. I find that the obvious interpretation of these results is that functions of daily usefulness prevail. Goals which are related to academic studies turned out to be much less popular. Typical Web 2.0 activities were relegated to the bottom of the range:

- Sharing my pictures/photos with others
- Contributing to discussion forums
- Expressing my ideas to other people
- Publishing my own work

Findings Concerning Media Use

We are not only interested in how students use the internet for private purposes, but also in their opinion about internet use in education, and if media use has influenced their studies.

Table 14. Interests in using the internet

Interest in the Internet			
	N	Percent	Percent of Cases
Publishing my own work	106	1.7%	5.1%
Exchanging ideas for scholarly topics	507	8.1%	24.2%
Having access to thousands of photos and films	764	12.1%	36.4%
Sharing my pictures/photos with others	196	3.1%	9.3%
Keeping track of scholarly topics	735	11.7%	35.1%
Contributing to discussion forums	181	2.9%	8.6%
Meeting people with similar interests	396	6.3%	18.9%
Expressing my ideas to other people	213	3.4%	10.2%
Finding sources comfortably and quickly	1967	31.3%	93.8%
Shopping comfortably and cost-effectively	1226	19.5%	58.5%
Total	6291	100.0%	300.0%

Question 3F: To what extent do you agree with the following statements concerning media use in your studies?

The following questions were asked:

- I would like more seminars to use LMSs more intensively.
- I prefer courses which do not use learning technology
- I think that a moderate use of information technology is desirable.
- I wish there were seminars which were exclusively virtual.
- I do well with the present internet use and do not need any special software surroundings.
- I very much enjoy using the opportunities of communication with other students via email and chatting.

In order to have a basis of comparison, I used questions from the EDUCAUSE-Survey of Kvavik et al (2004) and Kvavik et al (2005), which determined through repeated studies that students prefer a moderate amount of media use in their studies and teaching (Kvavik, 2005). The scale chosen for this purpose can be regarded as an interval scale running between "not at all true"(1) through "completely agree"(5).

The result is obvious: the highest student approval exists for moderate media use. The approval of seminars which use a LMS is about 40%; however, 35% of the students answered in the negative and 25% were undecided, so that the standard deviation is highest here. The disapproval is equally clear for virtual seminars with 78%, with 14% undecided and 8% approving. Emailing and chatting received a high approval rating with 70% (17% undecided and 13% against).

A control question which could only be answered with "yes" or "no" was included:

3H. Do you have any experience with the use of LMSs and /or virtual classrooms (web-conferencing, web-meetings) in your courses?

LMSs and virtual classrooms are items which arose in the previous questions. This question

Table 15. Attitude towards media use in teaching (rng-study)

Attitude towards Media Use in University Teaching					
	Sex	N	Mean	SD	Standard error
Seminars using LMSs	male	883	3.04	1.255	.042
	female	1189	2.98	1.154	.033
Seminars which do not use information technology	male	884	2.34	1.143	.038
	female	1189	2.43	1.045	.030
Moderate use of information technology	male	881	3.82	1.009	.034
	female	1188	3.86	.862	.025
Virtual seminars	male	882	1.89	1.041	.035
	female	1184	1.80	980	.028
Sufficient internet use	male	881	3.04	1.125	.038
	female	1183	3.21	1.050	.031
Communication via Email und Chat	male	877	3.77	1.107	.037
	female	1183	3.86	1.069	.031

was intended to determine if a similar frequency distribution could be determined.

The question did not only address LMSs but rather the spectrum of possibilities was broadened to include a larger number of users. One can debate whether the result is encouraging or disappointing: Nearly 60% did not previously know any of the systems. However 42.4% did already have experience with LMS etc.

Question 3I: Have the following methods influenced your learning habits?

The scale basically only had three values. The values ranged between "Did not help me" to "Helped me very much." Respondents who had no input to these questions were to be identified through the responses "Not familiar to me" or "Never used."

This question generated a large number of missing values, namely constantly either 1214 or 1216 people = 58%. We were not able to assess a reason for this. The question was not de-pendent on answering a previous screening question. Fewer than half of the participants an-swered the question. They did not use the option of ticking off "Not familiar to me" or "Never used," but evaded the question. Since the mode (see note 3) was nevertheless "never used" and furthermore many others responded "not familiar to me," only between 10% and 22% remain who found the method helpful.

Considering this information, the question can unfortunately only be answered with the reservation that the question about the influence on one's own learning habits was not understood (or accepted). All of the following percentages must consider that only 42% of the respondents answered the question. Furthermore, of those who did answer, with 91% to 18% that they were not familiar with the method or did not use it or with 3.6% to 72.7% that the method helped them (Note: 50% of the 42% who answered this question amount to only 21% of the random sampling!) Since these percentages are quite problematic, the table below only states the frequencies.

I was astonished by the finding that so few students have used or are familiar with online learning materials to date. We have always assumed that at least this relatively low-threshold measure had already caught on, even if the somewhat more

Table 16. Experience with learning management systems (rng-study)

Experience with LMSs					
		Frequency	Percent	Valid percentage	Cumulative percentage
Valid	yes	889	42.4	42.4	42.4
	no	1207	57,5	57.6	100.0
	total	2096	99,9	100.0	
Missing	System	2	.1		
Total		2098	100.0		

Table 17.

Online learning materials	Discussions in forums	Tests online
Contact per Chat	Online Group projects	Visualisations
Interactive exercises	Podcasts	Simulations

Table 18. Missing values in question 31 (rng-study)

Statistics										
		Learning materials online	Discussions in forums	Tests online	Contacts per Chat	Online Group projects	Visualisa-tions	Interactive Excercises	Pod-casts	Simula-tions
N	Valid	884	884	882	882	882	882	881	882	882
	missing	1214	1214	1216	1216	1216	1216	1217	1216	1216

complex eLearning methods had not yet gained acceptance. And the majority of those few students who have had exposure to this method answered that the learning materials did not help them. In the HIS-study, a completely different impression arose from this question: "Whereas in 2004, 84% of all students responded that digital internet-supported learning materials have accompanied the courses in their respective fields of study, 86% attest to that statement today." (translation, R.S.)

CONCLUSION

The study presents a rather disappointing overview – it reflects negatively on of our efforts to introduce eLearning. We have not yet accomplished what we set out to do. The results are also sobering for anyone – deceived by the steep rise of user numbers in Web 2.0 Communities – who assumed that a new era of university education was dawning with the rise of interactive environments. Based on the myth of the "net generation" which I have dismantled in another study, a vast army of internet-enthusiasts was expected to descend upon the universities, but it has not yet appeared. On the contrary, regarding the students' careful use of Internet services and their distribution over time (see table 9) one might assume that students today have a very realistic time management and a rather pragmatic way of using services when they need them, while others suffer from information overload.

Rational faculty members who would like to employ eLearning methods in their instruction may, however, find some realistic toeholds. It has become apparent that those applications which are especially helpful in communication and information searches enjoy high positive user numbers and frequencies (Schulmeister, 2008). It

Table 19. How helpful was ...? (rng-study)

	Helped me very much	Helped me	Did not help me	I did not use this method	Not available/ I am not familiar with it
Learning Materials	5	27	44	456	352
Discussions in Forums	15	242	191	359	77
Tests online	82	279	117	316	88
Contact per Chat	34	366	127	265	90
Online group projects	69	436	146	182	49
Visualisations	79	241	68	362	132
Interactive exercises	73	298	101	310	99
Podcasts	163	478	86	125	30
Simulations	124	415	65	222	56

has become apparent that we are still encountering gender difficulties and digital divides with the new media. It has also become apparent that interest in and use of media change with age and that the older generation plays a special role for the younger generation (Herring, 2008). And it has also become apparent that education is not the primary purpose of media use and that there is no transfer from extensive computer experience to learning (see the three EDUCAUSE studies by Kvavik and others). These are the deficits which must be the starting points for further work.

REFERENCES

Bennett, S., Maton, K., & Kervin, L. (2008). The 'digital natives' debate: A critical review of the evidence. *British Journal of Educational Technology*, *39*(5), 775–786. doi:10.1111/j.1467-8535.2007.00793.x

CIBER. (2007). An evaluation of BL Learning: a website for younger scholars. *University College London, School of Library, Archive and Information Studies: Information Behaviour of the Researcher of the Future*. Retrieved from http://www.ucl.ac.uk/slais/research/ciber/

Deci, E. L., & Ryan, R. M. (1985). *Intrinsic motivation and self-determination in human behavior*. New York: Plenum.

Evans, J. (2007). Tomorrow's students: Are we ready for the new 21st-century learners? Video Podcast. *Educause Conference 2007*. Retrieved from http://hosted.mediasite.com/hosted4/Viewer/Viewers/Viewer320TL.aspx?mode=Default&peid=ce8f0201-7d54-4abb-b1b0-4f8a0479f481&pid=06155cca-0a78-4cd5-880f-d4c5ce23ba9c&playerType=WM64Lite

Herring, S. C. (2008). Questioning the generational divide: Technological exoticism and adult constructions of online youth identity. In D. Buckingham (Ed.), *Youth, Identity, and Digital Media* (pp. 71-92). Cambridge, MA: MIT Press.

Howe, N., & Strauss, W. (2000). *Millennials rising*. London: Vintage Books.

Kleimann, B., Özkilic, M., & Göcks, M. (2008). Studieren im Web 2.0. Studienbezogene Web und E-Learning-Dienste. *HISBUS Kurzinformation, 21*.

Kohlert, C., Schlickum, S., & Brübach, M. (2008). Die Entmystifizierung eines Phänomens — Die Generation Y?! Recruiting the Next Generation (rng-Studie). *DEGW Deutschland*. Retrieved from http://www.recruitingthenextgeneration.de/index.php?article_id=62&clang=1

Kvavik, R. (2005). Convenience, communications, and control: How students use technology. In D.G. Oblinger & J.L. Oblinger (Eds.), *Educating the Net Generation*. Boulder, CO: Educause.

Kvavik, R. B., & Caruso, J. B. (2005). *ECAR study of students and information technology 2005: Convenience, connection, and control, Vol. 6*. Retrieved from http://www.educause.edu/ecar

Kvavik, R. B., Caruso, J. B., & Morgan, G. (2004). *ECAR study of students and information technology 2004: Convenience, connection, and control, Vol. 5*. Retrieved from http://www.educause.edu/ecar

Oblinger, D. G., & Oblinger, J. L. (2005). Is it age or IT: First steps toward understanding the net generation. In D.G. Oblinger & J.L. Oblinger (Eds.), *Educating the Net Generation*. Boulder, CO: Educause.

Oehmichen, E., & Ridder, C.-M. (2003). Die MedienNutzerTypologie. Ein neuer Ansatz der Publikumsanalyse. *Media Perspektiven, 17*.

Oehmichen, E., & Schröter, C. (2007). Zur typologischen Struktur medienübergreifender Nutzungsmuster. *Media Perspektiven*, *8*, 406–421.

Opaschowski, H. W. (1999). *Generation @: die Medienrevolution entläßt ihre Kinder: Leben im Informationszeitalter.* Hamburg, Germany: BAT.

Paechter, M., Fritz, B., Maier, B., & Manhal, S. (2007). *eSTUDY - eLearning im Studium: Wie beurteilen und nutzen Studierende eLearning?* Retrieved from http://www.e-science.at/dokumente/eSTUDY_Endbericht.pdf

Palloff, R. M., & Pratt, K. (2003). *Virtual student: A profile an guide to working with online learners.* San Francisco, CA: Jossey-Bass.

Pedró, F. (2006). The new millennium learners: Challenging our views on ICT and learning. *OECD-CERI.* Retrieved from http://www.oecd.org/dataoecd/1/1/38358359.pdf

Prensky, M. (2001a). Digital natives, digital immigrants. *On the Horizon, 9*(5). Retrieved from http://www.marcprensky.com/writing/Prensky%20-%20Digital%20Natives,%20Digital%20 Immigrants%20-%20Part1.pdf

Prensky, M. (2001b). Digital natives, digital immigrants, part II: Do they really think differently? *On the Horizon, 9*(6). Retrieved from http://www.marcprensky.com/writing/Prensky%20-%20Digital%20Natives,%20Digital%20Immigrants%20 -%20Part2.pdf

Schulmeister, R. (2008a). *Gibt es eine Net Generation?* Retrieved from http://www.zhw.uni-hamburg.de/uploads/schulmeister-net-generation_v2.pdf

Schulmeister, R. (2008b). Gibt es eine Net Generation? Widerlegung einer Mystifizierung. In S. Seehusen, U. Lucke & S. Fischer (Eds.), *DeLFI 2008: Die 6. E-Learning Fachtagung Informatik der Gesellschaft für Informatik* (Vol. 7-10, pp. 15-28). Bonn, Germany: GI.

Schulmeister, R. (2008c). Is There a Net Generation in the House? Dispelling a Mystification (Trans.). *eLeed.* Retrieved from http://eleed.campussource.de/

Schweiger, W. (2004). Mythen der Internet-Nutzung — Ursachen und Folgen. In U. Hasebrink, L. Mikos & E. Prommer (Eds.), *Mediennutzung in konvergierenden Medienumgebungen* (pp. 89-113). München, Germany: Verlag Reinhard Fischer.

Tapscott, D. (1997). Growing up digital: The rise of the net generation. New York: McGraw-Hill.

Treumann, K. P., Meister, D. M., Sander, U., et al. (2007). *Medienhandeln Jugendlicher. Mediennutzung und Medienkompetenz. Bielefelder Medienkompetenzmodell.* Wiesbaden, Germany: VS Verlag für Sozialwissenschaften.

KEY TERMS AND DEFINITIONS

Podcast: Also known as audio podcast, video podcast. Similar to teleteaching, broadcast, online-lecture. Associated in the manuscript with Internet method for transmission of lectures by distributing or streaming audio or video media files

ePortfolio: Also known as electronic portfolio. Similar to personal documents, dossier, map. Associated in the manuscript with collection of personal documents in electronic format, assembled by the author or owner of these documents in a special software

Weblog: Also known as Web-based log file. Similar to: website, diary. Associated in the manuscript with websites that are used as diary, for journalistic purposes, or to disseminate opinions. Weblogs are open for comments by others contrary to normal websites

Diversity: Also known as variety of species, attitudes, social behaviour. Similar to difference, dissimilarity, variety. Associated in the manuscript with distinction of individuals and groups with regard to spending leisure time and developing lifestyle attitudes differently.

Factor analysis: Also known as principal component analysis. Similar to: cluster analysis. Associated in the manuscript with statistical multivariate methods used to investigate variations between variables and within samples and to describe the diversity among members of social groups.

Digital Divide: Also known as discrimination. Similar to social divide, economic divide, usability divide. Associated in the manuscript with gap between those who own computers and those who do not, between those who have access to the internet and those who have not. It is more and more recognized that there develops a new divide between those who master an information competence and those who lack the competence to evaluate information critically.

Social Communities: Also known as social software. Similar to: association, club. Associated in the manuscript with Web-based software that grants users a membership and enables communication, file exchange and sometimes collaboration between them.

New Millenium Learner: Also known as net generation, digital natives, generation Y. Associated in the manuscript with literature that speculates about the attitudes and preferences of youth regarding computer usage and Internet use.

ENDNOTES

1. http://www.oecd.org/document/10/0,3343,en_2649_35845581_38358154_1_1_1_1,00.html; the term was adopted by Howe & Strauss (2000).
2. http://www.elearningpapers.eu/index.php?page=fix&id=14
3. Mode or modal value is the most frequent observed or measured value of a frequency distribution, whereby mode is not identified by its frequency but by the scale value with which it occurs.
4. Other examples of studies on media use that generated group characteristics of users by means of factor analysis or cluster analysis as well as the methodological aspects of these methods are discussed in Schulmeister (2008), e.g. Treumann, Meister, Sander et al (2007), ARD/ZDF-Nutzertypologie (Oehmichen & Ridder, 2003 und Oehmichen & Schröter, 2007).
5. In our study, of the 2096 respondents to the question about having experience with LMSs, 889 =42.4% answered "yes" and 1207=57.6% answered "no." The question how about how often they use LMSs was answered by 282 "I am not familiar with the method" and 1051 "never." These 1333 participants comprise 64%. The frequency of use of LMSs by the remaining 763=36% was rather evenly spread over the time scale: daily 76, weekly 265, monthly 209, every few months 213. Daily use is the least frequent case. In the HIS-study, LMSs are not offered at 31.6% of the respondents' own universities, and are not used by 21.2% (Total 52.8%). The distribution of uses of LMSs is also rather evenly spread over time in the HIS-study: very often: 11.2%, often: 23.5%, sometimes: 8.9%, rather seldom: 14.4%, and seldom: 7.9%.

6 The data of the HIS-study on social bookmarking: 37.8% are not familiar with social bookmarking and 45.2% don't use it. Only 17% use social bookmarking, varying from 0.3% very frequently through 11.7% very seldom.

7 The HIS-study reported for the question „Do you write articles in Wikipedia? ": 85.1% never do it; the remaining 15%, do it very seldom, 10.7%. If one considers that only those participants who know Wikipedia actually answered, then 86% actually never write articles. Similar distributions were found for "revising articles" and "participating in discussions about articles."

8 Data of the HIS-study for audio podcasts: 12.9% are not familiar with audio podcasts, 43.5% do not use them; the remaining 43.5% use them often (1.1%) to very seldom (23.0%). The mode here is also "never." Audio podcasts of presentations at the university: are not offered (63.4%), are never used (22.4%); use varies between very often (1%) and very rarely (4.6%).

9 Data of the HIS-study for video podcasts: 9.8% are not familiar with video podcasts, 41.6% do not use them; the remaining 48.5% use them often (1.2%) to very seldom (22.8%). The mode is "never." Video podcasts of presentations at the university: are not offered (62.0%), are never used (20.1%); use varies between very often (2.3%) and very rarely (4.5%).

10 Comparable data from the HIS-study: 7.2% are not familiar with weblogs, 46.4% do not use them; the remaining 46.3% use them often (1.9%) to very seldom (24.6%). The mode is "never." Weblogs used as a method of study at the university according to the HIS-study: are not offered (55.6%), are never used (28.9%); use varies between very often (0.3%) and very rarely (6.2%).

11 Comparable data from the HIS-study for Wikipedia: 60% use Wikipedia often and 40% seldom, but only 0.2% are not familiar with it, and 0.7% do not use it. HIS specifically inquired about domain specific Wikis: 5.8% are not familiar with them, 16.4% do not use them; only 3.9% use them often and 24.3% very seldom. Wikis are not offered for university courses 49%, are not used 20.8%; the use varies between very often (1.7%) and very seldom (6.8%).

Chapter 3

How to Improve Media Literacy and Media Skills of Secondary School Teachers in Order to Prepare Them for the Next Generation of Learners:

A New Type of In-Service Training for Teachers

Silke Weiß
Institute of Didactics of Chemistry, Germany

Hans Joachim Bader
Institute of Didactics of Chemistry, Germany

ABSTRACT

Students in schools should acquire media literacy, and the development of new media can promote self-directed learning and so enhance the quality of the learning process. It has been assumed that teachers lack sufficient media literacy. Therefore, we developed a new chemistry teacher in-service training based on blended-learning. These courses should familiarize teachers with the application of new media and acquaint them with their students' world, the world of the so-called "digital natives". Three studies were performed to explore its acceptability, suitability and effectiveness. Participants' ratings on self-report measures of self-rated skills and perceived competence improved significantly after the training. Participants had more favorable attitudes towards the use of electronic media than subjects from a control group. Among participants the attitudinal measure "perceived competence" predicted the use of blended-learning at 6-month follow up. It is concluded that attitudes play an important role for promoting teachers' media literacy and their intention to apply new media in teaching. In addition to training programs focusing on skills and knowledge, future interventions should target on teachers attitudes.

DOI: 10.4018/978-1-61520-678-0.ch003

INTRODUCTION

In the call for papers for this book there is an appeal to teach children how to cooperate worldwide. How can this be achieved in an ordinary secondary school if teachers do not even know what a bulletin board is or how to send an email? There is a difference between the demands and the reality.

This can be seen in the huge gap between the possibilities new media provide and the actual competences teachers have to use them in the classroom. It is often said in our school system that teachers ("digital immigrants") and learners ("digital natives") seem to speak different languages and they no longer understand each other. Teachers are characterized in their strategies to acquire knowledge that are nowadays possibly no longer valid because their students are differently structured in their learning behaviour. This study asks if it is possible to change this situation by teachers´ in-service training which acts like an interpreter, translating from one language into the other and explaining the different learning behaviours. A new course-model was therefore created. We will describe what theoretical background leads to the new structure and how this new method of further training of teachers was created and tested.

One goal of this study is to explore chemistry teachers' attitudes towards blended-learning and the use of electronic media in chemistry lessons. The questions were: what kind of teachers participate, what is the acceptance of and what is the satisfaction with this new model? Also, there was the question: what are the predictors of teachers' e-learning usage?

One part of the study focused on the measurement of three different aspects of attitudes: perceived competence, emotional valence and perceived necessity which are tested if they can explain teachers behavior. *Perceived competence* refers to the teachers' self-rated competence in the use of electronic media. *emotional valence* refers to the teacher's feelings towards the use of electronic media. *Perceived necessity* refers to the teacher's rating of the necessity of the use of electronic media. It is assumed that attitudes are related to e-learning usage and the acceptability, suitability and effectiveness of interventions focusing on e-learning (Wen & Shih, 2008).

Altogether three studies are presented here. An insight of the results will be given.

BACKGROUND

Digital Natives and the New Teaching Paradigm

It is often said, that nowadays teachers mostly belong to the so called "digital immigrants" while their students belong to the "net-generation" or the "digital natives". Prensky formulated this concept:

Our students today are all "native speakers" of the digital language of computers, video games and the internet. (Prensky 2008a, p.1)

According to Prensky, the "digital native" receives information quickly, likes to network, is multitasking, prefers games to serious work, is motivated in learning but no longer willing to listen to lecturing teachers (Prensky 2008a).

In contrast, the "digital immigrant", who grew up without the omnipresence of new media, is used to working linearly, is rarely networking etc. and principally has different strategies to learning.

This concept has been criticised due to lack of empirical support (Schulmeister 2008) and todays´ students do not (yet) belong to this species (Ebner 2008). Nevertheless there is evidence that teachers and students differ in their use of electronic media. For example, 83% of young people believe that they could not live without the internet. Over 50% start the computer immediately they get home. Nearly 25% never switch off the internet. They meet each other in communities and have their own profiles there (Microsoft, MTV 2007). In comparison, teachers use the internet to prepare for their classes, use platforms to get material and information. They are typical Web 1- users (Michel 2008). Teachers and their learners use the internet and new technology for different reasons, but both rarely use it in school. Possible ubiquitous learning stops in front of the classroom.

Empirical data suggest that teaching and learning of topics in chemistry can be improved by the use of computer-assisted teaching materials (Eilks et al. 2004, Pietzner 2005, Pietzner & Schmidkunz 2006, p.11 ff, Özmen 2008). Despite substantial evidence of beneficial effects of the use of electronic media for educational purposes, only seven percent of chemistry teachers said they use computers in class more than once a month. ([N]onliner-atlas 2006).

Good lessons should not depend on the use of a particular kind of media. However, new media could help to develop a new kind of teaching by moving from a teacher-centered approach towards one which is learner-centered (Röll 2005). So working with new media a teacher risks losing the role of the dominating person in class because the computer skills of students are almost invariably far more advanced than those of their teachers, and this means losing authority and hence leads to anxiety. This can be seen as one reason why changes towards using new media are so slow:

But it seems that hardware and infrastructure are not the biggest barriers. The main difficulty is transforming teaching. (Jenkins 1999, p.3, see also Koistinen, K. 2000)

Another anxiety, so called "computer anxiety" leads to the avoidance of the use of computers, even if the means are given (Rosen & Weil 1995).

In our study two aspects related to "computer anxiety" are assessed using the attitudinal measures *"perceived competence"* and *"emotional valence"*.

Another fact is that learner's motivation and commitment seems to decrease, while an increasing number of teachers are suffering from psychological problems like burn-out syndrome, tinnitus or depression. Studies about the health of teachers reveal alarming results, for example, 88% of Bavarian teachers retire early. One reason which makes teaching such a stressful job is being centered on the attention of the students (Klippert 2006, p. 16 ff). So transform teacher-centered instruction to a more learner-centered process could be helpful for both sides, for the teachers to assume a new position in the learning process und so fulfill the demanded change in teaching paradigm (from the "sage on stage" to the "guide on the side" (Prensky 2008c, p.1). For students it is to acquire knowledge in a more constructive way.

A first step towards the new paradigm of learner-centered teaching in Germany (with or without new media) comes from the German ministry of education. It is a definition of competences (KMK 2004, Bildungsstandards Chemie 2005) instead of content-based qualifications formulated in the actual curriculum.

Teacher's Apprenticeship and In-Service Training and the Demands in School

Neither during studying at university, nor in traineeship (or in in-service training) for teachers new media plays an important role. In Germany, teacher-training and in-service training is not standardized. It is up to the individual's interest to acquire knowledge about new media, new skills and competencies. There are educational standards for the use of new media for students, but not for teachers. (For more information see Weiß & Bader, in press.)

To some small extend, education in this area nowadays takes place in university and traineeship, but rarely in in-service training. So, new teacher generations will be more and more familiar with new media. But teachers who are already in school have few possibilities to improve their knowledge. The question is: do students need teachers with a high level of media literacy? At the moment, they don't possess it, as Schorb (2007) states:

Generally, media literacy is a buzzword on everyone's lips, but it is not always available to everyone and its development is required first of all at the functional level, then in the mediation of technical skills. But neither can schools nor the education of teachers rely on the curriculum for its widespread uptake. (p. 17)

Another question is: why should children learn about new media in school rather than in their leisure time, like other hobbies? In fact, German students acquire their computer-skills mainly in their free time, not at school (Bildungsbericht 2006). But those skills are dependent on social class and the accessibility of computers. In comparison to upper class students, students from lower classes acquire a greater part of their computer skills at school. But school has to be a place where all students have the same chance to acquire media literacy, which is very important for their later professional life. When children do not have the possibility to gain this at school, this will lead to the disadvantage of lower class students.

Media Literacy

What kind of media literacy do teachers need? There are many different definitions of media literacy. Gapsky reports about 104 different ones in the time between 1996 and 2001! (Gapsky 2001)

The competence models of Tulodziecki and Moser reveal different fragments of competences concerning media literacy (Moser 2006, Tulodziecki 2007.) For example Tulodzieckis´ model distinguishes between 5 main competencies:

- choosing adequate media tools and using them
- creating own media productions and broadcasting them
- understanding compositions of new media and evaluating them
- realizing media's influences and dealing with them
- understanding conditions for publishing media productions and evaluating them

and every competence is subdivided in different levels that a person can achieve.

Fundamental knowledge about the basic issues belongs to a rather lower level than in these models. But this is what teachers often don't possess. They can't evaluate ways of communication when they never logged on to a chat room and do not even know how to do so.

A New Kind of Teachers' In-Service Training to Improve Chemistry Teachers' Media Literacy

One aim of these courses is to get teachers familiar with the use of new media. People who often use a computer are less anxious than those who use it rarely. By practicing computer skills, anxiety should decrease. This should increase the likelihood that computers will be more frequently used in class.

To achieve this, the developed in-service training course model uses structures with which the teachers of the digital immigration-generation are familiar. At the same time the participants practice modern working methods during the course. These courses were created in the "Lehrerfortbildungszentrum Frankfurt" (Centre of teacher in-service training), situated at the Institute of Didactics of Chemistry (http://www.chemiedidaktik.uni-frankfurt.de/index.html.) Here, "normal" in-service training consists of one to three laboratory-days dedicated to a special theme, e.g., pharmaceuticals or separation of substances. Usually the course begins with an introductory presentation on the topic to be covered. After this lead-in there is a practical phase in the laboratory where teachers can test school-experiments.

The new courses combine these elements with the integration of new media and parts of self-regulated learning. The idea is to swap teachers' classical, more-passive role to a more active one. They have to participate actively to acquire new knowledge constructively. By answering questions and fulfilling tasks by means of using new media tools, teachers can acclimatize to new technology. In a kind of protected room they can experiment and exchange experiences. The course can be seen in the same way as an interpreter, who translates some aspects of the new "language" of the students to that one of their teachers.

To improve the extrinsic motivation to participate in these courses, teachers can get a significant number of credit points for their portfolio. (For more detail see Weiß & Bader 2008.)

The Design of the Environments for Teachers´ In-Service Training

The teachers´ in-service training was designed as blended-learning courses with two attendance days and an intermediate online phase of 3-4 weeks.

The first day of attendance is one of familiarization, as it is important to get to know each other. Another blended-learning course in chemistry teachers' advanced training designed by Aljanazrah began with the online phase. In these courses, communication between participants and the tutor rarely took place during the online-phase and teachers justified this by saying that they did not feel comfortable communicating with someone they did not know (Aljanazrah & Bader 2006).

This day also serves to transfer information on how to work with the new tools. While here the "teacher" – the leader of the training - is in the centre, he disappears in the second part, the online phase. There he remains in the background, helps and solves technical problems and gives hints and feedback to the teachers' tasks. This way, he is assuming a new position in the progression of learning and the participants can experience this mode of teaching. Behind that is the hope that the teachers transfer this way of acquiring knowledge to their classrooms.

During the online-phase, participants receive information in form of specially created online modules with which they have to solve several tasks. New media tools or methods on how to work with the computer in the classroom are integrated, e.g. doing a webquest, or learning how to make an electronic mindmap. The participants do not learn about chatting, but they chat about what they have learned!

On the second attendance day, teachers can test experiments for school use, related to the topics of the course, for example "synthetic polymers" or "chemical equilibrium".

Tools for the courses were chosen for their intuitive handling, thus lowering the users' anxieties, for example, BSCW as the platform.

Five courses were created which have the same structure but different contents, methods, and tools. Four of them were content-based with chemistry-related topics combined with using new media. The themes of the courses are more or less relevant to the demands of the curriculum. The fifth course is called "Making Webquests". It has the same structure as the others but without a chemistry-related subject because the focus is on the method itself (information: http://www.lehrer-online.de/webquest-frankfurt.php and Weiß & Bader, 2007).

EXECUTION, EVALUATION AND RESULTS OF THE TREATMENT

Objectives

Three studies were performed to explore the acceptability, suitability and effectiveness of a new chemistry teacher in-service training model based on blended-learning.

The main objectives are:

1) To identify the obstacles preventing chemistry teachers from the use of electronic media in chemistry lessons and from participating in a blended-learning form of in-service training.
2) To identify the reasons explaining teachers' lack of use of electronic media in chemistry lessons and of the participation in a blended-learning in-service training.
3) To clarify the role of attitudes towards the use of electronic media and of self-rated skills in the use of electronic media in the prediction of the use of electronic media in chemistry lessons and the participation in a blended-learning in-service training.
4) To find out whether an in-service training based on blended-learning has beneficial effects on self-rated skills in the use of electronic media and on attitudes towards the use of electronic media in chemistry lessons.
5) To explore the participants' attitudes towards the blending-learning course including their acceptance of the course and their satisfaction with it.

First Study: Representativeness of the Treatment Sample Compared to Teachers from the General Population

Methods

The first study aimed to reveal whether the treatment sample is representative for the general population of chemistry teachers.

Samples

Two samples of chemistry teachers were compared on self-report measures of attitudes towards the use of electronic media, on self-rated skills in the use of new media and on sociodemographic variables. The first sample (further referred as "participants") comprises 127 participants of five different blended-learning courses of our new chemistry teacher in-service training program. (Data on the effectiveness of the intervention will be presented in the next section).

The second sample comprises chemistry teachers from the general population (further referred as "non-participants".) Questionnaires were sent to all heads of the chemistry departments at secondary schools in the federal state of Hessen via e-mail with the request to pass them on to all chemistry teachers in the school. The teachers were asked to fill them in and send them back. This took place in December 2007. Altogether 71 completed questionnaires from chemistry teachers were returned.

Measures

Self-rated skills in the use of electronic media were measured with several items covering the teachers' knowledge of e-learning-tools like bulletin boards, chat rooms, searching engines and learning-platforms. Each item was rated using a 6-point Likert scale ranging from 1 (extremely good) to 6 (extremely bad).

Attitudes towards the use of electronic media in chemistry lessons were assessed with 12 items measuring three different aspects: perceived competence, emotional valence and perceived necessity. Each item was rated using a 4-point Likert scale ranging from 1 (it doesn't apply at all) to 4 (it applies a lot).

A principal components analysis with varimax rotation was performed on these 12 items. This analysis revealed three factors with eigenvalues greater than 1 (4.63, 1.59, and 1.17), accounting for 61.6% of the total variance. To demonstrate good simple structure, only items that loaded over 0.50 on one factor and less than 0.50 on all other factors were assigned to factors. These items and their loadings are displayed in Table 2. The empirically derived scales have an acceptable internal consistency. The Cronbach's alphas for

Table 1. Group differences between participants and non-participants on items measuring self-rated skills in the use of electronic media: Sample size (n), Means (M), standard deviations (SD), and t-tests (t = t-value; df = degree of freedom, p = p-value), p values ≤ 0.05 are statistical significant Each item was rated using a 6-point Likert scale ranging from 1 (extremely good) to 6 (extremely bad)

Item		n	M	SD	t df	p
Bulletin board	Non-participants	68	4.41	1.48	1.355	0.177
	Participants	115	4.11	1.42	181	
Chat	Non-participants	69	4.48	1.44	0.624	0.534
	Participants	115	4.35	1.33	182	
Searching engines	Non-participants	71	2.20	0.92	-0.728	0.468
	Participants	120	2.29	.83	189	
Learning- platform	Non-participants	70	4.54	1.45	1.146	0.253
	Participants	116	4.30	1.35	186	

the scales were 0.81 (perceived competence), 0.75 (emotional valence), and 0.66 (perceived necessity).

Results

Independent samples t-tests showed that non-participants and participants did not differ on age (non-participants: M = 45.26; SD = 10.7; participants: M = 45.13; SD = 9,18) and years of service (non-participants: M = 17,25; SD = 11.00; participants: M = 14.79; SD = 10,83.) Chi-square tests showed no significant differences in the gender distribution of the two groups (non participants: 38 women, 32 men; participants: 72 women, 48 men.)

As table 1 shows, independent samples t-tests revealed no significant mean differences between the two groups on items measuring self-rated skills in the use of electronic media. From all e-learning-tools, both groups knew most about search engines and their use.

Table 2 shows the 12 items measuring attitudes towards the use of electronic media in chemistry lessons. The subscale *perceived competence* contained four items (Items 5, 6, 9, and 10), the subscale *emotional valence* contained four items (Items 1, 2, 3, and 7), and subscale *perceived necessity* contained three items (Items 4,11,12).

Independent samples t-tests revealed significant differences between participants and non-participants on the subscales "emotional valence" and "perceived necessity" (see Table 3). Participants accepted and valued the computer more than the non-participants.

The results of independent samples t-tests (data are omitted for the sake of brevity) show that participants and non-participants differ significantly on two items measuring the teachers' intention to use computers in the classroom and to use a computer for preparation of the lessons in the future. Participants had a greater intention than non-participants.

The effects of gender and age on teachers' attitudes towards the use of electronic media and self-rated skills in the use of electronic media were explored in further analyses:

Independent samples t-tests show significant differences between women and men on the subscales "perceived competence" and "perceived necessity". Men rate their competence higher and their ratings of the necessity of the use of electronic media in chemistry lessons are also higher.

Table 2. Attitudes towards the use of electronic media in chemistry lessons: Factor matrix following varimax rotation. 1 = item of subscale perceived competence 2 = item of subscale emotional valence, 3 = item of subscale perceived necessity

No. of Item		Factor loadings		
		Factor 1	Factor 2	Factor 3
1	Working with computers is a necessary evil [2]	-0.017	0.726	0.149
2	I use the internet for the preparation of my lessons [2]	-0.327	0.659	-0.021
3	The computer plays an important role for the preparation of my lessons [2]	0.363	0.680	0.156
4	The computer plays an important role in my lessons [3]	0.376	0.246	0.540
5	By working with computers I feel competent [1]	0.577	0.483	0.132
6	My students are more self-confident using computers than I am [1]	0.853	0.073	0.139
7	I find working with computers amusing [2]	0.069	0.758	0.226
8	I like to work with my students on the internet	0.366	0.465	0.458
9	I feel competent working on the internet [1]	0.681	0.353	0.026
10	My students are more self-confident using the internet than I am [1]	0.859	0.055	0.037
11	The computer is out of place in an experimentally-orientated subject like chemistry [3]	0.071	0.150	0.755
12	Lessons involving computers have the same status as traditional chemistry lessons [3]	-0.059	0.048	0.854

Age correlates significantly with perceived knowledge of the use of bulletin boards ($r^1 = 0.28$), chat ($r = 0.33$), searching engines ($r = 0.15$) and learning-platforms ($r = 0.22$). Younger subjects rate their knowledge more favourably. Age is also related to perceived competence ($r = -0.31$) and "emotional valence" ($r = -0.26$). Younger subjects rate their competence higher and have more positive feelings towards the use of electronic media than older subjects.

Second Study: Evaluation of the In-Service Training with Blended-Learning Courses with Questionnaires and Interviews

Methods

Five different blended-learning courses were offered to chemistry teachers in Hessen and Niedersachsen (two federal states of Germany)

Table 3. Group differences between participants and non-participants on scales measuring attitudes towards the use of electronic media in chemistry lessons: Sample size (n), Means (M), standard deviations (SD), and t-tests (t = t-value; df = degree of freedom, p = p-value), p-values ≤ 0.05 are statistical significant

Subscale		n	M	SD	t df	p
perceived competence	Non-participants	61	10.60	2.57	0.448	0.665
	Participants	111	10.43	2.25	176	
emotional valence	Non-participants	61	12.54	2.64	-2.454	0.015
	Participants	111	13.42	2.11	176	
perceived necessity	Non-participants	61	7.29	1,63	-3.814	0.000
	Participants	111	8.18	1.43	176	

between May 2006 and July 2008. There was not a call for a specific group of participants to get an impression of the general appreciation of these topics. Questionnaires for all courses were designed with a similar structure, varying only in the questions about the certain topics and tools used in different courses. There was a pre-, post- and follow-up- questionnaire. Besides general demographic data, the participants were asked for attitudes towards new media and their further plans to use it.

The participants completed the first questionnaire (Measurement time T1; pre-questionnaire) at the first attendance day before the course started. The second one (Measurement time T2; post-questionnaire) they filled in at the end of the second attendance day. After 6 months the third one (Measurement time T3, follow-up questionnaire) was sent to their home-addresses with a self-addressed envelope. The responses were always anonymous. The questionnaires were quantitatively analyzed. The results refer to self-estimated data, because compiling a test from a teachers' in-service training course is not normal and there is the danger, that teachers would not attend such a course. The perceived competence in this case is very important because the application of new media depends on one's own self-confidence.

Interviews concerning the course were conducted with participants at the second attendance day. They were chosen randomly and the participation was voluntary. These interviews were transliterated and evaluated qualitatively.

Results

General Data

Altogether 14 blended-learning in-service training sessions took place in Hessen between May 2006 and July 2008 with a total of 127 participants, age 26 - 62, 60% women and 40% men. In Niedersachsen all courses were cancelled because there were not enough registrations. Many courses in Hessen also didn't take place, especially from the beginning of 2008. The cancelled courses were basically those without direct relation to the curriculum's obligatory contents, e.g. "renewable primary products". The course with the subject "chemical equilibrium" on the other hand, received sufficient participants every time. The 23 interviews from the second day of attendance completed the evaluation of the courses in a qualitative way.

Quantitative Results

Table 4 shows the difference of self-rated skills and attitudes towards new media before and after the treatment.

The teachers' expectations were fulfilled and the teachers attested a general improvement of their knowledge about media tools and their media literacy. They were satisfied with the results (see below table 5).

At the same time they attest immense workload and amounts of time they had to invest as it is shown in table 6. There was an intensive deal with the subjects.

Further analyses tested whether attitudes towards the use of electronic media predict the teachers' intention to use computers in lessons.

There were significant correlations between "emotional valence" (time of measurement: after the training T2) and

- the intention to use the computer in future chemistry lessons (time of measurement: after the training T2).
- the intention to use the computer for the preparation of lessons ($r = 0.22$, time of measurement: after the training T2).
- the motivation to use new media in the future ($r = 0.29$, time of measurement: after the training T2).

"Perceived competence" predicted the application of blended-learning during chemistry lessons at the 6–month follow-up ($r = 0.43$). Teachers with

Table 4. Changes of self-rated skills in the use of new media and attitudes towards the use of new media in chemistry lessons. Means (M), standard deviations (SD), and t-tests (t = t-value; df = degree of freedom, p = p-value), p-values ≤ 0,05 are statistical significant.

Item/Subscale	Time of measurement	M	SD	t df	P
Bulletin board	T1	4.18	1.47	9.737	0.000
(self-rated skills)	T2	2.58	0.95	77	
Chat	T1	4.44	1.41	10.236	0.000
(self-rated skills)	T2	2.93	1.08	79	
Search engines	T1	2.33	0.83	5.640	0.000
(self-rated skills)	T2	1.95	0.67	83	
Learning- platform	T1	4.32	1.34	11.678	0.000
(self-rated skills)	T2	2.55	0.80	77	
perceived competence	T1	10.49	2.34	-3.094	0.003
(attitudes subscale)	T2	11.09	2.51	75	
emotional valence	T1	13.50	2.19	-1.246	0.216
(attitudes subscale)	T2	13.73	2.31	79	
perceived necessity	T1	8.09	1.45	-1.180	0.242
(attitudes subscale)	T2	8.27	1.31	66	

Measurements were taken at the beginning and at the end of the in-service training programs.
T1 = before training, T2 = after training.

a high level of perceived competence answered in the follow-up-questionnaire that they have worked with their students in a blended-learning-mode.

But in general, the subjects of a blended-learning-course who deal with new media were applied rarely (in comparison to the experiments they also got to know). As reasons for the non-application of the new elements in class they claimed the lack of equipment in their schools. Also they often didn't have the chance because they didn't teach the right class for this in the meantime.

Table 5. Statistical frequencies (%) of the responses towards items concerning the results of the in-service training

	it doesn´t apply at all (%)	it doesn't apply much (%)	it applies to some degree (%)	it applies a lot (%)
My media literacy has improved	1,9	4,9	53,4	39,8
The advanced training motivated me to work more with new media	3,9	9,7	50,5	35,9
I´m satisfied with the results of the advanced training.	1	5	65,3	28,7
I want to work increasingly with computers with my students	3,9	10,8	67,6	17,6
I want to use the computer more for the preparation of my lessons	4,9	14,7	55,9	24,5

Table 6. Statistical frequencies (%) of the responses towards items concerning the workload in the in-service training

	it doesn´t apply at all (%)	it doesn´t apply much (%)	it applies to some degree (%)	it applies a lot (%)
I had to work hard work for my credit points	5,1	18,2	46,5	30,3
The advanced training was labour-intensive for me	1	15,7	49	34,3

Qualitative Results

In the following, some answers in the interviews at the end of the second attendance day are reported. Concerning the structure of the courses and the used methods, the participants mentioned in the interviews:

This structure, first the attendance day, then the online-phase and then another attendance day, is actually super, because at the first attendance day we got to know each other and we developed a relationship.

Of course it was more work than "classic" teacher in-service training [...]. Because we didn't get everything prepared, we had to be more involved with the subject.

In the courses, the participants were communicating via the platform and began to take a liking to networking and using electronic media!

Actually, the bulletin board was really helpful. We exchanged experiences...

My confidence concerning the use of computers, I would say, it is at best middle rate. Yes, and it took quite a while to get used to it. But I've learned a lot. I really know now at the end how to deal with the program, how to post something on a bulletin board.

In our school, we have Kappenberg (a data-logging system, annotation of translator), which I discovered accidentally, but nobody knows how to work with it. And now I´m willing to get it started.

On the second attendance day, the teachers already had doubts concerning the application and gave reasons as to why they probably won't use their new skills in a classroom.

I got to know about additional media through the Webquest, and the chat room was also very interesting. But I have doubts that I will be able to apply it, because the technical equipment in our school and at home isn't very good.

And the other thing, concerning E-Learning and Webquest, that will surely take more time, I daren't take the risk. I need to look for more teacher-training, if I am going to participate in this area.

Teachers were asked about their opinion as to why the interest in such blended-learning courses is apparently low. The following citation is a typical example:

I think the main issue is that teachers are "lone warriors" and not used to working in groups. And everyone is working for himself and there are many older colleagues that are practically afraid of computers.

(All results will be published in the doctoral dissertation of Silke Weiß.)

Third Study: Interview-Study Concerning the Acceptance of the Blended-Learning Course Model

Methods

The interview-study concerning the acceptance took place between October 2007 and July 2008. The interview partners were chosen randomly from participants of "classical" courses at the Lehrerfortbildungszentrum and were asked for voluntary participation. The participating teachers in this study could be characterized as those who were generally interested in teachers′ in-service training because they were doing one at the time the interview was taken. But they are not automatically interested in blended-learning courses. There was a qualitative and quantitative analysis.

The participants were asked general questions about their habits about how they prepare for their classes, their preferences for in-service training organisations, the importance of new media in their classes and their knowledge about blended-learning. Then they got a text about the organisation of the blended-learning teacher-training and were asked about the concept.

Results

The interview-study concerning acceptance of these courses contains 21 interviews. In the following, the number of mentions to the questions in the half open interviews are presented.

Criteria of choice of content for their classes

- curriculum named first (17 teachers)
- orientation on students′ interest (14)
- orientation on relation to everyday-life (10)
- personal interests (2).

Media used for preparation:

- internet (14)
- schoolbooks (12)
- didactic material like special journals or worksheets (12)
- textbooks (11)

New media plays a role in classes (21)

- low priority (10)
- higher level of significance (4)
- priority not specified (7)

Advantages of new media:

- utilization for homework (6)
- motivation for students (4)
- better visualization (3)
- better comprehensibility (2)

Reasons for non-application of new media:

- equipment (12)
- lack of knowledge (6)
- lacking acceptance/necessity (6)
- bad correlation between time and usefulness (4)
- lacking support (4)
- being frustrated (4)
- being anxious (4)
- lacking interest (2)

Reasons for choosing a certain form of teacher-training:

- possibility for the direct implementation in class (18)
- interesting content (10)
- location (7)
- focus on laboratory-work/experiments (6)
- receipt of credit-points (2)

Reasons for non-participation

- personal overload (8)
- lack of permission (4).

Content for future teacher training to be

- chemical content (16)
- new media (7).

Preconditions one should have before participating a blended-learning-course

- good computer-knowledge (14)
- good equipment (6)
- interest (5)

Advantages of a blended-learning course

- flexible working time (12
- more intensive training (9)
- better learning effects (7)
- individuality (5).

The disadvantages were named mostly as higher workload at home (9).

Teachers were asked if they were familiar with the term "blended-learning and 19 teachers confirmed, yes. Only 4 teachers had ever attended a blended-learning-course, but they all agreed that they would do it again. Of the 17 teachers who had not yet attended, 14 indicated a willing interest to participate.

After the presentation of the blended-learning course concept, 10 teachers evaluated it as good or very good (8: good, 2: very good). 14 Teachers appreciated the combination between chemical themes and methods.

Concerning the use of new media, 11 participants gave some critical responses. The use is seen critically, especially in comparison with the use of experiments. In 7 Interviews, the participants expressed the opinion that in chemistry lessons, the experiment has a favoured position over the use of computers.

(...) I prefer using computers in other subjects, because in chemistry experiments, working with real glassware is much more important.

And secondly, as a chemistry teacher I'm lucky when I'm able to do an experiment. That means, if I had the choice between use of a computer and an experiment, I'd choose the experiment.

DISCUSSION

As seen in the results of the questionnaires and the interviews, participants were satisfied with the courses and their increase of knowledge. At the same time, they had a large workload what can be a reason for the former. A positive correlation between perceived competence and the use is shown, so it seems to be a precondition. This result fits together with studies of Sun and Liaw. Mounting evidence shows the important role of attitudes in predicting and improving the use of e-learning (Sun et al. 2008). Liaw showed that perceived enjoyment of e-learning, perceived usefulness and perceived self-efficacy are positively related to the behavioural intention to use e-learning (Liaw et al. 2007). The measured hypothetical constructs of perceived competence, emotional valence and perceived necessity share many similarities with the constructs of perceived self-efficacy and perceived usefulness.

Although the teachers were willing to, they often did not apply their new skills in class. There are several reasons, but the period of six months is perhaps too short to make a final statement. Such changes will take more time.

In the interviews with the participants another reason for non-application came to light: they want to become more confident with the handling of new media before using them with students. For the teachers are familiar with "telling and testing", being the most competent person in the taught subject is normal. But when it comes to media literacy, they are about to lose this race with their much more skilled students as mentioned above. Here it is the risk that they draw back from the use of new media and focus on more traditional methods instead.

Despite the general satisfaction, many courses did not take place due to insufficient registrations. In Niedersachsen, all courses were cancelled. In Hessen those without direct relation to the curriculum were also cancelled. One reason for the difference of these two states in Germany might be that teachers´ in-service training became obligatory for teachers in Hessen (from 2005 - 2008). In Niedersachsen there was no obligation.

The course "chemical equilibrium" which always took place deals with an obligatory subject in the final two years at grammar school. The introduction of the "Zentralabitur" (centralized A-Levels) in Hessen seems to force the teachers to focus on the curriculum's main subjects. According to this, in the interviews concerning the acceptance, 81% of the teachers questioned replied that the main criterion for picking the content for teaching is focusing on the national curriculum's content. Therefore they select their courses by the criteria of their direct applicability in class - and not their personal interests.

Another issue is the rising need for a great variety of advanced training sessions as a result of the many reforms that took place during the last few years. Media literacy is only one of these many topics. Schools have increased their workload by taking on more responsibilities. Participating in a time-consuming blended-learning course might just be the extra workload teachers are not willing to take on. The great workload at home is a perceived disadvantage of a blended-learning course.

The comparative survey concerning media literacy reveals that most teachers who participate in our courses already have a positive attitude towards new media in which they differ from the compared group of non-participants. This raises the question: how we can reach the others who do not share this attitude? Or how to work on the teachers´ attitude, as a positive emotional value is related to the further plans of using computers in class.

FUTURE RESEARCH DIRECTIONS

As the results show, the direct possibility to implement the subjects in chemical classes is important. For further courses, this means that the chemical topics have to be related to the curriculum if teachers are to become more interested.

With the results of the represented study, final statements about the application in class or the change of teaching in general cannot be made. For this, there has to be a study in which teachers were accompanied for a longer time after their participation in the course.

In Hessen, now that teachers' in-service training is no longer mandatory, participation in in-service training is again voluntary, as is the case in most other federal states.

It would be helpful to augment extrinsic motivation. Here in Frankfurt, a concept of a media literacy certificate will be developed. Tasks for gaining this certificate can spread throughout the entire teachers' education. Perhaps, Moser's and Tulodeziecki's models for media literacy competencies can help in defining certain levels of competence.

Support from institutional sources would also be helpful. Emphasizing more significance on new media, or mandatory advanced training in this sector would be welcomed from our side. Giving teachers more time and releasing them from some of their workload to give them the opportunity for participating in advanced training would be an improvement as well. If learning new media skills is an extra workload for teachers, motivation will be reduced to some extent. This could be tested in a pilot scheme.

One needs to consider how to influence attitudes towards new media, for this is the reason to participate in the in-service training and also a precondition for further use in the classroom. Participation in in-service training is up to the participant's personal interests. But as mentioned above, the personal interests are restricted by the needs of the curriculum. A fundamental problem concerning the curriculum and working with new media and using learner-based methods is that there is no correlation between them. New media are predestined for self-centered learning. This is also demanded by the new "Bildungsstandards", so called "educational standards" in Germany, which are supposed to replace the national curriculum at some stage in the future. But the valid curriculum provides the criteria for learning according to the old teaching paradigm of telling and testing. So there is the problem of no correspondence between new directions in education and possibilities for realizing them in school. When taking their final exams, the German "Abitur" (A-Level), students are still asked for information and knowledge, not for competencies - in most parts of the final exam. New forms of exam where students do not only show what they have learned, but also present their working progress, why they chose certain topics etc are coming up. Here self-reflection abilities are a part of, and competencies begin to play a role in grading. This has to be more transparent for teachers, in all phases of their education.

There is a need to develop new learning methods, which emphasize learning together and from each other. Teachers and students, trainee teachers and students, teachers and students, students and students, they should all find ways to learn from each other in a cooperative way, in universities as well as in schools. These methods may create less stressful jobs for teachers. This development might lead to an improvement of the health of teachers, which is discussed (and is of concern) nationwide. Even though Klippert illuminates reasons which led to the current situation and how teachers can reduce their workload by using less teacher-centered methods, he does not mention new media and its possible use as a significant possibility in helping to deal with this situation. At the moment, we are developing a new kind of teacher-training, dealing with the classical role that teachers play in school and the anxieties they possess to change it in order to raise the awareness of this problem.

To underline the discussion about the importance to let students participate in the process of establish new media in school, some research should focus on their opinion how the situation can be improved.

The developed in-service training is still offered with certain modifications. It is planned to expand the courses from those interested volunteers to students and teacher-training as well. In the "Projekt Lehr@mt"[2],) a teacher-training which combines different phases is being developed. Teachers, trainee teachers and university students should be learning together with new media and practising networking. Additionally, with "Lehrer-online" (http://www.lehrer-online.de) it is planned to build a platform for all chemistry teachers in all phases that allows exchange of materials and experiences.

CONCLUSION

Above, it is asked whether students need media-literate teachers. I think, the answer is "yes!", to a certain degree. That means to educate and train teachers in all phases (studies, traineeship, further training) to improve their media competence. To reach them, some possibilities are discussed above. But that will not be enough; training of teachers alone can not guarantee success. The number of trainers and training sessions, and also the resource of time are all insufficient. Since the development of new media is so fast, there would be a permanent lack of in-service training.

It's infeasible to educate teachers in order to make them the most competent person in class concerning new media before they allow it in their classrooms. To deal with this problem, teachers have to adopt a new self-image of the teacher's role. Letting students work independently with new media means losing control over them to some extent. We have to work on teachers´ illusion that traditional teaching means having everything under control or have more disciplined classes.

Their reluctant attitude has to be replaced with an open-minded one. It's time to learn how to learn from our students and with our students. This can be a winning situation for both sides. Whether teachers are improving their media literacy together or with their students, in-service training is taking place on a day-to-day basis. This everyday use cannot be provided by teacher-training alone. Lifelong learning becomes a new significance for teachers, lifelong learning in the classroom! And so, ubiquitous learning becomes a new dimension.

We think, for the future, we have to focus more on the general change of the attitude towards new media, as it seems to be an important factor, if teachers are willing to expand their knowledge - or not. To continue with our courses can be seen as a first step. We are creating space where teachers can experience on their own how much fun self-directed learning with new media can be. We also hope that these teachers will use their newly-acquired techniques in class, if not today, then maybe soon.

REFERENCES

Aljanazrah, A. M., & Bader, H. J. (2006). Chemielehrerfortbildung durch E-Learning und Labortag – Entwicklung, Erprobung und erste Erfahrungen. *CHEMKON*, *13*(2), 69. doi:10.1002/ckon.200610040

Bildungsbericht2006: Bildung in Deutschland, 2. nationaler Bildungsbericht. (n.d.). Retrieved October 23, 2008, from http://www.bildungsbericht.de/zeigen.html?seite=6129

Bildungsstandards Chemie. (2005). Retrieved October 25, 2009, from http://www.kmk.org/fileadmin/veroeffentlichungen_beschluesse/2004/2004_12_16-Bildungsstandards-Chemie.pdf

Ebner, M. (2008). *Has the net-generation arrived at the university? - oder der Student von Heute, ein digital native?* Retrieved October 25, 2009, from http://lamp.tu-graz.ac.at/~i203/ebner/publication/08_gmw.pdf

Eilks, I., Krilla, B., Flintjer, B., Möllencamp, H., & Wagner, W. (2004). *Computer und Multimedia im Chemieunterricht heute - Eine Einordnung aus didaktischer und lerntheoretischer Sicht*. Retrieved October 25, 2009, from http://www.uni-muenster.de/imperia/md/content/didaktik_der_chemie/computerkurs/fachgruppe_chemieunterricht___stellungnahme.pdf

Gapski, H. (2001). *Medienkompetenz: Eine Bestandsaufnahme und Vorüberlegungen zu einem systemtheoretischen Rahmenkonzept*. Wiesbaden, Germany: Westdeutscher. Verl.

Jenkins, J. (1999). *Teaching for tomorrow: The changing role of teachers in the connected classroom*. Retrieved October 25, 2009, from http://www.eden-online.org/papers/jenkins.pdf

Klippert, H. (2007). *Lehrerentlastung: Strategien zur wirksamen Arbeitserleichterung in Schule und Unterricht*. Weinheim, Germany: Beltz Verl.

KMK. (2004). *Standards für die Lehrerbildung: Bildungswissenschaften*. Retrieved October 25, 2009 from http://download.bildung.hessen.de/lakk/stsem_gym/fulda/modul/standards_lehrerbildung.pdf

Koistinen, K. (2002). Towards virtual academy – teacher's changing role. In *FIG XXII International Congress, TS2.4, Virtual Academy and New Teaching and Learning Methods*. Retrieved October 25, 2009, from http://www.fig.net/pub/fig_2002/Ts2-4/TS2_4_koistinen.pdf

Liaw, S.-S. (2007). An activity-theoretical approach to investigate learners' factors toward e-learning systems. *Computers in Human Behavior*, *23*, 1909–1920.

Michel, L. (2008). Digitale Schule – wie Lehrer Angebote im Internet nutzen: Eine Bestandsaufnahme im Auftrag des Bundesministeriums für Bildung und Forschung (BMBF). *MMB-Institut für Medien- und Kompetenzforschung, Essen.* Retrieved October 25, 2009, from http://www.dlr.de/pt/Portaldata/45/Resources/dokumente/bildungsforschung/MMB_Veroeffentlichung_Lehrer_Online_20080505_final.pdf

Microsoft, & MTV. (2007). *Circuits of Cool - Germany*. Retrieved October 25, 2009, from http://www.viacombrandsolutions.de/de/research/studien/national/index.html

Moser, H. (2006). Standards für die Medienbildung . *Computer & Unterricht*, *16-18*(63), 49–55.

(N)ONLINER Atlas. (2006). *Lehre oder Leere?* Retrieved January 30, 2009, from http://www.nonliner-atlas.de/

Özmen, H. (2008). The influence of computer-assisted instruction on students' conceptual understanding of chemical bonding and attitude toward chemistry: A case for Turkey. *Computers & Education*, *51*, 423–438. doi:10.1016/j.compedu.2007.06.002

Pietzner, V., & Lutz, B. (2005). Themenheft Lernen mit dem Computer, *Naturwissenschaften im Unterricht – Chemie*, 16 (90).

Pietzner, V., & Schmidkunz, H. (2006). *Computer im Chemieunterricht: Eine praxisorientierte Einführung*. Köln, Germany: Aulis-Verl. Deubner.

Prensky, M. (2008a). *Digital natives, digital immigrants, part I*. Retrieved October 25, 2009, from http://www.marcprensky.com/writing/Prensky%20-%20Digital%20Natives,%20Digital%20Immigrants%20-%20Part1.pdf

Prensky, M. (2008c). *The role of technology in teaching and the classroom: They got gameplay*. Retrieved October 25, 2009, from http://www.marcprensky.com/writing/Prensky-The_Role_of_Technology-ET-11-12-08.pdf

Röll, F. J. (2005). Hinweise zur Notwendigkeit einer neuen Lernkultur. *Seelsorge - Ergebnisse aus Sozialwissenschaft und Theologie*, (2), 2–6.

Rosen, L. D., & Weil, M. M. (1995). Computer availability, computer experience and technophobia among public school teachers. *Computers in Human Behavior*, *11*(1), 9–31. doi:10.1016/0747-5632(94)00018-D

Schorb, B. (2007). *Mit eLearning zu Medienkompetenz: Modelle für Curriculumgestaltung, Didaktik und Kooperation* (Vol. 2). München, Germany: Kopaed Verl.

Schulmeister, R. (2008). *Gibt es eine Net Generation? Version 2.0*. Retrieved Oktober, 25, 2009, from http://www.zhw.uni-hamburg.de/uploads/schulmeister-net-generation_v2.pdf

Sun, P.-C. (2008). What drives a successful e-Learning? An empirical investigation of the critical factors influencing learner satisfaction. *Computers & Education*, *50*, 1183–1202. doi:10.1016/j.compedu.2006.11.007

Tulodziecki, G. (2007): Entwicklung eines Kompetenzmodells für die Medienbildung - Grundlagen für die Formulierung von Bildungsstandards. *Computer & Unterricht*,(65), 50-54.

Weiß, S. (n.d.). *Blended-Learning Kurse in der Chemielehrerfortbildung zur Erhöhung der Medienkompetenz*. Unpublished doctoral dissertation, University of Frankfurt, Germany.

Weiß, S., & Bader, H.J.(2007). Wie kommen WebQuests in den Chemieunterricht? Erfolgreiche Ansätze in der Lehrerfortbildung. *Computer & Unterricht*, (67), 52-53.

Weiß, S., & Bader, H. J. (2008). Mehr Medienkompetenz für Chemielehrer: Das Drei-Fliegen-Konzept. In D. Höttecke (Ed.), *Kompetenzen, Kompetenzmodelle, Kompetenzentwicklung: Jahrestagung in Essen* (Vol. 28). Münster, Germany: LIT-Verl.

Weiß, S., & Bader, H. J. (in press). Wodurch erwerben Lehrkräfte Medienkompetenz? Auf der Suche nach geeigneten Fortbildungsmodellen. *Jahrbuch Medienpädagogik, 8*, Germany . *VS Verl.*

Wen, J. R., & Shih, W. L. (2008). Exploring the information literacy competence standards for elementary and high school teachers. *Computers & Education, 50*(3), 787–806. doi:10.1016/j.compedu.2006.08.011

ENDNOTES

1 r = correlation coefficient

2 Cooperation between the University of Frankfurt and the AfL (Amt für Lehrerbildung, department for teacher training). This project aims to support media literacy during all phases of teacher training and to enable the different institutes of teachers´ education to cooperate.

Chapter 4
Navigation and Visualisation Techniques in eLearning and Internet Research

Sue Fenley
University of Oxford, UK

ABSTRACT

Research into investigating how users navigate through internet and multimedia resources in an educational context has revealed distinct preferences in how they approach the resource, their methods of interrogating it and both the quantity and quality of the information they obtain. Using highly sophisticated software even for digital natives involves learning a series of methods or techniques for easily manoeuvring through the vast quantities of data and developing schemas to do this efficiently and accurately. This chapter analyses methods that have been used for navigating through multimedia packages, explores users' preferences for navigation and visualisation, investigates design errors in multimedia that prevent good navigation and details newer visualisation methods and navigational tools. The chapter should give educational users a fresh perspective of issues of navigation and visualisation and allow them to develop these techniques in order to improve their use of internet and web resources and teaching materials.

INTRODUCTION

This chapter reports on the observational sessions of users individual preferences using multimedia and online resources. It investigates how they chose to move through the software, their choices and options and how these are related to their methods of working and ways of learning. Allowing the students access to the methods that have been used, and compiling this into a predictable tool, is valuable and may allow students to use their preferred method(s) through a number of similar resources without having to relearn new tools or methods. Linking these methods to an intelligent tutor or agent will permit this knowledge to be used both by other students but also by academic staff to deliver courses, and to view students' progress. This would also help the course developer as knowing which sections of

DOI: 10.4018/978-1-61520-678-0.ch004

the resource are most used, gives an indication of which should be updated first and which can be discarded or updated less frequently.

The chapter analyses a series of tools for navigation and visualisation and supports the provision of a toolkit of specified navigational components for use both by educationalists and by designers for internet and multimedia resources.

The aim of the chapter is to investigate navigational patterns employed by users while exploring multimedia and internet resources. The objectives of the chapter are:

- to see how these navigation patterns affect the learning potential of the resources,
- to investigate which navigational patterns digital natives use,
- to find the most beneficial methods of utilising the resource,
- to encourage the use of newer or more efficient methods of navigating within resources,
- to promote a toolkit of specified navigational tools as a transferable toolkit or palette for users,
- To demonstrate how visualisation techniques can inform users, tutors and software designers of the methods that have been used to interrogate resources.

The chapter commences with a short background section on previous research in this area. Then the five key issues of audit trails, navigational patterns, navigational tools, newer tools and design issues are discussed in detail. This last issue here briefly details some of the problems encountered in multimedia in order to give readers an understanding of the type of issues that occur in digital resources. The next solutions and recommendations section looks at intelligent tutors and network maps/charts before exploring visualisation techniques that can both demonstrate and compare different methods of navigation. This is followed by an investigation of future research directions and a short conclusions section.

BACKGROUND

Digital Natives Research

The Digital natives debate was started by Prensky in 2001 when he stated that the Digital Natives had "spent their entire lives surrounded by and using computers, videogames, digital music players, video cams, cell phones, and all the other toys and tools of the digital age" (Prensky, 2001, p.1). Prensky proposed that the Natives exposure to digital culture and environment had changed the way they think: "It is now clear that as a result of this ubiquitous environment and the sheer volume of their interaction with it, today's students think and process information fundamentally differently from their predecessors." (p.1). Prensky's digital natives are meant to: prefer receiving information quickly; be adept at processing information rapidly; prefer multi-tasking and non-linear access to information; have a low tolerance for lectures; prefer active rather than passive learning, and rely heavily on communications technologies to access information and to carry out social and professional interactions.

Prensky also had a view on these student's educators, terming them Digital Immigrants – foreigners in the land of the Net Generation. Prensky's view, which has been supported by other researchers such as Oblinger (2003) and earlier work by Frand (2000) along the same lines, that educators need to adjust their pedagogical models to suit these new kinds of learners. Students according to Prensky are already "adopting new systems for communicating (instant messaging), sharing (blogs), buying and selling (eBay), exchanging (peer-to-peer technology), creating (Flash), meeting (3D worlds), collecting (downloads), coordinating (wikis), evaluating (reputation systems), searching (Google), analysing (SETI), reporting (camera phones), programming (modding), socialising (chat rooms), and even learning (Web surfing)" (p8).

Many researchers are now harnessing the technologies that students are finding more comfortable. These include the expected mobile technologies, social networking software such as Facebook and MySpace, sharing digital files and web usage. However, the information on producing (rather than reading) blogs, RSS feeds usage, and conferencing is more variable and may have different skill levels. It is arguable that students would have better skills at the social software and less developed skills with the more work/education oriented systems such as virtual learning environments, immersive environments, virtual reality, role play, strategy games (such as economic modellers), interviewing skills and intelligent tutors. If Prensky is to be followed completely we as educators may overestimate the abilities and skills of the Digital Natives and their skill at accessing and manipulating software which may camouflage their reduced ability to understand and be creative within a totally new environment. Having the prior knowledge of a range of software may though lessen the learning curve and enable rapid uptake of any new technology, and students may not necessarily judge which technology is best for a specific purpose or to be able to assess how useful a new technology is for a specific educational activity.

Incoming university students are using and reading blogs, are taking photos with their mobile phones, are regularly using social networking software such as *MySpace*, are communicating via web conferencing, and are sharing all sorts of digital files using both their mobile phones and the web. The question of whether students who use a particular technology in their everyday lives also want to use it in their studies was also discussed. For some emerging technologies (blogs, instant messaging, texting, social networking, RSS feeds and downloading MP3s) the answer is positive. However, 'early adopters' who extensively use non-educational purposes may also consider that these same technologies as have a wider education value, while more limited users may fail to see potential uses. It is also difficult to expect students to have the expertise to judge how to best use emerging technologies for educational purposes

Navigational Patterns Research

Research undertaken by Horney (1993), and Canter, River and Storrs (1985), both recorded and discussed the navigational paths of individual users. Research by Simpson and McKnight (1990) on how users preferred to navigate looked at different structures within a hypertext system. They varied the structures and cues for the subjects from alphabetical indexing to hierarchical structuring, using typographical cues and giving provision for position indicators. Their results showed users had preferences for hierarchies. When researching different navigation methods, Henderson (1993) commented that the prevalent characteristic of the modern worldview was the dependence on the conceptual view of information as being hierarchical, and that this conflicted with an alternative conceptual view, that of time, which produced a linear and sequential pattern. It was this dichotomy that Henderson considered made the investigation of multimedia packages more difficult, as users wanted to use the resource hierarchically, but moved through it sequentially. The user's perspective and gradual acquisition of navigational skills and awareness were emphasised by McKnight, Dillon and Richardson (1990): "Acquisition of navigational knowledge proceeds through several development phases from the initial identification of landmarks in the environment to a fully formed mental map" (p.69).

Horney (1993) investigated hypertext by looking at the individual user's experiences and describing the navigational patterns that emerged. These users or authors (as Horney referred to them) were creating hypertext and were experts or competent users of the system, but Horney investigated how they used the software and the patterns these experts had chosen to use. His work mitigated the lack of research on differences in novice and expert behaviour in multimedia and methods of analysing these, as he used experts but defined a very specific method of tracking users, which could be used in further research. Horney employed a software program that allowed each user's exact route to be recorded. Horney stated: "Reader navigation is constrained by the prior decisions of authors who force readers into particular styles of navigation....software design that incorporates set or explicit routes and therefore less choice, restricts the navigational preferences of the user" (p.267).

Horney classified the patterns of access to hypermedia documents in six major categories: linear, side trip, star, star extended, ring and chaotic. He further made a distinction between chaotic patterns to attain a purposeful goal and chaotic patterns that are caused by confusion. Orey and Nelson (1994) however identified four types of navigation patterns using a measure that was based on the number of times a learner visits a screen (e.g. 'visits most screens twice'). Horney (1993) and Orey and Nelson asserted that design decisions might favour particular styles of navigation. Lawless and Kulikowich (1996) recorded user's log files in their work on user's navigational routes. They used cluster analysis, rather than Horney's method of comparing nodes visited and the duration of the visit, to see if there were any similar patterns. They found three navigational performance patterns: Knowledge seekers, Feature explorers and Apathetic hypertext users. They thought that the ability to look at individual differences without obtruding on the individual's use of the computer was very constructive.

Canter, Rivers and Storrs (1985), investigated user navigation through interactive databases and developed a set of indices in order to characterise each user's search sequences. They proposed that these indices could be used for precisely defining search strategies such as browsing and scanning. They started with the premise that users were already aware of how to navigate through concrete environments, such as a city, and how to navigate through data. They argued that it was constructive to explore whether or not there was an analogy in the psychological processes involved in user navigational patterns. They considered several factors crucial to understanding user's navigation patterns; such as the task the user was performing (directly or indirectly affecting the path), and the user's preferred strategies. This area brings in another area of my research, that of using landmarks within multimedia and Internet research. These enable users to navigate within the resource and to be aware of their physical place within the resource, again in much the same way as a games user can fix their position in a game either by geographical landmarks or by placing themselves within a maze or 3D map. The concept of a mental map related to navigation patterns to the mental processes involved in working through software, and with physical awareness of where the user was in the package. Shum (1990), discussing navigating in multimedia and the user's acquisition of spatial knowledge as a two-step process, produced similar results to Simpson and McKnight. Shum explained the first step as the acquisition of route knowledge, where the information was context dependent, and the second step as the acquisition of map knowledge, in which the individual understood the global spatial relationships, navigation was then world centred.

Learning Strategies Research

There has been considerable research in multimedia and internet research, and in particular, on how users learn from resources and the strategies they employ to do this. Qui (1994) emphasised the importance of this research when investigating the strategies learners employ when navigating through hypermedia material with various structural designs. Misanchuk and Schwier (1993) contended that descriptions of navigational strategies provide very useful information for formative evaluation on the instructional design of multimedia materials. Recker (1994) conducted research in which students were asked to use a hypertext-based environment to study recursivity in LISP programming. The study showed that novices tend to use a more linear navigational strategy that precludes backtracking, whereas more advanced students seem to prefer a top-down, non-linear approach. The multimedia research cited in this chapter however found that both novices and experts used linear and non-linear methods at particular times of the search. Like Canter et al. (1985), Recker suggested that the choice of navigation patterns is influenced not only by constraints in the design of the environment but also by the learner's goals. Beasley and Waugh (1997) used a fully constrained hypermedia environment, which had been developed to provide learners with an overview of the different ways computers could be used in a classroom. They found that the participants tend to use a systematic top-down, left-to-right navigation strategy and suggested that this preference was not only due to the constraints in the design of the environment but also to a strong cultural bias. The children in Study 1 of my multimedia research definitely preferred a top down left-to right approach but this may simply reflect the way they had been taught to interrogate material. Beasley and Vila (1992) had conducted a similar study in which university students were asked to study fundamental concepts of artificial intelligence using a multimedia instructional module. One of the objectives of their study was to determine the relationship between navigation patterns and gender. Navigation patterns were qualified in terms of degree of linearity. They found that females were more linear as they had spent significantly less time exploring the program.

Cognitive Strategies Research

Work by Chen and Macredie (2001) has determined that cognitive styles have a significant effect on student learning bin hypermedia systems. They investigated several different themes within hypermedia learning such as nonlinear learning, learner control, navigation in hyperspace, matching and mismatching, and learning effectiveness. They stated that although there has been an increased growth in the use of these systems there is still a need for research on how different learners perceive such systems. They proposed a learning model and gave a series of implications for the design of learning systems. Investigating how students physically use these systems is also important, even with digital natives, who despite their increased awareness of interactive environments may not have encountered specific types before. Jih and Reeves (1992) have emphasised the need for more user-friendly hardware and software and that a well-designed computer based system "permits users to experience mastery of the system, ease of using it, competence in performance of practical tasks, enjoyment and even eagerness to show it off to others". Software user-friendliness they considered to be of major concern to the designers of interactive learning systems and users often have difficulties in understanding the structure and functions of applications and the operating procedures for using them. Jih and Reeves consider that although using basic packages such as word processing and spreadsheets have a degree of difficulty, the difficulties experienced in using specialist education and training is especially detrimental. Research by Ford and Chen again in hypermedia investigated cognitive style, levels of prior experience, motivation, age and gender. They found that students with different cognitive styles (Classified as field dependent/independent) used strategically different methods of navigation, and students' prior experience affected both the navigation behaviour and the learning performance. Their research focused on the user's navigation of information structuring afforded by hypermedia. As hypermedia can allow non-sequential access patterns as well as sequential patterns this can give the designer a range of options with learning material packages.

Boyle has been concerned with the need to make learning resources interoperable across different systems. He proposes the use of defined learning objects[1] and a facility to convert these into different systems such as VLE's. The principal aim of his research was "to explore and delineate principles underlying authoring for reuse and repurposing". His work again has considerable resonance with the research in this chapter as using a topology of learning objects could be done in much the same way as a topology of navigation patterns, i.e. a classification of these and then usage and deployment information, so that the same specific pattern can be used in a number of contexts. A similar aim is involved in the research work of Avgeriou et al (2003) who propose the development of a pattern language for learning management systems. The need to re-use and re-purpose elements of learning systems is again topical. Added to the increasing use of open source and open educational resource material, it becomes necessary to make not only the learning components flexible and adaptable but also the tools to use them and the learning environments themselves. The design of these systems is complex as they involve the use of organizational, administrative, instructional and technological components. A systematic, disciplined approach such as design patterns would enable re-useable design experience to be developed to further new systems.

Perception Research

Gibson's work on perception (*The Ecological Approach to Visual Perception* (1979)) is important here as he invented the phrase affordances, which referred to the interactive possibilities of a particular object or environment. Gibson pioneered the concept of direct perception or direct realism as opposed to the cognitivist indirect realism. Information pickup theory is regarded usually as a general theory of perception although this area is usually concerned with research on the visual system. Gibson investigated the implications of this theory for research in still and motion pictures, which has some relevance to visually rich multimedia. Much of Gibson's practical work involved investigation into how pilots orientated themselves with the ground during flying, so the variables of the terrain and the sky determined perception rather than sensory perception. This obviously relates closely to navigation, as users often perceive the multimedia world as a 3D world, which has to be negotiated. Users employ landmarks or fixed points enables the user to navigate within a large resource both more quickly and more satisfactorily in terms of the user's perceptions of the amount of information covered and their own interpretation of it. Gibson developed this into a general theory of visual perception, with three key elements:

1) Optic Array – patterns of light reaching the eye giving unambiguous information about objects
2) Textured Gradients – the gradients of what you perceive in terms of distance, speed, involving little cognitive information processing
3) Affordance – attaching particular meaning to visual information

Reed (1988) states: "For centuries philosophers and scientists alike have taught that we are directly aware not of the things surrounding us, but only of our subjective representations. ... Gibson's theory of direct perception challenged this scientific dogma by showing that perception is not purely a subjective matter. Gibson denied that perception was based on sensory inputs or stimuli at all. Instead, he claimed that perception was based on ecological information, which is external to organisms, and, unlike sensory inputs, specific to its environmental sources". His work was further developed by Norman, who worked with him and adapted several of his ideas into his own developed theories. Neisser (1976) also worked on a theory of cognition, which had a strong developmental link to Gibson's work.

MAIN FOCUS OF THE CHAPTER

Having investigated some of the extensive literature on navigation within multimedia resources the chapter will now detail the multimedia research that I have completed. This is dealt with under five main issues using audit trails, the development of the navigation patterns, developing navigational tools and new navigational tools and design aspects of multimedia packages.

ISSUE 1: USING AUDIT TRAILS

Research was conducted into the methods users employ in navigating through multimedia and internet resources. The three elements of the research into these patterns consisted of:

1) A taxonomy of multimedia packages – concentrating on the navigation paths and available tools
2) A First Study – of children in primary and secondary schools using multimedia packages (2-3 packages for each pair – 23 pairs)
3) A Second Study – of adults using a specific encyclopaedic multimedia resource – 20 individuals.

The taxonomy was useful as it revealed how the design of a range of multimedia packages affected how these resources could be used. The second study on children fits in well with the scope of this chapter as the children could be termed digital natives but as they were young in age, they had not experienced the full effect of the digital revolution, in terms of access to and use of computers, mobile devices and the Internet. The third study looked at adults and although they ranged from novice to expert, they ranged from being digital natives to the digital immigrant range of Prensky's work (2001). An interesting point here is that novices were able to benefit from the more experienced experts and it is possible that digital immigrants could learn usage and navigation techniques from digital immigrants in the same way. The other key aspect of this research is the nature and amount of learning that took place, and how the navigation patterns used affected what information was retrieved and the sections that were used within the resources.

The most important of these three areas of study for this chapter is the last of these. In this research, each user was given three tasks within the same extensive encyclopaedic package. For each of these tasks a 2D chart was produced. From these navigation charts (60 in all) each users navigation patterns and preferences were assessed. These charts also enabled comparison of different users across each task. An example of one of the charts is included (Figure 1). Using the scanned records of each user's progression through the software and these navigation charts, it was possible to create a range of the different types of navigation pattern found. The list of navigation types was then compared to the other patterns, which are shown in Table 1 below. From these scanned records or audit trails of each user and the subsequent charts it was possible to build a taxonomy of navigation patterns. These included some nine main types (together with several sub types). A diagram demonstrating a selection of these navigational patterns is given overleaf.

In Figure 1, a navigational chart for one user is shown with their use of specific tools (left hand bar) and their movement through the resource for each of three tasks – each in a different colour. The graph is also timed in minutes across the time bar

Figure 1. Diagram of a navigation chart from one of the participants in the research

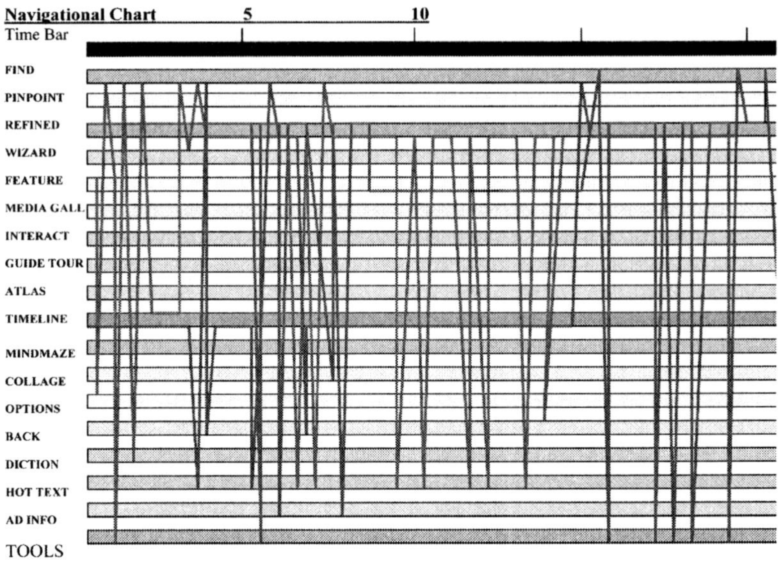

at the top. This enables the charts for each user to be compared. In Figure 2 (overleaf 2 pages) Each of the navigation patterns has been divided into several sub types (detailed in Table 2) and as this extends even in its simplest form over three pages only one of these pages has been included in the chapter. The previous two pages of diagrams (not included here) are simpler forms of these diagrams and explore the range of types of patterns, which are given in Table 2.

Further work was done on each user and their preferences, in terms of their navigational preferences – how they preferred to navigate, whether they always chose the same tools, whether they used a full range of tools etc. by means of an interview after the end of the multimedia session.

Table 1. Comparison between Fenley and other researcher's navigation patterns

Fenley	Parunak	Canter, Rivers & Storrs	Horney
Linear	Linear	Path (Pathiness) any route not crossing node twice	Linear Traversal
Linear Extra	-	Loop (Loopiness) ring, which contains no other rings	Side Trip
Circular	Ring	Ring (Ringiness) Returns to start node, May include other rings	-
Star	-	-	Star
Star Extra	-	Spike (Spikeness) retraces path back	Extended Star
Hierarchical	Hierarchical	-	-
Hierarchical Extra	DAG	-	-
Complex -Chaotic	Arbitrary	-	Chaotic
Complex -Planned	Hypercube Hypertorus	-	-

Figure 2. Diagram of a section of the navigational pattern types, in graphical form (overleaf)

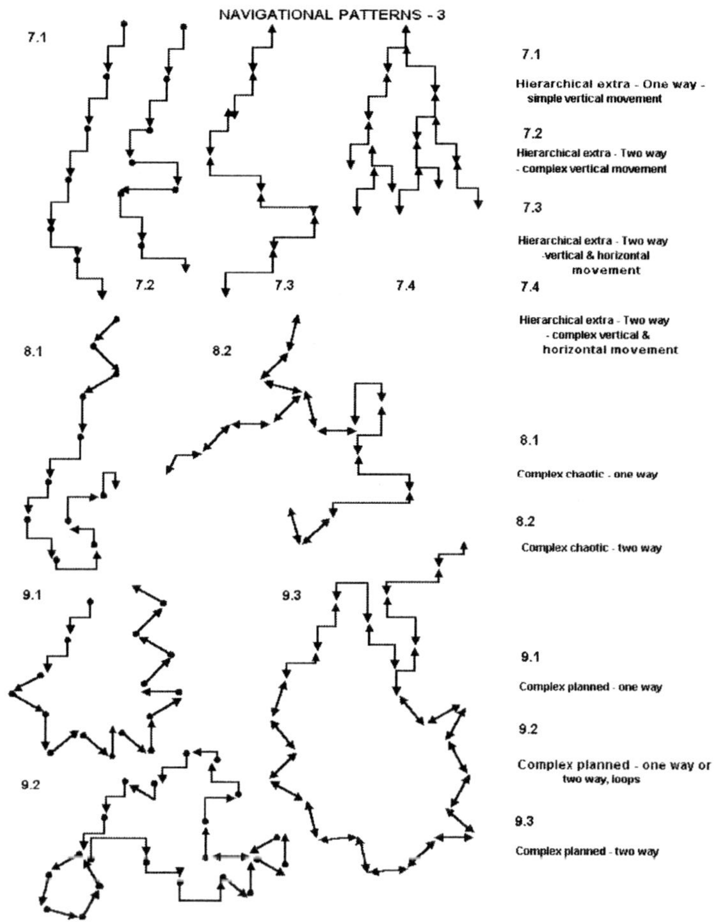

There are various ways of visualising navigation trails; several examples are included later in the chapter.

ISSUE 2 - DEVELOPMENT OF THE NAVIGATION PATTERNS

Further development of the navigational patterns will involve using more participants and further developing the earlier findings that most users have preferences for which patterns they prefer to use. The use of Net generation students is interesting here as both children – pre Net Generation/Digital natives and post this group the adults are represented here. It is possible that the Digital natives may relate better to the adults and the experts in this study rather than the novices or relatively low to medium computer literate children. The navigation tools provided with the package included a tour, a guide, an advanced search mechanism, and several specific tools such as a wizard, which allowed users to be guided through selection processes. Further developments of this would be to develop a similar large resource and to provide arrange of different tools such as 2D and 3D maps of the resource. Some of these features would also develop techniques used in games programming, e.g. mazes, position maps, where you are signs and a depiction of the route followed. This may again

Table 2. List of the navigational patterns identified in the research with their sub divisions

1 Linear	1.1) One way - uni-directional (no return) 1.2) Two way - bi-directional (return possible)
2 Linear Extra	2.1) One way (along path and extended path - no return) 2.2) One way (along path but may return from extended path back to original) 2.3) Two way (path and extended path)
3 Circular	3.1) One way - clockwise - single circle 3.2) One way - anti clockwise 3.3) One way - + multiple circle/loop still one way - not complete - no repeats 3.4) One way - + multiple circle/loop, complete circle, returns to starting point, no repeat 3.5) Two way - but not repeating loops - no repetition of path 3.6) Two way - with repeats on loops - multiple circles
4 Star	4.1) One way 4.2) Two way
5 Star Extra	5.1) Star extra/ Extended - One way 5.2) Star extra – Extended One way + return on extended path only - back to formal star 5.3) Star extra - Two way - star and return on extended star 5.4) Star complete star pattern, with return to starting point
6 Hierarchical	6.1) Hierarchical one way - no returns vertical path - no branching 6.2) Hierarchical one way - branching off same tree - no returns 6.3) Hierarchical two way - vertical tree 6.4) Hierarchical two way - branching off basic tree
Hierarchical Extra	7.1) Hierarchical - one way /no returns - vertical branching - possible multiple trees - vertical - unidirectional route 7.2) Hierarchical - one way - loops to other trees - return to main tree 7.3) Hierarchical - two way - vertical branching - more than one tree 7.4) Hierarchical - two way - vertical & horizontal branching - can return – multiple trees
8 Complex -Chaotic	8.1) Complex - unidirectional- no fit to above patterns - or mixture of above 8.2) Complex - two way - erratic - could loop/ cross hierarchies /stars etc. no set patterns
9 Complex - Planned	9.1) Controlled one way route - several search strategies, unidirectional no returns/ loops 9.2) Unidirectional - short loops off main plan, return to set pattern 9.3) Two way - planned includes loops/returns/different patterns-formalised path

be representative of digital native's behaviour as these are areas where digital natives are extremely comfortable. The topology of the navigation maps was considered to be important and further work in this area is continuing.

Navigation Patterns

The following navigation patterns were recognised from the initial empirical work and these were then further tested in the second study. These navigational patterns were then put into a definitive list (overleaf) and then the graphical version of the patterns was prepared (Figure 1)

1. **Linear** - path on one level, using tools e.g. index, time line, or word search, one direction
2. **Linear extra** - paths lead away from basic linear pattern, returning to the linear path, usually at the same place or the next node to their original leaving point.
3. **Circular** - initially recognised as linear, but circular if completed, one/two-way dependent on software design, may be represented by an ellipse/multifaceted shape e.g. an octagon.
4. **Star** - movement initially linear but implies a change in level, going into second level areas from the first level and returning, one way or two way. Complete star pattern can

represent continuous topic selection through multimedia going into each item in turn to the next level and returning to starting level, especially with circular or thematic structures.

5. **Star extra** - a development or extension of the star pattern, movement into the second or third level of the package, i.e. into an additional level, beyond the usual star pattern, one or two way, and the extra depth may only be used for part of the route.
6. **Hierarchical** - movement down the hierarchy, with a possible return along the same path, to go down one or more branches of a tree structure. Progressing one way down the structure and across to the next branch of the tree, can be two-way, but unusually returning to the original starting point, but may retrace path.
7. **Hierarchical -Extra** - movement along multiple hierarchies usually with different subject/themes, usually in the same way, returning to the same tree structure or continuing onto a linked or associated tree. The hierarchical and extra patterns are differentiated by changes in depth and width as the extra extension may involve more than one tree structure, while the basic hierarchical pattern is confined to one tree structure.
8. **Complex - Chaotic** - movement follows a series of different paths, usually in rapid succession, random and erratic navigation, frequent changes of route and searching method, may be a mixture of the above types.
9. **Complex -Planned** - sequence of moves following established path, sometimes including definite patterns, using a mixture of different types, but following an ordered route. Types can be mixed within routes - with some recognition of each type but too confused/short for full classification. The complex patterns are the most difficult to recognize and analyse, as these may be hybrid forms of other patterns or result from rapid use of pattern types

The list of navigational patterns above shows all the subdivisions of each pattern type. These have been developed to prevent any misunderstanding of what constitutes an actual pattern and this classification together with detailed charts of each pattern type (an example of one of these charts is shown in Figure 1) should mean that the navigational patterns are clear and that the classification can be used with many different types of digital resources. This is especially useful for educational resources when the user may not be aware of how the package/ resource is structured or how to find the information required.

ISSUE 3: DEVELOPING NAVIGATION TOOLS

Further development of the navigation tools would necessitate having knowing information on each node and where the information is found within the resource. This information proved difficult to find for commercial resources and so a new resource would need to be developed around this basis.

Recent research by McGuffin and Schraefel (2004) on Hyperstructures has involved representing information on the web. Hyperstructures, which include component models such as Zzstructures and mSpaces, are described using graph theory. These structures use hypertext structures like the web and hypertext links to show links between pages but also the multiple relationships between information within the pages. The example they give is of a group of musicians who might show they are from a particular country or how they created a specific style of music or that they were all child prodigies. The INTENTS project from the University of Dublin (2007) involves the design of a series of intelligent knowledge based tools to assist in the construction, navigation and management of hypertext documents. Examples of these tools are 1) Creation of a framework which gives conceptual structure to a document corpus which can then be interrogated by an intelligent hypertext browser or 2) A knowledge based browser, using metadata from other tools in the series, as well as document management and authoring tools, and user behaviour tools. Developments of this nature would allow further exploration of individual's preferences and behaviour when using navigation tools.

The next part of my research was to develop a list of the most essential navigational tools to be used by designers in the construction of multimedia/Internet resources. This list gives an overview of the necessary component parts of good quality interactive multimedia. These resources are a good example of how digital natives could be used to determine the nature and extent of what they would prefer to have in their own toolkit.

1. Navigational tool Diagrams or Map
2. Known material
3. History
4. Audit Trails - navigational paths
5. Time line
6. Activities - Worksheet/ Tasks
7. Index tutorial/tour
8. User levels
9. Individual student records/personal histories
10. Customobility issues
11. Curriculum/ research links
12. Off-line facilities
13. Internet links
14. Expert guide, induction/introductory
15. Intelligent Tutor

This list can be used by designers as a check to ensure that as many of these as feasible are built into the new software package. Some of these are reasonably straightforward but other items such as the intelligent tutor involve more detailed construction and facilities and substantial input from the tutor(s) to make this effective. If the navigation tools are produced as a series of device independent software tools then these could be added onto each resource and the user allowed to select from the available palette, which tools they would like to use in a specific resource.

ISSUE 4: NEW NAVIGATION TOOLS

Investigation of some of the newer navigation tools was done as part of this multimedia research project; however there are few available resources, especially educational resources where this type of tool selection is possible to bring in and use. For educational resources, there is a need for an intelligent tutor approach which could remember the previous routes taken and navigational preferences and suggest future routes, areas for further study or searching or the type of tools or methods preferred by the individual user.

The newer navigational tools consist of the following: Beacons, Landmarks, Breadcrumb trails, Searchlights, intelligent agents, 2D and 3D maps and interactive guides. Beacons allow significant items or areas to be highlighted or lit up for particular students, or for whole classes or for specific search areas. Landmarks relate to the resource in the same way as physical resources, by providing points at which users can recognise that they have been there or they have gone past this point. These can be colour markers or set up as points within the resources so that users can find them again easily. A simple map could involve reproducing a schematic image of these and putting these landmarks on to a virtual map of the entire resource. Searchlights can be used with or without a search engine and can highlight just the relevant section or be used within areas where specific references are made to the search term. Breadcrumb trails enable a series of markers (with the breadcrumbs left at strategic points, i.e. whenever a user may wish to flag this area or page/

screen, or would want to return to it. These trails could be set up either with different markers/ objects or colours or for specific trails. For instance, while searching for a particular set of images the user may find several that are useful for another project and they could then use several different breadcrumb trails while researching in the same resource. Intelligent agents are increasingly used in educational or training resources. These agents can be pre-programmed with a series of items on which to gather information or they can be set up to capture information. Examples of this are where the user has been, how long they have taken, or more pedagogically which section of the work they have completed, how well they have done, which parts they need to redo/repeat/ practice and so on. This information can be relayed back to the user (and to the human tutor) either on request or at the end of the session.

The example shown in Figure 3 is of a geographical resource with breadcrumb trails in different colours. It should be possible to create a similar navigation tool within a multimedia or internet based resource so that individual routes through the resource are detailed as a distinct route and can then be viewed on an overview map such as this one. New technologies such as geo location, the facilities of smart phones and usage knowledge by digital natives could all be used to make learning more interesting, relevant and available ubiquitously and whenever needed.

ISSUE 5: DESIGN ISSUES WITH MULTIMEDIA AND INTERNET RESOURCES

Research into multimedia packages has revealed a wide range of structures and an even wider range of both the number and facilities for navigating and visualising information within these packages. Most of the multimedia software reviewed as part of the multimedia research detailed at the beginning of the chapter – a taxonomy of 100 packages showed that each package had some form of navigation facility, although this might simply mean some form of index and /or a simple search facility. Few packages had sophisticated navigation tools, fewer still had tools that could be shared across several resources and very few

Figure 3. An example of one of the new navigational tools, Breadcrumbs trails (from http://wiki.openstreetmap.org/images/1/19/Weekend_traces_cropped.png)

had a linked series of tools which enabled easy navigation and an awareness of where the user was in the package. This situation can also be mirrored in internet searching and the lost in hyperspace situation is still a frequent problem especially with novices.

Much of the research in this area has been in the field of human computer interaction or interface design. If we are intending, as seems to be an important move forward, to promote an exchangeable and stand alone series of navigational tools then it is essential that the HCI aspects of the software packages are able to match this, and the structure of the underlying resource can be adapted or is developed to enable these navigational tools to be used effectively. The issue of personalization – the development of each individual's preferences in terms of the type of software to use need experienced educators to assess the relative merits pedagogically for their courses. The development of a type of Apps store for educational applications suitable for use on smart phones or hand held devices may both interest digital natives but also enthuse them into providing new apps specifically for their generation. Creating, using, distributing and updating educational apps (or mini applications) could allow students to get involved and to develop and enhance the educational world to make it more similar to their own social world. Using blogs, wikis, social networking, and graphics/photo sites would expand the potential methods of involving and getting feedback from students, as well as recording the exact role of each student.

During the analysis phase of the research, several packages were identified as having specific areas or problems, which would inhibit full navigational movement through the resource. These can be classified as educational constraints on how the packages should be used and design constraints. These two areas will be discussed with the use of specific examples.

Educational Constraints on Navigational Patterns

Many educational resources have been designed for specific courses, although in some cases a large amount of resource is developed for a limited range of activities. Developing these more carefully would expand their potential use and allow different views or areas for specific user groups.

Homer

The Homer package from the Open University has a front end that pushes the user into a linked and sequential series of weekly work plans. Completing one of these would allow access onto the next and so one. Underneath this rigid framework is a rich resource of the homer poems, maps and information on Mycenae and other Greek sites, an archaeological skills section and a wealth of written and historical information. The rigid structure of the package limits its use and forcing students along a specific path, although this may help them complete the required work, limits their potential usage of the resource. The solution to this would have been in allowing a flexible access to the resource and the option of going into the formal course information would have allowed much more exploration and self-development and could have allowed the resource to be used by many more educational groups and other courses.

Sonoran Desert

The Sonoran Desert package produced by the BBC, used a rigid compass-based method of navigation with a series of geographical routes through the resource which resembled trails. As there was a strong route bias most of the students using this followed a top down approach and selected the north route at the top of the screen. They would then usually go clockwise and so follow east, south and west routes. Having this information could enable the designer to put much of the introductory material to the north, however this route is not selected by every use and so these people would miss this introduction. There are problems with a resource if the same route is always follow although again that would help the designer who would need to update these first, but it becomes limiting to returning users. This has a similar effect to software which uses a metaphor structure. An example of this is where information is placed in a house or museum metaphor as users may not realize that each room or gallery has a specific collection. If the users had been given a freer approach or the resource had been tested some of these constraints may have been removed.

Medieval Realms

The Medieval Realms package published by the British Library has a huge amount of material with a challenging search structure imposed upon it. Although this has now been substantially improved, the requirements from the user of knowing which area and which specific item within this would yield what they wanted made this package a very difficult one for the average user. Aimed at GCSE students who covered areas of this in their humanities and history topics, this would have benefited from a user friendly and flexible interface. The impressive resource was only investigated in very peripheral ways, many of the students did not fully investigate any aspect of the resource and few navigational tools were available.

A better navigation method to allow exploration or simple browsing may have helped introduce users to the structure of the resource, as well as breadcrumb trails to remember their searcher, or even a sampler session where aspects of each type of media – music, sounds, text, and manuscripts could be displayed and users could have searched a specific area in depth.

Design Constraints on Navigation

The design of the resource also affects how and what the user can navigate. Most resources are structured on a series of menus where each level has more specific and detailed information, however few resources use standard navigation tools (common in games software) of an inset map, plan, current location indicator or an indicator of how far or to what depth the user has ventured.

Two common problems are outlined here, the first is where the interface and content are mismatched, which is a common problem with primary/secondary level software (less so with HE level) and design issues where there is a specific need to process through the resource in a particular sequence.

Interface and Content Mismatches

There are several packages where the resource and the design of the interface are not well enough matched. Examples of this are: - the Way Things Work package which has a cartoon interface but a much higher level information on machines and how these work; the Eyewitness History of the World which has a sophisticated interface, a reasonable starting point but very little depth; and Encarta where users investigating the collages are left within it but not where the link should have taken them. This inability to link aspects of the design is unfortunately common and the only satisfactory way to deal with it is to do sufficient testing with the groups who are intended to use it. There are many extensive multimedia resources where little thought or design has been given and the material is made available, possibly even sorted into areas but not linked sufficiently to allow ease of use. Again, these issues could be partially resolved with a standardized set of navigational tools which the user has at their disposal.

Figure 4. Front end of the Open University Carbon Cycle Software package

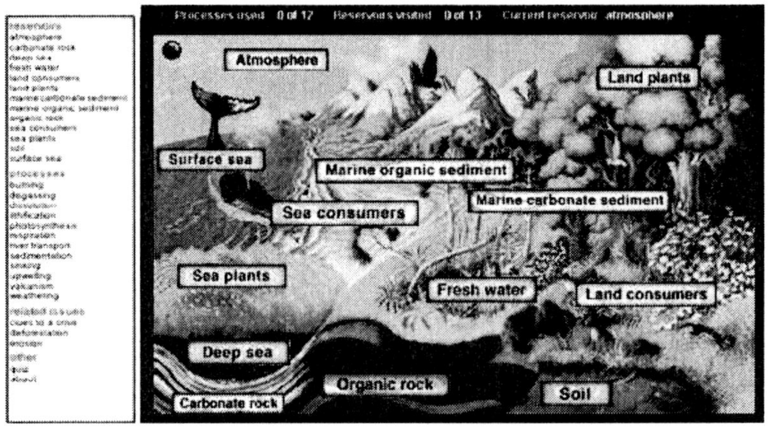

The Carbon Cycle

The Carbon cycle package produced by the Open University is part of a large series of science-based software designed for university level courses. This design went through several iterations as the front end (Figure 4), needed to be changed as users did not follow the necessary sequence. In the initial design many users went straight down into the sea on the left side - following a top down approach.

This sequence created problems with the carbon cycle as this necessitated going over the land and then down to form the cycle i.e. along the top, down and then into the sea. Placing the whale in the sea, where is had previously been an inviting blue, meant that the users' eye line carried along to the right and then continued down and around, thus allowing the completion of the sequence. Testing this fully with users meant that the interface could match the method of navigation needed for the science session.

DISCUSSION

Analysing the packages has highlighted several problems, which were common across many packages. Insufficient or inadequate capabilities for navigation, the lack of awareness of where the user is in the package, and misconceptions of the amount of the resource they had investigated were all common problems. Many of these problems could be resolved with better interfaces and more adequate testing; however allowing the users to develop navigational skills and providing them with a known set of facilities to do this may have longer term and more developmental benefits. The next section looks at some of the newer tools for investigating navigation and then some of the visualisation tools, which may help to improve further the users' perceptions and understanding of the digital resources.

SOLUTIONS AND RECOMMENDATIONS

The solutions and recommendations section covers the areas that have been discussed already by presenting some possible solutions to the issues and problems encountered. This section first investigates newer navigational tools that are being developed for multimedia resources and also briefly discusses the use of intelligent agents. These navigation tools are also meant to give an ability to the user to navigate on a physical level, and to do physical actions such as they might do in exploring a physical resource. Common actions in this environment would be walk, look around, zoom, pan, orbit, examine (as well as pick up/ inspect) fly – or bird's eye view, and turntable. Using this type of physical approach may lessen the need for specific navigational tools although as users are not familiar with these should be seen as additional facilities within a whole toolbox or palette of navigational tools. Developing the ability and skills to use these is another whole area of research, but the time investment needed is reduced if these tools are re-usable over a wide array of resources.

The outline in the first part of the chapter listed the standard types of navigational tool. These include indexes, search engines, maps, plans, timelines, histories and directional devices. There is however, a whole range of more innovative tools that could be developed for multimedia and Internet resources. The development of Open source software has meant that it would be possible to develop a set of tools, which conform to XML or Java formats. This would mean that these tools could be freely available and could be added in with the minimum of effort. The newer tools include breadcrumbs, searchlights, beacons, landmarks, 3-D mapping, trackers, location finders, compasses, and route maps. Breadcrumbs are paths selected by the user of the key screens they have visited and can be set up to record different aspects of the search or information retrieval, Searchlights and beacons allow selected searches to be highlighted. There are whole ranges of direction/ map finders that have emanated from the games software where compass type location finders, and 2-D plans of the whole resource, help locate the user and allow them to find specific areas of the resource. There are a series of additional features that can be created within the digital resource. These features include:

- Reconstructions: building or site reconstructions, drawings, views, structures, plans, schematic drawings, schemas, aspects
- Walkthroughs: paths through the building, which appear as you walk through them, the perspective changes as you progress giving a real awareness of size and shape
- Timelines: comparative views of different periods sites and artifacts through time, scrollable and showing comparative developments/ civilizations through set periods of time
- Day in the life: Outline of what a particular person would be doing during the day, where they would go, places they would visit, particularly important for children's understanding
- Event reconstructions: using multimedia or video clips or sound reconstruct or re-enact events, could use commercial film or video clips if relevant and with copyright
- 3-D plans: reconstructions give a 3-D view of buildings so that these can be realised in terms of their structure, possible materials and colour, outward appearance, internal design and content.
- Mashups – overlays of student based research onto the existing resource
- Social networking – could be used for role-play, splitting up the assignment, sharing additional work, critiquing other students, bringing in new material etc.
- Individual experiences – blogs of how the student created the information, live recordings, interviews (with the correct permissions) could be used to enhance presentations

Using some or all of these features will help in the comprehension and understanding of the digital resource. It may be expensive and time-consuming to create these for all potential scenarios but the use of some of these techniques would develop interest in the resource and some of these features such as schematic drawings, plans and even reconstruct ions may already be available. The reason these new facilities need to be added to multimedia and digital resources is the potential added benefits that are given by these new media formats. These benefits include interactivity, individual selection and progress and even the ability to select (by both the designer and the user) multiple or the most suitable, methods for conveying the required message. Multimedia and Internet resources would also be improved with an array of visualisation tools. These would include the standard zoom and turning facilities, but also allow different objects, maps, plans, reconstructions and digital resources to be viewed and compared. Different views of each object or plan could be requested, their location, a 3-D site map, reconstruction of the setting, and associated objects. Being able to select how the information is presented, viewing a timeline, using zoomable interfaces, would help the users understand electronic resources and these techniques are accessible and available, although there is a significant cost of setting these up.

Using Intelligent Agents: Intelligent Tutor Concept

From these requirements there develops a need to expand these further into a full intelligent tutor system, which is built into the multimedia and Internet software, again aimed at the individual and with an objective of developing the individual's skills and abilities. There is a need for continued research on intelligent tutoring systems and development of this area is not detailed in this paper, although there are implications on learning such as Wright and Likorish's work on user's choice of less demanding routes (1994), McGrath's work on learner control (1992), Mischanchuk and Schwier (1992) on learning using audit trails and Canter, River and Storrs (1985) whose five search strategies were related to ways of learning. Zaiane (2002) looked at recommender systems in e-learning that would intelligently recommend actions to a learner based on the actions of previous learners. He suggested using web mining techniques to build the agent so that it could then recommend learning activities or shortcuts to students. This was intended to improve both navigation and the online learning process. The use of the overview sections and holistic processing skills also enhanced the knowledge representation in the form of maps. Their results supported the belief that individual differences can affect hypermedia navigation, even thought their role in learning is complex, but the impact of cognitive style on learning outcomes was found to be less important than was originally thought. Brusilovsky and Rizzo (2005) research investigated issues on problems of building links from closed to open corpus Web pages in the context of Web-based education. They suggested that using landmark-based navigation using semantic information space maps was beneficial. Their research work explains the technical aspects of this work by presenting a system Knowledge Sea that implements this approach. They then describe the mechanism behind the system, and report some results of a classroom evaluation of this system.

Using intelligent tutors could again be angled for the individual student and the results of all the students in terms of their pathways through a resource could be shown, and (anonymously) the fastest route to the information, most effective route, most common one and for future students the routes the best/most effective users employed.

FURTHER RESEARCH WORK AND DISCUSSION

Using Tools

Tan and Kumar (2002) describe the development of Web robots which are software programs that automatically traverse the hyperlink structure of the World Wide Web to locate and retrieve information. While many researchers and commercial organisations believe that these robots are deployed for unauthorised uses such as for gathering business intelligence of their Web sites and dislike the network bandwidth problems they cause these Web robots could be used to give valuable information on where users navigate, how easy it is for them to do so and how quickly they obtain the information they want. Srivastava, Cooley, Dashpande and Tan (2000) investigated web usage mining where data mining techniques are applied in order to discover usage patterns from Web data. They determined three distinct phases in this usage namely prepossessing, pattern discovery and pattern analysis. They thought that these techniques would have relevance to both research and practice communities. Applying these types of data mining was considered beneficial for students and may help their learning within Web based resources. The existing tools which have been used to build web applications are often not sufficiently robust and flexible to last and be continuously upgradable. These tools need to be flexible within a rapidly changing software environment and the proliferation of different tools, settings and combinations of these make a complexing task for even digitally aware or digital native students. In order to enhance the learning process from these software resources there needs to be a tools desktop or palette which is separate from the actual resources but which can be bolted on to a series of resources. This would enable students to familiarise themselves with the tools they find most useful and to continue using them through a series of different resources. The concept of the navigation tool such as the IE flower (see below) which would be transferable and easily recognisable across a series of resources is likely to become more common.

New Technologies

Gomez, Cachero, and & Pastor (2001) determined that as new technologies are continuously emerging there is a need for the web developer to create new approaches which encompass the whole software lifecycle from initial concept and design through development and even through the deployment stage into the continued maintenance so that the software packages would remain up-to-date. One outcome of this is that developers need to produce device independent applications so that new techniques or tools can be added at any stage in their development and use. The issues of navigation whether this is through hyperspace or through a more limited resources are very important, not only for software and interface designers but also for tutors concerned with computer mediated learning and for authors of hypermedia and multimedia information resources.

Navigating in Complex Information Resources

Problems with navigating in complex information spaces have been subjected to a wide array of research techniques such as think-aloud protocols, as well as more traditional questionnaires – such as pre and post questionnaires and interviews – often again before and after the multimedia/ Internet session, (which were all used in this multimedia research) (Chen & Rada, 1996). Using audit trails or server log files it is possible to back up this more esoteric research with objective behavioural data however, these data files are not easy to capture, analyse and interpret. The multimedia research described within this chapter initially used simple audio files to capture the respondents' comments but these did not prove sufficient, either in quality of content and a more sophisticated scanning method was deployed on the later adult research study that captured each screen display, how long they stayed on this screen and where they moved within it. This timed sequence of moves within a multimedia resources meant that it was possible to determine a user's specific navigation path but also a temporal perspective on how they wanted to spend their time within a restricted framework (as in a normal practical or tutored session).

The greatest problem to these scanned and audio files though is the time that it takes to analyse these sufficiently in order that robust statements can be made backed by actual data. This problem has been recognized by other researchers (c.f. Spiliopoulou, et al. 1999) who developed methodological procedures for visualising and analysing log file data for data mining purposes. However, there are a few methods that have been developed which would enable the navigational behaviour of individuals to be analysed using the methods of the psychological researcher, such as using a range of different task demands and conditions (Unz & Hesse, 1999). Berendt and Brenstein (2001) gave a new approach to the classification and visualisation of navigation behaviour, which was intended to give the researcher a series of quantitative measures, and a straightforward method of analysing the quantitative and qualitative data. In their research, they presented their requirements analysis and then their tool STRATDYN. They also demonstrate that individual differences in the student's attention during their web navigation can also be analysed.

Berendt and Brenstein discussed navigation behaviour and considered that it was often formalised in term of measures. They cited certain measures as being typical of this such as one-dimensional variables from a recorded navigation history and thought that their method of analysing this data – Web server logs was the most efficient. Other measures used by other researchers included the total number of pages visited to solve a task (Park & Kim, 2000), the total time needed to complete a task, the average time spent on specific pages (Hall, Balestra & Davis, 2000) or the extent to which pages which were supposed to be accessed together were actually accessed in that way. These measures of navigation behaviour may make the individual components of the navigation through software quantifiable but it is the whole route and the methods tools used that is the most useful in terms of the preferences of each individual user. The additional question of how much is learnt by doing this is a much more difficult area to assess. Students bring different amounts and recall of prior knowledge with them to a multimedia session and the variability between students together with their own preferences for both searching and learning make this a difficult area to accurately measure. Pre and posttests have been applied to this by several researchers, which may indicate how good the student's recall is, but again this can be affected by their familiarity with the material or the system, the tools they use and their ability to store and remember information quickly and accurately. Using a recall test one week after their session in this research revealed a wide range of differences with some students having a detailed sequence of pages and areas researched while others recalled very little. Beredt and Brenstein then demonstrated the usefulness of this new approach by reporting their results of two studies (with 44 students in education and vocational training). These studies indicated that navigational effectiveness is positively related to the ability to concentrate and selectively focus attention, as measured by a series of specific and recognized tests in this area.

User Behaviour

Research by Shapiro and Niederhauser investigated user behaviour and the results indicate that certain user behaviours such as the choice of links, the navigation patterns used and the metacognitive practice are mediators of learning. This research strongly supports my research in that navigation patterns in terms of both the understanding and the knowledge of their use are important for the learning when using multimedia. Mor and Minguillon (2004) further support this hypothesis when they state that e Learning, SCORM, data mining, navigational patterns and personalisation which are now being customarily included in good quality multimedia, are becoming necessary in e-learning standards and preferences for the tools and components of their design. In their research, they presented a practical framework for studying the navigational behaviour of the users of an e-learning environment integrated within a virtual campus. The students were tasked with navigating through a web based virtual campus. They were asked to interact with a series of e-learning resources, which had been created within a SCORM e-learning standard. The goal of the researchers was to develop a data or usage mining tool, which would enable them to analyse the students' navigational behaviour. This tool would then allow them to extract relevant data and validate the design of the virtual campus as well as its usability. An additional aim of the research was to determine the optimal scheduling for each course, which they based on the user profiles. The final aspect of the research was that they were then intending to feed back this information into the system so that the sequence capabilities of the system would also allow a recommended itinerary, which combined the teachers expertise with the learned experience gathered from an analysis of the systems usage.

Niederhauser, Reynolds, Salmen and Skolmoski (2000) are concerned over the ever increasing spread of hypertext based instructional materials in schools and businesses and have queried the technological infrastructure to support their use and the utility of this type of presentation medium. They examined the effects of the cognitive load associated with using hypertext-linking capabilities which 'criss-cross the conceptual landscape'. Their results suggested that the extensive use of hyperlinks to compare and contrast concepts when reading within hypertext resources may actually inhibit the learning to be gained from them. They attribute the problems with this form of instructional media to the cognitive load theory and discuss this in detail as a possible reason behind their research results. Another research project investigating cognitive load by Rossi, Schwabe, and Lyardet (2000) involved the difficulties behind designing high quality visual interfaces for hypermedia applications. These they classified as: organising different kinds of interface objects (i.e. those that prompted navigation) and methods used to prevent the user from having problems with high cognitive load while using the resources. They found that as interface design methods do not capture the actual design decisions or the rationale behind a specific method of organising the resource, it is difficult to both record and inform users of interface design expertise decisions. Rossi et al wanted to reuse interface designs and suggested interface patterns as a method of doing this. They present the context of the patterns they discovered, then a rational for their use and also a series of 'simple but effective' patterns created using a standard template. These templates could then be used by future designers. This concept of re-use is again linked to the navigation patterns people use and to the previous discussion on navigational tools. If these patterns could be expressed as a series of possible templates than the interface mechanisms, navigational methods and learning components – including specific tools, could be shared across series of multimedia and internet resources.

Cognitive Style Research and Application to Digital Natives

Cognitive style research is also represented amongst those researchers investigating the use of multimedia resources. Chen and Macredie and Calcaterra et al. have investigated this area. Chen and Macredie (2002/2004) feel that there is a lot still to be learned about how different learners perceive hypermedia, despite the increased growth in its use. They believe it is essential to build robust learning models that demonstrate how hypermedia features are in fact used by different learners. The individual difference research literature proposes that cognitive style has a significant effect on how students learn within a hypermedia system. Chen and Macredie investigated issues such as field dependence and reviewed empirical studies of hypermedia learning. Their review of this field resulted in a classification into five themes: nonlinear learning, learner control, navigation in hyperspace, matching and mismatching, and learning effectiveness. From this classification, they produced a learning model, based on previous work and then discussed the design implications of this model for designing hypermedia-learning systems.

The research by Calcaterra, Antonietti and Underwood (2005) investigated the influences that cognitive style, spatial orientation and computer expertise have on the usage of hypertext navigation patterns and the subsequent learning outcomes when users interacted with a hypermedia package. A large sample of 306 undergraduates was given a pre-test on their cognitive style and the frequency and ability they thought they had while using computers. From this sample, 40 students were selected in four groups (a) 10 high computer users – sequential thinkers, (b) 10 high computer users – holistic thinkers, (c) 10 low computer users – sequential thinkers and (d) 10 low computer users – holistic thinkers. The research involved a questionnaire on spatial orientation and then a session browsing a hypermedia resource, followed by a posttest assessing recall of the resource and the cognitive organisation of the acquired knowledge. The outcomes of the research allowed them to propose that hypermedia navigation behaviour was linked to computer skills rather than cognitive style and that learning outcomes were not changed by either cognitive style or by computer skills. They further stated that outcomes for learning were affected positively by specific search patterns, especially in revisiting sections and viewing overviews initially.

Learning Strategies

Prensky (2001) considered that it was important that students had learnt techniques not through expensive graphics or multimedia, but through what the kids call "gameplay." We need to incorporate into our classrooms the same combination of desirable goals, interesting choices, immediate and useful feedback, and opportunities to "level up" (that is, to see yourself improve) that engage kids in their favorite complex computer games. Prensky also advocated collaborating with students, using them to decide what software worked best and as "21st century educators, we can no longer decide *for* our students; we must decide *with* them, as strange as that may feel to many of us. We need to include our students in everything we do in the classroom, involving them in discussions about curriculum development, teaching methods, school organization, discipline, and assignments"(Prensky (p.3)

Outcomes from Digital Natives' Research

Researchers such as Prensky have commented that the Digital natives use of ICTs differentiates them from previous generations of students and from their teachers, and that the differences are so significant that the nature of education itself must fundamentally change to accommodate the skills and interests of these 'digital natives' (Prensky, 2001). However, Bennett, Maton and Kervin (2008) state that these claims have had little critical assessment and they do not have a sound empirical backing. These native users are meant to learn differently from previous generations, they are active experiential learners, should be proficient in multi-tasking, and are dependent on communications technologies for accessing information and for interacting with others (Frand, 2000; Oblinger & Oblinger, 2005; Prensky 2001). Tapscott (1998), stated "There is growing appreciation that the old approach [of didactic teaching] is ill-suited to the intellectual, social, motivational, and emotional needs of the new generation" (p. 131), which was enforced later by Prensky's comments that the students had changed radically, and that these people are not the same as those which the educational system was designed to teach.

Visser (2007) gives another important perspective by stating that *digital natives* developed their first information literacy skills "in the digital world

Table 3.

Behaviors of digital immigrant	The behaviors of the digital native learners
Slow/ controlled release of information from limited sources. Singular processing and single or limited tasking. To provide text before pictures, sounds, and video. To provide information linearly, logically, & sequentially. Students work independently not network and interact. To teach "just-in-case" (it's on the exam). To teach to the curriculum guide and standardized tests. Deferred gratification and deferred rewards.	Receiving information quickly from multiple multimedia sources. Parallel processing and multitasking. Processing pictures, sounds, and video before text. Random access to hyperlinked multimedia information. To interact/network simultaneously with many others. Instant gratification and instant rewards. Learning that is relevant, instantly useful, and fun. To learn "just-in-time

with computers, videos, and the Internet" *Digital immigrants*, though formed their information literacy skills "in the print world" (p. 4).

Digital Natives and Digital Immigrants

Jukes and Dosaj (2006) gave descriptions of behaviours, which they thought differentiated native learners from immigrant teachers. Some of the teachers prefer:

Several models have developed embellishments of Prensky's original categories. Coburn (2004b) suggested the addition of an "Analogists" group. Feeney (2007), in her article *Digital Denizens*, thinks that adding additional categories would be useful. Her continuum is as follows:

- *Digital recluse*: use of technology is a result of the need to function in the current environment, not used by choice; computers are prohibited in his/her home.
- *Digital refugee*: unwillingly forced to use technology; prefers hard copies, does not trust electronic resources; seeks assistance; may have grown up with technology or adopted it as an adult.
- *Digital immigrant*: willingly uses technology, but not familiar with its potential; believes technology can be used successfully for some tasks; may have grown up with technology or adopted it as an adult.
- *Digital native*: chooses to use technology for numerous tasks; adapts as the tools change; may have grown up with technology or adopted it as an adult.
- *Digital explorer*: uses technology to push the envelope; seeks new tools that provide more work, faster, and easier.
- *Digital innovator*: adapts and changes old tools for new tasks; creates new tools.
- *Digital addict*: dependent on technology; will go through withdrawal when technology is not available.

Methods of Visualising Navigation

The final section in the chapter investigates methods of visualising information, in particular with respect to how users navigate and how they use digital resources. Several of the examples shown here have been used for social networking. The analyses show the contacts over a period of time and the relationships between individuals. The six examples show a range of techniques that could be applied to data and provide useful visualisations which would help to explain and demonstrate navigational techniques.

New Visualisation Techniques

Figure 5 (after Tauscher and Greenberg) demonstrates a sequence of web searches and a specific method of analysing these. The graph shows counts

Figure 5. Revisitation patterns in World Wide Web navigation

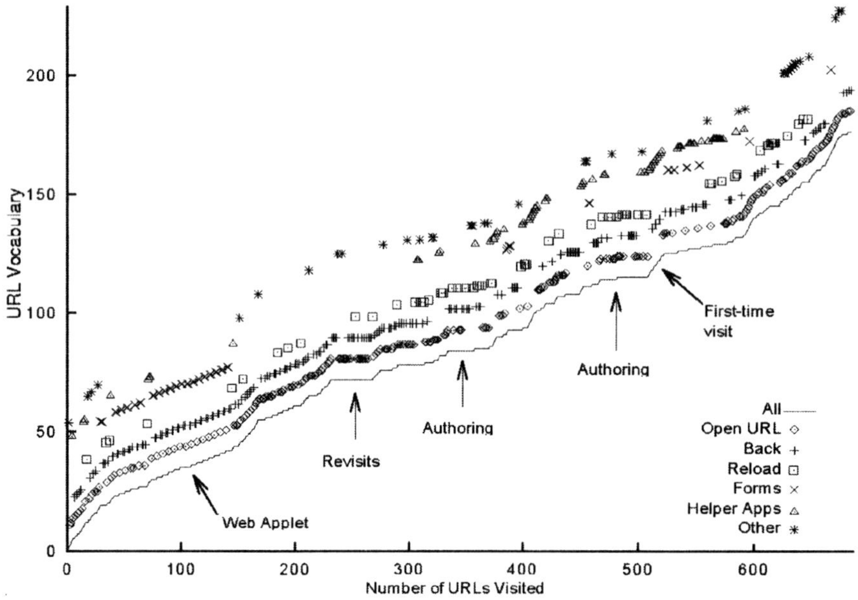

of the number of URL's visited, revisits, reloads, first time visits, forms and helper applications. This type of chart can be used to compare users and to investigate how many screens they visit and other issues such as returns, having to go back to the main menu, revisiting specific information, the amount of text read and the amount of time and content of the URL's visited.

Figure 6. Internet Explorer flower

IE Flower (Figure 6. after Internet Explorer)

The IE Flower is a simple navigation tool for Internet Explorer, which can be used with a mouse or touchpad. There are a series of commands that can be performed using the flower such as a double click with the left mouse button, using the right button as a shift feature enables more functions to be selected. Combinations of moves such as holding the left button and rotating the wheel enables horizontal or vertical scrolling.

The yFiles project (Figure 7)

The yFiles project is a series of software components, which together provide methods of visualising networks and diagrams. In the diagram below (left) an example of a graph showing network links with the darker colours more intensive activity. yFiles is effectively a library of algorthims allow-

Figure 7. yFiles project

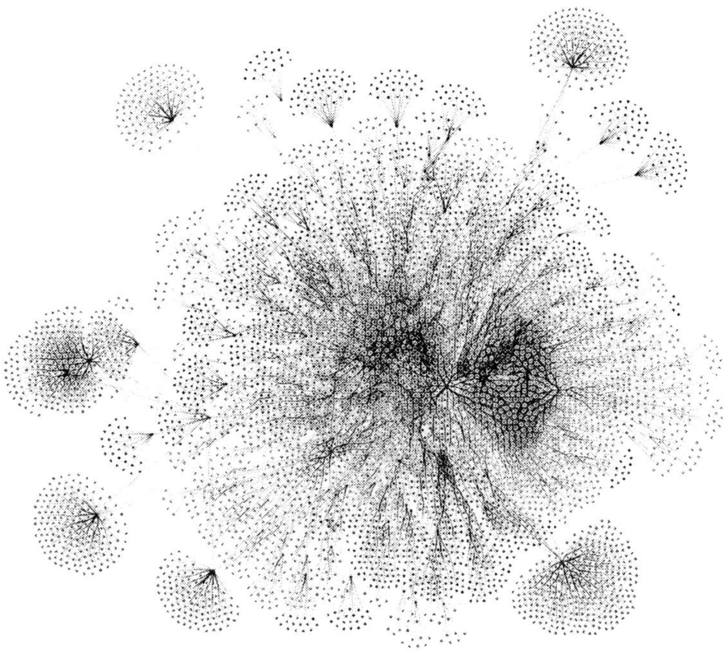

Figure 8. System data mining and analysis

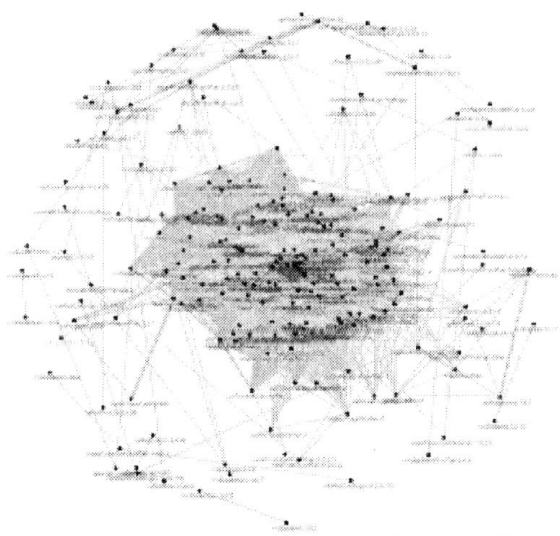

ing analysis, visualisation and layout of graphs, diagrams and networks.

System Data Mining and Analysis (Figure 8)

In the diagram above the network shows a large amount of collected during system operation. This data is then analysed to provide information about the systems operational status. Various types of data files can be used as the basis for this analysis such as software log files, audit trails, and network traffic statistics. The projects goal was to create 'advanced system management technology' by analysing mining and modelling large data sets of system measurement statistics. They have dealt with 'system invariants' which can cause problems that need to have fault detection, and have considered other problematic areas such as resource managements, performance tuning, configuration set up and debugging.

Tulip Project (Figure 9)

The Tulip software system has been designed to visualize very large graphs. It is capable of dealing with up to 500,000 elements on a personal computer. The technology allows 3D visualisations, 3D modifications, plug-in support, support for clusters and navigation, automatic graph drawing, automatic clustering of graphs, and finally automatic selection and colouring of elements

Model Based Clustering (WebCANVAS, Figure 10)

Cadez, Heckerman, Meek, Smyth and White (2000) have produced a methodology, which presents visualized navigation patterns on a web site. Users are first put into clusters so that users with similar navigation paths are grouped together. Then within each cluster, the navigational paths are displayed so that they can be compared. The model based clustering approach clusters users according to the order they select web sites. Their algorithm scales linearly with the number of user and the number of clusters, and ca deal with millions of users and thousands of clusters. The diagram below demonstrates one of these comparisons across several clusters.

FUTURE RESEARCH DIRECTIONS

The previous sections detailed current research on navigation patterns, new navigation tools and

Figure 9. The Tulip project

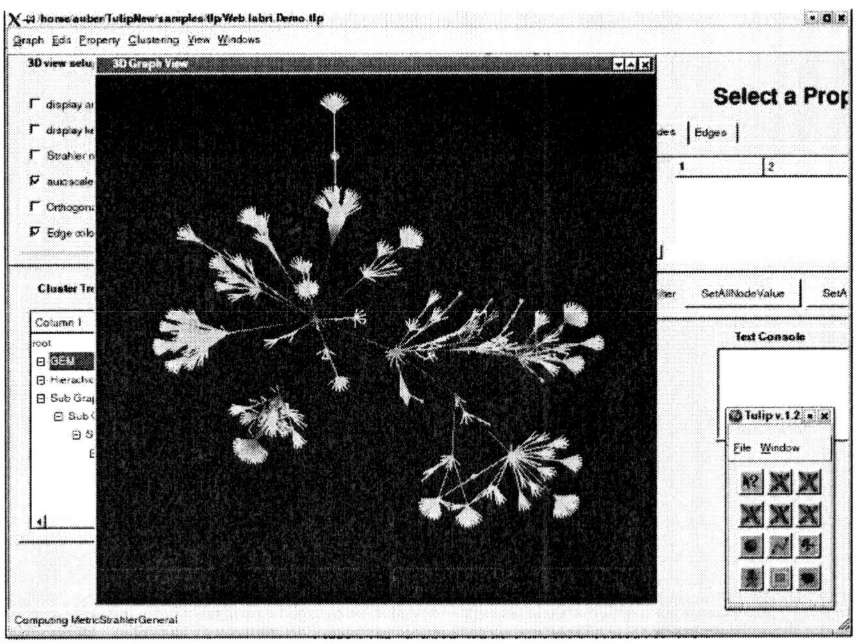

an outline of possible directions in visualising these with some visualisation examples across a range of disciplines. These new areas of research in visualisation which would have significant impact when applied to multimedia and internet resources and these techniques would allow an expansion of the possible views or investigations possible within interactive media resources. Much of this work is being done in the field of social networking. In this research the connections that people make over work or research is mapped and different methods of visualising these as maps, charts, patterns etc. give a different perspective on potential analysis methods. The key point of the chapter is the need to assess navigation abilities of students, even of digital natives, to develop their skills and abilities in this area and to give them a set of device independent navigation tools that they can use in many different resources.

It has proved very difficult to assess the amount of learning being done during multimedia and internet sessions. Pre and posttests do assess some of this however, the background knowledge of each individual is very varied and this prior knowledge makes comparisons across a student body very difficult. The important aspect of this is rather to ensure that the student is using the resource well and is actually learning while using it. The benefits of the visualisations are that these are easy to understand and to remember and a graphical image is easier to retain in the memory. Allowing students to link work areas together and to see the benefit of the work they have done is very important. Allowing them the facility to re-use information and skills is equally essential and developing an appropriate set of tools into a tool bag or palette would be a useful skill set to take with them into employment or further study. The Internet will remain a source of information resources and users need to be fully equipped to use these and to make the best use of limited time.

Figure 10. Web CANVAS

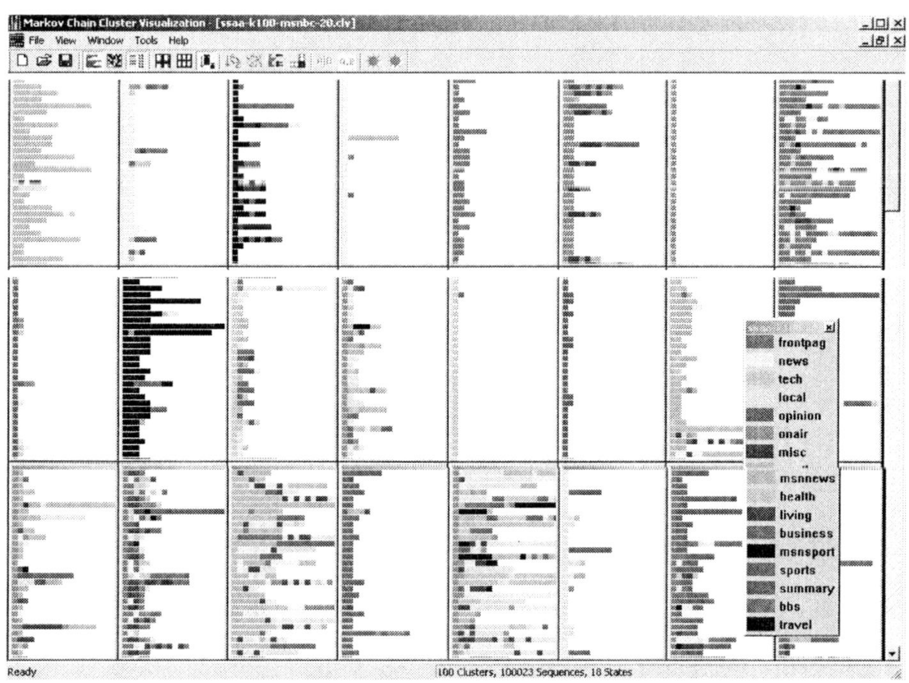

CONCLUSION

The present work on navigation patterns discussed in the chapter has shown that for all groups – children and adults there were distinct preferences in how they preferred to navigate. These findings have significant importance in education and especially in learning, as giving users the tools to navigate how they prefer but also how they are used to navigating imposes less cognitive load. It also allows them to develop their learning and skills with the minimum amount of interference – having to find out how something works rather than finding the information required. There were differences in particular between novices and experts, and with those with little and high levels of experience (not necessarily synonomous groups). Most of the users enjoyed using the navigation tools and when shown how to use a specific tool they would re-use this tool in their own open sources. This would happen either with the tools they had been using initially or in some cases to the exclusion of everything else they had used, e.g. with the wizards. The users were keen to use tools they had not used before or were not aware of their existence. They were particularly keen to find out about and also to try out the newer tools, especially if they saved time and effort. This promotes the view that developing navigational tools is an issue of importance to users and further expansion of these tools and knowledge of using them would both speed up the process of searching and make the search more varied and interesting.

This chapter has significance for digital natives as they may be able to use a wider range of tools but may not be aware of specific educational tools, or be able to determine exactly which tool would be the best for a particular resource. The research has shown how vital it is for educators and for digital natives to work together, to educate each other and to provide facilities, which both personalise, and individualise learning. This chapter has argued for the development of a series of navigational tools that are stand alone, totally device independent, flexible and can be assembled as a toolkit or palette, which the user would employ on a series of different multimedia and internet resources.

REFERENCES

Avgeriou, P., Papasalouros, A., Retalis, S., & Skordalakis, M. (2003). Towards a Pattern Language for Learning Management Systems. *Educational Technology & Society*, *6*(2), 11–24.

Barry, C., & Lang, M. (2001). A survey of multimedia and Web development techniques and methodology usage. *IEEE MultiMedia*, *8*(3), 52–60. doi:10.1109/93.917971

Beasley, R., & Vila, J. (1992). The identification of navigation patterns in a multimedia environment: A Case Study. *Journal of Educational Multimedia and Hypermedia*, *1*, 209–222.

Beasley, R., & Waugh, M. (1997). Predominant initial and review patterns of navigation in a fully constrained hypermedia hierarchy. *Journal of Educational Multimedia and Hypermedia*.

Bennett, S., Maton, K., & Kervin, L. (2008). The 'digital natives' debate: A critical review of the evidence. *British Journal of Educational Technology*, *39*(5), 775–786. doi:10.1111/j.1467-8535.2007.00793.x

Berendt, B., & Brenstein, E. (2001). Visualizing individual differences in Web navigation: STRATDYN, a tool for analyzing navigation patterns. *Behavior Research Methods, Instruments, & Computers*, *33*(2), 243–257.

Boyle, T. (2003). Design principles for authoring dynamic, reusable learning objects. *Australian Journal of Educational Technology*, 19(1), 46-58. *Breadcrumbs image.* (n.d.). Retrieved from http://wiki.openstreetmap.org/images/1/19/Weekend_traces_cropped.png

Brusilovsky, P., & Rizzo, R. (2005). Using Maps and Landmarks for Navigation between Closed and Open Corpus Hyperspace in Web-based Education. *Computers & Education*, *44*(4), 441–457. doi:10.1016/j.compedu.2004.04.007

Cadez, I., Heckerman, D., Meek, C., Smyth, P., & White, S. (2003). Visualization of navigation patterns on a web site using model based clustering. *Journal of Data Mining and Knowledge Discovery*, *7*(4), 399–424. doi:10.1023/A:1024992613384

Calcaterra, A., Antonietti, A., & Underwood, J. (2005). Cognitive style, hypermedia navigation and learning. *Computers & Education*, *44*(4), 441–457. doi:10.1016/j.compedu.2004.04.007

Canter, D., Powell, J., Wishart, J., & Roderick, C. (1986). User navigation in complex database systems. *Behaviour & Information Technology*, *5*(3), 249–257. doi:10.1080/01449298608914518

Canter, D., Rivers, R., & Storrs, G. (1985). Characterising user navigation through complex data structures. *Behaviour & Information Technology*, *4*(2), 93–102. doi:10.1080/01449298508901791

Chen, C., & Rada, R. (1996). Interacting With Hypertext: A Meta-Analysis of Experimental Studies. *Human-Computer Interaction*, *11*, 125–156. doi:10.1207/s15327051hci1102_2

Chen, S. Y., Fan, J. P., & Macredie, R. D. (2006). Navigation in Hypermedia Learning Systems: Experts vs. Novices. *Computers in Human Behavior*, *22*(2), 251–266. doi:10.1016/j.chb.2004.06.004

Chen, S. Y., & Macredie, R. D. (2002). Cognitive Styles and Hypermedia Navigation: Development of a Learning Model. *Journal of the American Society for Information Science and Technology*, *53*(1), 3–15. doi:10.1002/asi.10023

Chen, S. Y., & Macredie, R. D. (2004). Cognitive Modelling of Student Learning in Web-Based Instructional Programs. *International Journal of Human-Computer Interaction*, *17*(3), 375–402. doi:10.1207/s15327590ijhc1703_5

Coburn, P. (2004). The change function. *Always on: The Insider's Network*. Retrieved April 19, 2006, from http://www.alwaysonnetwork.com/comments.php

Conklin, J. (1987). Hypertext: An introduction and survey. *IEEE Computer*, *20*(9), 17–41.

Edwards, D., Hardman, L., & McAleese, R. (1989). Lost in hyperspace: cognitive mapping and navigation in a hypertext environment. In *Hypertext: Theory into Practice* (pp. 90-105). London: Intellect Books.

Fast, K., & Sedig, K. (2005). The INVENT framework: Examining the role of information visualisation in the reconceptualization of digital libraries. *Journal of Digital Information*, *6*(3).

Feeney, L. (2007). Digital denizens. In *Instructional technology resources: In the spotlight*. Retrieved May 16, 2007, from http://loki.stockton.edu/~intech/spotlight-digital-denizens.htm

Fenley, S. (1997). Educational objectives and the promotion of learning in the construction of multimedia packages. In *Proceedings of Euro AI-ED*, Lisbon

Fenley, S. (1998). Navigational issues in interactive multimedia. In *Proceedings of ICCE 1998 Conference, International Conference on Computers in Education*, Beijing, China.

Fenley, S. (2006). *Navigational patterns in interactive multimedia.* PhD thesis, Open University.

Ford, N., & Chen, S. (2000). Individual Differences, Hypermedia Navigation, and Learning: An Empirical Study. *Journal of Educational Multimedia and Hypermedia*, *9*(4), 441–457.

Frand, J. L. (2000). The information-age mindset. Changes in students and implications for higher education. *EDUCAUSE Review,* 35(5), 15-24. Retrieved from http://www.educause.edu/ir/library/pdf/ERM0051.pdf

Gibson, J. J. (1979). *The Ecological Approach to Visual Perception*. Boston: Houghton Mifflin.

Gibson's Theory of Direct perception – Optic Flow. (n.d.). Retrieved from http://www.users.totalise.co.uk/~kbroom/Lectures/gibson.htm

Gomez, J., Cachero, C., & Pastor, O. (2001). On Conceptual Modeling of Device-Independent Web Applications: Towards a Web Engineering Approach. *IEEE MultiMedia, 8*(2), 26–39. doi:10.1109/93.917969

Gregory, R. (1974). Distortion of visual space as inappropriate constancy scaling. In R. Gregory (Ed.), *Concepts and mechanisms of perception* (pp. 342-349). New York: Charles Scribner's Sons.

Hall, R., Balestra, J., & Davis, M. (2000). *A Navigational Analysis of Linear and Non-Linear Hypermedia Interfaces*. American Educational Research Association, New Orleans, LA.

Henderson, L. (1993). Interactive multimedia computer courseware and culturally appropriate ways of learning. In C. Latchem, J. Williamson & L. Henderson-Lancett (Eds.), *Interactive multimedia: Practice and promise* (pp. 189-203). London: Kogan Page.

Horney, M. A. (1993). Case Studies of Navigational Patterns in Constructive Hypertext. *Computers & Education,* 20(3), 257-270. Hutchings, G., Hall, W., & Colbourn, C. (1992). *The Effect of Navigation Tool Presentation on Hypermedia Navigation Strategies and User Disorientation.* Technical Report, University of Southampton. Retrieved from http://eprints.ecs.soton.ac.uk/4410/

Jih, H., & Reeves, T. (1992). Mental Models: A Research Focus for Interactive Learning Systems. *ETR&D, 40*(3), 39–53. doi:10.1007/BF02296841

Jukes, I., & Dosaj, A. (2006). *Understanding digital children (DKS): Teaching and Learning in the new digital landscape.* Retrieved April 1, 2009, from http://www.ibo.org/ibap/conference/documents/IanJukes-UnderstandingDigitalKids.pdf

Kennedy, G., Judd, T., Churchward, A., Gray, K., & Krause, K. (2008). First year students' experiences with technology: Are they really digital natives? *Australasian Journal of Educational Technology, 24*(1), 108–122.

Lawless, K. A., & Kulikowich, J. M. (1996). Understanding hypertext navigation through cluster analysis. *Journal of Educational Computing Research, 14*(4), 385–399.

Mat-Hassan, M., & Levene, M. (2003). *Understanding Web Searching & Navigation Patterns.* Retrieved from http://www2003.org/cdrom/papers/poster/p061/p61-mathassan.html

Mayes, J., Draper, S., McGregor, A., & Oatley, K. (1988). Information flow in a user interface: the effect of experience and context on the recall of Macwrite screens. In D. Jones & R. Winder (Eds.), *People and Computers IV*. Cambridge, UK: Cambridge University Press.

McGrath, D. (1992). Hypertext, CAI, paper, or program control: Do learners benefit from choices? *Journal of Research on Computing in Education, 24*, 513–532.

McGuffin, M. J., & Schraefel, M. C. (2004) A Comparison of Hyperstructures: Zzstructures, mSpaces, and Polyarchies. In: *ACM Conference on Hypertext and Hypermedia, 2004*, Santa Cruz, California, USA, 153-162

McKnight, C., Dillon, A. P., & Richardson, J. H. (Eds.). (1993). *Hypertext: A Psychological Perspective*. Chichester, UK: Ellis Horwood.

Misanchuk, E. R., & Schwier, R. A. (1992). Representing Interactive Multimedia and Hypermedia Audit Trails. *Journal of Educational Multimedia and Hypermedia, 1*, 355–372.

Mor, E., & Minguillón, J. (2004). E-learning Personalization based on Itineraries and Long-term Navigational Behavior. In *Proceedings of the 13th International . World Wide Web (Bussum), 2004*, 264–265.

Neisser, U. (1976). *Cognition and Reality*. San Francisco: W.H. Freeman.

Niederhauser, D., Reynolds, R., Salmen, D., & Skolmoski, P. (2000). The Influence of Cognitive Load on Learning from Hypertext. *Journal of Educational Computing Research, 23*(3), 237–255. doi:10.2190/81BG-RPDJ-9FA0-Q7PA

Oblinger, D. (2003). Boomers, Gen-Xers & Millennials. Understanding the new students. *EDUCAUSE Review,* 38(4), 37-47. Retrieved from http://www.educause.edu/ir/library/pdf/ERM0342.pdf

Orey, M. A., & Nelson, W. A. (1994). *Visualizing Techniques for Examining Learner Interactions with Hypermedia Environments*. ERIC Document Reproduction Service . *No. ED, 373*, 747.

Park, J., & Kim, J. (2000). Contextual Navigation Aids for Two World Wide Web Systems. *International Journal of Human-Computer Interaction, 12*(2), 193–217. doi:10.1207/S15327590IJHC1202_3

Prensky, M. (2003). Digital game-based learning Computers in Entertainment (CIE). Retrieved from http://portal.acm.org Qui, L. (1994). Frequency Distribution of Hypertext Path Patterns: A Pragmatic Approach. *Information Processing & Management,* 30, 131–40.

Prensky, M. (2005). *Listen to the natives Educational Leadership*. Retrieved from http://centre4.core-ed.net

Recker, M. M. (1994). *A Methodology for Analysing Students' Interactions within Educational Hypertext*. ERIC Document Reproduction Service . *No. ED, 388*, 288.

Reed, S. *(1988)*. James J. Gibson and the Psychology of Perception. *New Haven, CT: Yale University Press*.

Rossi, G., Schwabe, D., & Lyardet, F. (2000). User interface patterns for hypermedia applications AVI. In *Proceedings of the working conference on Advanced visual interfaces,* Palermo, Italy, 136 - 142.

Shapiro, A., & Niederhauser, D. (2004). *Handbook of research on educational communications*.

Shum, S. (1990). Real and Virtual Spaces: Mapping from Spatial Cognition to Hypertext. *Hypermedia, 2*(2), 133–158.

Simpson, A., & McKnight, C. (1990). Navigation in hypertext: structural cues and mental maps. In R. McAleese & C. Green (Eds.), *Hypertext: State of the Art*, 73-83. Oxford, UK: Intellect.

Spiliopoulou, M., Faulstich, L. C., & Winkler, K. (1999). A Data Miner analyzing the Navigational Behaviour of Web Users. In *Proc. of the Workshop on Machine Learning in User Modelling of the ACAI'99*, Greece.

Srivastava, J., Cooley, R., Deshpande, M., & Tan, P. N. (2000). Web usage mining: discovery and applications of usage patterns from Web data. *ACM SIGKDD Explorations Newsletter, 1*(2), 12–23. doi:10.1145/846183.846188

System Data mining and Analysis. (n.d.). Retrieved from http://www.nec-labs.com/research/robust/robust_ASM-website/main/projects.php

Tan, P. N., & Kumar, V. (2002). Discovery of web robot sessions based on their navigational patterns. *Data Mining and Knowledge Discovery, 6*(1), 9–35. doi:10.1023/A:1013228602957

Tapscott, D. (1998). *Growing Up Digital. The Rise of the Net Generation*. New York: McGraw-Hill.

Tauscher, L., & Greenberg, S. (1996). *Revisitation Patterns in World Wide Web Navigation*. Technical Report Research report 96-587-07, University of Calgary, Calgary, USA.

The Tulip project. (n.d.). Retrieved from http://www.linuxsoft.cz/screenshot_img/4150-a.jpg

The INTENTS Project. (2007). Dublin, Ireland: University of Dublin.

Unz, D., & Hesse, F. (1999). The use of hypertext for learning. *Journal of Educational Computing Research, 20*(3), 279–295.

Visser, K. (2007). *Digital immigrants abroad: Learning the language of e-learning*. Retrieved May 16, 2007, from http://web.archive.org/web/20050616154156/http://ilp.anu.edu.au/Digital_natives.htm

Wagner, H., & Weibel, S. (2005). The Dublin Core Metadata Registry: Requirements, Implementation and Experience. *Journal of Digital Information, 6*(2).

Wright, P. (1991). Designing and evaluating documentation for IT users. In B. Shackel & S. J. Richardson (Eds.), *Human factors for informatics usability*. Cambridge, UK: Cambridge University Press.

Wright, P., & Lickorish, A. (1994). Menus and memory load: Navigation strategies in interactive search tasks. *International Journal of Human-Computer Studies, 40*, 968–1008. doi:10.1006/ijhc.1994.1045

yWorks. (n.d.). Retrieved from http://www.yworks.com/

Zaiane, O. R. (2002). Building a recommender agent for e-learning systems, In . *Proceedings of the International Conference on Computers in Education, 1*, 55–59. doi:10.1109/CIE.2002.1185862

ENDNOTE

1 A learning object is defined as any entity, digital or non-digital, that may be used for learning, education or training, IEEE March, 2002

Section 3
Context of Learning

Chapter 5
Building a Global E-Community: Intercultural Courses on Human Rights Education

Sandra Reitz
Amnesty International & Goethe University Frankfurt, Germany

ABSTRACT

Traditional E-Learning programs mostly focus on disseminating knowledge. Motivation and the transfer to behavior in everyday situations are often neglected. Human Rights Education specifically encompasses attitudes and behavior, but the challenge is to bring this into a virtual setting. The Intercultural Courses on Human Rights Education were conducted with 80 learners from five different countries: USA, the Dominican Republic, Morocco, Germany, and Mongolia. The chapter first describes the practical background of these courses as well as theoretical considerations regarding computer-mediated communication and social constructivist learning approaches. The main focus lies on giving practical examples from the course, which include forum discussions, working with pseudonyms, internet research, and building a human rights conformant society in a simulation. A pre- and post-test enabled a thorough evaluation for all three learning areas: knowledge, attitudes and skills. The results of this evaluation, several lessons learned and a future learning scenario will be shared.

INTRODUCTION

After the "hype" of E-Learning in the past few years, a distinct disenchantment can be observed. Extremely high cancellation rates (Tyler-Smith, 2006) and a loss of motivation due to a lack of exchange with other learners contribute to this disenchantment. On the one hand, E-Learning–just like distance learning in general - requires a high motivation and a high competence for self-learning. The feeling of being "lost in hyperspace" makes it more difficult for the learners to keep an overview of the extent of the program, and previous knowledge of the learner is hardly taken into account. On the other hand, E-Learning environments can be more individualized than classroom trainings, and the combination of different media and learning paths

DOI: 10.4018/978-1-61520-678-0.ch005

enable the consideration of different learning styles and preferences.

Still, the majority of E-Learning programs in the past have stuck to a more traditional approach, focusing on transferring knowledge and "page-turning". Motivation and the transfer to behavior in everyday situations have often been neglected. The setting has mostly been an isolated learner going through textual wasteland of material, and sometimes completing quizzes afterwards to ensure that a knowledge transfer has taken place.

This chapter wishes to show an alternative to this traditional approach. In 2007, Intercultural Courses on Human Rights Education were conducted with learning groups from all over the globe. Learners were not isolated, but members of an e-community exchanging ideas, questions and opinions while at the same time working in small virtual project teams. Even though there were also drop-outs in this course, the building of a virtual community and the importance of exchange as opposed to an isolated learning as well as some responsibility for the success of the project teams increased the motivation of the learners. The courses specifically focused not only on knowledge, but also on the formation and reflection of attitudes and on the acquisition of skills. Working on attitudes and skills was the real challenge for these courses, as hardly any E-Learning programs have tried to do that so far.

Whereas the used technology does not include the latest state of the art, it is the setting of an intercultural course and the inclusion of attitudes and behavior which makes the approach future-oriented. The focus lies clearly on didactic approaches for the world of tomorrow.

BACKGROUND

The Intercultural Courses on Human Rights Education were conducted as a part of a dissertation (Reitz, 2009) at the UNESCO-Chair for Human Rights Education at the University of Magdeburg, and with the support of Amnesty International Germany.

About 80 learners between 16 and 25 years from five different countries participated in the course. Exchange was fostered between all groups of students who came from Michigan State University (USA), and schools in Göttingen (Germany), Marrakesh (Morocco), Salcedo (Dominican Republic) and Ulanbaator (Mongolia). The learners were in various local settings and with variable access to the internet, which of course was a challenge. The learner groups were acquired through their educators – most of these educators had participated in a previously conducted multipliers' course on Human Rights Education and E-Learning. The virtual learning environment was realized with the open-source platform "Moodle" (Moodle, 2008).

The initial situation for the sub-groups was very heterogeneous, especially in form of access to the virtual learning environment, whether the course for them was part of a school setting, and in terms of their level of English. The learners from Germany and the USA were the groups with the easiest access (from home or from school) to the virtual learning environment, while also being the ones most embedded in a school or university setting. The majority of the learners from Morocco, the Dominican Republic and Mongolia were voluntary participants in the project and usually had to go to an internet cafe to access the virtual learning environment, which of course led to a difference in the time and effort they spent on the project.

Before going into the details of the course, some theoretical clarifications and considerations are necessary that will be laid out in the next three sub-chapters.

WHAT IS HUMAN RIGHTS EDUCATION? OR: WORKING ON ATTITUDES AND SKILLS WITHOUT INDOCTRINATION AND MANIPULATION

Human Rights Education is a relatively new field established with the Universal Declaration of Human Rights by the United Nations in 1948, trying to foster human dignity, peace, respect, freedom and equality after the horrors of the Nazi regime and the Second World War (Suarez & Ramirez, 2004). Human Rights Education is embedded in the fields of education, political sciences and law, and therefore has moral as well as political and judicial aspects. It is also closely related to a number of similar pedagogical concepts. The Council of Europe lists a number of those in Figure 1.

Most definitions of Human Rights Education share the same general understanding, as could be summed up by Flowers' (2000) definition: "all learning that develops the knowledge, skills and values of human rights" (p.17). These three areas of knowledge or cognition, skills or behavior, and values or attitudes area are in parallel to the three domains described in Bloom's taxonomy (Bloom 1956; Clark 1999).

Whereas the dissemination or gaining of knowledge seems to form the unproblematic part, questions around values and behavior must be asked: Are learners aware that their attitudes and behavior is to be changed? Do they want this change at all? If learners are unaware, there is the danger of manipulation and indoctrination. Teachers can use their power – their knowledge and their role of setting the content and presenting material in educational settings - to influence the learners without those learners even being aware. Therefore, it must be clear from the beginning that also attitudinal and behavioral aspects are a part of the educational program. In the context of Human Rights Education, it is relatively easy to shock the learners e.g. with film material about drastic human rights violations. Depending on the context in which this material is presented, such a film can be very manipulative. Respecting the learners' autonomy while at the same time achieving better long-term effects requires reflective questions – about film material, fictional questions, dilemma situations or about attitudes in general.

Similarly, behavior should also become a topic for general discussions, rather than creating pressure in order to evoke a certain action. For example class charters – rules how to behave in class that

Figure 1. Different fields related to Human Rights Education (Council of Europe, 2002, p. 27)

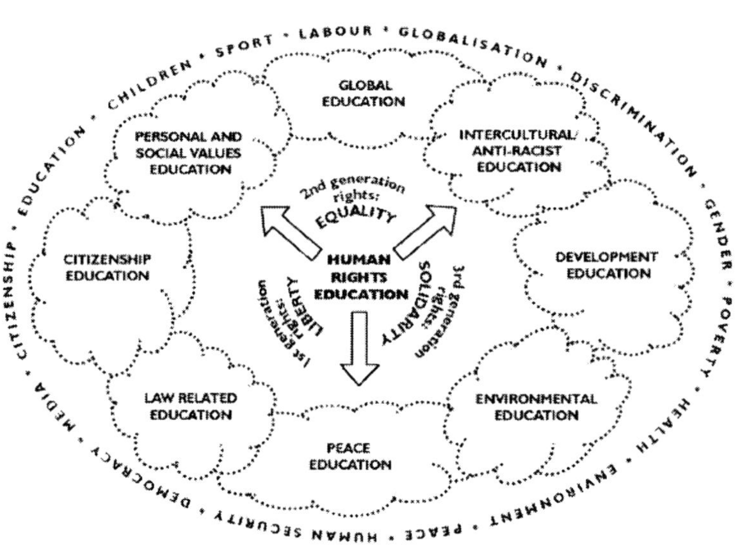

are developed by the whole class – often lead to the fact that the learners themselves remind one another about what kind of behavior they all wish to experience in class.

Only in such an open and participative environment can human rights and democracy be practiced, and "teaching and preaching" (Nations Decade for Human Rights Education No. 4, 2003, pp. 12-13) go hand in hand. Moreover, both empowerment and solidarity become the center of attention, as postulated by Fritzsche's definition of Human Rights Education, which includes the factors "Know and defend your rights" as well as "Acknowledge the rights of others (...) defend also the rights of others" (Fritzsche, 2004, p. 169). The challenge of course is to transfer this open, participative approach that specifically also addresses attitudes and behavior into an E-Learning setting.

Communicative Characteristics of E-Learning

When choosing E-Learning as a tool for education, or more specifically a virtual learning environment, some implications need to be considered, the more so when focusing on attitudes and skills. The most relevant implications relate to communication. Even though voice and video chat will soon become more widely used than nowadays due to improved technology and bandwidth, text-based communication will remain an important factor in E-Learning, especially since it is completely different to the kind of communication we are otherwise used to. A lot of context information is missing due to the form of this online communication, such as the appearance of the "speaker" including age, gender, status expressed through clothes, non-verbal signs such as mimic and gestures, the general communication context or the intonation. Strategies have evolved to cope with these difficulties, e.g. the smiley ":-)", acronyms such as "LOL" for "laughing out loud" or action words such as "*smile*" to express emotions and convey mimics. Yet these strategies can only partly compensate the missing communication channels. Even though the usage of avatars in 3D environments such as in "Second Life" or in online roleplays like "World of Warcraft" conveys appearance and mimic, it is not the natural appearance and mimic of the speaker, who can consciously choose these cues as opposed to a usually unconscious usage in real life.

Theories expecting these kinds of communication to be problematic, diffuse and instable have been disproven, as studies have shown that this kind of communication can actually be even more intense and personal than face-to-face communication (Beck, 2006, pp. 27, 170-172; Koehler, 1999; Thiedeke, 2003, p.9). Beck and Döring (Beck, 2006, pp. 27, 178; Döring, 2003, pp. 161-169) argue that this "channel reduction" can also be interpreted as a kind of liberation, and that the missing information is being imagined, projected and re-contextualized. They argue that exactly through this kind of shelter of pseudonymity, the communication can quickly come to more emotional and intimate topics.

It is important to note that we need to speak of "pseudonymity" rather than anonymity. Nicknames, avatars or e-mail addresses can convey much more than our real names, as they are voluntarily and deliberately chosen. They convey information about identity, and sometimes also about the communication purpose, especially when considering chat nicknames, names on dating platforms or the appearance in a roleplay. This can lead on the one hand to more participative and less status-driven communication, but on the other hand, it can also lead to more aggression and provocation than face-to-face communication (Thiedeke, 2003, pp. 25-29).

THE NEW LEARNING APPROACH: SOCIAL CONSTRUCTIVISM WITH WEB 2.0 TECHNOLOGY

Buzzwords such as Web 2.0 and E-Learning 2.0 underlined a change in the usage and perception of the internet. Social networking, more multimedia such as podcasts and video casts and especially user generated content, which seems to mix producers and consumers to "prosumers" (producer + consumer) or "produsers" (producer + user) were important factors. The shift went from publishing to participation, from personal homepages to blogs, from encyclopedias with editorial staff such as Britannica Online to encyclopedias to which each reader can contribute such as Wikipedia (O'Reilly, 2005). The term "web 2.0" has been criticized with some justifications. Some authors argue against such a shift, because the internet has had users generating content from the very beginning, and that even today, it is only a small number of users actually creating content (Nielsen, 1997; Swartz, 2006). Still, the development holds some important and promising benefits for constructivist learning models. The possibilities to collaborate and participate have increased enormously, and it has become much easier to publish on the internet (Jörissen & Marotzki, 2008; Pütz, 2006).

Constructivism assumes that only little can be taught via traditional teaching. On the contrary, the assumption is that learners construct "their own" reality based on subjective experience structures. Learning is an individual process and happens through the exchange of learners, which is emphasized by the term "social constructivism". A number of didactic requirements have been deducted from constructivism, most prominently a different role of the teacher as a learning consultant, project methodologies and authentic contexts (Holzinger, 2000, pp. 146-164; Kammerl, 2000, pp. 13-14; Kerres, 2001, pp. 74-84).

THE DIDACTIC CONCEPT OF THE INTERCULTURAL COURSES ON HUMAN RIGHTS EDUCATION

Using web 2.0 technology as authoring tools or generally for constructing knowledge in a group clearly supports this learning approach. Moreover, a social-constructivist, participatory E-Learning approach is perfectly adequate for the previously mentioned attitudinal and behavioral areas. Only with such an approach can changes in the attitudinal and behavioral area be planned without using manipulation or indoctrination. Learning in groups is encouraged rather than an isolated self-learning, and an active construction rather than a passive consummation. A prominent virtual learning environment supporting social constructivism is "Moodle" (Moodle, 2008), an open-source application that has been adapted for the E-Learning courses on Human Rights Education. The decision for Moodle is based on an evaluation that looked at previously conducted comparative studies, such as the ones conducted by Schulmeister (2003), Baumgartner, Häfele & Maier-Häfele (2005) and Edutech (2005). This is by no means a general recommendation: for other purposes, other products may have been the better choice, and even the Human Rights Education Courses could certainly have been conducted with other platforms. Still, the availability of a large number of different learning activities, a very active support forum, and an intuitive navigation compared especially to other open-source products were factors in favor of Moodle when looking at tools to support social constructivist learning.

As far as the understanding of intercultural learning is concerned, the term "culture" is by no means to be understood as something homogeneous or static, or something that defines an individual on its own. Intercultural education in a more modern sense means to sensitize the learners for other beliefs and social norms, for their own prejudices and for how they react to "otherness". Consequently, the course did not concentrate on the differences between the cultures, but fostered general exchange between different cultures, with a focus on the discussion of values, ethics and human rights. New media and specifically the internet offers enormous opportunities for intercultural learnings: Allemann-Ghionda (2008) shows how new media such as films can serve as a basis for discussion about culture, beliefs, and prejudices, as they often show "another world", e.g. the Bollywood films if they are watched and analysed in Europe or other non-Indian cultures. Rus (2008) goes a step further by describing an intercultural learning scenario via the internet, even though only in an inter-European context. Seen in this way, the internet not only shows this "other world", it also holds the easiest ways for communication with this "other world".

The didactic concept of the Intercultural Courses on Human Rights Education are based on the theoretical background described in the previous sections: due to the implications in the section "Working on attitudes and skills without indoctrination and manipulation", a participative approach is chosen with the teacher acting as a facilitator, and communication being fostered within the learning group as opposed to a more teacher-centered approach. Pseudonymity and other phenomena described in the section on "Communicative Characteristics of E-Learning" serve as a background; the course will try to use the advantages of this kind of communication, as will be explained in "Example 1" below. Finally, the social constructivist approach described in the section on "Web 2.0" is chosen, which mirrors the implications about a participative approach and the focus on communication and exchange between the learners. Attitudes and behavior play an important part in this course, which is mirrored by the discussion of values (Example 2) and a Mars Mission simulation (Example 3).

As far as the didactic sequence is concerned, different stage models for E-Learning have been proposed. For example, Kerres (2001, pp. 188f) suggests adapting instructional events based on Gagné, but these very much focus on cognitive aspects and less on exchange between the learners. The five-stage framework developed by Salmon (Figure 2) seems more appropriate to the social constructivist learning approach used in the Human Rights Education Courses:

This structure was followed in a broad framework, as the learners were be introduced to the course with special care through individual messages and easier tasks, before fostering socialisation through guided forum discussions. Informa-

Figure 2. Five-stage framework model by Salmon (2002, p. 11)

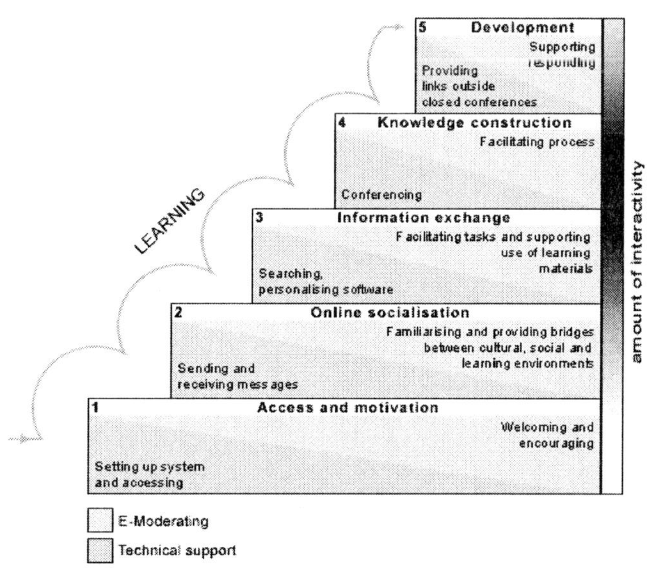

tion exchange was also realized in forums, but for knowledge construction and development, special groupwork forums and chat sessions were used.

Depending on their local situations, learners were required to spend around two hours per week in the virtual learning environment, for a total of eight weeks. Local support was given through the local multipliers, who had a special forum and phone conferences for their questions and exchange with the other multipliers. It was also necessary to adapt to the local limitations regarding technology using a certain bandwidth or CPU power, such as video chat or 3D environments. Therefore, the technology used in this case study is not really future-oriented from a Western perspective, but the inclusion of different cultures, the social constructivist approach and the conscious inclusion of attitudes and behaviour as learning goals certainly is. The "digital divide" is likely to remain an important factor for intercultural courses, as statistics show, in spite of a remarkable growth in the developing countries, that only 20% of the worldwide population had access to the internet in 2006, and around 24% in 2008 (BITKOM 2006; Internet World Stats, 2008).

The following sections give more details about the course, including screenshots taken from the Intercultural Courses on Human Rights Education.

EXAMPLE 1: WORKING WITH PSEUDONYMS

Learners of the E-Learning courses on Human rights Education did not log on with their real names, but with pseudonyms. The idea behind this was twofold: On the one hand, according to the theoretical implications of pseudonimity discussed above, the learners should focus more on the content of the discussion, and not so much on who said something. Especially since learners of the same sub-group or country knew one another, these learners were encouraged to overcome the usual divide between introverted and extroverted learners, between learner stereotypes such as "the mouse" or "the clown". Personal sympathies and antipathies were to step back. On the other hand, the pseudonyms were not chosen by the learners or arbitrarily. The learners were assigned to names of human rights activists. They were not only given the task to find out more about their pseudonyms, but these activists should indirectly also serve as role models.

Learners were encouraged to look at the other learners' pseudonyms. Apart from the clear purpose of getting to know the other learners – who were also allowed to write additional personal information into their profiles – learners should also learn more about other human rights activ-

Figure 3. Overview site of the E-Learning Course on Human Rights Education, realized with Moodle

Figure 4. Example for a profile filled with a description of a Human Rights Activist

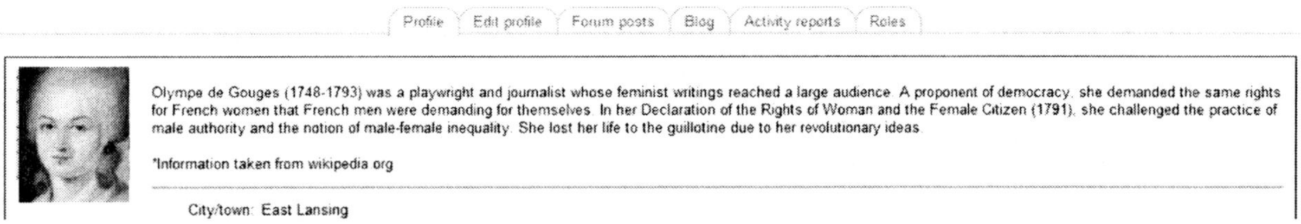

ists. A few matching exercises realized with the Hot Potato Module were introduced, in which the learners had to match the names of human rights activists with the correct description (see Figure 5).

Based on the informal feedback gathered, the learners liked both learning about human rights activists and working with pseudonyms in general. The matching exercise shown above was completed by the majority of the learners even though it was declared as an optional activity.

EXAMPLE 2: FORUM DISCUSSIONS

Figure 6 shows the different forums that were incorporated into the course to ensure learner participation. As suggested by Salmon (2002, p.24) this included an informal forum in order to foster the building on an e-community. As can already be seen by the number of discussions (which means "discussion threads", each discussion could have one or many more posts), learners made heavy use of this opportunity and discussed about their families, friends, hobbies, and popular sports in their countries. However, also more serious topics were posted here, such as why human rights are necessary, what can be done against racism at school, or what the purpose of life is. Except the group work forums, none of these discussions needed much moderation, the learners were focused on the content and did not post anything inappropriate. In the following, the special case of the dilemma forums will be described in a bit more detail.

In order to enable discussions about attitudes and values, moral dilemma discussions were introduced to the E-Learning course. Moral dilemmas are situations in which a person has to choose between two actions, but either way, the person will do something unethical. The most prominent moral dilemma is the Heinz dilemma used by Lawrence Kohlberg (Colby, Kohlberg, Speicher, Hewer, Candee, Gibbs & Power, 1987).

Important from a moral development point of view is not the choice a person would take, but the kind of arguments they use to justify their decision, as these arguments indicate the moral stage the person is in, and for what kind of (counter-) arguments the person might be open. The purpose of moral dilemmas in the E-Learning course was not to diagnose the moral stage the learners were in, but to enable an exchange of arguments, and, consequently, reflection about values, attitudes and human rights as well as a possible development towards "higher stage" arguments. The following examples show those dilemmas that led to some controversy, and they also illustrate what kind of arguments were exchanged and how the learners reacted to one another.

Example 2a

Moderator: "The government of country X has suggested to use the genetic data of all criminals to fight sexual offenses. The government wants to take the data of all criminals who are in prison, and to store their data centrally. So if there is an unsolved sexual offense, police could identify the criminal much quicker, if that person has been

Figure 5. Matching exercise about human rights activists

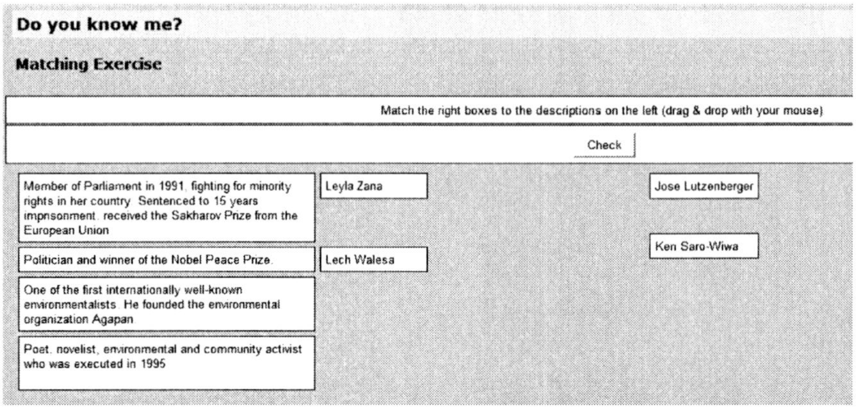

in prison before. Some critics ague that forcing someone to take a DNA test is a serious violation of personal rights. Imagine you are a member of the parliament voting about this suggestion. How would you vote and why?" (dilemma adapted from Rolf, 2001)

Learner A: "I would vote in favor of this suggestion. After committing a crime, a person voluntarily gives up many of his freedoms, including the right to vote in most cases. If storing someone's genetic information could further the resolution of heinous crimes, I believe it is worth having a convicted criminal give up one more right. If someone doesn't want his DNA stored by the police, he should not commit a crime in the first place."

Learner B: "Coming back and reading this topic again has sort of changed my mind on this. I agree with you that I would vote yes. I think that solving crimes and making them do DNA testing is more important than the rights of the criminals. They have lost so many rights by committing crimes that really what is one more for the benefit of all?"

Learner C: "I agree with you. I don't think that getting someone's DNA is as serious as the other rights people actually have to give up when they go to jail."

Figure 6. Overview of discussion forums

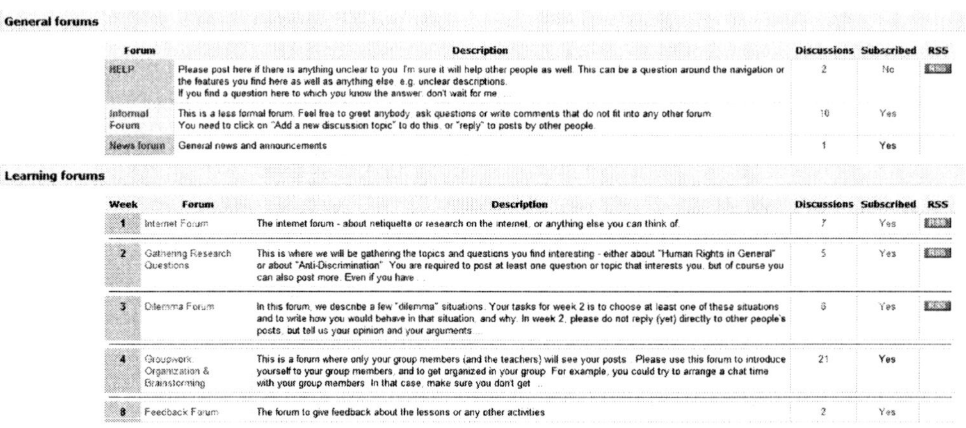

Learner D: "I personally would agree with the critics. To force someone to take a DNA test is a violation of personal rights, no different than forcing someone to have something injected into their body.

I do not agree that prisoners should lose so many rights. The little opportunity that they have present day is ridiculous, and regardless of crime they are still human beings. Many people are in prison for crimes they never committed, like Efren Paredes, Jr., simply because the jury was all white in a very race-conscious area. He has suffered 19 years in prison because he was Mexican and accused of a crime. See http://www.4efren.com for more info. I feel that taking away ALL of their rights (I understand removing some) is counter-productive as far as making them better citizens.

As far the argument for identifying sex offenders, this country's government fails to recognize that most sexual offenses are committed by someone that the victim/survivor was acquainted with already or knew well. Usually sex offenders are not strangers in long cloaks coming out of dark alleys. They are mostly men, and sometimes friends, boyfriends, husbands, fathers, uncles, or brothers. The DNA collection seems to me like it would barely do enough help to make it even considerable to violate so many people's rights."

Important arguments are being exchanged in this example, such as the fact that the prisoners have already committed a crime and therefore lost other, maybe more important rights, learner B arguing "for the benefit of all", and learner D defending prisoners' rights, making the other learners aware of innocent prisoners, paraphrasing statistics, and even referencing other websites. The post from learner B proves that the learners actually change their mind while reading each others' posts – and that they are aware of this shift.

Example 2b

Learner E: "As we all know from the past violence at schools has increased enormously and the gun rampage of 17 years old Robert Steinhäuser in Erfurt is a deterrent example to realize how cruel pupils can be. He killed 16 people with his gun and afterwards he killed himself. There are other deterrent examples in the US. Do you think that we should install bodyguards at the entrance of schools who search all pupils for guns?"

Learner F: "I think it is not necessary to put bodyguards at the school entrance, because it is very seldom that there is an violence act like this at the school. The school should be a peaceful place to learn and not guarded like the white house."

Learner G: "Yes, I think you are right!! If there would be bodyguards at the school entrance, nobody would feel saver I think. I mean: planned violence couldn't stop with this method; just violence in form of a brawl or something like that. And therefore you need not a bodyguard!"

(…)

Learner H: "I thinks so too. In some countries bodyguards are really necessary because attacks and terroristic threats belong to their daily life. It would help to save innocent children who suffer from the political system of their country."

What is important to note in this last example is that the "dilemma" was not introduced by the moderator, but by a learner. Even though one may argue that this case is not necessarily a moral dilemma in the narrow sense, it obviously is on the learners' minds as a question to which there is no clear answer, and which affects their basic rights. It also shows that the learners bring their everyday experiences into the course, start thinking about these experiences in terms of basic rights and dilemma situations, and experience their cultural differences ("in some countries..."). Moreover, they obviously want to discuss these dilemmas with their peers and read each other's opinion.

EXAMPLE 3: MISSION TO MARS – BUILDING A HUMAN-RIGHTS CONFORMANT SOCIETY

The "Mission to Mars" task was one of two group work tasks to be completed in small groups consisting of 5-7 participants each. The learners were introduced to the following scenario:

"It is 2030. The climate crisis has become worse and worse, and the world continues to be full of conflicts and wars. However, the technical development enabled the Mars Mission, and you have been chosen to participate. The goal is to enable permanent living on Mars. We want to avoid the problems that exist on the Earth. Therefore, we want to find a way of life that is as human rights conformant as possible. You have almost absolute power in the beginning - you only need to agree with your group members...

Each group represents a basis station on Mars. Regard the group members as members of the government. Each member of the government is responsible for one Human Right as follows (...)"

The idea of this activity was that each learner is made responsible for a certain human right. Through the scenario, each learner argues for the importance of this human right – in order to receive more money. Some competition for the money is introduced in order to enable a discussion about which human right is regarded as more important than another one. This does by no means speak against the indivisibility of all human rights, but by identifying with a human right and by trying to argue for its importance, the learners are getting emotionally involved and again reflect their attitudes and values. Going into the same direction was a task that asked the learners to create a poster advertisement for "their" human right that was later presented to the whole group, and the best poster was elected by the group.

Finally, the learners should use their creativity in the small group and describe methods how to achieve a human rights conformant society. In a second round, a Mars newspaper article showed the progress of each group and introduced a second element: It turns out that other intelligent life on Mars already exists, and the group has to decide how they behave towards the aggressive Mars inhabitants, who have already started a war with another Mars station...

After having made their decisions, each group analyzed the decisions of another group and wrote an article in the Mars Newspaper about it, in which they could criticize or compliment these decisions while at the same time continuing the story with the fictional development of that Mars station.

The experience with this activity is twofold. Whereas more active groups enjoyed the tasks and the openness with which they could use their creativity, groups with more mixed participants had their problems understanding the approach and completing the tasks. Obviously the different background of the learners and the different embeddedness in the school setting created some issues, with some group members being very active and others not writing a single post. Still, the posters created for this activity to promote "their" human right became very popular among the learners, and the behavior towards the aliens was revealing and thoroughly reflected among the groups while writing the Mars newspaper articles.

OTHER EXAMPLES: CHAT SESSIONS, VOTING, INTERNET RESEARCH, AND SHORT LESSONS

The mixture of different, learner-centered activities turned the course into a truly interactive experience, even though some activities were much more popular than others. Two short, easy-to-prepare, but very interactive actions were the chat sessions and the voting. The chat sessions were always open, and learners could either meet spontaneously with other learners, which was made feasible through a list of currently active learners. The learners could also agree in the group work forum with their 4-6 other group members on a time to meet and discuss the group work. Based on the experience with this course, specific time slots when to meet in the chat are the preferred option for the next course, as hardly any learners met in the chat. Another way to improve the chat session would be to give them more structure, e.g. a special topic to discuss, possibly combined with experts participating in the chat as well and thereby making those chat sessions more attractive.

The voting was another very short, but interactive and participative activity. Learners could vote on the topics or questions to be researched in the course, and they could also vote their favorite posters created in the Mars Mission activity described above. This voting activity only took a minimum of time – both to prepare and for the learners to vote – but gave the learners more influence and supported the participative, interactive approach.

One of the most popular, though less innovative activities was the internet research. In the beginning, learners could gather questions they were interested in. This also included political events at that time, e.g. the demonstration of the Burmese monks, and the so called "Jena 6" incident about racist attacks in a school in the small town of Jena, Louisiana. Afterwards, these plus other questions were listed and the learners could choose topics they would like to work on. After receiving the topic, learners completed their research task independently – mostly with the help of the internet, but in some cases also with books. They also had to formulate a question around that topic that was later to be answered by the other learners. What turned this activity into a very successful activity for the learners were three important factors:

a) The learners participated in the process of gathering the research questions and had influence on the topic they worked on.
b) They received detailed feedback during the course, so they could improve their piece of work before finally submitting it.
c) Their final pieces of work were transformed into short lessons for the other learners. This included the text plus pictures, but also the question for the readers to answer, e.g. in the lesson about the discrimination of homosexuals: "Why you think this discrimination started in the first place? What can we do, as individuals, to stop it?"

Through these factors, and through the activities in total, the role of the learners was different than in traditional classroom settings. They had influence on the topics the group in total worked upon as well as on the individual task they were given. They received detailed feedback which was not directly related to their grades, but to the quality of the product they created, and, most of all, the products were not only for the teachers to read and grade, but to share with their peers who worked through a number of lessons and answered the questions. So instead of being passive consumers of knowledge, learners constructed their own research questions and their own pieces of knowledge. By becoming "experts" for their topic and creating these lessons, they became teachers for one another. This also contributed to the building of an e-community. They exchanged opinions, e.g. in the dilemma forums, with one another rather than arguing towards and for the teacher. The role of the moderator or teacher changed into a learning consultant – basically the idea of the social constructivist learning approach discussed above.

EVALUATION RESULTS

In total, the Intercultural Courses on Human Rights Education were regarded a success by all teachers and most learners involved. Even though some tasks proved very difficult, especially the virtual project work in such a short time frame and with the different settings in the different countries, the vast majority enjoyed the course and the open exchange with learners from other cultures. Reflections about human rights in their own countries as well as abroad, in everyday life and as a philosophical idea, concerning governments and one's own morale were a key factor. A pre- and post-test enabled a thorough evaluation for all three learning areas: knowledge, attitudes and behavior.

The self-reported results showed that

- There were no significant differences between the countries in how often the learners used the internet or how comfortable they felt using new media
- 64% of the learners found the project "good" or "very good", compared to 19% "bad" or "very bad"
- 74% of the learners stated they had learned "a whole lot" or "a lot" about Human Rights Education (13% "not so much" or "nothing")
- 50% of the learners stated they had learned "a whole lot" or "a lot" about communication and virtual teamwork (32% "not so much" or "nothing")
- 48% of the learners answered they had learned "a whole lot" or "a lot" about cultures and cultural barriers (22% "not so much" or "nothing")

In addition to these self-evaluation questions, a questionnaire with cognitive, attitudinal and behavioral elements was used as a pre- and post-test with the learners. Some of these questions need to be revised based on the mixed outcome, but some others show that changes took place in spite of the short time frame of eight weeks.

The knowledge questions evaluated through a paired samples t-test are summarized in Figure 8 and reveal significant differences before and

Figure 7. "I feel I have learned a lot about Human Rights..."

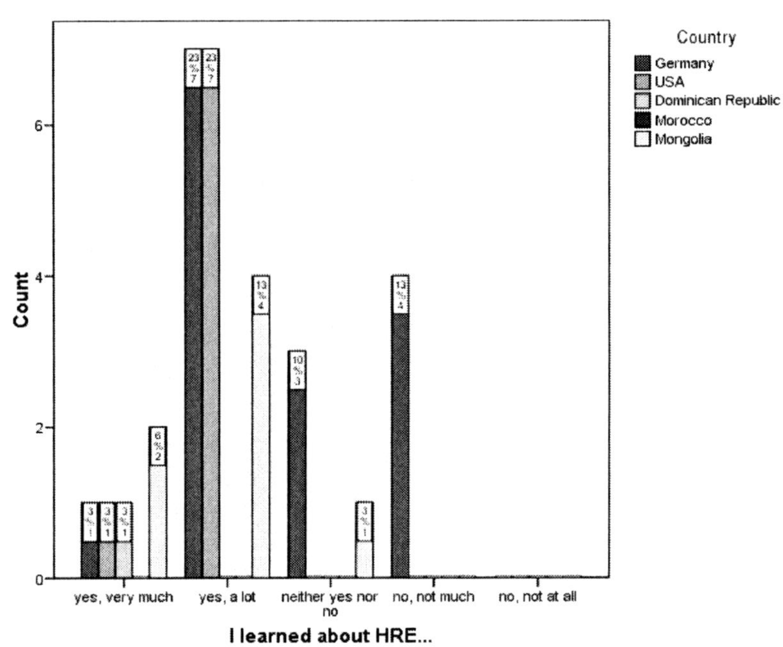

Figure 8. Paired t-test results for the cognitive area

Paired Samples Test

		Paired Differences					t	df	Sig. (2-tailed)
					95% Confidence Interval of the Difference				
		Mean	Std. Deviation	Std. Error Mean	Lower	Upper			
Pair 1	Pre: List of HR - Post: List of HR	-,750	1,713	,324	-1,414	-,086	-2,316	27	,028
Pair 2	Pre: Difference HR - Post: Difference HR	-,778	2,044	,393	-1,587	,031	-1,977	26	,059
Pair 3	Pre: History of HR - Post: History of HR	-,300	1,867	,417	-1,174	,574	-,719	19	,481
Pair 4	Pre: Define Discrimination - Post: Define Discrimination	-1,160	2,249	,450	-2,088	-,232	-2,579	24	,016
Pair 5	Pre: Skin Question - Post: Skin Question	,033	,183	,033	-,035	,102	1,000	29	,326

after the course especially for three knowledge questions:

a) listing human rights
b) describing differences between human rights and other rights
c) (less significant) defining discrimination

Questions related to attitudes and behavior required partly quantitative and partly qualitative answers. As could be expected, the number of significant differences was not as high as in the cognitive area, as attitudinal and behavioral changes take more time than the increase of knowledge. Even though the correlation and paired t-test evaluation shows only weak evidence of changes in the attitudinal and behavioral area, the evaluation also indicates generally positive changes, especially changed means as the following areas:

Attitudes:

a) learners show more agreement to the statement that disabled people should have a right to vote in political elections
b) learners find less situations to be justifying torture

Behavior:

a) increased willingness to join a political organization
b) increased willingness to donate money to an organization that supports human rights and/ or the anti-discrimination movement
c) increased willingness to participate in a non-violent protest march or rally

As indicated above, learners tended to find less situations justifying torture in the post-test than in the pre-test. The original question was: "In which cases do you personally think torture is justified? This question cannot be answered "correctly" or "incorrectly", only your opinion counts" (question adapted from Amnesty International, 1995). The free text learners could enter reveals some interesting arguments, such as the following examples:

Mongolians say that if you tortured your child. Your child will torture his/her child. It mean torture cultivates more advanced torture.

I know, that I am contradictory with my choices. So on one hand I think torture is never justified.

But on the other hand I can understand that people need to be tortured because it helps to save other lives.

If somebody does something bad and you torture him, you make the same mistake like the actor. That's the sole point!

All in all, evidences for significant changes were found to a larger degree in the cognitive field, and to a lesser degree in the attitudinal and the behavioral field. A few changes both in the course material – as described in the examples sections – and in the questionnaire to try and find more appropriate questions – would certainly improve the results. Also, a more long-term oriented evaluation would be helpful to analyze whether these changes are sustainable, even though such an evaluation is difficult to realize in a global, distributed setting. It would also be interesting to see how sustainable such an e-community can be after the course has finished. In spite of these limitations, bearing in mind that both the course material and the questionnaire were freshly developed, and taking into account that all evaluations trying to measure changes in the attitudinal and behavioral area have their difficulties, the results are very encouraging, because they prove that significant changes can happen in a relatively short E-Learning course, and that these changes are not only happening in the cognitive, but also in the attitudinal and behavioral area.

FUTURE RESEARCH DIRECTIONS

The intercultural courses in Human Rights Education represent trends that are likely to grow in the future years: On the one hand, we have changes on a societal level. Globalization will continue, and intercultural settings will become more and more normal. That does not mean that these intercultural settings are unproblematic, and therefore, courses in which learners can exchange their opinions across cultures will become more important. In parallel to this development, human rights and common values across all cultures will most likely become a widely debated topic. We can already see an enormous increase of the debate since the Universal Declaration of Human Rights in 1948. Human Rights are much more in the news, wars or military interventions are being justified with human rights or their violations. It is only natural that in the process of globalization, people are trying to find values they all can share, and in spite of arguments against the universality of human rights, they are the most accepted values and norms we currently have. Therefore, Human Rights Education will also continue to be a growing field in the future, possibly expanded with forms of global education.

Learning and teaching will continue to change. We will experience dramatic changes in the technical field. Ubiquitous computing and ubiquitous learning is already advancing, so we will have to find ways of teaching and learning that make use of these new ways of communications. That does not mean that we will have to invent completely new ways of teaching, but the focus on certain methodologies are likely to shift. Interactivity as well as the new forms of communication will have to be incorporated into our approaches. The shift from teacher-centered to learner-centered and participative approaches will continue. We already have an information overflow, but the learners need to learn how to turn information into knowledge – which is not a question of more factual information, but a question of methodological and process knowledge. This will not only shift the focus from purely cognitive to attitudinal and behavior approaches, it will also strengthen learner-centered approaches as opposed to teacher-centered approaches. More and more importance will lie on how to evaluate sources, how to critically question statements and how to transfer information into knowledge that can be used in everyday situations. This is an individual process, and therefore, the individual learning processes will have to be supported rather than applying a teacher-centered "teach-test-reply" approach, which might still be useful for disseminating purely factual knowledge. What is important is that we do not get carried away – neither with technological gimmicks that appear appealing and shiny, but do not follow any logic learning approach – nor with our educational methods without taking our learners with us.

A FUTURE SCENARIO FOR INTERCULTURAL E-LEARNING COURSES

Based on the theoretical implications discussed in the beginning of this chapter and on the lessons learned described in the examples, a future scenario for Intercultural E-Learning Courses on Human Rights Education could look like this:

Young learners from all over the globe use their mobile devices to log onto the course – with only minimal costs. This results in more log-ons, but probably for a shorter period of time spent in the environment per log-on. Therefore, short, interactive elements not needing too much concentration – such as the voting example described here – are needed. Another consequence is that the E-Learning course becomes more embedded into the everyday life of the learners. They may watch a relevant report on the news and log on for a minute to hear from the peers in other parts of the world if they have heard similar information and share their own views. We have already seen this happening in the case study with learners being very interested in exchange on school shooting sprees, the demonstrations of the Burmese monks or the Jena 6 event in the USA. Finally, time differences are less problematic due to the possibilities of ubiquitous learning.

Even though the world "comes together" through easier ways of communication, the different values systems in each culture are very stable and require an exchange about these values and possibly universal norms such as human rights. Consequently, attitudes and behavior play a more important role than knowledge, and a participative, collaborative learning approach is still best suited. In addition to posting in forums, 3D environments with self-created avatars and synchronous chat are popular environments for learning. This changes the communicative characteristics of E-Learning, but still enables a kind of pseudonimity, possibly a more realistic one. Especially the area of behavior enters a new dimension through the use of 3D environments and avatars, as behavior can be tried out even more realistically in such a virtual, sheltered environment. As a further development of 3D environments, augmented reality (a combination of real-world and computer-generated data, the Star Trek "Holodeck" being the most popular example) goes even one step further towards reality. Also, the difference between games and learning simulations such as the Mars Mission become less obvious, and learners enjoy both the cultural exchange and the creativity they can bring into the course. On the other hand, more "traditional" learning approaches such as the internet research, in combination with a truly participative approach that includes constant feedback, remains both important and popular for the learners. Just like in the Web 2.0 philosophy, learners become not only produsers, but experts and teachers for a certain piece of the course. In the future scenario, their research products certainly include more multimedia elements, such as podcasts, videocasts, or simulations in the 3D environment.

The experiences gained in this case study – the fact that in spite of some language problems, learners were able to communicate with each other about their values and felt at ease with the learning environment leads to an optimistic outlook: All in all, new forms of technology will help coping with a globalized world and thereby overcoming cultural barriers.

CONCLUSION

The courses described in this chapter show one approach of dealing with these challenges. The Intercultural Courses on Human Rights Education reached students who might not otherwise see the relevance of understanding human rights from the perspectives of other nations and cultures. The learners developed new skills in online learning, increased awareness and knowledge about the strengths and challenges of conducting projects in small, and large, online groups. This was an enriched environment because of the cultural diversity and e-setting. Most significantly, the course provided an enriching opportunity for students to re-conceptualize and approach broader aspects of learning, their values and their relationships with others and the systems inherent to their national context.

It is an approach that can certainly still be improved, but it not only shows that such an approach can be successful, it also gives empirical evidence. We need much more evaluation of our educational approaches – not to prove which way is "the best" - too much depends on the context and on individual preferences on parts of the learners and teachers to realistically assume there is a "best way" - but to prove that educational programs can be successful while at the same time finding out where improvement is needed.

Certainly the combination of the attitudinal and behavioral areas with E-Learning will be a growing field for research. The buzzword social competence is an indicator for this, as well as the challenges we face in schools, like mobbing or general violence. Educational programs facing these challenges will focus on learner-centered and participative approaches. New media can help us using innovative approaches, including pseudonimity, while at the same time preparing the learners for their future life, which will certainly encompass more technology and more contact with other cultures.

REFERENCES

Allemann-Ghionda, C. (2008). Vom Postulat zur bildungspolitischen und didaktischen Umsetzung? In L. Rosen & S. Farrokhzad (Eds.), *Macht – Kultur – Bildung* (pp. 147-163). Münster, Germany: Waxmann Verlag.

Amnesty International. (1995). *Unterrichtspraxis Menschenrechte. Folter und Gewalt.* Solothurn, Switzerland: Amnesty International.

Baumgartner, P., Häfele, H., & Maier-Häfele, K. (2005). *Evaluation von Lernplattformen: Verfahren, Ergebnisse und Empfelhungen (Version 1.3).* Retrieved January 5, 2009 from http://www.bildung.at/filedatabase/downloader.php?file_code=6d0873c599c24c0a7f302fba323d8065&filedb_dir=/bmbwk/dateidb/bildung2

Beck, K. (2006). *Computervermittelte Kommunikation im Internet.* München, Germany: Oldenbourg.

BITKOM - Bundesverband Informationswirtschaft. Telekommunikation und neue Medien e.V. (2007). *Fast jeder fünfte Mensch ist online.* Retrieved October 20, 2008, from http://www.bitkom.org/46074.aspx

Bloom, B. S. (1956). *Taxonomy of educational objectives: The classification of educational goals.* Chicago, IL: Susan Fauer Company, Inc.

Clark, D. R. (1999). Learning *domains or Bloom's taxonomy: The three types of learning.* Retrieved January 7, 2009, from http://www.nwlink.com/~donclark/hrd/bloom.html

Colby, A., Kohlberg, L., Speicher, B., Hewer, A., Candee, D., Gibbs, J., & Power, C. (1987). *The measurement of moral judgment (Vol. 2), standard issue scoring manual.* Cambridge, UK: Cambridge University Press.

Council of Europe. (2002). *Compass. A manual on human rights education with young people.* Strasbourg, France: Council of Europe Publishing.

Döring, N. (2003). Sozialpsychologie des Internet. In Göttingen et al., *Die Bedeutung des Internet für Kommunikationsprozesse, Identitäten, soziale Beziehungen und Gruppen (2nd ed.)*. Göttingen, Germany: Hogrefe.

Edutech. (2005). *Course platform evaluation report*. Retrieved January 5, 2009 from http://www.edutech.ch/lms/ev3/index.php

Flowers, N. (2000). *The human rights education handbook. Effective practices for learning, action, and change*. Minneapolis, MN: Human Rights Resource Center, University of Minnesota. Retrieved February 3, 2007, from http://www1.umn.edu/humanrts/edumat/hreduseries/hrhandbook/toc.html

Fritzsche, K. P. (2004). *Menschenrechte. Eine Einführung mit Dokumenten*. Paderborn, Germany: Schönigh.

Holzinger, A. (2000). *Basiswissen Multimedia. Band 2: Lernen. Kognitive Grundlagen multimedialer Informationssysteme*. Würzburg, Germany: Vogel Buchverlag.

Internet World Stats. (2008). *Internet usage statistics. The Internet big picture. World Internet users and population stats*. Retrieved October 20, 2008, from http://www.internetworldstats.com/stats.htm

Jörissen, B., & Marotzki, W. (2008). Neue Bildungskulturen im "Web 2.0": Artikulation, Partizipation, Syndikation. In F. von Gross, W. Marotzki & U. Sander (Eds.), *Internet – Bildung – Gemeinschaft* (pp. 203-225). Wiesbaden, Germany: VS Verlag für Sozialwissenschaft.

Kammerl, R. (2001). Computerunterstütztes Lernen – Eine Einführung. In: R. Kammerl (Ed.), *Computergestütztes Lernen* (pp. 7-22). München, Germany: Oldenbourg.

Kerres, M. (2001). *Multimediale und telemediale Lernumgebungen. Konzeption und Entwicklung*. München, Germany: Oldenbourg.

Koehler, T. (1999). Sozialwissenschaftliche Theorien und Befunde zur computervermittelten Kommunication. In W. Frindte & T. Koehler (Eds.), *Kommunikation im Internet* (pp. 137-182). Frankfurt, Germany: Peter Lang.

Moodle. (2008). *Philosophy*. Retrieved January 24, 2009, from http://docs.moodle.org/en/Philosophy

Nielsen, J. (1997). *Community is dead; long live mega-collaboration*. Retrieved December 2, 2008, from http://www.useit.com/alertbox/9708b.html

O'Reilly, T. (2005). *What is Web 2.0? Design patterns and business models for the next generation of software*. Retrieved December 2, 2008, from http://www.oreillynet.com/pub/a/oreilly/tim/news/2005/09/30/what-is-web-20.html

Pütz, M. (2006). *E-Learning 2.0 - Buzzword oder ernstzunehmende Entwicklung?* Retrieved December 2, 2008, from http://www.fortbildung-bw.de/wb/09_bildungsanbieter/05_e-learning/zwei_null.php

Reitz, S. (2004). Menschenrechtsbildung als E-Learning. In C. Mahler & A. Mihr (Eds.). *Menschenrechtsbildung. Bilanz und Perspektiven* (pp. 265-278). Wiesbaden, Germany: VS Verlag für Sozialwissenschaften.

Reitz, S. (2009). *Improving social competence via e-learning: The example of human rights education*. Unpublished Doctoral Dissertation, Otto-von-Guericke University, Magdeburg.

Rolf, B. (2001). *Eine kleine Sammlung von Dilemmata*. Retrieved January 29, 2009, from http://www.learn-line.nrw.de/angebote/praktphilo/didaktik/dilemma_slg.pdf

Rus, C. (2008). Intercultural and citizenship education through the use of information technologies. In V. B. Georgi (Ed.), *The Making of Citizens in Europe: New Perspectives on Citizenship Education* (pp. 148-152). Bonn, Germany: Bundeszentrale für politische Bildung.

Salmon, G. (2002). *E-tivities. The key to active online learning*. London and New York: Routledge.

Schulmeister, R. (2003). *Lernplattformen für das virtuelle Lernen. Evaluation und Didaktik*. München, Germany: Oldenbourg.

Suarez, D., & Ramirez, F. (2004). *Human rights and citizenship: the emergence of human rights education. center on democracy, development and the rule of law*. Stanford, CA: Stanford Institute for International Studies. Retrieved November 22, 2006, from http://iis-db.stanford.edu/pubs/20682/ramirez_suarez_6.25.2004.pdf

Swartz, A. (2006). *Who writes Wikipedia?* Retrieved December 3, 2008, from http://www.aaronsw.com/weblog/whowriteswikipedia

Thiedeke, U. (2003a). Einleitung. In U. Thiedeke (Ed.), *Virtuelle Gruppen. Charakteristika und Problemdimensionen (2nd. Ed.)* (pp. 7-19). Wiesbaden, Germany: Westdeutscher Verlag.

Thiedeke, U. (2003b). Virtuelle Gruppen: Begriff und Charakteristik. In U. Thiedeke (Ed.), *Virtuelle Gruppen. Charakteristika und Problemdimensionen (2nd. Ed.)* (pp.23-67). Wiesbaden, Germany: Westdeutscher Verlag.

Tyler-Smith, K. (2006). Early attrition among first time e-learners: A review of factors that contribute to drop-out, withdrawal and non-completion rates of adult learners undertaking e-learning programmes. *Journal of Online Learning and Teaching, 2(2)*. Retrieved October 20, 2008, from http://jolt.merlot.org/Vol2_No2_TylerSmith.htm

United Nations Decade for Human Rights Education No. 4. (2003). *ABC: Teaching human rights. Practical activities for primary and secondary schools*. New York: United Nations Publications. Retrieved Jan 20, 2009, from http://www.unhchr.ch/html/menu6/2/abc.htm

Chapter 6
Technology Infused Service Learning:
Changing Our World

Janet Holland
Emporia State University, USA

ABSTRACT

It seems like everyone is so busy today, it is easy to miss opportunities to reach out and make a positive difference. Though we are all experiencing the impact of tight economic times there is one lesson we are learning internationally: by putting our minds and actions towards mutual goals we all can benefit. What better way to live, learn, and work together than to share our knowledge and skills to improve our communities, both the one we live in immediately, and the one we thrive in globally. When we leave behind a legacy, will it be one of teaching service to our students to improve both academic learning and making valuable contributions to our communities for generations to follow? With the prevalence of computer-based technologies and the desire of youth to be digitally connected, it is an optimal time to share technology knowledge and skills for service learning opportunities.

We only think when we are confronted with problems. - John Dewey

INTRODUCTION

Service Learning History

Service learning is a curriculum approach combining academic learning with serving the community. This is in contrast to community service where the focus is on providing assistance alone. In contrast, service learning places the focus on the acquisition of knowledge, skills, and experiences related to learning goals and objectives as a critical component. According to Titlebaum, Williamson, Daprano, Baer and Brahler (2004) service learning began in 1862 with the establishment of the Morrill Act Land Grant Institutions teaching agriculture and mechanic arts. In 1916, John Dewey who was an advocate of learning through experience viewed service as a way to improve education by learning

DOI: 10.4018/978-1-61520-678-0.ch006

more effectively and becoming better citizens. Even though service has been in existence for a long time the current term service learning was not put into place until the mid 1980s (Stanton, Giles, & Cruz, 1999). The incorporation of service learning seemed to really take hold in the 1970s, and is currently undergoing extensive reform and growth.

As to the chapter organization the first section provides a brief description of service learning, cases of service learning benefits, defining service learning elements and issues, demonstrating connections to experiential instructional methods, and technological enhancements of the service learning experience. The following sections provide additional background information on service learning, design and implementation, connections to service and technology standards, instructional technology tools, assessment of outcomes, discussions on some of the challenges, success factors, future challenges, and final conclusions.

Case studies of successful service learning initiatives integrating technology are severely lacking in the research literature. The use of technology in learning environments is still in the development stages and remains impacted by geographic locations, economic conditions, and level of technology experience. Most educational environments, both domestic and even more so in developing countries, are struggling to obtain sufficient numbers of computers, appropriate software, and needed training. With these issues in mind, we suggest how commonly available and current technologies can be used for technology enhanced service learning. Service learning has often been associated with acts of charity, volunteer work, or non-profit organizations and with current financial strains the need to offer service is even greater.

Service Learning Defined

Service learning can be defined as linking academic learning in specific ways to meet curriculum goals and objectives while serving community needs. Service learning allows students to have the opportunity to develop an equal reciprocal relationship with the community for mutual gains by sharing knowledge, skills, and experience.

Service learning in the K-12 school setting is a growing area of interest to educators.

Legislative reform during the past 10 years demonstrates a growing national emphasis on increasing students' involvement with their community and linking this service to academic study through service learning. From a study of 6-12 grade students in 1996, the data demonstrated service learning had grown significantly since the 1980s. In 1984, researchers found 27 percent of all high schools (public and private) in the United States offered some type of community service and 9 percent of all high schools offered service learning. In 1996 National Center for Education Statistics, found 49 percent of all students in grades 6-12 participated in community service with 56 percent reporting service was incorporated into the curriculum (NCES, 1999).

Cases of Service Learning Benefits

Research on positive academic learning outcomes of service learning identified by Eyler, Giles, Stenson, & Gray (2001) include 1) better understanding of the course concepts, 2) improved communication and problem-solving skills, and 3) increased understanding of responsibility of citizenship. Others such as (Gray, Ondaatje, Fricker, & Geschwind, 2000), have cited academic gains, personal and civic development (Sax & Astin, 1997; Eyler & Giles, 1999; Eyler, Giles, Stenson, & Gray, 2001), student perceptions of increased learning, more likely to graduate (Osborne, Hammerich, and Hensley, 1998), increase in perceived engagement, satisfaction, and retention (Sax & Astin, 1997), and learners ability to see the relevance of learning as related to authentic experiences and issues (Dewey, 1938). Several case studies have reported higher levels of motivation, commitment, attendance, paying attention, completing homework on time, sharing what was learned with others, cognitive complexity, problem solving, increased grade point averages, and higher test scores. When quality service learning was connected to academic learning many positive results were reported.

Service learning is often written into University and school districts' mission statements to foster students with ethics and social responsibility. When students are connected in meaningful ways and satisfied with their college learning experiences they tend to later support the university as alumni. By reaching out to help the community to solve problems, it helps students to gain authentic work experiences, and helps the community to thrive and build long-term productive relationships.

Service Learning Elements

Key service learning elements can vary depending on the specific goals and objectives targeted. The California Department of Education (2009) cites the following five elements 1) meets a real community need, 2) integrates into and enhances the curriculum, 3) coordinates with a community agency, another school, or the community at large, 4) helps foster civic responsibility, and 5) provides structured time for reflection.

The National Service-Learning Cooperative (1999) refers to the following essential elements of effective service-learning practices. Within the learning category the following three elements are included 1) the application of concepts, content, and skills from the academic disciplines and actively involves students in their own learning, 2) engages students in tasks that challenge and stretch them cognitively and developmentally, and 3) uses assessment as a way to enhance student learning as well as to document and evaluate how well students have met content and skills standards. In the service category two elements are included 1) engages students in service tasks that have clear goals, meet genuine needs in the school or community, and have significant consequences for themselves and others, and 2) employs systematic evaluation of the service effort and its outcomes through formative and summative methods. In the key critical components that support learning and service category 6 elements are included 1) seeks to maximize student voice in selecting, designing, implementing, and evaluating the service project, 2) values diversity through its participants, its practice, and its outcomes, 3) promotes communication and interaction with the community and encourages partnerships and collaboration, 4) prepares student for all aspects of their service experience including understanding their role, the skills and information required, safety precautions, and sensitivity to the people with whom they will be working, 5) includes student reflection as a central force in the fulfillment of curricular objective and is done before, during, and after service using multiple methods that encourage critical thinking, and 6) acknowledges, celebrates, and further validates students' service. Having an awareness of the overall key elements helps in clarifying the goals and objectives for service learning projects prior to implementation in any content area.

Service Learning Issues

As great as service learning sounds, like anything it is not without issues or concerns to consider and address in the planning and design phase prior to implementation. Before beginning, if any special funding is needed it will need to be set up with expenditures clearly outlined and identified. It is important students want to participate and volunteer or be provided other alternative projects. If the student does not want to be involved, a negative attitude and lack luster effort could harm the good efforts of others and the long-term relationship and success of the overall program. Planning and management problems can serve as a guide for adding clarity and quality design in the implementation of service learning in the areas of 1) locating service learning contacts, screening, and written agreements, 2) training and instructional materials needed to provide learners with the needed knowledge and skills, 3) scope agreements for meaningful learning and service assistance, 4) instructor time for facilitation, guidance, and monitoring, 5) goals and objectives, 6) problem identification, 7) setting up collaborative teams, 8) credit, 9) grading rubric or checklist and weighting, 10) time requirements and weekly contact schedule, 11) synchronous and asynchronous communications, 12) due dates, 13) written recommendation report, 14) presentation, 15) reflection paper, 16) peer evaluation feedback, and 17) evaluation survey.

Experiential Learning

Within the field of instructional design and technology more emphasis is being placed on using experiential instructional methods for providing authentic real world learning experiences to students. When students can apply the knowledge and skills they have gained in the classroom to making valuable contributions in the field to help solve community problems they gain a realistic and deeper understanding for academic applications and support. When students offer their knowledge, skills, time and effort by volunteering, reciprocal learning, a key component of service learning can be met. In the current competitive job market it gives students additional opportunities to gain additional authentic knowledge, skills, and experiences to be successful in the workforce and help land jobs with required and needed experiences upon graduation. As we all know with great opportunities many challenges must be met with regards to setting up and managing the service experience. It will require facilitating advanced planning with the selected organizations, coordination of schedules, agreements on the scope, determining learning goals and objectives, and reflection and assessment of the desired outcomes.

The David Kolb and Fry (1975) model of experiential learning provides the theoretical foundation for integrating service learning. The stages include 1) concrete experiences, 2) observation and reflection, 3) forming abstract concepts, and 4) testing in new situations. It is easy to see how experiential learning can easily be merged with service learning opportunities.

Technological Enhancements of the Service Learning Experience

To date, when the use of technology has been discussed as a part of service learning, it has been limited to the generation of e-mail to those involved in coordinating actions, and for creating newsletters, brochures, and posters to inform others of what is being done. However, with the rapid development of newer collaborative technologies we can expand options for making successful contributions in the area of service learning by identifying current technology tools and how they can be effectively implemented for teaching, learning, and serving the community.

BACKGROUND

Service learning can provide a great way to enhance interest in studying real world problems and challenging learners to excel in the outcome goals. Service learning can be used to bridge knowledge and experiences related to the students' own areas of interest. By "connecting academic instruction to the social, political and economic conditions of students' lived experiences" (Hart, 2006, p. 18), instructors can then assist students in making powerful personal connections to the topic fostering authentic hands-on learning. When students are actively and meaningfully engaged with the topic, the framework is set for a satisfying and memorable learning experience. Classroom learning can then be transformed "well beyond the walls of the classroom" (Steffes, 2004, p. 46). The knowledge gained can be put into action for making positive changes. "Our systematic processes too often stop at the acquisition of knowledge. The much harder and more meaningful process is to facilitate understanding and wisdom, leading to…informed thought and action" (Steffes, 2004, p. 46).

Instructors can serve as facilitators assisting students to identify problems, examine why the need exists and the potential causes for that need, formulate appropriate questions, research, examine policies, laws, interview, collaborate with community members, brainstorm options, analyze action choices, lobby, petition, make decisions, develop and implement action plans, to sustain long term, collectively solve problems, promote the cause, fundraise if needed, work alongside community members to effect positive change, strive for mutual empowerment, reflection, and analysis. Educators can "help students articulate their own vision of social justice" (Hart, 2006, p. 23). When students are allowed to find their own voice and take positive action to successful completion they discover they can make a difference.

Learners can be active participants in the roles of brainstorming, researching, discussing, organizing, and synthesizing to create digital presentations to garner the needed support. Digital presentations can be used to tap diverse student learning styles and preferences using a wide-range of media options including text, images, audio, video, and even a web presence, if desired. Digital presentations align nicely within the constructivist approach of teaching and learning through discovery, exploration, construction, problem solving, and shared ideas (Alessi & Trollip, 2001). Additionally, students can work together collaboratively to reach service-learning objectives.

"Service learning is a grassroots movement that is springing up in community after community" (Silcox & Leek, 1997, p. 615). Statistics from CompactCampus, (2001) clearly demonstrates the increasing growth of service learning. One survey including 349 universities respondents between 1999-2000 they reported 712,000 students participating in community service, 12.2% of the faculty offered courses, 6,272 courses were taught, and 9% required service learning for graduation. The National Center for Education Statistics (NCES) cited between 1984 and 1997 service learning at the K-12 level rose from 900,000 to over 12.6 million. During the 2000-2001 school year more than 13 million K-12 students were involved in service and service learning. A growing trend can clearly be seen at both the college and K-12 levels. It has been speculated the reason these activities are increasing is because of "a disenchantment of youth with formal political processes and structures; a feeling of remoteness from influence and a desire to make a difference" (Mohan, 1995, p. 131). For university level students, making connections to career interests can enhance important future job knowledge and skills.

DESIGN AND IMPLEMENTATION

Service Practice Standards

From Learn and Serve (2008), we obtain standards and indicators for effective service-learning practice to help in guiding curriculum integration into various content areas. The standards are divided within several categories of service learning to 1) actively engage participants in meaningful and personally relevant service activities, 2) intentionally used as an instructional strategy to meet learning goals and/or content standards, 3) incorporates multiple challenging reflection activities that are ongoing and that prompt deep thinking and analysis about oneself and one's relationship to society, 4) promotes understanding of diversity and mutual respect among all participants, 5) provides youth with a strong voice in planning, implementing, and evaluating service-learning experiences with guidance from adults, 6) partnerships are collaborative, mutually beneficial, and address community needs, 7) engages participants in an ongoing process to assess the quality of implementation and progress toward meeting specified goals, and uses results for improvement and sustainability, and 8) has sufficient duration and intensity to address community needs and meet specified outcomes.

The research needed for service learning can easily encompass any content area desired and be aligned to meet content specific International, National, State, Regional, or district content standards. Often, a combination of standards can be included from the specific content areas of interest. Service learning allows "students to both learn and apply skills and knowledge" in any content area "toward the goal of creating a socially just society" (Wade, 2001, p. 26).

The 2008 International Society for Technology in Education (ISTE) and the National Educational Technology Standards (NETS) for teachers provide additional resources to effectively use technology to support both service learning as a communication tool, as when writing reports or creating presentations, and for offering instructional technology knowledge and skills for service learning opportunities. The standards include 1) facilitate and inspire student learning and creativity, 2) design and develop digital-age learning experiences and assessments, 3) model digital-age work and learning, 4) promote and model digital citizenship and responsibility, and 5) engage in professional growth and leadership.

Instructional Technology Tools

My interest in service learning stems from my responsibility as an assistant professor in Instructional Design and Technology teaching pre-service and master's degree students to become effective instructors. We want our learners to be able to assist their own students in making authentic connections to content so it becomes personally meaningful and relevant. Then, through practice, the concepts become better understood, remembered, and applied to new situations for high-level teaching and learning opportunities. Why not have students move beyond individual learning goals and knowledge acquisition, to move towards authentic applications solving community problems and have a positive impact on relevant meaningful issues in our communities?

Instructional technology can be integrated with service learning in several different ways such as 1) supporting any content area, 2) tools used to support service learning communications, reports, and presentations, and 3) offering instructional technology knowledge and skills for service learning projects.

Graphic Organizer Tools

Instructors can assist students' service learning efforts with the use of graphic organizers so students can identify service problem main topic areas of need, subset categories, supporting details, underlying relationships, action plan steps, and sequencing order. The semantic map or storyboard can serve as the foundation for the service learning project to determine the structure, relationships, plans, and supporting content specific information to be included. Options can range from using simple word processors, slide presentations, or specific mapping software programs. The graphic organizers can bridge the gap between what the learner already knows and what they need to know before successfully learning the task at hand (Ausubel, 1968). Having students use graphic organizers is a way to scaffold knowledge acquisition and detail retention for successful project completion.

Problem Solving Process

Problem-based service learning often includes teams of students working for service organizations in the role of consultants working for an employer or client. The team works to understand the problem or issues to be addressed. Students then work collaboratively to solve the problems using their classroom academic knowledge and skills, often supplemented with additional research related to the specific issues at hand. Students then make recommendations to the client to solve their community problems through reports and presentations. Some examples might be business students assisting with promotional plans, science students helping with environmental issues, instructional design and technology students developing a website for the organization or assisting with technology training or distance learning for the organization.

The problem solving process may include students discussing potential problems, conducting additional research on the topic, brainstorming possible solutions, selecting one or more issues to address, determining a logical sequence for problem resolution, forming a scope of coverage, researching and analyzing options, examining current policy, identifying best approaches, then report the findings in an interesting and informative way using multimedia presentations. The processes of thinking, reflecting, and reasoning assist students in moving concepts from theory to practical application. When the problems are personally meaningful real world issues, students have the opportunity to learn what it takes to ask relevant questions, contribute to the goals, research and solve problems. Some of the typical problem-solving task applications often include planning, reading, designing, and constructing (Smith & Ragan, 1999). "The ideal task should confront each student with a problem for which that student has no immediate solution" (Grabe & Grabe, 2007). Good problems encourage student decision-making, spark questions, inspire dialogue, and contribute to informative digital service learning presentations. Project problem-based learning is a great way to provide learners with additional practice when acquiring new knowledge to "deepen their understanding and skills relative to content" (Marzano, Pickering, & Pollock, 2001, p.60).

Creative Digital Presentations

Service learning is a great way to harness student creativity by helping learners to make personal connections to the problems at hand. Through problem analysis, research, brainstorming, synthesizing solutions, and presenting the findings through the use of digital media presentation processes, students can put their thinking into action with the use of writing, images, editing, and arranging the content to communicate their needs, plans, and project goals. Using pre-made digital templates can make the process faster and easier.

When the service-learning goals are well suited to the students by being personally relevant, they serve as a catalyst to inspire creative high-level thinking. Students can then be in a position to transfer classroom theories to real world applications by devising creative solutions.

Collaboration

Service learning provides opportunities for students to communicate and share common goals conducive to building positive social relationships with peers and community members. "When these features are present in social networks, they are likely to have a high capacity for cooperative problem solving" (Root & Schmidt, 2008, p. 125). As educators, we want learners to be able to work together collaboratively towards reaching common goals. When students interact on an equal level with community members and learn from each other, the combined collective knowledge can be mutually beneficial.

Research by Slavin (1996) cites small interactive group benefits of increasing 1) motivation, 2) social cohesion, 3) development through high-level peer modeling, 4) cognitive practice and elaboration. Some students prefer to "learn through speaking and listening processes (oral language) as well as through reading and writing processes (written language)" (Orlich, Harder,

Callahan, Trevisan, & Brown, 2007, p. 274). For students, collaborative learning can improve both academic and social learning through immediate sharing, support, and feedback. The literature cites many positive benefits ranging from providing support, engagement, problem solving, improved relations, well-being, self-esteem, coping skills, positive attitudes, trust, self-expression, communication skills, caring, and productivity making a good case for collaborative efforts (Orlich, et al., 2007). Collaborative service learning can be used to facilitate students' brainstorming, discussions, provide additional ideas and positive peer feedback.

Digital Imaging

Graphic images are often used for service learning training, communications, reporting, and promotions and can come from many different sources. Students can use digital cameras, scanners, clip art images or other copyright free online resources, purchase CD's or DVDs from retail stores or online.

Many age appropriate image-editing programs are available if any of the images need modifications. By searching online, one can locate what is currently available then download a free trial version to be sure it will perform, as needed, on either a Mac or PC platform. The Adobe Photoshop Elements image-editing program currently costs about $69, with teacher or student discounts, and operates on both Mac and PC platforms. Paint.net is a free program, also capable of running on either platform. Some of the commonly used image editing techniques include, cropping the image to remove unwanted areas, enlarging to create a focal point, reducing the size, adjusting the color, brightness, contrast, flipping the image, erasing, sharpening, reducing red-eye, repairing, fading the watermark image, texture filtering, and adding special effects.

Some additional considerations include paying attention to the lighting, stabilizing the camera with a tripod, and taking extra images to get a good shot. Be sure to experiment with some unique camera angles including having the camera looking down from above, below looking up, from the side, and tilted. For additional interest, try a variety of shots from close up, mid-range, and far away to tell the story visually. The photos can also be collaged prior to placement in the layout, if desired. If the photographs will eventually be placed on the web, they should be saved in the .jpg file format. If the camera does not save in this format, the images can be taken into an image-editing program to save for the web.

Designing Instructional Materials

The basic elements and principles of design apply to creating an aesthetically pleasing digital presentation. Design elements include effective use of line, color, shape, form, value, size, and texture. Principles of design include; balance, repetition, contrast, harmony, focal point, direction, rhythm, and unity. The color scheme selected will set the tone or mood and should coordinate with any images included. The key design element is to be sure the design allows for high readability and effective communications.

Content

Service learning goals can easily be integrated into research efforts and presented using a wide range of multimedia. Combining student selected goals with cutting edge technologies can result in an enriched approach towards teaching students to generate questions, conduct in-depth research using a wide variety of resources, solve authentic problems, and formulate effective plans of action. Service learning can include one area or a multidisciplinary approach. Table 1 and Table 2 list some service learning topics and digital communication project ideas to help one to get started.

Service learning images can be digital, printed on paper, or printed on a wide variety of objects

Table 1. Service Learning Topic Ideas (Holland, 2009)

School	Home	Community	Social	Neighborhood
Violence	Water Quality	Elderly	Literacy	Equality
Bully/Gang	Safety	Homeless	Economic	Health
Graduation	Environment	Food & Hunger	Disasters	Disabilities
Academic	Utilities	Disadvantaged	Abuse	Animals
Drugs	Preservation	Business	Business	Medical
Transportation	Beautification	Crime	Rights/Justice	

for an additional fee. In addition to the educational purpose, promotional objects can be used for fundraising projects to further support service learning efforts. Searching online, one can find many sites like http://www.snapfish.com/ or http://www.zazzle.com/ in addition to many others for media sharing products.

Integrating Writing

Service learning can involve writing in many different ways. Students can conduct research and report on the findings, promote the cause through letter writing, create training materials, promote, support, and write journals about their experiences while reflecting on the outcomes as a part of the assessment process. The narrative style can include details such as who, what, when, where, how, and why. Journaling can be used to motivate student writing, editing, and publishing skills. The writing can be from the author's perspective, the perspective of others, interviewer/ interviewee, narrative, dialogue, and can even include poetry, related song lyrics, quotes, definitions, historical documentary, letter, e-mail, chronological, news reporter, compare and contrast, changes over time, one point in time, explanatory, factual, humorous, question answer, and change or growth.

Digital authoring should include a title in the largest size of font, subtitles in medium or normal size, and the body text in a normal paragraph size to designate the order of importance of the text. Bullets can be used to list key content. Table 3 provides a list of possible writing topics related to service learning.

Technology and Service

The use of electronic media for service learning allows students to more fully engage in active hands-on authentic learning experiences. Multimedia tools can be used to enhance learning,

Table 2. Service Learning Digital Technology Communication Ideas (Holland, 2009)

Portfolio	Book	Newsletter	Brochure	Proposal
Poster	Report	Presentation	Display	Kiosk
Journal	Graph	Mailer	Podcast/Vodcast	Editorial
Letter	Website	Timeline	Audio/Video	Exhibit/Demo
Map	Wiki	Chart	Conferencing	Scrapbooking
Blog	Blackboard	Virtual Reality	Second Life	Animations
Chat	Moodle	360 Degree View	Facebook	T-Shirt, Mug
Illustration	Organizer	Graphics/Photos	Survey	Calendar

Table 3. Service learning writing integration ideas (Holland, 2008)

Brochure	Petition	News Release	Proclamation	Proposal
Research	Public Service Announcement	School Resolution	Political Resolution	Lobby
Lobby State Laws	Survey	City Ordinance	State Funding	Fundraising
Lobby Federal Laws	Discussion Forums	Web Page	Interview Questions & Responses	Speech Writing
Ad Campaign	Support/Oppose a Law	Phone Script	Report	Online/Distance Learning

promote creativity, increase student collaboration, and improve communication and publication skills (Green & Brown, 2002). The technology tools used for creating digital reports, teaching and learning materials, communications, sharing, and presentations allow students to develop both visual and media literacy skills while enhancing capabilities with computer technologies and content knowledge simultaneously. Many digital software tools are open-ended and can be easily integrated into any topic area. Digital presentations can draw upon the use of a wide range of multimedia skills in the manipulation of text, images, audio, and video.

Technology Software Tools

The choices of technology software tools are widespread and constantly changing and evolving. Below are some common widespread tools to facilitate service learning technology training and service learning project tools for organization, writing, illustration, communications, demonstration, promotion, and reporting.

Graphic organizers are great to assist in the early stages of the service learning project to storyboard out the issues, organizational planning, demonstrating relationships, making comparisons, and brainstorming possible solutions using tools such as Inspiration for young students. Or, by searching online one can find many free template options for sharing ideas.

For writing documents and reports one popular tool widely available is the use of Microsoft Word. Some of the free writing tools are also growing in use such as Google Docs, Zoho, and others. Many of the newer online versions have also built in document sharing features and Writeboards.

Slide presentation tools are great for demonstrating concepts, charts, graphs, and kiosk shows using Microsoft PowerPoint (PC), or Keynote (Mac). For creative presentations Scrapbook Factory (PC) or iScrapbook (Mac) can be integrated for a creative flair.

Some of the most common image editing tools include Adobe Photoshop (PC/Mac fee) or Paint.net (free) for older students and Kid Pix (PC/Mac fee) for working with younger students. Sometimes it is helpful to be able to take screen captures during the image editing process and SnagIt (PC fee) or Grab (Mac free) can be a valuable tool. To take it one step further video screen captures are another option for recording computer actions often used for tutorial demonstrations with programs such as Camtasia (fee), Jing (free), and many others.

If you are on a tight budget, the Flip Video is a very affordable video recording option. Two inexpensive video editing tools include Microsoft Movie Maker (PC free), and iMovie (Mac fee). If you need to add additional or separate audio, Audacity (PC/Mac free) is a great audio editing tool. GarageBand (Mac fee) is another audio editing alternative. The audio and videos can be posted to a website, a video site such as YouTube or TeacherTube, Podcast, or Vodcast can be hosted on sites like Podomatic.com (PC/Mac) or iWeb podcast authoring (Mac fee) combined with a .Mac (Mac fee) account to host the site.

To create your own websites, one premium web-authoring program is Adobe Dreamweaver (PC/Mac fee). For tight budgets, good alternatives include NVU (PC/Mac free), or Mozilla SeaMonkey (PC/Mac free). For web based tagging, social bookmarking like Furl, and sharing web resources sites like del.icio.us can be useful. When using the web for getting the word out many are now using Facebook, EduSpace, MySpace, Twitter, Ning, and others for social networking sites. Wikis are another alternative web-based collaboration tools for sharing online documents, sites, and illustrations at a distance.

Digital communications offer many choices such as e-mail, Blogger.com collaborative discussion forums within distance learning course management programs such as Moodle (free), Blackboard, Angel and digital surveys are also included, or separate surveys sites such as Survey Monkey is also available, or live audio and video communication tools such as Skype (PC/Mac), iChat (Mac free), and Horizon Wimba (fee) for video conferencing.

Some fun special effect tools of possible interest depending on the type of service learning project, include simulations and virtual reality worlds such as Second Life, Active Worlds, and Quest Atlantis. One can create 360 degree virtual reality objects and panoramas using VR Worx, or for humorous promotions try Comic Book Creator (PC) or Comic Life (Mac), educational games, science probes for data measurements, and many others are available to fit special application needs.

Showcasing Student Learning

Having students create service-learning presentations assists learners in synthesizing and elaborating on newly acquired knowledge. Presentations successfully showcase student research and learning efforts. Digital presentations provide an outlet to "knowledge that is both of interest and helpful to others" (Morrison & Lowther, 2005). By placing content online to share with instructors, classmates, peers, family, friends, and the community, the amount of support greatly increases.

Since the final photo images are in a .jpg file format, they work on any photo-sharing site and can easily be placed on a website, as desired. Some sites even offer a discussion blog so viewers can post comments. As needed, the instructor sets up a private classroom account to control who has access and who can leave comments and instructions for students. Below are resources to help one get started sharing students' creative efforts or search online to find more.

Digital Showcase Resources

1. Blogs http://www.blogger.com/
2. Podcasts http://www.podomatic.com/
3. Photo Sharing http://flickr.com/
4. My Photo Album http://www.myphotoalbum.com/
5. Student Generated Website using Dreamweaver, NVU, or Mozilla SeaMonkey
6. Course Management Programs, Moodle (free), Angel, Blackboard (fee)

Assessment of Outcomes

Authentic project-based service learning activities can include research efforts, recommendation reports, presentation materials, and reflective journals. Some other tools that may be helpful to use are task checklist criteria and or quality rubrics to inform students of the desired outcomes. When assessment instruments are well constructed, they can provide learners with quality guidelines to strive to achieve. The evaluation instruments should align to the desired learning goals, objectives, and standards. The assessments can include

1) research paper, 2) recommendation report, 3) reflective journal, 4) digital portfolio, 5) digital presentations, 6) project documentation, or any combination serving the intended purpose and audience. The digital media documentation used can include letters, interviews, observations, reflections, and presentations to record learner progress over time.

When designed effectively, students can be evaluated using 1) written documentation, 2) content specific objectives, 3) service objectives, or other targeted outcome goals. Some of the positive outcomes identified specifically from service learning research includes the development of leadership, interpersonal social intelligence, reasoning, communication, cultural awareness, tolerance, citizenship, community building, reward in helping others, self-esteem, social self-confidence, viewing oneself as a person of values, public speaking, and commitment to social responsibility (Kezar, 2002).

Current "survey instrumentation appears to be limited in assessing interpersonal skills, social responsibility, discrimination, moral decision making, empathy, and personal development" (Kezar, 2002, p. 17). With this in mind, reflective journaling and more project-based assessments seem to be a logical approach to evaluation. Howard Gardner's Theory of Multiple Intelligences (MI) provides a framework for assessing community service learning especially in the area of intrapersonal and interpersonal intelligence "not currently even being considered as part of most standard assessment tools" Kezar, 2002, p. 18). As one can see, the use of digital portfolios with samples of the service learning actions demonstrated through the use of; illustrations, audio, video, graphics, animations, simulations, presentations, brochures, posters, writings, letters, papers, reports, interviews, observations, petitions, reflections of change over time, and other documents provide a broader alternative to community service learning pedagogy and assessment options.

DISCUSSION

Challenges

Service learning has often been used in the teaching of Science, Civics, History, Business, Marketing, and other areas. As interest continues to grow within the field, more and more content areas are working to make service-learning connections. Opening up new content areas requires being somewhat of a pioneer when developing the needed content specific training materials required. Instructional design and technology knowledge and skills can be used to assist in preparing needed instructional content, support the service communication tools, and serve as a bridge to participation in community service learning projects surrounding technology needs.

Success Factors

The potential for positive outcomes from service learning is possible with quality implementation. If it is not well planned out in advance using current best practices, the desired good outcomes may not be realized. Service learning is not telling students today is service learning day and we are going to go outside to pick up trash on the school grounds. If students do not have input into valuable and meaningful service learning choices to improve their school and or community they will not be thrilled at the prospect of participating. If there is not the needed connection to sharing their academic knowledge and skills, the success possible may not materialize. If the student skills are not matched to the service organizations' needs, it may flop rather than flourish. If the proper amount of time, communications, facilitation, and guidance is not in place, students may loose interest and focus. Advanced planning and commitment is essential to realize the positive benefits possible.

Future Challenges

It is important to continue our examination of the service-learning pedagogy and how it can be used to increase knowledge across disciplines. Educators and students will benefit from comprehensive research on how knowledge can be leveraged when establishing service learning as an effective way to facilitate knowledge acquisition, personal development, and civic involvement. Constructs such as attitudes, civic responsibility, and critical thinking are prime candidates for further investigations. Fostering on-going innovative research has a proven potential to uncover deeper understandings of the value of service learning related to instruction.

CONCLUSION

Service learning opens up an important avenue for learning and making positive contributions to the community. Students can gain valuable knowledge and experience while providing a needed service "to some of these most pressing problems" (Jacoby, 2004, p. 550). Potential gains for students include increasing leadership skills, cultural awareness, tolerance, social skills, improved communications, collaboration, self-esteem through helping others, reasoning, analysis, problem solving, ethics, by becoming active and informed responsible citizens. Integrating service learning in the classroom in a meaningful way to assist students to "become effective workers and concerned, knowledgeable citizens" (Steffes, 2004, p. 50). When setting up service learning projects within the community it is important to identify; "a clear sense of identity and purpose (e.g., a mission statement, program priorities, strategic plan, learning objectives), procedures (e.g., policies, service-learning contracts, liability issues, evaluation of student performance), and resources (e.g., personnel, facilities, time) need to exist and be effectively communicated to the other party" (Bringle & Hatcher, 2002, p. 507) with a defined start, and ending dates. Reciprocal learning allows opportunities to "arrive at innovative solutions to community problems" (Reardon, 1998, p. 63). By transforming students to "active participants and contributors – we may begin to give them insights into the causes of and solutions to social problems, the contribution they, as individuals, might make to solving those problems, and their responsibilities as citizens" (Mohan, 1995, p. 129).

Below are some additional resources to help you to implement service learning into the classroom.

Service Learning Online Resources

1. America's Promise http://www.americaspromise.org/
2. Campus Compact http://www.compact.org/
3. Learn and Serve http://www.servicelearning.org/
4. National Center for Learning and Citizenship http://www.ecs.org/ecsmain.asp?page=/html/ProjectsPartners/nclc/nclc_main.htm
5. National Community Service http://www.nationalservice.org/
6. National Service Learning Partnership http://www.service-learningpartnership.org/site/PageServer?pagename=reus_homepage
7. National Society for Experiential Education http://www.nsee.org/
8. National Youth Leadership Council http://www.nylc.org/
9. Points of Light Institute http://www.pointsoflight.org/
10. Students in Service to America http://www.studentsinservicetoamerica.org/tools_resources/national.html#service
11. Youth Serve America http://www.ysa.org/
12. Youth Volunteer Corps of America http://www.yvca.org/

REFERENCES

Alessi, S., & Trollip, S. (2001). *Third edition multimedia for learning: Methods and development.* Needham Heights, MA: Pearson Education.

Ausubel, D. P. (1968). *Educational psychology: A cognitive view*. New York: Holt, Rinehart & Winston.

Bingle, R. G., & Hatcher, J. A. (2002). Campus-community partnerships: The terms of engagement. *The Journal of Social Issues*, *58*(3).

California Department of Education. (2009). *Key elements of service learning*. Retrieved March 28, 2009, from http://www.cde.ca.gov/ci/cr/sl/keyelements.asp

CompactCampus. (2001). Retrieved July 30, 2008, from

Dewey, J. (1938). *Experience and education*. New York: Macmillian.

Eyler, J., Giles, D., Stenson, C., & Gray, C. (2001). At a glance: What we know about the effects of service-learning on college students, faculty, institutions and communities, 1993-2000 (3rd ed.). *Learn and Serve America National Service-Learning Clearinghouse.*

Eyler, J., & Giles, D. E. (1999). *Where's the learning in service learning?* San Francisco, CA: Jossey-Bass.

Grabe, M., & Grabe, C. (2007). *Integrating technology for meaningful learning (5th ed.).* Boston, MA: Houghton Mifflin Comp.

Gray, M. J., Ondaatje, E. H., Fricker, R. D., & Geschwind, S. A. (2000). Assessing service-learning: Results from a survey of 'Learn and serve America, higher education.' . *Change*, *32*, 30–39.

Green, T., & Brown, A. (2002). *Multimedia projects in the classroom: A guide to development and evaluation.* Thousand Oaks, CA: Corwin Press, Inc.

Hamilton, B. (2007). *It's elementary! Integrating technology in the primary grades.* Washington, DC: International Society for Technology in Education (ISTE).

Hart, S. (2006). Breaking literacy boundaries through critical service-learning: Education for the silenced and marginalized. *Mentoring & Tutoring*, *14*(1). doi:10.1080/13611260500432236

http://servicelearning.org/what_is_service-learning/service-learning_is/index.php

International Society for Technology in Education. (2008). *NETS for teachers*. Retrieved March 28, 2009, from http://www.iste.org/AM/Template.cfm?Section=NETS

Jacoby, B. (2006). Public work and the academy: An academic administrator's guide to civic engagement and service-learning. *The Journal of Higher Education*, *77*(3). doi:10.1353/jhe.2006.0022

Kaye, C. B. (2004). *The complete guide to service learning*. Minneapolis, MN: Free Spirit Publishing Inc.

Kezar, A. (2002). Assessing community service learning. *About Campus*, *7*(2).

Kolb, D. (1975). *David A. Kolb on experiential learning.* Retrieved March 28, 2009, from http://www.infed.org/biblio/b-explrn.htm

Krueger, C. (2006 January). Shared futures: Two universities' global learning initiatives. *Academic Leader, (1).*

Learn and Serve, America's National Service-Learning Clearinghouse. (2008). *Standards and indicators for effective service-learning practice.* Retrieved March 28, 2009, from http://www.servicelearning.org/instant_info/fact_sheets/k-12_facts/standards/index.php

Lewis, B. A. (1995). *The kid's guide to service projects.* Minneapolis, MN: Free Spirit Publishing Inc.

Lewis, B. A. (1998). *The kid's guide to social action*. Minneapolis, MN: Free Spirit Publishing Inc.

Marzano, R., Pickering, D., & Pollock, J. (2001). *Classroom instruction that works:* Research-based strategies for increasing student achievement. Alexandria, VA: Association for Supervision and Curriculum Development (ASCD).

Mohan, J. (1995). Thinking local: Service-learning, education for citizenship and geography. Journal of Geography in Higher Education, July, 19(2).

Morrison, G., & Lowther, D. (2005). *Integrating computer technology into the classroom (3rd ed.).* Upper Saddle River, NJ: Prentice Hall.

National Center for Education Statistics. (1999 September). *Service-learning and community service in K-12 public schools, report number 1999043.* Retrieved March 28, 2009 from http://nces.ed.gov/surveys/frss/publications/1999043/

National Educational Technology Standards. (2008). *NETS for teachers*. Retrieved March 28, 2009, from http://www.iste.org/AM/Template.cfm?Section=NETS

National Service Learning Cooperative. (1999). *Essential elements of service-learning for effective practice, organizational support.* Retrieved March 28, 2009 from http://servicelearning.org/filemanager/download/203_Essential_Elements_of_Service-Learning,Revised.pdf

Orlich, D., Harder, R., Callahan, R., Trevisan, M., & Brown, A. (2007). *Teaching Strategies: A guide to effective instruction (8th ed.)*. Boston, MA: Houghton Mifflin Company.

Osborne, R. E., Hammerich, S., & Hensley, C. (1998). Student effects of service-learning: Tracking change across a semester. *Michigan Journal of Community Service Learning*, *5*, 5–13.

Reardon, K. M. (1998). Participatory action research as service learning. *New Directions for Teaching and Learning*, 73.

Roberts, P. (2002). *Kids taking action: Community service learning projects, K-8.* Turner Falls, MA: Northeast Foundation for Children.

Sax, L. J., & Astin, A. W. (1997). The benefits of service: Evidence from undergraduates. *The Educational Record*, *78*, 25–32.

Schoenfeld, R. M. (2003). *Service-learning – Student's guide & journal.* Seattle, WA: Guide and Journal Publications.

Silcox, H., & Leek, T. E. (1997). International service learning. *Phi Delta Kappan*, *78*(8).

Slavin, R. E. (1996). Research on cooperative learning and achievement: What we know, what we need to know. *Contemporary Educational Psychology*, *21*, 43–69. doi:10.1006/ceps.1996.0004

Smith, P., & Ragan, T. (1999). *Instructional Design (2nd ed.).* Upper Saddle River, NJ: Prentice-Hall, Inc.

Stanton, T. K., Giles, D. E., & Cruz, N. I. (1999). *Service learning: A movement's pioneers reflect on its origins, practice, and future*. San Francisco, CA: Jossey-Bass.

Steffes, J. (2004). Creative powerful learning environments beyond the classroom. *Change*, *36*(3).

Wade, R. C. (2001). Social action in the social studies: From the ideal to the real. *Theory into Practice*, *40*(1). doi:10.1207/s15430421tip4001_4

ADDITIONAL READINGS

Kaye, C. B. (2004). *The complete guide to service learning.* Minneapolis, MN: Free Spirit Publishing Inc.

Lewis, B. A. (1995). *The kid's guide to service projects*. Minneapolis, MN: Free Spirit Publishing Inc.

Lewis, B. A. (1998). *The kid's guide to social action*. Minneapolis, MN: Free Spirit Publishing Inc.

Roberts, P. (2002). *Kids taking action: Community service learning projects, K-8*. Turner Falls, MA: Northeast Foundation for Children.

Schoenfeld, R. M. (2003). *Service-learning – Student's guide & journal.* Seattle, WA: Guide and Journal Publications.

Titlebaum, P., Williamson, G., Daprano, C., Baer, J., & Brahler, J. (2004). *Annotated History of Service Learning 1862-2002*. Retrieved March 28, 2009 from http://www.servicelearning.org/page/index.php?detailed=311

Chapter 7
OLnet:
A New Approach to Supporting the Design and Use of Open Educational Resources

Gráinne Conole
The Open University, UK

Patrick McAndrew
The Open University, UK

ABSTRACT

The web 2.0 practices of user participation and experimentation have created models for social networking that influence the way people communicate and interact online. This chapter describes an initiative, OLnet, that is creating a technical environment based on web 2.0 principles to support the sharing of experiences around the design and use of Open Educational Resources (OER) in order to facilitate closer links between researchers and users. The aim is to combine online functionality, face-to-face events and research activities so that research outputs can inform users and users can help steer future areas for research work. This chapter sets out the challenges and background that have motivated OLnet before looking at two of the tools that form part of the initial OLnet technical infrastructure; a tool for visualising OER designs – CompendiumLD, and a social networking tool for exchange of ideas – Cloudworks.

INTRODUCTION

This chapter revisits the view that online technologies can change the way we learn and teach. In particular it sets out some actions that can be taken to meet four challenges that have emerged from previous research and discussion in the community. These challenges are, in brief, to understand why:

1. Despite the rhetoric around the potential application of technologies in education, their impact on practice has been limited.
2. Teachers seem to lack the design skills needed to exploit the potential of technologies within their teaching.
3. There is an abundance of free resources (learning objects and Open Educational Resources) now available, but the majority of teachers do not use them.

DOI: 10.4018/978-1-61520-678-0.ch007

4. Research into the use of technologies in education and into OER, on the whole, does not inform practice and vice versa.

These challenges are reflected in the concerns that others in the community have expressed but are also linked to our previous work in two areas - the development and evaluation of OER through the OpenLearn project[1] and Learning Design research as part of the OU Learning Design Initiative[2]

The structure we follow in this chapter is to first consider the background to the first challenge: what are the promises of online learning and what steps are needed to move those forward? Secondly a review of OER research and the associated challenges. Thirdly a description of the OpenLearn project. Fourthly an outline of the OU Learning Design Initiative. Finally we discuss the OLnet activity and how we aim through OLnet to bring together learning design and OER research within a community structure showing examples of how social networking approaches are starting to help us address the fourth challenge: linking researchers in OER to practice in OER.

Key Terms and Definitions

Terminology in this field is contested and varied; therefore it is worth clarifying our meaning of the key terms used in this chapter.

- A learning object can range from a simple digital asset (such as a piece of text or an audio file) through to a more complex learning resource incorporating a range of media and designed to support a particular learning activity.
- Open Educational Resources (OER) are teaching and learning materials made freely available for use and repurposing by teachers and learners. Potentially synergistic with learning objects, the emphasis is on the open licence allowing use and reuse of the resources.
- A learning activity consists of a set of tasks a learner undertakes, either individually or in a group, using a specific set of resources (which may include tools) to achieve a set of intended learning outcomes.
- Learning design is a research area developing methods, tools and resources to support teachers in making pedagogically informed, better use of technologies.

The Rhetoric around Technology Transformation

This section reviews the use of technologies in education, focusing in particular on why they have not had a great impact on the practice of education. The disruptive nature of technologies has long been heralded, many have argued that features and affordances of technology are poised to revolutionise education (Christensen et al., 2008; Sharples, 2002). Examples can be identified that show there is some truth in this statement in terms of the ways in which technology is used to support research, teaching and administrative activities within educational institutions. Institutional and departmental web sites are now standard, email is used as the main form of communication, Learner Management Systems (LMS)/Virtual Learning Environments (VLE) are now commonplace. There has also been a noticeable move towards a strategic recognition of the mission critical importance of technologies as part of wider institutional structures. These changes are evidence that technologies have had an increasing impact on education *processes* over the last couple of decades, however the impact on actual *practice* – on teaching and learning – is perhaps not as radical as might have been expected. Considered in terms of methods of teaching, models of work and the relations between teacher and learner, the impact of technologies has not been as transformative in education as it has been in other industries such as finance, tourism or online shopping.

A similar pattern occurred in terms of the lack of uptake of previous technologies in education (radio, TV, computer-based materials, early use of the web, etc.). The reasons for the lack of uptake are complex and multi-faceted (Lokken and Womer, 2007). Firstly, teachers lack the experience of using these new technologies. Secondly, they do not have the time to explore and experiment with using them in their teaching. Thirdly, they lack the skills needed to find, evaluate and repurpose resources. Fourthly, they need guidance on how to rethink their design processes to make better, more effective use of technologies. Fifthly, existing organisational structures and institutional cultures negate against inclusion of new technologies. For example current assessment practices which predominately focus on knowledge recall, are at odds in a technological environment where content is essentially free and practice is about user-generated content, active participation and a culture of mash ups and remixing.

Despite this lack of uptake, the emergence of web 2.0 technologies appears to potentially align well with good pedagogy practices. The emphasis on the social and collaborative characteristics of these new tools is very prominent (user-generated content, networked communities, interactivity, participation, sharing and remixing) – practices captured in phrases such as 'the wisdom of the crowds' (Soruwiecki, 2004) and 'the architecture of participation' (O'Reilly, 2004)). There are now enough tangible examples of the use of web 2.0 tools in an educational context (Ala-Mutka, 2009; Crook and Harrison, 2008) for us to be able to assess their impact and reflect on what particular new properties they might offer. There are numerous examples of innovation in the application of these technologies - the use of blogs as reflective diaries (Kerrawalla et al., 2009). wikis to create co-constructed reports (Lamb, 2004; Briggs, 2008). art exhibitions in Second Life (Educational uses of Second Life, 2007). experiential, problem-based learning through gaming technologies (Sancho et al., 2008).

There seems to be a tantalising alignment between the properties of new technologies (the focus on user-generated content, the emphasis on communication and collective collaboration) and the fundamentals of what is perceived to be good pedagogy (socio-constructivist approaches, personalised and experiential learning) (Conole, forthcoming). Despite this there is still a gap between the rhetoric (O'Reilly, 2004; Downes, 2006) about the potential impact and actual practice. In particular there is a very real disjuncture between web 2.0 technologies and current educational systems and practices.

The Open Educational Resource movement (Seely Brown and Adler, 2008) is synergistic with web 2.0 approaches with its focus on collective endeavour, sharing and promotion of free access to educational resources. There has been significant funding to support the development of major OER repositories, however, on the whole, the majority of teachers and learners are not using them. However finding *appropriate* resources and knowing how to use them is a specialised skill; many learners, despite being competent technology users, lack the appropriate academic literacy skills to appropriate these free resources for their learning (Lankshear and Knobel, 2007); similarly teachers lack the expertise needed to disaggregate resources and redesign them. McAndrew et al. (2009) considered web 2.0 characteristics and compared them against the way in which OER are developed and used, drawing on evaluation data on the use of the OpenLearn (http://openlearn.open.ac.uk) site. They argue that such sites align well with the long-tail phenomenon by providing access to specialist subjects. Similarly, the social tools associated with the site enables users to contribute ideas and adapt content providing an example of the web 2.0 user-generated content and the broader notion of users adding value within a web 2.0 context.

To summarise, new technologies appear to offer much for education, in particular utilisation of web 2.0 technologies and free educational resources.

However teachers lack the necessary skills to make effective use of these. As described above a good understanding of how these technologies can be used and illustrative examples of good practice are emerging from research work in the field, but this is not being disseminated effectively to teachers. Addressing these challenges has been the focus of our research on Open Educational Resources and Learning Design. The next two sections summarise this work before we move on to describing how this is now being used as the basis for the new OLnet initiative.

OPEN EDUCATIONAL RESOURCES AND THE OPENLEARN PROJECT

The first body of research that underpins the OLnet initiative is the work we have been doing at the OU on the development and evaluation of a repository of OER of OU material as part of the OpenLearn project. Before describing OpenLearn we will first contextualise this work and provide a brief history of the development of OER as a research area.

The Rise of the Open Educational Resource Movement

There has been a growing interest in recent years in making educational content freely available. Terms such as 'open content' and 'open educational resources' have gained currency and there is now a well-established international community of those interested in producing, using and researching OER. This section is not intended to provide a comprehensive review of the field, but simply to summarise some of the issues and highlight key references.

Commission by the Hewlett foundation, Atkins et al. (2007) provide a comprehensive review of the development of the OER movement, describing many of the major initiatives in the field and some of the key achievements. A complementary report emerged at around the same time, commissioned by OECD (2007). Both reports give a good overview of the field, the motivations and aspirations behind the OER movement, as well as reflecting on some of the challenges associated with this area. Iiyosh, Kumar and Seely Brown (2008). through an edited collection, consider the wider notion of 'openness' and what it might mean in an educational context.

The Hewlett foundation define OER[3] as:

teaching, learning, and research resources that reside in the public domain or have been released under an intellectual property license that permits their free use or re-purposing by others

digitised materials offered freely and openly for educators, students and self- learners to use and reuse for teaching, learning and research (OECD, 2007:133).

According to OECD (2007) over 300 universities worldwide are engaged in the development of OER with more than 3000 open access courses. There are numerous initiatives and consortia involved in this area; examples include the following:

- OpenCourseWare consortium (http://www.ocwconsortium.org/).
- China Open Resources for Education (CORE) consortium (http://www.core.org.cn/cn/jpkc/index_en.html).
- Japanese OCW Consortium. (http://www.jocw.jp/).
- ParisTech OCW project. (http://graduate-school.paristech.org/).
- Irish IREL-Open initiative (http://www.irel-open.ie/) and
- JORUM repository (http://www.jorum.ac.uk/).

The scale of effort and investment in the development of OER is impressive, as the following statement on the OpenCourseWare website[4] indicates:

OpenCourseWare Consortium is a collaboration of more than 200 higher education institutions and associated organizations from around the world creating a broad and deep body of open educational content using a shared mode.

In 2002 Hewlett initiated an extensive OER programme, the chief aim was to 'catalyze universal access to and use of high-quality academic content on a global scale' (Atkins et al., 2007:1). More recently, the UK, the Higher Education Academy (HEA) and the Joint Information Systems Committee (JISC) have initiated a large-scale call on the development of OER,[5] building on existing initiatives such as JORUM and OpenLearn.

The Cape Town Open Education Declaration[6] argues that the OER movement is based on 'the belief that everyone should have the freedom to use, customize, improve and redistribute educational resources without constraint'. It focuses on three suggested strategies to removing current barriers to the use of OER: teacher and learner engagement with OER, a general policy to publish openly and commitment to open approaches at institutional and government levels.

The OER movement has been successful in promoting the idea that knowledge is a public good, expanding the aspirations of organizations and individuals to publish OER. However as yet the potential of OER to transform practice has not being realised, there is a need for innovative forms of support on the creation and evaluation of OER, as well as an evolving empirical evidence-base about the effectiveness of OER. However, recognition of the importance of investment and effort into promotion of the use and uptake of OER is evident in the prominence given to OER developments in a recent major report on Cyber-learning, commissioned by the National Science Foundation (NSF, 2008). 'Adopt programs and policies to promote Open Educational Resources' is one of the five higher-level recommendations in the conclusion to the report.

Researching Open Educational Resources raises issues in how to address global connections, reuse, design and evaluation of world wide efforts to work with learning resources that are available for free use and alteration.

OER is not only a fascinating technological development and potentially a major educational tool. It accelerates the blurring of formal and informal learning, and of educational and broader cultural activities. It raises basic philosophical issues to do with the nature of ownership, with the validation of knowledge and with concepts such as altruism and collective goods. It reaches into issues of property and its distribution across the globe. It offers the prospect of a radically new approach to the sharing of knowledge, at a time when effective use of knowledge is seen more and more as the key to economic success, for both individuals and nations. How paradoxical this may turn out to be, and the form it will eventually take are entirely unforeseeable. The report offers some preliminary handles for understanding the issues raised. (OECD, 2007:9)

Open provision of course materials has become a more extended movement with many universities adopting the approach. There are indications of adoption of an open approach, however the diverse OER projects have not received much research attention to establish how best to move from existing provision to better structures for open operation. Our own work associated with the Open University's OER programme known as OpenLearn is described in the next section.

The OpenLearn Project

MIT was one of the first projects established to develop OER, attracting funding from The William and Flora Hewlett Foundation in 2000. The Open University in the UK successfully bid for support from the Hewlett Foundation to establish its Open Content Initiative, launched

Figure 1. LearningSpace in OpenLearn

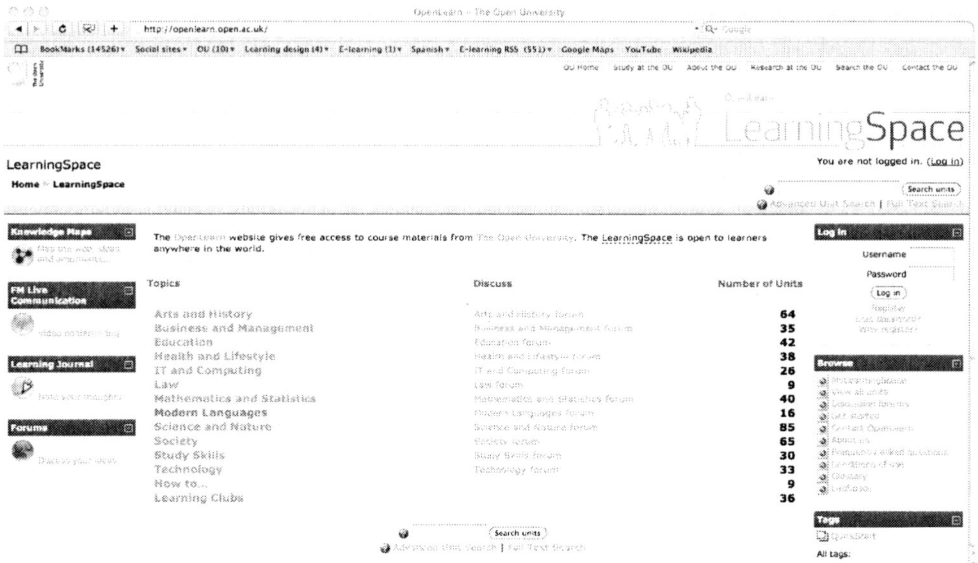

as OpenLearn in 2006. OpenLearn is an online repository of Open Educational Resources. The site aims to make a significant proportion of the Open University UK's educational materials freely available on the web.

The initial site was made publicly available in October 2006 and now offers a full range of Open University subject areas from access to postgraduate level, with over 3 million visitors since it was launched. The site is divided into two sides: LearningSpace (which provides access to the quality assured OER derived from Open University courses) and LabSpace (where users can download, repurpose and upload OER).

Figure 1 shows a screen shot of the site. In April 2008 OpenLearn reached its target of 5400 learning hours (based on designed time for student activity) of content in the LearningSpace and 8100 hours in the LabSpace. The site was built using the Open Source learning environment Moodle.[7] In addition to the OER, the site provides a variety of learning support and social networking tools. These include:

- Forums linked to individual OER to connect and discuss with others,
- An instant messaging and presence indicating tool (MSG),
- Compendium for visualizing and representing OER and the development of shared argumentation,
- Flashmeeting – for live video conferencing, and
- A learning journal – for users to reflect on and record their experiences.

Lane (2006) provides a commentary on the Openlearn experience and in particular gives an overview of many of the issues involved in initially setting up and running Openlearn. He sets out a conceptual framework for what the project was intending to achieve and then lays down the steps needed to move from the necessity of a fairly constrained re-purposing situation in the short term towards a more open and creative environment. McAndrew (2006) discusses the rationale for the Open University developing OpenLearn and in particular looks at how the initiative aligns with the practices associated with web 2.0 technologies. He argues that OpenLearn – with its associated tools for communication and collaboration provides a useful testbed to explore and research user behaviour in participating in new digital environments. This experimental aspect was identified as part of the rationale for OpenLearn which meant that as part of the research and evaluation work associated with the initiative a set of research issues were picked out:

- What are the most effective ways to develop OER?
- What intellectual properties arise from OER initiatives?
- What are the barriers and enables to the development and use of OER?
- What models are different initiatives adopting in terms of the production of OER?
- What are sustainable business models for OER?
- What accessibility and inclusion issues are arising in associated with OER?
- What new pedagogical models are needed to support the use of OER across both formal and informal learning contexts?
- What methods are appropriate to evaluate the effectiveness of OER and how can transfer of good practice be best achieved?

Although the research and evaluation work associated with OpenLearn made some process in addressing these issues, clearly these are big questions and cannot be addressed within a single initiative. There is a need for a collective understanding of the impact of OER, Olnet is in part a response to this. In the final research and evaluation report for the initiative McAndrew and Santos (2009) summarise the research findings from the evaluation of OpenLearn and reflect on the implications for future OER activities. An integrative approach was use for the evaluation; research activities included action research, direct and remote studies, trials and experiments, and surveys and interviews. The evaluation provided valuable insights into how users perceived the OpenLearn materials and more importantly how they were being used. Three main categories of users were identified based on their level of engagement with the site: enthusiasts, registered users and visitors.

Findings were both expected and surprising. Although the majority welcomed the concept of free educational resources, it was not always fully understood – many assumed there was an associated cost of some sort. A significant proportion said they would use the site again (there were over 100,000 unique visitors each month). Perhaps surprisingly users classified material as interactive even when it was text-based. Interest in downloading content was high, but evidence of reuse was low when measured in terms of content returned to the site. There appeared to be technical (lack of understanding of XML), pedagogical (lack of experience or redesigning) and cultural (not wanting to alter existing perceived 'good' content) barriers to reuse.

A need for a more explicit understanding of the inherent design associated with OER became evident; educators appeared wary of using content without first understanding it. In fact research exploring the design of educational materials and activities was being undertaken in parallel to the OpenLearn project, and although this work considered design more broadly in terms of learning and teaching, it was evident that a lot of the tools, methods and approaches being developed could be adapted and applied specifically to an OER context. This learning design work is described in the next section. The chapter then looks at how these two areas of research are now being combined as the basis of the Olnet initiative.

LEARNING DESIGN

Learning design has been defined earlier in this chapter as a research area developing methods, tools and resources to support teachers in making pedagogically informed, better use of technologies. In part this research is concerned with the format and representation of learning events, typically consider as Learning Design (with initial capital letters) and in part with the process and methods of designing learning experiences, often written with lower case as learning design. For more information on the origins of learning design as a research area and for an brief overview of current work in the area see Cross and Conole (2009). Beetham and Sharpe (2007) and Lockyer at al. (2008) provide recent edited collections of research and development activities in the field.

The Open University Learning Design Initiative (OULDI)

The OU Learning Design Initiative[2] has being developing and applying a methodology for learning design. The project was initially funded through strategic development funding from the Open University and in September 2008 secured additional funding (of £400 K) from the JISC through its Curriculum Design programme,[8] to look at extending the work to date and cascading findings, tools and resources to other institutions.

The initiative aims to provide support for the entire design process; from gathering initial ideas, through consolidating, producing and using designs, to sharing, reuse and community engagement. These are complex and challenging processes that involve a range of stakeholders with different interests; issues and representations are different depending on whether design occurs at the level of individual activity, course or curriculum. The vision is of a learning design methodology and suite of practical tools and resources that bridge between good pedagogic practice and effective use of new technologies.

Surprisingly, despite the fact that designing courses is a core teaching activity, the design process and how teachers go about designing and representing their ideas is poorly understood (Cross et al., 2008). Therefore within OULDI we adopt an empirical evidence-based approach to our activities. This includes gathering data about existing teaching practices (such as: how do teachers go about designing and representing learning activities? where do they get new ideas or support and advice from? how do they evaluate the effectiveness of their designs?). In addition we run an ongoing programme of activities and events to validate and discuss research findings with others and to trial out the tools and approaches we are developing. Tools and approaches are clustered around three main aspects of design: visualising and representing pedagogy, guiding and supporting the design process, and sharing and discussing ideas; each informed by an evolving understanding of the design process (Figure 2).

The initiative has developed a visualisation tool for design, CompendiumLD [9](Conole, Brasher et al., 2008; Brasher et al., 2008) and a social networking site, Cloudworks[10], for sharing learning and teaching ideas linked to designs (Conole, Culver et al., 2008, Conole and Culver, 2009, Conole and Culver, forthcoming).

CompendiumLD Learning Design Construction Tool

CompendiumLD[11] enables users to visualise a design sequence. It also provides in situ help, for example on how particular tools can be used to support different types of learning activities or suggestions of case studies or examples. The resulting design representations can be saved in a variety of formats – as simple visual jpegs, as

Figure 2. The four interconnected aspects of OULDI

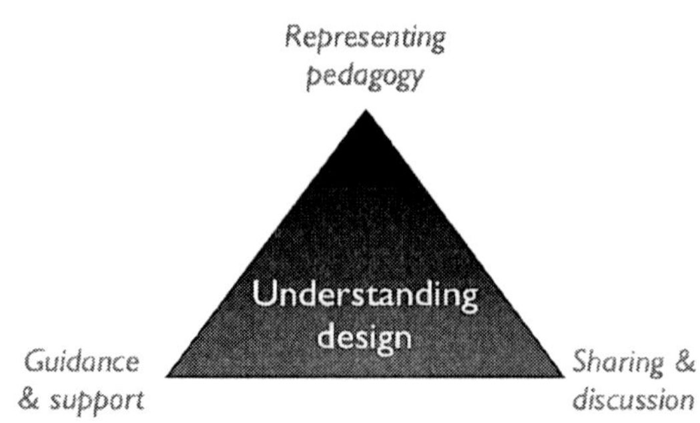

XML or as a set of connected, interactive webpages. Evaluation from user trials and workshops indicates that users find the tool easy to use and that it provides a valuable way of articulating their design activities and as a means of guiding them through the design process. It enables them to develop a shared language for discussing ideas with others and as a means of making the design process more explicit. CompendiumLD can be used flexibly with a typical representation such as that shown in Figure 3 consisting of strands of learner activity, resources, and tutor activity containing instructions, linked resources and tools. The result can be seen as a picture similar to a concept map, however any of the objects can be linked to externally hosted resources via URLs or embedded content.

CompendiumLD has enabled us to build up a rich understanding of the nature of the design lifecycle and of the different kinds of representation that are possible (see Cross et al., 2008; Brasher et al., 2008; Conole and Mulholland, 2007 for more detailed discussion of different forms of representation). It is evident that design occurs at different levels of granularity; from the design of small-scale learning activities or OER, through to sequences of activities (such as a block of several weeks worth of activities) up to programme or whole curriculum level. The nature of design is also different depending on when it occurs – brainstorming ideas for a new course for example is very different from refining a course taking account of student feedback.

Cloudworks Social Networking Site

The production of designs forms one aspect of our research, the other is to provide the right set-

Figure 3. Visual representation of a design developed in CompendiumLD

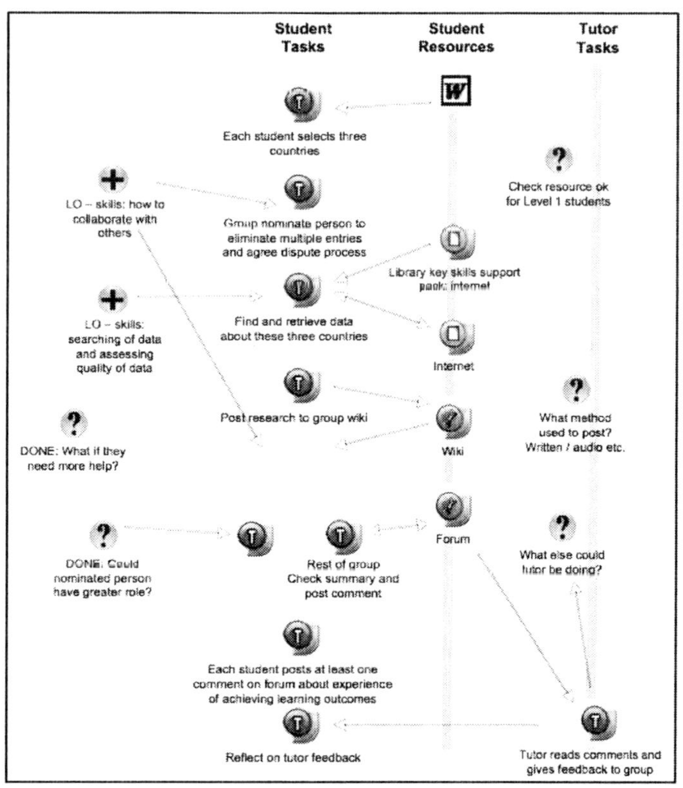

ting for sharing and discussing design ideas. To help achieve this we are also developing a social networking site for finding, sharing and discussing learning and teaching ideas, Cloudworks[10]. The site is based on web 2.0 principles and it is intended that there is a low barrier to use. Figure 4 provides a screenshot of the site. There are two key concepts associated with Cloudworks: 'clouds' and 'cloudscapes'.

The core object in cloudworks is a 'cloud'. This could be: a short description of a learning and teaching idea, information about resources or tools for learning and teaching or more detailed learning designs or case studies of practice. Each cloud is a 'social object' (Engeström, 2005) in that it is possible to have a conversation around the cloud. Clouds can be aggregated into 'cloudscapes' associated with a particular event, purpose or interest. For example you can have cloudscapes associated with a conference aggregating clouds about conference presentations or tools and resources referenced. A cloudscape can be set up for a workshop where clouds might include workshop resources, tools or activities.

Cloudscapes can also be more general; for example to stimulate debate about a particular teaching approach. Clouds can be associated with more than one cloudscape. Using the notion of 'following' common in many social networking sites (such as twitter.com). you can follow both people and cloudscapes, helping to build the sense of community engagement. Each person registered on the site automatically has all the clouds they have input associated with them and a list of the people and cloudscapes they are following. Each has their own 'cloudstream', listing all their clouds chronologically.

A series of 'cloudfests' were run during the initial development of the site. Lasting around one and a half hours, participants were presented

Figure 4. The Cloudworks homepage showing featured cloudscapes, active clouds and the activity stream for the site

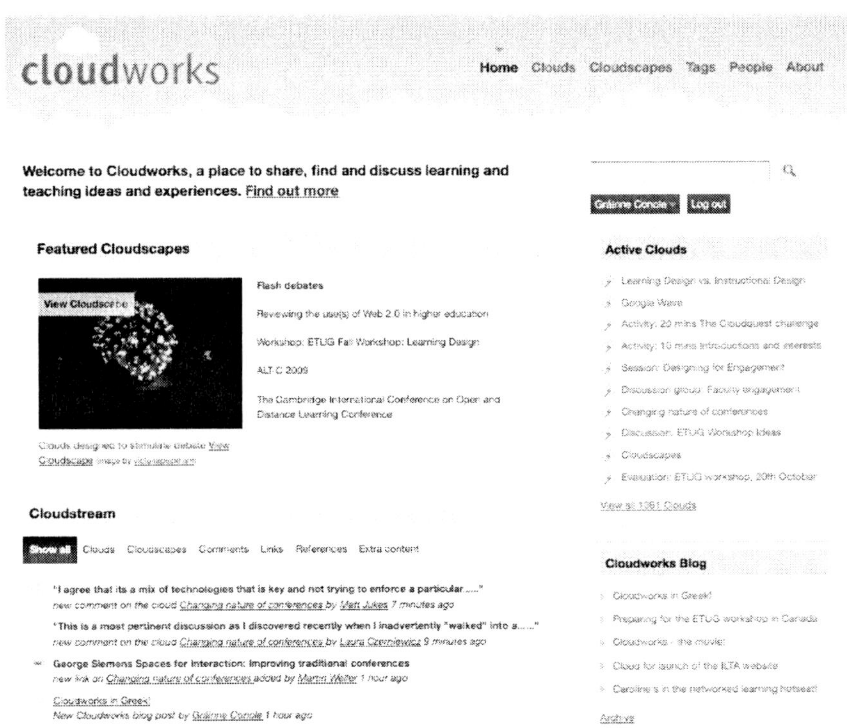

with a series of clouds from the site. They read and rated the clouds. They were then asked to write their own cloud, describing a learning and teaching activity they had designed or someone else's that they thought was good. These cloudfest events have given us a valuable insight into the challenges around encouraging practitioners to share and discuss learning and teaching ideas. Some of the issues discussed included:

- How effective are abstract vs. more concrete clouds, how much detail should be included?
- Who owns a design and hence has the right to include it in the site? Is it ok to include descriptions of other peoples' ideas?
- How is the site quality controlled, will an evolving user-generated folksonomy provide enough structure?

They also felt there was a need for transferable designs and practical suggestions on what worked and what didn't. Participants stated that seeing comments attached to clouds helped make them come alive, which resonated closely with our notion of the site being built on social objects. One participant stated [the site is] 'not just a repository but a conversation'. This is the key challenge we are addressing in forthcoming development activities for the site.

In addition to the tools described above, OULDI has been experimenting with the development of a range of events to foster and develop community engagement around learning design:

- Cloudfests as a means of critiquing existing content and getting users feedback Design summits with peer researchers in the field, to discuss some of the key research challenges to get a collective sense of where the field was going.
- Design challenges as targeted time-intensive events to support the initial planning and visualisation of a new course. One 'Design challenge' has also been run to date. The challenge was for teams to devise a short course in a day; they were provided with a structured outline to guide them through the design process, a range of physical resources and a series of 'resource stalls' of experts around the room. Participants reported finding the resource stalls valuable and that the structure of the day enabled them to develop their thinking and designs far more that they would ordinarily have. Ideas to build on the success of this event, include running similar events in other faculties or pan-university and trialling the notion of a 'Design-lite challenge', where the expertise and resource stalls would be available virtually using the cloudworks site.

We have also been working on the development of 'pedagogical schema' or 'design methods' that provide specific guidance on different pedagogical approaches. Figure 5 gives an example that shows a matrix where designers can create a set of principles for a course and map these to four overarching aspects of pedagogy. (This matrix has been used to map Openlearn in Conole, 2008).

We have also produced a pedagogy profile widget, which enables teachers to map types of student activities against blocks of time (http://cloudworks.ac.uk/index.php/cloud/view/2459). Our evolving set of tools, resources and activities for the OU Learning Design Initiative are available as a cloudscape in cloudworks (http://cloudworks.ac.uk/cloudscape/view/1882).

THE OLNET INITIATIVE

The experience of building OpenLearn and our learning design research work through OULDI and led us to revisit the challenges of the introduction: it seemed as if the open activity in OER together with a social network approach to design could

Figure 5. Mapping principles to pedagogy

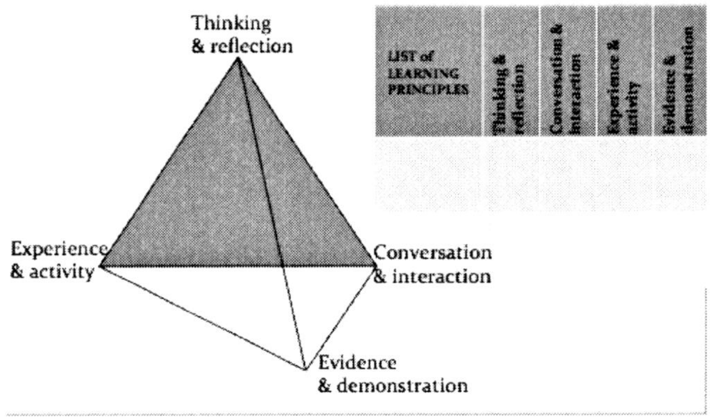

be adapted to provide a good basis for further research to both refine the challenges and start to address them. The result has been to construct a progamme of activity embodied in the OLnet initiative. The Open Learning Network (OLnet) is a partnership between the OU and Carnegie Melon University funded by The William and Flora Hewlett Foundation, as a means of building on and learning from the experiences gained through OpenLearn and Carnegie Mellon's Open Learning Initiative.[12]

Aims of OLnet

OLnet aims to provide a global network for researchers, users and producers of OER. In particular it aims to better articulate the design and evaluation of OER and to facilitate a greater degree of transfer of good practice. The network will foster closer links between those researching OER and those producing and using them. However as the proposal[13] for the initiative to the Hewlett Foundation states:

The very openness of OER means that we cannot be sure how they are being used, what ways people are getting the best out of them, or if they are meeting the original goals of the developers. OER authors are often not in the best position to address these questions, partly because their position inhibits neutrality and partly because of the need for expertise and resources to do the research. (McAndrew, 2008: 3)

Previous evaluations of OER initiatives, as described earlier, highlight the challenges to realising the vision inherent in the OER movement of free educational resources which teachers and learners can adapt and repurpose. It is clear that just producing the OER is not enough; teachers and learners need more guidance on how to deconstruct and redesign OER for their own context and easy access to summarizes of the research findings on effective use of OER. We see OLnet as being the next evolutionary step in the OER movement and to this effect our core research question is:

- How can we build a robust evidence base to support and enhance the design, evaluation and use of OER? With three sub-questions:
  1. How to improve the process of OER reuse/design, delivery, evaluation and data analysis?
  2. How to make the associated design processes and products more easily shared?
  3. How to build a socio-technical infrastructure to serve as a collective evolving intelligence for the community?

OLnet intends to build on the evaluation findings from the OpenLearn project and use these as a basis for adapting the tools developed through OULDI to an OER context. OLnet aims to provide a basis for gathering evidence, developing methodologies, supporting involvement and gaining value by aggregating and sharing information through appropriate infrastructure. It offers a community-based solution: a researcher/practitioner network, supported by Web tools, for aggregating, sharing, debating and improving OER. Adopting a Community of Practice approach (Wenger, 1998). the aim is to build on existing communities and the needs that they have for evidence and investigation, rather than attempt either to create a new community or provide catalogues of existing efforts.

We aim to address the questions outline above through an integrative, iterative approach to gaining an understanding of the nature of information sharing about OER and by developing a series of research studies focusing on how to improve the design and use of OER. The research studies are intended to act as threads that feed information into the network of OER developers and users. Likewise, the discussions in the human network of OER developers and users will feed information back about the kind of research that still needs to be designed and performed.

To initiate these cycles of information exchange, OLnet is building an evolving socio-technical infrastructure to support the development of a collective intelligence in a social network designed to become self-sustaining. The initial, 'day-one' platform is adapted from the previous tools and approaches we developed in OULDI and Openlearn (such as Cloudworks, CompendiumLD and Cohere[11]). but we fully anticipate that this platform will develop and adapt as we learn from the OLnet research studies and evaluation of activities associated with the network.

We see capacity building, practice and research as essentially parallel and interacting strands that build on the base of technology and activities shared among the participants. Therefore the platform is complemented by a range of capacity-building activities and support for communities interested in improving OER design and applying methods for assessing robustness of OER. Through its activities, OLnet aims to encourage adoption of evaluative techniques to provide evidence on the effectiveness of OER in use. Experiences gained across OLnet will be distilled, synthesised and repurposed in a range of formats. For example by aggregating methods and approaches to evaluating and research OER, by synthesising collective knowledge of the design process, through creation of generic OER pedagogical patterns and models, and through an evolving roadmap of research questions to define the OER research domain. The next two sections look at the role for design in OLnet and provide specific examples of OLnet activities using tools from OULDI.

Focusing on Learning Design

As described earlier one strand of Olnet activities is a set of specific research projects. One of the initial ones is focusing on exploring specifically how the OULDI research work in particular, as well as learning design research more broadly, can be applied to an OER context.

As discussed earlier, learning design is an approach that considers learning materials as having a final product (the educational resource). and a design that captures the intent of the product. This design is often implicit and has not been valued as a product in itself. OER challenge that position as it becomes important to communicate why material has been developed so that users can make best use of it and also see the designs as shareable in themselves. Designs matter both to educators, to understand potential reuse, and to learners to help them select material relevant to their context. We see design is an important part of an overall OER effectiveness cycle (see later).

The research question the learning design project intends to address is at two levels.

On the specific OER level:

1. Design-based description in a shareable representation.
2. Data on the interpretation of design and how it can support reuse.
3. Materials to capture the approach and enhance participation.
4. Use data on designs in relation to OERs

On the network level:

1. A collection of social objects that enable research discussions.
2. Community building through sharing of representations and interlinking with the OER community.
3. Integration of tools (e.g. from Cloudworks) within the OLnet framework.

Putting the Vision into Practice

The first opportunity to test out the OLnet approach to working with the OER community occurred in March 2009, at two related OER conferences in Monterey, CA held over four days (See http://cloudworks.ac.uk/index.php/cloudscape/view/873 and http://cloudworks.ac.uk/index.php/cloudscape/view/863). Cloudworks was used as the basis for the conference website and delegates were encouraged to use the site as a means of sharing ideas and synthesizing discussions at the conference. A conference Cloudscape was set up which summarized details about the conference; delegates could choose to follow the Cloudscape

Figure 6. The Monterey Cloudscape, as it appeared in March 2009

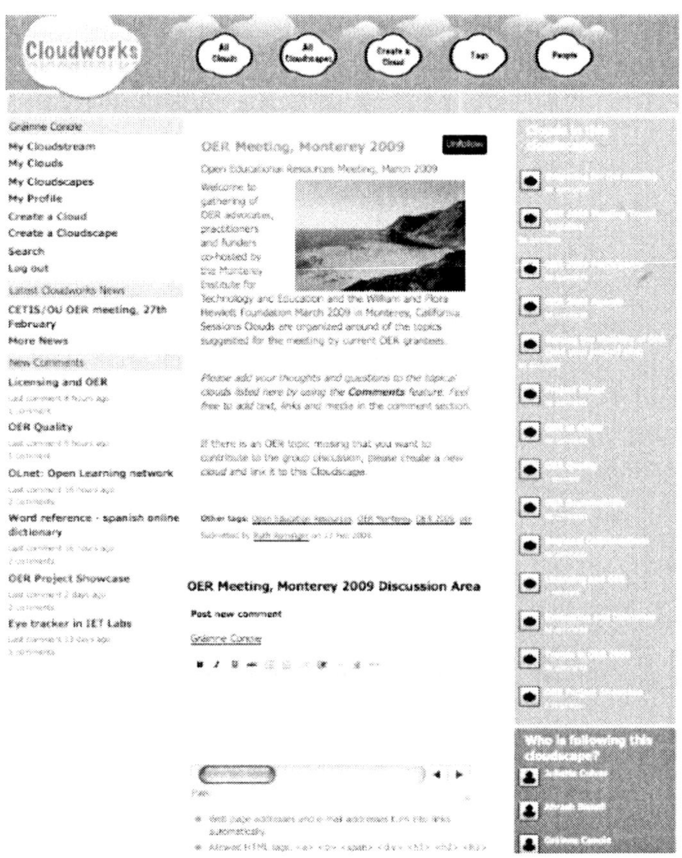

and would then be listed on the side. New Clouds created in the Cloudscape appeared on the right hand side of the screen, along with an indication of any associated comments (Figure 6).

Each session at the conference had a dedicated Cloud and delegates were encouraged to feed in conference discussions into the site. The explicit aim was to encourage new forms of participation and to explore different forms of representation for capturing ideas and discussions. The suggestion to use CLoudworks came from the OLnet team, the implementation was carried out by the conference organisers who involved a set of student reporters. Those students live blogged sessions and included the summaries they produced as Clouds in the conference website. Arguments and discussion threads were also visualized as Compendium diagrams produced by OLnet team members as participants in the conferences. The Compendium diagrams provide an alternative, complementary representation to the text-based reports (Figure 7).

A twitter tag was agreed and live tweets aggregated dynamically within Cloudworks. Similarly photos associated with the conference were tagged and aggregated on Flickr[15]. Wordle[16] was used to visual summarise plenary discussions and media embedding enabled the incorporation of SlideShare[17] presentations and video clips. Around 150 delegates attended the conference. Figure 8 illustrates some of the different types of Clouds created during the conference.

Four interconnected Cloudscapes were associated with the conferences. One for each of the conferences, one for a series of interviews carried out with delegates and one specifically related to OLnet.

The experience was very positive, with Cloudworks being described as "a very flexible addition" as a "layer that enabled people to reflect as we went along". Nearly 100 clouds were generated and over 500 comments from across the participants alongside a further 200 tweets on the twitter backchannel. 37 people elected to 'follow' the 'NROC Networking meeting Cloudscape' and 73 people the 'OER Meeting, Monterey March 2009' Cloudscape. The use of Cloudworks meant that normally sequential activities of brainstorming, noting and collating could occur in parallel. Some clouds essentially acted as discussion forums. For example a session where project ideas was requested led to 37 comments giving project ideas.

Figure 7. Compendium visualisation of a plenary session at the Monterey conference

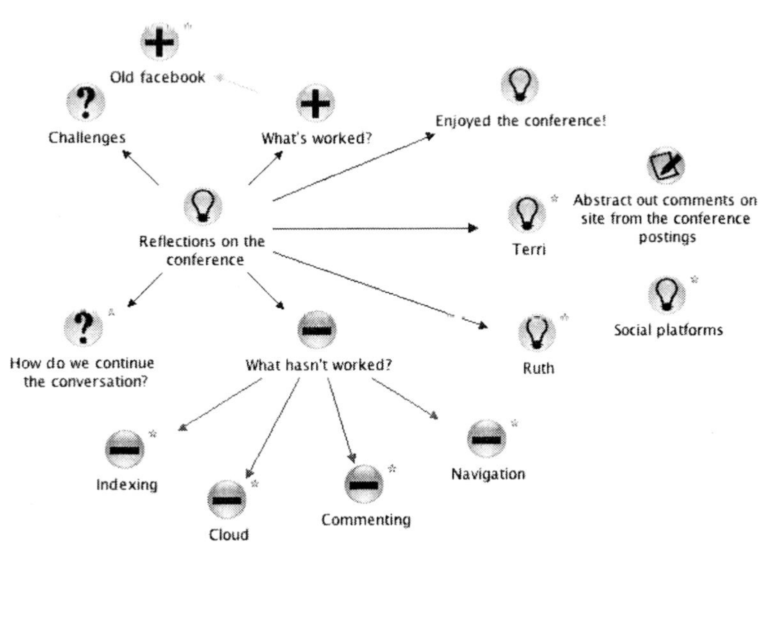

Figure 8. Video clouds, blog aggregators and the conference Flickr stream

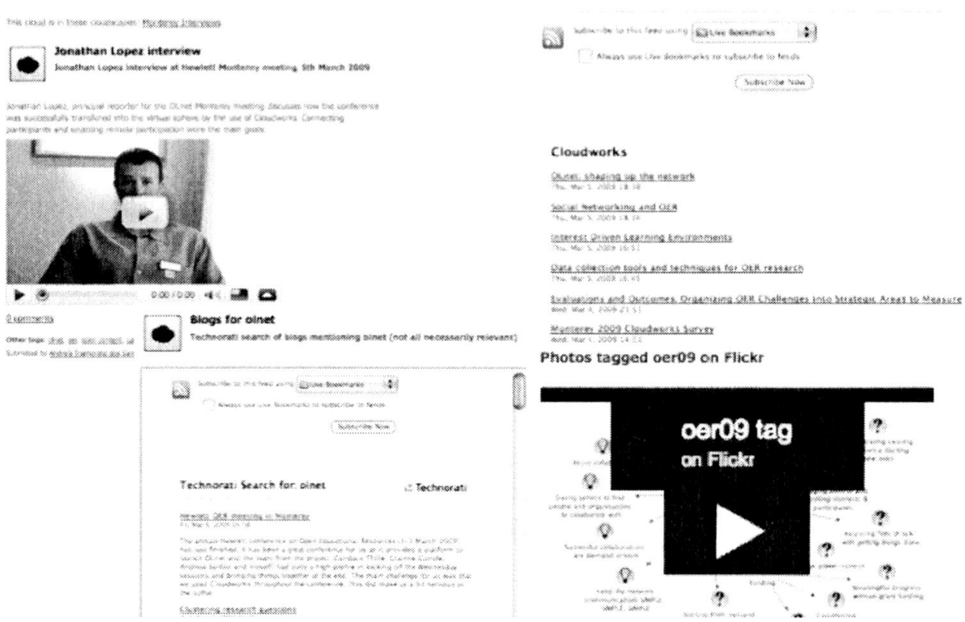

Similarly, the 'Trends in OER research' generated 23 comments and the Cloud on 'Evaluations and outcomes' research related to OER generated 13 comments. These could then be quickly analysed using Compendium and Wordle to feedback to the community through visualization of the data. 18 delegates completed an online survey about the use of the tool, positive comments were that it was felt the tool provided a useful mechanism for enhancing discussion and debate at the conference, however navigation and usability were cited as areas for improvement.

This early experience has given us some confidence that we have tools that can help support social networking aspects of researching OER and to add value to existing activities. We need to take this further to extend beyond use in conferences and connect with models for how OER are used. A tentative model for effect use and reuse of OER and OLnet itself is described in the next section.

THE OER EFFECTIVENESS CYCLE

A core concept underpinning OLnet is the notion of an OER effectiveness lifecycle (Figure 9). The lifecycle consists of four stages: select, design, use and evaluate. As the figure illustrates, these are not seen as distinct, but as inter-locking. It is possible to start at any point in the cycle. This cycle can be used to describe both small-scale interventions such as an individual teacher choosing and using an OER in their own practice (for example the OER case study project[18] is supporting a range of individual OER initiatives, through to large-scale, research-focused interventions (Lovett et al., 2008).

OLnet aims to make explicit relevant tools, resources and schema to help the user make informed choices about each stage in the cycle. This will include describing how generic tools (such as Google or analytic tools) can be used, as well as identifying and describing specific resources or tools of relevance to the OER cycle (such as the CompendiumLD tool and the Cloudworks site, and the OpenLearn OER repository).

Figure 9. The OER effectiveness cycle

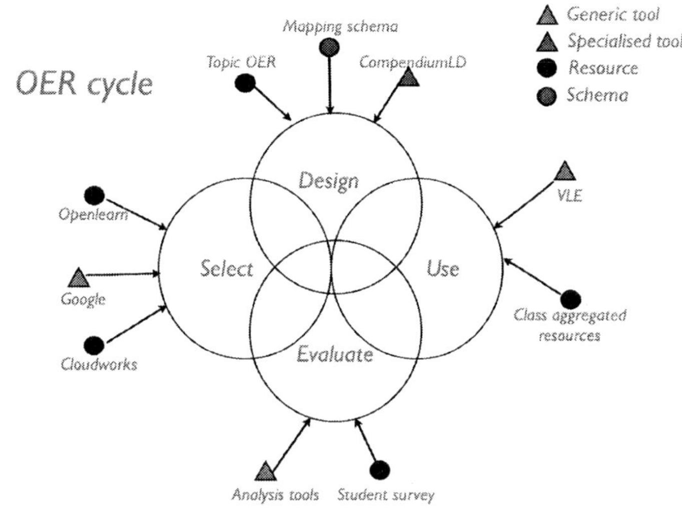

Our central argument is that all too often, the feedback loop that links from evaluation, to data collection, to cumulative design improvement is broken, and that those links should be forged and nurtured. This design cycle is focused on OER as the objects of interest, with other tools facilitating its transition at different stages, hence the label 'OER Effectiveness Cycle' at the component, or sub-system, level.

We believe that user engagement is also an important ingredient in the OER effectiveness cycle. Therefore any one OER cycle is surrounded by a range of potential tools, resources and schema that can be drawn on to support the cycle along with the users engaged with the cycle – either through design of the OER (for example teachers). use of the OER (students) or evaluation of the effectiveness of the OER against its intended purpose (researchers) (Figure 10).

We want to emphasis that we see the cycle as reflexive: OER are not the only objects of interest. Any of the design representations or other artefacts generated, or used to analyze, OER design can themselves become 'social objects', that is, artefacts shared, deployed, evaluated and improved on by the community. Each stage in the cycle can therefore generate specific outputs such as a design representation or new evaluation instruments, which can be put back into the OLnet community for others to use. So for example a user might query an existing OER repository such as OpenLearn as a means of selecting an OER for use. Another user might develop a new survey instrument for evaluating the use of a science-focused OER which they then make available to the OLnet community, and yet another user might then use that instrument to evaluate their own use of a Science OER. Thus, the very infrastructure that we use to accomplish this process – OLnet – becomes the object of reflection, hence the same effectiveness cycle applies to OLnet itself at the system level.

Figure 11 shows how we see knowledge and experience gained within individual OER cycles being passed around the network. Five OER effectiveness cycles are shown. It shows how OLnet provides a facilitative infrastructure and network to enable connections to be made across different OER cycles, so that outputs from one activity can be taken up and reused by another activity. So for example a design representation in one cycle can be picked up and used as a starting point for a dif-

Figure 10. The OER cycle and associated community

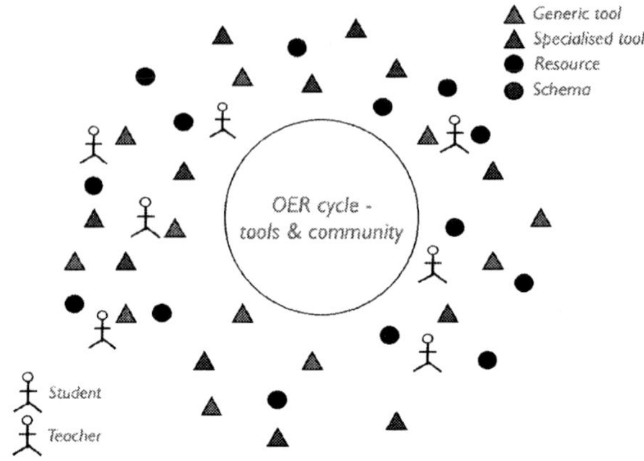

ferent OER cycle, or evaluation findings on the use of one OER can be used to inform and shape the design of a different OER. In addition to this transfer of knowledge and outputs between OER cycles, OLnet also plans to aggregates outputs in different ways, for example by providing a means to group people and sub-communities in different ways, aggregating tools and resources, collating designs, evaluations and case studies and performing a range of relevant meta-synthesis studies. This will ensure that the sum is greater than the parts and that maximum benefit is derived at the level of individual OER cycles and the overall OLnet.

CONCLUSION

At the time of writing OLnet is focusing on setting up the socio-technical infrastructure, capacity building and initiating specific research projects as described above. The initial socio-technical infrastructure for OLnet went live in March 2009,[19] with specific links to Cloudworks and CompendiumLD. A fellowship scheme has been initiated and the first visiting professor started in April 2009. A series of workshops and summits are planned, a precursor workshop to the establishment of OLnet held in February 2009 focused on the topic 'Researcher 2.0' and explored what researching in a web 2.0 environment means. Two research projects have been initiated – 'Integrating pedagogies and technologies that support individual learning and group knowledge building' (led by Carnegie Melon) and 'Learning design of OER' (led by the OU as described earlier). The conferences with other OER researchers in the field in March 2009 in Monterey proved to be a useful point to launch OLnet and to test out some of the approaches we are planning to develop.

OLnet is an ambitious initiative that aims to learn from our experience in the development of OER to date and harness the best in emergent practices of the use of new technologies to create an evolving knowledge network on the state of the art in OER design and effectiveness. We believe that it will provide valuable insights into the success factors associated with creating and sustaining such networks, but also insights more broadly into addressing some of the challenges with the uptake and use of technology more generally in education.

Figure 11. The OLnet network

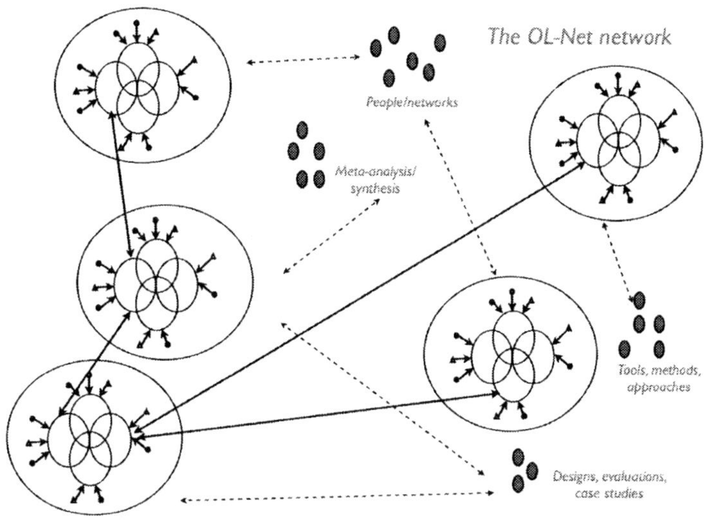

ACKNOWLEDGMENT

We would like to acknowledge The William and Flora Hewlett Foundation for funding OLnet and also OpenLearn and to the JISC for funding aspects of the OULDI work. The work described in this chapter spans contributions from a large number of individuals, we would like in particular to acknowledge the following: Andrew Brasher, Simon Buckingham Shum, Paul Clark, Simon Cross, Juliette Culver, Rebecca Galley, Paul Mundin, Andreia Inamorato de Santos, Martin Weller, and Tina Wilson. Also thanks to OLnet visiting professor Yannis Dimitriadis for extensive comments on this chapter.

REFERENCES

Ala-Mutka, K., Bacigalupo, M., Kluzer, S., Pascu, C., Punie, Y., & Redecker, C. (2009). Review of Learning 2.0 Practices. In IPTS technical report prepared for publication. Seville, Spain: IPTS. Retrieved April 18, 2009 from http://ipts.jrc.ec.europa.eu/publications/pub.cfm?id=2139

Atkins, D., Seely Brown, J., & Hammond, A. L. (2007). *A review of the Open Educational Resource movement: achievements, challenges and new opportunities, report to the William and Flora Hewlett Foundation.* Retrieved May 2, 2009, from http://www.hewlett.org/NR/rdonlyres/5D2E3386-3974-4314-8F67-5C2F22EC4F9B/0/AReviewoftheOpenEducationalResourcesOERMovement_BlogLink.pdf

Becta. (2008). *Harnessing technology: next generation learning.*Retrieved Augusat http://publications.becta.org.uk/display.cfm?resID=37348&page=1835, last accessed 8/2/09.

Beetham, H., & Sharpe, R. (Eds.). (2007). *Rethinking pedagogy for a digital age: designing and delivering e-learning.* Oxford, UK: Routledge.

Brasher, A., Conole, G., Cross, S., Clark, P., Brasher, A., & Weller, M. (2008). CompendiumLD – a tool for effective, efficient and creative learning design. In *Proceedings of LAMS conference*, Cadiz, Spain.

Briggs, L. (2008). The power of wikis in higher education. *Campus Technology*. Retrieved February 9, 2009, from http://campustechnology.com/Articles/2008/08/The-Power-of-Wikis-in-Higher-Ed.aspx

Christensen, C., Johnson, C. W., & Horn, M. B. (2008). *Disrupting class – how disruptive innovation will change the way the world learns*. New York: McGraw Hill.

Conole, G. (2006). What impact are technologies having and how are they changing practice? In I. McNay (Ed.), *Beyond Mass Higher Education: Building on Experience* (pp. 81-95). New York: McGraw-Hill Education.

Conole, G. (2008). New schemas for mapping pedagogies and technologies. *Ariadne*. Retrieved from http://www.ariadne.ac.uk/

Conole, G. (in press). Stepping over the edge: the implications of new technologies for education. In M. Lee & C. McLoughin, *Web 2.0-based e-learning: applying social informatics for tertiary teaching*. Hersey, PA: IGI Global.

Conole, G., Brasher, A., Cross, S., Weller, M., Clark, P., & White, J. (2008). Visualising learning design to foster and support good practice and creativity. *Educational Media International*.

Conole, G. and Culver, J. (2009), The design of Cloudworks: applying social networking practice to foster the exchange of learning and teaching ideas and designs, Computers and Education, doi: 1-.1016/j.compedu.2009.09.013

Conole, G., Culver, J., Well, M., Williams, P., Cross, S., Clark, P., & Brasher, A. (n.d). *Cloudworks: social networking for learning design*. Melbourne, Australia: Ascilite Conference.

Conole, G., & Mulholland, P. (2007). *Using the concepts of design and narrative. PI working paper No. 2.* Milton Keynes, UK: The Open University.

Conole and Culver. (forthcoming). Cloudworks: social networking for learning design, Australian Journal of Educational Technology Cross, S. & Conole, G. (2009). *Learn about learning design (OU Learn About Series).* Milton Keynes, UK . *The Open University.*

Cross, S., Conole, G., Clark, P., Brasher, A., & Weller, M. (2008). Mapping a landscape of learning design: Identifying key trends in current practice at the Open University. In *LAMS Conference*, Cadiz, Spain.

Downes, S. (2006). E-learning 2.0. *eLearning magazine: education and technology in perspective.* Retrieved April 20, 2007 from http://elearnmag.org/subpage.cfm?section=articlesandarticle=29-1

Educational Uses of Second Life. (2007). Retrieved June 26, 2007, from http://sleducation.wikispaces.com/educationaluses?f=print

Engeström, J. (2005, April 13). Why some social network services work and others don't — Or: the case for object-centered sociality. Retrieved August 8, 2008, from http://www.zengestrom.com/blog/2005/04/why_some_social.html

Iiyoshi, T., & Kumar, M. S. V. (Eds.). (2008). *Opening up education – the collective advancement of education through open technology, open content and open knowledge.* Cambridge, MA: MIT Press.

Iiyoshi, T., Kumar, M. S. V., & Seely Brown, J. (2008). *Opening up education: the collective advancement of education through open technology.* Cambridge, MA: MIT Press.

Jeffreys, A., Falconer, I., Conole, G., & Littlejohn, A. (2006). *LADIE project final repost – Learning Activity Design in Education – reference model project*. Retrieved February 5, 2009, from http://www.jisc.ac.uk/media/documents/programmes/elearningframework/ladie_finalreport.pdf

Kerawalla, L., Minocha, S., Kirkup, G., & Conole, G. (2009). A framework for blogging in Higher Education. *Journal of Computer Assisted Learning, special issue on Web 2.0 technologies*. Retrieved from http://www.blackwell-synergy.com/doi/abs/10.1111/j.1365-2729.2008.00286.x

Lamb, B. (2004). Wide open spaces: Wikis, ready or not. *Educause Review, 39*(5), 36–48. Retrieved January 12, 2007, from http://www.educause.edu/pub/er/erm04/erm0452.asp

Lane, A. (2006). *From pillar to post: Exploring the issues involved in re-purposing distance learning materials for use as Open Educational Resources*. Retrieved fromhttp://kn.open.ac.uk/public/document.cfm?docid=9724

Lockyer, L., Bennett, S., Agostinho, S., & Harper, B. (2008). *Handbook of research on learning design and learning objects*. New York: Information Science Reference.

Lokken, F., & Womer, L. (2007). *Trends in e-Learning: Tracking the Impact of e-learning in Higher Education*. Washington, DC: Instructional Technology Council.

Lovett, M., Meyer, O., & Thille, C. (2008). The Open Learning Initiative: the effectiveness of the OLI statistics course in accelerating student learning. *Journal of Interactive Media in Education,* (14). Retrieved from http://jime.open.ac.uk/2008/14/jime-2008-14.pdf

McAndrew, P. (2006). Motivations for OpenLearn: the Open University's Open Content Initiative, OpenLearning workshop paper, the OECD experts meeting on Open Educational Resources 26-27 October 2006 in Barcelona, Open University: Milton Keynes, http://kn.open.ac.uk/public/document.cfm?docid=8816

McAndrew, P. (2008). *OLnet network to support sharing methodologies and evidence on the effectiveness of OER*. Milton Keynes, UK: The Open University.

McAndrew, P., Conole, G., Clow, D., Buckingham Shum, S., & Wilson, T. (in press). *Sharing designs for Open Learning: applying learning design to support open participation.* Paper submitted for special issue.

McAndrew, P., & Santos, A. I. (Eds.). (2009). *Learning from OpenLearn: Research Report 2006-2008*. Milton Keynes, UK: The Open University.

NSF. (2008). *Fostering learning in the networked world: learning opportunity and challenge. A 21st Century agenda for the National Science Foundation*. Retrieved August 2, 200, from http://www.nsf.gov/publications/pub_summ.jsp?ods_key=nsf08204

O'Reilly, T. (2004). *The architecture of participation.* Retrieved November 12, 2008, from http://www.oreillynet.com/pub/a/oreilly/tim/articles/architecture_of_participation.html

OECD. (2007). Giving knowledge for free – the emergence of open educational resources, report for OECD. *Centre for Educational Research and Innovation.* Retrieved May 2, 2009, from http://www.oecd.org/dataoecd/35/7/38654317.pdf

Sancho, P., Gómez-Martín, P. P., & Fernández-Manjón, B. (2008). Multiplayer role games applied to problem based learning. In *DIMEA '08: Proceedings of the 3rd international conference on Digital Interactive Media in Entertainment and Arts* (pp. 69-76). New York: ACM.

Sharples, M. (2002). Disruptive devices: mobile technology for conversational learning. *International Journal of Continuing Engineering Education and Lifelong Learning, 12*(506), 504–520. doi:10.1504/IJCEELL.2002.002148

Surowiecki, J. (2004, May). *The wisdom of crowds*. New York: Bantam Books

Wenger, E. (1998). *Communities of practice.* Cambridge, UK: Cambridge University Press.

ENDNOTES

1 http://openlearn.open.ac.uk

2 http://ouldi.open.ac.uk

3 Definition on the Hewlett website, http://www.hewlett.org/Programs/Education/OER/

4 http://www.ocwconsortium.org/about-us/about-us.html

5 See http://www.jisc.ac.uk/fundingopportunities/funding_calls/2008/12/grant1408.aspx for details of the call and associated documentation

6 http://www.capetowndeclaration.org/

7 http://moodle.org/

8 http://www.jisc.ac.uk/whatwedo/programmes/elearningcapital/curriculumdesign.aspx

9 CompendiumLD is an adaptation of an existing tool, Compendium (http://compendium.open.ac.uk/institute/)

10 http://cloudworks.ac.uk

11 CompeniumLD is available to download from http://compendiumld.open.ac.uk

12 http://www.cmu.edu/oli/index.shtml

13 It is interesting to note that the process of working up the bid was done in the spirit of openness too – a wiki was established with a draft of the proposal and people were invited to contribute and comment, http://iet-public-wiki.open.ac.uk/index.php/OPLRN_proposal

14 Like Compendium, Cohere is an argumentation tool. It is web-based and can be used to build up rich, semantically meaningful connections of ideas, http://cohere.open.ac.uk/

15 http://flickr.com

16 http://www.wordle.net

17 http://www.slideshare.net

18 http://wiki.oercommons.org/mediawiki/index.php/OER_Case_Study_Project

19 http://olnet.org/

Chapter 8

iCyborg:
Shifting Out of Neutral and the Pedagogical Road Ahead

Catherine Adams
University of Alberta, Canada

ABSTRACT

Teachers may no longer envision their educational technologies as powerful yet essentially neutral tools plied to accomplish their own pedagogical ends. Rather, these technologies are more accurately theorized as vocative objects that prereflectively engage and invite us into their world, and mimetic interventions that scaffold, transform, and sustain new teaching and learning practices and ways of thinking regardless of teacherly intentions. This chapter explores some of the significances and implications of a ubiquitous technologizing of educational lifeworlds in light of this understanding.

Digital technologies are transforming how we learn, what we know, and how we understand the world around us. New media, Virtual Learning Environments, electronic whiteboards and new software tools are significantly changing the processes of teaching and learning in primary, secondary and postsecondary education settings. Few are surprised that in virtually every classroom in schools, training institutions and universities, information and communication technologies (ICTs) are commonplace. Students supplement textbooks by accessing their assignments and readings online, they word-process their course papers, download PowerPoint presentations and class notes, keep in touch via online social networks, discussion boards and texting on their smart phones. Yet, we have barely begun to grasp the profoundly co-constitutive relationships we share with our digital technologies, relationships that simultaneously open new worlds of possibilities while silently closing down others (Introna, 2007).

This chapter explores some of the pedagogical significances and implications of this ubiquitous technologizing of the lifeworld, and suggests that as educators we may no longer view the digital technologies we adopt in our classrooms as neutral tools. I aim to show how these new technologies are more accurately comprehended as *evocative*

DOI: 10.4018/978-1-61520-678-0.ch008

objects (Turkle, 2004) and *mimetic vehicles* (Benjamin, 1978) that invite, scaffold, and sustain new practices and patterns of thinking, and thus carry significant *effective* as well as *affective* implications for students and teachers alike. This recommendation to theorize digital technologies anew precipitates from a hermeneutic phenomenological study I conducted exploring students' and teachers' lived experiences of PowerPoint in the classroom (Adams, 2006, 2008, in press). This research investigated how students and teachers are not only aided and "enhanced" by the particular digital media technology in use, they are also enmeshed, constrained by and relinquished to the language, imagery, framing, at-handedness, and sensuality of their materiality and design.

At the hand of teachers' everyday experience of PowerPoint in their classrooms, I will demonstrate how "our existence changes with the appropriation of a fresh instrument" (Merleau-Ponty, 1962/2002, p. 143). From this simple example, familiar to every teacher and student who has experienced the world of digital-technology-enhanced education, I then wonder what transformations of perception occur, what translations of action manifest any time we take up a "fresh instrument" of digital technology, be it PowerPoint or Smartphone, Second Life or Web 2.0, wiki or Wii, in the lived space of the classroom. Mark Hansen suggests that new media technologies are "poised on the cusp between phenomenology and materiality" and as such have introduced "a theoretical oscillation that promises to displace the empirical-transcendental divide" (Hansen, 2006, p. 297) that has long structured western thinking. This chapter is situated in the midst of this difficult theoretical divide, and attempts to make visible some of the tight intimacies, primordial interminglings, and, at times, acute dependencies teachers find themselves living with their educational technologies everyday.

VOCATIVE OBJECTS

The totality of the immediate environment that we inhabit, our lifeworld, is best described as "a *milieu*—a field of intensive forces, vibrant according to their own inner codes" (Lingis, 2004, p. 278). Ivan Illich (1997) coins the phrase *le milieu technique* to refer to the irresistible embrace of the high technology lifeworlds we find ourselves dwelling in today. The technological milieu is shaping substantially—insinuating itself, habituating us and simultaneously reinterpreting—how we act in and perceive the world. To gain access to the unique tenor and structure of this new milieu, Illich suggests we look beyond what technological objects *do*, and attend more carefully to what they *say* to us, to what they *invite* us to do. Within the situated, relational, embodied context of lived space, each object or place presents a unique evocation or "pathic" appeal to us: "cool water invites us to drink, the sandy beach invites the child to play, an easy chair invites our tired body to sink in it" (van Manen, 1997, p. 21). Of course, beaches and easy chairs do not "speak" to us in the same way as people do:

> *Pathic knowing inheres in the sense and sensuality of our practical actions, in encounters with others and in the ways that our bodies are responsive to the things of our world and to the situations and relations in which we find ourselves.* (van Manen, 2007, p. 12)

Orienting to pathic or lived sensibilities, we are positioned to catch glimpse of the nature and quality of the intimate rapport enacted between human beings and their technologies every day.

The pathic or invitational quality of a thing is always "heard" in light of our *intentionality* or indissoluble connection and orientation to the world as child, parent, teacher, etc. The sandy beach commands the child differently than the watchful parent, or the teenage sibling in the company of friends. Intentionality expresses the phenomenological insight that we do not exist apart from our world, but are always already intimately intertwined, caught up in and tacitly informed by it: "human experience and consciousness necessarily involve some aspect of the world as their object, which, reciprocally, provides the context for the meaning of experience and consciousness" (Seamon, 2002). Too, how a thing shows up to us in our world as well as what it simultaneously "says" to us rests on our cultural pre-understandings and meaning structures. The cultural ground of our existence pre-reflectively provides the "conditions whereby we experience something—whereby what we encounter says something to us" (Gadamer, 1976, p. 9). Similarly, the world discloses itself differently to us depending on the historical (onto-theological) epoch we find ourselves living in. According to Martin Heidegger, we currently suffer (and enjoy) the sway of *das Gestell*, the technological way of being: the things of our world tend to appear and speak to us as resources to be used and manipulated (Heidegger, 1977).

Heidegger, one of the earliest philosophers of technology, shows that each thing (or place) opens a new world to us, revealing novel structures of experience and meaning; every technology discloses a new horizon of possibilities to us. Human beings are "the be-thinged" (Heidegger, 1971, p. 181): we are prereflectively inhabited, conditioned, and creatively provoked by the things of our world. Having pre-reflectively responded to the invitational quality of a thing, we enter into a "rapport" with it (Heidegger, 1971); we become ontologically and hermeneutically engaged. From a phenomenological perspective, we may thus seek to describe the *vocative* appeal digital technologies make to teacher and student in the lived space of the classroom. Using the example of PowerPoint, we might inquire: What invitation does PowerPoint issue to a teacher as s/he is preparing for a class? What is the nature of the rapport that is enacted between, with and through the teacher and this tool? What practices are newly informed, reformed, and transformed, and what habits of mind are prescribed, subscribed to, and subsequently inscribed?

INHABITING POWERPOINT

PowerPoint is an intentionally architected form; a windowed milieu that the teacher traverses with her eyes upon screen, fingertips on keyboard, hand on mouse. Heidegger (1972) tells us, "When we handle a thing, for example, our hand must fit itself to the thing. Use implies a fitting response" (p. 187). Reaching out with anticipation of PowerPoint's promise to help her point powerfully, the teacher orients herself toward her windowed screen; her being is drawn in and gently caught up in the "draft" of PowerPoint, the unique horizon of possibilities it brightly offers. The teacher responds fittingly. The pathic call or vocative appeal PowerPoint makes to the teacher consists of both *explicit* linguistic gestures ("Click to add title", "• Click to add text") as well as *implicit* suggestions and prohibitions (you may do this but not that). Bruno Latour (1992) calls this collection of imperative statements "prescriptions" that are encoded in the design of artifacts[1] and subsequently "uttered (silently and continuously) by the mechanisms for the benefit of those who are mechanized" (p. 232). Gathered together, PowerPoint's overall vocative script to the teacher is a promisingly familiar and easy-to-use digital environment for designing and delivering presentations.

One teacher describes how she constructs a lesson using PowerPoint:

I insert an image, add some text, then try them in different positions on the slide. I'm looking for balance. I like using compelling images, with minimal, carefully chosen text for impact. As I work, I do not, cannot separate the composition of slides themselves from the subject matter at hand, the vision of my students, and the appeal I am trying to make. I sit back and look (perhaps trying to see the slide as my students might), then adjust, and adjust things again. I try out different fonts, sample background colors from my images, wanting to give the whole presentation a sense of visual cohesion. I take a certain pleasure and satisfaction in this. I move to Slide Sorter View [where all the slide thumbprints are laid out across the window] to grasp the whole so far, to visualize the general flow of the presentation. From here, I move a few slides to a different place in the sequence to see how that flows, then return to Normal view. I find I am variously engaged with trying to represent the content, the purpose of this teaching presentation, visually, in text, or both, and thinking about, imagining presenting the slides to my class.[2]

Within the PowerPoint environment or milieu, the teacher's work materializes as an accumulating series of slides. The basic elements of each slide are text, images, color, and animation. She composes, adjusts, tries out new fonts, samples colors, switches "views," plays with order. She is engaged representing content as slides, then imagining the presentation in the immediacy of a classroom with her students. Slides, subject matter, the vision of her students, and her presentational and teacherly intentions intermingle. In performing this preparatory work, the teacher sits in her office with computer, screen, keyboard and mouse; texts and papers litter the desk. Her screen shows numerous windows open: a web browser, email, a Word document, as well as PowerPoint. Occasionally her eyes wander from the screen, and stare thoughtfully out her office window into the distance. She turns back to the PowerPoint window, pulls her keyboard a little closer, nudges her mouse and continues work. Once the teacher is engaged in her preparation work, her office, desk, screen, keyboard and mouse recede into the background. PowerPoint too withdraws from full view, fading to a translucent framework or scaffold, a sophisticated but peripherally present set of tools that she may variously call upon to perform her presentation design activities in this digital world.

Phenomenologically speaking, we do not usually engage a tool as a discrete, obvious object, that is, in what Heidegger calls its present-at-hand mode (*vorhandenheit*). Rather we tend to encounter a tool through using it, in its handiness (*zuhandenheit*). In this handy encounter, the tool is essentially invisible to us, taken-for-granted. It is, as Sartre says about the everyday experience of our own bodies, passed over in silence—"*passé sous silence*" (Sartre in Bleeker & Mulderij, 2002).

Consider the example (used by Wittgenstein, Polyani, and Merleau-Ponty) of the blind man's cane. We hand the blind man a cane and ask him to tell us what properties it has. After hefting and feeling it, he tells us that it is light, smooth, about three feet long, and so on; it is occurrent for him. But when the man starts to manipulate the cane, he loses his awareness of the cane itself; he is aware only of the curb (or whatever object the cane touches); or, if all is going well, he is not even aware of that....Precisely when it is most genuinely appropriated equipment becomes transparent. (Dreyfus, 1991, p. 65)

When we are writing a scholarly paper or an email, we are barely aware of our typing fingers or the keyboard. Our fingers serve us silently, falling transparently on the vaguely present keyboard, while we are primarily engaged in the higher-level business at hand: writing. The video-gamer is only prereflectively aware of the controller held confidently in her hands, the Bluetooth mic and headset in her ear, the bright screen directly before her; rather, she is immersed in playing with her virtually-present friends in the space opened by the videogame. Only when the Bluetooth connection is lost, or the battery dies in her controller, does she suddenly awaken to the headset or controller as obvious objects. Too, until our fingers know how to type, the keyboard stands as an insurmountable obstacle. But, as Heidegger (1962) describes, "the less we just stare at the [tool], and the more we seize hold of it and use it, the more primordial does our relationship to it become" (p. 98). To be what it is, a tool must recede from visibility.

The work-object or focal project of our instructor is thus not PowerPoint. Her project is the classroom situation she will find herself in a few days hence. As a teacher, her primary intention is to creatively assist her students in learning the particular subject matter at-hand. For this purpose, for this subject matter, she has chosen to use PowerPoint. Thus while the presentation software frames and facilitates her activity of planning a lesson, PowerPoint is not the main objective and intention, anymore than canvas and paint palette are the object and intention of the artist. Nonetheless, we must also notice how the instructor's activity patterns and meaning structures are also being quietly *in-formed*—conformed, deformed, and reformed—by the architecture of the particular software she finds herself *inhabiting*.

Post-phenomenologist Don Ihde (1990) observes that "technologies, by providing a framework for action,...form intentionalities and inclinations within which use-patterns take dominant shape" (p. 141). *In* PowerPoint, the teacher "does not, cannot separate" the software's possibilities and designs from her own: the aims and inscriptions of the Microsoft programming team and the teacher intentionalities and inclinations intertwine, enmesh and reorient. The teacher's world is translated into new vocabularies and presentation genres, expanding her possibilities of action while simultaneously framing and constraining the world as a screenic succession of 4:3 slides.

Having answered the call of PowerPoint—its invitational qualities or affordances—the teacher enters a mode of human-technology engagement that Chesher (in Suchman, 2007) describes as "managed indeterminacy" or *invocation*. "Invocation involves those actions that define the terms of engagement written into the design script or discovered by the participating user" (Suchman, 2007, p. 282). The teacher is now conversationally engaged, enfolded and intertwined with PowerPoint. The teacher-technology relational boundaries blur and a hermeneutically rich but "silent" corporeal rapport sets in.

A Sensorium of New Vocabularies: Aural, Visual, Corporeal, Haptic

Looking toward the future of technology-enhanced teaching and learning environments, what are the implications of theorizing tomorrow's technologies as *vocative objects* that prereflectively engage and invite us into their world? Hermeneutically speaking, we may begin to glimpse the startling articulation and surround of iconic and gestural languages occurring, the growth of new digital literacies that interweave and subsume orality and text with image and icon, manual and corporeal gesture. Tomorrow's teachers and students will be called upon to master these evolving languages of interface, the facility to converse with and navigate the multiplying cadre of nonhuman entities that increasingly mediate our everyday lives. Like touch-typing, our inter-facing with technologies must become "second nature" in order to traverse with ease each new digital landscape. Unlike touch-typing however, the interfacial "keyboards" that mediate our human-technology relations will continue to shift beneath our fingertips. The task will involve continuous adaptations to the particularized dialects of the machine—aural, visual, corporeal, and haptic; vernaculars that may only be apprehended via (prereflective) manipulation and direct use, rather than through (reflectively) reading a user manual. To comprehend today's vocabularies of texting and twittering, or tomorrow's tactile Siftables (Merrill, Kalanithi & Maes, 2007) and Sixth Sense technologies (Mistry, Maes & Chang, forthcoming), we must *grasp* hold of each new technology, play with it, use it. Only in the midst of a technology-in-play may its potentials unfold and new meaning structures manifest.

However, in striving for such fluency, both teacher and student are necessarily prereflectively enfolded and enmeshed in the designs—the extensions, potentials, as well as the constraints—of each new technology. As Walter Ong (1982) amply demonstrates through his landmark study of orality and writing, "technologies are not merely exterior aids but also interior transformations of consciousness" (p. 81). Learning to "speak" the language of the machine, we increasingly meld with its constructs and prescriptions, expanding but also perturbing our own intentionalities along the flow lines afforded by the technologies-in-use. As educators we must carefully weigh these questions: what ways of knowing, what habits of mind, what forms of community do we wish to promote in tomorrow's world? What transformations of consciousness are we intending to set in motion? There is nothing neutral about digital technologies: each issues its own unique vocative appeal, opening us to new ways of thinking, being, and doing in the world, while simultaneously attenuating others.

MIMETIC INTERVENTIONS

Returning to the familiar example of PowerPoint: enter teacher with trolley replete with laptop, mouse and data projector. Untangling the garage-band knot of electrical cords and connector cables, the teacher connects, plugs in, and turns on laptop and projector. This process is sometimes accompanied by palpable anxiety surrounding the stages of equipment hook-up, and worries about self-competence in the face of difficulties or breakdown and the implications of "no PowerPoint" to the fate of the class. The projector hums at last, the slides are cued up, the teacher breathes a quiet sigh of relief.

The simple act of drawing the blinds or switching off the light, darkens perceptibly the hue of the wall, softens the faces of students. The teacher becomes less visible; the projected slide shines brighter. The mood changes, the classroom atmosphere shifts. PowerPoint reconfigures the classroom as a cinematic space: the students settle in as spectators, the teacher as orator, narrates the slides from the side. When the teacher turns to the opening slide, the students are cued to sit back, get comfortable and (hopefully) "enjoy" and learn from the PowerPoint presentation with a certain sense of passivity. A subtle change occurs in the students' attitude and orientation: students listen to a talk or lecture, look at overheads, but seem to watch a set of PowerPoint slides. The large, bright slideshow reminds students they may become a particular kind of audience, "invigorated or drowsy, [but] a generally passive audience that is rarely called upon to really interrogate the images" (Crang, 2003, p. 242). As students are drawn into the PowerPoint show as spectators, what of the teacher?

The Vocal Rhythm of PowerPoint

I notice when I turn to begin my PowerPoint, I shift my role slightly—I'm less conversational, more oratorical. PowerPoint locks you into a gait in your speech, a kind of vocal rhythm.

The teacher with-PowerPoint finds himself standing somewhat differently in relationship to his class: less dialogic, more monologic; less open to interruption and discussion, fastening to a vocal pattern that rhythmically signals oration not conversation. Vocal rhythm may also synchronize with slide rhythm.

The arrival of a new slide is the occasion to take a breath, a momentary pause to look at the slide, allow its meaning to prompt me: a reminder of what to say next, what direction to pursue. But too, I must somehow find connection with what I have just said. Or not. It tells me what comes next. I feel I must press on.

Like walking and talking with a good friend, footfalls—breath and slidefalls—find a mutually comfortable rhythm and pace. Here a special kind of pathic relation is hosted, not between teacher and students, but between teacher and projected slides. This human-technology relational dialogue is less mechanically complex and nuanced than the one taken up during the planning and design phase. Here, the slide "speaks," and the teacher responds; then the next slide "speaks" again regardless of what the teacher says. Of course, this is most simply because in "View Show" mode, the PowerPoint machinery only responds to a few select fingertaps on the keyboard or manipulations of the remote. More specifically, the slides are no longer in the midst of being created and manipulated. In "View Show" mode, the teacher cannot change the slides themselves, he can only control the direction of movement between the slides and animation moments—forward, backward—as well as access preset links and buttons. This predicament of being instructionally captivated in a slide set may also be the consequence of the teacher planning the lesson with a series of headlines or points to "talk to".

I am committed to do this PowerPoint.

As soon as I clicked to the next slide, I knew immediately it was the wrong thing. Seeing their eyes, I felt: I simply can't go on. It was the same sinking feeling you get realizing the person you are having a conversation with isn't listening to you. I had spent all this time preparing this PowerPoint presentation and then the problem with PowerPoint is you just can't simply jump ahead, be extemporaneous—"just ignore this and this while I find the right slide." I was stuck with my plan.

This college instructor recalls a time when he suddenly felt that, in the lived context of his class, his choice of using PowerPoint to address a particular topic was misjudged. Of course, any lesson plan or teaching approach can go awry or fall flat. In such moments, the teacher may decide to "stick with the plan" or diverge and improvise. The seasoned teacher usually has a few other "tricks" at-hand. Yet, is there something about PowerPoint that complicates the move to diverge in response to one's felt sensibilities? One teacher describes her PowerPoint dilemma like this:

In the classroom, PowerPoint is a representation of my anticipated presentation—an imagining of what my presentation would be, could be. But in the actual moment of teaching, things are often otherwise. In the midst of teaching, my slides and I sometimes come into conflict with one another. Then I feel fragmented, forced to choose this particular outcome—what is represented up there on the slides—over the felt relation with my students—what seems to present itself to me in the moment. I am committed to do this PowerPoint. I cannot now easily choose to do something else.

When a teacher uses PowerPoint in her classroom, she commits to the unfolding of a particular form of teaching and learning, a predetermined story wending its reckoned path to a decided conclusion. A PowerPoint presentation prepared beforehand is also an investment, visible proof of preparation and organization in the face of the contingent, indeterminate lifeworld of the classroom. To abandon such obvious evidence of competence may strike as foolhardy, exposing oneself to an uncertain, unprepared-for future. As Howell (2007) laments,

From the moment I walk into the lecture theatre I feel the pressure from my students to line up my thinking with their PowerPoint notes, without which they seem to be lost. I usually succumb by connecting them to the screen rather than to myself, each other, and the subject matter. In giving precedence to the object of PowerPoint, where the slides take on a language and world of their own, ...students may subconsciously be encouraged to zoom out of the teacher's presence in favor of the rectangle on the screen. (p. 139)

The Times-Square-like surround of slick and easy possibilities is so appealing and omnipresent, our inner compass as teachers may be quietly lifted from us and replaced by the veneer of "powerful" solutions. As sociologist Daniel Bell prophetically wrote in the early 1970s, the new "intellectual technologies"—tools that specifically extend our cognitive reach—substitute "algorithms (problem-solving rules) for intuitive judgments" (1973, p. 29). Here, a digital technology is given unintentional proxy for professional knowing.

The Technologizing of the Lifeworld

Our corporeal being—our lived body—is increasingly and intimately enhanced by, enmeshed with, and enfolded into new digital technologies. These paratextual[3] machines mediate our lived experience with astonishing immediacy and complexity, lending us novel sensory worlds, and pre-scribed ways of knowing and doing that are increasingly shared globally. The moniker "digital" is signaling a radical change in our material world, but also in our human selves.

Techno-utopian thinkers like Hans Moravec and Ray Kurzweil predict human-technology fusions where the "software" of our minds will one day be uploadable to more durable, faster hardware, thus rendering our "mere jelly" (Moravec, 1988, p. 117) bodies—the "old slow carbon-based neural-computing machinery" (Kurzweil, 1999, p. 129)—obsolete. In the wake of such euphoric, science-fiction claims of transcendence, philosopher N. Katherine Hayles (1999) reminds us that the "human mind without human body is not human mind. More to the point, it doesn't exist" (p. 246). Our human self is intimately tethered to the possibilities as well as the limits of our flesh-and-blood, human body. Thus, as the "mere jelly" body is gradually being relinquished in these technology turf wars, a new version of human being has been conceived: the post-human, "whose basic capabilities so radically exceed those of present humans as to be no longer human by our current standards" (Bostrom, 2003, p. 5).

What does this mean for educators of tomorrow's children? We must begin to discern and "focus on our own embodiment as the material site—the bearer—of technology's otherwise wholly inhuman impact" (Hansen, 2000, p. 263). Digital technologies are locally deployed "mimetic vehicles" (Benjamin, 1978) that prereflectively shape our embodied agency. "Software quite literally conditions existence" (Thrift, 2005, p. 241), an habituation process that occurs primarily outside of the phenomenal field of subjectivity. One of the difficulties in grasping the mediating influence of software is that its texts do not fit the usual model of representation, wherein humans and objects represent each other via words and images. Instead, software texts concern words *doing* things in particular contexts: the language of the machine has direct material effects.

Our interactions with software, often via a screen and keyboard/mouse/controller, are direct, sensuous and mimetic. Software "affects our experience first and foremost through its infrastructural role, its import occurs prior to and independently of our production of representations" (Hansen, 2000, p. 4). In this way, our lived experience is being radically, but prereflectively re-habilitated; our intentional involvements perturbed and reinscribed via the constraints and dispensations of pre-fabricated digital architectures. We are now well into an era of technological-becoming, our sensuous bodies quietly adapting to the inhuman rhythms of an evolving, digitally inscribed and intensifying mechanosphere. Today's brick and mortar classrooms may persist for decades in one form or another, but tomorrow's digitally-enhanced students will increasingly interface, enfold into and inhabit digitally-enhanced environs and virtual spaces. As we grasp hold of these powerful new technologies with growing vigor, they too take hold of us, adumbrating new ways of being, doing and thinking in the world.

It is imperative that we attend mindfully to the material, hermeneutic, and existential shifts that are transpiring as our worlds are daily extended, intensified, and complicated by digital technologies. The continued promotion of digital technologies as neutral agents—a foundational belief or "posit" of our current ontological epoch—imperils the normative project of pedagogy by concealing the instrumental constructs they materialize. Rather, these paratextual machines must be recognized as effective and affective *mimetic interventions* that prereflectively in-form our being, knowing and doing in the world. Such a view necessarily burdens tomorrow's teachers with a renewed sense of professional responsibility, one sensitive to the fragile ecology of our classrooms in the wake of digital technology "integration," but more importantly, for the future well-being of our "post-human" children living in the midst of this brave new world.

Digital Literacy: Acquiring Digital Fluency Both With and Beneath the Surface of the Interface

Recalling the profoundly vocative quality of human-technology relations outlined above, Mark Prensky's (2001) terms "digital native" and "digital immigrant" seem to gain new credibility.

> Our students today are all "native speakers" of the digital language of computers, video games and the Internet... *our Digital Immigrant instructors, who speak an outdated language (that of the pre-digital age), are struggling to teach a population that speaks an entirely new language.* (p. 1, 2)

On the other hand, the bifurcation of human-technology relations into a "native" and "immigrant" binary does little to address the deeper issues that promise to trouble educational futures. Given the necessarily evolving nature of dialects that will continue to proliferate and redefine the complex worlds of ubiquitous digital technologies, we all (digital immigrants and natives alike) are more aptly conceived as *digital migrants* or *nomads* caught in the perpetual flux and flow of migrancy. Dwelling too long in any given world, the scene inevitably changes, the lived space shifts, and "naturalized" digital inhabitants find themselves once more "deterritorialized" (Deleuze & Guattari, 1987). Digital worlds resist "old-fashioned attempts to put down roots, ways of being that sink into the earth in search of a sturdy foundation on which to erect a new life" (Buchanan, 2005). Rather, we must each learn the supple art of swimming through these vocative landscapes, the difficult task of re-territorializing in new environments, and an open willingness to enter the flow again as the world shifts once more.

To develop this facility, tomorrow's students and teachers (1) will continue to need experience with a broad repertoire of digital vocabularies—text and image, iconic and haptic; but more essentially, they (2) will need to learn the codes and design patterns undergirding and adumbrating their movement and activity in and through these digital spaces. The former recommendation implies regular, but pedagogically thoughtful and critically reflective immersion opportunities with a variety of new technologies across the curriculum. The second recommendation suggests a different but more fundamental curricular response. Beyond the traditional literacy domains of language arts, music, fine arts, mathematics, and sciences (each characterized by its own language spheres), tomorrow's *digital literacy* requires that children also be schooled in the basic vocabularies and languages of the machine itself. For this, it is critical that the theoretical and practical discipline of computing science be adopted as a core subject area of the school curriculum, on par with language arts and mathematics. Such "computer" literacy is essential in facilitating our children's transparent understanding of and open-eyed fluency with the multiple worlds they will find themselves participating in. Learning the language beneath the surface of human-machinic interfaces positions us and our children to critically assess, and democratically reshape and transform the digitally-enhanced spaces we will increasingly inhabit.

REFERENCES

Adams, C. (2006). PowerPoint, habits of mind, and classroom culture. *Journal of Curriculum Studies, 38*(4), 389–411. doi:10.1080/00220270600579141

Adams, C. (2008). PowerPoint's pedagogy. *Phenomenology and Practice, 2*(1), 63–79.

Adams, C. (in press). The poetics of PowerPoint. *Explorations in Media Ecology, 7*(4), 43-58.

Bell, D. (1973). *The coming of post-industrial society: a venture in social forecasting*. New York: Basic Books.

Benjamin, W. (1978). On the mimetic faculty. In P. Demetz (Ed.), *Reflections: essays, aphorisms, autobiographical writings* (pp. 333–36). (E. Jephcott, Trans.). New York: Random House.

Bleeker, H., & Mulderij, K. J. (2002). The experience of motor disability. *Phenomenology + Pedagogy*. Retrieved from http://www.phenomenologyonline.com/articles/bleeker.html

Bostrom, N. (2003). *The transhumanist FAQ: a general introduction*. Retrieved from http://www.transhumanism.org/resources/FAQv21.pdf

Buchanan, I. (2005). Space in the age of non-place. In I. Buchanan & G. Lambert (Eds.), *Deleuze and Space*. Edinburgh, Scotland: Edinburgh University Press.

Crang, M. (2003). The hair in the gate: Visuality and geographical knowledge. *Antipode, 35*, 238–243. doi:10.1111/1467-8330.00321

Deleuze, G., & Guattari, F. (1987). *A thousand plateaus: Capitalism and schizophrenia.* (B. Massumi, Trans.). Minneapolis: University of Minnesota Press.

Dreyfus, H. (1991). *Being-in-the-world: A commentary on Heidegger's Being and Time, div. 1*. Cambridge, MA: MIT Press.

Gadamer, H. G. (1976). *Philosophical hermeneutics.* (D. E. Linge, Trans.). Berkeley, CA: University of California Press.

Hansen, M. (2000). *Embodying technesis: technology beyond writing*. Ann Arbor, MI: University of Michigan Press.

Hansen, M. (2006). Media theory. *Theory, Culture & Society, 23*(2-3), 297–306. doi:10.1177/026327640602300256

Hayles, N. K. (1999). *How we became posthuman: virtual bodies in cybernetics, literature, and informatics*. Chicago: University of Chicago Press.

Heidegger, M. (1962). *Being and Time.* (J. Macquarrie & E. Robinson, Trans.). New York: Harper & Row.

Heidegger, M. (1971). *Poetry, language, and thought.* (A. Hofstadter, Trans). New York: Harper Colophon Books.

Heidegger, M. (1972). *What is called thinking* (F. D. Wieck & J. Grey, Trans.). New York: Harper and Row.

Heidegger, M. (1977). *The question concerning technology.* (W. Lovitt, Trans.). New York: Harper and Row.

Howells, K. (2007). PowerPoint: friend or foe? In J. Sigafoos & V. Green (Eds.), *Technology and Teaching* (pp. 137-146). New York: Nova Science Publishers.

Ihde, D. (1990). *Technology and the lifeworld: From garden to earth*. Bloomington, IN: Indiana University Press.

Illich, I. (1997). Philosophy... artifacts... friendship—and the history of the gaze. In T.-A. Druart (Ed.), *Philosophy of Technology: Proceedings of the American Catholic Philosophical Association, 70* (pp. 61-82). Washington, DC: Catholic University of America.

Introna, L. (2007). Maintaining the reversibility of foldings: Making the ethics (politics) of information technology visible. *Ethics and Information Technology*, *9*, 11–25. doi:10.1007/s10676-006-9133-z

Latour, B. (1992). Where are the missing masses? A sociology of a few mundane artefacts. In W. E. Bijker & J. Law (Ed.), *Shaping Technology/Building Society: Studies in sociotechnical change* (pp. 225-258). Cambridge, MA: MIT Press.

Lingis, A. (2004). *Trust*. Minneapolis, MI: University of Minnesota.

McLuhan, M. (1964). *Understanding media: the extensions of man*. New York: McGraw-Hill.

Merleau-Ponty, M. (2002). *Phenomenology of perception*. (C. Smith, Trans.). New York: Routledge. (Original work published in 1962).

Merrill, D., Kalanithi, J., & Maes, P. (2007). Siftables: Towards sensor network user interfaces. In *Proceedings of the First International Conference on Tangible and Embedded Interaction (TEI'07)*, Baton Rouge, Louisiana. Retrieved from http://web.media.mit.edu/~dmerrill/siftables.html

Mistry, P., Maes, P., & Chang, L. (2009). WUW - Wear Ur World - A wearable gestural interface. In *CHI '09 extended abstracts on Human factors in computing systems*, Boston, MA. Retrieved from http://www.pranavmistry.com/projects/sixthsense/

Moravec, H. (1988). *Mind children: The future of robot and human intelligence*. Harvard University Press: Cambridge, MA.

Ong, W. (1982). *Orality and literacy: The technologizing of the word*. New York: Routledge.

Prensky, M. (2001). Digital natives, digital immigrants. *On the Horizon, 9*(5), 1–2. Retrieved from www.marcprensky.com/writing/Prensky%20-%20Digital%20Natives,%20Digital%20Immigrants%20-%20Part1.pdf

Seamon, D. (2002). *Phenomenology, place, environment, and architecture: a review of the literature*. Retrieved from http://www.phenomenologyonline.com/articles/seamon1.html

Suchman, L. A. (2007). *Human-machine reconfigurations: plans and situated actions (2nd ed.)*. New York, NY: Cambridge University Press.

Thrift, N. (2005). Beyond mediation: three new material registers and their consequences. In D. Miller (Ed.), *Materiality* (pp. 231–56). Durham, NC: Duke University Press.

Turkle, S. (2004). The fellowship of the microchip: global technologies as evocative objects. In M. M. Suárez-Orozco & D. B. Qin-Hilliard (Eds.), *Globalization: Culture and Education in the New Millennium* (pp. 97–113). Berkeley, CA: University of California Press.

Van Manen, M. (1997). *Researching lived experience: human science for an action sensitive pedagogy (2nd ed.)*. London, Ontario: The Althouse Press.

Van Manen, M. (2007). The phenomenology of practice. *Phenomenology & Practice*, *1*, 11–30.

ENDNOTES

1 Rather than "artifacts", Latour more usually employs the term "nonhumans" to describe human constructed objects. "Nonhuman" signals the agency that Latour and other Actor Network Theorists attribute to objects in co-constituting social assemblages.

2 The italicized text represents phenomenological research material drawn from interviews conducted with twelve university and college instructors regarding their lived experiences of PowerPoint.

3 The term "paratextual" is used by Gerard Genette in his book *Palimpsestes* (1982) to describe "accompanying productions" that bind the text and the reader together. He lists the following as examples of paratexts: "title, subtitle, intertitles; prefaces, postfaces, notices, forewords, etc; marginal, infrapaginal, terminal notes; epigraphs; illustrations; blurbs, book covers, dust jackets, and many other kinds of secondary signals."

Section 4
Learning Approaches

Chapter 9
Digital Game-Based Learning: New Horizons of Educational Technology

Michael D. Kickmeier-Rust
University of Graz, Austria

Elke Mattheiss
University of Graz, Austria

Christina Steiner
University of Graz, Austria

Dietrich Albert
University of Graz, Austria

ABSTRACT

Computer games are an incredibly successful technology; due to the dynamic and active nature they are perhaps even more successful and appealing than TV or movies. Facing this success and the significant amount of time young people spend on playing computer games, it is a compelling idea of educators, developers, and researchers to utilize this technology for educational purposes. In this chapter we focus on the emerging technology of digital educational games, we attempt to give a brief summary of the state-of-the-art, and we emphasize leading-edge research in this genre. Moreover, we discuss the psycho-pedagogical foundations of "good" educational computer games. Finally, we provide an outlook to the future of educational technologies.

INTRODUCTION

If certain researchers and educators are right, computer games and the MTV culture changed the way young people perceive and process information and, therefore, the way those young people learn. "Twitch speed" computer games and fast moving video clips and films emphasized specific cognitive aspects and deemphasized others (Prensky, 2001). According to many authors, the genre of actively played, dynamic computer games affect cognitive aspects as well as individual preferences probably even more than TV or movies does. The generation that grew up with computer technology, the Internet, and digital games – the so-called digital natives – has different demands on educational technology. The consequence is that future educational technology requires a dramatic change of its nature, particularly

DOI: 10.4018/978-1-61520-678-0.ch009

since learning and knowledge is becoming more and more important. So it is not a big surprise that the idea of using the same genre – computer games – for educational purposes is becoming increasingly popular amongst educators.

Computer games are a tremendously successful and popular genre. Since the 1990s research and development has increasingly addressed learning aspects of playing recreational games and also the realisation of computer games for primarily educational purposes. At the beginning of our journey towards successful digital educational games (DEGs) we have to ask why (computer) games are so successful, popular, and important. A great many scientific and philosophical works addressed such factors. According to the work of Lepper and Malone (e.g., Lepper & Malone, 1987; Malone, 1981) four key factors are challenge, curiosity, control, and fantasy. Very briefly, the motivational effect of a *challenge* is seen in the potential to engage a learner's self-esteem using personally meaningful goals with "uncertain" outcomes. According to Habgood, Ainsworth, and Benford (2005) uncertainty can be achieved through variable difficulty levels, multiple goals, hidden information, and randomness. The effect of *curiosity* is seen in the emotional appeal of narrative and game play, stimulating sensory and cognitive components. Curiosity is aroused by the feeling that one's own knowledge is incomplete or inconsistent – in terms of subject matter, game play, or narrative. The effect of *control* is seen in a self-empowerment, an increase of a learner's own control over the events in the game. This perception is triggered by the range of choices offered by a game, by the extent to which the events in the game depend on the actions of the learners, and the inherent power of these responses (Habgood, Ainsworth, & Benford, 2005). A specifically important factor is *fantasy*, which is a type of fictional narrative (e.g., Gee, 2003) and it is either intrinsic or extrinsic to game play. Intrinsic fantasy refers to the degree with which the learning is embedding the fantasy context. Intrinsic fantasy is more relevant to educational games since it might be "*designed to indicate how a skill might be used in the real-world setting, and may provide metaphors or analogies to aid in understanding*" (Dickey, 2006, p. 254).

The idea of using this motivational potential and the rich and appealing virtual worlds for educational purposes appears to be convincing. As mentioned, modern computer game technology could be used as a novel technology for education that can meet aforementioned new requirements and, even more, that can establish a link between learners and education, which is stronger, more enduring, and more effective than "all" existing educational technology could realize so far. The question is whether learning and gaming, which sometimes are considered being two entirely different concepts, can be merged at all. From a psycho-pedagogical point of view the answer is simple: Playing is (one of) the most natural forms of learning, children start learning to talk by playing with noises or they learn collaboration and strategic thinking when playing *Cowboys and Indians*. Computer games can combine this fact with leading-edge technological possibilities for presenting, practising, and testing knowledge and skills. In addition to these "natural" advantages of digital games, an origin for the increasingly popular idea of game-based learning is the misgiving (fact?) that the majority of current approaches to technology-enhanced learning are based on traditional, unexciting 2D user interfaces. At the same time, this view is compounded by the proliferation of high quality commercial computer games the learners are used to. In addition, traditional interfaces for educational applications have distinct weaknesses from the perspectives of learning psychology and didactics. For example, it is difficult to retain a learner's interest, to provide a meaningful context throughout learning episodes, or to activate prior knowledge in a meaningful context as a basis for learning. Moreover, it is not always possible to provide "real-world" problems for practicing new knowledge and for a purposeful application. Computer games can achieve all that (at least potentially) in a very natural and compelling and credible way.

The second stage of the journey towards the new horizons of learning technology is to ask for the educational advantages and scientific foundations of learning games. In the broadest sense, it is based on two challenges; one concerns the appropriate balance between learning and gaming and the other concerns the psycho-pedagogical foundations.

A subtle balance between learning and gaming and between challenge and ability (in terms of gaming as well as learning) is a prerequisite for fun and educational effectiveness. It is important to maintain fun, immersion, flow experience, and motivation. Moreover, it is important to realize a gaming experience that can compete with that of commercial, non-educational games. Successful DEGs must be able to adapt to the learner's knowledge, skills, and abilities, motivation, and consider pedagogical implications. Also in traditional forms of technology-enhanced learning, concepts of adaptivity, adaptability, and personalization are increasingly important. Generally, these approaches contest the one-fits-all approach of traditional learning environments, trying to tailor learning to individual needs and preferences. For example, an adaptive system may only provide learning objects which are suitable for an individual's learning progress - learning objects either too difficult or too easy might not be displayed. In the context of immersive DEGs, existing approaches to adaptivity must be extended in order to maintain an immersive gaming experience. A special challenge in this context arises from the need for pedagogical support during learning, which must be strongly embedded in gaming. Considering the importance of not destroying immersion, flow, and engagement in the game, the assessment of the learning progress and psycho-pedagogical interventions must occur in a non-invasive way. This, however, requires an intelligent system that is capable of assessing individual competences and learning progress by observing and interpreting the learner's behaviour in the learning situations within the game. We will briefly outline a leading-edge approach for this type of adaptation and personalization in the following sections.

A second pillar concerns the psycho-pedagogical aspects of game-based learning and teaching. In the field of technology-enhanced learning per se and DEGs in particular, it is still not unusual to find quite an imbalance between technology and pedagogy; a predominant portion of current e-learning materials and environments is still lacking sound pedagogical principles and instructional concepts. Decades of psycho-pedagogical research on the principles of teaching, learning, and cognition need to be taken up and utilised to ensure successful and effective learning experiences. This involves, for instance, considerations on cognition development and cognitive processing, learning theories, as well as research on motivational aspects of learning. In an in-depth overview we will link instructional design and didactic models, emotional and motivational psychology, and (educational) game design. In addition, we will describe a transformation of the existing instructional design guidelines and didactics, which quite naturally focus on traditional learning (software), to the genre of DEGs. To complete the picture, we will describe the identification and articulation of requirements in the course of the design and development processes.

Talking Digital Educational Games

To elucidate the area of digital educational games, we do need a description of computer (or video) games in general. Several definitions, taxonomies, and classifications have been proposed. A popular and still valid definition of the term game came from the Dutch culture-anthropologist Johan Huizinga in his famous work *Homo ludens* (1938, p.132). He stated, a game "*is an activity which proceeds within certain limits of time and space, in a visible order, according to rules freely accepted, and outside the sphere of necessity or material utility. The play-mood is one of rapture and enthusiasm, and is sacred or festive in accordance with the occasion. A feeling of exaltation and tension accompanies the action, mirth and relaxation follow*". This definition is old, we grant, however, it comprises the most important aspects of games, that is, gratuitousness, enjoyment, rules, and the absence of a purpose. Ludwig Wittgenstein (1953) emphasized that too simple approaches to defining what a game is, fail to comprise the entire concept. He argued that it could not be contained by any single definition; rather games must be considered a "family resemblance" of a series of definitions. A more recent approach came from Chris Crawford (1984) who tried to describe the term game along several dimensions such as art, entertainment, play, interaction, etc. This approach may be summarized as an interactive, goal-oriented activity within which players (including virtual characters) can interfere with each other. An attempt to formalize the definition of game on the pillars of challenge, conflict, and play came from Smed and Hakonen (2003). These authors argue that the main components are linked together in a subtle way by the representation form (medium), by rules, by the goal definition, and by the absence or presence of opponents. A special case is serious or educational games where the aspect of the absence of a specific purpose and - in parts - the voluntariness, must be reconsidered. An issue we want to point out is the fact that, in an evolutionary and anthropological sense, playing is a purposeful activity, already in animals. The act of playing has the purpose of practicing certain skills, which in turn closes the circle towards educational games. Over the past 40 years, a tremendous diversity of computer game types emerged. This diversity makes it difficult to establish a sound or complete taxonomy of computer games. An attempt to classify current approaches to DEGs comes from Kickmeier-Rust, Hockemeyer, Albert, and Augustin (2008) which is based on the psycho-pedagogical and technical level of games.

Mini Games for Young Children

The most common and likely most successful form of educational games are mini games for the preschool age and the primary education level. Generally, those games are based on Flash or Shockwave technology, are distributed through online platforms, and have a child-oriented comic-like design and game-play. In many cases they are associated with characters known from movies, television series, or books. Essentially, the games attempt to teach young children basic knowledge and skills like knowing numbers, letters, simple math, reading, or biology – just to mention a few. Often the game genre is based on trivia, puzzle, memory, or drill and practice (in a positive sense) styles. These games are very successful; they are entertaining and instructional for their target audience.

Simulation Games

Simulation games basically pursue a drill and practice approach to certain procedural, strategic, or tactic skills. The instant feedback and risk-free environment invite exploration and experimentation, stimulating curiosity, discovery learning and perseverance (Kirriemuir, 2002). The game character and intensity are varying depending on the context and application. Flight simulators, for example, are used in professional pilot training but almost the same simulations are sold for pure gaming or edutainment purposes (e.g., Microsoft's Flight Simulator). Further examples are military training promoting simulation (games) for practicing specific warfare skills or simulations in medical training (e.g., to enable surgery training in safe virtual environments). From a technical perspective, simulations and simulation games are on a high level; from an educational perspective, simulations are generally virtual representations of the real world and sparsely implement – if any – sound didactic or pedagogical strategies.

Off-the-Shelf Games / Moddings

A third approach to using games for educational purposes is using commercial off-the-shelf games. A prominent example is "Teaching with games", which was a one-year project by *Futurelab* (www.futurelab.org.uk). Basically, the scope of the project was to research the capabilities of off-the-shelf games for application in schools. The educational objectives of using such games, however, are limited, basically comprising the promotion of collaboration, fostering engagement and motivation, and developing thinking skills. In many cases off-the-shelf games are used as supplementary material or as incentives for learning.

Modding (a term for modifying software or hardware) is an extension of the off-the-shelf approach. In such cases commercial games are modified using level editors in order to realize certain educational objectives (cf. de Freitas, 2006). An example is *Revolution*, a modding of the game *Neverwinter Nights* (*BioWare*, http://nwn.bioware.com/), which is supposed to teach and illustrate social aspects of history.

Game-like Enhancements for Learning Material

A large part of educational games applied successfully in practice is game-like enhancements to digital learning material; Sara de Freitas (2006) classified such games as "tools". Generally, such approaches incorporate sound instructional theories and provide goal-oriented learning situations (LeS). However, in most cases the level of educational objectives, narrative, game-play, and audio-visual realization is limited. In other words, such approach incorporates small games as training for a specific limited set of skills.

Competitive Educational Games

What we mean with competitive educational games is games with a primarily educational purpose that – at the same time – can compete with commercial entertainment games as well as with conventional learning environments. Such games are characterized by a convincing narrative and game-play, an appealing audio-visual design, sound instructional design, and clear educational objectives. The most significant characteristic of such games is that learning is embedded in the narrative and the game-play. Among the most advanced learning games are *Global Conflicts: Palestine* and *Global Conflicts: Latin America* (*Serious Games Interactive*), games dedicated to journalism and the problems of crisis regions (www.globalconflicts.eu), *Peacemake* (*Impact Games*), a commercial game simulation of the Palestine conflict, designed to promote dialog and understanding (www.peacemakergame.com), or *NanoMission* (*Playgen*), a scientifically accurate 3D action adventure teaching nanotechnology through real world practical applications ranging from microelectronics to drug delivery (www.nanomission.org).

TODAY ...

Over the past years, serious games and DEGs have become serious business. Several commercial online platforms are distributing (semi-) educational mini games (e.g., www.funbrain.com or www.primarygames.com), Nintendo DS' "Dr Kawashima's Brain Training: How Old Is Your Brain?" is a best seller, and a growing number of companies concentrate on educational simulation and game software as well as (e.g., www.braingames.de). DEGs arrived at higher education also. Besides the growing number of use cases for off-the-shelf games and moddings in schools, a Dutch college holding (www.rocwb.nl) deploys serious games in the area of business strategies, English, and mathematics. But, summarizing the existing approaches, the largest part of today's DEGs are simple games, limited in their educational impact. They generally do not relate to school curricula nor do they attempt to provide sound knowledge or learning progress assessment methods. According to many authors in the field of game-based learning, DEGs are still at an early stage. Diana Oblinger (2006, p.5), for example, describes today's use of games in education as follows: "*Although [digital games] may educate, that is not their primary goal or their most important design feature. Moving forward, educators must hope for games based on learning theory and research*".

Significant drawbacks of current DEGs are seen in difficulties in providing an appropriate balance between gaming and learning activities or between challenge and ability, in embedding 'education' in a convincing game-play, or the extensive costs of developing high quality games. In addition, many learning games do not rely on instructional/pedagogical models, leading to a separation of learning from gaming; often they provide gaming actions only as reward for learning. Many of the existing DEGs do not differ substantially from conventional multimedia (e-)learning objects and applications. As a consequence, there is considerable debate about the power of games for educational purposes, the advantages, disadvantages, costs, and risks. Also the psycho-pedagogical viewpoint contributes to the list of existing teething troubles. As a result, today's DEGs – most often – cannot compete with their commercial counterparts and they cannot utilize the full potential of immersive digital games in terms of gaming experience, immersive and interactive environments, narrative, or motivation to play.

... AND TOMORROW

It is not trivial to address the described challenges concerning essentially didactically sound and fanciful educational game design as well as scientifically sound methods for adaptation and personalization. Major efforts in this direction were accomplished by the *ELEKTRA* project (www.elektra-project.org). ELEKTRA was a European research project, running from 2006 to 2008 and addressing the challenges of fully utilizing the advantages of computer games and their design fundamentals for educational purposes. Moreover, the project addressed psychologically sound methods for an intelligent adaptation and personalization in the gaming context. As a result, the project developed a methodology that is a combination of game design principles, instructional design principles, media psychology principles, and pedagogy. However, the sum of the principles must be considered being more than the sum of its parts, the methodology refers to a novel genre, the *learning game design* (cf. Kickmeier-Rust, Marte, Linek, Lalonde, & Albert, 2008a, 2008b; Kickmeier-Rust, Peirce, Conlan, Schwarz, Verpoorten, & Albert, 2007).

A further major achievement of ELEKTRA was the concept of *micro adaptivity*. As mentioned above, the aim of adaptation and personalization is having a technology that provides each learner with a tailored learning experience in order to optimize learning effectiveness. In contrast to conventional adaptive tutoring and knowledge testing, within a DEG assessment is restricted by the game's narrative, the gameplay, and the game flow. Common methods for adaptation (e.g., curriculum sequencing or adaptive presentation) or knowledge assessment fail to adapt to individual learners and most likely they break the game's narrative, what in turn weakens the "natural" advantages of educational games. Within an educationally adaptive game such as the ELEKTRA prototype (Figure 1), the learning tasks are so integrated with the games narrative that the reordering of learning tasks in order to personalize learning experience would result in a corresponding reordering of narrative plot elements. With a linear narrative this would result in a nonsensical narrative that is implausible. Micro adaptivity is a continuous

Figure 1. Screenshots of ELEKTRA's demonstrator game, which supports learning of high school physics according to European curricula.

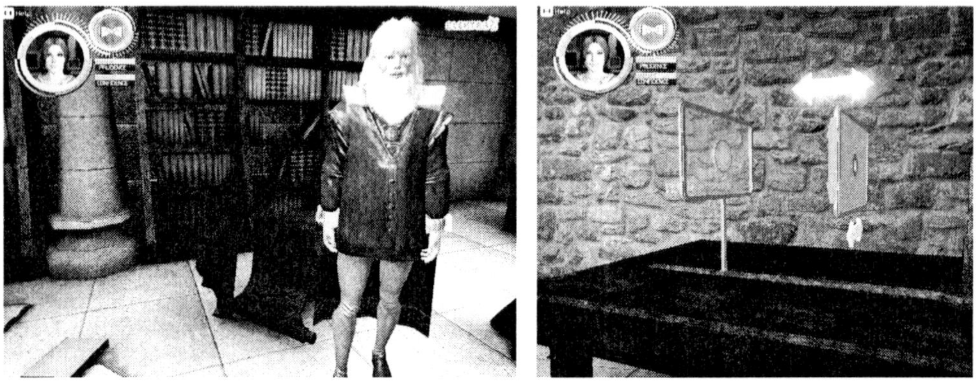

assessment by non-invasively interpreting the learner's behaviour in the game and a subsequent adaptation and intervention within learning situations. The work of ELEKTRA is continued by a successor project named *80Days* that is running from 2008 to 2010, addressing aspects of integrating interactive storytelling and emergent game design. Moreover, a main objective is merging virtual game environments with existing learning resources, thus reducing development costs and time. The project is inspired by Jules Verne's novel "Around the world in eighty days" (the project's full title is "Around an inspiring virtual learning world in eighty days") and it is concerned with theories, methodologies, and technologies for game-based learning.

WARNING SCIENCE CONTENT: THE FOUNDATIONS OF DIGITAL EDUCATIONAL GAMES

Personalization, it is All about Balance

Game-based learning requires a healthy balance between gaming and learning, since these two concepts seem to be contradictory in parts. The crucial purpose of a learning game is that the learner actually acquires knowledge or skills but at the same time it should be fun. Garris, Ahlers, and Driskell (2002) forecasted aptly about the development of instructional games: "*If we succeed, we will be able to develop games that instruct and instruction that engages the student. If we fail, we end up with games that are dull and instructional programs that do not teach*". In very simple words, if the aim is that a learner plays voluntarily and with high engagement, then we have to find the right amount of learning activities in comparison with pure gaming activities, moreover, we have to embed learning in the game in a compelling way. Of course, motivation is not only driven by the typical characteristics of the game (as for example described by Malone, 1981), the "educational part" strongly influences motivation as well. If we overburden the learner with too complex or difficult subject matter, motivation will decrease quickly. Vice versa, if the demands are too easy, the learner will be bored very soon and – very likely – will quit gaming quickly. This type of balance cannot be accomplished by a general one-fits-all approach; it requires a dynamic adaptation to each individual learner. This basic idea of personalization, of course, is not new, it is a significant part of research and development in the context of technology-enhanced learning per se.

To give a very brief overview, techniques of adaptation and individualisation are primarily adaptive presentation of learning objects, adaptive navigation support, and adaptive problem solving support (cf. De Bra, 2008 for a review). A prominent approach to adaptive tutoring is *Competence-based Knowledge Space Theory* (CbKST; cf. Albert & Lukas, 1999). It is a cognitive framework, extending the originally behavioural *Knowledge Space Theory* (Doignon & Falmagne, 1985), where a knowledge domain is characterised by a set of problems and *prerequisite relations* among them, establishing a *knowledge space*. The basic idea of CbKST is to separate observable performance and underlying latent skills or competencies (e.g., Albert & Lukas, 1999; Korossy 1997). The relationships between the skills/competencies and problems/tasks are established by so-called *skill functions* and *problem functions*. By associating skills and competencies with the problems of a domain, a *knowledge structure* on the set of problems is induced. Basically, this theoretical framework was used for adaptive assessment and adaptive navigation support (in terms of individualized curriculum sequencing). Recently, this theoretical framework has been elaborated by integrating an ontological approach including conceptual structures, didactic strategies, and by connecting the competence approach with problem solving models in order to interpret a learner's behaviour in various learning and assessment situations (Kickmeier-Rust & Albert, 2008).

However, in the context of narrative learning environments and particularly educational games, this type of adaptation/personalization is not realizable in its original sense. As already mentioned, curriculum sequencing means a re-ordering of learning objects (which is identical to specific learning situations in a DEG) and maybe skipping specific ones (since the learner might already have the related knowledge/ability). Unfortunately, when skipping a specific situation in a game, most likely the red thread through the game's story will be corrupted, ending up in a weird and implausible sequence of situations and events. Similar problems concern the knowledge assessment. In conventional learning environments, knowledge assessment occurs through typical computer-supported test items such as multiple choice questions or cloze texts. Unfortunately, this can (or rather should) not be realized in a DEG. If the learner is immersed in the game's flow, a sudden pop-up of a couple of multiple choice questions would impair the gaming experience significantly. Both problems must be considered in relation to each other since each adaptation requires an assessment of knowledge/learning progress or other internal states of the learner (e.g., motivation).

In the context of the ELEKTRA project a novel approach was introduced, tailored to learning environments with large degrees of freedom, namely adaptivity on macro and micro levels (Kickmeier-Rust, Göbel, & Albert, 2008; Kickmeier-Rust, Hockemeyer, Albert, & Augustin, 2008). While *macro adaptivity* refers to traditional techniques of adaptation such as adaptive presentation and adaptive navigation on the level of learning objects (or learning situations in a DEG), *micro adaptivity* is non-invasive, meaning that an overall narrative is not compromised. Micro adaptivity attempts to monitor the learner's actions in the game and, subsequently, to interpret the behaviour in terms of available and lacking knowledge, learning progress, motivation or other characteristics of the gaming and learning progress. On the basis of those conclusions subtle, non-invasive interventions are made, for example, the learner could be provided with hints or feedback (see Kickmeier-Rust, Hockemeyer, Albert, and Augustin, 2008 for details).

The 80Days project endeavours to extend the existing state-of-the-art by strongly integrating motivational/emotional aspects, adaptive storytelling, and dynamic processes of learning and navigation into a sound cognitive framework for personalization (cf. Kickmeier-Rust, Göbel, & Albert, 2008; Law & Kickmeier-Rust, 2008). Particularly adaptive and interactive storytelling is an interesting field for educational adaptation.

What we can achieve with interactive storytelling is an adaptation on the macro level without the result of an incomplete or implausible storyline. We can re-order or even skip learning situations; the idea of adaptive storytelling enables the game technology to automatically adapt the storyline to the new requirements, retaining a plausible yet exciting red thread. Even more, we can adapt the game's story, ambience, or pace to the individual preferences or requirements of the learner.

The challenge of creating dynamic yet plausible adaptive narratives is considerable and requires arduous manual editing of branching narratives. Experimental systems such as *Façade* (Mateas & Stern, 1997) or *Virtual Human* (Göbel, Iurgel, Rössler, Hülsken, & Eckes, 2006) exemplify the pitfalls of creating adaptive narratives. Therefore, 80Days is working on a theoretical basis for generic yet engaging, immersive, and plausible storytelling in educational games. Hereby, the key challenge is to find a right and fair balance between the initially created story and 'exceptions' caused by user interactions (unforeseen or at least not intended by the author). Examples for such exceptions are wrong paths (not following the instructions of a virtual guide), skipped stations (passing artefacts without interacting), or too long or short interactions at artefacts (causing problems with external and internal time constraints). To accomplish the linkage between educational adaptation and story adaptation we merged formal *story structures* (i.e., the set of meaningful paths through a story on the basis of a given pool of story elements) with formal *knowledge structures* (i.e., educationally meaningful sequences in which the learner should proceed through the learning situations). Therefore, from *competence spaces* and story plot we can derive a "*game space*", the set of admissible and meaningful paths through story and game (cf. Kickmeier-Rust, Göbel, & Albert, 2008).

Communicating with the Learner: Interventions and Feedback

An important role in the personalization of DEGs plays an appropriate response to the learner's behavior. From the "micro" perspective this primarily refers to didactic interventions such as giving hints in problem solution processes, giving feedback about the learning progress, or adjusting game parameters (e.g., the difficulty). In educational games it is not enough to find an intervention method, which is appropriate in the specific situation to facilitate the learning process but interventions need to occur smoothly and non-invasively such that game flow and learning situation are not disrupted. In the end there are two questions game-based learning and the related research has to address (cf. Kickmeier-Rust, Marte, Linek, Lalonde & Albert, 2008a, 2008b):

- Can interventions such as feedback in gaming situations facilitate the learning progress or do they increase the learner's cognitive load?
- Do educational interventions, although designed to be non-invasive, impair gaming experience?

The former apparently is a question of appropriate design for the specific learning situation, because an instructional situation as a whole should not overwhelm the cognitive resources of the learner. The latter addresses a basic challenge in game-based learning: playing and learning are considered to be two different things, so how can they be merged reasonably? We have to keep in mind that we want to create an educational game in terms of using the encouraging features of games to learn something.

General guidelines for feedback in a learning context can be found for example in Pivec, Koubek, and Dondi (2004) or Shute (2008) and are based on a comprehensive literature review. Some of these guidelines can help to adapt feedback to the actual learning situation and the specific learner. Some guidelines relate to the timing of feedback, which can be immediate or delayed. Immediate feedback is preferable when errors should be fixed in real time, for difficult tasks, to avoid frustration and enhance retention of procedural or conceptual knowledge. Delayed feedback is better for simple tasks, to avoid feedback intrusion or annoyance and is beneficial for learning transfer. Another set of guidelines refers to the learner's high or low achievement. For high-achieving learners delayed, facilitative, and verification feedback are eligible, whereas low-achieving learners profit the most from immediate, directive, scaffolding, and elaboration feedback. To give an example for research in this area, Narciss and Huth (2004) advice on form and mode of informative tutorial feedback, which is potentially useful in adaptive educational games:

- avoid presearch availability;
- do not immediately present the correct response;
- use stepwise presentation of feedback information;
- check prerequisite knowledge before moving on in the learning process;
- present feedback rather acoustically than textually;

These authors demonstrated the benefit of the above presented guidelines for error correction, mastery, performance on a delayed test and positive motivational beliefs in a multi-media learning environment for written subtraction.

With regard to motivation, feedback mechanisms establishing a motivational training based on attribution theory (Weiner, 1974; Dresel & Ziegler, 2006) have proven useful in learning contexts. They also appear to be suitable for realizing adaptive motivational feedback in game-based learning. Causal attribution in a learning situation is motivationally advantageous if success is attributed internally and if failure is attributed variably. Motivational feedback should therefore guide the learner to attribute in this desired way. Based on empirical results Dresel and Ziegler (2006) recommend using effort attributions for success at the beginning of the learning process, when the learner has few skills in the specific learning domain. Later, after the learner has acquired a certain amount of knowledge, it is more effective to encourage ability attribution for success. The selection of failure feedback should be suggestive of attributing failure to a variable reason, that is, lacking effort or bad luck (Weiner, 1974).

Adaptation to the motivational state of learners through feedback was also investigated; Song and Keller (2001) developed a model in computer-assisted instruction systems to carry out a frequent motivational assessment and to provide appropriate motivation strategies. A motivationally adaptive instruction system for the topic genetics was developed and the authors suggested that it would be better in motivating a learner than a system which includes all possible motivational strategies at each point because if a learner is already motivated to learn s/he could be annoyed by such tactics. The developed system frequently analyzed the learner's motivational state by self-assessment of their current motivation and strategies to sustain or enhance motivation provided adaptively to the learner dependent on his/her answers. The comparison with versions, which included no and all motivation strategies regardless of the motivational state of the learner showed a superiority of the motivationally adaptive instruction system to enhance overall motivation and attention.

Motivation to Play and Motivation to Learn

Motivation is key to many activities and so it is for education and learning. Playing is normally motivating in nature and usually results in an engaging gaming experience. But the goal of many instructional tactics is to enhance the motivation

Figure 2. The extended cognitive motivation model (adapted from Heckhausen & Heckhausen, 2006 and Rheinberg, 2006).

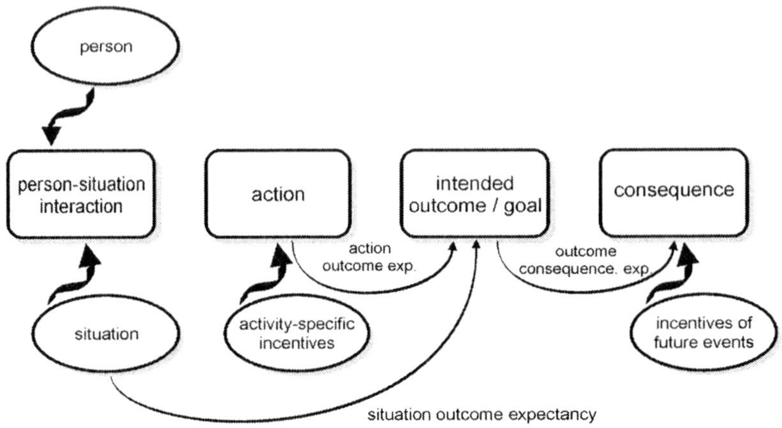

to learn by setting clear goals or promising worthwhile rewards. A model including a multitude of motivational aspects is the *cognitive model of motivation to learn* (Heckhausen & Heckhausen, 2006; Rheinberg, 1989; Rheinberg, Vollmeyer, & Burns, 2000). As shown in Figure 2, the model basically consists of the person-situation interaction, the action to be considered, the intended outcome, and the consequences of the intended goal. Additionally, there are three kinds of expectancies (i.e., situation-outcome expectancy, action-outcome expectancy, and outcome-consequence expectancy) and three different incentives (i.e., incentives of the situation, activity-specific incentives, and incentives of future events). The formal character and the extent of the model make it a good starting point for motivational design as well as for dynamic interventions in DEGs.

As mentioned before, play usually needs no external motivator but is appealing by the actions associated with it. In this context "*flow experience*" is frequently considered in research on game-based learning. The concept of flow refers to the motivation to do something, which is caused by the execution of this activity itself and not by its consequences (Rheinberg, 2006). Csikszentmihalyi (1992) defines flow as a state in which the person is fully immersed in an activity, does not reflect about his/her actions, and mostly has a complete loss of sense of time. This state can occur e.g. while interacting with a computer, it is referred to the optimal experience and is sensed very positively (Kiili, 2005). Several attributes characterize a flow experience:

- The level of ability and demand fit, such that the person is challenged in an optimal way but has at the same time the feeling to have personal control over what is happening. If, on the contrary, the challenge is higher than the person's skills s/he will feel anxiety or, respectively, the person will be bored if the skills are higher than the challenge.
- Action demand and feedback are completely clear and the person always knows what to do.
- The action flow is experienced fluently and one step fades to the next one.
- The person is concentrated and focuses his/her attention on a limited field.
- The sense of time is altered, mostly accelerated.
- The person loses the feeling of self-consciousness; awareness and action are merged.

There has been research on the influence of flow experience on achievement but no clear relationship could be identified (Schiefele, & Rheinberg, 1997). Nevertheless, some authors assume that flow is not only experienced very positively but also enhances achievement (Kiili, 2005). This plays an important role when implementing flow related considerations in game-based learning. In sum, provoking flow is undoubtedly a reasonable goal of an instructional game, since it can hold the learners in the activity for a sufficiently long time that they potentially develop a personal interest in the subject.

Another strategy to motivate a user to play an instructional game is to design it in an interesting way. A model which stresses the question how instruction can be designed to stimulate the learner's interest is Keller's (1987) *ARCS model*. ARCS is an acronym for the concepts attention, relevance, confidence and satisfaction, which all four are essential to engage a person in a learning task. The ARCS model "*...helps an educator to identify the component of instruction that either increases or decreases student motivation to learn and also provides motivational strategies which an educator can use to make instruction responsive to the interests and needs of students*" (Wongwiwatthanaukit & Popovich, 2000, p. 190). The original model was recently expanded by *volition* and *self-regulation* (Keller, 2008). An overview on the ARCS concepts is given in the following (Keller, 1987, 2008):

- *Attention: "...refers to gaining attention, building curiosity, and sustaining active engagement in the learning activity"* (Keller, 2008, p. 176). Opportunities to realize this are the usage of interesting graphics or animations, mystery and unresolved problems. To keep attention it is important to use varying learning approaches.
- *Relevance:* The motivation to learn is higher if the learner considers a personally relevant knowledge to be learned. Therefore, the learning environment should be related to the learner's goals, learning styles, and past experiences.
- *Confidence:* In order to motivate a person to learn, it is important that the learner believes s/he is able to succeed in the task. A way to enhance confidence is to bring the person in situations where s/he can build a positive expectancy for success and can attribute success to internal factors like his/her own ability (Bandura, 1977; Weiner, 1974).
- *Satisfaction:* To allow a person to have a continuous motivation to learn, s/he should experience satisfying consequences of the learning task. Such outcomes can be extrinsic reinforcement (like rewards) or outcomes that excite intrinsic motivation (like applying the learned knowledge). Another important condition to enable satisfaction is that the learner experiences equity, e.g. regarding the amount of work and grading.
- *Volition and self-regulation:* To assure a continuous working on a learning task until some kind of learning goal is achieved, it is often necessary to use volitional or self-regulatory strategies. These strategies help a person not to be distracted from the goal by other things

The three concepts and models of motivational psychology presented in this chapter are different approaches to describe and consequentially enhance motivation in DEGs.

Psycho-Pedagogical Principles

Besides finding the balance between learning and gaming to motivate the user to play an instructional game, also pedagogical and instructional aspects have to be considered to create a valuable educational game. To ensure that an instructional game has a learning effect, relevant concepts and theories from cognitive psychology need to be considered.

"*Cognitive load theory is concerned with the manner in which cognitive resources are focused and used during learning and problem solving*" (Chandler & Sweller, 1991, p. 294). The major point statement of this theory is that capacity of working memory is limited. This bears the possibility of cognitive overload, which should be avoided by an intelligent instructional design. The theory describes the three different additive cognitive loads: intrinsic, germane, and extraneous cognitive load (Paas, Renkl, & Sweller, 2003; Sweller, van Merrienboer, & Paas, 1998).

In short a well designed instruction increases the germane cognitive load but decreases the extraneous cognitive load, to enhance the learning process. A comprehensive model, which also considers the issue of cognitive load, is the *cognitive-affective theory of learning with media* (CATLM, Moreno & Mayer, 2007). In the CATLM research and theories from cognitive science are joined together and enriched by additional features. Mayer and Moreno (2003) assume that the human information-processing system consists of an auditory and a visual channel, which are separated from each other and have both a limited capacity (Pavio, 1990; Baddeley, 1998). Relating to the cognitive load theory Mayer and Moreno (2003) defined three kinds of cognitive demands tailored to multimedia learning:

- essential processing;
- incidental processing;
- representational holding;

Essential processing is used to make sense of the presented information by selecting, organizing, and integrating words and images. Incidental processing is caused by the design of the learning task (e.g. background music) but not by processes of sense-making. Representational holding refers to maintaining a mental representation in working memory for a particular time, which is necessary if parts of information which belong together (e.g. an illustration and its explanation) are presented successively. These three demands build the total processing in multimedia learning. A significant concern in learning from interactive multimodal environments is to avoid a cognitive overload, which occurs when the total processing overshoots the learner's cognitive capacity. Another important assumption of the CATLM is that deep learning requires a substantial amount of cognitive processing (essential processing), like selecting information, organizing it into a coherent structure, and integrating it with existing knowledge (Mayer & Moreno, 2003). In summary, the theory provides an explanation how instructional media is cognitively processed (Figure 3). Narrations and sounds are transferred into the auditory channel, and text and pictures are transferred in the visual channel of the sensory memory, which have both a limited capacity. Observed information which is selected and carried forward in the working memory, where it is organized and integrated with prior knowledge stored in the long-term memory. From there it can be retrieved and is (as same as motivation and affect) able to influence the perception and processing of new information.

From the psycho-pedagogical point of view, furthermore, instructional principles and considerations of constructivism appear highly relevant to game-based learning. Constructivism sees learners in the centre of the learning process, actively constructing and discovering their knowledge instead of being passively exposed to teaching (Ally, 2004). Games by nature possess almost all key features of constructivist learning environments (Tsai, Yu, & Hsiao, 2007). Active exploration and involvement are inherent characteristics of computer games. This is in line with the concept of self-regulated learning (SRL), which can be seen as a didactical approach in the tradition of constructivism.

SRL describes the ways in which individuals regulate their own cognitive processes in educa-

Figure 3. The cognitive-affective model of learning with media (adapted from Moreno & Mayer, 2007).

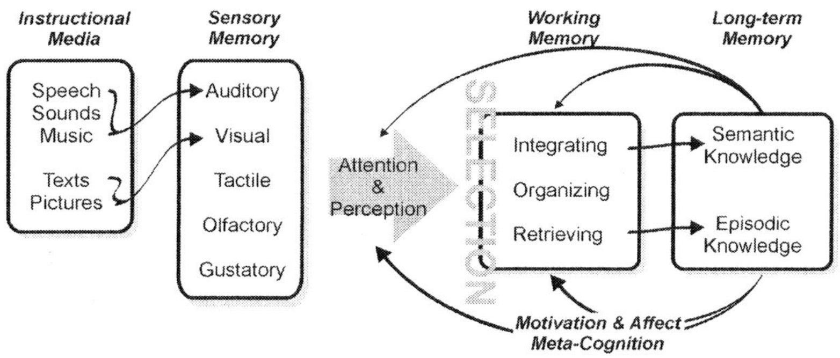

tional settings and therefore refers to learning experiences that are directed by the learner (Puustinen & Pulkkinen, 2001). Zimmerman (2002) views SRL as an activity that learners carry out for themselves in a proactive manner. Self-regulation is considered as self-generated thoughts, feelings, and actual behavior for attaining goals. SRL can be seen as a cyclical process consisting of three phases: forethought, performance, and self-reflection. The forethought phase involves activities of goal setting and strategic planning carried out before learning. Furthermore, it involves processes of self-motivation based on self-efficacy beliefs (Bandura, 1977), outcome expectations, intrinsic interest, and learning goal orientation. The performance phase refers to the actual process of learning and involves strategies aimed at fostering the quality and quantity of learning performance through self-control and self-observation. The self-reflection phase involves processes of self-evaluation (the comparison with some kind of standard) and causal attribution (beliefs about cause of error and success), and self-reaction (self-satisfaction and adaptive/defensive reactions). These reflection processes influence the forethought with respect to subsequent learning efforts. In sum, SRL can be seen as learning that is guided by meta-cognition, strategic action, and motivation to learn. SRL fosters self-satisfaction and motivation of learners to continue improving their learning methods (Zimmerman, 2002).

Implications for Instructional Design

Considerations from motivational psychology, cognitive science, and pedagogy lead to instructional design guidelines, which are consistently referenced in the literature on multimedia learning and are summarized in the following paragraphs:

Some recommendations concern the obviation of *cognitive overload*, which inhibits learning. It is important not to present all information visually, but to address also the auditory channel. To decrease the cognitive load in general it is advantageous to present instructional material successively in small portions, to provide the learner with a pre-training, to be parsimonious with interesting but extraneous features (like background music), to present the information in a logical matter, and arrange the different parts accordingly (Mayer & Moreno, 2003). Furthermore instructional material is easier to process, if the learner is confronted with a guided activity and not with direct instruction or pure discovery, if s/he has to reflect upon a given answer, and if s/he gets explanatory feedback instead of just a corrective one (Moreno & Mayer, 1999).

Research on *flow experience* (Csikzentmihalyi, 1992; Kiili, 2005) suggests delivering clear feedback, allowing a fluent action procedure, and considering the fit of ability and challenge, which also has a motivational advantage in terms of a low situation-outcome and high action-outcome expectancy (Rheinberg, 1989; Rheinberg, Vollmeyer, & Burns, 2000).

There are several guidelines aimed at enhancing an interesting instructional design in terms of *attention, relevance, confidence*, and *satisfaction* (Keller, 1987), which are in part also suitable for the educational game design and are selected and summarized by Garris, Ahlers, and Driskell (2002), Keller (1987), Song and Keller (2001), or Wongwiwatthananukit and Popovich (2000). To sustain or enhance the player's *attention* to the instructional material it is feasible to use flashing or inverse text, animations, and surprising or unfamiliar sounds. However, these features should not be used excessively as they may distract the learner's concentration. Further attention can be supported by question-response-feedback interactions, problem-solving situations, humor, contradictory or bizarre content, visual presentations, and examples of taught concepts, role plays, and simulations. To let the student experience the learning content as *relevant* for him-/herself, the material should provide clear goals and suggest future usefulness. It should be presented in a familiar way by using concrete language, personal pronouns, and the learner's name. To sustain a self-*confident* user, s/he should have control over navigation and pacing. Further the game's requirements should fit the learner's knowledge, challenges should be organized with an increasing level of difficulty, and the player should be provided with attributional feedback that relates a success to the personal ability or effort. The *satisfaction* of a player who is engaged in an instructional game can be positively influenced by using verbal praise and external rewards judiciously (immediately following the task, not too often, not for easy or intrinsically interesting tasks but while the mastering new skills or boring tasks), by allowing the student to apply acquired knowledge in a realistic setting and difficult task, and by forcing equity and consistent measurement standards for all accomplishments.

Based on a review of literature Garris, Ahlers and Driskell (2002) deduced six key features for a successful educational game. First of all, the game needs to occur in a specific time and place and include fixed *rules and goals*. This provides a good basis for learning, because a clear, specific, and difficult goal leads to higher performance (Locke, & Latham, 1990), since it allows the learner to perceive goal-feedback discrepancies. This perception can lead to greater attention and motivation to reduce discrepancies and achieve the goals, which should be structured hierarchically. Possible actions in the game should be flexible and not restricted because of rules and goals. In this way, the learner may apply own specific strategies to solve the task. Second, games should include different kinds of *sensory stimuli* like sounds, graphics, and animations which can be surprising or unfamiliar and further catch the learner's attention. The third characteristic of an educationally sound game is *challenge*, which is also related to the enhancement of the action-outcome expectancy (Rheinberg, 1989; Rheinberg, Vollmeyer, & Burns, 2000), flow experience (Csikzentmihalyi, 1992), and confidence of the ARCS model (Keller, 1987). A learner prefers a challenging task, which is neither too easy nor too difficult; goals should be clear but the outcome uncertain. Possibilities to obtain a challenging game experience are multiple goals, progressive difficulty levels, ambiguity. It is important to provide the learner with a performance feedback or score to figure out the progress toward his/her goal. The feature of *mystery* is able to produce curiosity, which can evoke in us the desire to close a (not too simple nor to complex gap) in our existing knowledge. It can be aroused by incongruent, incomplete, incompatible or inconsistent information/ideas, novelty, surprise, violation of expectations, and unpredictability of the future. The final point is *control*, referring to the importance for a player to experience personal control while using an instructional game. This can be enabled by allowing the user to select strategies, to manage the direction of activity, and to make decisions, which directly affect outcomes. Taking all those implications into account is a promising starting point for developing engaging, immersive, yet effective DEGS.

THE FUTURE OF EDUCATIONAL TECHNOLOGIES

Using computer games for teaching and learning is undoubtedly a promising idea. One reason is that the characteristics of modern computer games enable to transmit knowledge and skills in a very natural and discreet way. Moreover, characteristics of computer games amazingly match instructional design principles (e.g., the provision of a credible and meaningful context for new knowledge). Another reason is that computer games facilitate reaching young people, particularly those that are difficult to reach by other means of education. An idea that is considered too sparsely in the educational technology research community is that a significant amount of young people are not interested in or not willing to learn at all. For those young people it is regardless if certain features of conventional tutorial systems improve or not. Computer games do have the potential of making learning, making knowledge and skills important for those young people.

Still, the technological baseline is at an early level. Generally speaking, existing educational games either cannot compete with their commercial counterparts in terms of game quality (e.g., visual appearance, gameplay, or narrative) or they cannot compete with other educational technology in terms of educational quality (e.g., effectiveness, extent of learning, or didactic background). Although the first and the second steps are done, research must and will increasingly address the foundations of game-based learning and learning-game design. Moreover, the technology for intelligent adaptation and personalization must be substantially advanced in the future. Not least, the enormous cost factor of competitive educational games must be considered.

The way to educational games that can compete with their commercial, non-educational counterparts is long but there is a promising movement towards serious games becoming a mainstream genre of educational, scientific, and commercial spheres. Current trends in gaming support this vision. Online gaming and casual games increasingly equal the AAA games in popularity, massively multiplayer online games are a major genre, and mobile gaming (e.g., with Nintendo DS, PSP, or smart phones) is hitting the big time. These trends strengthen the educational potential of games, since casual and mobile games are realizable with significantly less development budget, they serve the ideas of collaborative learning, and they increase pervasiveness and hardware requirements (so that in-class gaming finds an acceptable technological basis).

The step towards learning in virtual worlds and learning by gaming – including an adaptation to the learners' culture, habits, and preferences – is very natural and logical. This step will open up new horizons for educational technology because "*if you tell me, I'll forget; if you show me, I may remember; if you involve me, I'll understand*" (Chinese proverb).

ACKNOWLEDGMENT

The research and development introduced in this work was co-funded by the European Commission under the sixth framework programme in the IST research priority, contract number 027986 (ELEKTRA, www.elektra-project.org) as well as under the seventh framework programme in the ICT research priority, contract number 215918 (80Days, www.eightydays.eu).

REFERENCES

Albert, D., & Lukas, J. (Eds.). (1999). *Knowledge spaces: Theories, empirical research, and applications*. Mahwah, NJ: Lawrence Erlbaum Associates.

Ally, M. (2004). Foundations of educational theory for online learning. In T. Anderson & F. Elloumi (Eds.), *Theory and practice of online learning* (pp. 3-31). Athabasca: Athabasca University.

Baddeley, A. (1998). Working memory. *Comptes Rendus de l'Académie des Sciences. Série III, Sciences de la Vie, 321*(2-3), 167–173. doi:10.1016/S0764-4469(97)89817-4

Bandura, A. (1977). Self-efficacy: Toward a unifying theory of behavioral change. *Psychological Review, 84*(2), 191–215. doi:10.1037/0033-295X.84.2.191

Chandler, P., & Sweller, J. (1991). Cognitive load theory and the format of instruction. *Cognition and Instruction, 8*, 293–332.

Crawford, C. (1984). *The art of computer game design*. Berkeley, CA: McGraw-Hill.

Csikszentmihalyi, M. (1992). *Flow - the psychology of optimal experience*. Stuttgart, Germany: Klett-Cotta.

De Bra, P. M. E. (2008). Adaptive hypermedia. In H. H. Adelsberger, Kinshuk, J. M. Pawlowski, & D. Sampson, (Eds.), *Handbook on Information Technologies for Education and Training* (pp. 29-46). Berlin, Germany: Springer.

de Freitas, S. (2006). *Learning in immersive worlds. A review of game-based learning*. Retrieved August 28, 2007 from http://www.jisc.ac.uk/media/documents/ programmes/elearning_innovation/gaming%20report_v3.3.pdf

Dickey, M. D. (2006). Game design narrative for learning: Appropriating adventure game design narrative devices and techniques for the design of interactive learning environments. *Educational Technology Research and Development, 54*(3), 245–263. doi:10.1007/s11423-006-8806-y

Doignon, J.-P., & Falmagne, J.-C. (1985). Spaces for the assessment of knowledge. *International Journal of Man-Machine Studies, 23*, 175–196. doi:10.1016/S0020-7373(85)80031-6

Dresel, M., & Ziegler, A. (2006). Langfristige Förderung von Fähigkeitsselbstkonzept und impliziter Fähigkeitstheorie durch computerbasiertes attributionales Feedback. *Zeitschrift fur Padagogische Psychologie, 20*(1-2), 49–63. doi:10.1024/1010-0652.20.12.49

Garris, R., Ahlers, R., & Driskell, J. E. (2002). Games, motivation, and learning: A research and practice model. *Simulation & Gaming, 33*(4), 441–467. doi:10.1177/1046878102238607

Gee, J. P. (2003). *What video games have to teach us about learning and literacy*. New York: Palgrave Macmillan.

Göbel, S., Iurgel, I., Rössler, M., Hülsken, F., & Eckes, C. (2006). Design and narrative structure for the Virtual Human scenarios. *International Journal of Virtual Reality, 5*(3), 1–10.

Habgood, M. P. J., Ainsworth, S. E., & Benford, S. (2005). Endogenous fantasy and learning in digital games. *Simulation & Gaming, 36*(4), 483–498. doi:10.1177/1046878105282276

Heckhausen, J., & Heckhausen, H. (2006). Motivation und Handeln: Einführung und Überblick. In J. Heckhausen & H. Heckhausen (Eds.), *Motivation und Handeln* (p. 1-8). Heidelberg, Germany: Springer Verlag.

Huizinga, J. (1947). *Homo ludens. Proeve eener bepaling van het spelelement der cultuur.* (R.F.C. Hull, Trans.). New York: Roy Publishers. (Original work published in 1938).

Keller, J. M. (1987). Development and use of the ARCS model of motivational design. *Journal of Instructional Development, 10*(3), 2–10. doi:10.1007/BF02905780

Keller, J. M. (2008). First principles of motivation to learn and e3-learning. *Distance Education, 29*(2), 175–185. doi:10.1080/01587910802154970

Kickmeier-Rust, M. D., & Albert, D. (2008). The ELEKTRA ontology model: A learner-centred approach to resource description. In *Advances in Web Based Learning – ICWL 2007* (LNCS 4823, pp. 78-89). Berlin, Germany: Springer.

Kickmeier-Rust, M. D., Göbel, S., & Albert, D. (2008). 80Days: Melding adaptive educational technology and adaptive and interactive storytelling in digital educational games. In R. Klamma, N. Sharda, B. Fernández-Manjòn, H. Kosch, & M. Spaniol (Eds.), *Proceedings of the First International Workshop on Story-Telling and Educational Games (STEG '08) - The power of narration and imagination in technology enhanced learning*, Maastricht, The Netherlands.

Kickmeier-Rust, M. D., Hockemeyer, C., Albert, D., & Augustin, T. (2008). Micro adaptive, non-invasive assessment in educational games. In M. Eisenberg, Kinshuk, M. Chang, & R. McGreal (Eds.), *Proceedings of the second IEEE International Conference on Digital Game and Intelligent Toy Enhanced Learning*, Banff, Canada (pp. 135-138).

Kickmeier-Rust, M. D., Marte, B., Linek, S. B., Lalonde, T., & Albert, D. (2008a). Learning with computer games: Micro level feedback and interventions. In M. E. Auer (Ed.), *Proceedings of the International Conference on Interactive Computer Aided Learning (ICL),* Villach, Austria. Kassel, Germany: Kassel University Press.

Kickmeier-Rust, M. D., Marte, B., Linek, S. B., Lalonde, T., & Albert, D. (2008b). The effects of individualized feedback in digital educational games. In T. Conolly & M. Stansfield (Eds.), *Proceedings of the 2nd European Conference on Games Based Learning*, Barcelona, Spain (pp. 227-236). Reading, UK: Academic Publishing Limited.

Kickmeier-Rust, M. D., Peirce, N., Conlan, O., Schwarz, D., Verpoorten, D., & Albert, D. (2007). Immersive digital games: The interfaces for next-generation e-learning? In C. Stephanidis (Ed.), *Universal Access in Human-Computer Interaction. Applications and Services* (LNCS, 4556, pp. 647-656). Berlin, Germany: Springer.

Kiili, K. (2005). Digital game-based learning: Towards an experiential gaming model. *The Internet and Higher Education, 8*, 13–24. doi:10.1016/j.iheduc.2004.12.001

Kirriemuir, J. (2002). A survey of the use of computer and video games in classrooms. *Internal report for Becta (British Educational Communications and Technology Agency)*. Retrieved August, 12, 2008 from http://www.slideshare.net/silversprite/use-of-computer-and-video-games-in-the-classroom

Korossy, K. (1997). Extending the theory of knowledge spaces: A competence-performance-approach. *Zeitschrift fur Psychologie mit Zeitschrift fur Angewandte Psychologie, 205*, 53–82.

Law, E. L.-C., & Kickmeier-Rust, M. D. (2008). 80Days: Immersive digital educational games with adaptive storytelling. In R. Klamma, N. Sharda, B. Fernández-Manjòn, H. Kosch, & M. Spaniol (Eds.), *Proceedings of the First International Workshop on Story-Telling and Educational Games (STEG '08) - The power of narration and imagination in technology enhanced learning*, Maastricht, The Netherlands.

Lepper, M. R., & Malone, T. W. (1987). Intrinsic motivation and instructional effectiveness in computer-based education. In R. E. Farr (Ed.), *Aptitude, learning and instruction* (pp. 255-287). Hillsdale, NJ: Lawrence Erlbaum.

Locke, E. A., & Latham, G. P. (1990). *A theory of goal setting and task performance.* Englewood Cliffs, NJ: Prentice Hall.

Malone, T. W. (1981). Towards a theory of intrinsically motivating instruction. *Cognitive Science, 3*(4), 333–369.

Mateas, M., & Stern, A. (1997). *Façade, an artificial intelligence-based art/research experiment in electronic narrative.* Retrieved February 5, 2007 from http://www.interactivestory.net/

Mayer, R. E., & Moreno, R. (2003). Nine ways to reduce cognitive load in multimedia learning. *Educational Psychologist, 38*(1), 43–52. doi:10.1207/S15326985EP3801_6

Moreno, R., & Mayer, R. E. (1999). Cognitive principles of multimedia learning: The role of modality and contiguity. *Journal of Educational Psychology, 91*, 358–368. doi:10.1037/0022-0663.91.2.358

Moreno, R., & Mayer, R. E. (2007). Interactive multimodal learning environments - special issue on interactive learning environments: Contemporary issues and trends. *Educational Psychology Review, 19*, 309–326. doi:10.1007/s10648-007-9047-2

Narciss, S., & Huth, K. (2004). How to design informative tutoring feedback for multi-media learning. In H. M. Niegemann, D. Leutner, & R. Brunken (Eds.), *Instructional design for multimedia learning* (pp.181-195). Munster, NY: Waxmann.

Oblinger, D. (2006 May). *Simulations, games, and learning.* ELI White Paper. Retrieved August 28, 2007 from http://www.educause.edu/ir/library/pdf/ELI3004.pdf

Paas, F., Renkl, A., & Sweller, J. (2003). Cognitive load theory and instructional design: Recent developments. *Educational Psychologist, 38*(1), 1–4. doi:10.1207/S15326985EP3801_1

Paivio, A. (1990). *Mental representations: A dual coding approach.* New York: Oxford University Press.

Pivec, M., Koubek, A., & Dondi, C. (Eds.). (2004). *Guidelines for game-based learning.* Lengerich, Germany: Pabst.

Prensky, M. (2001). *Digital game-based learning.* New York: McGraw-Hill.

Puustinen, M., & Pulkkinen, L. (2001). Models of self-regulated learning: A review. *Scandinavian Journal of Educational Research, 45*, 269–286. doi:10.1080/00313830120074206

Rheinberg, F. (1989). *Zweck und Tätigkeit.* Göttingen, Germany: Hogrefe.

Rheinberg, F. (2006). *Motivation.* Stuttgart, Germany: Verlag W. Kohlhammer.

Rheinberg, F., Vollmeyer, R., & Burns, B. D. (2000). Motivation and self-regulated learning. In J. Heckhausen (Ed.), *Motivational Psychology of human development: Developing motivation and motivating development* (pp. 81-108). Amsterdam: Elsevier Science Publisher.

Schiefele, U., & Rheinberg, F. (1997). Motivation and knowledge acquisition: Searching for mediating processes. In M. L. Maehr & P. P. Pintrich (Eds.), *Advances in motivation and achievement* (Vol. 10, pp. 251-301). Greenwich, CT: JAI Press.

Shute, V. J. (2008). Focus on formative feedback. *Review of Educational Research, 78*(1), 153–189. doi:10.3102/0034654307313795

Smed, J., & Hakonen, H. (2003). *Towards a definition of a computer game. Technical Report 553*. Turku, Finland: Turku Centre for Computer Science.

Song, S. H., & Keller, J. M. (2001). Effectiveness of motivationally adaptive computer-assisted instruction on the dynamic aspects of motivation. *Educational Technology Research and Development, 49*(2), 5–22. doi:10.1007/BF02504925

Sweller, J., van Marrienboer, J. J. G., & Paas, F. W. C. (1998). Cognitive architecture and instructional design. *Educational Psychology Review, 10*, 251–296. doi:10.1023/A:1022193728205

Tsai, F. H., Yu, K. C., & Hsiao, H. S. (2007). Designing constructivist learning environment in online game. In *Proceedings of the First IEEE International Workshop On Digital Game And Intelligent Toy Enhanced Learning*, Jhongli, Taiwan.

Weiner, B. (1974). *Achievement motivation and attribution theory*. Morristown, NJ: General Learning Press.

Wittgenstein, L. (1953). *Philosophical investigations*. (G. E. Anscombe & R. Rhees, Eds., G. E. Anscombe, Trans.). Oxford, UK: Blackwell.

Wongwiwatthananukit, S., & Popovich, N. G. (2000). Applying the ARCS model of motivational design to pharmaceutical education. *American Journal of Pharmaceutical Education, 64*, 188–196.

Zimmerman, B. J. (2002). Becoming a self-regulated learner: An overview. *Theory into Practice, 41*, 64–70. doi:10.1207/s15430421tip4102_2

Chapter 10
A Case Study of Augmented Reality Serious Games

Fotis Liarokapis
Coventry University, UK

Sara de Freitas
Coventry University, UK

ABSTRACT

The study introduced in this paper examines some of the issues involved in the design and implementation of serious games that make use of tangible AR environments. Our motivation is to understand how augmented reality serious games (ARSG) can be applied to some very difficult problems in the real gaming world. Emphasis is given on the interface and the interactions between the players and the serious games themselves. In particular, two case studies are presented, ARPuzzle and ARBreakout. Results from both case studies indicate that AR gaming has the potential of revolutionizing the way that current games are played and used as well as that it can help educate players while playing.

INTRODUCTION

Serious games are part of a new emerging field that focuses on computer games that are designed for non-leisure and often educational purposes. During the past few years there has been an explosion of serious games mainly because of the evolution of computers, communications, intelligent software agents and accurate physics models. Their main advantage over traditional games is that they can be reused for other simulations in a number of commercial areas such as military operations, medical education, emergency management training, and many others. This allows modern game technology to make a bridge between entertainment and work changing their image from 'toys' to 'serious tools'.

Serious games evolve from military games originally conceptualized around simulated play and role play, and as a result are particularly used in training and pre-live training situations at present. However, as the tools evolve uses in medical training, cross- agency training and business training are becoming more widely used. The term serious games has developed as a rebuttal to the idea that games are purely for leisure purposes and its use

DOI: 10.4018/978-1-61520-678-0.ch010

goes back to Plato's work on the importance of play as a teaching method. Recently, the serious games movement has emerged from academic communities identifying the power of play for supporting non-leisure activities such as education and training. Recent case studies have identified the power of games technologies for supporting online communities and distributed training groups, for explaining difficult concepts and for engaging and motivating learners (de Freitas & Neumann, 2008; de Freitas & Jarvis, 2008). The power of the formats to engage and motivate in particular has attracted interest from schools and tertiary education institutions, leading to a re-conceptualization of what learning is and stimulating debate around how games might be applied to support specific user groups.

These immersive tools together are offering greater advantages for teaching and training particularly with respect to supporting collaborative learning, supporting social interactions and illustrating complex environments and concepts. The tools certainly do not imply the end of traditional teaching they do however necessitate a re-evaluation about learning and a need to revisit traditional models and modes of learning. One of the authors argues elsewhere (de Freitas & Neumann, 2008) that a new form of learning theory is needed to support these more 'immersive' technologies, and has proposed a model of exploratory learning that focuses upon learning considered as sets of immersive experiences. The work extends from the constructivist models of Kolb's experiential learning, and experimental work being undertaken as part of the UK Technology Strategy Board part-funded Serious Games – Engaging Training Solutions (SG-ETS) research project (with partners Blitz Games Studios and Selex Systems) (de Freitas & Jarvis, 2007; de Freitas & Jarvis, 2008).

The model extends from Kolb's experiential learning cycle with more emphasis upon the role of learner control and exploration and upon social and peer interactions as underpinning effective approaches to learning with immersive tools. Through a consideration of learning as sets of immersive experiences, we can focus upon learning design as crafting these experiences through role plays, modeling specific processes from real life into virtual environments and editing scenarios that allow for multiple outcomes. Serious games come in many different formats, from simple Flash quizzes animations to high fidelity first person style challenge games. Studies are revealing that the range of games used also have distinct appeal to certain gender and age groups. Although this is changing, on the whole the differences are central to designing the most effective game for the particular target group.

On the other hand, augmented reality (AR) has existed for a few decades now and it refers to a technology that combines virtual information onto the real environment in real-time performance. AR technology is developing rapidly, but it is still in its infancy. The main characteristics of AR, includes accurate registration and seamless interaction between the users and the superimposed information. This information may be any available format that can be digitally reproduced. Users can visualize the superimposed information with a selection of display technologies and can interact with it in a natural manner by employing software interfaces, physical markers and hardware interaction devices. Up to now a number of experimental prototypes have been developed mainly from universities and research institutes targeting numerous application domains including gaming, but commercial applications are not widely available.

The study introduced in this paper examines some of the issues involved in the design and implementation of serious games that make use of tangible AR environments. Emphasis is given on the AR interface, the presentation as well as the natural interactions between the players and the serious games themselves. Our motivation is to investigate whether augmented reality serious games (ARSG) can be used effectively in the real gaming world. The main objective is to understand whether a combination of educational and entertainment experiences while playing serious games in AR environments can be beneficial. To address these issues, two diverse case studies in ARSGs are presented, ARPuzzle (Liarokapis et al., 2005) and ARBreakout (Liarokapis, 2006) using a previously implemented AR platform (Liarokapis, 2007). The former is a simple 3D game designed for geography students that consists of six physical pieces and focuses on tangible interaction and collaboration between the players. For the purpose of the interactive ARPuzzle a big part of City University campus in London was accurately modeled and geo-referenced in correspondence to cognitive tuning. Then the 3D map was split into six equal 3D pieces and players can first visualize the 3D geographic information in both VR and AR interfaces and then try to reconstruct the puzzle which is in essence the 3D map of City University campus. Using the interface menu, they can receive audio-visual feedback in various formats including text, images and spatial sound (Liarokapis, 2007). Furthermore, to address accessibility issues, the size and the color of the superimposed text can be changed interactively by the users using the interface menu or predefined keyboard keys. The latter is a 3D arcade game that includes a physics engine and focuses more on user centreed interface that provides accurate and reliable control of the game. A traditional 2D video game was implemented first in VR and then transformed into AR. The traditional 2D Breakout is one of the first interactive video games available on personal computers. The main idea is to knock down a set of 2D bricks using a 2D racket and a ball moving at constant speed. As soon as the ball collides with a brick then it vanishes. The goal of the game is to make all bricks disappear from the game arena.

Both games were exposed to undergraduate students at City University and Coventry University. The ARPuzzle was evaluated with 30 students whereas the ARBreakout with 30 students. Results from both case studies indicate that AR gaming has the potential of revolutionizing the way that current games are played and used as well as helping to educate players while playing. In particular, the ARPuzzle game seemed to be much more appropriate as far as AR serious games are concerned in terms of visualization, interaction, collaboration and learning. We also considered that AR could help learners to understand and learn difficult concepts (like topology and geography) much quicker than traditional methods (i.e. paper maps). On the other hand, for the ARBreakout results indicate that with AR games it is much easier to familiarize with and adapt to the gameplay compared to VR games.

BACKGROUND

The aim of this section is to provide a background of *serious games* methodologies and *virtual and augmented reality* case studies relevant to the study presented here.

Serious Games

The gaming industry grew enormously during the past decade ranging from console, pc and mobile based games. However, most of them are not designed to have any educational flavor. Serious games are computer games that have an educational and learning aspect and are not used just for entertainment purposes. The addition of pedagogy also plays a significant role to makes games serious. However, according to Zyda (2005), pedagogy must be subordinate to story and that the entertainment component comes first. Previous studies illustrated that games can promote learning (e.g. van Eck, 2006). It is worth mentioning, that spatial abilities can be also improved by playing arcade games (de Lisi & Wolford, 2002). Further potential benefits of games include improved self-monitoring, problem recognition and problem-solving, decision making, better short-term and long-term memory, and increased social skills such as collaboration, negotiation, and shared decision-making (Rieber, 1996; Mitchell & Savill-Smith, 2004).

Moreover, Mingoville (Sørensen, & Meyer, 2007) is a serious game based on the idea that children learn and are motivated by problem-solving and game activities rather than traditional skills-based and textbook based material focusing on reading, writing, spelling and listening. The project intends to explore, build and implement prototypes in collaboration with companies, using their products and experience to develop knowledge about serious game challenges, educational design, and assessment with the aim of innovation. In another study, content was combined with pedagogy through a multi-player educational gamming platform designed for students (Annetta et al., 2006). Evaluation results showed potentials to advance gaming theories and problem-based solving approached in multi-player educational gamming platforms. Furthermore, a good overview of serious games has been recently documented (Susi et al., 2007).

A very popular platform for serious games is online gaming. The availability of various online platforms such as Second Life (Linden Research, 2008), Active Worlds (Active Words, 2008) and the OLIVE platform (Forterra Systems, 2008), allows for a number of operations in virtual environments. Some of them include: social networking, collaboration, learning, training, experimentation as well as custom-based applications. A recent application of the Olive platform by Stanford Medical School project involves practice innovation through supporting training for cardio-pulmonary resusitation (CPR), mass casualty and assessment in acute-care medicine (de Freitas & Neumann, 2008). However, the main disadvantage of these platforms is that they do not support high-level graphics or advanced interaction techniques. In addition, a number of serious games are using game engines. One of the most popular areas is in training situations. A characteristic example of a serious gaming application developed based in game engines, to train traffic accident investigators how to attend a virtual traffic accident (BinSubaih et al., 2006). To measure the system's effectiveness it was empirically evaluated with 56 police officers.

Serious games are currently being used in a range of different contexts. One study, the SG-ETS project is developing three serious games demonstrators. As part of the study, one user group nurses and ambulance workers have been polled to establish more about their game-playing attitudes and preferences. The study found distinct gender and age differences with respect to game type favored and levels of gaming. As part of the study, we surveyed 223 nurses and ambulance workers in the UK. 89% were female and 11% were male reflecting the demographic audience. The full results of the study are compiled in (de Freitas & Jarvis, 2008). The largest positive response came from males under the age of 30 (81%) played games. This dropped to 26% for the female over-40 group. The frequency of game players is significantly affected by both age and gender. The work indicates both the distinct preferences for game-play and the strengths of games for allowing active involvement of the learners thereby making serious games a powerful tool for training and education. However, there are specific design challenges with making engaging content, and ongoing work with the UK's Serious Games Institute research group is assessing the best methods, frameworks and metrics for evaluating and validating the efficacy of serious games (de Freitas & Oliver, 2006).

Virtual and Augmented Reality

In the past a number of AR games have been designed in different areas including education, learning, enhanced entertainment and training. One of the earliest examples of education was the MagicBook (Billinghurst et al., 2001). This is a real book which shows how AR can be used in schools for educational purposes providing an interesting method of teaching. It enables users to read the book either like any traditional book or with a handheld display allowing the reader to see virtual 3D images 'popping out' of the pages. The MagicBook was also used as a template for a number of serious applications in numerous educational and training domains. Moreover, the BBC's research identified how children aged five and six responded positively to AR learning. The team argued that AR learning enables children to be more imaginative as he discovered children were becoming the characters and making stories of their own, therefore enabling children to play as they naturally would but also to learn at the same time (Thomas, 2006). Many other research projects have been undertaken with older children. One example is the earth, sun and moon project where children aged 10 years old can understand how the sun and earth interact together. This project showed the acceptance of learning via this method by children aged 10+ and also suggested it is a suitable teaching tool (Kerawalla et al., 2006). In another study, the design and development of AR applications for educational purposes from the area of human medicine was presented (Nischelwitzer et al., 2007). Usability studies with children and the elderly showed that this technology has potential and can be of great benefit. Moreover, examples exist of AR educational applications used to support and simplify teaching and learning techniques currently applied in the higher education sector (Liarokapis, 2007) as well as on learning and performance (Holzinger et al., 2008; Holzinger et al., 2009).

Also AR can be applied successfully for educational and learning purposes in archaeology and cultural heritage settings. One of the earliest examples is the Virtual Showcase (Bimber et al., 2001) which is an AR display device that has the same form factor as a real showcase traditionally used for museum exhibits and can be used for gaming. The potential of AR interfaces in museum environments and other cultural heritage institutions (Liarokapis, 2007) as well as outdoor heritage sites (Vlahakis et al., 2002) have been also briefly explored for potential educational applications. A more specific gaming example is the MAGIC and TROC systems (Renevier et al., 2004) which were based on a study of the tasks of archaeological fieldwork, interviews and observations in Alexandria. The mobile game allowed the players to discover archaeological objects while moving around the site.

In terms of enhanced entertainment outdoor AR gaming can play a significant role. A characteristic example is the Human Pacman project (Cheok et al., 2003) that was built upon position and perspective sensing via GPS, inertia sensors and tangible human-computer interfacing with the use of Bluetooth and capacitive sensors. The game strives to bring the computer gaming experience to a new level of emotional and sensory gratification by embedding the natural physical world ubiquitously and seamlessly with a fantasy virtual playground. AR Tennis (Henrysson et al., 2006) is the first example of a face-to-face collaborative AR application developed for mobile phones. Two players sit across a table from each other, while computer vision techniques are used to track the phone position relative to the tracking markers. When the player points the phone camera at the markers they see a virtual tennis court overlaid on live video of the real world.

Another interesting project is STARS (Magerkurth et al., 2004) which focused on the nature of state representation in augmented game designs and developed several games based on these principles. Moreover, Mixed Fantasy (Stapleton et al., 2003) presents a MR experience that applies basic research to the media industries of entertainment, training and informal education. As far as training is concerned, the US Army paid more than $5 million to design an educational game based on the Xbox platform to train troops in urban combat (Korris, 2004). Another example is the MR OUT project (Hughes et al., 2005) which uses extreme and complex layered representations of combat reality, using all the simulation domains such as live, virtual, and constructive by applying advanced video see-through mixed reality (MR) technologies. MR OUT is installed at the US Army's Research Development and Engineering Command and focuses on a layered representation of combat reality.

Important Design Issues

One of the issues arising from the relatively new technologies emerging is the need to develop consistent guidelines and frameworks to support more effective design of games. Towards this end, one model being developed by the Serious Games Institute is the four dimensional framework (de Freitas and Oliver, 2006). The tool is being used both for selection of serious games and for supporting development and evaluation of serious games (de Freitas & Jarvis, 2008). The four dimensional framework (Figure 1) supports a participatory design approach that brings together detailing learner modelling, a consistent use and consideration of the pedagogic models adopted with the game, a consideration of the representational elements of game design including levels of required interactivity and immersion and the context in which the game will be used (e.g. blended, task centred).

The four dimensional framework is being further developed in the exploratory learning model. An overview of the exploratory learning model (de Freitas & Jarvis, 2008) developed in the Serious Games Engaging Training Solutions project is presented in Figure 2. The exploratory learning model includes three levels: the processes of game design, the principles of game design and the tools and techniques for using these. The processes include the development processes driven by the business need, and include the analysis, specification, design, development and testing processes, modeling the learning processes and evaluating the overall process. The game principles include: considerations for selecting the game type (in line with users needs), usability and efficacy of learning. The tools we have developed include: learning needs analysis, human factors analysis, pre-prototypes and the four dimensional framework (de Freitas & Jarvis, 2008).

Figure 1. The four dimensional framework

Four Dimensional Framework	
Learner Specifics Profile Role Competencies	**Pedagogy** Associative Cognitive Social/Situative
Representation Fidelity Interactivity Immersion	**Context** Environment Access to learning Supporting resources

CASE STUDIES

This section presents first two ARSGs, a puzzle called ARPuzzle (Liarokapis et al., 2005) and an arcade game ARBreakout (Liarokapis, 2006) which satisfy the Four Dimensional Framework presented above. Both games have been designed on top of a previously implemented AR platform (Liarokapis, 2007). A comparative study between these two tangible AR games is presented illustrating the strengths of each type of game.

ARPuzzle

The ARPuzzle, is based on an earlier prototype (Liarokapis et al., 2005) and it is a simple game that consists of six equal parts that represent parts of City University campus in London. During the session and as long as the camera is in sight of sight with them, the virtual components of City Campus together is superimposed onto the table-top environment. For the purpose of the interactive ARPuzzle a big part of City University campus in London was accurately modelled and

Figure 2. The exploratory game-based learning model

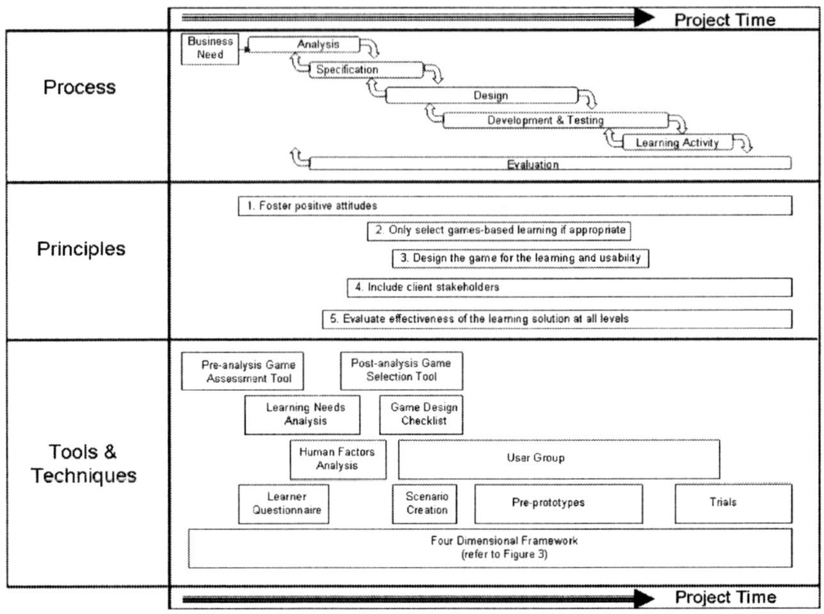

geo-referenced in correspondence to cognitive tuning. Then the 3D map was split into six equal 3D pieces and players can first visualize the 3D geographic information in both VR and AR interfaces and then try to reconstruct the puzzle which is in essence the 3D map of City University campus. Using the interface menu, they can receive audio-visual feedback in various formats including text, images and spatial sound (Liarokapis, 2007). Furthermore, to address accessibility issues, the size and the color of the superimposed text can be changed interactively by the users by using the interface menu or predefined keyboard keys. Figure 3 illustrates an overview of the ARPuzzle. Players can pick up the marker cards and examine the geometrical and geographical information in a tangible manner. An advantage of this game is that it is possible to collaborate with other players that could stand around the table-top environment and either give advice or play the game. Multiple users can naturally experiment with different combinations by randomly placing the marker cards close to each other.

ARBreakout

Breakout is an old arcade game which was ported into a tangible AR environment. The goal of the game is to make all the bricks disappear from the game arena. To increase the level of difficulty and game-play, later versions make use of multiple rackets and balls and vary the speed of the ball. Collision detection is supported between the graphics components of the application based on Newton laws of physics. The ARBreakout presents a more exciting way of playing video games, by allowing some extra features in terms of visualization as well as interaction experiences. In terms of software infrastructure, the game engine was ported onto a high-level AR interface (Liarokapis, 2007). Implementation details about ARBreakout have been previously published (Liarokapis, 2006). From the visualization (or augmentation) point of view, the game can be positioned anywhere in the real-environment using the reference point (which is the marker card). The player can use a handheld device which is equipped with a camera to superimpose the Breakout game into the

Figure 3. ARPuzzle unsolved (left image) solved (right image)

physical world. An obvious advantage of the AR visualization technique is that it makes the users feel more immersed into the gaming scenario as well as promoting collaboration between multiple users. As far as the interaction techniques are concerned, players can manipulate the gaming environment using the controls of the handheld device (keyboard or mouse) or through tangible ways. Figure 4 illustrates how a user can rotate the ARBreakout scene, using his hand to physically rotate the marker cards. This allows getting the best viewpoint in a natural and realistic manner. Similarly, the player can move the scene closer to the camera (and vice-versa) to zoom into the scene instead of scaling the game.

Analysis

The end-user evaluation took place at City University and Coventry University with undergraduate and postgraduate students studying Information Science and Computer Science respectively. A total of 60 end users took part in this pilot testing at both Universities. The ARPuzzle was evaluated with 30 students whereas the ARBreakout with 30 students. The average time for each assessment was 45 minutes and participants had to complete questionnaires with rating between 1 (= not very good) to 5 (= excellent). Although a number of questions were asked, this section presents only these ones which were relevant to both ARSGs. These include important issues of gaming such as: visualization of the game, interaction techniques, collaboration with other players and education and learning.

In terms of visualization in both games the ARPuzzle (Mean = 3.93, SD = 0.91, SE = 0.17) received much better feedback compared to the ARBreakout (Mean = 3.13, SD = 1.19, SE = 0.22). An overview of the visualization results are illustrated in Figure 5. In particular, the majority of users agreed that the ARPuzzle contains simpler graphics but because the purpose of the game was different, ARBreakout scored less. However, all users agreed that more realism would

Figure 4. ARBreakout

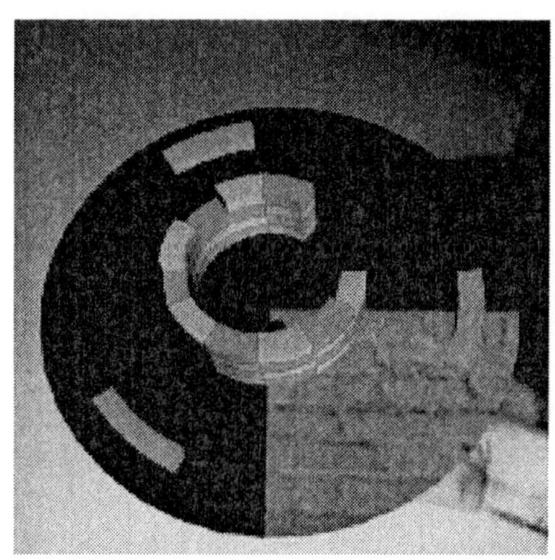

Figure 5. Visualization comparison for ARPuzzle vs. ARBreakout

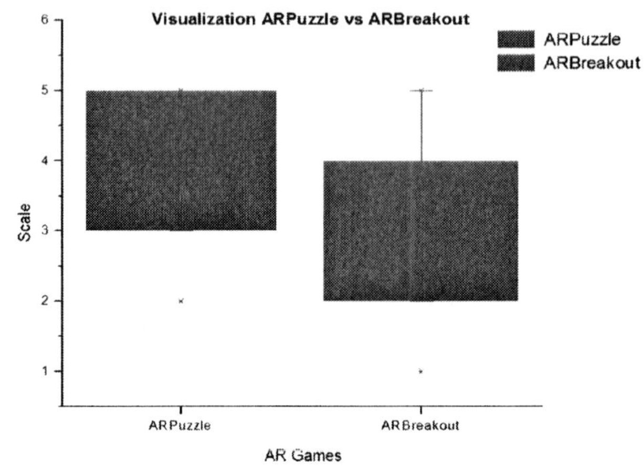

help improving the immersion in both games. As far as the interaction techniques are concerned, the ARPuzzle (Mean = 4, SD = 0.95, SE = 0.17) received again much better feedback compared to the ARBreakout (Mean = 3.17, SD = 1.05, SE = 0.19). On the puzzle game, the users did not have to use any input devices (keyboard or mouse) to interact with the game whereas user input was essential in the arcade game. This made the puzzle game much more attractive and 'easy' to play allowing for a wider age-range. An overview of the interaction results are illustrated in Figure 6.

Next, the level of collaboration in both games was tested. It is worth mentioning here, that to finish either game, collaboration is not required. The ARPuzzle (Mean = 4.07, SD = 1.01, SE = 0.19) is a more collaborative game compared to the ARBreakout (Mean = 2.77, SD = 1.01, SE = 0.18). Participants felt that it is more important to collaborate in a table-top environment in order to solve the puzzle rather than play an arcade game. On the contrary the arcade game requires less space and can be positioned almost anywhere in the real environment but participants mentioned that collaboration might confuse users instead of helping them. An overview of the collaboration results are illustrated in Figure 7.

Finally, the educational and learning aspect of both games were measured. As expected, the ARPuzzle (Mean = 3.97, SD = 0.85, SE = 0.16) received much more positive feedback compared to the ARBreakout (Mean = 2.77, SD = 1.07, SE = 0.20) mainly because users learned about geography and GIS. On the contrary the arcade game educational value was more into the novel interaction techniques in such types of games. An overview of education and learning results are illustrated in Figure 8.

Based on the above results, it is obvious that the ARPuzzle is a more effective educational game compared to ARBreakout for the above-mentioned reasons. For the ARBreakout game, participants indicated that it is much easier to familiarize and adapt to the game-play compared to VR or video games. Regarding the ARPuzzle they found it very interesting, easy to use and good as a learning tool. In general it was recorded that tangible AR interactions are preferred compared to traditional ways of playing games. This was verified according to the game type preferences, puzzle games are preferred by larger numbers of people than arcade games, according to a previous study (de Freitas & Jarvis, 2008). This would seem to indicate that in AR environments puzzle types of games may

Figure 6. Interaction comparison for ARPuzzle vs. ARBreakout

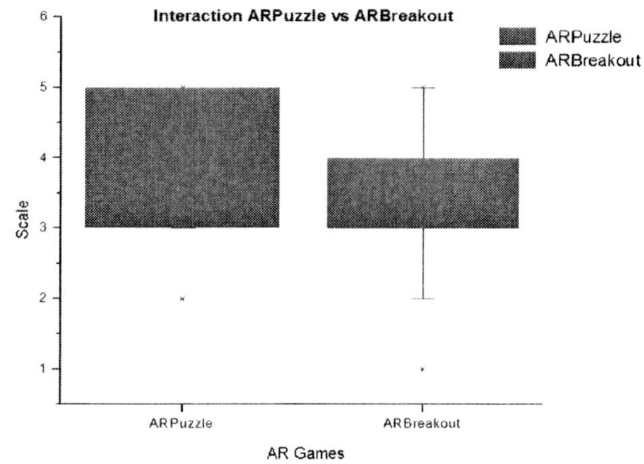

Figure 7. Collaboration comparison for ARPuzzle vs. ARBreakout

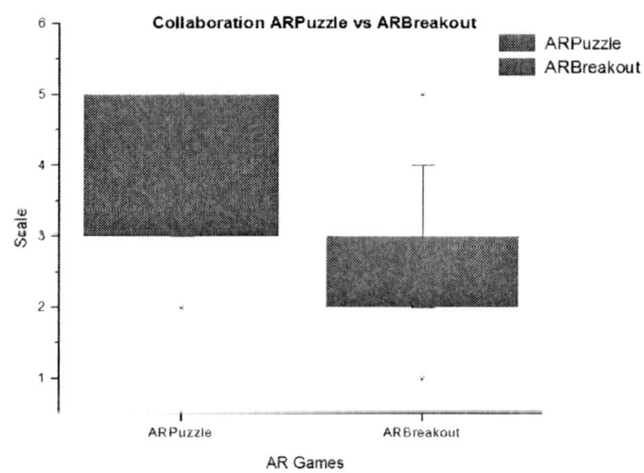

be most appropriate in terms of preferred learning method over other game types tested.

CONCLUSIONS AND FUTURE DIRECTIONS

This paper has presented an overview of two diverse ARSGs based on an evaluation of the Four Dimensional Framework. In particular, two case studies were presented, a puzzle game called ARPuzzle and an arcade game called ARBreakout. An evaluation with 60 users was performed and important issues of ARSGs were asked including: visualization of the game, interaction techniques, collaboration with other players and education and learning and results clearly illustrated that the puzzle is a more appropriate serious game. If applied properly, AR gaming seems to have the potential of changing the way that serious

Figure 8. Education and learning comparison for ARPuzzle vs. ARBreakout

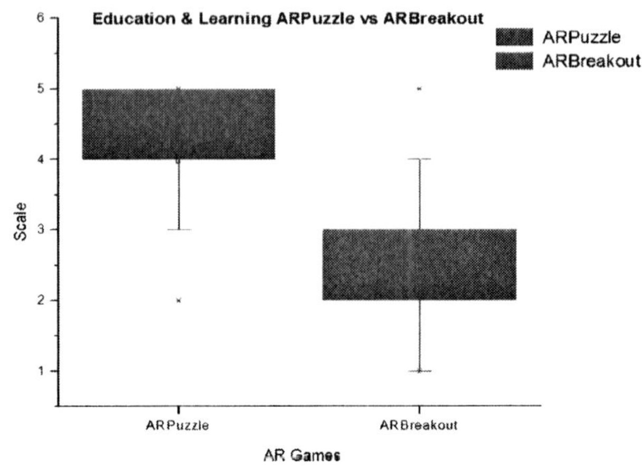

games are played and used as well as helping to educate players while playing. The value of AR applications in serious games has the potential of transforming the way we perceive training and multimodal learning.

The future of serious gaming includes three significant aspects: convergent technologies, widening application areas and efficacy proofs that together will power the wider uptake of these applications over the next three to five years. The video game sector is due to grow at an annual compound rate of 11.4% according to PriceWaterhouse Coopers Global Entertainment and Media Outlook: 2006-2010 analysis of the video games sector. Alongside this, significant growth of leisure games, the use of mash-up applications such as of games with mirror worlds (representations of the real world) like Google Maps, and the use of social software tools such as Facebook, will together fuel a wide range of future applications.

The proliferation of different formats of games as a whole including mobile games will present a diverse range of applications for every client need and learning requirement. The widening application areas for the technologies are presenting unique global reach and potential markets for well developed tools. The studies being undertaken at the Serious Games Institute and elsewhere are beginning to provide evidenced proof of the efficacy of serious games, contributing to metrics and frameworks that can be used to support better development and design of serious games and the potential for benchmarking efficacy via specified metrics. Future research and development work will focus upon the potential of using these emerging tools for testing and validating other formats of serious games.

In the future, the technical characteristics of both games will be improved. Both games will include alternative methods of interaction, such as the Wiimote control and a 3D mouse for the arcade and a virtual glove for the puzzle. The ARPuzzle will also contain more pieces and the 3D buildings will be textured appropriately (according to the actual urban environment). Also, the ARBreakout game will include multiple levels of difficulty. In addition, the tracking component of the AR platform will be combined with a six degree-of-freedom tracker allowing a wider gaming area as well as gestures and voice recognition. Finally, more AR serious games are currently being implemented and future research will focus more user-studies with larger sample sizes.

ACKNOWLEDGMENT

Part of this work was conducted within the LOCUS project, funded by EPSRC through Location and Timing KTN. The authors would also like to thank Kamaljit Kaur for performing part of the evaluation studies as well as the participants who took part in the studies.

REFERENCES

Active Words Inc. (2008). Active Words. Retrieved September 18, 2008, from http://www.activeworlds.com

Annetta, L. A., & Murray, M. R. (2006). Serious games: Incorporating video games in the classroom. *EDUCAUSE Review*, *3*, 16–22.

Billinghurst, M., Kato, H., & Poupyrev, I. (2001). The MagicBook: A transitional AR interface. *Computers & Graphics, Elsevier*, *25*(5), 745–753. doi:10.1016/S0097-8493(01)00117-0

Bimber, O., Fröhlich, B., Schmalstieg, D., & Encarnação, L. M. (2001). The Virtual Showcase. *IEEE Computer Graphics and Applications*, *21*(6), 48–55. doi:10.1109/38.963460

BinSubaih A. Maddock S., Romano D.M. (2006). An architecture for portable serious games. In *Doctoral Symposium hosted at the 20th European Conference on Object-Oriented Programming ECOOP 2006*, Nantes, France.

Cheok, A. D., Fong, S. W., et al. (2003). Human Pacman: a sensing-based mobile entertainment system with ubiquitous computing and tangible interaction. In *Proc. of the 2nd Workshop on Network and System Support for Games*, California (pp. 106-117). New York: ACM Press.

de Freitas, S., & Jarvis, S. (2007). Serious games – Engaging training solutions: A research and development project for supporting training needs. *British Journal of Educational Technology*, *38*(3), 523–525. doi:10.1111/j.1467-8535.2007.00716.x

de Freitas, S., & Jarvis, S. (2008). Towards a development approach for serious games. In T.M. Connolly, M. Stansfield, & E. Boyle (Ed.), *Games-based learning advancements for multi-sensory human-computer interfaces: Techniques and effective practices*. Hershey, PA: IGI Global.

de Freitas, S., & Neumann, T. (2008). The use of 'exploratory learning' for supporting immersive learning in virtual environments. *Computers and Education*.

de Freitas, S., & Oliver, M. (2006). How can exploratory learning with games and simulations within the curriculum be most effectively evaluated? *Computers & Education*, *46*, 249–264. doi:10.1016/j.compedu.2005.11.007

de Lisi, R., & Wolford, J. L. (2002). Improving children's mental rotation accuracy with computer game playing. *The Journal of Genetic Psychology*, *163*(3), 172–182.

Forterra Systems Inc. (2008). OLIVE - Purpose driven virtual worlds for everyone. Retrieved September 18, 2008, from http://www.forterrainc.com/images/stories/pdf/OLIVE_Dec07_Final_Rev.pdf

Henrysson, A., Billinghurst, M., & Ollila, M. (2006). AR tennis. In *International Conference on Computer Graphics and Interactive Techniques archive ACM SIGGRAPH 2006 Sketches*. New York: ACM Press.

Holzinger, A., Kickmeier-Rust, M., & Albert, D. (2008). Dynamic media in computer science education; content complexity and learning performance: Is less more? *Educational Technology & Society*, *11*(1), 279–290.

Holzinger, A., Kickmeier-Rust, M., Wassertheurer, S., & Hessinger, M. (2009). Learning performance with interactive simulations in medical education: Lessons learned from results of learning complex physiological models with the HAEMOdynamics SIMulator. *Computers & Education*, *52*(1), 292–301. doi:10.1016/j.compedu.2008.08.008

Hughes, C. E. (2005). Mixed reality in education, entertainment, and training. *IEEE Computer Graphics and Applications*, 24–30. doi:10.1109/MCG.2005.139

Kerawalla, L., Luckin, R., Seljeflot, S., & Woolard, A. (2006). Making it real: exploring the potential of augmented reality for teaching primary school science. *Virtual Reality (Waltham Cross)*, *10*(3), 163–174. doi:10.1007/s10055-006-0036-4

Korris, J. (2004). Full spectrum warrior: How the Institute for Creative Technologies built a cognitive training tool for the Xbox. In *24th Army Science Conference*, Orlando, Florida.

Liarokapis, F. (2006). An exploration from virtual to augmented reality gaming. *Simulation and Gaming, Symposium: Virtual Reality Simulation, 37*(4), 507-533.

Liarokapis, F. (2007). An augmented reality interface for visualising and interacting with virtual content. *Virtual Reality (Waltham Cross)*, *11*(1), 23–43. doi:10.1007/s10055-006-0055-1

Liarokapis, F., Greatbatch, I., et al. (2005). Mobile augmented reality techniques for geovisualisation. In *Proc. of the 9th Int'l Conference on Information Visualisation*, London (pp. 745-751).

Linden Research. (2008). *Second Life*. Retrieved September 18, 2008 from http://www.secondlife.com

Magerkurth, C., Engelke, T., & Memisoglu, M. (2004). Augmenting the virtual domain with physical and social elements: towards a paradigm shift in computer entertainment technology. *Computers in Entertainment*, *2*(4), 12. doi:10.1145/1037851.1037870

Mitchell, A., & Savill-Smith, C. (2004). The use of computer and video games for learning: A review of the literature. *Learning and Skills Development Agency*. Retrieved October 10, 2008, from http://www.lsda.org.uk/

Nischelwitzer, A., Lenz, F.-J., Searle, G., & Holzinger, A. (2007). Some aspects of the development of low-cost augmented reality learning environments as examples for future interfaces in technology enhanced learning. In *Universal Access to Applications and Services (LNCS 4556)* (pp. 728-737). New York: Springer.

Renevier, P., Nigay, L., Bouchet, J., & Pasqualetti, L. (2004). Generic interaction techniques for mobile collaborative mixed systems. In *Proc. of the International Conference on Computer-Aided Design of User Interfaces (CADUI'2004)*, Funchal, Portugal (pp. 314-327).

Rieber, L. P. (1996). Seriously considering play: Designing interactive learning environments based on the blending of microworlds, simulations, and games. *Educational Technology Research and Development*, *44*(2), 43–58. doi:10.1007/BF02300540

Sørensen, B. H., & Meyer, B. (2007). Serious games in language learning and teaching – a theoretical perspective. In *Proc. of the 3rd International Conference of the Digital Games Research Association*, Tokyo, Japan (pp. 559-566).

Stapleton, C. B., Hughes, C. E., & Moshell, J. M. (2003). Mixed fantasy: Exhibition of entertainment research for mixed reality. In *Proc. of the 2nd International Symposium on Mixed and Augmented Reality (ISMAR 2003)*, Tokyo, Japan (pp. 354-355).

Susi, T., Johannesson, M., & Backlund, P. (2007). Serious games - an overview. *Technical Report HS-IKI-TR-07-001*. Retrieved October 10, 2008, from http://www.his.se/upload/19354/HS-%20IKI%20-TR-07-001.pdf

Thomas, K. (2006). Augmented reality: a new approach to learning. *FutureLab*. Retrieved January 8, 2008, from http://www.futurelab.org.uk/resources/publications_reports_articles/web_articles/Web_Article496

van Eck, R. (2006, March). Digital game-based learning: It's not just the digital natives who are restless. *EDUCAUSE Review*, 16–30.

Vlahakis, V., & Ioannidis, N. (2002). Archeoguide: An augmented reality guide for archaeological sites. *IEEE Computer Graphics and Applications*, *22*(5), 52–60. doi:10.1109/MCG.2002.1028726

Zyda, M. (2005). From visual simulation to virtual reality to games. *Computer*, *38*(9), 25–32. doi:10.1109/MC.2005.297

Chapter 11
Web 2.0 Meets Conference:
The EduCamp as a New Format of Participation and Exchange in the World of Education

Thomas Bernhardt
University of Bremen, Germany

Marcel Kirchner
University of Technology Ilmenau, Germany

ABSTRACT

Admittedly the usual conference format stays in opposite to the thoughts of participation and equality in Web 2.0. The EduCamp is a special BarCamp for trends in teaching and learning. It is focused on the educational context and considers important topics like E-Learning 2.0 in schools, universities or business and many others. The main intention of an EduCamp will become obvious which aims on conversations and discussions about different problem areas, searching and finding solutions together and exchanging on application scenarios or appropriate tools for education. It is based on a new concept that finally offers potentials for developing a conference culture with improved participation.

1 INTRODUCTION

The ideas of using social software in educational context, also known as e-learning 2.0, had a great circulation in the internet since 2005 when Stephen Downes mentioned this term first (cp. Downes, 2005). Social software increasingly is used by teachers and scientists supporting their lessons and courses, also students and even sometimes pupils use them for their personal learning. But in the current context of education still mostly the already web-affine educators, knowledge workers and young digital learners are reached and accomplished in implementing these tools with different learning methods. To get a broader audience especially the mostly non-digitals it is necessary to use other diffusion formats like conferences and symposiums to design the future of education. Out of the cognition of many conference participants that the most interesting discussions take place at the coffee break and not in the 20 to 30 minutes of presentation emerges the concept of BarCamps.

The new event format EduCamp developed from the requirement of exchange in a permanently

DOI: 10.4018/978-1-61520-678-0.ch011

growing edu-community in the internet and also from the ambition to get more people in contact with new trends in education. The EduCamp wants to bring together all education-interested people, especially scientists, teachers as well as enterpreneurs and is increasingly reaching the young digital generation, too.

In the following article there will be given information about the origins and development of a dynamically evolving community which has established an open unconference format for exchange and discussion. Furthermore the key principles and main important aspects of managing and planning an EduCamp will be clarified. Moreover it will be pointed out which distinctions towards traditional conferences exist, which elements from this are combined with the EduCamp principles and which challenges of arranging such an event have to be considered. At least the future aspects in giving perspectives for the next EduCamps and showing some examples of resulting projects will be explained.

2 BACKGROUND AND ORIGINS

To give an overview about the current situation of the EduCamp there should be an explanation over the roots of this conference concept at first. Therefor BarCamps and their origins are characterized and afterwards the development of EduCamps in international context and in German-speaking regions are represented.

2.1 What is a BarCamp?

As mentioned the foundations of EduCamp go back to the concept of BarCamps which are described as "an open and participative unconference whose order procedure and topics are predefined by the participants themself." (Wikipedia, 2009a) All people who can bring useful aspects in or learn informative things from the developing web community are invited to become participants of this events.

Originally BarCamps were established as counter events to the Foo Camps of the publisher and web 2.0-term inventor Tim O'Reilly who arranged his annual conference only for exclusive invited guests the so called "Friends of O'Reilly" (Foo) since 2003. As the two terms "foo" and "bar" are both placeholder in programming languages the initiators named their open meeting BarCamp to clarify the contrast in both concepts. The first Barcamp took place in August 2005 in Palo Alto, California. From there on the number increased exponentially and then differentiated in their thematic focusing (HealthCamps, TourismusCamps, Wordcamps, Bibcamps etc.)(Figure 1).

In 2006 also the first BarCamps in Germany and German-speaking regions were organized at the same time in Berlin and Wien (cp. Gassner, 2006; Patzig, 2007a; Wikipedia, 2009a).

"BarCamps are organized from enthusiasts for enthusiasts who want to learn and share their knowledge in an open environment." This is how Franz Patzig (2007a) one of the first BarCamp organisers in Germany describes the principles. Organisers coordinate the scope but the main content is realized by the participants themselves. The aim is a non-passive audience. All BarCampers are considered as more or less active players in the event by giving a session, moderating a discussion, blog or twitter about it, stream and record it and so on. The topics mainly concentrate on web trends. A special session plan evolves initially on location itself in a welcome round after everybody gave a short introduction of his person in about three keywords, called tags. Then every speaker who wants to give a session offers his topic and asks for interested persons. Afterwards the time slots and rooms are assigned. In general it is possible to set as many parallel sessions as rooms are available. Typically they last 30 minutes. Locations and catering are regularly supported by sponsoring of firms and the attendance is free (cp. Gassner, 2006; Patzig 2007a).

Figure 1. The BarCamp Swarm by Franz Patzig (2007b)

Finally the circulation and differentiation of the concept leaded into the consideration of bringing together the topic education and BarCamps to an EduCamp.

2.2 The First EduCamps in Colombia

Diego Leal, researcher and advisor at the Colombian Ministry of Education, developed an unconference format in August 2007 that he finally called EduCamp. In a discussion with other educators the idea to organize workshops raised that foster the "over-the-shoulder" learning. A learning we all know from reading someones newspaper in the bus or let us explain something from a colleague (cp. Leal, 2008a). Considering other unconference formats like BarCamp and Open Space, he tried to "model practices of collaboration between perfect strangers, in an environment that would allow them to discover that we all can be teachers and learners at the same time." (Leal, 2008a)

Leals design differs from the German EduCamp. The workshop day of his concept starts with the registration, a welcome round and a presentation of the schedule. In this opening session the "game rules" will be defined which show some parallels to those of an Open Space (cp. Wikipedia, 2009b; see also chapter 4):

- "Upon arrival, be prepared to share with other participants.
- When you leave, be prepared to share with the world.
- We are all learners.
- No one is a tourist.
- Whatever happens is the only thing that could have happened." (Leal, 2008b)

After that follows a 45 to 60 minutes talk of an expert on the concept of personal learning environments (PLE) and the use of social software "to provide a conceptual framework for the activities of the day." (Leal, 2008b) Then the participants discuss in small groups how their PLE looks like and which tools they use. Afterwards they have to write down these tools on an adhesive label and put them on a white t-shirt which every participant got at the beginning (moderators got a black one and supporting students a red one). Finally every participant wears his/her PLE and the labels represent tools they know and could teach about. In a more informal process the participants can search people with tools, they do not know already, on given criteria to manage learning. Subsequently the "over-the-shoulder" coaching starts. Important for this setting is that everybody has his own laptop to be able to show and to practise the tools (cp. Leal, 2008b).

In the afternoon more or less the procedure of an Open Space unconference with tables for several topics follows on which the participants only have to stay as long as they learn something or could give some input in the discussion (cp. chapter 4). The workshop ends with a closing discussion where all results of the topic tables are presented. The first EduCamps on this procedure took place in Bogotá and Medellín Colombia in December 2007. Then a second series followed at the end of 2008.

Out of the experience of the past EduCamps in Colombia Leal did several improvements of the format. The actual design can be found in Spanish language in his wiki.[1]

2.3 The Development in Germany and German-Speaking Regions

In June 2007 Steffen Büffel, freelancer and media scientist, asked in his weblog media-ocean, if there is somebody interested in organizing a BarCamp with the focus on "teaching and learning 2.0" similar to the other topic focused BarCamps (cp. Büffel, 2007).

Together with the authors of this article he developed the idea to the German EduCamp. They considered the BarCamp concept as the suitable format for bringing together experts and students to let them discuss the possibilities of using social software in educational context. Finally the first EduCamp took place from April 18th to April 20th 2008 at the Ilmenau University of Technology and was visited by 180 participants. Because of the unexpected and positive response on and after the event a second EduCamp was organized in October 2008 at the Humboldt University of Berlin where nearly 90 participants discussed education trends.

While in the first one the emphasis was on the BarCamp concept and its conditions accompanied by a traditional panel discussion in the second one an OpenSpace was added on Sunday due to the experiences of discussion potential for certain topics while this was opened again in the third one (detailed information cp. chapter 4).

Prominent topics of EduCamps are Web 2.0 in the classroom, corporate learning, information overload, serious games, virtual worlds, mobile and micro learning as well as online reputation and privacy. Through the open atmosphere and the trend setting topics especially young web affine people take part in these event and contribute meaningful input for the discussions in technology enhanced learning.

The following chapters concentrate in form and content on the events which were organized and enhanced in Germany and the German-speaking regions but are of course applicable in all other parts of the world.

3 THE EDUCAMP: EDUCATION 2.0 IN A NEW CONFERENCE STYLE

To characterize the EduCamp some main aspects should be pointed out. At first it is reasonable to describe the key principles by considering form and content as well as presenting some helpful rules. Moreover essential organizational things, important tools and techniques for planning and arranging the event will be emphasized.

3.1 The Key Principles

The event as already described is mainly based on the formal principles of BarCamps and focused on trends in e-learning and corporate learning. Every participant is requested to bring a topic from his educational context to the EduCamp for presenting and discussion – with regard to the read-write and participation activities in Web 2.0. This can be realized in short lectures, workshops, round tables or other methods of scientific exchange. Due to the experiences from the first event session slots were generally extended to 45 till 60 minutes with a break option at the end of about 15 minutes. As it is barcamp-typical the day´s schedule results from the theme introduction by all presenters after a short welcome round (cp. Patzig, 2007a; Wikipedia, 2009a).

With regards to content it concentrates on the adoption of social software like Weblogs, Podcasts, Wikis, Microblogs and other web applications in schools and universities as well as in enterprise environments. Furthermore other trends like mobile or micro-learning, digital games and virtual worlds which are in direct coherence with the implementation in educational context can be brought in. The aim is to accomplish people which are engaged in the different educational branches and deal with innovative forms, formats or strategies of media-supported learning to discuss whose future.

Long frontal speeches are not typical. Visiting an EduCamp means to speak about concrete problems in daily teach or learn routines, search for solutions together or exchange about implementation examples and adequate tools for different didactically scenarios. Sessions can be planned before the event or emerge from ideas or initiatives on location.

For first ideas or impulses and as an accommodation a panel discussion with experts about the main topics on the opening eve takes place followed by an informal gathering to get to know each other and begin networking. Further cultural highlights like the EduCamp Party on the second evening can help socializing in a more solute atmosphere.

Also the main principles have been successful approved in past EduCamps there are some aspects that still could be added or improved in future events. The traditional creation of the session plan by sticking notes on a prepared poster could be professionalized by using a smartboard for example to digitize the entries directly and optimize the visualization. To support a consistent documentation concepts of creating a conference transcript for certain contributions could be take into consideration. For getting more input from other parts and networks in the world an increased international alignment is planned. Supplementary points therefor can be also found in chapter 6.

Moreover there are a few helpful rules which were originally developed for BarCamps as a parody to the Fight Club rules and can be adapted also for the EduCamp.

- **1st Rule:** You do talk about EduCamp.
- **2nd Rule:** You do spread the idea of EduCamp (by blogging, twittering, streaming and so on).
- **3rd Rule:** If you want to present, you must write your topic and name in a presentation slot.
- **4th Rule:** Introduce yourself by three tags about your relation to education.
- **5th Rule:** As many presentations at a time as facilities allow for.
- **6th Rule:** Normally no pre-scheduled presentations, except planned connections to experts from other time zones.
- **7th Rule:** Presentations will go on as long as they have to or until they run into another presentation slot. Additional slots are possible and topics can be immersed.
- **8th Rule:** No tourists. EduCamp means "balance of give and take".
- **9th Rule:** If this is your first time at EduCamp, you SHOULD present.
- **10th Rule:** You don't really HAVE to, but try to find someone to present with, or at least ask questions and be an active participant. (cp. barcamp.org, 2008)

Basically apart from one or two persons who are on location the organization is established by a geographically wide spread team which uses social software like Google Docs, Wikis and Skype for coordination and planning.

3.2 The Main Important Things to Organize an EduCamp

As it is typically for a BarCamp everybody is appealed to organize such an open event. According to this principles also the EduCamp has to consider some important things.

- **Make the planned Camp public on time especially in the blogosphere and other online communities!** For announcement and coverage also use the traditional offline media like newspapers, TV or radio.
- **Organize the location and required rooms as early as possible!** It is important to search for sponsored or low-priced rooms by contacting possible cooperation partners. Often there is no extensive technical equipment needed because the participants bring their laptops or other things with oneself. However installed video projectors in the rooms are very useful!
- **Provide a page for topic recommendation and tools for exchange (e.g. forum and wiki) in the established network!** (cp. chapter 3.3) This helps the participants to plan and discuss their sessions as well as to get more interested persons informed about the themes and activities on the event.
- **Find more sponsors and convince them of the EduCamp idea!** Sponsors are essential for the realisation of the EduCamp. They give the financial support for providing all participants the free entrance and catering. It is recommendable to use the available and individual contacts of many persons in the network to explain the idea and intentions directly. In the current organization special sponsoring packages are offered which define clearly all services and equivalents. Basically every sponsor is allowed to hold a session like all participants.
- **Start early with the overall content planning!** It has to be clarified which main concept the EduCamp should trace. Is it organized completely as a Barcamp or are their elements like panel discussion and Open Space integrated? Is there a special motto and which cultural highlights should be planned? But keep in mind that only the scope has to be prepared and the programme will be actively formed by the participants themselves on the event!
- **Use adequate PR and Marketing instruments to announce the event!** Important instruments can be flyers and posters which should be send on time to educational institutions and distributed on other conferences and BarCamps. Additional merchandising products are e.g. buttons, t-shirts, batchholder and name badges which can enhance the identification with the event. Also an attendant medial coverage fostered by dedicated participants during the event (e.g. live streaming, recordings and interviews) could be very useful and public-oriented.
- **Think of the preparation of W-LAN and important materials!** Very important is the availability of an open W-LAN network for all participants so they can twitter, blog and exchange about current developments! Furthermore ask the participants which materials they need respectively consider hints they give - for example pinboards, control desks, multiple sockets or office equipment.
- **Consider further organisational aspects!** Provide all participants on time with information about arrival and overnight stay. Not until shortly before the beginning of the event the main organisation starts. This means for example the naming of the rooms the attaching of sponsoring poster and session plan and so on.

3.3 More Meaningful Aspects: Tools, Techniques and Planning

In contrast to common conferences BarCamps and especially the EduCamp lives from an active community. A network of people interested in the topic and the event itself. The success of the first EduCamp in large parts was the merit of the established educational network in the run-up of the event.

For that purpose very early it was necessary to find a suitable platform to combine the possibilities of registration, reach all members with email, giving information at a front page, letting the members discuss the upcoming topics and describe their topics of interest easily. The right tool for that was found in mixxt - a social networking platform like ning.com - which supports creating and managing a network. The EduCamp network[2] quickly became the central point for everything around the EduCamp.

At Mixxt there are features like a wiki, a forum, members management functions, internal e-mail and event management among others. Especially through the forum a community of like minded people grew very fast. Between the events in presence the platform was used to prepare and to document sessions and to care about contacts.

Since the end of 2008 also an EduCamp weblog was established[3] which informs all EduCampers about current developments in the preparation, to involve the community in the planning and to provide interested persons who also plan to organise an EduCamp with background information.

At the event also other tools play an important role. For quick information from the organisation team and live reports from the sessions the microblogging service Twitter[4] is used. At past events there was a separately Twitter-account and all participants used a unique hashtag (e.g. #ec08) in their tweets. The hashtag allows to follow the actions on the EduCamp over a Twitter wall solved for example with the web application Monitter[5] – a tool which enables you to show all tweets with a specific hashtag - which is visualized for all on a central point of the event.

Furthermore Skype[6], the Voice over IP service, can be used for the realisation of connections to international experts. With Skype Video the experts are presented via video projector to the audience and get a back-channel via webcam. Also live video broadcasting tools like Mogulus[7] can be used for offering people the possibility of live streams from several sessions and give input via chat even if they could not attend directly on the EduCamp.

Beside the used tools which are mostly free and online available the organisation-team has to ensure a stable internet connection via Wi-Fi and provide video projectors in every single room as already mentioned. In most cases the participants bring their own laptops, but its recommendable to have some on hand.

Because of the fast developing tool landscape for communication and collaboration in the internet it seems difficult to predict which further tools will play a role in next EduCamps. But the variety offers great potentials to flexibly support such events by dedication of many participants which fosters the join in character again. Furthermore upcoming events could think about a stronger interconnectedness between different locations and maybe can contemplate representations in virtual environments like Second Life.

4 DISTINCTIONS OF TRADITIONAL CONFERENCES TOWARDS THE EDUCAMP PRINCIPLES

Traditional conferences are characterised by several critical points which let it become interesting to think about alternative formats:

- Long preparation stages with calls for submission of more than a half year before the event cause that topics and results have to be presented which sometimes seem outdated compared to the current developments in the networked internet world.
- High fees create unnecessary barriers to access especially for people who are actually also the subject of the discussion itself (e.g. pupils and students) and therefore

could provide important input. This is certainly relevant particularly in the educational context.

- The fixed time table with often very short presentation slots followed by mostly even shorter discussion times prevent the potential of a topic to be discussed and enhanced adequately.
- Often a clear separation between presenters and audience is recognizable on the most common conferences which can also affect a casual discussion atmosphere.

Lately these points led to the experience of many participants that the coffee breaks - so to say the informal situations - are the really creative parts of a conference. Thus was born the idea for a conference type with a more informal nature which does not artificially restrict the chances of creating ideas and network with people who have the same interests or fields of work.

The unconference delivers the alternative: There is no long preparation phase and it is possible to discuss topics that evolve from ideas already at the Camp itself. There are usually no fees, everybody serious interested in the topic is welcome. Only a matrix with time slots and room names is given, a schedule which is filled by the participants on the event. Therefor everybody is equal.

Especially the German EduCamp has developed some specific characteristics in fact of the educational background which differs from the normal BarCamp format. The EduCamp tries to combine classic elements of a conference, like the panel discussion with typical unconference elements like BarCamp and Open Space.

The panel discussion takes place on the beginning of the event. Only for this part some key speakers are officially invited. It should deliver inspiration for the upcoming event (cp. chapter 3.1). The second part is like a normal BarCamp and the third part could be leant on an Open space setting. This format was integrated in the second EduCamp in Berlin in fact of the determination of many participants that some of the topics could not be discussed sufficiently in depth during one or event two BarCamp sessions.

Open Space is more or less a method to run meetings of any size. At the beginning all participants have the possibility to present a topic on which he/she wants to speak. If there are enough interested people the person will become the moderator of this topic till the end of the Open Space.

The common Open Space only has four principles and one rule that should ensure the success of this unconference format. They are presented during the opening session. For the EduCamp the following two principles of an Open Space seem to be very important:

1. Whoever is interested in education is the right people: This alerts the participants that attendees of a topic table are "right" simply because they care to attend.
2. When it's over, it's over: encourages the participants not to waste time, but to move on to something else when the fruitful discussion ends (cp. Wikipedia, 2009b; Böttger, 2001).

The relevant rule is the "Law of Two Feet" (or "The Law of Mobility"), which means: "If at any time during our time together you find yourself in any situation where you are neither learning nor contributing, use your two feet. Go to some other place where you may learn and contribute." (Wikipedia, 2009b)

At last there is another principle that goes along with an Open Space. Normally everyone decides to be a "bee" or a "butterfly". Bees are free to fly from one topic table to another. They give important input and have a stimulating effect on the topics. The butterflies are more relaxed. They also fly from one to another table, do not go in the depth of a topic but they also give some useful hints (cp. Böttger, 2001).

The first workshop part starts and every moderator takes a flip chart to document the results of the discussion in a room and starts the so called topic table. All other participants have now the chance to chose one topic of interest.

After a short break for presenting the interim results and getting useful input through the other groups the second workshop follows. Here the moderators should come to a final outcome perhaps some concrete projects or collaborations with attendees of the topic table. At the end all groups present their results in a final discussion round.

Finally it has to be exposed that the EduCamp is not a rigid institution. It is certainly always a subject to change and may be supplemented by new and innovative formats in its further development. Due to the major opinion of a blog survey in the run-up of the third EduCamp in Ilmenau the Open Space was rejected by the opportunity to extend sessions on two time slots.

5 CHALLENGES OF ARRANGING AN OPEN UNCONFERENCE FORMAT

While planning an unconference like the EduCamp the great advantage of setting up the schedule on location is simultaneously a big risk. There is a reduced guarantee for high quality presentations and workshops as well as other inputs that will be given. On the one hand it stays doubtful to a certain degree who will come with which topics or if there will be enough or even too many who want to hold a session. Also on the other hand people who do not know exactly what the EduCamp is all about rethink their participation when it isn't clear which detailed sessions and contents they can expect from the event, especially for professionals with a chronic lack of time. Furthermore this could lead to quality problems what is often linked to the Web 2.0 philosophy that unsecured knowledge could be presented by every participant. But at the same time this is the chance for collecting new perspectives and ideas in practice and research fields.

As organiser there are two ways to reduce this risk: At first motivating the participants to point out the topics which should be introduced on a recommendation page in the wiki and discussed in the forum. So attendees can suggest announce topics that should be presented and the other way round they could show in the run-up which topics they want to present or talk about. In the forum remains the possibility to discuss the topic before and after the event. A second way - successfully used in the first EduCamps 2008 - is to invite several international experts to take part via video conferencing or give background information about the key speakers and topics at the panel discussion. So you could guarantee a rudimentary program.

In contrast to usual BarCamps the expected output of the event is even higher. But the expectations differ by the participants. On a BarCamp the participants are often guided by the topics other people bring in. So the participants like the high degree of flexibility and diversity. For those attendees - so to say the "spectators" - the output lies in getting new ideas and over all making contact with like-minded people for future projects. But there is on the other hand a different type of participants - so to say the "creators". They intensively use the possibilities of exchange in forum and wiki as well as in their blogs and Twitter accounts in the run-up to the event to increase their participation competence and net sensibility (cp. Martin, 2008). The main advantage in this approach is the possibility to get in very productive topic discussions on the event because a common foundation of terms and thoughts by the involved participants is already given, special explanations are not needed. A disadvantage could be that other attendees getting interested in the topic on the event have difficulties to enter into the discussions. But the main improvement of the open EduCamp format seems to be that both versions of participation are specifically fostered and can be combined within one event. The participants are free to decide for themselves how they gain the highest output from the event.

Another critical aspect is the more adequate sustainability on conventional conferences through the conference transcript. There are mostly survey reports of the complete event in the blogosphere, but only sometimes on specific sessions. Since the first EduCamp the use of the wiki for documentation and the forum for further discussions was advised but only some of the presenters used it to summarize their sessions pleasant as a discussion fundament after the event. Probably this might be the biggest challenge for upcoming EduCamps to improve and guarantee a comprehensive documentation of the results and encourage ongoing activities between the Camps.

6 THE FUTURE OF EDUCAMP

The EduCamp is the result of an ongoing discussion about the challenges in the future of education. As the discussion itself also the EduCamp format will still have further changes. In the following chapter these future aspects will be described by characterising the next planned EduCamps and mentioning first sustainable projects out of the events.

6.1 The EduCamp Series: New Interests and Locations

After the first EduCamps many participants in the community manifested their interest to arrange the event in their educational point of origin. First ideas of establishing educational camps focussed on specific branches (schools and universities) arised. For the year 2009 two further EduCamps were realized - one again in April back to the traditional first location at the Ilmenau University of Technology and one at the Graz University of Technology in Austria in the beginning of November. The future of the EduCamp format seems assured, especially since other universities also announced their interest to organize it. Summarized the EduCamp movement had a successful start and released a series of events.

With regards to content the EduCamp should keep their main topical centre on the trends of teaching and learning but focussings on different target groups e.g. school, university or business with crosslinking between parallel camps could be possible. As mentioned in chapter 3.3 the organization of two or more simultaneous organized EduCamps in German-speaking or international regions could have special potentials. A connection could be realized with shared live streams of experts or combined sessions via video- or audio-conferencing.

In the run-up of the third EduCamp the first time Online Round Tables (ORTs) were organized to discuss the main topics of the upcoming event. In these monthly online sessions, so to say pre-events, the invited experts present their thoughts on a given educational trend issue like Personal Learning Environments (PLEs) or online reputation and afterwards debate on this with the audience. The ORTs were planned together with the EVOLVE network[8] supported by JISC[9] in English language. These pre-events turned out as a pleasant way to increase the attention in advance of the EduCamp.

Another special feature was also first used for the preparation of the third EduCamp. The organisers set up main topics for the panel discussion with several subitems. Over the EduCamp weblog the edu-community was invited to vote for the items on which the podium should discuss. This additionally supported the join in character of the concept as the participants could co-determine the podium and to a certain degree its experts.

6.2 Resulting Projects

As in chapter 5 mentioned there are different types of attendees. One of the most active creators was

Jean-Pol Martin, a teacher and professor of french didactics at the Catholic University of Eichstätt, who built up a very engaged network of education enthused people. He used the wiki and the forum on the Mixxt platform in an exemplary manner. Already some months before the first EduCamp he fostered a living network in which the participants discussed the new and alternative method of "Lernen durch Lehren (LdL)" (learning through teaching)[10] by his challenging way of knowledge construction. Under the label "Weltverbesserung" (making a better world) he motivated the attendees to contribute own new ideas and projects. After the first EduCamp a new community-platform for this raised, called "Neuron".[11]

Also other communities were built up out of this projects after the second EduCamp like "Maschendraht" (netting wire)[12] with focus of connecting teachers to share their experience in computer mediated learning with web 2.0 and LdL[13], a community for discussing the correspondent method. Furthermore the junior professor for informatic didactics at the Pedagogic University of Ludwigsburg Christian Spannagel developed the concept of Open Scientist [14] out of the EduCamp and Neuron community which cultivates the nearly complete openness of thoughts and science work on the internet (vgl. Spannagel, 2008).

Finally on the second EduCamp in Berlin one group developed at the Open Space the seven requirements for a modern education, which can be found in German language in the Mixxt wiki and was supported by all participants.[15]

In the future the EduCamps certainly will be used to generate new projects and perhaps overall to create a global network. For the next events the focus on generating common project ideas should be enhanced.

6.3 Possible Impact on the Future of Education

The EduCamp can be seen as a platform for all different target groups in educational context. Representatives of the educational branches should be brought together in discussion rounds to bring in especially the perspectives of teachers and learners in their traditional sense as well as to clarify and re-define their roles in the current state and future of education.

Next to the researchers and scientists, who typically talk about theoretical background or the evaluation of implementations on educational conferences, many students get participants who are normally underrepresented because of restrictions like fees or peer-reviews for submissions. Particularly the use of internet technologies seems to be an interesting topical aspect to reach this target group and gives valuable additional views on the discussions. Furthermore and perhaps because of this the EduCamp is relevant also for young creatives who use their energy to built-up ideas in new start-ups and talk about this with the other participants. Last but not least lots of practitioners like school teachers take part in the event and report promptly on their experiences in using technologies and social software in their lessons and courses. This convention fosters the exchange between scientific and practical oriented experts, handlers and newbies who create new ideas, projects and technologies.

Finally with the conference format also formal and informal learning processes are enhanced by establishing long-ranging, active and emerging community networks between each Camp. Therefor the EduCamp can make important contributions to the constructive discussion of further developments in education.

7 CONCLUSION

The EduCamp format with unconference style seems to be a flexible solution for the rapidly changing world of education in which web 2.0 communities and the ambitious digital generation increasingly gains ground, non-digitals have to be leaded towards new social tools as well as the combined didactic scenarios and the common, inflexible conference formats cannot keep pace with. In times where two month old information could be outdated it is more and more important to deliver platforms where new educational trends could be discussed immediately. Moreover the EduCamp reflects the typical melting borders between producer and recipient. On a join-in conference like this all are attendees and presenters at the same time and everybody is fostered to participate in the origin sense of the word: take part and be a part of the event. Make the most of it.

The EduCamp therewith creates potentials for a conference culture that supports and raises active involvement even stronger. It will be very interesting to see how this format will develop especially because it is primarily organized by volunteers.

REFERENCES

barcamp.org. (2008). *The rules of BarCamp*. Retrieved February 6, 2009, from http://barcamp.org/TheRulesOfBarCamp

Böttger, I. (2001). *Methodenlexikon - Open Space*. Retrieved February 6, 2009, from http://www.sowi-online.de/methoden/lexikon/open-space-boettger.htm

Büffel, S. (2007). *Dokumentation zum Skypecast*. Retrieved February 4, 2009, from http://www.media-ocean.de/2007/06/21/dokumentation-zum-skypecast-vorlesung-20-online/

Downes, S. (2005). E-learning 2.0. *eLearn magazine*. Retrieved February 7, 2009, from http://elearnmag.org/subpage.cfm?section=articles&article=29-1

E-Learning 2.0-Blog. (2007). *Online round table: E-Learning 2.0*. Retrieved January 8, 2009, from http://www.elearning2null.de/online-round-table-e-learning-20/

Gassner, O. (2006). *Happy campers*. Retrieved February 5, 2009, from http://www.heise.de/tp/r4/artikel/24/24251/1.html

Leal, D. (2008a). *EduCamp Colombia*. Retrieved February 4, 2009, from http://www.diegoleal.org/social/blog/blogs/dotedu-dotco/index.php/2008/11/16/educamp-colombia-1

Leal, D. (2008b). *EduCamp Colombia 2007: Bogotá*. Retrieved February 4, 2009, from http://www.diegoleal.org/social/blog/blogs/dotedu-dotco/index.php/2008/11/16/educamp-colombia-2007-bogota-1

Martin, J.-P. (2008). *LdL (Lernen durch Lehren) goes global: Paradigmenwechsel in der Fremdsprachendidaktik unter Beruecksichtigung kulturspezifischer Lerntraditionen*. Retrieved February 7, 2009, from http://de.wikiversity.org/wiki/Benutzer:Jeanpol/guido

Patzig, F. (2007a). *Was ist eigentlich BarCamp?* Retrieved January 8, 2009, from http://www.franztoo.de/?p=113

Patzig, F. (2007b). Swarm (Picture) Retrieved January 8, 2009, from http://www.flickr.com/photos/franzlife/390044262/(permission granted)

Spannagel, C. (2008). *Der öffentliche Wissenschaftler*. Retrieved February 7, 2009, from http://cspannagel.wordpress.com/2008/05/18/der-offentliche-wissenschaftler/

Wikipedia. (2009a). *BarCamp*. Retrieved January 8, 2009, from http://de.wikipedia.org/wiki/BarCamp

Wikipedia. (2009b). Open Space Technology. Retrieved February 4, 2009, from http://en.wikipedia.org/w/index.php?title=Open_Space_Technology&oldid=266025253

ENDNOTES

[1] http://www.diegoleal.org/social/wiki/mediawiki/index.php5?title=Diseño_Educamp
[2] http://educamp.mixxt.de
[3] http://www.educamps.de
[4] http://twitter.com
[5] http://monitter.com
[6] http://skype.com
[7] http://mogulus.com
[8] http://www.evolvecommunity.org/
[9] http://www.jisc.ac.uk/
[10] http://www.ku-eichstaett.de/Forschung/forschungsprojekte/ldl/
[11] http://neuron.mixxt.de/
[12] http://maschendraht.mixxt.de/
[13] http://ldl.mixxt.de/
[14] http://www.ph-ludwigsburg.de/wp/spannagel/openscientists/
[15] http://educamp.mixxt.de/networks/wiki/index.10forderungen

Chapter 12
Authentic Tasks:
The Key to Harnessing the Drive to Learn in Members of "Generation Me"

Thomas C. Reeves
The University of Georgia, USA

Jan Herrington
Murdoch University, Australia

ABSTRACT

Regardless of whether one thinks of today's higher education students as "digital natives" or members of "Generation Me," it is obvious that traditional instructional methods are failing to engage them adequately in developing the kinds of higher order learning outcomes necessary in the 21st Century. These outcomes should encompass the conative learning domain as well as the traditional cognitive, affective, and psychomotor domains. This chapter describes a set of ten authentic tasks learning design principles that can be used to create and support the kind of engaging learning experiences that today's learners must have if they are to achieve a full range of cognitive, affective, conative, and psychomotor outcomes for the 21st Century. A case study of a graduate level online course that exemplifies these design principles is described. Responding to the needs of Generation Me learners requires far more of a pedagogical revolution than it does the widespread adoption of Web 2.0 technologies.

INTRODUCTION

For us, the term "Digital Natives" represents an overly simplistic portrayal of the younger students enrolled in today's colleges and universities. Prensky (2001a, b) coined the term "digital natives" to describe a new generation of students who are native speakers in the digital language of the Internet, video games, cell phones, and computers, and distinguished them from "digital immigrants" who are members of an older generation of students and their teachers who were not born into a society where digital technologies were as ubiquitous as they are now. One problem with Prensky's definition of "digital natives" is that it seriously over-estimates the information literacy of the digital natives as opposed to their technological fluency. As Oblinger and Oblinger (2005) noted:

DOI: 10.4018/978-1-61520-678-0.ch012

Having grown up with widespread access to technology, the New Gen is able to intuitively use a variety of IT devices and navigate the Internet. Although they are comfortable using technology without an instruction manual, their understanding of the technology or source quality may be shallow. (p. 2.5)

In 2009, Prensky himself admitted that the distinction between digital natives and digital immigrants was becoming less relevant. However, Prensky and others (cf. Tapscott, 2008) still appear to us to over-emphasize the technological advantages of the world in which the new generation of students have lived while underestimating the enormous changes in the social, economic, and environmental aspects of their world. In light of this, we prefer to use the term "Generation Me" (GenMe) created by Twenge (2006) to describe the majority of students born since 1990 that are in or about to enter postsecondary education in the second decade of the 21st Century. Although GenMe is usually thought of as an American construct, it can be extended to encompass young people in most developed countries in Europe as well as to Australia and New Zealand. Based upon rigorous research studies going back to the 1950s and extending into the early 2000s, Twenge (2006) presented convincing evidence that most of today's young people, especially in the USA, have been raised to think that they will be highly successful, even stars, although the reality is that they will find it harder than ever to get into and afford the best colleges, find a high-paying, personally-rewarding job, and buy a decent home. On her *Generation Me* book website, she summarized the plight of GenMe as follows:

Today's young people have been raised to aim for the stars at a time when it is more difficult than ever to get into college, find a good job, and afford a house. Their expectations are very high just as the world is becoming more competitive, so there's a huge clash between their expectations and reality. (http://www.generationme.org/aboutbook.html)

Twenge (2006) made her observations about GenMe two years before the current global financial crisis became evident. If her predictions seemed dire then, they are even more so now. Twenge (2006) painstakingly analyzed the results of studies that involved adolescents and college students completing well-designed, validated questionnaires in the 1950s, 60s, 70s, 80s, 90s, and today. This enabled her to compare, for example, the attitudes of the Baby Boomer generation expressed when they were adolescents with the attitudes of GenMe expressed during their adolescence. This approach distinguishes her research from the majority of generational studies that have relied upon respondents such as Baby Boomers' reporting memories of the attitudes they held in their younger years or on interviews with students selected from elite groups (cf. Howe & Strauss, 2000).

A sample of Twenge's (2006) findings derived from data collected from 1.3 million young Americans since the 1950s include:

- In 2002, 74% of high school students admitted to cheating whereas in 1969 only 34% admitted such a failing.
- In 1967, 86% of incoming college students said that "developing a meaningful philosophy of life" was an essential life goal whereas in 2004 only 42% of GenMe freshmen agreed.
- In 2004, 48% of American college freshmen reported earning an A average in high school whereas in 1968 only 18% of freshmen reported being an A student in high school.
- In the 1950s, only 12% of young teens agreed with the statement "I am an important person" whereas by the late 1980s, 80% claimed they were important.
- In the 1960s, 42% of high school students expected to work in professional

jobs whereas in the late 1990s, 70% of high school students expected to work as a professional.

- In a recent poll, 53% of GenMe mothers agreed with the statement that a person's main responsibility is to themselves and their children rather than making the world a better place, whereas only 28% of Boomer mothers agreed.

Regardless of whether we think of them as Digital Natives or GenMe, the challenges of preparing these new learners to have the strongest possible 21st Century skills so that they will have a better chance of successful and fulfilling lives in the face of economic, environmental, and social barriers may be greater than any time since the development of the modern university. Friedman (2008) describes the world Generation Me graduates will confront as:

The world also has a problem: It is getting hot, flat, and crowded. That is, global warming, the stunning rise of middle classes all over the world, and rapid population growth have converged in a way that could make our planet dangerously unstable. In particular, the convergence of hot, flat, and crowded is tightening energy supplies, intensifying the extinction of plants and animals, deepening energy poverty, strengthening petrodictatorship, and accelerating climate change. (p. 5)

We believe that Friedman (2008) accurately describes the harsh realities of the global society at least for the next decade. This raises an important question. What are the outcomes we in higher education should be addressing to prepare GenMe learners to live in this world?

21ST CENTURY OUTCOMES

Today, it has become commonplace to assume that members of the so-called Net Generation have sophisticated technology skills simply because they are the first generation to grow up with computers and ubiquitous Internet access (Prensky, 2008; Tapscott, 2008). Although it is clear that middle and upper class students are more likely to possess and use the latest high tech gear such as iPods, video phones, and game boxes, their information literacy, especially with respect to judging the quality of information obtained on the Internet through search engines such as Google, is unacceptably weak (Bauerline, 2008; Oblinger & Oblinger, 2005; Reeves & Oh, 2007). Information literacy encompasses far more than the ability to find information. Most importantly, it includes the capacity to judge the quality of information, to identify the underlying values inherent in diverse information resources, to communicate clear interpretations of the information found, and to use information to solve problems and accomplish tasks (Breivik, 2005).

The ability to establish a Facebook page, post a video on YouTube, or engage in Twittering says little if anything about the information literacy of today's higher education students. The National Academies (http://www.nationalacademics.org/) issued a report that questions the presumed technological prowess of today's younger generations (Committee on Science, Engineering, and Public Policy, 2006). The authors of this alarming report concluded that:

It is easy to be complacent about America's competitiveness and preeminence in science and technology. We have led the world for decades, and we continue to do so in many research fields today. But the world is changing rapidly and our advantages are no longer unique. Without a renewed effort to bolster the foundations of our competitiveness, we can expect to lose our privileged position. For the first time in generations, the nation's children could face poorer prospects than their parents and grandparents did. (p. 8)

Figure 1. 21st century student outcomes and support systems

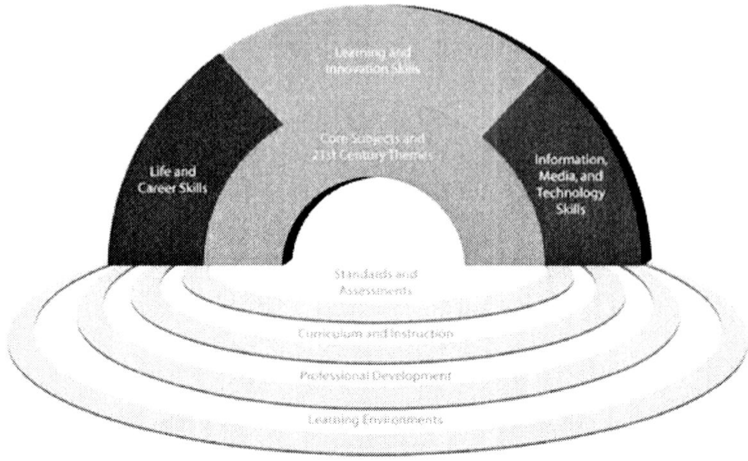

Salpeter (2003) describes the outcomes prescribed by the Partnership for 21st Century Skills (http://www.21stcenturyskills.org), a public-private coalition of education and business leaders founded in 2002. As illustrated in the rainbow sections of Figure 1, the outcomes prescribed by the Partnership encompass core content knowledge as well as life and career skills, learning and innovation skills, and information, media, and technology skills. (The pool sections of Figure 1 represent the support systems required by schools and universities to help students accomplish the 21st Century outcomes.) The Partnership outcomes are similar to earlier specifications of 21st Century skills delineated by others such as the "1991 SCANS Report (Secretary's Commission on Achieving Necessary Skills) or later reports issued by the CEO Forum" (Salpeter, 2003, p. 18).

The outcomes prescribed by the Partnership for 21st Century Skills, the CEO Forum, and SCANS are improvements over earlier conceptions of the most important learning outcomes, but they still leave out an important construct, specifically, the conative domain (Reeves, 2006). Student learning outcomes in both K-12 and postsecondary education are traditionally defined in relationship to three primary domains: cognitive, affective, and psychomotor. The cognitive domain relates to the capacity to think or one's mental skills (Anderson, Krathwohl, Airasian, Cruikshank, Mayer, Pintrich, Raths, and Wittrock, 2001; Bloom, Engelhart, Furst, Hill, and Krathwohl, 1956). The affective domain (Krathwohl, Bloom, & Masia, 1964) is about emotions and feelings, especially in relationship to a set of values. The psychomotor domain (Harrow, 1972) is concerned with the mastery of physical skills ranging from reflexive movements to exhibiting appropriate body language.

The neglected conative domain (Snow, Corno, & Jackson, 1996) is associated with action. It is clear that although someone may possess the cognitive capacity, affective values, and physical skills to perform a given task, whether the person possesses the will, desire, drive, level of effort, mental energy, intention, striving, and self-determination to actually perform at the highest standards possible remains an unanswered question. The conative domain focuses on conation or the act of striving to perform at the highest levels. With rare exceptions, the literature on higher education teaching, learning, and assessment is not informed by consideration of the conative domain. However, the roots of conation can be traced all the way back to Aristotle who used the Greek word "orexis" to signify striving, desire, or the conative state of mind. Kolbe (1990) contrasted

Figure 2. Kolbe's (1990) comparison of cognitive, affective, and conative domains

Cognitive	Affective	Conative
• To know	• To feel	• To act
• Thinking	• Feeling	• Willing
• Thought	• Emotion	• Volition
• Epistemology	• Esthetics	• Ethics
• Knowing	• Caring	• Doing

the cognitive, affective, and conative domains as illustrated in Figure 2.

Given the "hot, flat, and crowded" world in which GenMe learners must live (Friedman, 2008), those of us involved in higher education must help these students develop their conative dispositions, especially their drive for learning. The purpose of this chapter is to describe an approach to developing effective learning environments that address 21st Century outcomes as well as the conative domain through the learning design principles of authentic tasks (Herrington, Reeves, & Oliver, 2006; Herrington, Reeves, Oliver, & Woo, 2004). We argue that fundamental pedagogical change must underlie any attempts to reform higher education using Web 2.0 tools. We also maintain that the widespread adoption of Web 2.0 tools without significant pedagogical change may have detrimental effects on student achievement. For example, a new study conducted by Karpinski and Duberstein (2009) at Ohio State University found that students who use the popular social networking site, Facebook, spend less time studying and have lower grades than students who don't spend time on Facebook.

GENERATION ME LEARNERS

Do GenMe students learn in fundamentally different ways than the students of earlier generation? Some such as Prensky (2006) clearly believe that GenMe is fundamentally different from previous generations in ways that require new approaches to teaching and learning. Prensky (2001a) defined one side of this issue as follows:

Our students have changed radically. Today's students are no longer the people our educational system was designed to teach. Today's students have not just changed incrementally from those of the past, nor simply changed their slang, clothes, body adornments, or styles, as has happened between generations previously. A really big discontinuity has taken place. One might even call it a 'singularity' - an event which changes things so fundamentally that there is absolutely no going back. This so-called 'singularity' is the arrival and rapid dissemination of digital technology in the last decades of the 20th century. (p. 1)

To support his contentions, Prensky (2001b) summarizes the findings of neuroscience studies from which he concludes that his so-called digital natives really do think and learn differently from the digital immigrants of earlier generations:

Based on the latest research in neurobiology, there is no longer any question that stimulation of various kinds actually changes brain structures and affects the way people think, and that these transformations go on throughout life. The brain is, to an extent not at all understood or believed to be when Baby Boomers were growing up, massively plastic. It can be, and is, constantly reorganized. (Although the popular term rewired is somewhat misleading, the overall idea is right—the brain changes and organizes itself differently based on the inputs it receives.) The old idea that we have a fixed number of brain cells that die off one by one has been replaced by research showing that our supply of brain cells is replenished constantly. The brain constantly reorganizes itself all our child and adult lives, a phenomenon technically known as neuroplasticity. One of the earliest pioneers in this field of neurological research found that rats in "enriched" environments showed brain changes compared with those in "impoverished" environments after as little as two weeks. Sensory areas of their brains were thicker, other layers heavier. Changes showed consistent overall growth, leading to the conclusion that the brain maintains its plasticity for life. (p. 1)

Other scholars challenge Prensky's optimistic interpretations of the findings of contemporary brain science done with rats (Kennedy, Judd, Churchward, Gray, & Krause, 2008; VanSlyke, 2003). Owen (2004) maintains that setting up dichotomies such as digital natives and digital immigrants can lead to poor decisions about the design of new teaching and learning environments. In support of this contention, Owen cites an influential book by John Seely Brown and Paul Duguid (2000) titled *The Social Life of Information*:

Brown and Duguid's central theme is that access to information does not equate to knowledge. Brown and Duguid note, much of what we recognize as learning comes from informal social interactions between learners and mentors. These social interactions are difficult to achieve in mediated instruction. They recognize that technology can enhance instruction in remarkable ways; however, it cannot replace the insights that students receive by struggling to make sense of information with both peers and mentors. They contend that the gung-ho tunnel vision of commentators like Prensky - seeing only one way ahead (if all you have is a hammer, everything looks like a nail!), has led to erroneously simplified and unrealistic expectations of what our future in the information age will be like.

Regarding higher order learning outcomes, Healy (1998) maintains that the development of abstract reasoning ability requires the physical experience of action, the kind of experience that is decreased when children are placed in passive modes for many hours by television. She also expressed concerns about the lack of language stimulation and the accompanying decline in linguistic capabilities that stem from over-exposure to video games. Whereas Prensky (2006) argued that video games stimulate children's creativity, Healey (1998) worried that today's interactive media actually stifles their intellectual curiosity. A decade later, Bauerline (2008) concluded that too few of the members of GenMe "master the skills to negotiate an information-heavy, communication-based society and economy" (p. 16).

Will members of GenMe leave our universities equipped with superior information literacy that matches their purported strong technology skills as some have predicted? Or will their technology skills remain shallow and superficial? Is their information literacy limited in fundamental ways that actually reduces their powers to reflect, reason, and make decisions? The research literature in this area provides no clear answers, and so the debate continues. On the one hand, some researchers and pundits suggest that the information literacy of GenMe (digital natives) far exceeds that of earlier generations (digital immigrants), and that this has profound implications for how they should be educated. On the other hand, some argue that the media-saturated environment in which today's youth have grown up has actually stifled some of the fundamental thinking and social interaction skills that derive from human-to-human interaction, including a decline in the capacity to reason, engage in critical reflection, and exhibit intellectual curiosity.

There is, of course, a middle ground in this debate. We support this middle ground because we believe that how people learn, reason, reflect, and create are robust human capacities that are not unduly influenced by new media and technology for better or for worse. Postman (2003) wrote:

To my knowledge, there does not exist any compelling evidence that PCs or any other manifestation of computer technology can do for children what good, well-paid, unburdened teachers can do. Nor is there any evidence whatsoever that children in wired classrooms do any better than children who aren't. (p. 193)

GENERATION ME AND GAME-BASED LEARNING

Some have tried to make the case that GenMe students have been positively affected by the sophisticated interactive games and simulations they have spent much of their youth playing. Gee (2003) maintained that playing contemporary video games has positive outcomes with respect to many cognitive skills. He identified 36 important learning principles that are inherent in good video games. These include enhancing the ability to detect patterns in seemingly chaotic events and learning to think like a scientist. In a similar vein, Beck and Wade (2004) wrote:

How hard this new cohort works, how they try to compete, how they fit into teams. How they take risks – all are different in statistically verifiable ways. And those differences are driven by one central factor: growing up with video games. (p. 2)

GenMe members who play interactive games regularly appear to believe that they are learning important things through their interactive play, and not just wasting their time. For example, Beedle (2004) surveyed players of the popular online game, *Everquest*, and found that the majority of the players believe that playing this game increases their creativity and problem-solving abilities. Of course, there is a great leap from someone believing that playing a game increases creativity to providing demonstrative evidence that playing a game increases creativity. The latter, more desirable, research evidence does not yet exist. Other studies have detected adult-like expert behaviors among children who frequently play video games. For example, VanDenventer and White (2002) reported that observations of children teaching adults how to play video games exhibited expert behaviors such as:

...actively seeks new information; incorporates new information; assesses situations using multiple pieces of data; organizes, classifies, and categorizes information; consistently applies successful behaviors; is confident about one's own knowledge; is willing to take risks; employs corrective action when needed; can consider input from multiple sources; recognizes patterns; uses holistic thinking; is able to integrate information with behaviors; uses inductive thinking; strategizes; thinks critically; and recognizes constraints and misinformation. (p. 46)

Steinkuehler (2008) investigated the cognitive effects of playing massively multiplayer online games and found that players exhibit many skills that most universities would want their graduates to exhibit in the 21st Century:

[Massively multiplayer gaming] communities instantiate their collective intelligence (Levy, 1999) in the form of unofficial user manuals that are far more accurate than official ones, authoring and maintaining database-backed websites that function as "how to" manuals for the game (Squire & Steinkuehler, 2005; Steinkuehler, 2005e),

and they create in-game apprenticeship systems (Galarneau, 2005) that enculturate newcomers into valued cultural practices: Gamers who have already mastered the social and material practices requisite to gameplay apprentice, through scaffolded and supported interactions, newer gamers who lack such knowledge and skill. (p. 619)

Slator and Associates (2006) provide evidence of the effectiveness of multi-user role playing games in subjects as diverse as geology and microeconomics. Mitchell and Savill-Smith (2004) reviewed the literature on gaming in education and concluded that well-designed interactive games have the potential to:

- engage unmotivated learners
- engage learners who lack confidence in ability to learn
- develop skills in literacy
- develop mathematical skills
- develop skills in visualization
- develop capacity for strategic and tactical decision making
- develop critical thinking and problem solving skills

Unfortunately, whether playing interactive games has bad or good effects is the subject of much more speculation than robust research. Indeed, computer play is generally not well researched or understood. It is "the first qualitatively different form of play that has been introduced in at least several hundred years, ...it merits an especially careful examination of its role in the lives of children" (Salonius-Pasternak & Gelfond, 2005, p. 6). Even when research has been done, there is substantial debate about its quality and interpretation. For example, several prominent psychologists (e.g., Anderson & Bushman, 2001; Bensley & Eenwyk, 2001; Gentile & Anderson, 2003) have presented research that indicates that some popular video games such as *Doom*, *Grand Theft Auto* and *Tomb Raider* encourage antisocial and even violent behavior, but other researchers have called such research into question (Cassell & Jenkins, 1998; Greenfield & Cocking, 1996; Griffiths, Davies, & Chappell, 2003; Sherry, 2001; Squire & Jenkins, 2003; Wolf & Perron, 2003). It should be clear that determining whether the members of GenMe have unique learning capacities stemming from playing online games and using other digital tools that are fundamentally different from the learning capacities of earlier generations has not been definitely established.

THE NEED FOR PEDAGOGICAL CHANGE IN HIGHER EDUCATION

Instead of concluding that the teaching methods of higher education need to be adjusted to accommodate the learning styles and preferences of GenMe, we prefer to argue that the pedagogy of higher education needs to be enhanced for other reasons. First, there is woefully little evidence that higher education is effective in the first place. Although virtually everyone directly involved in higher education (students, professors, parents, and alumni) seem convinced that high quality teaching and learning are occurring in our universities and colleges, the evidence for this belief is sorely lacking (Hersh & Merrow, 2005). Indeed, Schneider (2005) concludes that unquestioned belief in the efficacy of higher education is naïve:

Americans are increasingly cynical about their public institutions and public leaders. But their skepticism does not extend to the content of a higher education. Most students–and the public as a whole–assume without question that whatever students choose to study in college, they will learn what they need to know for today's competitive and complex environment. But in practice, college figures in the public imagination as something of a magical mystery tour. It is important to be admitted; it is also important to graduate with a degree. But what one does in between, what students actually learn in college, is largely unknown and largely unchallenged. (p. 62)

In the absence of compelling evidence that higher education does yield effective learning through its primary pedagogical methods of lecturing, textbook reading, and multiple-choice testing, we conclude that pedagogical change is needed.

The National Survey of Student Engagement (NSSE) (http://nsse.iub.edu/) conducted by Indiana University indicates that undergraduate students are much less engaged in learning activities known to foster academic achievement than expected by their professors (Kuh, 2003). NSSE surveys have been conducted every year since 2000. In 2008, the survey collected data at more than 750 colleges and universities in the USA and Canada. According to NSSE, the average professor expects undergraduate students to be engaged in classes or labs 10-15 hours per week and out-of-class studying for another 25-30 hours per week. This does not seem like an unreasonable expectation, but the NSSE data shows that 20% of students spend less than 5 hours per week studying, 25% spend 6-10 hours per week, 48% spend 11-30 hours per week, and only 7% exceed the 30 hours per week expected by faculty members. Traditional pedagogical methods are not engaging the learners of any generation sufficiently, and thus fundamental pedagogical change is imperative.

AUTHENTIC TASKS TO ENGAGE GENERATION ME

The NSSE studies have delineated five essential strategies for increasing student engagement in their university studies (Kuh, Laird, & Umbach, 2004):

- Increasing student – faculty interaction,
- Engaging students in active, collaborative learning activities,
- Encouraging more achievement-oriented "time-on-task" among students,
- Setting high academic challenge, and
- Providing continuous timely feedback.

The five NSSE strategies are important, but they do not spell out in sufficient detail the kind of learning design principles that professors and others who desire to develop and implement more effective learning environments in higher education require. In our research, we have previously identified the critical characteristics of the learning designs that can create and support the kind of authentic learning experiences that GenMe learners should have if they are to achieve a full range of cognitive, affective, conative, and psychomotor outcomes for the 21st Century. Ten specific learning design principles related to authentic tasks have been identified (Herrington, Reeves, Oliver, & Woo, 2004). These principles are:

1. *Authentic tasks require real-world relevance:* The learning tasks set for GenMe learners should match as nearly as possible the real-world tasks of professionals in practice rather than de-contextualized or academic tasks (Brown, Collins & Duguid, 1989). Authentic tasks should address the realistic economic, environmental, and social problems that GenMe must learn to solve if they are to thrive, not just survive, in the 21st Century.
2. *Authentic tasks are ill-defined, requiring students to define the tasks and sub-tasks needed to complete the activity:* Problems inherent in the tasks set for GenMe learners should be ill-defined and open to multiple interpretations rather than easily solved by the application of existing algorithms. In the face of problems that approximate

the complexity of the real world, learners must identify their own unique tasks and sub-tasks in order to complete the major task (Cognition and Technology Group at Vanderbilt, 1990).

3. *Authentic tasks comprise complex tasks to be investigated by students over a sustained period of time:* Tasks developed for GenMe learners should require work over days, weeks, and months rather than minutes or hours. These tasks should require significant investment of time and intellectual resources (Bransford, Vye, Kinzer, & Risko, 1990). The design of authentic task-based learning environments must break out of the rigid semester and course hour structures that limit contemporary innovations in higher education.
4. *Authentic tasks provide opportunities for students to examine the task from different perspectives, using a variety of resources:* Authentic tasks should be developed in ways that afford GenMe learners the opportunity to examine the problem from a variety of theoretical and practical perspectives, rather than encouraging a single perspective that learners simply imitate to be successful. The use of a variety of resources rather than a limited number of preselected references requires students to distinguish relevant from irrelevant information and thus develop the high levels of information literacy as well as technological fluency they will need in the years to come (Young, 1993).
5. *Authentic tasks provide the opportunity to collaborate:* Collaboration should be integral to the tasks that GenMe learners must complete, both within the course and the real world, rather than achievable by an individual learner (Lebow & Wager, 1994). Developing the ability to lead and work in groups is essential for GenMe learners.
6. *Authentic tasks provide the opportunity to reflect:* Tasks should be designed to enable GenMe learners to make choices and reflect on their learning both individually and socially (Gordon, 1998). Self-reflection, meta-cognition, and self-regulated learning must be fostered.
7. *Authentic tasks can be integrated and applied across different subject areas and lead beyond domain-specific outcomes:* Tasks for GenMe learners should be designed to encourage interdisciplinary perspectives and enable students to play diverse roles thus building robust expertise rather than knowledge limited to a single well-defined field or domain (Jonassen, 1991). Traditional course and discipline structures will need to be redefined for GenMe learners.
8. *Authentic tasks are seamlessly integrated with assessment:* Assessment of how GenMe learners perform in the face of an authentic task should be seamlessly integrated with that major task in a manner that reflects real world assessment, rather than separate artificial assessment removed from the nature of the task (Herrington & Herrington, 1998). Grades that fail to represent the richness of achievements that GenMe learners must accomplish should be abolished and replaced with rich descriptions of the cognitive, affective, conative, and psychomotor progress made by these learners.
9. *Authentic tasks create polished products valuable in their own right rather than as preparation for something else:* The tasks set for GenMe learners should culminate in the creation of a whole product rather than an exercise or sub-step in preparation for something else (Barab, Squire & Dueber, 2000). Integrated with the principles of service learning (Jacoby, 1996), these products should contribute to society at large whenever possible.
10. *Authentic tasks allow competing solutions and diversity of outcome:* Authentic tasks should allow a range and diversity of

> outcomes open to multiple solutions of an original nature, rather than a single correct response obtained by the application of rules and procedures (Duchastel, 1997). Expert, peer, self, and public review of the solutions that GenMe create to the problems inherent in the authentic tasks set for them should be enabled and encouraged.

Tasks such as these are not distinguished from learning games and simulations simply by being real—indeed, they do not need to be real to be authentic. If these principles are used as a design guide, the tasks will be 'cognitively real' (Smith, 1987; Herrington, Reeves, & Oliver, 2007). Smith (1987) in a review of research related to simulations concluded that the 'physical fidelity' of the learning environment is of less importance than 'realistic problem-solving processes' (p. 409), a process Smith described as the 'cognitive realism' of the task. Scenarios and simulations can effectively be presented as realistic contexts for the investigation of complex problems in both games and in authentic tasks. However, in contrast to the more tacit learning that may occur in games, authentic tasks require realistic and polished products as outcomes. Such outputs require considerable intellectual effort in collaboration with others.

AUTHENTIC TASKS EXAMPLE

What does a learning environment based upon authentic tasks look like? The first author of this paper teaches a graduate level course online called "e-learning evaluation" in which students work in small groups to plan, conduct, and report an evaluation of an actual e-learning program for real world clients. The major task in this course approximates the real-world work of professional evaluators. The task is not a de-contextualized, academic one. The challenges of planning, conducting, and reporting an evaluation of an e-learning program in the real world are by their very nature ill-defined and open to multiple solutions rather than easily solved by the application of existing formulas. The learners in this online course must identify their own unique activities and sub-activities in order to complete the major task.

The e-learning evaluation course requires 10-15 hours per week of sustained effort over the length of a 16 week semester. The overall task requires significant investments of time and intellectual resources. This task affords learners the opportunity to approach the problem from a variety of perspectives, rather than a single set of steps that learners imitate to be successful. The use of multiple resources rather than a limited number of preselected references requires students to detect relevant from irrelevant information. Collaboration is integral to successful evaluation projects, both within the course and the real world, rather than achievable by an individual learner or evaluator. Effective group work is essential to most evaluation projects, and thus collaborative work is required in this course.

The complexities of the realistic and often unpredictable activities inherent in e-learning evaluation require learners to make choices and reflect upon and self-regulate own their learning. The activities that must be accomplished for a successful e-learning evaluation encourage interdisciplinary perspectives and enable students to play diverse roles such as project manager, data collector, statistician, and report writer. Playing these different roles allow students to develop robust expertise rather than inert knowledge. Assessment in the e-learning evaluation online course is seamlessly integrated with the major task in a manner that reflects real world assessment, rather than separate artificial assessment removed from the nature of the task. The final evaluation report is submitted to the real world client after several rounds of expert and peer assessment. The final evaluation report becomes a key part of each learner's professional portfolio. Rubrics and models are provided to scaffold learners' efforts in this e-learning evaluation course, but there are multiple more or less successful outcomes.

Putting the e-learning evaluation course online has opened the course up to learners from around the world, and the course has attracted learners from Australia, Canada, Europe, and South Africa as well as the USA. Widely dispersed, the students work in virtual teams to accomplish the authentic tasks of planning, conducting, and reporting an e-learning evaluation. The evaluation clients are also widely distributed, and none of them are co-located with the learners in the course. This e-learning evaluation online course is implemented asynchronously mode using the open-access course management system Moodle (http://www.moodle.org).

Although this e-learning evaluation course is intended for graduate students, there are other examples of similar authentic task-based courses for undergraduates. For example, Herrington et al. (2006) describe:

- a humanities course about American Film and Fiction in which students edit a real journal that reports their analyses of the relevant literature and film,
- a business communication skills course in which students are "hired" at a virtual communications company where they carry out realistic tasks for a virtual employer, and
- an ecology course in which students prepare a report of the environmental impact of a new marina based on real world data.

CONCLUSION

There are many creative ways to design high quality authentic tasks for GenMe learners. Web 2.0 innovations such as podcasts, wikis, and social networking sites will surely have a role, but revolutionary pedagogy is required far more than new software and communication tools. Exemplary examples of higher education learning environments that incorporate many of the learning design principles outlined above can be found on our authentic tasks research project website (http://www.authentictasks.uow.edu.au/). Of course, the form and nature of the tasks will vary considerably between learning environments depending on the learning outcomes being sought.

Despite the intuitive appeal of authentic learning environments, and the considerable evidence that they are effective in promoting higher order learning (Herrington, Reeves, & Oliver, 2007), these learning environments often appear too complex to instructors who seek to design and to implement alternative approaches in their teaching. We believe that the solution to the promotion and support of authentic learning tasks can be found by enhancing their accessibility and visibility, two factors strongly influenced by the availability of appropriate representations of these learning designs. In addition, more and better research is needed. Instead of worrying about whether GenMe will learn more from virtual reality games or online communities, instructional designers and educational technology researchers should work closely with instructors and subject matter experts to identify the needs of GenMe learners, design the best possible prototype learning environments *in situ*, and then conduct iterative cycles of formative evaluation and refinement to optimize the solution and reveal ever more-refined design principles. These are the features of "design research" (Reeves, 2006).

One thing is clear. Adopting Web 2.0 technologies to serve out-dated instructional methods is sure to fail. Direct instruction of the kind advocated by Kirschner, Sweller, and Clark (2006) will not be sufficient with GenMe learners. The solution proposed by Kirschner et al. (2006) is to provide 'information that fully explains the concepts and procedures that students are required to learn' (p. 75). Bransford, Brown, and Cocking (2000) demonstrate clearly that superficial coverage of concepts and an over-emphasis on the teaching of facts occurs far too much in all levels of education, including universities. University instructors often focus more on covering content found in textbooks or embedded in classroom lectures than on learning. They primarily aim to present students with numerous facts and predictable textbook problems, and rarely attempt to engage students in the tasks involving complex, ill-structured problems of the kind encountered in the real world. This has not worked well with previous generations of students, and it surely won't work with GenMe learners.

REFERENCES

Anderson, C. A., & Bushman, B. J. (2001). Effects of violent video games on aggressive behavior, aggressive cognition, aggressive affect, physiological arousal, and prosocial behavior: A meta-analytic review of the scientific literature. *Psychological Science*, *12*, 353–359. doi:10.1111/1467-9280.00366

Anderson, L. W. (Ed.). Krathwohl, D.R. (Ed.), Airasian, P.W., Cruikshank, K.A., Mayer, R.E., Pintrich, P.R., Raths, J., & Wittrock, M.C. (2001). *A taxonomy for learning, teaching, and assessing: A revision of Bloom's Taxonomy of Educational Objectives* (Complete edition). New York: Longman.

Barab, S. A., Squire, K. D., & Dueber, W. (2000). A co-evolutionary model for supporting the emergence of authenticity. *Educational Technology Research and Development*, *48*(2), 37–62. doi:10.1007/BF02313400

Bauerline, M. (2008). *The dumbest generation: How the digital age stupefies young Americans and jeopardizes our future*. New York: Tarcher/Penguin.

Beck, J. C., & Wade, M. (2004). *Got game: How the gamer generation is reshaping business forever*. Boston, MA: Harvard Business School Press.

Beedle, J. B. (2004). *What educators can learn from multiplayer computer gaming: A study of who is playing and their perceptions of learning*. Dissertations Abstracts International, AAT 3155858.

Bensley, L., & Eenwyk, J. (2001). Video games and real-life aggression: Review of the literature. *The Journal of Adolescent Health*, *29*, 244–257. doi:10.1016/S1054-139X(01)00239-7

Bloom, B. S. (Ed.). Engelhart, M. D., Furst, E. J., Hill, W. H., & Krathwohl, D. R. (1956). *Taxonomy of educational objectives: The classification of educational goals. Handbook 1: Cognitive domain*. New York: David McKay.

Bransford, J. D., Brown, A. L., & Cocking, R. R. (2000). *How people learn: Brain, mind, experience, and schoo*l. Washington, D.C.: National Academy Press.

Bransford, J. D., Vye, N., Kinzer, C., & Risko, V. (1990). Teaching thinking and content knowledge: Toward an integrated approach. In B.F. Jones & L. Idol (Eds.), *Dimensions of thinking and cognitive instruction* (pp. 381-413). Hillsdale, NJ: Lawrence Erlbaum Associates.

Breivik, P. S. (2005, March/April). 21st century learning and information literacy. *Change*, *37*(2), 20–27. doi:10.3200/CHNG.37.2.21-27

Brown, J. S., Collins, A., & Duguid, P. (1989). Situated cognition and the culture of learning. *Educational Researcher*, *18*(1), 32–42.

Brown, J. S., & Duguid, P. (2000). *The social life of information*. Cambridge, MA: Harvard Business School Press.

Cassell, J., & Jenkins, H. (1998). *From Barbie to Mortal Kombat: Gender and computer games*. Cambridge, MA: MIT Press.

CEO Forum on Education and Technology. (2001). *Student achievement in the 21st Century. Assessment, alignment, accountability, access, analysis.* Retrieved February 12, 2009, http://www.ceoforum.org/

Cognition and Technology Group at Vanderbilt. (1990). Anchored instruction and its relationship to situated cognition. *Educational Researcher*, *19*(6), 2–10.

Committee on Science. Engineering, and Public Policy. (2006). *Rising above the gathering storm: Energizing and employing America for a brighter economic future*. Washington, DC: National Academies Press. Retrieved June 8, 2006, from http://www.nap.edu/books/0309100399/html

Duchastel, P. (1997). A web-based model for university instruction. *Journal of Educational Technology Systems*, *25*, 221–228. doi:10.2190/UFF9-KB1X-NGG4-UHKL

Friedman, T. (2008). *Hot, flat, and crowded: Why we need a green revolution--and how it can renew America*. New York: Farrar, Straus and Giroux.

Gee, J. P. (2003). *What video games have to teach us about learning and literacy*. New York: Palgrave Macmillan.

Gentile, D. A., & Anderson, C. A. (2003). Violent video games: The newest media violence hazard. In D. A. Gentile (Ed.), *Media violence and children* (pp. 131-152). Westport, CT: Praeger Publishing.

Gordon, R. (1998). Balancing real-world problems with real-world results. *Phi Delta Kappan*, *79*, 390–393.

Greenfield, P. M., & Cocking, R. R. (1996). *Interacting with video*. Norwood, NJ: Ablex.

Griffiths, M. D., Davies, M. N. O., & Chappell, D. (2003). Breaking the stereotype: The case of online gaming. *Cyberpsychology & Behavior*, *6*, 81–91. doi:10.1089/109493103321167992

Harrow, A. J. (1972). *A taxonomy of the psychomotor domain: A guide for developing behavioral objectives*. New York: David McKay.

Herrington, J., & Herrington, A. (1998). Authentic assessment and multimedia: How university students respond to a model of authentic assessment. *Higher Education Research & Development*, *17*(3), 305–322. doi:10.1080/0729436980170304

Herrington, J., Reeves, T. C., & Oliver, R. (2006). A model of authentic activities for online learning. In C. Juwah (Ed.), *Interactions in online learning: Implications for theory and practice* (pp. 91-103). New York: Routledge.

Herrington, J., Reeves, T. C., & Oliver, R. (2007). Immersive learning technologies: Realism and online authentic learning. *Journal of Computing in Higher Education*, *19*(1), 65–84. doi:10.1007/BF03033421

Herrington, J., Reeves, T. C., Oliver, R., & Woo, Y. (2004). Designing authentic activities in web-based courses. *Journal of Computing in Higher Education*, *16*(1), 3–29. doi:10.1007/BF02960280

Hersh, R. H., & Merrow, J. (Eds.). (2005). *Declining by degrees: Higher education at risk*. New York: Palgrave Macmillan.

Howe, N., & Strauss, W. (2000). *Millennials rising: The next great generation*. New York: Vintage Books.

Jacoby, B. (1996). *Service-learning in higher education: Concepts and practices*. San Francisco: Jossey-Bass.

Jonassen, D. (2000). Toward a design theory of problem solving. *Educational Technology Research and Development*, *48*(4), 63–85. doi:10.1007/BF02300500

Karpinski, A. C., & Duberstein, A. (2009, April). *A description of Facebook use and academic performance among undergraduate and graduate students*. Paper presented at the Annual Meeting of the American Educational Research Association, San Diego, CA. Retrieved April 18, 2009, from http://www.aera.net/

Kennedy, G. E., Judd, T. S., Churchward, A., Gray, K., & Krause, K. (2008). First year students' experience with technology: Are they really digital natives? *Australian Journal of Educational Technology, 24*(1), 108–122.

Kirschner, P. A., Sweller, J., & Clark, R. E. (2006). Why minimal guidance during instruction does not work: An analysis of the failure of constructivist, discovery, problem-based, experiential, and inquiry-based teaching. *Educational Psychologist, 41*(2), 75–86. doi:10.1207/s15326985ep4102_1

Kolbe, K. (1990). *The conative connection: Acting on instinct*. Reading, MA: Addison-Wesley.

Krathwohl, D. R., Bloom, B. S., & Masia, B. B. (1964). *Taxonomy of educational objectives: The classification of educational goals, handbook II: The affective domain*. New York: David McKay.

Kuh, G. D. (2003). What we're learning about student engagement from NSSE. *Change, 35*(2), 24–32.

Kuh, G. D., Laird, T. N., & Umbach, P. (2004). Aligning faculty activities and student behavior: Realizing the promise of greater expectations. *Liberal Education, 90*(4), 24–31.

Lebow, D., & Wager, W. W. (1994). Authentic activity as a model for appropriate learning activity: Implications for emerging instructional technologies. *Canadian Journal of Educational Communication, 23*(3), 231–144.

Mitchell, A., & Savill-Smith, C. (2004). *The use of computer and video games for learning: A review of the literature*. London: Learning and Skills Development Agency.

Oblinger, D., & Oblinger, J. (Eds.). (2005). *Educating the Net generation*. Washington, DC: EDUCAUSE.

Owen, M. (2004). *The myth of the digital native*. Retrieved February 10, 2009, from http://www.futurelab.org.uk/resources/publications-reports-articles/web-articles/Web-Article561

Postman, N. (2003). Questioning media. In M. S. Pittinsky (Ed.), *The wired tower: Perspectives on the impact of the internet on higher education* (pp.181-200). Upper Saddle River, NJ: Prentice Hall.

Prensky, M. (2001a). Digital natives, digital immigrants. *On the Horizon, 9*(5). Retrieved January 11, 2006, from http://www.marcprensky.com/writing/

Prensky, M. (2001b). Digital natives, digital immigrants, part II: Do they really think differently? *On the Horizon, 9*(6). Retrieved January 11, 2006, from http://www.marcprensky.com/writing/

Prensky, M. (2006). *Don't bother me, mom – I'm learning: How computer and video games are preparing your kids for twenty-first century success*. St. Paul, MN: Paragon House.

Prensky, M. (2009). H. sapiens digital: From digital immigrants and digital natives to digital wisdom. *Innovate: Journal of Online Education, 5*(3). Retrieved February 12, 2009, from http://www.innovateonline.info

Reeves, T. C. (2006). How do you know they are learning?: The importance of alignment in higher education. *International Journal of Learning Technology, 2*(4), 294–309. doi:10.1504/IJLT.2006.011336

Reeves, T. C., & Oh, E. J. (2007). Generation differences and educational technology research. In J. M. Spector, M. D. Merrill, J. J. G. van Merriënboer, & M. Driscoll. (Eds.) *Handbook of research on educational communications and technology* (pp. 295-303). Mahwah, NJ: Lawrence Erlbaum Associates.

Salonius-Pasternak, D. E., & Gelfond, H. S. (2005). The next level of research on electronic play: Potential benefits and contextual influences for children and adolescents. *Human Technology, 1*(1), 5–22.

Salpeter, J. (2003). 21st century skills: Will our students be prepared? *Technology & Learning, 24*(3), 17–26.

Secretary's Commission on Achieving Necessary Skills. (1991). *What work requires of schools: A SCANS report for America 2000*. Washington, DC: Government Printing Office. Retrieved January 11, 2009, from http://wdr.doleta.gov/SCANS/

Sherry, J. L. (2001). The effects of violent video games on aggression: A meta-analysis. *Human Communication Research, 27*, 409–431.

Slator, B. M., & Associates. (2006). *Electric worlds in the classroom: Teaching and learning with role-based computer games*. New York: Teachers College Press.

Smith, P. E. (1987). Simulating the classroom with media and computers. *Simulation & Games, 18*(3), 395–413. doi:10.1177/104687818701800306

Snow, R. E., Corno, L., & Jackson, D. (1996). Individual differences in affective and conative functions. In D. C. Berliner & R. C. Calfee (Eds.), *Handbook of educational psychology* (pp. 243-310). New York: Macmillan.

Squire, K., & Jenkins, H. (2004). Harnessing the power of games in education. *Insight (American Society of Ophthalmic Registered Nurses), 3*(1), 5–33.

Steinkuehler, C. A. (2008). Cognition and literacy in massively multiplayer online games. In J. Coiro, M. Knobel, C. Lankshear, & D. Leu (Eds.), *Handbook of Research on New Literacies* (pp. 611-634). Mahwah NJ: Erlbaum.

Tapscott, D. (2008). *Grown up digital: How the net generation is changing your world*. New York: McGraw-Hill.

Twenge, J. M. (2006). *Generation me: Why today's young Americans are more confident, assertive, entitled -- and more miserable than ever before*. New York: Free Press.

VanDeventer, S. S., & White, J. A. (2002). Expert behavior in children's video game play. *Simulation & Gaming, 33*(1), 28–28. doi:10.1177/1046878102033001002

VanSlyke, T. (2003, May/June). Digital natives, digital immigrants: Some thoughts from the generation gap. *The Technology Source*. Retrieved February 12, 2009, from http://technologysource.org/?view=article&id=77

Wolf, M. J. P., & Perron, B. (Eds.). (2003). *The video game theory reader*. New York: Routledge.

Young, M. F. (1993). Instructional design for situated learning. *Educational Technology Research and Development, 41*(1), 43–58. doi:10.1007/BF02297091

Section 5
Learning Technologies

Section 5.1
Mobile Learning

Chapter 13
Mobile Learning:
Didactical Scenarios in the Context of Learning on the Job

Sandro Mengel
University of Dortmund, Germany

Maciej Kuszpa
University of Hagen, Germany

Claudia de Witt
University of Hagen, Germany

ABSTRACT

Mobile learning extends the media dissemination of knowledge and learning in extremely varying educational contexts with mobility and independence of location. The chapter describes possibilities of mobile learning for situation-oriented, personalised and collaborative learning. It explains on the one hand existing conceptions and application scenarios with regard to learning theory backgrounds, and on the other thematises possibilities of Web 2.0 for mobile learning. In doing this, it presents in particular didactical scenarios for mobile learning situations in the context of learning on the job.

1 INTRODUCTION

As a result of the rapid technological developments of mobile communication technologies, but also as a result of the great distribution in everyday life of mobile devices such as mobile phones, smartphones and PDAs which now have almost the computer capacity of PCs, the next step in multimedia learning is predestined. Learning with the help of mobile devices (mobile learning) will gain considerable importance if this medium is used as an additional channel for deepening and extending educational content within existing blended learning arrangements. Because of the independence from a location and the mobility, the user has individually significant information available in his respective situation. He uses mobile devices without restrictions as to space and time, and uses the devices flexibly to gain qualifications, e.g. directly at the workplace. Information is therefore adapted to individual use and learning needs, and linked to this is a personalisation of information. Mobile learning conceptions refer to learning users with situation-based problems who recognise their learning targets and

DOI: 10.4018/978-1-61520-678-0.ch013

learning needs, and want to work through their own knowledge deficiencies as quickly as possibly. Mobile learning scenarios are not limited just to the dissemination of knowledge, or the presentation of teaching materials, but also comprise the interaction, communication and collaboration of all participants in the teaching/learning process. Mobile learning will differ from e-learning on the one hand through the characteristics of the location-independent devices, and on the other through new didactic scenarios. Therefore the chapter introduces into technical features and didactical settings with mobile devices, differentiates in this context mobile and e-learning. According to the perspective of lifelong learning, learning on the job becomes an important context of mobile learning. Against this background relevant didactical conceptions are presented, potentials of Web 2.0 applications, of mobile communication and of mobile internet are explained for mobile learning on the job. Finally didactical scenarios of mobile learning in different situations of learning on the job are described.

2 MOBILE LEARNING

If we look at the subject of 'mobile learning' (also: mobile computer-based learning, m-learning, mobile education, m-education, ubiquitous learning or microlearning), two different aspects have to be taken into account. The term 'mobile' illuminates the technological and the term 'learning' the didactical side of the aspect. The word 'mobile' can be assigned initially to the area of 'mobile communication'. Mobile communication is used to describe in general individual, group and mass communication that take place via portable, wire-bound and wireless devices (cf. Schiller, 2003).

2.1 Mobile Devices and Technical Features

On the technological level, mobile communication is based on specific devices, networks, services and applications. Because of its spread, mobile communication in the private field is based mainly on the mobile phone (smartphone) as the device, and at work on handheld device groups (also: PDA - Personal Digital Assistant or pocket PC) and portable computers such as (mini-)notebooks or tablet PCs (cf. Döring, 2008). In addition, there are the new e-book readers (e.g. Kindle from amazon.de). With these A5-size devices, which weigh about 250 g and were optimised specifically for reader-friendliness, books, texts and articles which have been put into electronic format can be downloaded in seconds to the reader, read and edited. The scope of functions of these e-book readers includes a text-to-speech function, which reads out books or websites automatically to headphones and in general enables audio files in MP3 format to be played (e.g. audio books and podcasts). The current appliance generations of so-called mini-notebooks, also known as netbooks or subnotebooks, can also be included among mobile devices, depending on their technical equipment. Their strengths for mobile learning are found in the relatively large display (8"-10"), the low total weight and the low total size, the computing output, which is sufficient for a PC, and the existing full-scale keypad. The long battery life, in comparison with traditional notebooks, of up to 6 hours, and integrated UMTS/HSDPA modems for wireless internet access, contribute somewhat to the factor 'mobility'. The development of netbooks which will satisfy even more the essential criterion of 'immediacy', in the sense of availability for mobile learning, is expected for the near future.

The media 'walkman' and 'newspaper', for example, do not count as mobile communication. While it is true that they can be used independently of a location, they do not have any technical interface to a communications network. Even the simple networking of several stationary desktop computers via a wireless connection (e.g. WLAN) is not counted as mobile communication (cf. Döring & Dietmar, 2005). According to Döring and Dietmar (ibid.), mobile communication devices (mobile devices) have in particular the following features:

- small size (in the optimum case palm-sized)
- low weight
- independence from power sources
- portable use, independent of location and time
- interface with a data or communication network.

Apart from the basic functions (telephony, SMS, address book, etc.), individual devices do in fact differ through the scope of functions (e.g. photo/film camera, media player, navigation system) and the capacity (e.g. memory size, processor output), but, for example, smartphones or PDAs are increasingly approaching the functional scope of a portable computer in their technical development (cf. Döring, 2005).[1] However, an existing zoom function for enlarging the display of content is now part of the basic equipment of most smartphones or PDAs.

Fundamentally, mobile devices have a whole bundle of very different computer, web and communication technologies which can be used for mobile learning as with e-learning. These technologies enable digital data to be shown, stored, processed and transmitted in standard platform-overlapping file formats which can be used for teaching and learning as well (e.g. HTML, PDF, DOC, JPEG, MP3, SWF, MPEG4). Internet pages for browsing during the search for information can be displayed by means of existing web technologies. Students and teachers can download/upload content, or exchange it with one another. In educational practice these may be files with learning content in the form of texts or presentations, images or graphics, as well as audio or video podcasts in collaborative and/or social networks. Those taking part in learning can communicate directly and interact with each other via email, chat rooms, web forums, moblog (weblog which is used from mobile devices and filled with contributions, e.g. moblog.net), SMS or (video-)telephony. Depending on the model, the devices are operated via an integrated keypad or a touch-sensitive screen (touch screen) that can be used with fingers or a pen. For space-saving reasons, touch screen operating appears to be gaining in popularity with regard to comfort and user-friendliness, e.g. the Apple iPhone. In the optimal case, a mobile phone has both a touch screen and a full-value writing keypad (e.g. the Google G1 mobile phone), which can be slid out when required, to save space, for the more comfortable input of email text. Put simply, the technical infrastructure for the above-mentioned applications is formed by the mobile device with corresponding technical and software-based equipment on the user side, and various servers, communication services and content-filled databases on the part of the education provider. Along with the handiness of the devices, above all user-friendly software equipment is decisive on the user or learner side for the acceptance and learning success of, and with, mobile learning.

Table 1 provides an overview of the essential technical features and tools of currently available mobile device generations that can also be used for mobile learning:

As an explanation for this figure it should be said in supplement that not all devices necessarily have all the functionalities. The figure shows an overview of available technologies with regard to the wireless technologies shown, whereby their difference is found mainly in the speed of data transmission, which may influence the functionality of individual education offers.

Not shown, but part of the technical features, are the different available operating systems for the devices. The operating system landscape is

Table 1. Overview of the technical equipment of mobile devices for didactical conceptions (Mengel, 2009)

Data processing and display		
Media formats	**Symbol systems**	**Applications**
Documents (HTML, EMAIL, PDF, DOC) Photos (JPEG) Videos (SWF, MPEG4) Audio files (MP3)	Text Image Graphics Sound	*Via software* Reading, writing, observing, listening, playing, recording, processing, saving, transmitting *Via photo camera* Photographing Video recording Barcode scanning *Via microphone or loudspeaker* Audio recording and playback
Communication and data exchange		
Wireless technologies		**Applications**
GSM/GPRS UMTS/HSDPA WLAN Bluetooth GPS		Network/internet access Data transfer/synchronisation Email transmission SMS/MMS transmission Textchat/microblogging Discussion forums (Video) telephony Speech transmission Topographical navigation Localising/position fixing
Wired technologies		**Applications**
USB Memory cards (SD/MicroSD)		Data transfer/synchronisation Data storage

very heterogeneous (Windows Mobile, Symbian, Blackberry RIM, Apple OS X or Android). The result is that it is difficult for software developers to produce platform-overlapping applications which can be run on all devices. With regard to compliance with general usability criteria, and depending on the technical equipment of the mobile devices, some other factors represent a challenge in the development and design of software or web-based learning applications which have to be taken into account:

- small screen
- limited input possibilities
- limited output
- limited memory
- limited possibilities for representing visual information
- limited bandwidths for the network interface (cf. Döring, 2008).

Along with the small screen, the limited input possibilities in particular are a hindrance. Text-based communication processes and typing long sentences on the small and mostly limited keypads may prove to be cumbersome for mobile learning. It remains interesting to see what the manufacturers of mobile devices will come up with in future for the effective use of the limited available space. However, the current input facilities are fully sufficient for short texts or messages in text chats, or in microblogging (e.g. in twitter.com). Further optimisation will probably also result through the behaviour of users who, for example, will make increasing use of speech-based communication with mobile devices.

2.2 Learning with Mobile Devices

The decisive advantage of mobile devices is that users are enable to access available information independently of location and time that refers specifically to their own situation and can be requested 'just' when it is required. It seems obvious that this information function in the interplay with mobile communication will make mobile devices interesting for teaching and learning as well (cf. Nösekabel, 2005; cf. Döring, 2005).

In common with e-learning, the learning form of mobile learning has the technological support of learning processes through information and communication technologies. However, in e-learning learners usually sit at stationary wired PCs, whereas in m-learning learners can move around in real-world contexts with their portable devices, independent of the location. Through the extended context of mobility, mobile learning could also be regarded as a specialisation of e-learning, because the main difference is to be found here, along with the technical properties of the devices used. However, this in fact creates the necessity of an adjustment of already existing learning theory approaches and models (cf. Nösekabel, 2005). Mobile learning is not to be understood (exclusively) as the transmission of e-learning on mobile devices, but, in comparison with computers or laptops as well, innovative functionalities of mobile devices, as described in the previous section, should be taken into account.

If learning and the acquisition of knowledge are regarded as a process in which knowledge-relevant information is obtained by learners, processed and classified in existing prior knowledge as a gain in understanding, the following exemplary learning situation can be imagined in which a learning process takes place at the simplest level: students are sitting together at lunch in the canteen and discussing the theory of evolution, which is relevant to their examinations. None of those present can remember the name of the developer of this theory. However, one of them mentions the possibility of checking briefly in an online knowledge database. Countless typical learning situations of this type exist in all conceivable subject areas, including those from the world of work.

The difference between m- and e-learning can be explained very simply at this point. To exaggerate, a learning participant in this situation, provided he has a mobile device with an internet connection, and also wants to fill the gap in his knowledge, will look up the name of the evolution theoretician online using the mobile device and will thus acquire the desired factual knowledge immediately and directly; on the other hand, if he has a notebook, even if he has it with him, he will probably not look the name up, because the time required before the notebook is ready for operation for this concrete and random learning situation is too long in comparison.

But where is the foundation for this assumption? In contrast to a notebook people nearly always have a mobile phone or smartphone with them, and this is usually ready for use immediately after being taken out of the pocket. This would bring us back to the factor of extended mobility, which also reduces the learner's path to the required information or knowledge because of the low threshold. In learning pro-cesses in which the respective knowledge is to be filtered deliberately from data networks on demand and just in time as a knowledge module, mobile learning using 'stationary' devices is more direct, more in real time, than e-learning. The factor of the differentiated learning situation must be emphasised at this point.

The differences between mobile learning and e-learning can be summarised as follows:

- Mobile devices enable a more time- and location-independent access to information and knowledge (theoretically, e-learning offers can also be used by means of mobile devices).
- Mobile learning is suitable for other learning situations which arise from the learner's

situative context. Information and knowledge can be retrieved more directly and in a timely manner.

- Mobile learning is more suitable in particular for imparting small, manageable knowledge units (e.g. factual knowledge) than for imparting complex knowledge contents (e.g. differences between learning theory currents).
- Mobile learning takes place in different didactical settings (e.g. situated or informal learning).

Various definitions of mobile learning can be found in the literature, though these are kept as general as possible, for example: "the ability to receive learning anytime, anywhere and on any device" (Chabra & Figueiredo, 2001). Along with the mobility, other definitions stress the technological support of learning: "m-learning is learning that can take place anytime, anywhere with the help of a mobile computer device" (Dye, Odingo & Solstad, 2003). Other versions are based on the understanding of Georgiev, Georgieva and Smrikarov (2004): "m-learning must include the ability to learn everywhere at every time without permanent physical connection to cable networks".

When the mobility of the learning location is taken into account, the focus lies in particular on the exclusive consideration of smaller devices such as mobile telephones, smartphones and PDAs. In this context, devices with a comparably larger size, such as laptops or notebooks, are deliberately not considered. The reason for this limitation is based on the consideration that, in comparison with mobile communication devices, far fewer portable personal computers (PCs) have a facility for data transmission via the internet without restriction, i.e. at all times and everywhere.

The definition of Nösekabel is the most precisely formulated one that can currently be found in the relevant literature and also contains a demarcation to e-learning. It is true that he uses the term 'mobile education' in his definition, but this can be understood as synonymous with 'mobile learning' (Nösekabel, 2005, p. 121): "Mobile education is the use of non-situation changing mobile (not necessarily wireless) technologies and devices through which teachers and learners can access electronic services independently of place and time for the purposes of teaching (mobile teaching), learning (mobile learning) or the administrative support of learning processes (mobile administration). Mobile education is a subspecies of e-learning, but, because of the technical limitations of the devices and the mobile use conception, requires an adjustment of the existing didactical conceptions, through which the advantages of mobility are used for the activities that are aimed for." The description 'non-situation changing' conditionally excludes notebooks or similar devices for mobile learning, because these are not always directly available in the learner's situative context or in the learning process. In contrast, MP3 players (e.g. Apple iPod) and future developments are included in Nösekabel's definition.

Nösekabel's definition can be currently extended further or defused by the consideration of including the generation of e-book readers and netbooks in mobile learning, because these also satisfy the criterion of 'non-situation changing' because of their small size and low weight, their independence of power sources and their permanent network connection.

If the didactical side is examined, a series of different methodological-didactical targets can be aimed for in the direct situative context of the learner in mobile learning, that is, learning which is independent of location and time (cf. Döring, 2005):

- PDAs and mobile phones can be used for telemobility and location-independent learning. The portable and networked device can serve as a source of information (e.g. navigation, access to knowledge

databases), a communication medium (e.g. collaborative exchange with other learners) and as a cognitive tool (production and exchange of notes, photos, videos or mind maps, etc.), e.g. on excursions or working processes in the real world.
- Mobile learning can be used for lifelong learning in so-called 'idle times' (e.g. waiting times), if suitable learning applications are structured and divided into short 5-minute learning units. For example, health education programmes are possible that provide regular instructions on taking medication, diet or health care via text messages to mobile phones.
- Mobile learning is suitable for reaching persons for learning processes who are unable to take part in formal education processes for reasons of time.

With regard to the potentials that Döring worked out it may be added that today there are more mobile phones or smartphones which are far more integrated in people's everyday lives than notebooks, for example. Accordingly, the use of mobile devices is taken for granted and has a greater nexus to everyday life. These points are also among the potentials which are to be exhausted for mobile learning scenarios.

However, a further consideration in learning in mobile environments has to be directed at the tendency towards fragmentary knowledge. In mobile learning, learning processes frequently take place in short disparate phases (30 seconds to 10 minutes) and requires well-trained concentration and reflection skills. The situations in which learning is done *on the fly* are really not suitable for memorising knowledge on a long-term basis and anchoring it in the memory. And in many cases the distractions during rail journeys or waiting periods are too great. Often, the abundance of information cannot be processed into significant knowledge because of a lack of time or because of limits to cognitive efficiency. For this reason, learners in mobile working and learning environments should be guided and supported by teachers as coordinators or facilitators (cf. Döring & Dietmar, 2005). In addition, configuration tips for the general KISS (keep it simple, stupid) approach can be derived from these framework conditions that apply to the so-called mobile internet but which can be transferred to mobile learning applications as well (cf. Chincholle, 2003).

2.3 Learning Theory Approaches for Mobile Learning

The use of (mobile) information and communication technologies for vocational training and further training requires a notion of this and an understanding of how learning functions. Within learning psychology there are different trends that have compiled their perceptions into learning theories and that are then included as the basis for computer- and technology-supported teaching/learning media. The understanding of the definition of learning is very much informed by the underlying learning theory. The three learning theory directions that have decisively characterised teaching and learning with new media are the *behaviourist*, the *cognitive* and the *constructivist learning theories*. Up to the present day, these three theories have had different effects on teaching and learning with digital media and in mobile learning (cf. Kerres, 2001; Kerres & de Witt, 2004; O'Malley & Vavoula et al., 2005). Constructivism is regarded here as the antithesis to behaviourism and cognitivism. For the advocates of the current approaches, which are adjudged as constructivism, it is important to offer learners the possibility of an active involvement with learning contents, which are prepared appropriately and adequately with regard to individual learning ability and content-related structure. With constructivist-oriented learning processes with more complex demands, communication between teachers and learners in mobile learning by means of mobile devices, for example, can be placed in the foreground. When a mobile learning application is designed on the basis of more behaviourist principles, learning contents would be subdivided into small sections and processed structurally. These can then be stored in the mobile device's memory and learners can then work through them on a task-oriented basis. Learning success is then tested by answering questions (e.g. multiple choice). An advanced flexibility of the learning process is achieved through the location-independent use of the mobile devices. (cf. Nösekabel, 2005). In both e-learning and m-learning the individual learning theories may not be seen as independent approaches, but should be treated as complementing each other. When mobile learning courses in vocational training and further training are being designed, the findings of the various knowledge and learning theories can be applied in different sub-areas depending on the target group and the learning goal. The situative conditions of the work processes in which the learners find themselves are crucial here.

3 MOBILE LEARNING AND LEARNING ON THE JOB

If mobile learning should be established in situations on the job, thinking about didactical settings have to be made in the run-up. Didactical scenarios should be designed orientated by the work processes of their respective industry focus on the one hand and by the basis of learning theory approaches on the other hand. Such conceptions have to be chosen which profits from the application of mobile technologies and does justice to the characteristics of mobile teaching and learning:

- Control and flexibility of the learner
- Relevance of the situation with regard to knowledge acquisition
- Computer technical support of the learning process

Mobile devices can be used independently from location and time by the user. As a consequence the user possesses control over the device and therefore over the flexible use for his qualification according to his workplace. This spatial flexibility allows teacher and learner as well to choose learning place and learning situation independend from technical limits. Thus conceptions based on situation oriented learning processes are significant for mobile learning conceptions (e.g. 'situated learning'). Mobile learning scenarios are not limited to instructions of knowledge or presentation of produced teaching materials but includes interaction, communication and cooperation (cf. Nösekabel, 2005, p. 11). These qualities are the basics of the didactical scenarios in mobile learning described in the following chapters.

3.1 Lifelong Learning and Learning on the Job

The conception of lifelong learning in Germany comes to the fore since 1995. In consequence of the requirements in a constantly changing society and of new working conditions abilities for lifelong learning get decisive competencies to cope with life in future. Lifelong learning is a conception to enable people to learn not for customizing to requirements in job life, but to learn because of individual and social reasons. Learning then takes place in different environments within as well as beyond formal education systems. So the concentration of situative learning in live and operation contexts is the didactical consequence for the future conditions of lifelong learning (cf. Höfling & Mandl, 1997, pp. 9; cf. BMBF, 2006). New knowledge and skills have to be developed self directed dependently on individual or situate necessity. The increase of knowledge and skills is a lifelong process which challenges the individuals to filter selective their knowledge as components 'on demand' from information worldwide stored in literature and data networks, with the aim to apply the new constructs of knowledge flexible and constructive for coping with current problems and challenges (cf. Dohmen, 1998; cf. Mayer, 2004).

For Nuissl von Rein some requirements and consequences result from this described development which have to be taken into account for the arrangement of vocational (further) learning products and for the support of lifelong, self directed learning.:

- Working and learning have to take place simultaneously.
- The learner can choose self-determined learning content relevant for his context.
- Qualification has to take place ad hoc (just in time) (cf. Nuissl von Rein, 2000).

Lifelong learning includes all formal and non-formal learning processes which need suitable new forms of teaching and learning. Consequently vocational education has to be conformed to the needs of lifelong learning. Knowledge becomes more quickly obsolete and the continuous reduction of the half-life of knowledge makes a situated and just-in-time qualification of apprentices and employees necessary. This fact demands self-directed and working place oriented processes of learning for this target group of an organisation or a company. Learning and working fall into place. Learning on the job demands therefore learner who are able to search for informations and knowledge directly in the process of their work and who acquire – at the same time integrated in a learning process – practice oriented knowledge (cf. Reinmann-Rothmeier & Mandl, 1998; cf. Probst et al., 2003; cf. BMBF, 2007). Learning situations are needed which – under the perspective of self-directed learning – offer such possibilities of learning to gain information and knowledge promptly and if required (cf. Thissen, 2005).

To allocate important knowledge at any time, at any place and for everybody and to comprehend quickly the necessary processes of accommodation and change the introduction of e-learning and technologies for information and communication in the last few years are becoming self-evident for vocational qualification. E-learning support processes of self-directed learning autonoumsly arranged from the learner (cf. Neubauer, 2002). It is seen as an effective possibility to supply the needs of lifelong and self-directed learning. Comparable potentials are also seen for mobile learning. However, the enhanced portability of the lower seized devices and the permanent access to the mobile internet will augmented the potentials of use and of self-direction in learning processes, not at least by an use more independent from location and time than in e-learning scenarios.

3.2 Didactical Conceptions for Mobile Learning on the Job

In the relevant literature and the internet sources some learning conceptions are taking shape that in the last few years have already been taken up in e-learning or vocational training in practice and that also possess potential for use in mobile learning scenarios. Depending on the learning targets and the subject area, these learning forms are suitable for specific, self-regulated and concrete learning situations and are located in moderately constructivistically oriented didactics. They fit equally into the approaches of *activity-oriented learning* and of *learning at the workplace*. These approaches of activity-oriented learning and of learning at the workplace, in which the acquisition of a capability for decision-making and responsibility is in the foreground, and which are particularly esteemed in vocational training, are closely linked to one another in the basic principles. Both models start from the principles of authenticity, situatedness and social embeddedness, and both models aim for the integration of working and learning, i.e. working and learning processes take place parallel (cf. BMBF, 2007).

Situated Learning

Situated learning is attributed to the constructivist learning approach and means action processes in social learning situations in which knowledge is reconstructed in each situation. Knowledge is always created through an active construction process on the part of the learner (cf. Mandl, Gruber & Renkl, 2002; cf. Schulmeister, 2001). The approaches to situated learning stress the representation of complex social reality instead of abstract contents and authentic activities by learners instead of activities by teachers in problem situations. They are characterised not only through their taking account of the situatedness of learning processes, but also by a marked problem orientation (see *problem-based learning* as well). The active solving of complex problems is intended to improve the application quality of the knowledge. Through the contextualising of the learning contents in realistic situations a connection is made to the everyday experiences of the learners and to the application. The focus is in imparting the capability for decision-making and responsibility (cf. de Witt & Czerwionka, 2007, p. 61-68). Situated learning represents the distinctive feature of constructivist instruction and is important for the development of media learning environments and scenarios (cf. Mandl et al., 2002). Situated learning is not only suitable for e-learning, but with the advantage of extended location independence is also predestined for mobile learning.

Problem-Based Learning

The terms 'problem-based' learning (PBL), or 'problem-centred' or 'problem-oriented' learning, describe a learning conception that confronts learners, as in situated learning, with authentic or comparable problems from, for example, their occupational or working lives. Reinmann-Rothmeier and Mandl see PBL as a moderately constructivist conception, in which there is a practical combination of constructivist elements with traditional components of imparting knowledge. This means that it implies as a middle way the compatibility of instruction and construction (cf. Reinmann-Rothmeier & Mandl, 1998). According to this, problem-based learning is an active, self-regulated, constructive, situative and social process, which always takes place in specific contexts, e.g. in the direct context of working processes in occupational practice. The demarcation of PBL as against situated, project- or activity-oriented learning conceptions is "more gradual, i.e. it is merely a displacement of the accentuation to group-borne learning experience in working out solutions for more complex problems" (Hoffmann, 2004, p. 245). It is also a gradually developed cooperative learning form, which includes in addition a reflection of the learning process and the learning results. For vocational training this learning conception enables ongoing and practically relevant learning as well as the targeted development of the capability for decision-making and responsibility. An example of PBL in vocational training and further training is 'learning on the job', in which employees acquire knowledge and skills directly in their working environment (cf. Gräsel & Mandl, 1999, p. 57).

Task-Oriented Learning

Task-oriented didactics stress the acquisition of the capability for decision-making and responsibility by learners. These didactics, which offer task-related learning contents and place the processing of tasks in the centre of learning processes, are a sub-section of the holistic approach of activity-oriented didactics, the use of which is widespread in vocational training (e.g. *learning island, guidance text methods*). The selection and structuring of the learning contents are oriented to the requirements of the tasks that learners are to solve in their work. Real work orders are carried over to systematically processed problems, which learners have to work on. Practical experience is to be linked to specialist theoretical knowledge and reflected on through the active involvement of learners with the problems (cf. Thillosen, 2005; cf. e-teaching.org, 2006). The principles of task-oriented learning are also reflected in current approaches to learning with digital media. "An e-learning module structured on a task-oriented basis thematises in a generalised form – possibly with concrete supplements specific to the company – the contents and methods of complex occupational tasks, [...]. The contents wise and methodological processing of the modular learning contents should take place in a hypertext structure, following the logic of task processing, so that the contents can be worked out in accordance with the individual learning logic on a self-organised basis and in cooperation with other learners. The structures must provide at the same time both content-wise and methodologically for on-demand telemedia support from mentors or specialists and the possibility of choosing between self-determined and recommended learning paths." (Zimmer, 2003, p. 4). The principles of task-oriented learning can not only be used for e-learning, but also, with the advantage of extended location independence, for mobile learning as well.

Informal Learning

The term *'informal learning'* is currently also increasingly used with regard to mobile learning, because it is regarded as being particularly suitable for mobile learning processes. Whereas formal learning comprises all learning processes that are organised and supported by state or company educational/training institutions on a target basis, with a clear structure and a timetable, informal learning describes learning processes that take place outside formalised educational measures. Informal learning can take place both on a planned and an unplanned basis, partly randomly and outside educational institutions in 'natural' life situations of the total environment. Learning usually results here from context-bound activities and from concrete (learning) situations. Dohmen describes informal learning as instrumental learning, as a means to an end. In contrast to formal learning, the end of learning is not learning itself but the solution of a specific or individual situation requirement or of a problem with the help of learning (cf. Dohmen, 2001, pp. 18). Pachler and Cook see informal learning as follows: "informal learning is a natural activity by a self-motivated learner 'under the radar' of a tutor, individually or in a group, intentionally or tacitly, in response to an immediate or recent situation or perceived need, or serendipitously with the learner mostly being (meta-cognitively) unaware of what is being learnt" (Pachler & Cook, 2008, p. 3). At a congress of the American Association for Adult and Continuing Education (AAACE) and Commission of Professors of Adult Education (CPAE) in October 1999 in San Antonio, USA, 'immediacy' was put forth as an additional supplementary criterion of informal learning ('learndirect'). Because informal learning mainly reproduces learning that is (self-) motivated through a concrete needs situation from everyday life or work, it requires information, answers and problem solutions that are immediately available and usable. Immediate, prompt, on the spot and without formal distractions (cf. Dohmen, 2001, p. 26). Learning contents that impart factual knowledge are particularly suitable for this. It is exactly against the background of this learning-related immediacy and the technical immediacy of mobile devices that a practical application link with mobile learning scenarios – naturally in a vocational further training context as well - is particularly obvious.

In the conception of e-learning or mobile learning offers that are to support informal learning processes, the challenge is to design the learning offers in such a way that, while they do not curtail the potentials of informal learning, they do bring in a certain amount of 'formality': for example, through tutorial learning support on the meta-level, which 'keeps an eye' on the informal learning processes and can provide support on the cognitive reflection of learning activities, for example, by initiating the communicative interexchange between teachers and learners (e.g. blogging and commenting) on what was learnt, or by regular subsequent surveys of knowledge to check whether the prior defined learning targets were reached. To support informal learning at the workplace in a mobile learning scenario one approach to a solution might be to implement Web 2.0 tools.

The models introduced in this section, which are similar to one another as far as the basic principles are concerned, should not be considered in isolation from one another, in the same way as the learning theory approaches should not be considered in isolation from one another. On the contrary, they can be used in learning arrangements as an interplay or method mix as well in which, for example, informal learning can also take place parallel to task-oriented learning processes.

3.3 Potentials of Web 2.0 Applications for Mobile Learning

The Web 2.0 conception and catchwords such as social software, Wikis, podcasts, weblogs, moblogs and RSS feeds are on everyone's lips today and the first mobile versions of these portals are already in existence. Users can edit their personal profiles on Web 2.0 portals and contact other like-minded users, form interest groups and swap ideas. In addition, they generate all types of media content and place it on the globally accessible internet.

The most characterising features of Web 2.0 are participation and collaboration. What is meant in particular is jointly preparing, sharing and using information and/or, in the educational field, jointly preparing and developing knowledge and competences. The forms of virtual participation in common knowledge connected with Web 2.0 appear to produce in this way a huge globally available encyclopaedia, in which everyone can find what is 'right' for his knowledge and his competences. Additional functions such as blogging, tagging or commenting are interactions that support active participation in the joint production and processing of contents and thereby suggest a type of quality assessment. The networking of computers through the internet is accompanied by the networking of participants, the formation of 'communities'. Social software also means active participation in social interaction processes. The dynamics of Web 2.0 are only partly driven by technology, because the technology has been present for years (http, html, web browsers, databases, Flash, web-based audio and video formats, etc.). It is the social factors (social software) that constitute Web 2.0 (cf. de Witt, 2008).

Web 2.0 applications are steadily increasing in the educational field and in e-learning. The didactical potential is described by Dalsgaard as follows: "The educational potential of social software is to facilitate self-governed, problem-based and collaborative activities by supplying students with loosely joined personal tools for independent construction, and by engaging them in social networks." (Dalsgaard, 2009). The various channels of Web 2.0 are used for educational purposes as well, to form a sense of social community and to use collected joint knowledge. Virtual communication on these different channels is central for teaching and learning with Web 2.0 and enables participation in the knowledge and competences of others.

Among the most popular and at the same time the most successful of such technologies are the so-called 'wiki webs', which are used in both the openly accessible internet and within organisations' own intranets. A wiki is an internet-based software that enables the simple preparation, publication, revision and interlinking of texts, images, graphics, videos or other multimedia contents through their users. Wikis are collections of intranet or internet pages that are both passively read by users and prepared actively online. They usually fulfil the function of a lexicon, a central knowledge database and a general work of reference. They are oriented to supporting the collaborative preparation and processing of page contents (cf. de Witt, 2008). From a technical aspect there is nothing more behind the wiki principle than the *hypertext technology* that has been in existence for some time.

The distribution of information and knowledge for learning and communication processes via this type of knowledge network is proving to be increasingly significant and makes its use interesting for mobile learning as well. For learners, wiki webs enable flexible, self-regulated access to information and knowledge. Access to information takes place by browsing or by means of a targeted search for keywords. From the pedagogical-didactical aspect, the use of wiki webs for learning processes is suitable in particular "if a subject area does not have clear structures, if a representation from specialist disciplines is practical for an understanding of the circumstances in focus, or if the subject area concerned can only be represented adequately using multiple forms of information coding" (Tergan, 2002, p. 107). In addition, the use of such learning environments always makes sense "if self-regulated, open and constructive learning is to be enabled, a multimodal, mental representation of knowledge supported, cognitive flexibility encouraged and knowledge use (knowledge transfer) in practical application situations facilitated" (Tergan, 2002, p. 107). Wiki webs are also equally predestined for supporting collaborative, informal and situated learning processes.

4 EXAMPLES OF INNOVATIVE APPLICATIONS FOR MOBILE LEARNING

At present, some innovative applications can be found in the areas of mobile communication and the mobile internet which can be used in the context of mobile learning.

QR-Codes

One trend, for example, is so-called 'mobile tagging' using a QR code (QR = quick response). In mobile tagging a 1D or 2D barcode is read out with the help of the integrated camera and a small software application on the mobile device, a barcode reader (e.g. from kaywa.com). In contrast to standard barcodes on goods and products, up to 4,000 text characters can be coded by means of QR codes. This conforms to about 1.5 typed A4 pages in a normal font size. After a QR code is written via a so-called barcode generator (e.g. http://qrcode.kaywa.com) this can be saved as graphics and printed for decoding by the users.

In the entertainment sector QR codes are used, for example, to print them as add-ons on film or concert posters. If they are interested, users usually access further information in the internet through the barcode. News magazines are also using QR codes increasingly in the print editions to enable specific articles, e.g. additional photo material or images, to be made available through the internet.

Figure 1. Mobile tagging. Source: adapted from: http://mobile-tagging.blogspot.com/2007/06/was-ist-mobile-tagging.html

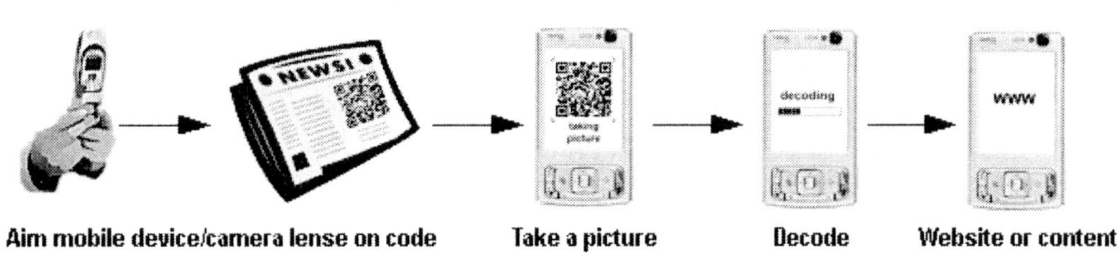

In mobile tagging, an internet address or URL is usually encoded to which the user is forwarded following decoding directly through the mobile phone's browser.

Frequently, the question of the purpose of coding internet addresses is raised. However, if the limited input facilities of mobile devices are considered, and the circumstance that internet addresses do not always consist simply of www, address name and top-level domain (e.g. .com) but often of many more, sometimes cryptic, sequences of characters (e.g. ?hl=de&q), QR codes can save a lot of typing time. The following illustration shows an example of a QR code which conceals the source address in Figure 2 and that, after decoding, links to this web page for further information on the subject of mobile tagging.

QR codes can also map complete information or learning texts. In the mobile learning environment, QR codes can be used to forward to complementary learning content (e.g. PDF documents). For example, a QR code could be generated on a PC and enclosed as graphics at the end of a lecture presentation. Listeners can photograph the barcode at the end and in this way obtain supplementary learning material in comfort. In a further possible use, QR codes, attached as small stickers, can be used in museum visits or other real world excursions for interaction with exhibits or objects.

Microblogging

So-called 'moblogs' and 'microblogging' are coming in for interpersonal communication via mobile device. Moblogs (e.g. moblog.net) and microblogging, pendants of weblogs which are widespread in the internet, are intended for use at mobile devices. In moblogs, registered users publish short blogs from mobile devices that in many cases are enriched with photos taken with a mobile phone camera. The most familiar representative of microblogging services is the social network, Twitter. Registered users can send and receive text messages with a maximum of 140 characters via the platform twitter.com. The basic idea, and the handling of microblogging services, is similar to that of a text chat or messenger tool on a PC and an SMS/MMS from a mobile phone. Users normally use Twitter to report on their daily environment, on personal experiences and on whatever they are doing at the moment. In addition, twitter has functions for community forming which enable users to enter into contact directly with like-minded persons who are also online.

Twitter, or similar services, could be used for the purposes of mobile learning in order to exchange information on learning content, learning experiences or suggestions within a learning group and its members via short messages. Links to learning processes which are regarded as worth reading can also be sent to the learning group. As an extension, the members of the community or learning group and their online status can be displayed. Another function would be desirable as a supplement which, together with text-based communication, supports or sets off, direct speech-based communication through a simple click on a member's name. Twitter and other microblogging services enable comfortable, device-overlapping integration in which they are included in the

Figure 2. Example of a QR code

users' devices as so-called widgets, or desktop applications.

Widgets are yet another trend that can be detected in internet applications for mobile devices. Along with Twitter, countless other providers offer a facility for installing their internet applications as widgets and 'little helpers' on the desktops of mobile devices or on their own mobile website. What will tomorrow's weather be like? What are the latest market prices, or what's the latest news? Appointment books or schedules of events, or a target group and subject-specific selection of videos or photos from the community platforms Youtube or flickr, can also be downloaded and integrated as widgets. Widgets, also known as applets or apps, are generally small tools which are used as a graphics interface and for a specific purpose in desktops.[2] The use of one of the Twitter widgets described above for communication purposes would be conceivable for mobile learning purposes. Another possibility might be widgets with an RSS feed reader function through which constantly up-to-date learning content is distributed, e.g. in the form of video or audio podcasts. Widgets or apps can also be small learning games. Own widgets for mobile devices can even be created through the platform STARmobi (www.starmobi.de). The advantages of widgets are that these small applications, or the appropriate source codes that providers supply, are downloaded in seconds and installed as graphical interfaces on the user's own mobile device.

Geo-Tagging

The cameras/camcorders integrated in the devices also come up with innovative technical and didactical facilities. New functions enable users to photograph objects (e.g. well-known buildings or museum exhibits) whose pictures are recognised by a server which provides appropriate information on them. In practice, these can be electronic city guides (the GPS function of the mobile devices is used here as well), or the photo take of a film poster brings a trailer of the film and displays the cinemas in which the film can be seen.

For mobile learning as well, innovative facilities for using the cameras integrated in the devices are being tried out that frequently enable not merely taking photographs but also recording short teaching/learning videos on all conceivable subjects. Learners and teachers can make the photo/video function useful, for example, for imparting implicit knowledge or an instrument for reflection. Learning contents which are difficult to describe can be shown by means of photos or videos, under the motto 'let me just show you' (e.g. tricks and knacks). One example of a scenario for in-company training and in the sense of collaborative learning processes in a Web 2.0 environment would be if trainees and trainers equally produce their own short learning videos on operational procedures or installation and repair manuals for machinery with the mobile devices and then upload them to a central server or a knowledge database for other learners.

RFID-Technologies

In addition, the interplay of mobile devices with RFID (Radio Frequency Identification) technology is being researched. RFID chips are millimetre-sized microchips which are invisible and can be embedded in objects or clothing. A mobile phone equipped with an RFID reader (wireless technology is used for reading out) enables interaction with objects. Users receive information concerning the object on their mobile device automatically, practically as they walk past. RFID readers in mobile devices are not yet standard. At the moment it is not possible to forecast whether, and how quickly, these developments will prevail on the mobile market. The areas of application of the navigation functions of the mobile devices are also being permanently further developed. In fashion are localising or location functions via GPS receivers, which notify the 'social location' of users. Embedded in map/navigation software, these functions show the location of friends and acquaintances in real time following the express consent of users. The function can also be used to exchange photos or videos.

Other forward-looking technologies which are practical for mobile learning processes are smartphones, which are equipped with a TV output for transmitting photos or videos with learning contents to a television receiver. Devices were presented at the GSMA Mobile World Congress in February 2009 in Barcelona which already have an integrated mini-beamer. Prior to this, centimetre-sized mini-beamers were only available as external adapters. In this way, 'larger' presentations in particular can be realised.

5 DIDACTICAL SCENARIOS FOR MOBILE LEARNING ON THE JOB

Up to now, there has been little research into mobile learning in work processes. Against the background of the increasing significance of education in society and technological progress in telecommunication, and the wide diffusion of mobile telephony, the bringing together of education and technology appears to be more interesting then ever for industry.

The methodological-didactical environment in which mobile learning takes place for the main part is problem-oriented, self-regulated and situated learning. Action-oriented learning is regarded as a suitable method for mobile learning (cf. Pehkonen & Turunen, 2004). In addition, along with the continuously increasing use of these mobile technologies in vastly different educational contests, Kukulska and Traxler (2005) see potentials in the combination of formal and informal learning. Apart from this, they stress the possibility of spontaneous and individual access to internet-based learning resources. Vavoula and Sharples assume that mobile and informal learning will grow together and that learners will prepare their own learning contents using their mobile devices, swap them and collaborate (cf. Vavoula & Sharples, 2002).

The learning theory approaches and didactical models explained here can be realised in the design of didactical scenarios for mobile learning in vocational (further) training. It is to be assumed here that a new didactics for mobile learning offers will not have to be developed initially, but that the existing conceptions can be applied on the principles, but require some modifications. On the whole, there is still relatively little practical experience and few theories on the use of mobile phones or smartphones in mobile learning situations at the workplace.

The didactical conception for mobile learning at the workplace that is to be applied depends in any case on the target group, the learning targets, the learning contents to be imparted and on the respective working environment. Starting from the specific target groups and their changing working environments and learning locations, and on the basis of the learning targets that have to be achieved, the following aspects, which add up to the script for a didactical scenario, should be included from conception through use in practice to the evaluation of mobile learning scenarios:

- choosing suitable learning contents,
- scope and type of representation of learning contents,
- didactical methods,
- interaction and communication factors,
- forms of learning support,
- facilities for checking learning success,
- technical infrastructure and
- acceptance of mobile devices (cf. Mengel, 2009).

The first pilot projects with mobile learning can already be found in various branches of industry, but even more training offers for mobile phones are conceivable. In manufacturing, for example, learning modules that serve both as works of reference as well as for training specialist knowledge 'on the road' could be used for the subject of materials for metalworkers or carpenters and joiners working on site. Because of safety at work, the subject of accident prevention, for example in the building industry, continues to be relevant. In this context as well, continual access via mobile devices to materials on health and safety at work can add extra value. For example, mobile learning can be used to impart behavioural rules with regard to health protection and they can be retrieved on demand, whether on unexpectedly occurring problems such as accidents with hazardous materials, or to prevent long-term complaints resulting from incorrect posture.

Learning contents on mobile devices regarding the prevention, detection and treatment of illness and injuries to persons are already used in medicine. For example, the innovation association '*PflegeWissen*' ('nursing knowledge') (www.projekt-pflegewissen.de) is pursuing the goal of promoting self-regulated and workplace-centred learning in nursing occupations through multimedia-processed learning modules. What is significant here is that the qualification is integrated systematically in the process of everyday nursing work and has been established as a firm component of in-house further and advanced training. Learning modules were developed for nursing staff involved with out-patients that can be retrieved from mobile phones and that comprise content wise situations that require critical action. The Helios Akademie (www.helios-akademie.de) offers short learning videos for mobile devices in supplement to its training and further training. The videos on anatomical and treatment subjects, which have been didactically reviewed specifically for mobile phones, are available not only to doctors but can also be accessed by nursing staff and even patients. Mobile learning is also applied in the pharmaceuticals industry, in particular in the framework of providing support for the marketing of medicines. For example, medical representatives can use longer journeys to extend their background knowledge and in this way to prepare themselves better for sales talks.

Reflections on mobile learning offers are possible analogously for other branches of industry, because mobile learning can be applied for practically all areas of knowledge. In the end, mobile learning can be considered for all occupations that require a certain amount of mobility. Three fields of application in vocational training will be described in more detail below; these refer to the branches: services, logistics and the energy industry.

Mobile Learning for Service Technicians in Facility Management

Facility management comprises the administration and management of buildings and facilities. This multi-faceted field of work used to be coordinated more through regional action plans and above all carried out by smaller work groups of service technicians. Employees in field service in manageable teams could carry out technical, infrastructural and commercial tasks in direct coordination and pass on personally all relevant improvements on maintenance at changing workplaces. However, today shorter and shorter innovation cycles and the increasing complexity of technologies demand multiplex competences and continuous further training, above all for field service employees who are always on the move and need learning possibilities independent of time and location. Instruction in theoretical knowledge is doubtless usually insufficient, and has to be supplemented with practical training for learners to deepen their knowledge and to make what they have learned workmanlike.

Mobile learning enables information and learning materials to be downloaded 'on the move' from the learning portal to the mobile device, for example on controlling and monitoring technical systems such as ventilation installations, in order to prepare before the consultancy interview with regard to a product and system selection that still has to be clarified. However, in situations of this nature the learning modules that are made available must be able to provide target-oriented cover for the learning demand in a short time of up to a maximum of 10 minutes. This does not mean that more extensive learning scenarios are excluded for mobile learning, but learning modules with a greater volume of up to one hour are more suitable for firmly planned learning phases. Facilitating learning periods would be advantageous not just on the way between company and job site but also in a service discussion on site. In this way, faults are not eliminated 'superficially' only, but if there is a problem the field worker can retrieve appropriate learning contents that are not only useful for him with regard to uncertainties that may occur in the framework of solving the problem, but also permit an additional optimisation of the technical installations. Learning videos on standard situations may prove here to be an important component of mobile learning. For example, specific assembly steps for a heating installation can be viewed at the individual's own learning speed and tried out on the appropriate installations.

The tasks of facility management are usually carried out in a team. Mobile learning makes suitable platforms available for this collaborative learning among field workers with time- and location-independent information and communication interfaces. It creates customised and flexible training measures in which, along with self-study and learning groups, target-group oriented support and control is guaranteed through the integration of teletutoring. If uncertainties arise during the operational and technical check of the preconditions for a new heating system, not only can detailed information be downloaded to the mobile device, gaps in knowledge can be eliminated directly as well through appropriate communication with a tutor. During the subsequent job planning on site on or the road the mobile device is used again for the analysis of the system requirements (obtaining information), planning work sequences and material requirements (working out), coordinating suppliers and employees (communicating) and more in-depth communication with the tutor (learning). In addition, useful tips for everyday business, for example for negotiation techniques or employee leadership, can enrich staff qualifications, if there are suitable framework conditions and the motivation for using waiting times as learning periods. A corresponding (voluntary or obligatory) check of learning and achievements in all these subject fields can also be carried out directly using the mobile device and evaluated centrally with a suitable test method. Today, field service workers in facility management often use so-called tablet PCs that are customised exactly for the multifaceted tasks in the constantly changing workplaces. These mobile devices are equipped with wireless connections such as wireless telephony or WLAN and in this way can be connected at any time via the intranet or internet with corresponding in-company learning management systems. With regard to the software, server-based communication and information applications should be used that facilitate cooperative learning in groups, for example with the help of web conferencing systems or learning blogs.

Mobile Learning for Commercial Drivers

The group of commercial drivers employed by transport companies that operate nationally and internationally is extremely characterised by changing hours of work and workplaces. As a result, this target group has a specific demand for assistance in training and further training, because its members are unable to take part easily in face-to-face instruction, for example. Nevertheless, lifelong learning affects this mobile occupational group as well, with subjects such as health and safety at work, which is in addition statutorily embedded in the obligations of transport companies.

Along with text-based communicating and looking up of job-related occupational safety and accident prevention regulations, learning modules can be used here as well with which, for example, the risks involved in driving and correct behaviour in emergencies are illustrated. Also conceivable for the realisation for mobile devices are learning modules from the 17 subject fields that the German Health and Safety at Work Act prescribes (e.g. guaranteeing the safety of loads through the application of the safety regulations and for preventing damage to health). Audio-visual learning modules can be produced in the form of learning videos lasting about three minutes with target-group oriented image and sound design, which learners work through as required in self-study. In order to guarantee the transport companies' duty to instruct, but also to deepen specific learning contents for the sake of comprehension through supplementary assistance from suitable specialists at head office, learning results should be reported back to a central learning management system, again for example by means of mobile telephony. In this way, learning progress can be established and evaluated on a regular basis and knowledge gaps closed specifically with additional learning modules. Interactive knowledge games can be used in this way for a diversion from the working day behind the wheel and motivate drivers to control and design their learning independently.

At the present time, the technical prerequisites for learning on the road in the driver's cab seem to be given. Navigation and mobile telephony devices are now part of standard equipment, in particular for long-distance drivers, so that at best further purchases for mobile learning are not necessary. As a consequence, knowledge and capacities for decision-making and responsibility can be acquired directly at the real workplace and with familiar learning media and the acquired skills can be applied immediately following the learning periods. The advantages, savings of training costs and the time variability of learning, can be used on the basis of the existing infrastructure for other subjects relevant to the transport sector. Learning modules for commercial drivers working in international transport would be conceivable for learning and extending their knowledge of languages, but also on road traffic regulations abroad, or on subjects involving the maintenance and care of the drivers' own vehicles.

Mobile Learning in Vocational Training for Electronics Technicians

The occupation of electronics technician is an approved training occupation in Germany and there is an apprenticeship lasting three and a half years in the so-called dual system. This means that apprentices are trained in a training company and attend vocational school during training. With the fact in mind that above all young persons start this vocational training after completing compulsory education, this means that in the first place an appropriately technophile target group can be addressed with mobile learning. The learning contents that are imparted in the framework of training (e.g. basics of mathematics and physics) are suitable at first glance for use on comparatively small devices. For example, calculations of mathematical formulas or percentage calculations by means of multiple choice tasks can also be trained in short learning phases of 5 to 10 minutes each. The correct allocation of graphical circuit symbols or knowledge of specialist vocabulary can also be deepened by means of a glossary and appropriate tests.

The use of mobile learning in vocational training for electronics technicians enables above all the individual learning demand to be satisfied more specifically in the often heterogeneous target group, which mainly covers all school types from the *Hauptschule* (lower secondary school) to the *Gymnasium* (higher secondary school). In addition to face-to-face teaching the target could be pursued of bringing about more security in the mastery and application of fundamental specialist knowledge in the comparatively young and mainly vocationally inexperienced trainees through self-regulated learning with regular repeats of the learning contents. Given corresponding learning motivation, it is conceivable that learners will learn their competences with the media, with which they are already very familiar, outside lessons, for example on the way to and from school and where appropriate in the company and in particular during their spare time. However, learning on the move should not be limited to mobile phones only but should also enable interactions. Prompt help from the vocational school teaching staff can be realised by generating a text message to the appropriate position from the learning module and sending it to a central server. This system supports in addition exchanges between trainees and enables virtual learning groups. Through the involvement of the teachers, manual and automated learning success checks can be realised in the form of short tests in which learners immediately receive a detailed explanation from the teachers if they answer incorrectly. Above and beyond pure text messages, learners can also take photos with the mobile telephone in the course of work if they are unable to progress in specific everyday situations, in order to discuss the uncertainties with others. The use of RFID chips and barcodes, with which mobile devices can identify objects and machines automatically, is conceivable in order to record and document the learning situation and uncertainties in greater detail.

While it is true that standard mobile phones are all that is required for the technical realisation of mobile learning, an appropriate server-based infrastructure must be set up, in particular to cater to the mobility of trainees: they have to commute between vocational school, work and, possibly, different job sites, for example, building sites. On the other hand, teachers have to have an administration and communication tool available, both to respond flexibly to the individual needs of learners and also to support the learning groups.

6 CONCLUSION

Today, the technological foundation for the employment of mobile learning appears to have matured. The technologies of the Apple iPhone and the Google G1 mobile phone, on which future developments will build, are regarded as serious and forward-looking. In addition, the intensive competition in mobile telephony has led to the costs of acquiring and operating the technologies required for mobile learning remaining manageable.

However, in order to realise the idea of learning on the mobile phone there are still some challenges that have to be overcome: methodological-didactical conceptions, design of user-friendly graphical interfaces, programming the applications and practical testing. However, it is foreseeable that mobile communication will make information available on a situation-specific and personalised basis and adequate for users' requirements. Informal learning processes at decentral learning locations during work, accompanied by activities and practical experience, will increase (cf. Ally, 2009). It remains to be seen whether the communication and collaboration potentials of mobile devices will be exhausted or whether individual learning forms prevail.

The personalisation of information promises the target-oriented acquisition of knowledge that demands appropriate competences: users must be in a position to handle them, to select information and to evaluate. With regard to Web 3.0, to the development of future generations of mobile telephony technologies and the resulting possibilities, the present potential for mobile learning will increase still further. The smaller and more mobile the devices become, the greater will be the prospect that users will always have them with them and arrive at knowledge more quickly, provided that they have a connection to a data network and are motivated to learn.

REFERENCES

Ally, M. (Ed.). (2009). *Mobile learning. Transforming the delivery of education and training.* Edmonton: AU Press (Athabasca University). Retrieved May, 2009, from http://www.aupress.ca/index.php/books/120155

Bundeministerium für Bildung und Forschung. (2007). Neue Medien in der beruflichen Bildung. In *Digitale Medien eröffnen der beruflichen Aus- und Weiterbildung neue Chancen,* Bonn, Germany (pp. 6-7).

Chabra, T., & Figueiredo, J. (2001). *How to design and deploy handheld learning*. Retrieved September, 2005, from http://www.empoweringtechnologies.net/eLearning/eLearning_expov5.htm

Chincholle, D. (2003). *Wireless service usability and design, tutorial 19*. Retrieved May, 2008, from http://www.chi2003.org/docs/t19.pdf

Dalsgaard, C. (2009). Social software: E-learning beyond learning management systems. *European Journal of Open, Distance and E-Learning.* Retrieved February, 2009, from http://www.eurodl.org/materials/contrib/2006/Christian_Dalsgaard.htm

de Witt, C. (2008, Januar 1). Vom Mängelwesen zum Superhirn? – Wissenserwerb und Kompetenzentwicklung durch Partizipation im Web 2.0. In *Vortrag auf der Learntec 2008*, Karlsruhe.

de Witt, C., & Czerwionka, T. (2007). *Mediendidaktik. Studientexte für Erwachsenenbildung.* Bielefeld, Deutschland: Bertelsmann.

didaktik/texte/aufgabenorientierte_didaktik_des_eLearning.pdf

Dohmen, G. (2001). Das informelle Lernen, Die internationale Erschließung einer bisher vernachlässigten Grundform menschlichen Lernens für das lebenslange Lernen aller. In *Bundesministerium für Bildung und Forschung, Das informelle Lernen*, Bonn, Deutschland (pp. 18-49).

Döring, N. (2005). Pädagogische Aspekte der Mobilkommunikation. In J. R. Höflich & J. Gebhardt (Hrsg.), *Mobile Kommunikation – Perspektiven und Forschungsfelder* (pp. 89-100). Frankfurt am Main, Deutschland: Peter Lang.

Döring, N. (2008). *M-Learning*. Retrieved May, 2008, from http://www4.tu-ilmenau.de/m-learning/index.html

Döring, N., & Dietmar, C. (2005). Medienproduktion für die Mobilkommunikation. In H. Krömker & P. Klimsa (Hrsg.), *Handbuch der Medienproduktion. Produktion von Film, Fernsehen, Hörfunk, Print, Internet, Mobilfunk und Musik* (pp. 545-577). Wiesbaden, Deutschland: VS Verlag für Sozialwissenschaften.

Dye, A. K'Odingo, J., & Solstad, B.-E. (2003). Mobile Education – A glance at a future. *Bekkestua.* Retrieved May, 2008, from http://nettskolen.nki.no/forskning/mobile_education.pdf

e-teaching.org. (2006). Didaktische Modelle. *Redaktionsteam PELe.* Retrieved May, 2008, from http://www.e-teaching.org/didaktik/theorie/didaktik_allg/Didaktische%20Modelle_19_07_06_bg.pdf

Georgiev, T., Georgieva, E., & Smrikarov, A. (2004). M-Learning – a new stage of e-learning. In *Proceedings of the 5th international conference on Computer Systems and Technologies (CompSysTech '04)*, Rousse, Bulgaria.

Gräsel, C., & Mandl, H. (1999). Problemorientiertes Lernen: Anwendbares Wissen fördern. In *Personalführung* (Vol. 6, pp. 54-62). Düsseldorf, Deutschland: Deutsche Gesellschaft für Personalführung.

Hoffmann, N. (2004). Problemorientiertes Lernen. In J. Haake, G. Schwabe, & M. Wessner (Hrsg.), *CSCL-Kompendium. Lehr und Handbuch zum computerunterstützten kooperativen Lernen.* München, Deutschland: Oldenbourg.

Kerres, M. (2001). *Multimediale und telemediale Lernumgebungen. Konzeption und Entwicklung.* München, Deutschland: Oldenbourg.

Kerres, M., & de Witt, C. (2004). Pragmatismus als theoretische Grundlage für die Konzeption von E-Learning. In H. O. Mayer & D. Treichel (Hrsg.), *Handlungsorientiertes Lernen und eLearning* (pp. 77-99). München, Deutschland: Oldenbourg.

Kukulska-Hulme, A., & Traxler, J. (2005). *Mobile Learning. A handbook for educators and trainers*. New York: Taylor & Francis.

Mandl, H., Gruber, H., & Renkl, A. (2002). Situiertes Lernen in multimedialen Lernumgebungen. In Issing, L.J. & Klimsa, P. (Hrsg.), *Information und Lernen mit Multimedia und Internet. Lehrbuch für Studium und Praxis, 3, vollständig überarbeitete Auflage*. Weinheim, Deutschland: BeltzPVU.

Mengel, S. (2009). *Beispielanwendungen und -szenarien für mobiles Lernen*. Unpublished paper, Hagen, Deutschland.

Nösekabel, H. (2005). *Mobile education*. Berlin, Germany: Gito.

O'Malley, C., Vavoulea, G., Glew, J. P., et al. (2005). *Mobilearn, WP 4 – Pedagogical methodologies and paradigms. Guidlines for learning/teaching/tutoring in a mobile environment (Report)*. Retrieved February, 2009, from http://www.mobilearn.org/download/results/guidelines.pdf

Pehkonen, M. & Turunen, H. (2004 Juli). A case study on the futures mobile work-based learning. *MLearn*, 5-6.

Reinmann-Rothmeier, G., & Mandl, H. (1998). Lernen in Unternehmen. Von einer gemeinsamen Vision zu einer effektiven Förderung des Lernens. In P. Dehnbostel, H.-H. Erbe, & H. Novak (Hrsg.), *Berufliche Bildung im lernenden Unternehmen: Zum Zusammenhang von betrieblicher Reorganisation, neuen Lernkonzepten und Persönlichkeitsentwicklung*. Berlin, Deutschland: Edition Sigma.

Schiller, J. (2003). *Mobilkommunikation*. München, Deutschland: Pearson Studium.

Schulmeister, R. (2001). *Virtuelle Universität – virtuelles Lernen*. München, Deutschland: Oldenbourg.

Tergan, S.-O. (2002). Hypertext und Hypermedia: Konzeption, Lernmöglichkeiten, Lernprobleme und Perspektiven. In Issing, L.J. & Klimsa, P. (Hrsg.), *Information und Lernen mit Multimedia und Internet. Lehrbuch für Studium und Praxis* (pp. 99-112). Weinheim, Deutschland: BeltzPVU.

Thillosen, A. (2005). Arbeits- und Lernaufgaben in der betrieblichen Ausbildung. *Literaturbericht*. Retrieved May, 2008, from www.ausbildernetz.de/media.php/2886/5738/Literaturbericht_ALA.pdf

Vavoula, G., & Sharples, M. (2002). KLeOS: A personal, mobile, knowledge and learning organisation system. In Milrad, M., Hoppe, U. & Kinshuk (Hrsg.), *Proceedings of the IEEE International Workshop on Mobile and Wireless Technologies in Education* (pp. 152-156). Växjö, Sweden: IEEE Computer Society Press.

Zimmer, G. (2003 April). Aufgabenorientierte Didaktik des E-Learning. In *Handbuch E-Learning*. Retrieved May, 2008, from http://www.weiterbildungsportal.ch/mas/ndkele/

ENDNOTES

1. There are countless mobile devices on the market that are subject to different technical restrictions, for example, display size, software equipment or facilities for data transmission, etc. With regard to display sizes - the majority of displays today are color displays - 340x320 pixel or larger are to be recommended for displaying mobile learning content.
2. A large selection of these widgets can be found on the website widgetbox.com.

Chapter 14
E-Learning Challenges for Polytechnic Institutions:
Bringing E-Mobility to Hands-on Learning

Martha Burkle
SAIT Polytechnic, Canada

ABSTRACT

Mobile technology use is a major issue in higher education institutions, and one that is increasing daily. While the new generation of students (the "digital natives") move across programs and courses, their learning expectations have started to emerge. It is with these expectations and needs in mind that educators around the world are recognizing the advantages of using mobile technologies to engage with students and make learning a more collaborative, interactive activity that can be engaged in at anytime, anywhere. Using a case study approach, this chapter explores the challenges of transforming static curricula into a mobile experience, and the ways in which these challenges were overcome within a polytechnic institution where hands-on learning takes place inside the classroom or the lab. In addition to presenting a literature review on the use of mobile technologies for teaching and learning, and an analysis of the relevance of connectivism theory to analyze students learning in the digital age, this chapter also includes an analysis of student surveys and interviews, as well as further opportunities for research.

INTRODUCTION

As 21st century students have started to arrive at colleges and universities, educators around the world have started to question whether their educational institutions are ready to respond to student needs and expectations. The reason for this hesitation is clear: these students are carrying with them an entirely different approach to learning, entertainment and life in general. The large majority of students in today's classrooms are the first generation to grow up with such a vast array of information technologies. They have spent their entire lives surrounded by and using computers, video games, digital music players, video cameras, cell phones, and all the other toys and tools of the digital age.

DOI: 10.4018/978-1-61520-678-0.ch014

As such, they are known as the Net Generation, or Net Gen-ers.

This chapter is about the learning desires and expectations that the Net Generation are bringing with them when they start higher education. It is also about the possibilities that mobile technologies offer to transform teaching and learning according to the Net Gen desires and expectations. In particular, the video iPod is analyzed in detail through a case study that involves a polytechnic institution using video iPods with students in the Avionics Program.

The main objectives of this chapter are to:

1. Present and analyze learning expectations of the Net Generation of students.
2. Discuss the need to transform curricula and content from a static to a mobile experience.
3. Analyze the challenges to the role of the instructor (from a 'knowledge holder' to a 'facilitator') that the use of mobile technologies brings with it.
4. Present research about student use of mobile technologies for accessing lab procedures, and for interacting with other students (in a collaborative way) and with the instructor. This is done with a case study of SAIT Polytechnic in Calgary, Alberta, Canada.
5. Examine and discuss student learning transformation since the introduction of mobile technologies into teaching and learning.
6. Point out further research in the topic.

In a framework that looks at the future role of mobile technologies to enhance education, this chapter discusses the way in which video iPods are transforming the ways in which students learn, as well as the ways in which this learning has been able to incorporate elements of fun and play while enhancing the acquisition of skills and hands-on learning.

1. NET GENERATION, DIGITAL NATIVES: THE NEW STUDENT GENERATION IN THE 21ST CENTURY

Today's average college graduates have spent less than 5,000 hours of their lives reading, but over 10,000 hours playing video games (not to mention 20,000 hours watching TV). Computer games, e-mail, the Internet, cell phones and instant messaging are integral parts of their lives (Gibson et al, 2008; Prensky 2001; Wesch, 2007). As a result of this ubiquitous technology, a number of social scientists sustain that today's students think and process information differently than their predecessors. Even more so, their entire system of beliefs and values are different from those in previous generations, and these differences usually go further and deeper that most educators realize. These are some of the reasons why Marc Prensky has dubbed today's students "digital natives". In coining this term, Prensky is making the analogy of natives to a homeland, in this case referring to the "digital land", or the Internet. Digital natives are those who have always known the Internet and a digital environment. Others have called this new generation of students the Net Gen, where Net refers to either networking or Internet use. Whether Digital natives or Net Gen-ers, this generation was born at a time when computers were an important part of the dynamics of a home, and where the Internet had become an integral part of daily activities.

Some argue that even if the digital natives have slight differences in speech and social interactions, they are fluent in digital communication forms that are prevalent in the new land (Jukes & Dosaj, 2004; Toledo, 2007). Oblinger (2005) characterizes the "millenials" (as she calls the generation of students born after 1982) this way: "They gravitate toward group activity and social networking; they identify with their parents' values and feel close to their parents; they spend more time doing homework and housework and less time watching TV, they believe "it's cool to be smart", they are fascinated by new technologies; they are racially and ethnically diverse…" (2005: 2)

Academic colleagues from different countries have begun to consider whether students around the world have similar experiences to those in North America. For example, Oliver and Goerke (2007) researched undergraduate students in Australia to find out whether their students confirm these assertions. They found that "ownership of laptops, mobile phones and music devices appears to be growing rapidly among this group, along with their use of tools such as instant messaging, blogs and podcasts" (Oliver and Goerke, 2007). Another example of this is the work done by Creanor, et al (2006) and published as the Lex (Learner Experience of E-learning) Report. A total of twenty-two interviews and six focus groups were conducted that evaluated students' experiences with e-learning in the UK. Findings of the report include the fact that learners involved in the research tended to be highly skilled networkers and often use technology to pull support when needed.

The significant changes that today's students bring with them (with some of these changes evident even in their brain structures, according to Tapscott, 2008) when they start their post-secondary education creates an urgent call to understanding the different ways they learn. In turn, this fact calls for a change in the way institutions educate them. It is time not only to radically change the way teaching takes place, but also to redesign curriculum, graduation processes, evaluation methods, infrastructure needs, and more.

The arrival of the Net Generation to today's classrooms and learning spaces is also the focus of a new emerging learning theory, Constructivism, proposed by George Siemens in 2004. Connectivism responds to the many changes in learning that the 21st century is experiencing: informal learning, learning for lifetime, technology influence in learning and thinking (Siemens, 2004). In the context of technologies for learning, where learners have immediate access to knowledge and where knowledge has multiple sources and forms, connectivism sustains that knowledge itself is the product of network connections, and learning is a function of conversations between the learners, rather than a product of content.

Together with a new learning theory, Web 2.0 technologies are here to test educational institutions making such a transformation (Anderson, 2007; Evans and Nation, 2000; Deal, 2007; Daniels, 1998; Mason, 1998). Techniques such as moving content from a static to a dynamic perspective; changing the lecture-centered relation of classroom teaching to a more student-centered one; breaking the old image of the instructor as the only knowledge holder; recognizing the network of processes and relations, and promoting collaborative approaches to teaching are some of the challenges these institutions have started to face.

Some of these possibilities will be analyzed in the next part of this chapter, and a case study will be presented that involves the Southern Alberta Institute of Technology (SAIT), a polytechnic institution in Canada that is working on the redesign of its curricula and implementing innovative ways for teaching and learning.

2. THE TRANSFORMATION PROCESS OF CURRICULA: FROM A STATIC TO A MOBILE CONTEXT

In the last decade, mobile technology has become an important part of our daily lives, transforming the ways in which we work and learn (Naismith et al, 2004). As technology now allows content to be mobile, the prospect of a mobile learner is also now possible. Mobile technologies (iPod, Blackberry, Tablet PCs, Palm Pilot, mobile phone, etc.) have started to transform the ways in which students access content, entertainment, and knowledge, making content portable, and in turn, transforming the physical limits of the classroom (Pasnik, 2007).

With the arrival of the digital natives (or Net Gen-ers) to higher education institutions, the use of mobile technologies to access learning content is being seen as an engaging way to provide content and knowledge exchange. The introduction of mobile technologies into the learning experience is expected to promote active learning by engaging students in the process and facilitating their interaction with learning and content. Used effectively, individual technologies have the potential to change the learning dynamic and foster new pedagogical approaches, enabling the instructor to promote collaborative, independent learning (Callaghan et al, 2006; Pasnik, 2007).

Portable audio and video players have, in fact, brought learning to a new dimension. Because of its capability to deliver rich media content, the iPod, for example, is seen as a "cognitive and cultural tool that allows students to explore symbols and meanings" (Pasnik 2007; 2).

A recent study in North America (Salaway, et al, 2008) showed how student use of information technologies is growing virtually day by day. Statistics from the report indicated that while in 2003 the number of students that owned cell phones was only 33 percent, two years later this figure had increased to 66.1 percent, an ownership that combines the use and possession of other gadgets, such as iPods, tablet PCs, etc. This phenomenon has caused some higher education institutions to start using mobile technologies to deliver content.

In parallel to the technology transformation, educators at nearly every level of instruction are examining the tools required to produce the 21st century skills that today's students need to be successful in their workplace. Furthermore, innovative instructors are working on ways to end the current disassociation of many of today's courses and academic programs with Net Gen students, technological capabilities, and technology engagement so that technology could be better integrated into course delivery and knowledge sharing. As University of Kansas anthropologist Michael Wesch mentioned in his digital ethnography work, today's students have to be prepared, if this is possible, for those jobs that they are going to get when they graduate, even though these jobs do not really exist in the present (Wesch, 2007; a).

It should be considered that the effective use and continued growth of new technologies inside and outside the classroom environment is dependent on two crucial factors:

1. Students' possibilities for learning engagement.
2. Instructors' technological skills and attitude towards change.

This is why reflecting on the challenges that students bring with them when they start their postsecondary instruction implies the analysis on how colleges, polytechnics and universities are evolving and transforming the ways in which they teach. This requires a constant evaluation of pedagogical models (student-centered alternatives) and the implementation of new educational goals and innovative strategies to deliver content and promote student engagement. In fact, mobile technologies have proved to be an attractive option for many instructors as a way to distribute their course lectures to students (Campbell, 2005; Frydenberg, 2006).

3. MOBILE TECHNOLOGIES AND THE CHANGING ROLE OF THE INSTRUCTOR

Mobile technologies support the new pedagogical model, where the instructor has become a facilitator of knowledge and is no longer the "knowledge holder". Laurillard (2002) examines the change from the instructor as a knowledge source to a facilitator providing a conversational framework for the evolution of learning. In order to enable the evaluation of the effectiveness of learning, she identifies the key elements of the process:

discussion (between the instructor and the student); interaction (between the student and some aspect of the world defined by the instructor); adaptation (of the world by instructor and action by the student); and reflection (on the student's performance by instructor and student). Furthermore, Laurillard believes that this framework can be applied to the evaluation of technologies in learning. In fact, one of the main goals for the use of technologies for teaching and learning should be to provide student-centered situations where instructors facilitate access to content in a horizontal, sharing environment.

The transformation of the instructor from a knowledge holder into a facilitator through the use of information technologies is further analysed by Sfard (1998). He identifies two teaching and learning models: the "acquisition model" and the "participation model". In the acquisition model, the role of the instructor is to deliver, convey, and clarify knowledge and concepts. With the acquisition model, the focus of learning activities is on acquiring pre-specified knowledge and on developing understanding of predetermined concepts.

In the participation model, he/she is a facilitator, mentor, expert participant, and guardian of practice/discourse. With the participation model, the focus of learning activities is on becoming a member of a community of practice, learning from the community but also contributing to it. As it will be shown in the case study analysis below, when students used video iPods to review the lab procedures, they became participants in the class content, learning from it and also contributing to it.

Sloman (2001) characterises the acquisition model as a 'transmission framework' where the instructor passes on a fixed body of information and the student interacts with pre-packaged content. In this model, Sloman argues that "the skill of the teacher lies in the selection of the content and teaching style to produce a specific outcome from the students" (p.113). He describes the participation model as a collaboration (transformation) framework that emphasises individual thinking and the construction of meaning.

The collaboration (transformation) framework necessarily emphasises individual thinking and construction of meaning. Teaching with this approach is more tentative, flexible and experimental – hence it is student-centred. In this context, a community of learners will improve learning through their interaction (Burkle, 2003; Perry, 2003).

Both Collis and Moonen (2001); and Sloman (2001) conclude their comparison of the two models by stating that a pedagogical theory means little if instructors do not apply it, and also that technological resources have no value if they are not used. In fact, the authors stress the fact that the number of instructors who choose to be innovators in technology and pedagogy is limited.

Both models are related to pedagogic theory where "behaviourist" models are compared with "constructivist principles". Sloman (2001) maintains that the acquisition model could be associated with behaviourist theory, while the participation model is related to a constructivist approach. This assumption is based on the fact that in the transmission model, a teacher (lecturer or instructor) can pass on a fixed body of information and the "student or learner interacts with a pre-packed content" (Sloman, 2001; 114), while the transformation framework implies individual thinking and constructing of meaning.

Holley & Haynes (2003) suggest that "such changes are most visible in the ongoing erosion of individual or small group teaching, and in the attempts to change the nature of contact time away from delivery of information towards more active participation" (p.4). The development and implementation of widely accessible communication and information technologies has been a key driving force in the move towards the adoption of social constructivism as a guiding principle in Higher Education Institutions HEIs (Laurillard, 2002). In other words, this change has resulted in a change in the role of the instructor from the

Figure 1. Structures and spaces, from a built to a nurtured environment (Siemens, 2006) (Source and © 2006 Complexive Systems Inc. -9- Google 2006 Training Summit: Learning in Synch with Life- permission TBD)

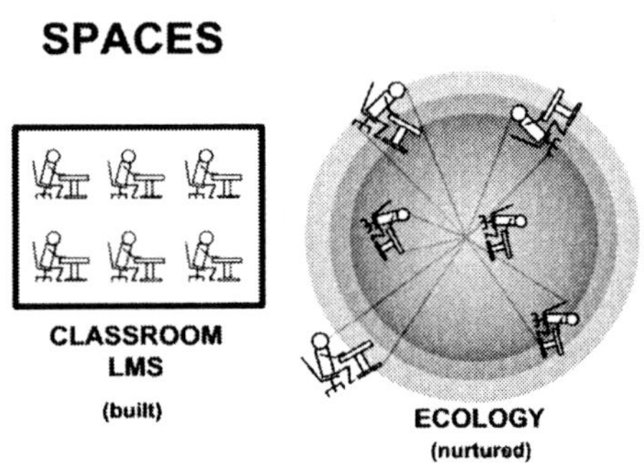

"sage of the stage", where transmissive, didactic learning took place, to the "guide on the side", where more student-centred learning takes place[1] (Harasim, 1990; Pasnik, 2007).

3.1. Connectivism Theory and the Changing Role of the Instructor

The instructor's role transformation should be further analyzed also from a connectivism perspective (Siemens, 2005, 2006) As referred above, in connectivism theory learning happens as a result not of a single mind (the instructor), but as a network of elements (in this case, other learners, and technology itself). Learning becomes a 'multi-faceted experience' (Siemens, 2006) where every participant in the network is the owner of a partial part of the knowledge experience. Moreover, in this model, the instructor shares his/her knowledge with the learner, with the technology and with the learning environment, as learners become participants in the learning ecology (Siemens, 2006). The challenge for the instructor and the learning context is then, to promote no rigid traditional classroom or learning management systems, but dynamic environments, where learning is nurtured by instructors, learners and connections.

4. MOBILE TECHNOLOGIES AND LEARNING

Innovative educators around the world are exploring how mobile technologies can serve as powerful educational tools in both the instructors' and the students' approach to teaching and learning. In fact, research has shown that among these mobile technologies, iPods have proved to be an effective and attractive option for teaching and learning (Naismith et al., 2004; Juniu, 2002; Chao, 2005). Because iPods are portable, their use in a higher education context can take the learning process beyond the boundaries of the classroom and can offer anytime/anywhere opportunities for teaching and learning (Burkle, et al, 2008).

Podcasting[2] use in higher education institutions is relatively new, and there are already some good examples (or best practices) where universities, colleges and polytechnics have made use of the technology in very efficient ways. In an academic setting, faculty have discovered the potential of creating podcasts of lectures and other course materials, and podcasting has become an accepted one-way channel of communication between instructors and students.

Moreover, since the recent upgrade of iPods to support video, the use of video podcasting has made this option even more attractive as a way for instructors to distribute their course lectures or to support the learning that happens inside the classroom. Following the pedagogical "coherence principle" (which states that students learn better as the corresponding words and pictures are presented simultaneously rather than successively), iPods make this possible in a mobile experience (Pasnik, 2007), facilitating what is called 'in situ' learning and allowing 'just in time' teaching, learning and training. Together, these technologies have the capacity to support the development of a wide range of learning skills and teaching strategies.

It should be noted that the novelty of this mobile technology brings with it the challenge of developing pedagogical understandings around the relationship between the use of the iPod itself and the educational context within contemporary society. There are still many questions to be answered with regard to what 'new' benefits the instructors and students will receive after using video podcasting for learning, or how we can usefully expand the learning opportunities so that a video iPod can become a valuable learning tool.

These connections do not exist yet in the literature (Kervin & Vardy, 2006), and that is why developing case studies around different uses of the technology should be accompanied by a continuous search of pedagogical models that could enrich the learning experience, or that could be brought/identified from a student's learning experience.

4.1. Mobile Technologies and Learning at the Southern Alberta Institute of Technology (SAIT Polytechnic): A Case Study of a Polytechnic Institution in Canada Using Mobile Technologies for Teaching

SAIT Polytechnic is a public two-year institution in Alberta with approximately 49, 000 learners distributed in full-time programs, apprenticeship programs, continuing education, and corporate training. Its annual budget is in the order of C$200 million (Bates, 2007).

SAIT first introduced e-learning in 1997 when it started delivering courses through the so-called "laptop program". Since then, laptop programs have been running in four of the seven Academic Schools (Business, Information and Communication Technology, Construction and Transportation). The laptop program strategy was part of the institution's vision to innovate the way teaching and learning processes took place and introduce a blended approach to learning.

By 2009, most of the seven academic schools at SAIT had a number of courses in the laptop program, or were using another learning technology such as the video iPods, YouTube videos, or Second Life virtual spaces to deliver courses and lab procedures. There are more than 90 fully wired classrooms at SAIT, and the number of computer ports on campus rose from 2,000 in 1997 to more than 15,000 in 2008.

In order to provide the leadership which resulted in SAIT's achievement of international recognition in the use of technologies for teaching and learning, and with the financial support of CISCO Systems, in 2004 SAIT opened the position of a research Chair (CISCO Chair in e-learning) and appointed Dr. Tony Bates to the position. Dr. Bates immediately reviewed e-learning strategies across campus and developed a strategic plan. At the end of the year, Dr. Bates produced the "SAIT Strategic e-Learning Plan", which proposed 82 recommendations to support student engagement with the use of e-learning technologies (Bates, 2007)*.

In June 2007, two innovative instructors in the Avionics and Aircraft Advance Systems Programs at SAIT decided to explore the possibilities of using mobile technologies for their students to learn and review the procedures happening inside the lab. This decision was based on the following instructors' needs and expectations:

1. Provide 'just-in-time training' to those students who were learning aircraft maintenance or complex avionics procedures.
2. Facilitate the memorization of complex lab procedures, in which students learn how to repair airplane radios or provide high quality maintenance to airplane fuselages, for example.
3. Reproduce in the lab a teaching practice that will imitate what is already happening in the avionics industry: Learning 'in situ' through mobile technologies.
4. Facilitate collaborative learning among students, by promoting critical thinking in a challenging and unique environment.

A team consisting of the curriculum coordinator of the Avionics and Aircraft Advance Systems Programs, the Faculty training advisor, and the CISCO Chair of e-learning was put together to design a working and research plan needed in order to identify the proper mobile technology to be used. This team will also measure student opinion on their readiness to use the technology, in a pilot research study that took place on December 2007. The plan's main objectives were to:

- Enhance the learning environment.
- Accommodate a variety of learning styles that will allow students to preview and review video demonstrations upon desire and demand.
- Enhance the use of technology in the educational process.
- Allow the instructor to spend more time with the learner who requires it.
- Allow learners to be more independent in controlling the pace and timing of their learning.
- Reinforce the student-centred nature of learning.
- Promote collaborative learning among students

After an in-depth literature review on the use of mobile technologies for teaching and learning, a decision to use video iPods for the research was taken. This decision was based on the following criteria:

1. Video iPods, which were new in the Canadian market as for December 2007, provided the capability of accessing videos in a mobile environment.
2. iPods in general were a familiar technology among students and one that will sound appealing to them.
3. SAIT had just signed an agreement with Apple to use iTunes U (an online service just created by Apple in May 2007) to manage, distribute and control its video production for SAIT students.
4. The expense of the video iPods could be supported by Curriculum Development funding in the School of Transportation, where the programs involved were located.

With this perspective in mind, research questions and methodologies were designed for a "Pilot Research Project" between September and October 2007, with these research goals:

1. To explore students current use and ownership of video iPods
2. To analyze student expectations of learning with video iPods
3. To target a learning strategy that will incorporate video iPods to students' expectations.

The research population for the Pilot stage of the research project included all students registered in the Avionics (20 in total) and Aircraft Advance Systems (60 in total) Programs. A total of 80 surveys were distributed in a printed format, on October 2007.

4.1.1. Research Pilot Findings

Surveys included 9 multiple choice questions and one open question. Findings are presented below:

1. Students' age: 75% of the students in the Research group had an average age of between 18 and 24 years old.
2. Students iPod ownership: 50% of the students had an iPod
3. Students' use of iPods (in time): 49% of the students used the iPod between 1 – 6 hours a day, while 4% of the group used the iPod between 13 – 18 hours a day.
4. Students´ use of iPods (use purposes): 58% of the students in the group used their iPods to listen music, 10% to watch

videos, and 8.75% to listen to podcasts or to study
5. 89% of the students surveyed stated they will find useful to have access to learning content through an iPod, while 96.5% thought it will be useful for them to review lab procedures with their iPods.
6. 88.75% of the group said the idea of using iPods to learning was appealing to them.

Research Pilot results were presented to the Deans Council, the Curriculum coordinator of the Program and the instructors involved in December 2007, and a decision was made to purchase 40 video iPods using Curriculum Development funding. Video iPods will be purchased through SAIT Computer and Technology Department (at a special price of $250 CDN), will be owned by the School of Transportation, and will be lent to students as a learning tool. Furthermore, the production of the videos was requested to SAIT Centre of Instructional Technology and Development (CITD) Multimedia team.

4.2. The Production and Use of Video iPods

Encouraged by the institution's wide range of technology strategies (Bates, 2000), the introduction of the video iPods was supported by the work done at SAIT Centre for Instructional Technology for Development (CITD). The Centre provided a team of instructional designers (IDs) and multimedia experts.

The IDs reviewed the videos of lab procedures and ensured that the content aligned with the learning outcomes and objectives so that learners could apply skills and knowledge required. The video production crew (videographers and new media specialists) reviewed lab demonstrations with subject matter experts (SMEs or faculty) and developed a bi-weekly shooting schedule.

The video iPod production started with the videographer and the subject matter expert (SME) reviewing each step in the lab. Notes were taken to define which parts of the lab demonstration could be covered in a wide shot, and which steps required close-ups to ensure students could see the details to successfully complete the labs on their own. Each lab was shot from beginning to end as a wide shot (WS) with the instructor presenting a short introduction and then walking students through a step-by-step process to complete each lab. The camera was then moved to capture the close-ups needed for each lab, eg; numbers on digital read-outs.

- Videos were captured on DVC Pro format and mini DV Format
- The instructors' narration was captured using a wireless Shure microphone
- Videos were transferred to Velocity HD hard drives and then edited using Velocity HD editing software

After the instructor had reviewed the video, the approved videos were compressed into Windows ".wmv" format with the highest data rate available with Velocity HD – 640 X 480 @ 2 Mb/s. Using a video converter software, the wmv files were converted to ".m4v", which is the video file format used by iPods. Once the videos were converted, they were copied into iTunes. A playlist in iTunes was created in order to keep the videos organized by course name, making the videos easy to find in the iPod's interface. Finally, the videos were transferred from iTunes to the video iPod, and these were then given to students so that they could use them throughout their course.

The video iPod Project was successfully implemented from January till May 2008. A total of eighty students in the Avionics and Aircraft Advance Systems Programs were involved in the project, two instructors, one instructional designer, and three multimedia experts.

Instructors required their students to the use of the videos for:

1. Review pre-recorded lab procedures.
2. Prepare content to be analyzed inside the classroom and/or the lab.
3. Memorize complex procedures individually and in teams.
4. Study the procedure in the video iPod, before applying a procedure in a real airplane.
5. Study before the hands-on exam.

A second stage in the research plan was developed by the CISCO Chair (author of this chapter) in order to:

1. Evaluate the impact of video iPods in students' learning strategies.
2. Observe students' using video iPods reaction to learning, interaction with instructors, interaction with peers (collaborative learning)
3. Analyze the experience of instructors teaching with video iPods.
4. Identify the challenges (problems and/or opportunities) in the use of video iPods among students
5. Suggest recommendations to the research team, curriculum coordinator and Deans Council of the potential benefits/challenges of using video iPods in other academic Schools

The second stage research plan included:

- A printed survey for all the eighty students involved in the experience.
- An interview questionnaire for selected students in the research population
- An interview with each of the instructors involved.
- A lab observation guide to record students' use of iPods and interaction with instructors and peers.

In the next section of the chapter, the data and opinions of students and instructors involved in the research pilot are presented.

4.3. Research Findings

Research findings are presented in this section and include the opinions and points of view of students participants in the research, 4 female and 76 male students in the Avionics and Aircraft Advance Systems Programs. Students ages fluctuated between 18-24 years old (75%), 25-35 years old (22%), and 35-44 years old (3%). More than half of them (51%) own an iPod, and 48% spend 6 hours daily listening to music or podcasts. A total of 88% of the students in the research found using iPods useful for learning, and 80% underlined the fact that they were enthusiastic about using the video iPod. After using iPods for the Avionics course, 95% of the students stated that they would like to use them in other courses and 60% of them watched the lab procedure video more than nine times.

4.3.1. Students' Perspectives on the Use of iPods

With regard to the impact of the video iPods in student learning, 47% of the students said that the iPods helped them to review what they had previously learned in the lab. For some others (45%), the video iPods helped them to have a clearer understanding of what was learned in the lab. From a collaborative learning approach, using video iPods helped the students to learn from each other, answering questions and solving complex procedures problems. Furthermore, students stated that after reviewing the videos, they were able to solve problems themselves, without the input of the instructor, which resulted in less time needed for questions inside the lab, and a more productive learning. These findings concur with what connectivism theory underlines regarding the use of technologies as a platform for collaboration and networking (Siemens, 2005).

Learning mobility and collaborative learning were an important issue for the researched students. A total of 38% stated that iPods gave them

Figure 2. Students at SAIT Avionics Program using video iPods to review lab procedures)

the opportunity to review their learning anywhere and at any time, while 15% of them said that iPods allow them to share what they learned in the lab with their classmates.

Qualitative analysis of students' interviews showed that students were extremely enthusiastic about using video iPods or learning and this factor influence their satisfaction and their learning curve. In their own words:

Video iPods are a 'good friend'. They give students a study plan and facilitate less confusion and frustration.

Video iPods allow 'play-by-play', step by step learning, and they are a good visual learning aid.

Video iPods facilitate information on demand. They are fun to study with.

Another important factor to analyze here is the impact video iPods had on instructor-student interaction both inside and outside the lab. According to Collis and Moonen (2001), in order to use technologies for teaching and learning, universities have to transform themselves in a number of areas, including the interaction between students and instructors and the ways in which students access knowledge. For 22% of the students in the research, the iPods helped them to raise new questions in relation to the learning material, while for 25% of them the iPods facilitate "less stress and demand on the instructor". Furthermore, the fact that students have a previous knowledge of the lab procedures allow them to reduce the questions to the instructors inside the lab so that instructors could focus more on those students who will have more difficulty with learning the procedure. As one student expressed it:

Video iPods allow students to answer their own questions and therefore reduce the demands on the instructor.

These findings concur with what is stated in the literature with regard to what information technologies in general can do to facilitate interaction with instructors (Hiltz, 1990; Moller, 1998; Holley & Haynes, 2003). For example, Moller (1998) remarks that when using technologies to interact with their instructors, students feel they are more involved and that they have learned more.

4.4. From Receivers to Active Learners: Using Video iPods to Promote Independent Learning Among Students

Another interesting finding from this research is that motivation was an important issue for students using video iPods. Motivation helped engage

Figure 3. The impact of video iPods on F2F mode instructor-student interaction

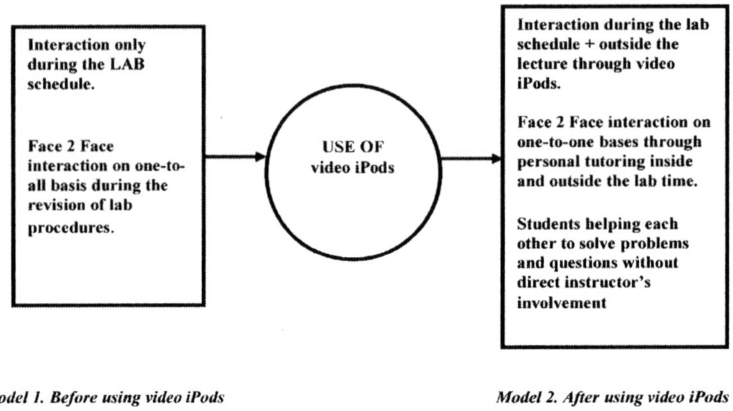

them in self-learning. Student participants in this research believed that their instructors encouraged their learning everywhere, breaking the limits of the classroom. Three students commented:

The instructors encourage us to learn on our own, therefore, we learn at our own pace, using the video IPod as a learning reference. (Interview with a student, Avionics Program, June 2008)

Video iPods are not going to substitute instructors, but they help them. Personal contact is extremely important in this teaching – learning process. The instructor does not tell us what to do for homework or what the topic of the next class is going to be. She assumes we are going to review what we learned in the lab using our video iPods and come to the next class ready to take the next topic. (Interview with a student, Avionics Program, June 2008)

It is a more participating model, the instructor is there more for us. It is no longer instructors giving us everything and we receiving it; we get involved. I think that instructors are more like a guide for us. (Interview with a student, Avionics Program, June 2008)

These findings are similar to research carried out in the United Kingdom and published by BECTA (British Educational Communications and Technology Agency) in 2007, where students' motivation was a determinant factor for the successful use of mobile technologies.

Motivation has also been noted in the literature with relation to the fact that technologies per se do not change settings, interaction, access to knowledge, or collaborative learning activities, etc. The use of mobile technologies to facilitate instructor-student interaction depends on the instructors' input and attitude towards the students, as well as the students' disposition and skill in using the technologies. As Holley and Haynes (2003) have noted, students who actively contact their instructors and participate in collaborative activities tend to be more motivated and are actually more familiar with mobile technologies. If these students encounter a problem, they approach the instructor to solve it.

4.5. Instructor's Perception of Role Change after the Use of Video iPods

Within the framework of this case study, it has been clear that instructors played a crucial role in bringing mobile technologies to their teaching experience. With the use of iPods to review learning contents of the lab, instructors become facilitators of knowledge rather than holders of it.

Figure 4. Students in the Avionics Program doing collaborative learning with the help of video iPods

Instructors interviewed for this research stressed the fact that the changes in the lab did not come only from the use of iPods, but from their use of different learning techniques and lab time. The fact that they knew that their students were familiar with the content review in the lab allowed instructors to let the students help each other solving problems in a collaborative way. Furthermore, instead of lecturing, instructors developed a "problem based" approach where students in the lab came to them only if they were not able to solve a particular problem on their own.

Instructors' pedagogic views are decisive when they use new technologies in teaching. For example, Bates (2000) underlines that new technologies need different teaching approaches and an understanding of the teaching process itself. The application of new pedagogic models has resulted in an ideological shift in the relationship between instructors and students (Collis and Moonen, 2001; Laurillard, 2002; Sloman, 2001). In this case study, the application of a new pedagogical framework was crucial for the success of the use of iPods inside and outside the lab.

One instructor using iPods with her students emphasized the fact that it was her personal challenge to use innovative pedagogic techniques that motivated her towards the use of video iPods inside her classroom. It was with the application of innovative pedagogic techniques that she made valuable use of video iPods to review lab procedures:

My challenge is more related to an innovative pedagogic practice, not to the use of the iPod. After coming from a conference, I was really motivated to use video iPods to complement the teaching process that happens inside the labs. It is true, iPods support the course, but the valuable thing about this innovation is the pedagogic design involved. (Interview with an innovative instructor, Avionics Program, May 2008)

This opinion was shared by another instructor who also was willing to change his approach to a centralized model of teaching:

From a technological point of view, my labs have not changed that much. What changed a lot was the introduction of pedagogic techniques such as personal learning. Since I began using the video iPods, the collaborative working in my lecture room has increased. (Interview with an instructor using video iPods, May 2008)

Figure 5 is a summary of instructor perception of changing roles:

5. FUTURE RESEARCH DIRECTIONS

Research presented in this chapter is only an example of how mobile technologies (video iPods in this case) can contribute to new pedagogical practices across colleges and universities and how they are responding to the Net Gen students' learning expectations. As we look into the future of technology enhanced education, we are led to wonder what the future holds for higher education institutions using mobile technologies as part of their curricula. What can institutions, instructors, and students expect to see over the next number

Figure 5. Instructor perception of role change

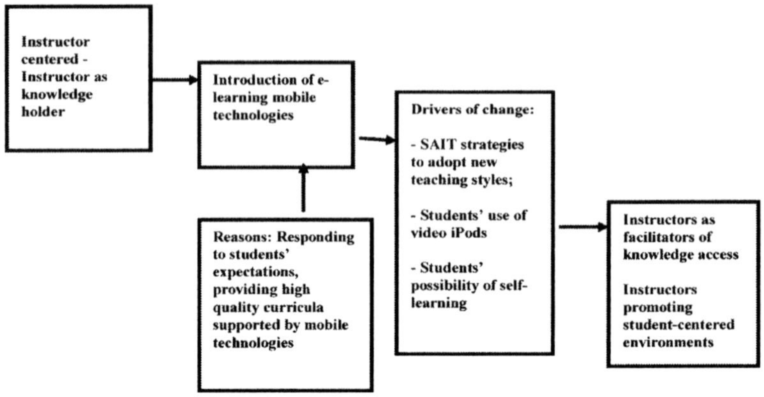

of years as mobile technologies become an even greater part of education contexts? Although there is not a certain answer to this question, we suspect that changes will be seen in all the areas connected to students' learning, including pedagogical practices, learning styles, faculty development, mobile technologies use and appropriation.

The mobility of learning that may result from portable devices (such as the video iPod) being given to students for their own use raises a lot of issues and potential areas of research. As higher education institutions analyze the possibility of using mobile technologies for teaching and learning in the near future, the following areas could be consider for further investigation:

1. Technology, infrastructure and services cost. Expenses should be considered when implementing mobile technologies for learning; not only the initial capital required to purchase devices and network equipment, but also the cost of technical support. Institutional analysis in this area should be considered.
2. Training requirements for all of those involved in the use of the mobile technology: students, instructors, curriculum developers, multimedia experts, etc. The successful use and implementation of the technology depends on each of these agents being properly trained for their use.
3. Research and assessment on which mobile technology is more suited to match institutional learning expectations. This assessment should include the pedagogical approach and the learning needs and goals.
4. Analysis and measurement of students' motivation in relation to the introduction of mobile technologies. As this chapter discussed, motivation has proved to be a determinant factor when using mobile technologies for learning.
5. Students' individual differences, such as age, gender, educational experience and learning style should also be explored when analyzing the potential use of mobile technologies.
6. Use of mobile technologies in non-academic areas, such as student administration tasks. Research on the use of mobile devices in different arenas can beneficial for classroom monitoring, student marks and personal information, etc.

The successful implementation of teaching and learning technologies in colleges and universities in the near future will depend on the planned research that is conducted before and during their application. As new technologies (those that we are familiar with at the present, and those that will become apparent in the future) make their presence known on the educational stage, institutions should be ready to evaluate them and research the technology's ability to be integrated into teaching and learning in the 21st century and beyond.

7. CONCLUSION

Using video iPods or any other mobile technology for teaching and learning in face to face or online environments is still a new issue for higher education institutions moving from traditional ways of course delivery to more student-centered models. The 'anytime, anywhere' capabilities of mobile devices encourage learning experiences outside the classroom, which in turn present significant challenges to conventional teaching practices in higher education institutions.

This chapter has provided a framework to help understand the participants and the processes of change in higher education institutions and the important role of mobile technologies in responding to Net Gen students' expectations for learning. An analysis of connectivism theory in relation to the use of new and innovative use of technologies for learning has also been included. Research presented here has shown that mobile devices such as cellular phones, video iPods, PDAs, games, and cameras have a great impact on learning. In the future, learning will move more and more outside the classroom and into the learner's environment, both real and virtual. Learning will involve making connections within these environments to resources and to other people. Learners will be able to manage the administration of their learning through consultations with their personal diaries and institution-based virtual learning environments.

This chapter has shown that there is a need for continuous research and evaluation within institutions using learning technologies. Bates (2000) and other authors in the area maintain that this is a topic that has to be further developed (Collis & Moonen, 2001; Palloff & Pratt, 2001; Salmon, 2001) and that not only quantitative but also qualitative explorations need to take place across higher education institutions that are using or are planning to use learning technologies.

Whether mobile technologies are welcome or rejected, the fact that they are finding their way into the classroom or the lab and into our student's pockets proves that educational institutions should see this as an opportunity to connect with the desires and dreams of the students. In the future (which has become the present already), the success of teaching and learning with mobile technologies will be measured by how educational institutions have incorporated them so that they become a part of our daily lives.

ACKNOWLEDGMENT

This project was possible thanks to the innovative ideas and dreams of two instructors in SAIT School of Transportation: Lisa Soderquist and Dean Radke. My gratitude goes to them and to their eighty students involved in the project. Finally, thanks also to CITD Multimedia team, led by the work of Nancy Miller.

REFERENCES

Anderson, P. (2007, February). What is Web 2.0? Ideas, technologies and implications for education. *JISC Technology and Standards Watch*. Retrieved December 9, 2008 from http://www.jisc.ac.uk/media/documents/techwatch/tsw0701b.pdf

Bates, A. (2000). *Managing technological change; Strategies for colleges and university leaders*. San Francisco, CA: Jossey-Bass Publishers.

Bates, A. (2007) Strategic planning for e-learning in a polytechnic. In M. Bullen & D. Janes (Eds.), *Making the transition into E-Learning: Strategies and Issues*. Hershey, PA: Information Science Publishing.

Burkle, M. (2003). *The impact of Information and Communication Technologies on Higher Education Systems*. Unpublished doctoral dissertation, University of Sussex, England.

Burkle, M., Miller, N., Soderquist, L., & Radke, D. (2008, May). *Using video iPods to support teaching and learning.* Paper presented at the Canadian Network of Innovation in Education Conference, Banff, AB, Canada.

Callaghan, M. J., Harkin, J., McGinnity, T. M., & Woods, D. N. (2006, November 8-10). Evaluation of technology supported pedagogy. In *Proceedings of APRU Distance Learning and the Internet Conference,* University of Tokyo, Japan.

Campbell, G. (2005, November). There's something in the Air. Podcasting in Education. *EDUCAUSE Review*. Retrieved January 10, 2008, from http://net.educause.edu/ir/library/pdf/erm0561.pdf

Chao, C. (2005). Evaluating teacher's attitudes towards the use of wireless-mobile technologies in supporting learning: an instrument development study. In *IEEE International Workshop, Wireless and Mobile technologies in Education,2005.*Retrieved March 27, 2008, from http://ieeexplore.ieee.org/xpl/freeabs_all.jsp?tp=&arnumber=1579245&isnumber=33360

Collis, B., & Moonen, J. (2001). *Flexible learning in a digital world.* London: Kogan Page.

Creanor, L., et al. (2006 August). *LEX: The learner experience of e-learning.* Final report presented at Glasgow Caledonian University, Scotland. Retrieved January 10, 2008, from http://www.jisc.ac.uk/uploaded_documents/LEX%20Final%20Report_August06.pdf

Daniels, J. S. (1998). *Mega universities and knowledge Media: Technology strategies for higher education*. London: Routledge.

Deal, A. (2007). Podcasting. A Teaching with Technology white paper. *Office of Technology for Education & Eberly Center for Teaching Excellence, Carnegie Mellon University*. Retrieved December 12, 2008, from http://connect.educause.edu/files/CMU_Podcasting_Jun07.pdf

Evans, T., & Nation, D. (2000). *Changing university teaching. Reflection on creating educational technologies*. London: Routledge.

Frydenberg, M. (2006). Principles and pedagogy: The two P's of podcasting in the information technology classroom. In *Proceedings of Information Systems Education Conference (ISECON)* (Vol. 23). Retrieved on December 10, 2008, from http://www.isedj.org/isecon/2006/3354/ISECON.2006.Frydenberg.pdf

Gibson, T., Koontz, D., & Van Den Hende, M. (2008, April 1-4) The digital generation: Teaching to a population that speaks an entirely new language. *Paper presented at the Chair Academy,* Denver, CO. Retrieved on January 12, 2009, from http://david.koontz.name/digital/Presentation_files/THE_DIGITAL_GENERATION.pdf

Harasim, L. (1990). *Online Education: Perspectives on a new environment*. New York: Praeger Publishers.

Hiltz, S. R. (1990). Evaluating the virtual classroom. In L. Harasim (Ed.), *Online education: Perspectives on a new environment*. New York: Praeger Publishers.

Holley, D., & Haynes, R. (2003). 'The INCOTERMS challenge': using multimedia to engage learners. *Education and Training*, *45*(7), 392–401. doi:10.1108/00400910310499965

International Journal of Teaching and Learning in Higher Education. Volume 19(1), 84-92. Retreived on Jan 16, 2008, from: http://www.isetl.org/ijtlhe/pdf/IJTLHE152.pdf

Jukes, I., & Dosaj, A. (2004). Understanding digital kids: Teaching and learning in the new digital landscape. *The InfoSavvy Group*. Retrieved January 15, 2009, from http://web.mac.com/iajukes/thecommittedsardine/Articles_files/ndl.pdf

Juniu, S. (2002). *Implementing Handheld computing technology in Education*. The Journal of Physical Education, Recreation and Dance, Vol. 73.

Kervin, L., & Vardy, J. (2006). A partnership for iPod pedagogy: Using technology of millennial learners across educational contexts. Proceedings of the 23rd Annual Ascilite conference. Sydney, Australia. Retrieved Dec 12, 2008, from: http://www.ascilite.org.au/conferences/sydney06/proceeding/pdf_papers/p111.pdf

Laurillard, D. (2002) *Rethinking University Teaching*. London: Routledge.

Mason, R. (1998). *Using Communications Media in Open and Flexible learning*. London: Kogan Page.

Moller, L. (1998). Designing Communities of Learners for Asynchronous Distance Education. *Educational Technology Research and Development*, *46*(1), 115–122. doi:10.1007/BF02299678

Naismith, L., Lonsdale, P., Giasemi, V., & Sharples, M. (2004). Literature Review in Mobile Technologies and Learning. Future Lab series. Retrieved online on March 31st, from: http://www.futurelab.org.uk/resources/documents/lit_reviews/Mobile_Review.pdf

Oblinger, D. (2005). Educating the Net generation. EDUCAUSE: Retreived on Jan 15, 2009, from: www.educause.edu/educatingthenetgen/

Oliver, B., & Goerke, V. (2007). Australian undergraduates' use and ownership of emerging technologies: Implications and opportunities for creating engaging learning experiences for the Net Generation. Australian Journal of Educational Technology 23 (2), 171 – 186. Retrieved on Jan 15, 2009, from: http://www.ascilite.org.au/ajet/ajet23/oliver.html

Palloff, R., & Pratt, K. (2001). Lessons from the Cyberspace Classroom. San Francisco: Jossey-Bass

Pasnik, S. (2007). iPod in Education: the Potential for Teaching and Learning. Series of iPod in Education white papers. Retreived Dec 12, 2008, from: http://edcommunity.apple.com/ali/galleryfiles/15300/ipod_in_educ_whitepaper.pdf

Perry, D. (2003). Hand-held computers (PDAs) in Schools. Coventry, UK: Becta.

Prensky, M. (2001) Digital Natives, Digital Immigrants. *On the Horizon* (MCB University Press, Vol. 9 (5) October. Retreived on Jan 15, 2009, from: http://helpdesk.muscatine.k12.ia.us/external/MPrensky.pdf

Prensky, M. (2007). How to teach with technology: keeping both teachers and students comfortable in an era of exponential change. *Emerging Technologies for Learning, Vol. 2*. British Educational Communications and Technology Agency (BECTA) (2007). http://partners.becta.org.uk/page_documents/research/emerging_technologies07_chapter4.pdf

Salaway., et al. (2008). The ECAR (Educause Center for Applied Research) Study of Undergraduate Students and Information Technology. Internet download Dec 10, 2008: http://net.educause.edu/ir/library/pdf/ers0808/rs/ers0808w.pdf

Salmon, G. (2001). E-Moderating: The key to teaching and learning online. London: Routlege/Falmer

Sfard, A. (1998). 'On two metaphors for learning and the dangers of choosing just one'. *Educational Researcher*, *27*(2), 4–13.

Siemens, G. (2005). Connectivism: A learning theory for the digital age. *International Journal of Instructional Technology & Distance Learning. Vol 2 (1).* Retrieved online on Mar 22, 2009 from Siemens, G (2006). *Learning in Sync with life: New Models, new processes. Google 2006 Training Summit white paper. Retrieved online on March 22, 2009 from:* http://www.elearnspace.org/Articles/google_whitepaper.pdf

Sloman, M. (2001). *The e-learning revolution*. London: Chartered Institute of Personnel and Development

Tapscott, D. (2008) Grown up digital. New York: McGraw-Hill.

Toledo, C. (2007) Digital Culture: Immigrants and Tourists. Responding to the Natives' Drumbeat

Wesch, M. (2007a). A vision of students today. YouTube video. Retrieved Dec 10, 2008, from: http://www.youtube.com/watch?v=dGCJ46vyR9o

Wesch, M. (2007b). The Machine is Us/ing us. YouTube video. Retrieved Dec 10, 2008, from: http://www.youtube.com/watch?v=6gmP4nk0EOE&feature=channel_page

Young, M. (1998). *The Curriculum of the Future. From the 'new sociology of education' to a critical theory of learning*. London: Falmer Press.

ENDNOTES

1 Young (1998) maintains that there are three models that determine educational policies priorities. These models could be compared with the discussion of the transmission versus participative model discussed in this section. The three models that Young defines are the 'schooling model', the 'credentialist model', and the 'access model'. The 'schooling model' puts the emphasis on the transmission framework, where learners are expected to have a high degree of participation in post-compulsory schooling. The 'credentialist model' places priority on the aim that learners should have the qualifications to achieve future employment. The 'access model' represents a vision of society where learners, freed from constraints, learn in any context they find themselves.

2 The process of 'podcasting' is defined as "a *collection of files (usually audio and video) residing at a unique Web feed address. The materials are prerecorded and users can check out the materials at their leisure time*". (Wikipedia, 2007; Deal, 2007; Frydenberg, 2006). Technically, the feed and subscription model of file delivery is what differentiates podcasting from posting files on the web.

* In 2006 the author of this chapter was appointed as the new CISCO Chair in e-learning. Dr. Burkle has continued the work that Dr. Bates started.

Chapter 15
M-Learning in the Field:
A Mobile Geospatial Wiki as an Example for Geo-Tagging in Civil Engineering Education

Christian Safran
Graz University of Technology, Austria

Martin Ebner
Graz University of Technology, Austria

Frank Kappe
Graz University of Technology, Austria

Andreas Holzinger
Graz University of Technology, Austria

ABSTRACT

In subjects such as Civil Engineering, Architecture, Geology etc., education is mostly based on visual information. For example, in Civil Engineering every building can be seen as a unique object at a certain location. During the education of Civil Engineers many field based studies and excursions take place, however, not only the images but also geographical coordinates are essential. Wikis have been in use for collaborative learning for more than ten years. Mobile phones provide access to them from nearly everywhere. The availability of those technologies has led to rapid advances in the area of m-Learning and the possibility to apply challenging constructive educational concepts. Consequently, in this paper we describe the user centered design, development and evaluation of a combination of these technologies to support collaborative learning in the field: A Wiki-based mobile geospatial information system, the so-called TUGeoWiki. The primary objective of this geowiki is to provide a user-friendly tool for mobile collaborative learning for all areas where geo-tagged information could be useful. Moreover, TUGeoWiki was developed in order to provide the integration of external map material via

DOI: 10.4018/978-1-61520-678-0.ch015

map APIs including information such as that delivered by Google Maps. Subsequently, it is possible to provide both highly detailed maps and satellite images without having the need to license such material. Furthermore, the user interfaces used by such tools is well established, due to the increasing number of mapping related mashups. The evaluation during an extensive field test within a large civil engineering excursion to various large-scale construction sites in Austria demonstrated that collaborative learning can be successfully supported by the application of TUGeoWiki.

GEOTAGGING AND CIVIL ENGINEERING

In subjects such as Civil Engineering, Architecture, Geology etc. education is mostly based on visual information. According to Brohn "the language of intuition is visual, just as the language of analysis is abstract and symbolic" (Brohn, 1983). This is especially true in the field of Civil Engineering where sketches and drawings are highly necessary, because there is a strong relationship between nature and mathematical models (Ebner, Scerbakov, & Maurer, 2006). Learning by studying existing load bearing models is essential for becoming a good engineer. Further, it must be pointed out that every building can be seen as a unique object at a precise location. So on-site excursions and field studies are common and are used to give learners more practical examples on how real-life situations look. One of the most difficult tasks is to find an appropriate physical relationship to describe an engineering model, because of the complex coherences. To represent nature with a simple and calculable structure is the first job of a structural engineer. However, all these arguments should show why visualizations are absolutely necessary for this work and are the basis for further work.But not only images help to plan and understand buildings, also geographical information is of interest:

- Where is a building located geographically?
- Which types of buildings are especially predominant in certain areas?
- In the case of large projects (streets, tunnels, hydraulic structures) where are the different contract sections?

Needless to say, that there are many more questions, which can be answered by providing global coordinates. From a technical perspective it must be pointed out, that nowadays mobile phones, such as the Nokia N95, with GPS modules on board, make it easy to add coordinates automatically to pictures. Access to the World Wide Web is available, in some shape or form, from nearly everywhere in Austria.

In this paper we would like to address the research question on how the learning behavior of structural engineering students can be enhanced by geotagged real-life, on-site, pictures. The main idea is that students, as well as lecturers, should take geotagged pictures with them during their field studies or excursions and upload them to a Wiki system in order to write collaborative articles about these pictures. Upon upload, the appropriate Google Maps section is automatically added to show the place on different maps. The questions that we would like to answer in the first phase are: How comfortable is the use of mobile phones in combination with GPS for lecturers on-site? How should the application look to allow user-centered collaborative work? How can global coordinates enhance the daily learning process of students?

This paper mainly concentrates on the implemented Wiki system and describes it from a technical point of view. Then, a preliminary field study is presented to show the general idea. Finally, problems as well as potentials are discussed and further work will be specified.

THEORETICAL BACKGROUND AND RELATED WORK

Today, the *organization of learning* is changing, especially in secondary schools and universities. However, in this context, new technologies offer the opportunity for pupils and students to communicate and interact with multimedia learning resources and simulated environments (A. Holzinger, 2002). Consequently, technology **can** enhance motivation, which is a vital aspect of learning (A. Holzinger, 1997), deliver information when needed, and encourage to *solve problems* and *satisfy curiosity* (Sharples, Corlett, & Westmancott, 2002). Most of all, new technologies also offer the possibility to *scaffold* learners through an extended process of capturing and organizing *situated activities* (Sharples, 2000).

To date, the use of computers in education has mostly been focused on enhancing learning in *formal settings,* typically in the traditional classroom or computer lab (Mifsud, 2002). However, learning does not only take place within such formal learning settings. The use of mobile devices could expand learning possibilities and solve the problem of being tied to a particular location.

Generally, the combination of e-Learning and mobile computing is called *mobile learning* (m-Learning) and promises the access to applications that support learning anywhere, anytime (Tatar, Roschelle, Vahey, & Penuel, 2003). Due to technological progress, meanwhile hardware is considered a solved problem. However, innovative, affordable and usable software remains still the greatest challenge. Handhelds, for example, should support **project-based learning in context,** that is, using the mobile as an integral part of a **learning activity** (Norris & Soloway, 2004). One of the central advantages of mobile learning is ongoing assessment and possible feedback, as demonstrated in (Klamma, et al., 2007), (Andreas Holzinger, Nischelwitzer, & Meisenberger, 2005), or (Robert, Paul, & Mark, 2007).

In m-Learning the issue of technology acceptance has been largely overlooked, although previous research showed that low-cost applications with low maintenance required are the most well-accepted (Tretiakov & Kinshuk, 2008).

An often-neglected issue is that the material offered is not attuned to learners' experience, expertise, and most of all their previous knowledge. It is important to acknowledge that distracting information and elements, which are not necessary to comprehend a concept, must be avoided as far as possible. The information provided to the learners must support the generation of appropriate mental models of the end-users. Moreover, the more complex and difficult the learning content is, the more important it is to direct cognitive and perceptual resources to intrinsic and germane processing, as i.e. argued in (Carroll & Mack, 1999), or (Kinshuk & Sampson, 2004). All those factors play an important role in contributing to is learners' satisfaction, which is a critical success factor in mobile device development (Chen, Lin, & Kinshuk, 2008). During development one can consider to include student modelling, which can be seen as important process for the design of learning environments. Such learner models include for example information about the end-users such as domain competence, learning style or cognitive traits (Graf, Lin, & Kinshuk, 2008).

Related Work

At Graz University of Technology Institute of Building Informatics a Wiki was used for lecturing and learning purposes for the first time in the beginning of 2005 (Ebner & Walder, 2008). The aim was to support lectures like Computer Science I, Computer Science II and Structural Concrete by creating a knowledge base for searching and retrieving information. Several studies were carried to show how Wiki-systems could be used for different learning processes. One of these studies was based on the identification and the establishment of those principles, that made Wikipedia successful (Ebner, Zechner, & Holzinger, 2006). Secondly Wikis were used as a tool to provide universal access in higher education (Ebner, Kickmeier-Rust, & Holzinger, 2008). Amongst others students wrote a civil engineering encyclopaedia, and there the problem of missing coordinates has been pointed out for the first time (Ebner & Walder, 2007).

One example for the use of mobile technologies for teaching purposes is the EU project RAFT (Remote Accessible Field Trips), which was conducted from 2002 to 2005. The target of the project was the support of school classes with virtual excursions using portable Internet-conferencing tools (Kravcik, Specht, Kaibel, & Terrenghi, 2003). In later stages the technology was incorporated in learning content management systems (Specht, Kaibel, & Apelt, 2005).

The term *geowiki* is already a well established term, which applies to geographically contextualized wikis (Priedhorsky, Jordan, & Terveen, 2007). Existing approaches focus on the aspect of a collaboratively editable and annotable map material[1].

REQUIREMENTS FOR TUGeoWiki

In order to cope with the previously defined requirements, a geowiki application was developed, which focuses on the description of the individual locations and the connections between them. The design of the TUGeoWiki server-side and client-side application was based on four central requirements.

Geotagging Interface

The first requirement was to provide a system, which is based solely on geotagged information. Several available geotagging applications allow subsequent geotagging of existing images, which is prone for mistakes. In the better case these mistakes result in inaccurate coordinates, which are just slightly off but preserve the relation to a place. In the worse case these coordinates are completely wrong and the relation to a place is broken, or a relation to a different place is created. Such misplacements can usually be corrected, but require that the user realizes the mistake, performs an additional action, and is knowledgeable about the correct position.

In order to avoid such misplacements from the outset, the information added to the TUGeoWiki must be properly geotagged. The two accepted alternatives to achieve this are the inclusion of the current location of the user (in a mobile setting) or the inclusion of the location stored within existing images (in a desktop setting). Both scenarios rely on a GPS receiver for providing information either about the current position or the position that should be included into the image files.

Mobile and Desktop Interface

The second requirement of the system is that it should be useful both while in the field and equally useful when post processing in a desktop environment. The first scenario makes it possible to retrieve information on the current location, upload images, and to create and edit location articles in TUGeoWiki. Although information retrieval is a fundamental feature while the user is in the field, image upload and article editing are intended for limited use only, due to possible bandwidth restrictions, and due to the general restrictions of mobile phones as input devices.

The second scenario is focused on discussion input, batch uploading of images, report writing, adding location information articles, and information retrieval.

Environment for Collaboration

In order to improve the impact on learning (in the desktop scenarios) a collaborative environment was identified as the third core requirement. Due to the positive results from its application in education, as shown in (Fucks-Kittowski, Köhler, & Fuhr, 2004), a Wiki was chosen for this task. Although there are several other Wiki systems available we decided to use Mediawiki[2]. Mediawiki is a software package originally developed for Wikipedia.

This decision was supported by the fact that Mediawiki is free software and therefore can be modified to fit the requirements for TUGeoWiki. Moreover, as it is used in Wikipedia, the user interface is probably familiar to the average user. Third, Mediawiki offers a well-defined framework for expansion. On the one hand a developer can implement extensions known as *special pages*, which are not-editable pages created on demand to perform a task (Mediawiki, 2008b). On the other hand the possibility to write *templates,* for the inclusion of standard texts, which can be edited by all users, allows the inclusion of additional material for the articles (Mediawiki, 2008a).

Map Mashup

The final requirement was to provide the integration of external location-based material based on the coordinates available for location articles in TUGeoWiki. This enables the integration of highly detailed material from external sources without the need to provide such material within TUGeoWiki itself, a concept known as a mashup. The term was coined by the music community and was used to describe when vocals and music from different songs were mixed to produce a new sound. In technology, the term refers to applications that combine contents from different sources and present them to the users seamlessly. The most obvious use for a mashup in the TUGeoWiki's case would be to integrate mapping material using an API such as the Google Maps API[3]. Numerous other map APIs are available and the integration of further material, such as geological data, could also be considered.

DEVELOPMENT OF THE TUGeoWiki APPLICATION

The final TUGeoWiki application consists of two independent systems that fulfill the requirements detailed above. Most of the interaction is performed using a Web application (a Mediawiki, with specially developed extensions) within a mobile and/or desktop browser. In order to make this extended functionality available on a mobile device in the field, an additional mobile client was implemented. Furthermore, as detailed above, several external applications were included in the final mashup.

Figure 1 depicts the components of the desktop application scenario and the interaction flow

Figure 1. Desktop scenario

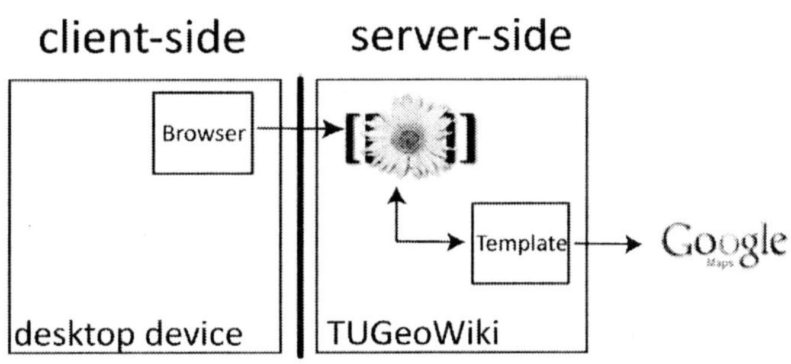

within them. On the client side all of the interaction is done with a browser, which connects to a Mediawiki on the TUGeoWiki server. The original Mediawiki is extended with two special pages. The first offers a list of all geotagged articles in the Wiki. More specifically, this page implements the functionality for the creation of new locations based on geographical coordinates. The second special page supports the image inclusion coordinates.

Within JPEG images additional information can be stored in a so-called EXIF header (Japan Electronics an Information Technology Industries Association, 2002). Besides metadata regarding a broad range of standard information such as date, time, or camera model, the EXIF header may also contain the geographical coordinates of the image. This information can either be added with a camera, while a photo is taken, or added at a later date. In order for the camera to be able to do this, it must have access to a (built-in) GPS receiver, such as the Ricoh 500SE camera or the Nokia N-95 high-end mobile phone. To add this information to the JPEG later, the user's coordinates must be recorded using a separate GPS tracker such as the Holux M-241 Datalogger[4] while the photo was taken. The coordinate information can later be merged with the images based on the image's and GPS coordinate's timestamps.

The server-side Mediawiki is further extended by a *template*, which is applied to all newly created location articles. The template contains a Google Map of the area around its coordinates and it links to the corresponding location on Google Maps and Microsoft Live Maps. Also, the template links to another Mediawiki extension called *GeoHack* which constructs links to various geographical services for the coordinates (Wikipedia, 2008). Finally, all location articles are added to a common *category*.

The mobile scenario extends the desktop scenario by integrating an additional application, which is on the mobile device, as depicted in figure 2. This application is responsible for accessing an internal or external GPS receiver and for relaying these coordinates to the TUGeoWiki application opened in the mobile phone's browser. For compatibility reasons the *Java Platform, Micro Edition*[5] (J2ME) was chosen for the development of this application. The application itself was designed using a model-view-controller pattern. It provides features to access the current location, to take an image and integrate this location, to search for location articles in a radius of 10-100 metres around the current position, and to upload images on the TUGeoWiki server. Figure 3 depicts three screenshots from the mobile application on the way to create a geotagged image. In the first step the source for the GPS coordinates is chosen. The second image depicts the main menu and the "take photo" tasks. The last image shows the usage of the mobile device's camera to take the image.

Upon uploading an image the user may then search for existing locations within a 10 to 100-metre radius of the coordinates embedded in the image. The image can subsequently be added to an existing location article, or a new article stub can be created containing just this image and

Figure 2. Mobile scenario

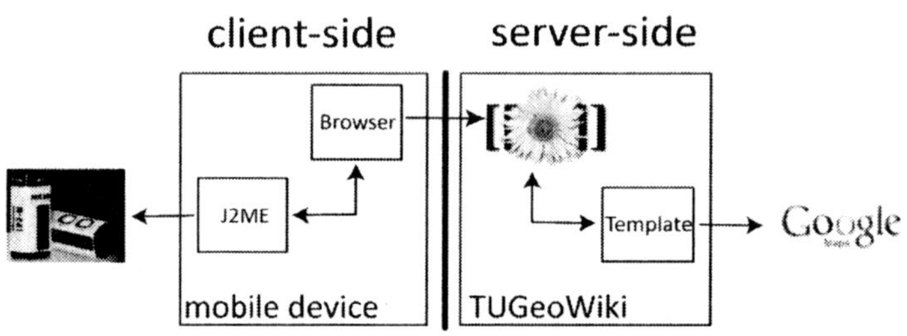

a *template* (previously described). This article stub can later be expanded, either in the mobile or desktop scenario. As mentioned above, the uploading of images, which are not geotagged is not permitted by the system in order to restrict the information contained in location articles to properly geotagged information.

The same restriction also affects the search for existing location articles. If no article within the chosen radius can be found, the user is presented with the option to create a new article stub containing only a location name and a *template* for further expansion.

EXPERIMENTAL SETTING AND METHODS: FIELD STUDY

In April 2008 the first field study with the TUGeoWiki prototype was conducted in the course of a civil engineering excursion. The goal of this study was to investigate the basic usefulness of the application within the scenario of an excursion in higher education. In order to provide this basic feedback for the developers, the lecturer was equipped with a Nokia N95 mobile phone with an integrated GPS receiver and was encouraged to take geotagged photos during the course of the excursion. The images were later uploaded to TUGeoWiki in the desktop scenario (see figure 4).

The experiment was concluded with a short interview with the lecture on his first impressions and the possible usefulness of the tool in future excursions. Furthermore also the limits and potentials of the software were carried out.

Following crucial factors can be pointed out:

- Geotagging by mobile phone: From a technical point of view the lecturer reported that using the mobile phone for taking geotagged pictures was easily possible. Only waiting for the GPS-signal for the first time seems to be cumbersomely in the same way as losing the signal indoors. In such cases manually geotagging or using the last coordinates maybe overcomes this situation.
- Easy Upload: The user also mentioned that the upload to the TUGeoWiki is easy and encouraged using the system. Due to the fact that each file must be uploaded one by one, a bulk upload of high number of files should be realized.
- Number of mobile phones with built-in GPS: One problem in the near future will be that of course not each student will own a mobile phone with built-in GPS. It may take some time until such devices are standard equipment. Especially for collaboration all pictures of the lecturers and learners should be gathered to present a lot

Figure 3. Screenshots from mobile scenario

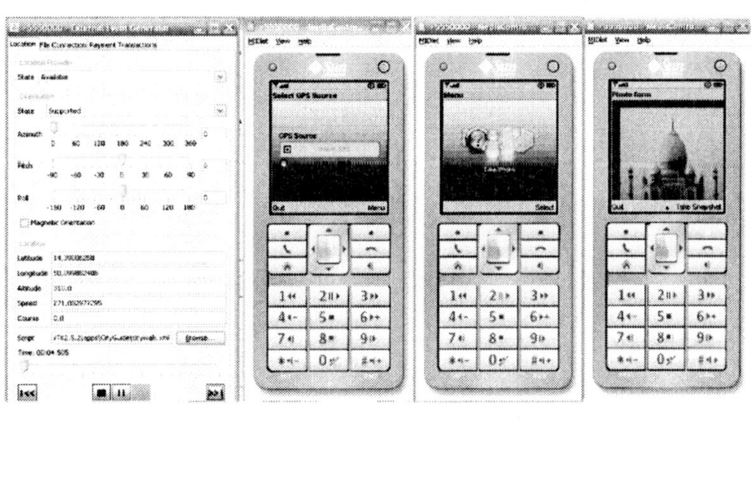

Figure 4. Example article from experimental study

of different details seen on-site. With the help of a GPS tracker this situation could be improved. The lecturer will record the location automatically in predefined time steps. These coordinates are subsequently synchronized with the timestamps of the images.

- Radius-depended upload: The lecturer pointed out that the radius-depended upload is extremely useful. By defining a radius (currently between 10-100 metres) all pictures within this distance are placed within one wiki page. Especially in the case of taking pictures of an object from different views and places the TUGeoWiki allows to put it one site instead of several pages. Concerning the dimension of building sites this is an absolutely necessary feature to avoid a huge amount of pictures loosing the connection to the corresponding location.
- Geological information: Another advantage of providing global coordinates for an object is that also geological information can be made available as well as hydraulic data. The combination of this data offers additional information, which helps analyzing different building measures. From a didactical point of view the lecturer can make the complex coherences between an object and its surrounding environment visible.
- Collaboration: Using TUGeoWiki for writing the students' reports should enhance collaboration in future. Furthermore by collecting a high number of pictures of different building sites a database for teaching can be established.

In the end it should be pointed out that though several images could not be extended with geographical coordinates, because they were indoor scenarios, and the study was restricted to a non-collaborative scenario, the feedback from the instructor confirmed the usefulness of the TU-GeoWiki approach for the intended application. A follow-up study will be conducted to test the functionality of the TUGeoWiki while working outdoors with student participants. The students participating in the excursion will be equipped with cameras and a GPS tracker, as well as several mobile phones with internal or external GPS receivers. The usefulness of these different approaches to add geotagged information into the TUGeoWiki will be surveyed. Finally the students will be assigned reports about different locations of the excursion, which will have to be collaboratively created based on the existing location stubs created from the images.

FUTURE DEVELOPMENT AND CONCLUSION

Mobile phones with built-in electronic magnetic compasses have been around for some time (e.g. the Nokia 5140), but not in combination with a GPS sensor. Together, these two sensors would allow us to determine not only where a picture was taken, but also the direction in which the device or person was facing, i.e., which building was actually being photographed. This would, of course, significantly enhance the usefulness and quality of the tags attached to a given picture.

From a didactical point of view the use of the TUGeoWiki in learning and teaching scenarios must be researched to see further potentials. Main buildings as well as famous ones can be described, located and discussed in a more collaborative way. Lecturers have to change their role towards a more steering and leading one.

However, subsequently the impact of this additional data has to be proven by using it in real-life scenarios. Of course also other departments like architecture should be supported in the future.

REFERENCES

Brohn, D. (1983). Academic priorities in structural engineering - the importance of a visual schema. *The Structural Engineer, 61 A*(1), 13-16.

Carroll, J. M., & Mack, R. L. (1999). Metaphor, computing systems, and active learning. *International Journal of Human-Computer Studies*, *51*(2), 385–403. doi:10.1006/ijhc.1984.0316

Chen, N. S., & Lin, K. M., & Kinshuk. (2008). Analysing users' satisfaction with e-learning using a negative critical incidents approach. *Innovations in Education and Teaching International*, *45*(2), 115–126. doi:10.1080/14703290801950286

Ebner, M., Kickmeier-Rust, M. D., & Holzinger, A. (2008). Utilizing Wiki-Systems in higher education classes: a chance for universal access? In *Universal Access in the Information Society*. New York: Springer.

Ebner, M., Scerbakov, N., & Maurer, H. (2006). New Features for eLearning in higher education for civil engineering. *Journal of Universal Computer Science*, *0*(0), 93–106.

Ebner, M., & Walder, U. (2007). *e-Learning in Civil Engineering - Six years of experience at Graz University of Technology*. Paper presented at the 24th W78 Conference.

Ebner, M., & Walder, U. (2008). *E-Education in civil engineering - A promise for the future?* Paper presented at the 6th AECEF Symposium Education in Changing Europe.

Ebner, M., Zechner, J., & Holzinger, A. (2006). *Why is Wikipedia so successful? Experiences in establishing the principles in higher education*. Paper presented at the 6th International Conference on Knowledge Management (I-Know'06).

Electronics, J. an Information Technology Industries Association. (2002). *Exchangable image file format for digital still cameras: Exif version 2.2*. Retrieved from http://www.exif.org/Exif2-2.PDF

Fucks-Kittowski, F., Köhler, A., & Fuhr, D. (2004). *Roughing up processes the wiki way - Knowlede communities in the context of work and learning processes.* Paper presented at the I-Know 2004.

Graf, S., Lin, T., & Kinshuk, J. (2008). The relationship between learning styles and cognitive traits - Getting additional information for improving student modelling. *Computers in Human Behavior, 24*(2), 122–137. doi:10.1016/j.chb.2007.01.004

Holzinger, A. (1997). Computer-aided Mathematics Instruction with Mathematica 3.0. *Mathematica in Education and Research, 6*(4), 37–40.

Holzinger, A. (2002). *Multimedia Basics, Vol. 2: Learning. Cognitive Fundamentals of multimedia Information Systems*. New Delhi, India: Laxmi.

Holzinger, A., Nischelwitzer, A., & Meisenberger, M. (2005, March 8-12). *Mobile phones as a challenge for m-learning: Examples of mobile interactive learning objects (MILOs).* Paper presented at the Third Annual IEEE International Conference on Pervasive Computing and Communications, Kauai Island, HI.

Kinshuk, D., & Sampson, G. (2004). Special issue on cognition and exploratory learning in the digital age. *Innovations in Education and Teaching International, 43*(2), 105–108.

Klamma, R., Chatti, M. A., Duval, E., Hummel, H., Hvannberg, E. T., & Kravcik, M. (2007). Social software for life-long learning. *Educational Technology & Society, 10*(3), 72–83.

Kravcik, M., Specht, M., Kaibel, A., & Terrenghi, L. (2003). *Collecting data on field trips - RAFT approach.* Paper presented at the The 3rd IEEE International Conference on Advanced Learning Technologies.

Mediawiki. (2008a). *Help:Templates*. Retrieved March 24, 2009, from http://www.mediawiki.org/w/index.php?title=Help:Templates&oldid=163132

Mediawiki. (2008b). *Manual:Special pages*. Retrieved March 24, 2009, from http://www.mediawiki.org/w/index.php?title=Manual:Special_pages&oldid=171875

Mifsud, L. (2002). *Alternative learning arenas - Pedagogical challenges to mobile learning technology in education.* Paper presented at the IEEE International Workshop on Wireless and Mobile Technologies in Education (WMTE'02), Växjö, Sweden.

Norris, C., & Soloway, E. (2004). Envisioning the handheld-centric classroom. *Journal of Educational Computing Research, 30*(4), 281–294. doi:10.2190/MBPJ-L35D-C4K6-AQB8

Priedhorsky, R., Jordan, B., & Terveen, L. (2007). *How a personalized geowiki can help bicyclists share information more effectively*. Paper presented at the 2007 International Symposium in Wikis (WikiSym).

Robert, C. P., Paul, D. C., & Mark, S. (2007). *Geo-tagging for imprecise regions of different sizes*. Paper presented at the Proceedings of the 4th ACM workshop on Geographical information retrieval.

Sharples, M. (2000). The design of personal mobile technologies for lifelong learning. *Computers & Education, 34*, 177–193. doi:10.1016/S0360-1315(99)00044-5

Sharples, M., Corlett, D., & Westmancott, O. (2002). The design and implementation of a mobile learning resource. *Personal and Ubiquitous Computing*, *6*(3), 220–234. doi:10.1007/s007790200021

Specht, M., Kaibel, A., & Apelt, S. (2005). *Extending LCMS for remote accessible field trips in RAFT.* Paper presented at the Third IEEE International Conference on Pervasive Computing and Communications Workshops.

Tatar, D., Roschelle, J., Vahey, P., & Penuel, W. R. (2003). Handhelds go to school: Lessons learned. *Computer*, *36*(9), 30–37. doi:10.1109/MC.2003.1231192

Tretiakov, A., & Kinshuk. (2008). Towards designing m-learning systems for maximal likelihood of acceptance. *International Journal of Engineering Education*, *24*(1), 79–83.

Wikipedia. (2008). *WikiProject Geographical coordinates*. Retrieved from http://en.wikipedia.org/w/index.php?title=Wikipedia:WikiProject_Geographical_coordinates&oldid=174960235

ENDNOTES

1 http://www.geowiki.com/ (accessed 2009-03-24), and http://worldkit.org/doc/geowiki.php, (accessed 2009-03-24)

2 http://www.mediawiki.org/wiki/MediaWiki/de (accessed 2009-03-24)

3 http://maps.google.com (accessed 2009-03-24)

4 http://www.holux.com/JCore/en/products/products_content.jsp?pno=341 (accessed 2009-03-24)

5 http://java.sun.com/javame/index.jsp (accessed 2008-03-24)

Section 5.2
Use of Collaboration Tools

Chapter 16
Learning in an Active, Collaborative Space

Michele P. Notari
University of Teacher Education, Switzerland

Beat Döbeli Honegger
University of Teacher Education, Switzerland

ABSTRACT

Based on the implications of technological progress and socioconstructivist learning theory, trends are being developed for tools to promote learning in the information society of the 21st century. The future promises a massive increase in information and its ubiquitous availability, along with an increase in computer-mediated communication. It is particularly important to understand that the communication requests placed on the individual and the range of available communication channels will increase in coming years. Tools must therefore be conceptualized to manage the communication and information glut of the future in an "intelligent" way permitting a collaborative way of learning. Looking ahead, lifelong, rather informal and problem-based learning could become significantly more important than formal learning. The characteristics of wikis will be presented as a possible representative example and explored based on the above criteria. The chapter concludes with prognoses on the nature of ICT supported learning in coming years.

The current search for new educational funnels must be reversed into the search for their institutional inverse: educational webs which heighten the opportunity for each one to transform each moment of his living into one of learning, sharing, and caring. (Illich, 1970, p. 2)

DOI: 10.4018/978-1-61520-678-0.ch016

1. INTRODUCTION

In this section a number of prognoses are presented concerning the future characteristics of ICT-supported learning tools based on current trends towards an information society. The discussion will address technological developments as well as their technological and social consequences while also the exploring the competences required for living in an information society. After describing a possible conception of learning and showing a didactic method that can be derived from it, some characteristics that learning tools may possess in the future will be inferred.

This section attempts to extrapolate these characteristics to their logical limits. Despite this fundamental approach, certain important aspects of living and learning in the 21st century will not be explored in depth. The discussion will not be extended, for example, to the consequences of globalization and dwindling natural resources, nor to the challenges posed by these developments (e.g., living and working in multicultural societies; sustainable development).

Figure 1 provides a structured overview of the considerations in this section in the form of a concept map (Novak, Gowin 1985). An enlarged version of the presented map can be found at the following url: http://beat.doebe.li/publications/liaacs/. The elements of the map discussed in the individual subsections are displayed in enlarged resolution. An introductory caveat is appropriate at this juncture: Although the concept map – which graphically displays the key aspects of each section – may convey a picture of reality that is highly deterministic, the authors do not endorse this conception. Reality is extremely complex, and eludes accurate schematization in a concept map. This form of presentation is useful, however, and has been selected in order to shed light on key developments and interrelationships.

In addition, as the goal of this section is to infer the future characteristics of learning tools, no attempt has been made incorporate reciprocal effects and feedback mechanisms between the displayed concepts, despite the fact that such mechanisms and effects do surely exist. Please try to keep in mind the concept map presented as figure 1 while reading the whole section. The map figures as leitmotiv, all terms, descriptions and definitions mentioned in the subsections refer to elements and connections of the map. Even if parts of the map are shown in the related subsections the 'whole picture' is crucial to understand the presented ideas.

2. HOW ICT CHANGES EDUCATION GOALS AND EDUCATIONAL TOOLS

2.1 Moore's Law

In 1965, Gordon Moore, a co-founder of Intel, the world's largest manufacturer of semiconductors, predicted in the magazine Electronics that, in coming years, it would be possible to double the number of transistors in an integrated circuit every year (Moore 1965). Moore pointed out that, on average, transistor counts had doubled every year in previous years and that the laws of physics did not prevent this trend from continuing unabated (Figure 2). While the amount of time required to double the density of transistors on a microchip has increased over past decades (up to about 18 months), Moore's law has remained valid to this day. According to experts, computing power will continue to grow at a nearly exponential rate until about 2020, when physical and economic limitations will be reached.

2.2 Technological Consequences of Moore's Law

With the increasing availability of computing power for the storage, processing, and transmission of digital data, information and communication technology (ICT) is playing an ever-more prominent role in our lives. Data are available in digital format everywhere and can be processed automatically.

The universal coding of data in binary format is leading to the convergence of previously distinct tools and media (Negroponte 1995): the computer, for example, combines the typewriter, adding machine, and file cabinet in one device, while the internet unites the traditional media of the

Figure 1. Outline of the section as a concept map

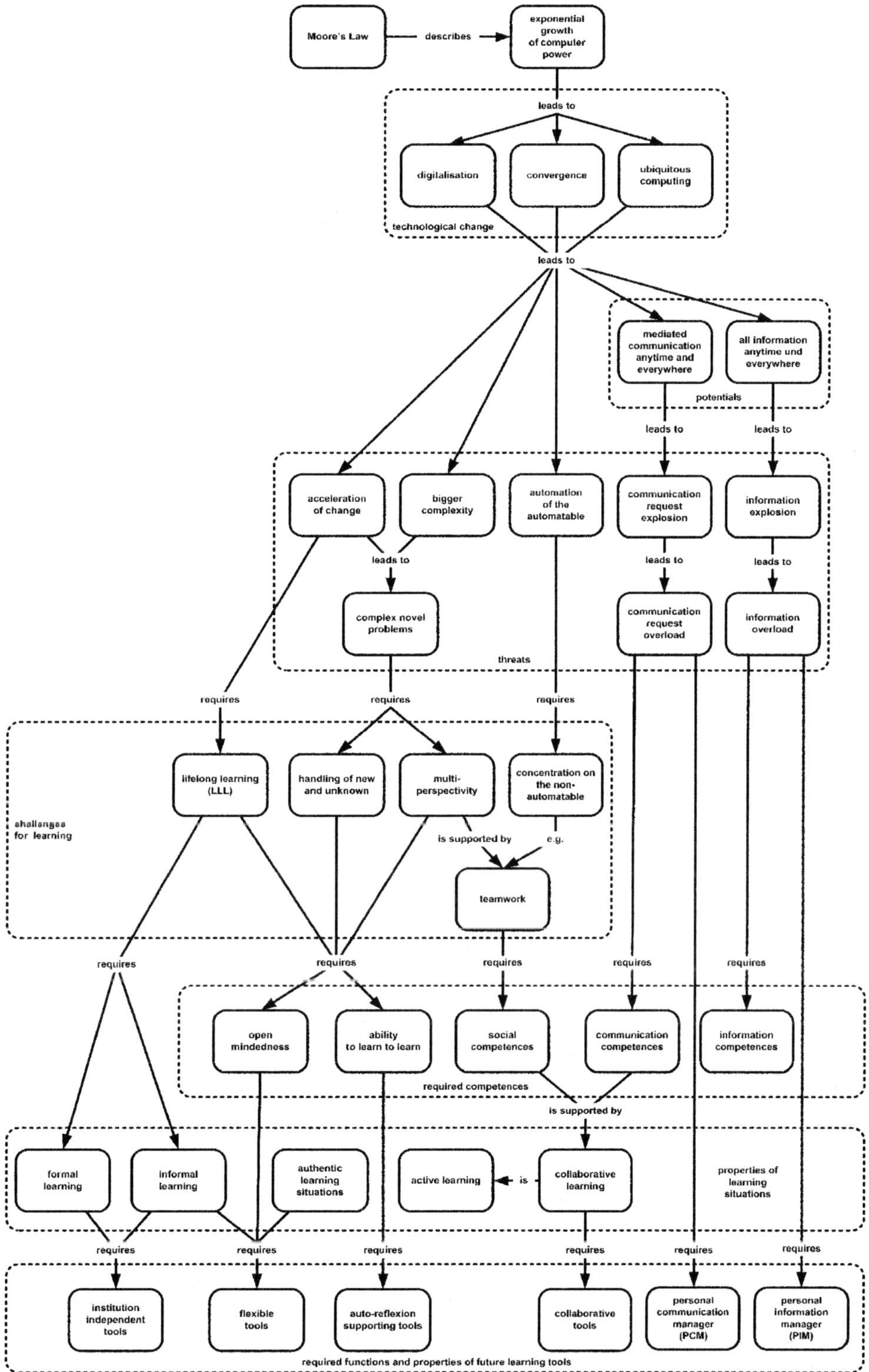

Figure 2. Technological change

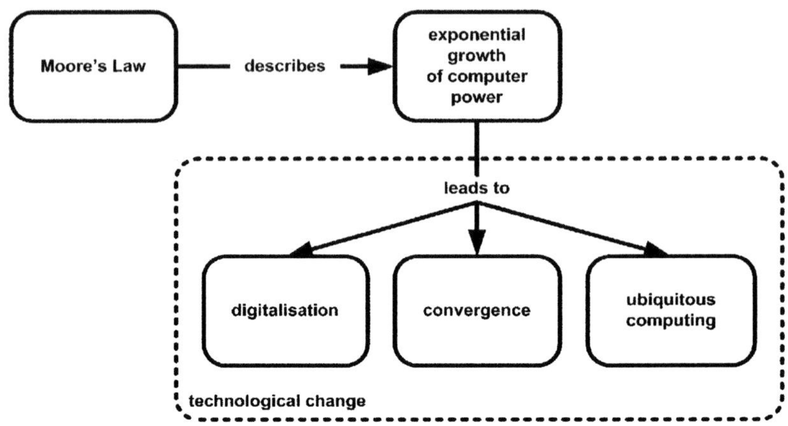

newspaper, radio, and television in a new medium. Therefore Kay and Goldberg call the computer a metamedium (Kay & Goldberg, 1977).

There are four possibilities as to how new digital tools and media can impact existing tools and media:

- Extinction: The new digital tools and media replace existing tools and media. Digital photography, for example, has largely replaced analog photography.
- Convergence: ICT combines previously distinct tools and media in a new, unified format.
- Coexistence: The new possibilities offered by ICT are used in tandem with existing tools and media.
- Evolution: While new tools and media are typically used at first as an imitation of existing tools and media, with time new and previously unknown forms of use can develop.

To the present day the computer remains a visible emblem of the trend towards an increasingly information-based society. Yet as early as 1991, Marc Weiser was using the term ubiquitous computing to prophesize a future in which computers would become an omnipresent but hidden feature of our environment, as they would be integrated in everyday items (Weiser 1991). The future envisioned by Weiser is already becoming a reality: A modern passenger car boasts more computing power than the first desktop computer, yet no one would view their car as a computer on wheels. State-of-the-art cellular telephones also have massive data processing and storage capacity, but are not perceived as computers in a standard sense. The majority of experts also see a trend in the direction of mobile computing. In a survey of 578 experts, 77% agreed that the mobile phone is the primary connection tool for most people in the world (Anderson & Rainie 2008).

The computer scientist Klaus Haefner postulated in 1982 that the increasing availability of information and communication technologies would lead to ever-greater automation. For economic reasons, everything that can be automated will be automated (Haefner 1982). This viewpoint – originally formulated in the early 1980s – is still shared by experts such as Thomas Friedman (Friedman 2005).

2.3 The Effects of Technological Development on Professional and Private Life

The developments described above are leading to a situation in which all of the world's information is increasingly available at any time, from any

Figure 3. Potentials and threats of technological change

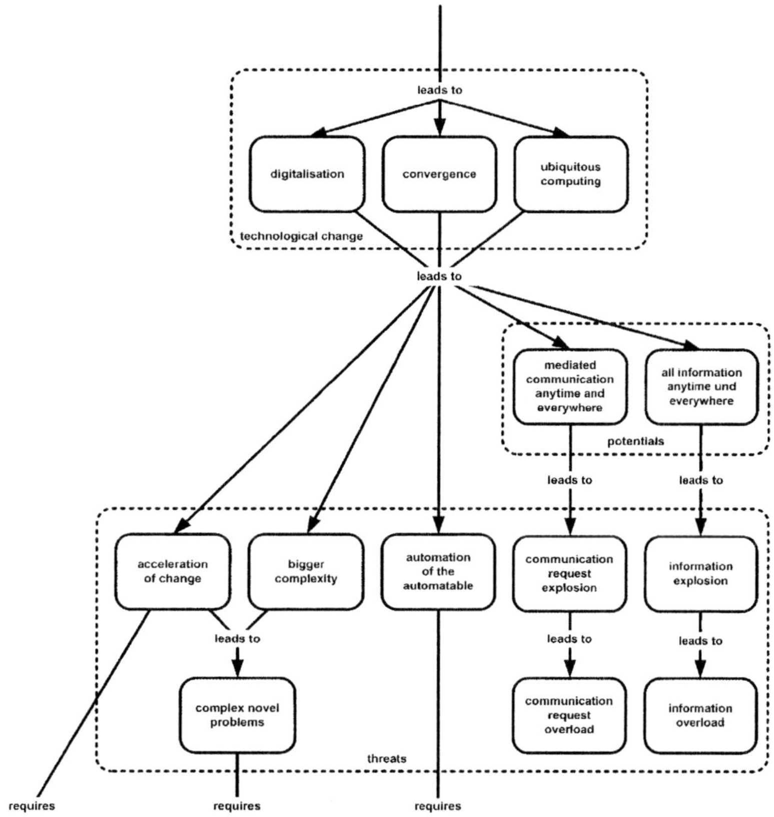

place. In addition, individuals can communicate through digital channels with increasing ease, and automation is on the rise. Our professional and private lives are impacted tremendously by these trends.

The resulting challenges can be described under the rubric of more, faster, and greater complexity (Figure 3):

- More: With the increasing availability of information and options for digital communication, the individual is faced by the latent danger of an information and communication-request overload.
- Faster: The availability of information at all times and places as well as the increasing automation of processes are causing developments to move at an accelerated pace, as less time is required to complete tasks. The free time thus attained is used to develop new processes.
- Greater complexity: The newly developed processes are often more complex as existing ones, as existing data and processes form the basis for new ones. This makes complex processes easier to manage and attracts users.

2.4 Challenges for the Individual

As a result the above, the individual is confronted by new challenges. The ubiquitous availability of digital information and communications poses the threat of an information and communication-request overload. To manage this threat, information and communication competences are required.

Figure 4. Challenges for learning

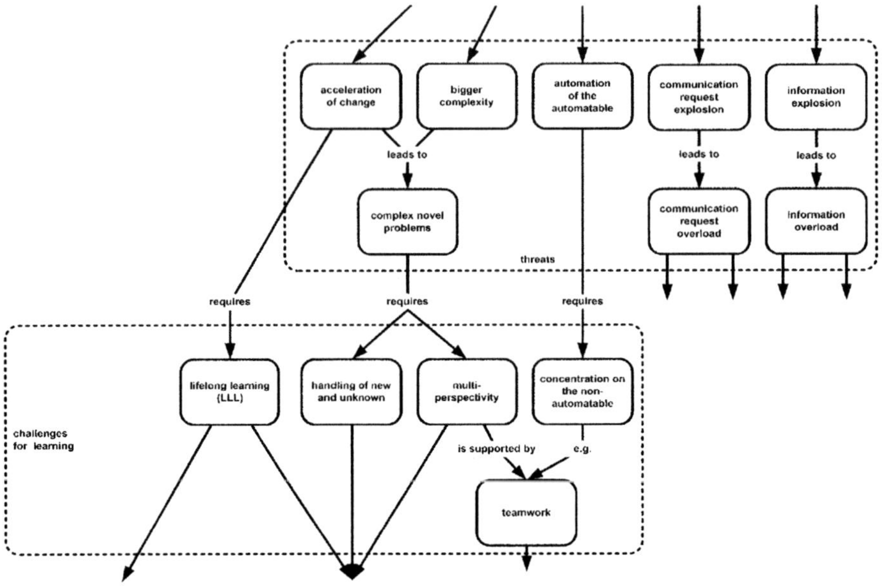

The accelerated rate of change requires lifelong learning and the proper handling of new and unknown problems. To thrive in an information society, the individual thus needs the ability to see things from multiple perspectives and to retain an open mind (Figure 4).

Haefner and Friedman both advance the view that it is fruitless to resist increasing automation. Rather, it is necessary to concentrate on the non-automatable. Haefner envisions two such occupational groups: The first group consists of the autonomes, who complete their work without the use of ICT. The second group consists of the Unberechenbaren ("non-computables"), who, with the help of ICT, fulfill complex jobs that rely heavily on communication and cannot be automated (Haefner 1992, p. 192) Friedman has formulated a similar concept and describes this second occupational group as the "untouchables" (Friedman 2005).

3. NECESSARY COMPETENCES FOR THE INFORMATION SOCIETY OF THE 21ST CENTURY

Globalisation will increase diversity and interconnection within the world. Individuals need to master changing technologies and to make sense of large amounts of available information. In these contexts, the **competences** the individuals need to meet their goals have become more complex, requiring more than the mastery of certain narrowly defined skills (Rychen & Salganik 2001).

According to Weinert, a competence is not reducible to cognitive skills, but instead also contains social, emotional, motivational, and behavioral components (Weinert 2001). The OECD project "Defining and Selecting Key Competencies (DeSeCo)" examined which *key competencies* would be essential in the future (Figure 5). Three categories of competencies were identified by the study: dealing with socially heterogeneous groups; autonomous action and creativity; and the interactive use of media and tools (Rychen & Salganik 2001).

Figure 5. Required competences

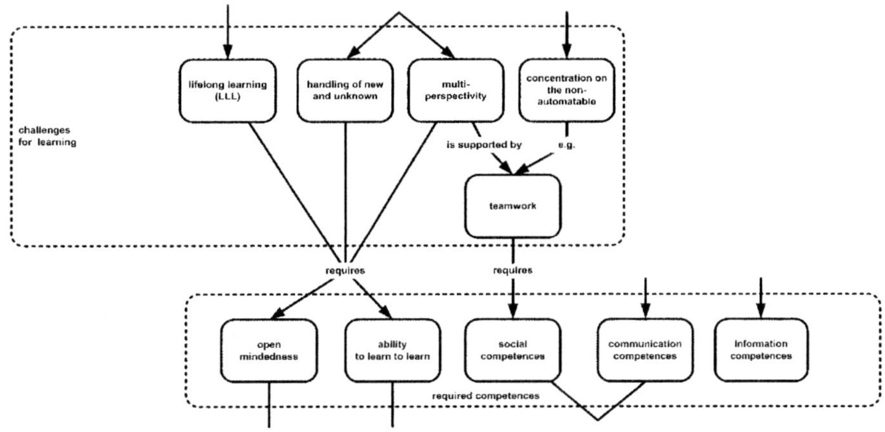

In pedagogy, the concept of competence goes back to the competence-model of Klafki (2000). Euler (2006) proposed a possible way to operationalize Klafki's model in the form of a matrix of competences. Table 1 shows this matrix filled in with the concepts proposed in Figure 5.

A short description of some terms may help understanding the importance of the different competences: Self-competence is a term described by Susan Harter (1982) referring to perceived ability in subject areas as a whole. This makes the definition very similar to self-concept, a term associated with Rosenberg (1965), Shavelson et al. (1976), and Marsh (1990). However, while self-concept also addresses students' beliefs about academic difficulties and student affect, self-competence refers only to their perceptions related to success. The term 'social competence' or 'social competences' refer to the social, emotional and cognitive skills and behaviors that persons need for successful social adaptation (Fiedler, 2003). Open mindedness has been pointed out by several researchers as one of the most likely characteristics associated with successful cross-cultural adjustment (Caligiuri, Jacobs, & Farr 2000, Van Oudenhoven, Van der Zee, & Van Kooten 2001, Yamazaki & Kayes 2004)

4. A CONTEMPORARY UNDERSTANDING OF LEARNING

Nowadays, learning is described, defined, and interpreted in very different ways. In the following passage a short overview of one of many concepts of learning is presented. We have chosen

Table 1. Organization of proposed competencies from the concept map (Fig. 1. and 5.) in Euler's matrix of competences (2006)

Dimensions of action / Areas of competence	Knowledge	Skills	Attitudes
Subject competence	*Information competences*	*Learning to learn; Information competences*	*Open mindedness*
Social competences	*Social competences; Communicative competences*	*Social competences; Communicative competences*	*Open mindedness; Social competences; Communicative competences*
Self-competence		*Learning to learn*	*Open mindedness*

a 'concept-mix' we suppose to be relevant for the evolving characteristics of future learning tools. Of course many other understandings of contemporary learning concepts and theories exist.

We start from the idea that learning is a social and active process. We then describe a motivational learning strategy and provide an overview regarding different types of learning. From these types of learning, we point out two learning methods (active, collaborative learning) and a didactic concept (problem based learning). The acquisition of competences in a world of increasing complexity and the fast-pace of change, is a lifelong learning process. Since formal learning occurs mostly in childhood and young adulthood, the role of informal learning has grown in significance. Information technologies also offer supplemental possibilities for informal education during childhood and young adulthood (Sefton-Green 2004).

4.1 Learning as Active, Constructive and Social Process

Using the theoretical work of Lev Vygotsky, an authority on socioconstructive learning theory and Albert Bandura, representing the behaviourist movement, learners activity and the importance of social interaction to learning processes are discussed:

The social cognitive theory explains how people acquire and maintain certain behavioral patterns, while also providing the basis for intervention strategies (Bandura 1997). It emphasizes the importance of observing and modeling the behaviors, attitudes, and emotional reactions of others. Evaluating behavioral change depends on the factors environment, people, and their behavior.

Vygotsky's theory of social cognitive development is complementary to Bandura's social learning theory. Its major thematic thrust is that "social interaction plays a fundamental role in the development of cognition" (Kearsley 1994). Vygotsky focused on the connections between people and the sociocultural context in which they act and interact in shared experiences (Crawford, 1996). According to Vygotsky, humans use tools that develop from a culture, such as speech and writing, to mediate their social environments (Crawford, 1996). Vygotsky's theory promotes learning settings where learners play an active role in learning. The role of learning manager (teacher) and learner are therefore shifted, as the teacher should not transmit instructions but rather collaborate with the learners in order to facilitate **meaning construction** in learners (Crawford, 1996).

The learning act is described above as an active, social and constructive process. In contemporary and in future learning scenarios the social interactions are intended to happen directly (face to face) or mediated by technology. Not only the interaction can be enhanced or sustained by technology but also the construction or co-construction of knowledge and learners activity. Mechanisms enhancing social interaction might be represented by communication and collaboration tools. Tools permitting and facilitating editing and sharing of meanings enhance (co-) construction of knowledge. Self determination theory and personal motivation may help to understand and enhance learners activity.

4.2 Self-Determination and Personal Motivation

Informal learning requires a high level of intrinsic motivation. The self-determination theory of Deci and Ryan describes three psychological needs that motivate one to engage in this behavior, namely, the need for competence, need for autonomy, and the need for relatedness (Deci & Ryan, 2002).

- Need for competence: refers to the need to actively experience oneself as competent in controlling the environment (Deci & Ryan 2002).

- Need for autonomy (or self-determination): refers to the need to participate in determining one's own behavior. It includes the need to experience one's actions as result of autonomous choice (Deci & Ryan 2002).
- Need for relatedness: refers to need to care for and be related to others. It includes the need to experience authentic relatedness from others and to experience satisfaction in participation and involvement with the social world (Deci & Ryan 2002).

The described needs underpin the importance of the predictions of the future tools: relatedness refers to the importance of being involved within a social environment. Learning in a social environment is a collaborative process, and the need for competence relates to the importance of being up to date with the changing world and induces active lifelong learning activities. The need for autonomy refers to independence from formal (learning) frameworks. Autonomy and environment control also enhances learners motivation and self determination which has an impact on his behavior / his learning activity.

4.3 More than Formal Learning

The necessity of lifelong learning has the consequence that a one-time educational program in school and college is no longer sufficient. Instead, continuous learning outside institutions is also necessary. For this reason, a distinction is drawn between two different types of learning:

- "**Formal learning** is accomplished in school, courses, classrooms, and workshops. It's official, it's usually scheduled, and it teaches a curriculum. Most of the time, it's top-down: learners are evaluated and graded on mastering material someone else deems important. Those who have good memories or test well receive gold stars and privileged placement. Graduates receive diplomas, degrees, and certificates." (Cross 2006, p. 16)
- "**Informal learning:** It can happen intentionally or inadvertently. No one takes attendance, for there are no classes. No one assigns grades, for success in life and work is the measure of its effectiveness. No one graduates, because learning never ends. Examples are learning through observing, trial-and-error, calling the help line, asking a neighbor, traveling to a new place, reading a magazine, conversing with others, taking part in a group, composing a story, reflecting on the day's events, burning your finger on a hot stove, awakening with an inspiration, raising a child, visiting a museum, or pursuing a hobby." (Cross 2006, p.16)

The new technologies affect both formal and informal learning. Due to the acceleration of change (see Figure 1) the "half-life of knowledge" — i.e. its validity in terms of being up-to-date and accurate — decreases. To keep abreast of developments, lifelong learning is therefore indispensable. Formal education (i.e. formal learning) normally stops at the age of 20-25. Because of the necessity of lifelong learning and rising life expectancy, **informal** learning will increase in importance.

4.4 Collaborative Learning

The first findings concerning factors that enhance collaborative learning evolved from the works of Piaget (1926) and Vygotsky (1978), who contended that learning occurs more effectively through interpersonal interactions in a cooperative rather than competitive context. Compared to individual learning, research on traditional face-to-face collaborative learning has revealed numerous benefits: better performance, better motivation, higher test scores and achievement, the development of high-level thinking skills, as well as higher student satisfaction, etc. (Dansereau

Figure 6. Properties of learning situations

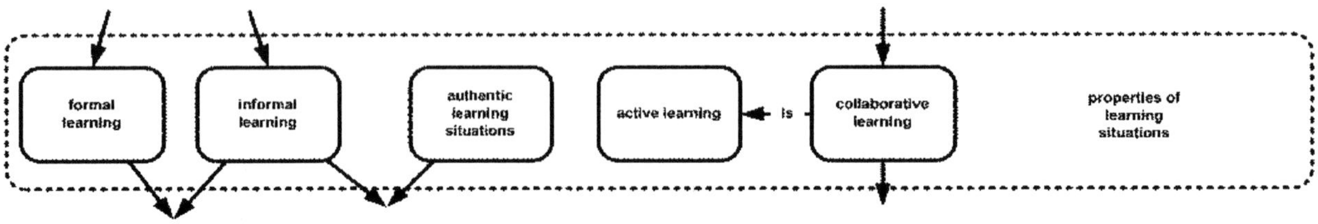

1983, Slavin 1987; Sharon 1990). More recent research on computer-supported collaborative learning (CSCL) has confirmed these benefits and has shown that they can be enhanced even further through adequate technological support (see e.g. Alavi 1994, Hiltz 1995, Huynh 1999, Suthers 2006, Hoppe et al. 2007). While these are important and very encouraging results, a deeper understanding of the "inside" of the collaborative learning process is still missing.

4.5 Problem-Based Learning (PBL) as an Example for authentic Learning Situations

Problem Based Learning (PBL) is a student-centered didactical concept to promote active learning while learners investigate authentic problems (David 2009). According to MacDonald and Isaacs (2001): "The characteristic that distinguishes PBL (..) is that the problem comes before the knowledge (in the broadest sense) needed to solve or resolve it." (p. 317) Some key principles of a problem-based curriculum (based on Engel 1991 & 1992) are:

- Active learning: Students take control of their own learning, pose and answer their own questions.
- Integrated learning: Students do not study different disciplines or sub-disciplines separately, do not view knowledge, understanding, and skills as distinct elements but rather as integrated; they put the problem into the focus and make every attempt to link the classroom and the real world of practice.
- Cumulative learning: No topic or problem is studied to the depth of the final learning outcome in a single block; rather topics are revisited in progressively greater depth.
- Learning for understanding: For students the processes of inquiry are more important than the facts delivered; knowledge must be tested by application, feedback is central and reflection is an integral part of the learning process.

There is a general agreement that problem-based learning provides an environment rich in potential for the development of a range of skills. Among the skills *usually* identified are: Problem-solving skills; skills in posing useful questions; thinking skills; teamwork skills; communication skills; time management skills; research and information handling skills; and computing skills (Figure 6).

Informal, problem-based, active, constructive, collaborative learning in authentic learning situations may indicate characteristics of emerging learning scenarios (see Figure 6).

4.6 The Role of Communication in an Active, Collaborative Learning Environment

Collaboration implies an interaction between the collaborating persons and "collaborative learning" is not always effective (Dillenbourg 1999). Its effects depend on the richness and intensity of interactions engaged in by group members while collaborating (Dillenbourg et al. 1996). Based on common theoretical backgrounds, collaborative learning takes place when learners get involved in knowledge-productive interactions such as argumentation, explanation, and mutual regulation (Dillenbourg 2008). The "knowledge-productive interactions" take place whenever the involved persons communicate to each other. Some communicative actions lead to explanation, some to argumentation, and some to mutual regulation of the collaborating group. The most open definition of communicative action given is that it is action in which "the actors seek to reach an understanding about the action situation and their plans of action in order to coordinate their actions by way of agreement. … (It is) a type of interaction that is coordinated through speech acts and does not coincide with them." (Habermas 1981, p. 101). Communicative action is based on an analysis of the social use of language oriented to reaching common understanding when action is coordinated by the validity claims offered in speech acts (Habermas 1981)

We will now turn to computer-mediated human-human communication like e-mail, chat, instant messaging, newsgroups, forums, tweets etc. Computer-mediated communication helps bridging spatial, social, and temporal distances and permits the tracking of past acts of communication.

Asynchronous communication gives the opportunity to rethink and correct the content of a message before it is sent and so promoting reflective learning (Hiltz and Goldman (2005). Computer-mediated communication (CMC) has become a part of everyday life. Research suggests that CMC is not inert as a social force, but that it can cause many changes in the way people communicate with one another, influencing communication patterns and social networks (see e.g. Fulk & Collins-Jarvis 2001). Rice & Gattiker (2001) state that CMC limits the level of synchronicity when interacting, which may cause a reduction of interactivity.

What features might we expect of the next generation of learning tools? As mentioned, ever-greater demands will be placed on the individual to engage in acts of communication in the future (see Figure 7). As a result, CMC tools might evolve to resemble face-to-face communication, including all its stimuli. It may also be that CMC tools merge all of the advantages of CMC with the advantages of face-to-face communication. Communication tools of the future will also presumably be better at managing large numbers of communication requests. Such tools may provide for the intelligent selection of relevant communication requests. To tailor such tools, further research is necessary on communication needs (see self-determination theory: Deci & Ryan 2002; see section above) as well as on the communication patterns of learners in active, collaborative learning environments

Figure 7. Communication request explosion requires communication competences

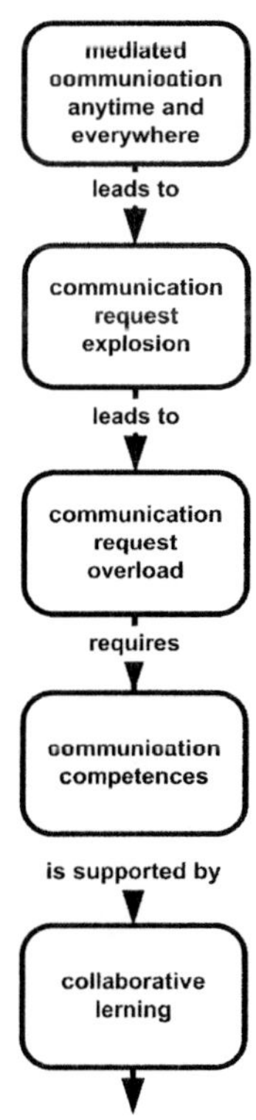

(Notari 2008), has described factors influencing computer-mediated written communication; research on communication needs and communication patterns is ongoing).

5. CHARACTERISTICS OF FUTURE LEARNING TOOLS

After elucidating some underlying principles from learning theory and describing models that appear applicable from our perspective, we can begin to formulate an overview of requirements placed on the learning tools of the future (see Figure 8).

An initial, perhaps banal and purely pragmatic requirement that we neither dealt with in theory nor as part of a model, but that seems nevertheless to be quite essential is the reliability and usability of the learning tool. Along with steady improvements in computer hardware and applications there has also been a concomitant increase in complexity, which potentially leads to the increased instability of learning tools.

In view of the latent dangers of information overload, the implementation of learning tools will become ever more important in the management of information, which could be transformed by a personal information manager (PIM) of the future with the following requirements: intelligent filtering, prioritization, and visualization of information, as well as the ability to link associations to existing information and an intelligent storage system for later retrieval. New concepts for solving problems raised by the flood of new information already exist in rudimentary fashion: statistical methods are increasingly available to make information management more logical, such as self-learning spam filters, and user-generated taxonomies (folksonomies).

Not only the quantity of information is increasing, but also, in similar fashion, the volume of communication requests directed at the individual is rising. In the modern world, we are bombarded by communication requests from a wide range of channels, including telephone, mail, VOIP, wall posts at social networking sites, and micro-

Figure 8. Required functions and properties of future learning tools

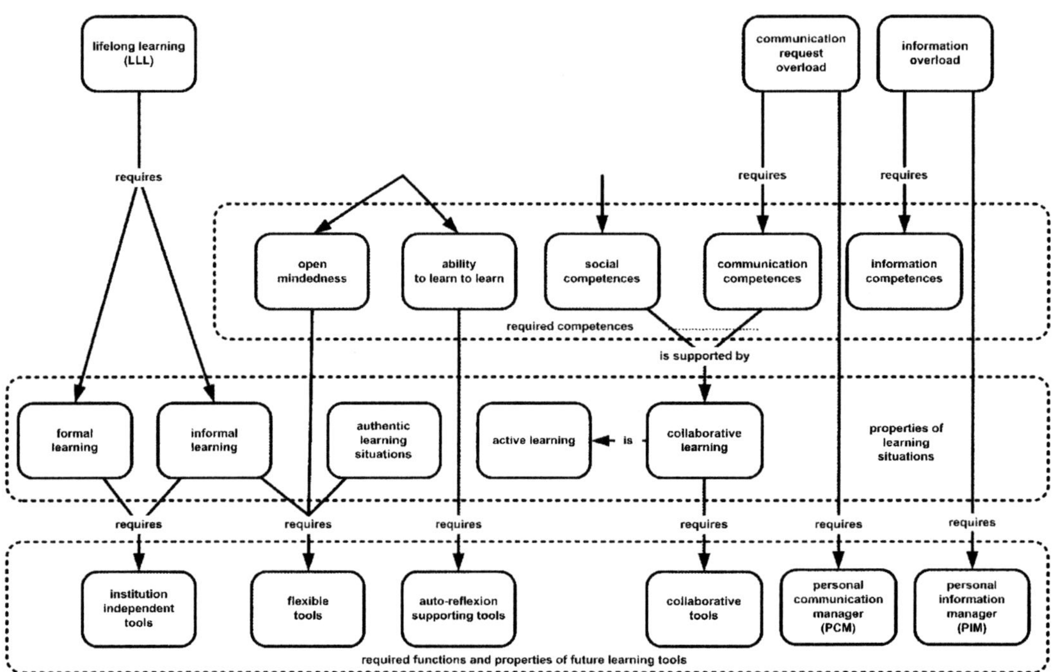

blogging comments. The escalating frequency of requests from an ever-increasing variety of communication channels requires a new form of communication management. Today, there are already services available that merge different communication channels. This helps raise efficiency by reducing the number of channels: the same quantity of communication may no longer be experienced as a flood of communication, because each communication channel no longer has to be checked individually. Adequate, active engagement in communication is an additional help for managing the flood of communication requests. Today, this kind of active "communication agent" already exists in the form of intelligent-email absence announcements. Some agents, for example, are able to limit announcing the absence of the message recipient to one occasion per message sender. Obviously, an additional aspect of communication management includes enhanced learning tool features such as filtering, prioritization, visualization, association and the integrated storage of new data.

A reliable learning tool must enable a high level of collaboration, and must make collaboration easier (Figure 8). We will speak in more depth about collaboration as a characteristic of learning tools with reference to wikis in the next section. As additional requisite properties we would postulate flexibility and organizational independence. Flexibility consists of actions that do not depend on time or place, and in the ability to use the same tool to tackle different problems in different ways. Organizational independence must be promoted in order to facilitate informal learning, which is becoming of such paramount importance to lifelong learning. Flexibility and organizational independence are also important characteristics of wiki tools, which will be described in the following section.

6. WIKI AS A REPRESENTATIVE EXAMPLE

In order to substantiate the theoretical considerations we focused, we will look at a tool that is currently available and used for learning purposes both in formal and informal settings. Our goal is to examine which of the projected requirements the selected tool satisfies.

Because of the fast pace of technical developments, tools will develop and change. Therefore the properties of a tool, but not the tool itself are relevant in the following discussion!

We have chosen wiki as example because it is well known, has a long and documented history of educational use (Guzdial 1999, Guzdial et al. 2000, Guzdial et al. 2001, Leuf & Cunningham 2001, Guzdial & Rick 2006, Schwartz et al. 2004, Bruns & Humphreys 2005, Forte & Bruckman 2006, Schaffert et al. 2006, Richardson 2006, Konieczny 2007, Parker & Chao 2007), and because several properties of wikis can be found in other tools like weblogs, Google Docs, sketchpad etc. There even exists a book called *"Wikinomics"* (Tapscott & Williams 2007), which tries to explain developments in economy and society with properties and the philosophy behind wikis.

As wiki is only a representative for a group of already existing of new and innovative tools, we will only provide one example of wikis in education. Much more and extended descriptions can be found in the literature cited above.

6.1 Potentials of Wikis

A **wiki** is the simplest form of content management system, and were invented by Ward Cunningham in 1995 (Leuf 2001). It didn't take long until their potential for education was discovered (Guzdial 1999). A wiki may be defined as follows: A wiki is a web server with version control on the Internet, where everybody can create, change, and link web pages without additional tools and without HTML knowledge (Döbeli Honegger 2007).

Using this definition, we can describe some of the potentials of wikis (Döbeli Honegger 2007):

- Create: creating content activates and motivates learners, two important prerequisites for learning
- Change: Wikis ease the modification of content (like all computer-based editors). This allows more revisions of a text which fosters re-reading and re-thinking the text and therefore can enhance the learning effect.
- Link: Wikis allow links between different parts of a text (like all hypertext systems). This requires that learners read and understand the parts they want to link and find fitting relationships. This enhances the discussion about the topic.
- Everybody: Wikis ease collaborative content creation and therefore ease working in interest-groups.
- Revision control: The integrated revision control of wikis not only lowers the danger and damage of vandalism. The revision control can also be used to look at the creation process by the teacher and the students. This can foster reflection about working and learning strategies (so called history pages).
- On the internet: As wikis can be hosted on a server on the internet, schools don't have to install hardware in their own buildings and the wiki can be accessed from everywhere
- Without additional tools: As wikis only need a web browser as a tool, there is no need for software installation on the learners' computers. This lowers the barriers for using **wiki**s as a learning tool.

6.2 Wikis and the Needs of Future Learners

In the following we will examine which of the required characteristics of future learning tools are already available in today's **wiki**s. Table 2 shows a comparison between the rudimentary properties of existing **wiki**s and the required properties of future learning tools.

The openness of wikis reflects the requirement for institution-independent tools. Unlike other groupware tools or learning management systems, wikis do not try to reproduce organizational structures. In addition, little about the architecture of the tool would stand in the way of broad uses across multiple organizations. The requirement for auto-reflection is supported by wikis in a number of respects. In wikis, revision control enables the documentation of the development process and thereby enables historical reflection. In a similar fashion, discussion pages on certain wiki engines promote meta-reflection on the part of the authors, as an explicit place is provided for such levels. The 'lack of predefined structures' may rise questions about effectiveness of the tool for active collaborative learning purposes. Following Jadin and Batinic (2006) students working with structured tools like a forum or a weblog worked more effectively than people using a wiki. The results of Jadin and Batinic relate to a formal university learning unit where the wiki was used for the first time. Tools used in the future might consider this fact and offer 'intelligent' structuring possibilities following specific learners needs or users might learn how to cope with the freedom of unstructuredness.

Wikis are rightly considered the most flexible content management systems, because they impose only the most minimal structure and leave the rest to the users. Wikis also fulfill the requirement for collaborative tools to a considerable degree, as Wikis were designed from the beginning to be multi-user systems. Correspondingly, it has been a fundamental goal of Wikis to promote and simplify

Table 2. Requirements placed on future tools

Required properties of future tools	Properties of existing Wikis
Institutional independence	wiki architecture is open and allows institutional independence
Supporting auto-reflection	version control and discussion pages support auto-reflection
Flexible	Lack of predefined structures fosters flexible use
Collaborative	wiki architecture is designed for collaboration
Personal information management	Is only supported to a limited extent by wikis at present
Personal communication management	Is hardly supported at all by wikis at present

the process of collaborative work. The situation with respect to personal information management is more ambiguous. On the one hand, wikis could certainly be used for this purpose, but offer very little automation toward this end. Current research in the area of semantic wikis and the visualization of wikis (see, for example, Schaffert et.al. 2006, Stickel, Ebner & Holzinger 2008), could ameliorate this deficit in the near future. Wikis offer hardly any practical support for personal communication management. In this respect, it is important to recall that no single tool is likely to be able to meet all requirements placed on future learning tools.

6.3 Example: Collaborative Authoring of Wikipedia Articles as a Learning Process

The previous theoretical considerations can now be illustrated by the exercise of collectively composing a Wikipedia article. The creation of a Wikipedia article can be conceptualized as a problem-oriented collaborative learning situation (Lawler 2006). The authors of a Wikipedia article can learn something themselves, even if they originally approach the situation with the idea of documenting something already known to them. On the one hand, the process of writing can itself lead to a deeper level of understanding, because implicit knowledge must thereby be made explicit. In particular, however, the collaboration and criticism of other authors can lead to the "perturbation" of one's own understanding and, as a result, to a learning process (Lawler 2006).

Writing a Wikipedia article can relate to formal and also informal learning. Learners can have the assignment to create or revise a Wikipedia article in a formal learning setting (Konieczny 2007). It is also possible that something is learned in the course of writing an article in an informal context. Finally, there are also Wikipedia authors who deliberately write articles in the hope of learning something about the topic involved (Forte, Bruckman 2007).

Revision control in Wikipedia permits an author to follow the evolution of the articles. With articles that have multiple authors, established modifications may be rescinded from time to time following consultation with the original authors.

Communication between Wikipedia authors most often takes place within the confines of Wikipedia itself, since for every article there also exists an associated discussion page. Within this discussion site, individual comments and viewpoints of the authors are debated. An enormous learning potential can be attributed to this process of discussion and debate (see the section on Collaborative learning). Even when individual authors do not have the impression that they have learned from creating or modifying their articles, in the process of discussion one's own perspective is necessarily juxtaposed with other viewpoints. Ideally, the confrontation leads to compromise and the article will be adapted accordingly. This adaptation of texts may lead to a transformation of the mental model held by all participants. According to Piaget, this would constitute an accommodation in response to a discordant perturbation caused by a different perspective (Piaget 1937).

Over time, a Wikipedia article is linked to a number of related articles. This process of linking is in and of itself a learning process: an existing concept (content and meaning of a concept or facts relating to an article) is connected to another similar and already established concept. In addition, linking may lead to perturbations and related discussions that ultimately lead to a learning process.

A paper which has been often cited as of late, *Studying cooperation and conflict between authors with history flow visualizations*, by Viégas et al. (2004), quite clearly visualizes the never-ending, collaborative, generative process of creating Wikipedia articles described above, and, at the same time, is an example of a needed tool for the future, one that eases the individual's management of the challenges posed by a flood of information.

7. CONCLUSION

Due to the rising complexity of problems in the future and the increasing capacity of the technical tools available, the importance of communication and collaboration will rise and informal learning will become more important. Instruction-based approaches will decrease and constructivist methods like PBL will become more popular. The tools of the future will render many repetitive work processes obsolete. They will also help us manage complex problem-solving activities, while easing collaborative and communicative tasks.

Competences that allow us to manage information- and communication-based environments will become more important considering the rising tide of information and communication requests we will be forced to manage Tools sustaining information- and communication management in different learning settings should optimize the following properties: First of all collaboration and flexibility are crucial due to the complexities of upcoming problems to solve. We also predict the importance of institutional independence due to the increasing importance of informal learning. Such informal problem solving activities also call for tools improving auto reflection mechanisms.

In the dynamic and interdependent world in which we live, learning and communication capabilities are becoming as crucial as knowledge. A main goal of institutional design should be to increase the learning and communication capabilities of the system and its constituents.

REFERENCES

Alavi, M. (1994). Computer-mediated collaborative learning: An empirical evaluation. *MIS Quarterly*, *18*(2), 159–174. doi:10.2307/249763

Anderson, J. Q., & Rainie, L. (2008). The future of Internet III. *Pew Internet & American Life Project*. Retrieved May 1, 2009, from http://www.pewinternet.org/~/media//Files/Reports/2008/PIP_FutureInternet3.pdf.pdf

Bandura, A. (1997). *Self-efficacy: The exercise of control*. New York: W.H. Freeman.

Bruns, A., & Humphreys, S. (2005). Wikis in teaching and assessment. In *The M/Cyclopedia Project, WikiSym 2005*. New York: ACM Press.

Caligiuri, P. M., Jacobs, R. R., & Farr, J. L. (2000). The Attitudinal and Behavioural Openness Scale: Scale development and construct validation. *International Journal of Intercultural Relations*, *24*, 27–46. doi:10.1016/S0147-1767(99)00021-8

Crawford, K. (1996). Vygotskian approaches to human development in the information era. *Educational Studies in Mathematics*, (31): 43–62. doi:10.1007/BF00143926

Cross, J. (2006). *Informal Learning: Rediscovering the natural pathways that inspire innovation and performance*. San Francisco: Pfeiffer.

Dansereau, D. F. (1983). *Cooperative learning: Impact on acquisition of knowledge and skills (Report No.341)*. Abilene, TX: U.S. Army Research Institute for the Behavioral and Social Sciences.

David, T., Patel, L., Burdett, K., & Rangachari, P. (2009). *Problem- based learning in medicine: A practical guide for students & teachers*. London:Royal Society of Medicine Press.

Deci, E., & Ryan, R. (Eds.). (2002). *Handbook of self-determination research*. Rochester, NY: University of Rochester Press.

Dillenbourg, P. (1999). What do you mean by collaborative learning? In P. Dillenbourg (Ed.), *Collaborative-learning: Cognitive and Computational Approaches* (pp.1-19). Oxford, UK: Elsevier.

Dillenbourg, P., Baker, M., Blaye, A., & O'Malley, C. (1996). The evolution of research on collaborative learning. In E. Spada & P. Reiman (Eds.), *Learning in humans and machine: Towards an interdisciplinary learning science* (pp. 189–211). Oxford, UK: Elsevier.

Dillenbourg, P., & Hong, F. (2008). The mechanics of CSCL macro scripts in computer supported collaborative learning. *International Journal of Computer-Supported Collaborative Learning*, *3*(1). doi:10.1007/s11412-007-9033-1

Döbeli Honegger, B. (2007). Wiki und die starken Potenziale: Unterrichten mit Wikis als virtuellen Wandtafeln. In *Web 2.0 - Internet Interaktiv (Journal Computer und Unterricht)* (pp. 39-41) Retrieved May 1, 2009, from http://beat.doebe.li/publications/2007-doebeli-honegger-wiki-und-die-starken-potenziale.pdf

Engel, C. E. (1991). Not just a method but a way of learning. In D. Boud & G. Feletti (Eds.), *The Challenge of Problem Based Learning*. London: Kogan Page.

Engel, C. E. (1992). Problem-based learning. *British Journal of Hospital Medicine*, *48*, 325–329.

Euler, D., Hasanbegovic, J., & Kerres, M. Seufert, S. (2006). *Handbuch der Kompetenzentwicklung für E-Learning Innovationen*. Bern, Switzerland: Huber.

Fiedler, D. (2003). Soziale Kompetenz - Ein unvollständiger Begriff. *Verhaltenstherapie & Psychosoziale Praxis*, *35*, 87–95.

Forte, A., & Bruckman, A. (2006). From Wikipedia to the classroom. In *Proceedings of the International Conference of the Learning Sciences*. Retrieved May 1, 2009, from http://www-static.cc.gatech.edu/~aforte/ForteBruckmanFromWikipedia.pdf

Friedman, T. L. (2005). *The world is flat: A brief history of the globalized world in the twenty-first century*. New York: Farrar, Straus and Giroux.

Fulk, J., & Collins-Jarvis, L. (2001). Wired meetings: Technological mediation of organizational gatherings. In L.L. Putnam & F.M. Jablins (Eds.), *New handbook of organizational communication (2nd ed.)* (pp. 624-703). Newbury Park, CA: Sage.

Guzdial, M. (1999). *Teacher and student authoring on the Web for shifting agency*. Retrieved May 01, 2009, from http://guzdial.cc.gatech.edu/papers/aera99/default.html

Guzdial, M., Kehoe, C., Realff, M., & Morley, T. (2000). *A catalog of CoWeb uses*. Retrieved May 1, 2009, from http://guzdial.cc.gatech.edu/squeakers/coweb-catalog.pdf

Guzdial, M., & Rick, J. (2006). Situating CoWeb. *International Journal of Computer-Supported Collaborative Learning*, *1*(1).

Guzdial, M., Rick, J., & Kehoe, C. (2001). Beyond adoption to invention. *Journal of the Learning Sciences*, *10*(3). doi:10.1207/S15327809JLS1003_2

Habermas, J. (1981). *The Theory of Communicative Action*. London: Beacon Press.

Haefner, K. (1982). *Die neue Bildungskrise*. Basel, Switzerland: Birkhäuser.

Harter, S. (1982). The perceived competence scale for children. *Child Development*, *53*, 87–97. doi:10.2307/1129640

Hiltz, S. R. (1995). *The virtual classroom: Learning without limits via computer networks*. New York: Ablex Publishing Corp.

Hiltz, S. R., & Goldman, R. (2005). What are asynchronous learning networks? In Hiltz, S. R., & Goldman, R. (Eds.), *Learning together online: Research on asynchronous learning networks* (pp. 3–18).

Hoppe, H. U., Ogata, H., & Soller, H. (Eds.). (2007). *The role of technology in CSCL: studies in technology enhanced collaborative learning*. New York: Springer.

Huynh, M. Q. (1999). *A critical study of computer-supported collaborative learning*. Unpublished PhD, SUNY Binghamton, New York.

Illich, I. (1970). *Deschooling society*. New York: Harper and Row.

Jadin, T., & Batinic, B. (2006, May 23-24). Social Skills durch Social Software. In *Interdisziplinäre Fachtagung zu Bildungs- und Arbeitstechnologien im Semantic Web*, Salzburg. Retrieved May 1, 2009, from http://www.hotel-virgil.at/fileadmin/user_upload/downloads/jadintrack_1-3.pdf

Kay, A., & Goldberg, A. (1977). Personal dynamic media. *Computer*, *10*(3), 31–41. doi:10.1109/C-M.1977.217672

Kearsley, G. (1994). Social learning theory. Retrieved May 1, 2009, from http://www.gwu.edu/~tip/bandura.html

Klafki, W. (2000). Kritisch-konstruktive Pädagogik. Herkunft und Zukunft. In *Eierdanz, Jürgen / Kremer, Armin (Hrsg.): Weder erwartet noch gewollt – Kritische Erziehungswissenschaft und Pädagogik in der Bundesrepublik Deutschland zur Zeit des kalten Krieges*, Baltmannsweiler, Germany (pp. 152-178).

Konieczny, P. (2007). Wikis and Wikipedia as a teaching tool. *International Journal of Instructional Technology And Distance Learning,* 1. Retrieved May 1, 2009, from http://www.itdl.org/Journal/Jan_07/article02.htm

Lawler, C. (2006). Wikipedia as a learning community: content, conflict and the 'common good'. In B. Lutterbeck, M. Bärwolff, & R. A. Gehring (Eds.), *Open Source Jahrbuch 2006 - Zwischen Softwareentwicklung und Gesellschaftsmodell*. Berlin, Germany: Lehmanns Media. Retrieved May 1, 2009, from http://www.opensource-jahrbuch.de/portal/articles/pdfs/osjb2006-06-04-en-lawler.pdf

Leuf, B., & Cunningham, W. (2001). *The wiki way*. Reading, MA: Addison Wesley.

MacDonald, D., & Isaacs, G. (2001). Developing a professional identity through problem-based learning. *Teaching Education*, *12*, 315–333. doi:10.1080/10476210120096579

Marsh, H. W. (1990). The structure of academic self-concept: The Marsh/Shavelson model. *Journal of Educational Psychology*, *82*(4), 623–636. doi:10.1037/0022-0663.82.4.623

Moore, G. (1965). Cramming more components onto integrated circuits. *Electronics, 38*(8).

Negroponte, N. (1995). *Being digital*. New York: Alfred A. Knopf.

Notari, M. P., & Minder, S. (2008). Electronic messaging in collaborative e-learning environments. A method to assess two key factors of communication quality: HCI and language. In *Proceeding of World Conference on Educational Media, Hypermedia and Telecommunications (ED-Media)* (pp. 1098-1103).

Novak, J. D., & Gowin, D. B. (1985). *Learning how to learn*. Cambridge, UK: Cambridge University Press.

OECD. (2007). Participative Web and user-created content: Web 2.0, wikis and social networking. *Organisation for Economic Co-Operation and Development*. Retrieved January 30, 2009, from http://213.253.134.43/oecd/pdfs/browseit/9307031E.PDF

Parker, K. R., & Chao, J. T. (2007). Wiki as a teaching tool. *Interdisciplinary Journal of Knowledge and Learning Objects*, *3*, 57–72.

Piaget, J. (1926). *The language and thought of a child*. London: Routledge & Kegan Paul.

Piaget, J. (1937). *La construction du réel chez l'enfant*. Neuchatel, Switzerland: Delachcaux.

Rice, R. E., & Gattiker, U. E. (2001). New media and organizational structuring. In F.M. Jablin & L.L. Putnam (Eds.), *The new handbook of organizational communication* (pp. 544-581). Thousand Oaks, CA: Sage.

Richardson, W. (2006). *Blogs, wikis, podcasts, and other powerful web tools for classrooms*. Thousand Oaks, CA: Corwin Press.

Rosenberg, M. (1965). *Society and the adolescent self-image*. Princeton, NJ: Princeton University Press.

Rychen, D. S., & Salganik, L. H. (2001). *Defining and Selection Key Competencies*. Toronto, Canada: Hogrefe & Huber Publishing.

Schaffert, S., Bischof, D., Bürger, T., Gruber, A., Hilzensauer, W., & Schaffert, S. (2006 June 11-14). Learning with Semantic Wikis. In *3rd Annual European Semantic Web Conference (ESWC), First Workshop SemWiki2006 - From Wiki to Semantics*, Budva, Montenegro.

Schwartz, L., et al. (2004, April). Educational Wikis – features and selection criteria. *International Review of Research in Open and Distance Learning*. Retrieved May 6, 2009, from http://www.irrodl.org/index.php/irrodl/article/view/163/692

Sefton-Green, J. (2004). Literature review in informal learning with technology outside school. *VAC Performing Arts and Media College, Futurelab Series, Report 7*. Retrieved April 26, 2009, from http://hal.archives-ouvertes.fr/docs/00/19/02/22/PDF/Sefton-Green_2004.pdf

Sharon, S. (Ed.). (1990) *Cooperative learning: Theory and research*. New York: Praege.

Shavelson, R. G., Hubner, J. J., & Stanton, G. C. (1976). Validation of construct interpretations. *Review of Educational Research*, *46*, 407–441.

Slavin, R. E. (1987). *Cooperative learning: Student teams*. Washington, DC: National Educational Association.

Stickel, S., Ebner, M., & Holzinger, A. (2008). Useful oblivion versus information overload in e-learning examples in the context of wiki systems. *Journal of Computing and Information Technology*, *16*(4), 271–277.

Suthers, D. D. (2006). Technology affordances for intersubjective meaning making: A research agenda for CSCL. *International Journal of Computer-Supported Collaborative Learning*, *3*(1), 315–337. doi:10.1007/s11412-006-9660-y

Tapscott, D., & Williams, A. D. (2007). *Wikinomics: How mass collaboration changes everything*. New York: Portfolio Hardcover.

Van Oudenhoven, J. P., Van der Zee, K. I., & Van Kooten, M. (2001). Successful adaptation strategies according expatriates. *International Journal of Intercultural Relations*, *25*, 467–482. doi:10.1016/S0147-1767(01)00018-9

Viégas, F. B., Wattenberg, M., & Dave, K. (2004). Studying cooperation and conflict between authors with history flow visualizations. In *Proceedings of SIGCHI*, Vienna, Austria (pp. 575-582). New York: ACM Press.

Vygotsky, L. S. (1978). *Mind in society: The development of higher psychological processes.* Cambridge, MA: Harvard University Press.

Weinert, F. E. (2001). Leistungsmessung in Schulen – Eine umstrittene Selbstverständlichkeit. In *Leistungsmessung in Schulen.* Weinheim, Deutschland: Beltz.

Weiser, M. (1991). The Computer for the 21st Century. *Scientific American*, *65*(3), 94–104.

Yamazaki, Y., & Kayes, D. (2004). An experiential approach to cross-cultural learning: A review and integration of competencies for successful expatriate adaptation. *Academy of Management Learning & Education*, *3*, 362–379.

Chapter 17
Wikipedia in Academic Studies: Corrupting or Improving the Quality of Teaching and Learning?

Klaus Wannemacher
Consultant for Research and Teaching Management, HIS GmbH, Germany

Frank Schulenburg
Head of Public Outreach, Wikimedia Foundation, U.S.A.

ABSTRACT

Although Wikipedia has carved its way into the common vernacular, it faces resentments, particularly in higher education institutions, and many professors say students should think twice before turning to the free online encyclopedia for their academic work. "According to the criterion of scholarly standards, Wikipedia is citable on no account since authorship is not verifiable, and therefore an authentication of information is impossible." (Haber, 2007, p. 500). In spite of perceived quality deficits, Wikipedia is a popular information resource among students. Instructors increasingly take advantage of this student attitude through actively integrating Wikipedia as a learning tool into university courses in accordance with a constructivist teaching and learning paradigm. The chapter raises the question if Wikipedia is suited to make complex research, editing and bibliographic processes through which scholarship is produced transparent to students, and effectively improve their research and writing skills.

A WEB 2.0 PROJECT CHALLENGES UNIVERSITY INSTRUCTORS

Wikipedia as a Popular Information Resource

The founder of the free multilingual encyclopedia project Wikipedia, Jimmy Wales, anticipates considerable changes of the academic learning culture. He presumes that "teaching at universities will change, that professors will become mentors accompanying the development of their students" and that students will "discover the world for themselves following their own interest." (Wales, 2008). Since 2001, Wikipedia has become one of the most popular websites and Web 2.0 applications worldwide. While the use of open contents and encyclopedic information as provided by Wikipedia has caused considerable problems within the academic community (e.g. the plagiarism problem and

DOI: 10.4018/978-1-61520-678-0.ch017

the declining use of reliable published sources in term papers), Wikipedia has evolved into a general reference website. It has increasingly facilitated and contributed to processes of self-contained learning and knowledge construction inside and outside of universities as propagated by the online encyclopedia's founder.

The open content, multilingual encyclopedia project was launched in early 2001. The project is operated by the Wikimedia Foundation, a US-based non-profit organisation aiming at the free distribution of knowledge. As of early 2009, the English-language Wikipedia edition contained more than 2.8 million articles, while the German-language version, the second largest among more than 260 language editions, comprises some 900,000 articles (Wikipedia, 2009a). Despite criticism, Wikipedia has become one of the most frequented information resources on the web. A recent survey performed by the Allensbach Institute on the use of computer and technology showed that Wikipedia ranked third among the most popular German-language websites with 13.6 million users per week after Google and Ebay (Institut für Demoskopie Allensbach, 2008; Meyer-Lucht, 2008). With regard to its growing popularity, Wikipedia is sometimes considered a trend-setting medium even among a growing number of academic professionals (Lorenz, 2006, p. 84).

While academic research on Wikipedia has been focused on aspects such as collaborative processes of knowledge construction and knowledge management, community building and coordination processes, Wikipedia as a lexical semantic resource, or its quality management procedures (e.g. Grotjahn 2007; Jaschniok, 2007; Martin, 2006; Pentzold, 2007; Wolf, 2007), little research has been done on the potentials of utilising Wikipedia within university teaching. In a short field report Bendel (2006) describes seminar experiences with editing Wikipedia articles using tiered forms of online collaboration. Ebner (2007) analyses Wikipedia's use in seminars pointing out the decisive difference between voluntary communities of practise driven by corresponding interests and 'forced' learning communities using Wikipedia at universities. Hodel & Haber (2007) outline different phases of student experience occurring during a seminar using Wikipedia assignments from enthusiasm through outrage to disillusionment. Konieczny (2007) describes a range of approved Wikipedia assignment forms that have successfully been applied at US universities.

Linking to these earlier analyses, this chapter examines the students' perspective on Wikipedia based on results of a representative survey carried out in 2008. The survey documents how students use Wikipedia and other encyclopedic applications for self-study purposes. The chapter furthermore aggregates and interprets different types of Wikipedia in teaching projects and their contributions to the online encyclopedia based upon a comprehensive list of some 92 Wikipedia university projects that have been carried out worldwide since 2002. Finally, the potential of extending the use of shared knowledge portals for teaching purposes to several sister projects of Wikipedia will be discussed on the basis of initial seminar experiences.

Professional Scepticism Against Wikipedia

Within the university context Wikipedia is met with scepticism due to perceived conflicts with fundamental scientific standards. A serious value of Wikipedia is regularly negated for reasons of scientific validity: "According to the criterion of scholarly standards, Wikipedia is citable on no account since authorship is not verifiable, and therefore an authentification of information is impossible." (Haber, 2007, p. 500). By contrast, the online encyclopedia claims to exclusively compile material that is verifiable (Wikipedia, 2009b). For reasons of verification, Wikipedia authors are committed to using "reliable, third-party published sources with a reputation for fact-checking and accuracy". Wikipedia's verifiability directive states that "editors should provide a reliable source for quotations and for any material that is challenged or likely to be challenged, or the material may be removed." (Wikipedia, 2009b).

The quality of Wikipedia content is to be guaranteed through an internal peer review process of the Wikipedia community. US publicist James Surowiecki coined the concept of the "Wisdom of Crowds" (Surowiecki, 2004) for such mechanisms of distributed quality management. Wikipedia's quality management approaches cover a multi-stage procedure for evaluating selected articles as well as a system of discussion pages for encyclopedic entries. In contrast to academic standards, however, Wikipedia's quality management procedures predominantly apply not until the publication has already taken place (Hodel & Haber, 2007, p. 44).

Aspects such as the comparatively high professional quality of many Wikipedia contributions even in comparison to established print encyclopedias (Terdiman, 2005; Güntheroth, Schönert & Rodtmann, 2007), and the opportunity of using encyclopedic content free of charge account for the specific appeal of the digital encyclopedia for students. Students value Wikipedia as a useful tool for their research and paperwriting duties. An information resource that was initiated as a participatory community project and seemed to adhere to the paradigm of lifelong learning increasingly enters genuinely academic spheres and unintentionally influences the teaching and learning practice at universities.

A Students' Perspective on Wikipedia

Frequency of Wikipedia Use Among Students

Specific assets such as the easy access and broad coverage make Wikipedia a favorite medium for information seeking and for learning among students. A representative online survey performed in 2008 among some 4,400 students from German universities focused on the current development of "Studying in Web 2.0" (Kleimann, Özkilic & Göcks, 2008) and on the students' Wikipedia use. The survey was carried out by the Higher Education Information System (HIS) and the Multimedia Kontor Hamburg (MMKH) using the HISBUS student panel. The survey addressed the students' perception of new web-based forms of teaching and learning at universities impacted by new generation Internet technologies. The survey that received a return rate of 40 percent proved that "knowledge platforms that function according to Web 2.0 principles and try to mobilise the 'Wisdom of Crowds' attain high acceptance among students." (Kleimann, Özkilic & Göcks, 2008, p. 8). It reveals how frequently and in which ways students at German universities use Wikipedia and other encyclopedic portals for self-study purposes. Furthermore, it shows as to how reliable students regard those portals.

60 percent of the students stated that they use Wikipedia frequently or very frequently (the upper two of six possible answer categories were comprised). Only 15 percent of the students stated that they use Wikipedia seldom or very seldom (the lowest two answer categories were comprised). 0.7 percent replied that they never use Wikipedia and 0.2 percent stated they did not know it. Other Internet applications such as social communities (e.g. StudiVZ, FaceBook, MySpace, Xing, etc.) (51 percent), chat/instant messaging (36 percent), video communities (e.g. YouTube) (16 percent), other wikis (15 percent), and further applications were used less frequently by German students than Wikipedia (Kleimann, Özkilic & Göcks, 2008, p. 5).

An additional in-depth analysis showed that male students used Wikipedia slightly more often (65 percent within the upper two answer categories) than female students (55 percent within the upper two answer categories). The intensity of Wikipedia use differed considerably in relation to the field of study. Wikipedia was most frequently used by students of natural sciences (75 percent), agricultural science (73 percent), medical science (65 percent) and engineering science (62 percent). It was least frequently used by students of law and social sciences (52 percent each) and of economical science (47 percent).

Forms of Wikipedia Use and Assumed Reliability

The students were asked how often they passively or actively use Wikipedia for "reading articles" or "editing existing articles". 80 percent of the students stated that they read Wikipedia articles (very) regularly. While the online encyclopedia is regularly used intensely in a receptive way, forms of Wikipedia use that imply an active contribution rarely apply at all. 1 percent stated that they edit existing articles (very) frequently while 20 percent do this (very) seldomly. 77 percent never do it. Only 0.3 percent of students write new Wikipedia articles (very) frequently, 14 percent do this (very) seldomly. 85 percent never do this. 0.5 percent participate in discussions on articles (very) regularly, while 15 percent do this (very) seldomly. 83 percent never do so. 0.5 percent engage in the Wikipedia community (very) regularly while 10 percent do this (very) seldomly. 89 percent never do so (Kleimann, Özkilic & Göcks, 2008, p. 5).

Students were additionally asked as to how reliable they regard Wikipedia and other online knowledge portals. 52 percent of all students regarded Wikipedia as reliable or very reliable. Since many students felt unable to judge a majority of online knowledge portals, only the specific group of students that made a judgement on the different applications will be regarded subsequently, though. If a majority of students uttered a good judgement on a specific portal this was regarded as statistically more significant than a very good judgement made by only a small amount of students. Wikipedia was regarded as (very) reliable by 53 percent of those students that were able to judge it (merely 0.8 percent answered they could not rate Wikipedia).

A differentiation according to fields of study documented that those students that used Wikipedia most frequently also regarded it as most reliable. Wikipedia received the best reliability evaluations by students of agricultural studies (69 percent that thought they could judge it regarded it as reliable or very reliable), engineering studies (63 percent), medical studies (62 percent) and of natural sciences (61 percent). Wikipedia received less good evaluations by students of the humanities (43 percent), of social science (41 percent) and of philology (38 percent). The students' judgement on the general quality of Wikipedia is perhaps strongly influenced by the quality of the (German-language) Wikipedia contents. Not all areas of knowledge are represented at the same depth and quality within Wikipedia. Furthermore, different academic cultures may involve a different general inclination to use Web 2.0 applications.

Comparison to Other Knowledge Portals

Compared with other online encyclopedias or knowledge portals, Wikipedia received the best quality assessment rates in absolute numbers. Students were much less regularly able to assess applications other than Wikipedia, though. An analysis on the basis of those students providing an answer produced different results for Wikipedia in relation to other knowledge portals. 49 percent of students could judge the newspaper-related portal "Spiegel Wissen" which was considered as (very) reliable by 70 percent of those students rendering a judgement. 45 percent of the students made a judgement on the portal "Zeit Online" which was considered as (very) reliable by 77 percent of them. 43 percent of students delivered a judgement on "Microsoft Encarta" which was regarded as (very) reliable by 68 percent of them. 33 percent made a judgement on "Meyers Lexikon Online" which received the second best relative results with 79 percent regarding it as (very) reliable. Only 32 percent made a judgement on "Wissen.de" which was evaluated as least reliable with only 45 percent of those students regarding it as (very) reliable. A mere 30 percent made a judgement on Encyclopædia Britannica. Still, the Encyclopædia Britannica received the best relative reliability results with 86 percent of the commenting students rating it as (very) reliable.

In contrast to all other applications, almost all students regarded themselves as competent to judge the quality of Wikipedia. Wikipedia was being used by a vast majority of students more or less intensely, regardless of the students' impression of the average quality of Wikipedia articles. Their assessment of other encyclopedic portals seems to suggest a tendency that if students use other knowledge portals they do so due to the supposed high encyclopedic quality of their contents. Due to the comparatively low popularity of other encyclopedic portals, the judgement of other applications gets less significant the fewer students feel able to comment on them. A certain indeterminacy of the survey's results should be taken into account when considering that the portal "Spiegel Wissen" heavily draws on Wikipedia material and was still regarded as more reliable than Wikipedia by students who could judge it (Kleimann, Özkilic & Göcks, 2008, p. 7 et seq.). Moreover, regardless of excellent assessments "Microsoft Encarta" and "Meyers Lexikon Online" announced the discontinuation of their services in 2009 citing changes in the traditional encyclopedia and reference material market as the key reasons behind the termination.

WIKIPEDIA IN TEACHING PROJECTS

Improving Information and Writing Competency

The participatory character that has been regarded as a weakness of Wikipedia pertaining to its scientific validity by some is perceived as a specific didactic quality by others. In particular, the strong appreciation of students for Wikipedia prefigures the online encyclopedia's adequacy as a potential tool for e-teaching. Prolific ways of integrating and actively using Wikipedia for teaching in accord with a constructivist teaching and learning paradigm as layed out by Swiss philosopher Jean Piaget have been applied at universities worldwide. In different subject-related contexts, instructors use Wikipedia under the didactic proposition of an active self-organisation of knowledge as the basis for communicating different educational objectives such as strengthening the competency to assess and differentiate between diverse source materials. Instructors apply Wikipedia in university courses as the basis for work assignments such as the training of a good narrative style, the discussion and review of specific encyclopedic entries, or the complete or partial revision of selected articles as a precondition for performance records. Manifold forms of using Wikipedia in seminars have been conceived so far.

Emergence and Objective of Wikipedia in Teaching Projects

Basic and Advanced Forms of Use

The simplest form of including Wikipedia into university teaching is to incorporate it into syllabi with the intention of having students read encyclopedic entries for course preparation purposes. Instructors presume that general information being easily available on Wikipedia implies a higher likelihood that students will actually do Wikipedia-related than conventional assignments and prepare for a seminar. Of course, even lecturers incorporating Wikipedia into syllabi advise students and other instructors to treat it sceptically (Child, 2007).

Many universities have applied more demanding forms of Wikipedia use as well. The application of the online encyclopedia in teaching at universities has partly been self-reported and documented by instructors. Since such an extensive documentation solely exists within the English Wikipedia edition, consideration will be given to the comprehensive data provided there. The English Wikipedia's "school and university projects" page specifies some 92 genuine Wikipedia projects at international universities between 2002 and 2009 (reference date: January 15, 2009), among them projects at the Ivy League universities of Columbia, Cornell, Dartmouth, Harvard and Yale, and at the Massachusetts Institute of Technology (Wikipedia, 2009). The "school and university projects" pages of Wikipedia editions in other languages and an Internet search for further Wikipedia in teaching projects prove that the actual amount of projects is much larger, though. The English-language "school and university projects" page additionally contained three high school projects not being considered within this paper.

Statistical Data on Wikipedia in Teaching Projects

The possibilities of a quantitative analysis of the data on the "school and university projects" page are restricted to some general facts since the depth of information provided on different projects varies strongly. Some instructors present just a limited amount of general information on their courses such as the university and course name and the semester while other instructors additionally exhibit the course subject and course structure, assignment forms, a list of finalised articles, and specific course experiences. Therefore, valid statistical information on the seminars can only be provided on a few aspects such as the country, the subject area, the period of time, and the general assignment form. Additonal aspects such as the course objective, course preparation, teaching methods, feedback and course documentation forms, or course experiences could only be presented and interpreted on a qualitative basis.

Initially, some basic statistical information on the seminars will be presented, followed by a more comprehensive qualitative analysis of additional aspects such as the differing didactical approaches or the experiences made within those 92 projects. The Wikipedia in teaching projects documented on the "school and university projects" page of the English Wikipedia edition come from 19 different countries (additional projects documented on the Catalan, Czech, French, Polish, Russian, and Slovene Wikipedia editions could not be taken into account). As far as precise information is provided, a majority of 60 courses come from US universities, colleges or business schools. 5 projects each originate from higher education institutions in Canada and Hong Kong. Another 22 projects were carried out in 16 other countries such as Australia, Germany, or the United Kingdom.

The projects were carried out in undergraduate as well as in graduate classes. They came from diverse fields of study with a strong focus on the humanities. In contrast to the low-key evaluations of the German language Wikipedia by humanities' students in the HISBUS survey, almost half of the international projects (44 of 92 projects) had a background in the humanities such as English writing, history, or cultural studies classes. Perhaps, text-oriented seminar types and hermeneutic working methods common among humanities' scholars encourage and facilitate the utilisation of Wikipedia within collaborative text editing assignments. 12 projects came from natural science and 12 projects from social science, 8 projects from engineering science, 5 projects from economic science. 2 projects each came from law, medical science, and agricultural science. Some instructors gave no indication on the seminar topic, and many seminars had an interdisciplinary character.

Constant Increase in Wikipedia Projects

A strong increase in projects using Wikipedia in teaching has taken place since the first mentioned seminars. 4 of the documented projects took place between 2001 and 2003 (the "school and university projects" page has not been set up before the year 2003, though). 24 projects occurred in the period between 2004 and 2006. 59 projects took place between 2007 and 2009 so far which adds up to considerably more than a duplication of projects compared to the previous period of time. Some projects were counted several times if they took place in subsequent time periods.

The nature of course work with Wikipedia was diverse. 84 of 92 projects involved the editing of existing encyclopedic entries or the creation of new entries. 4 of the projects even envisaged improving articles with the final goal of nominating them within Wikipedia's quality assessment process for "Good Article" or "Featured Article" status (e.g. Jon Beasley-Murray's Spanish class "Murder, Madness, and Mayhem" at the University of British Columbia in spring 2008). 5 projects asked for participating in an appropriate "WikiProject", a collection of pages devoted to the management of a specific topic or family of topics within Wikipedia, or the participation in a Wikipedia portal on a specific topic. Only five projects expressly mentioned a focus on analysing Wikipedia as a Web 2.0 application and as an open content-related community. At least 8 projects involved work in language versions of Wikipedia other than English.

Objective of Wikipedia Projects

The objectives of the documented Wikipedia courses were manifold. Besides the ostensible aim of enhancing the students' state of knowledge, particular emphasis was put on propaedeutic aims such as making research, editing and bibliographic processes transparent. Many instructors wanted to help students develop an awareness of Wikipedia's specific nature of knowledge production, as well as of the required rigour and balance in writing encyclopedic articles. Work on Wikipedia articles requires the consideration of different perspectives on a subject (Wikipedia's "neutral point of view" principle), e.g. in creating a balanced version of a nation's history. The neutral point of view is fostered by the frequently chosen collaborative form of student work as well. A theoretical analysis of Wikipedia as a network phenomenon, of quality measurement issues, or Wikipedia-related aspects of collaborative knowledge management was intended by other instructors.

Moreover, instructors wanted to give students an opportunity to experience collaborative writing and online publication, and wanted to foster their research and writing skills. Motivational aspects played a major role in these courses since writing for a very large audience was strongly motivating many students and made them put more work into the project than they would have otherwise. Even though 6 of 92 instructors explicitly report that a majority of students enjoyed those projects, others relate mixed results. Some students regularly abandoned Wikipedia assignments and preferred to carry out conventional assignments instead. With regard to the collaboration aspect, many instructors wanted students to learn from the advice of their own teammates as well as to benefit from the feedback of regular Wikipedia contributors. Since regular "Wikipedians" often visited course articles, students got to experience feedback in many forms from someone else than the instructor. Instructors requested students to take all feedback into account.

A specific objective of some courses consisted in the overcoming of language barriers. Occasionally, students were allowed to work on different language editions of Wikipedia such as the Catalan, English, French, Italian, Russian or Spanish Wikipedia edition. This was made possible if a course was offered by universities from different countries cooperatively and if a cooperation between students from different universities was demanded (e.g. the cooperation between Barcelona University and Washington University in St. Louis within the WikiProject "History and Archaeology of Central Asia" in fall

2007). Students were expected to write or edit the articles agreed upon in either language edition. Discussion still took place on the English-language version of each article.

Seminar Practice and Assignments

Preparation by Instructors

The use of Wikipedia in university courses requires a thorough and extensive preparation by the instructor. In the courses depicted on the "school and university projects" page, several work packages were regularly carried out for course preparation. Many instructors created an introduction page for their students on Wikipedia. This page can serve to introduce students to the wiki system, to ensure that they are working within the bounds of Wikipedia guidelines, and to precisely advise them what they can do. Since article work on Wikipedia currently requires students to publish their texts under a free licence, some instructors requested their students to submit a letter to them stating that they understand the implications of licensing their own work, e.g. making their texts reusable by the general public. Students that did not want to publish their texts under these conditions could submit them at the discretion of the instructor.

Providing a choice of texts that should be produced or revised by students was another central preparatory task. The English Wikipedia provides a broad range of "open task" pages with assignment proposals for instructors that are accessible primarily through its "community portal" (Wikipedia, 2009c). Other "suggested exercises" are provided on the "school and university projects" page (Wikipedia, 2009). Additional support can be mobilised through a particular Wikipedia project. Instructors can contact the English Wikipedia's "WikiProject Classroom coordination". More than 40 volunteers offer assistance for course conception and carrying out specific course tasks on this project page. Through this WikiProject, instructors can involve more experienced Wikipedians in providing technical and general support for their students.

Teaching Methods

The Wikipedia courses documented on the "school and university projects" page exhibit a wide range of assignments forms. Some courses start with an overview on the development of encyclopedias from ancient world's Gaius Plinius Secundus until digital encyclopedias under consultation of research literature. Regularly, students are initially introduced to the Wikipedia site and to Wikipedia norms and conventions. Instructors let their students familiarise themselves with Wikipedia the resource as well as Wikipedia the community. Common 'warm-up assignments' include letting students create a Wikipedia login of their own, letting them make some basic edits to the individual user page, and having them practice article editing in the "sandbox", a so-called Wikipedia namespace page designed for testing and experimentation with the wiki syntax before real article work is carried out. Additional warm-up exercises consist of editing text, and adding citations to existing articles, or letting students exercise image management, and categorisation tasks.

A typical multi-level seminar layout as realised in the course "Introduction to Interdisciplinary Studies" by Scott Alberts at Truman State University, Missouri, in fall 2007 took advantage of so-called "Wiki Labs" (Wikipedia, 2009d). The course scheduled seven wiki labs out of which four were required. Three were voluntary labs. The labs consisted of the assignments 0) finding a short path from article A to article B, 1) setting up a user page, 2) getting busy, 3) working collaboratively on an article, 4) writing a real article, and 5 to 6) making an article "good", joining a project, or working on special pages. The class applied "contract grading" in which students signed a contract stating exactly what grade they would like to receive and how much work they would like to do. Carrying out labs 4 to 6 was required to receive an upper grade. Instructors in other seminars offered students an option to gain extra credit for minor additional tasks such as correcting mistakes, or adding references to articles.

Forms of Assignment

Early Wikipedia in seminar projects have occasionally focused on letting students analyse the content of Wikipedia articles and related discussion pages concerning a specific topic and verify the information in these articles using non-internet sources. Students had to evaluate the articles for accuracy, having up-to-date information, being too short or overly verbose, having useful and active links, references to print media, and whether they provided a good source for someone who wanted to learn about the issue. Other instructors had students compare Wikipedia articles with their equivalents in Encyclopædia Britannica, or compare articles in different language editions of Wikipedia.

The most commonly applied Wikipedia assignments is letting students edit articles. Students are asked to research, and critique an existing article with a focus on readability and accuracy, work up drafts of the proposed revision, and edit the article drawing on appropriate research literature. After having incorporated changes into the Wikipedia articles, students should observe and discuss in class subsequent comments and edits by other users. Different options of article work apply such as choosing and expanding so-called "stub-articles", i.e. short articles in need of expansion. Sometimes students individually work on separate articles, sometimes they collaborate on different segments of an article in groups of two to seven students. Students were also asked to add references to articles under use of at least one primary source, one encyclopedic source, and one scholarly book or article ("Roman Civilization" class at Northwestern University, spring 2007).

Instead of rewriting articles students can also contribute one or several preapproved new articles or sub-articles ("stubs") related to the course issue. While the initial revision of existing articles occasionally takes place offline under use of a standalone course wiki, prior to submitting the students' work to Wikipedia, new articles are usually generated in the students' userspace. After the draft is completed, it can be transferred over to Wikipedia mainspace. In most cases, article editing assignments in seminars optionally substituted writing a seminar paper or a final research paper. Sometimes a final class project consists of revising an article on the central course topic.

While text-related exercises dominate the list of Wikipedia assignments so far, this emphasis may change in the future since many not text-related assignments are already conceivable. Film students can incorporate short video files into Wikipedia articles under use of Wikimedia Commons, a repository of free content multimedia files. Only a few Wikipedia articles have been complemented by video files so far. Students of photography may find a challenge in contributing so-called "featured pictures" to Wikipedia while students of audio-engineering may find the "featured sounds" review process a rewarding test of their skills. However, seminars with audio-visual assignments have not been documented yet on the "school and university project" page.

Feedback, Documentation, and Analysis

The feedback process regularly involves instructors reviewing article revisions as well as regular Wikipedians providing critique. While some instructors regard the additional feedback of regular Wikipedians to their students and the experience of collaboratively editing texts as useful, others prefer to work on a stand-alone wiki to avoid external intervention (Brandt-Pook, 2007; Forte & Bruckman, 2006; Panke & Thillosen, 2008). Another form of making use of the collaboration opportunities of Wikipedia includes students evaluating and commenting on other student-written articles on their discussion pages (e.g. within a "Downstream Processing" class, Cornell University, fall 2006). After article drafts underwent peer review and the editing process, they are submitted to Wikipedia mainspace. Some instructors called students to present the articles they have been working on within individual or group presentations.

Many seminars included a documentation and analysis of Wikipedia course work. The documentation started before the beginning of a term with the creation of an assignment list on the instructor's user page. This introductory list later turns to a list of completed articles. Other forms of documenting Wikipedia use in seminars include using a course blog or a general blog (Möller, 2006). Occasionally, students had to document the research and changes made to articles as well as the experiences of having their articles edited in a course-accompanying report or an essay. Occasionally, students had to complete a brief follow-up online questionnaire about the course. Some instructors such as Betsy Colwill of San Diego State University subsequently presented the "lessons learned" of a Wikipedia seminar to their fellow faculty (Colwill, 2006).

Advantages and Disadvantages of Wikipedia Use

Authentic Learning Environments

Even though Wikipedia was initially not meant to be used for teaching, and Wikipedia founder Jimmy Wales strongly advises students against relying upon Wikipedia as authoritative (Young, 2006), the use of the collaborative encyclopedia offers many advantages such as the didactically activating method, the propaedeutic training of properly using scholarly secondary sources, intensive text work and the collaborative training of writing competencies as well as learning outcomes relevant to examinations. The "school and university projects" page additionally promotes as advantages of this seminar form that many

> *of these projects have resulted in both advancing the student's knowledge and useful content being added to Wikipedia. An advantage of this over regular homework is that the student is dealing with a real world situation, which is not only more educational but also makes it more interesting ("the world gets to see my work"), probably resulting in increased dedication. Besides, it will give the students a chance to collaborate on course notes and papers, and their effort might remain online for reference.* (Wikipedia, 2009d)

The advantages and disadvantages of writing articles on Wikipedia have regularly been discussed within Wikipedia courses. While the evaluations of many instructors on the "school and university projects" page seem to back many of the claims made in the above paragraph, learning outcome research on Wikipedia's use in university courses still remains a desideratum. As a positive result of the active integration of Wikipedia in teaching, in connection with a 2006 Yale University course on "History of Modern Science in Society", teaching assistant Sage Ross emphasised multiple positive effects of Wikipedia seminars such as

- the increased student motivation due to the perspective of an (anonymous) online publication and the further usefulness of their texts
- a better understanding of the proper use of scholarly secondary information sources
- as well as an advancement of the argumentation and negotiation culture.

Ross concludes that Wikipedia is "a very convenient forum for giving and receiving feedback from classmates, which can dramatically improve the quality of student writing" (Ross, 2006). Students benefit from the aspect of an improved research and writing competency while the coursework incidentally leads to a considerable increase in the quality of Wikipedia entries.

Critical Experiences

The quality of student contributions to Wikipedia in a university course context varies strongly. Sporadically, Wikipedia in teaching projects have produced minor response by students who were adding only little information to the pages involved. Some classes resulted in downright failure, perhaps due to the unfamiliarity with Wikipedia and a lack in pedagogical guidance. A "Global Economics" seminar from Marshall University, Huntington, West Virginia, caused extensive disputes between the Wikipedia community, the instructor and the students in early 2008. Of some 70 articles that were newly created within this seminar, only seven survived in anything like their original form. About half of the articles were swiftly deleted, others were merged, or redirected since community guidelines had not sufficiently been considered (Wikipedia, 2009e).

A decisive disadvantage of Wikipedia use for teaching is associated with the workload of instructors. Instructors have to invest a significant amount of time in enabling students to contribute to wikis and in the extensive review of student contributions to articles. This additional work relates to the necessity of revising errors in the students' wiki syntax. Further disadvantages consist in lacking digital competencies of students, unwanted external interventions by regular Wikipedians, the impermanence and changeability of texts, or in students producing inappropriate texts that have to be revised and "cleaned up". Difficulties can also occur in developing appropriate criteria for grading the students' intellectual output. Therefore, innovative forms of grading have been applied occasionally such as evaluating students not only on their written contributions, but also on the effectiveness of their editing (Wikipedia, 2009f).

OTHER WIKIMEDIA PROJECTS AS TEACHING TOOLS

Besides Wikimedia's flagship project Wikipedia, over the years a growing number of other projects have emerged to serve the same Wikimedia objective of collecting and distributing knowledge free of charge. While Wikipedia disposes of a significant advantage due to its strong popularity among Internet users, some of the other Wikimedia projects are generally suited for an adaptation to university teaching as well. Using other Wikimedia projects besides Wikipedia within teaching most notably allows instructors for more versatile work assignments than for merely letting students edit articles. Other projects of the Wikimedia Foundation besides Wikipedia include the dictionary Wiktionary, the collection of free content texts labelled Wikisource, a repository of textbooks and manuals called Wikibooks, or the news portal Wikinews. Not all of the Wikimedia projects appear equally suited for teaching purposes, though, since not all have overcome their "teething troubles" and have yet reached a critical mass of participants attracting instructors to use them for teaching.

Wikimedia's current user statistics provide insight into the level of acceptance, diffusion and development of different Wikimedia projects. Dutch statistics expert Erik Zachte derived the user statistics from a logfile analysis of the proxy servers in 2008 (Zachte, 2008). Wikipedia readers have accessed the online encyclopedia 10,175 billion times in September 2008. About half of the pageviews were concentrated on the English-language edition of Wikipedia (5,4 billion pageviews). All of Wikimedia's sister projects generated 456 million pageviews within the same month (about 5 percent of the overall traffic). The multimedia archive Wikimedia Commons was second most strongly accessed among the Wikimedia projects (173 million pageviews). The third position was taken by Wiktionary with 151 million pageviews. Wikibooks, Wikisource, Wikiquote, Wikinews, and Wikiversity received less user attention.

Early Adoption of Sister Projects and Perspectives

Initial seminar experience exists for the Wikimedia projects Wikibooks, Wikisource, and Wikiversity. The Wikibooks project aims at collaboratively creating free content teaching and textbooks and annotated online texts that anyone can edit. Wikibooks claims that it was "uniquely suited for use in classroom collaborative projects" and provides comprehensive "guidelines for class projects" (Wikibooks, 2009). Composing a textbook on the basis of a term paper can be realised through using the infrastructure of the Wikibooks project and under consideration of the "guidelines for class projects" provided by Wikibooks. A so-called "theory workshop" ("Theoriewerkstatt") at the University of Salzburg has made use of the Wikibooks infrastructure for producing a textbook on "Sociological Classics" in the fall term 2006/2007. The wiki textbook has repeatedly been revised in subsequent seminars.

A Wikisource project that focuses on building an online library of free content textual sources has been used in seminars as well to present "Slovene literary classics" at the University of Ljubljana since 2007. Another Wikimedia project relevant for e-learning purposes is Wikiversity, a community devoted to collaborative learning. Wikiversity participants build open educational resources from the ground up and link them to existing Internet resources. Wikiversity provides instructors with material which they can use in their seminars and students with learning materials to use as self-study materials. Wikiversity serves as a place to share ideas about how to teach, how to learn, and what the best ways of facilitating learning are. Wikiversity provides a "school and university projects" page of its own specifying some 30 past and current teaching projects at universities (Panke & Thillosen, 2008, p. 11–13; Wikiversity, 2009).

Research Perspectives

Instructors should be encouraged to place a stronger focus on documenting and analysing the results of their Wikipedia use in seminars. The documentation available so far on the "school and university projects" page on the English-language Wikipedia shows a clear need to be revised to make the results of past courses more comparable. More comprehensive course reports would help other instructors to benefit from the diverse didactical conceptions and course experiences of their colleagues. Moreover, future in-depth research on the didactic Wikipedia use should establish a data basis exceeding incidental course documentations and should be carried out in close cooperation with instructors using Wikipedia in their teaching. It could focus on the students' specific teaching and learning experiences to inquire which seminar forms and which specific tools are suited for different educational contexts and purposes. While this chapter made use of incidental data of varying quality, primarily the HISBUS survey and Wikipedia's "school and university projects" page, a future systematic empirical survey with a standardised set of parameters should be performed based on a group of Wikipedia using courses as well as on lecturer and student polls.

Such an analysis could contribute to a deepened understanding of aspects such as the changing attitudes of students towards the online encyclopedia, the adequacy of Wikipedia use in seminars of different disciplines, the impact and didactical sustainability of different seminar and assignment forms, the learning processes and learning outcomes within seminars using Wikipedia compared to seminars with conventional assignment forms, the resulting workload of instructors, and the adequacy of Wikimedia projects other than Wikipedia for academic teaching purposes. Since the didactic opportunities of Wikimedia projects have not been fully realised yet, such a survey could contribute to the development of further forms of applying Wikimedia projects at universities.

CONCLUSION

The professional scepticism of instructors against Wikipedia as a source of reliable information due to widespread student plagiarism or due to the problem of anonymous Wikipedia contributions has occasionally lead to the misconception of a general inappropriateness of Wikipedia as a teaching tool. The reports of a majority of instructors that incorporated Wikipedia into their teaching practice indicate that new didactical terrain was explored with predominantly positive results. The reports on many seminars show that the online encyclopedia can successfully contribute to the quality of knowledge acquisition at universities and to a training of methodical and collaborative writing techniques. A growing amount of articles contributed to the English-language Wikipedia edition during coursework as documented on the "articles as assignments" page (Wikipedia, 2009g) proves that good results have been achieved in a majority of seminars. The online encyclopedia has proved useful e.g. for methodically training research skills, for letting students take editorial feedback into account, or for letting them consider different perspectives on a controversial subject.

A constant increase in Wikipedia using seminars with different didactic approaches further backs the assumption of a basic usefulness of the encyclopedia in teaching. The HISBUS survey and the analysis of 92 brief seminar reports demonstrate that the students' considerable familiarity with Wikipedia and their positive attitude towards Web 2.0 media create beneficial conditions for a systematic utilisation of Wikipedia. Diverse factors such as the authentic learning environment, the didactically activating method of cooperative and collaborative work and the text production for a very large audience create strong motivational impulses and sustainably contribute to improving the students' research skills. When students are held accountable to a global audience for what they are doing, they feel more devoted to their work. That way, writing for Wikipedia helps students to realise how responsibility for scientific accuracy can be linked to the dissemination of knowledge.

Challenges for Instructors and the Wikimedia Foundation

The palpable affinity of text-focused humanities departments to using Wikipedia seems to indicate that this form of teaching may not be suited for all disciplines in an equal manner. However, the excellent Wikipedia assessments presented by students of engineering studies, of natural sciences and of medical studies within the HISBUS survey suggest that a willingness to work with Wikipedia is presumably given in these disciplines as well (at least for the encyclopedia's German-language edition). In order to translate Wikipedia's high frequency of usage and its positive perception among students into an actual methodic-didactical use of Wikipedia, diverse teaching and learning approaches will have to be developed for different disciplines.

Nevertheless, an essential precondition for a successful application of Wikipedia is that courses are diligently prepared in the real as well as in the virtual world. Only instructors willing to invest more time than they would for conventional courses will be able to take advantage of the full didactic potential of this popular Web 2.0 instrument. Course work with Wikipedia can only take place successfully if instructors are prepared to make themselves familiar with central Wikipedia conventions and if precepts are taken into consideration. However, with regard to the increasing use of Wikipedia through instructors at least since the year 2004, the lack of educational materials like best practice documents, lesson plans or printed recommendations for university lecturers is striking. The acceptance of Wikipedia as a learning tool will mainly depend on the availability of such materials which help to minimise the time and effort for instructors and the threat of failure.

If barriers or major difficulties emerge during a course, instructors can profit from the advantages of a social software network through falling back on the support services offered by the above-mentioned WikiProject Classroom coordination. Involving senior Wikipedia authors in the planning and execution of university courses can minimise the risk of failure. For this purpose, either the Wikimedia Foundation (as operator of the online encyclopedia) or Wikipedia's community of contributing authors has to find better ways how to bring together instructors and Wikipedia authors willing to help.

REFERENCES

Bendel, O. (2006). Wikipedia als Methode und Gegenstand der Lehre. In K. Hildebrand (Ed.), *Social Software* (pp. 82–88). Heidelberg: dpunkt. verlag.

Brandt-Pook, H. (2007 June). Geschlossene Wikis als aktivierendes Element in der Hochschullehre. *HMD – Praxis der Wirtschaftsinformatik*, 255.

Child, M. L. (2007, February 26). Professors split on wiki debate. *Thecrimson.com*. Retrieved January 15, 2009, from http://www.thecrimson.com/article.aspx?ref=517305

Cohen, N. (2007, February 21). A history department bans citing Wikipedia as a research source. *The New York Times*. Retrieved January 15, 2009, from http://www.nytimes.com/2007/02/21/education/21wikipedia.html?ex=1329714000&en=156f770bd93c4fa0&ei=5088&partner=rssnyt&emc=rss

Colwill, B. (2006, January 10). *Wikipedia and the feminist production of knowledge*. Retrieved January 15, 2009, from http://pict.sdsu.edu/Jan06/collwill/wikipedia%20presentation1.ppt.

Ebner, E. (2007). Wikipedia. Hype oder Zukunftshoffnung für die Hochschullehre. In *E-Learning: Strategische Implementierungen und Studiengang. Tagungsband zur 13. FNMA-Tagung* (pp. 139–146). Köln, Germany: Verlag Forum Neue Medien.

Forte, A., & Bruckman, A. (2006). From Wikipedia to the classroom: exploring online publication and learning. In . *Proceedings of the International Conference of the Learning Sciences*, *1*, 182–188.

Grotjahn, H. (2007). *Qualitätsmessungen an der Wikipedia: Konstruktion von Qualität – eine Metaanalyse*. Saarbrücken, Germany: VDN Verlag Dr. Müller.

Güntheroth, H., Schönert, U., & Rodtmann, E. (2007). Juni 12). Wikipedia. Wissen für alle. *Stern*, *50*, 30–44.

Haber, P. (2007). Weltbibliothek oder Diderots Erben? Traditionslinien von Wikipedia. In R. Koschke, O. Herzog, K. H. Rödiger et al. (Eds.), *Informatik 2007 – Informatik trifft Logistik. Bd. 2. Beiträge der 37. Jahrestagung der Gesellschaft für Informatik e.V. (GI)* (pp. 497–502). Bonn, Germany: Köllen.

Hodel, J., & Haber, P. (2007). Das kollaborative Schreiben von Geschichte als Lernprozess. Eigenheiten und Potential von Wiki-Systemen und Wikipedia. In M. Merkt, K. Mayrberger, R. Schulmeister et al. (Ed.), *Studieren neu erfinden – Hochschule neu denken* (pp. 43–53). Hamburg, Germany: Waxmann.

Institut für Demoskopie Allensbach. (2008). Allensbacher Computer- und Technik-Analyse. *Allensbach am Bodensee*.

Jaschniok, M. (2007). *Wikipedia und ihre Nutzer: Zum Bildungswert der Online-Enzyklopädie*. Marburg, Germany: Tectum.

Kleimann, B., Özkilic, M., & Göcks, M. (2008). *HISBUS-Kurzinformation Nr. 21. Studieren im Web 2.0. Studienbezogene Web- und E-Learning-Dienste*. Hannover, Germany: HIS-Projektbericht. Retrieved January 15, 2009, from https://hisbus.his.de/hisbus/docs/hisbus21.pdf

Konieczny, P. (2007). Wikis and Wikipedia as a teaching tool. *International Journal of Instructional Technology and Distance Learning, 1*, 15–34.

Lorenz, M. (2006). Wikipedia. Zum Verhältnis von Struktur und Wirkungsmacht eines heimlichen Leitmediums. *WerkstattGeschichte, 43*, 84–95.

Martin, J.-P. (2006). Gemeinsam Wissen konstruieren: am Beispiel der Wikipedia. In M. Klebl & M. Köck (Ed.), *Projekte und Perspektiven im Studium Digitale, Medienpädagogik,* (Vol. 3, pp. 157–164). Berlin, Germany: LIT.

Meyer-Lucht, R. (2008, October 16). So nutzen die Deutschen Internet, Zeitung und Fernsehen. *spiegel.de*. Retrieved January 15, 2009, from http://www.spiegel.de/netzwelt/web/0,1518,584572,00.html

Möller, E. (2006). *Die heimliche Medienrevolution – Wie Weblogs, Wikis und freie Software die Welt verändern*. Hannover, Germany: Heinz Heise.

Panke, S., & Thillosen, A. (2008). Unterwegs auf dem Wiki-Way. Wikis in Lehr- und Lernsettings. *e-teaching.org*. Retrieved January 15, 2009, from http://www.e-teaching.org/didaktik/kommunikation/wikis/08-09-12_Wiki_Panke-Thillosen.pdf.

Pentzold, C. (2007). *Wikipedia: Diskussionsraum und Informationsspeicher im neuen Netz*. München, Germany: R. Fischer.

Ross, S. (2006). *User: Ragesoss/Assignments*. Retrieved January 15, 2009, from http://en.wikipedia.org/wiki/User:Ragesoss/Assignments

Surowiecki, J. (2004). *The wisdom of crowds: Why the many are smarter than the few and how collective wisdom shapes business, economies, societies and nations*. New York: Doubleday.

Terdiman, D. (2005, December 16). Study: Wikipedia as accurate as Britannica. *CNET News*. Retrieved January 15, 2009, from http://news.cnet.co.uk/software/0,39029694,39195096,00.htm

Wales, J. (2008, December 11). Die Bildung wird revolutioniert. *DIE ZEIT, 51*. Retrieved January 15, 2009, from http://images.zeit.de/text/2008/51/Traum-51/

Wikibooks. (2009). *Wikibooks: Guidelines for class projects*. Retrieved January 15, 2009, from http://en.wikibooks.org/wiki/Wikibooks:Guidelines_for_class_projects

Wikipedia. (2009). *School and university projects*. Retrieved January 15, 2009, from http://en.wikipedia.org/wiki/Schools_and_universities_project

Wikipedia. (2009a). *Wikipedia: Statistics*. Retrieved January 15, 2009, from http://en.wikipedia.org/wiki/Wikipedia:Statistics

Wikipedia. (2009b). *Wikipedia: Verifiability*. Retrieved January 15, 2009, from http://en.wikipedia.org/wiki/Wikipedia:Verifiability

Wikipedia. (2009c). *Wikipedia: Community portal*. Retrieved January 15, 2009, from http://en.wikipedia.org/wiki/Wikipedia:Community_portal#help_out

Wikipedia. (2009d). *Wikipedia: School and university projects/Past projects. Truman State University (Fall 2007)*. Retrieved January 15, 2009, from http://en.wikipedia.org/wiki/Wikipedia:School_and_university_projects/Past_projects#Truman_State_University_.28Fall_2007.29

Wikipedia. (2009e). *Featured content from schools and universities*. Retrieved January 15, 2009, from http://en.wikipedia.org/wiki/Wikipedia:Wikipedia_Signpost/2008-05-09/Dispatches

Wikipedia. (2009f). *Wikipedia: School and university projects/Past projects. University of Hong Kong (Spring 2007)*. Retrieved January 15, 2009 from http://en.wikipedia.org/wiki/Wikipedia:School_and_university_projects/Past_projects#University_of_Hong_Kong_.28Spring_2007.29

Wikipedia. (2009g). *Category: Wikipedia_articles_as_assignments*. Retrieved January 15, 2009, from http://en.wikipedia.org/wiki/Category:Wikipedia_articles_as_assignments

Wikiversity. (2009). *Wikiversity: School and university projects*. Retrieved January 15, 2009, from http://en.wikiversity.org/wiki/Wikiversity:School_and_university_projects

Wolf, A. (2007). Wikipedia: Kollaboratives Arbeiten im Internet. In T. Hengartner & J. Moser (Ed.), *Grenzen und Differenzen. Zur Macht sozialer und kultureller Grenzziehungen* (pp. 639–650). Leipzig, Germany: Leipziger Universitätsverlag.

Young, J. R. (2006, June 12). Wikipedia founder discourages academic use of his creation. *Chronicle.com*. Retrieved January 15, 2009, from http://chronicle.com/wiredcampus/article/1328/wikipedia-founder-discourages-academic-use-of-his-creation

Zachte, E. (2008). Wikimedia page view stats I. *infodisiac.com*. Retrieved January 15, 2009 from http://infodisiac.com/blog/2008/10/wikimedia-page-view-stats-i/

Section 5.3

Virtual Environments and Virtual Worlds

Chapter 18
Instructional Design for Virtual Worlds:
Basic Principles for Learning Environments

Nadine Ojstersek
University Duisburg-Essen, Germany

Michael Kerres
University Duisburg-Essen, Germany

ABSTRACT

This paper gives an overview of the didactic elements relevant to foster learning in virtual worlds. The specific requirements of learning in virtual worlds are investigated in detail using the C3-model of didactic components. Following this model, the specifications of virtual worlds are illustrated with regard to the components "content", "communication" and "construction". The use of virtual worlds is often connected with the hope for stronger immersion, which is encouraged by the possibility of three-dimensionality and the representation of the learner by a virtual representative ("avatars"). However, learning-/teaching processes are not automatically improved by the use of virtual worlds. The possibilities offered by virtual worlds can only be honoured when a dedicated didactical concept is implemented. This means a complex composition process which has to take into consideration the specific features of virtual worlds.

INTRODUCTION

The introduction of new media technology for learning and teaching is frequently linked to hopes for "better" learning. However, previous experience has shown that many of these expectations regarding the "optimisation" of learning are doomed to be disappointing. Virtual worlds are showing quite a different trend: They are viewed with great scepticism as regards their use for teaching and learning. Nevertheless, this critical viewpoint offers the opportunity for a serious, systematic debate concerning its potential and limitations. Despite this scepticism, interest in virtual worlds for teaching and learning is rather large in schools, universities and advanced training institutions. This interest can be explained by the associated hope for new potentials of e-learning. The focus is on the possibilities for learners to create their own avatar, to

DOI: 10.4018/978-1-61520-678-0.ch018

explore the virtual world and to communicate and collaborate with other learners.

The following paper outlines the components that are relevant to designing meaningfull learning in virtual worlds from an educational point of view. To begin with, the term "virtual world" will be discussed. Then the framework of the C3-model as a tool for instructional design will be explained. The aim is to design immersive learning environments that tap into the full potential of virtual worlds. Finally, the paper looks ahead: It shows that increasingly the dividing line between real life and virtual worlds is blurring.

BACKGROUND

The ongoing technical developments in the area of virtual worlds and the increasing interest of education providers in the use of virtual worlds are accompanied by the question of how courses in virtual worlds can be designed in a way that is didactically meaningful and what kind of added value they offer compared to other means of e-learning.

The perspective of instructional design is that the medium should not only be used to "improve" teaching and learning, but also to (better) solve a certain educational problem or issue. It must be considered that the medium itself will not bring about "improved learning" (Kerres, 2001).

The question is raised as to what added value is associated with the use of virtual worlds and in which scenarios they could be used. Obviously, it does not make sense to merely transfer existing didactic media concepts and methods to virtual worlds.

Typically with the rise of each new media technology, the technical options for learning are investigated. The instructional design focus, however, looks at the principles and strategies relevant to structuring meaningful learning opportunities in the building virtual worlds. Here, the focus is not on the media technology as such or on evaluating "the" technology, but on the process of designing learning enviorments. For example, it is not sufficient to make learning material available in virtual worlds and to "put them onto the net". Learning environments in virtual worlds need to be purposefully planned and designed. The hope that the playful character of virtual worlds will be effective in itself is not grounded. If learners and teachers do not make use of learning opportunities in virtual worlds, their didactic benefit is minimal.

The quality of courses and e-learning environments offered on the internet depends on the quality of a didactical analysis, a thorough instructional design concept, its implementation and evaluation.

With regard to virtual worlds this, for example, means to analyse if learners have any experience with virtual worlds, which learning objectives shall be achieved, which instructional methods are suitable and how learners can be supported.

Currently, instead of a systematic debate on these didactical components of the instructional design process, the discussion focuses on the "general" potentials and limitations of virtual worlds in the teaching/learning context. The various and new possibilities of designing a 3D enviornment and options for integrating Web 2.0 are viewed as essential potentials (Müller & Leidl, 2007). Some virtual worlds offer the possibility to involve learners actively into the design – and learning process by letting them create and modify objects themselves (Cheal, 2007). Furthermore, processes and models can be stimulated, which would be very difficult to be carried out under real conditions (Müller & Leidl, 2007) (e. g. testing of business concepts, language training). Compared to other variants of e-learning, a stronger feeling of social presence and a more intensive "immersion" (Cheal, 2007; Joseph, 2007; The Horizon Report, 2007) (see chapter on immersion) can be expected by the interaction of human actors and between human actors and the physical artifacts in the virtual world.

Often, however, traditional instructional models simply are copied from "real life" to virtual worlds - with limited to no success. For example, lecturs in an auditorium in a virtual world often are not accepted by learners due to their passivity. Instead, the virtual world must be viewed as an environment for active learning: a place for people interacting with each other and with physical artificats in the virtual word. Activites, e.g., can relate to visiting interesting places and events in the virual worlds (Cheal, 2007).

Therefore, the implementation of virtual worlds does not automatically come along with an "improvement" of teaching-/learning processes, but they can provide an attractive tool to implement concepts for active and meaningful learning. This leads to the question as how such an enviornment can be planned and designed in order to provide such learning opportunities.

VIRTUAL WORLDS AND MASSIVELY MULTIPLAYER ONLINE GAMES

For the following chapter, we will differentiate between virtual worlds and massively multiplayer online games. Virtual worlds are persistent virtual 3D-world simulations, in which a variety of people can participate at the same time. A variety of synchronous and asynchronous possibilities are available for communication and cooperation (Gierke & Müller, 2008).

Moreover, there are several variations in technical terms (e.g. 2D-world simulations, single user environments). However, due to their limited options, this chapter will not observe them closer. Names like multi user environment, multi user virtual environment or massively multiplayer online environment are mostly used as synonyms. These world constructions are often administrated on servers, are both client- and browser based and can be joined and explored with different input devices (for example keyboard, data glove). Thus, presence in a virtual world is possible without physical attendance (Raschke, 2007).

Depending on the specific virtual world, a different extent of possibilities for action, design and interaction (with each other and the virtual environment) are available to the user, which leads to a dynamic, complex, unpredictable and unlimited companionship (Götzenbrucker, 2001).

Gierke & Müller (2008) and Schmidt (2006) view massively multiplayer online games (MMOGs) as a sub-category of virtual worlds, as they feature a specific game context. However, Rittman (2008) argues against a commitment to the games context, as with MMOGs diverse targets can be set and the user can experience the environment as a "world".

MMOGs are all online computer games where multiple people can play together at the same time. The embodiment of the user takes place as an avatar, which is the centre of movement and orientation (Thiedeke, 2004b). Amongst others, massively multiplayer online role-playing games (MMORPGs) such as "World of Warcraft" are included. These are persistent computer games without predictability and finiteness (Neuenhausen, 2004) with the users participating in their design. The major difference to virtual worlds is that MMOGs are mainly narrative game worlds (Rittmann, 2008).

Similarly to MMOGs, in virtual worlds like for example Second Life, which is currently the most popular and complex platform for avatar based interaction in the internet, users are producers and consumers at the same time. Virtual worlds are also persistent, unlimited and allow synchronous communication and interaction of multiple users via the internet connection. However, a virtual world does not feature the characteristics of a game, like for example highly complex rules, a background story, a winning definition and a goal (Gierke & Müller, 2008). Even if diverse game elements may be integrated, communication and interaction are in the foreground.

Virtual worlds can be described as world- or social simulations (Gierke & Müller, 2008), which – independent of their size – are perceived as such (Rittmann, 2008). In virtual worlds a reflection of human experiences of life such as life, death and reincarnation take place. Relationships, communication - and action restrictions are developed as well as sufferance and exercise of power (Götzenbrucker, 2001). Following Thiedeke (2004a), it is not a matter of simulating reality, as the user experiences an own substantial reality, which can be separated from the current physical reality.

Such simulation may also be viewed as the core concept of a game with the goal to see connections from the outside, to abandon established paradigms and to free up creativity (Schmidt, 2006). One variety are closed economic simulations, which offer more security and performance and either built separate own worlds, or may be integrated into closed sections of already existing virtual worlds like Second Life (Gierke & Müller, 2008).

Most of all, it depends on the goals of the users whether a virtual world or a MMOGS is mainly a game or a platform for collaboration and communication. By trend, social interaction is more and more in the foreground and the virtual world is increasingly changing through the users (Neuenhausen, 2004). Whilst targets and tasks are explicitly assigned in MMOGS (Schmidt, 2006), virtual worlds in contrast focus on much broader and more individual goals (Gierke & Müller, 2008).

The freedom of design regarding construction - and communication possibilities is different between virtual worlds and MMOGs (Götzenbrucker, 2001). A virtual world like Second Life offers a very open design, which allows the user to generate objects, to program them and to create an avatar. The scope for design depends on the own competencies. Currently, the scope for design in MMOGs is mostly limited to the adjustment of the interface; add-ons and mods are also possible to enhance the user friendliness and the optical design (Rittmann, 2008). According to Schmidt (2006), due to the user generated content in virtual worlds, established patterns of thought have to be removed to free up creativity. Whether an extensive scope for design is combined with a greater immersion and if immersion has a positive effect on teaching and learning processes has not been clarified yet. However, immersion is a central characteristic both for MMOGs (Neuenhausen, 2004) and virtual worlds (see chapter on immersion).

In MMOGs the complexity of the game unfolds very slowly. A limited form of playful exploration is encouraged, without being so complex that it can not be handled anymore. With an increasing amount of complexity in the simulation game, the scope for design is also growing. MMOGs do have specific goals. However, the solutions to get to those goals may differ. Closeness to reality is achieved through an unmanageable number of constantly changing variables, which are beyond the own influence. The users cannot rule this world completely; they are exposed to its unpredictability, however, without experiencing a complete loss of autonomy (Becker, 2004).

On the contrary, in virtual worlds these restrictions are much smaller and immediately after entrance all courses of action are open to the user. The question has to be asked, whether certain restrictions and preset tasks are conducive or repressive for beginners or how "secured" rooms for beginners can support their introduction to the virtual world step by step. The following figure illustrates the described similarities and differences.

In conclusion, a virtual world is a computer-based simulated environment intended for its users to interact via (three-dimensional) graphical representations (avatars). These virtual worlds allow multiple users and the user to manipulate elements of the virtual world. The communication is textual or/and real-time voice communication is possible. The size of the virtual world is not relevant. There may be individual rooms or complex worlds. Accordingly, virtual worlds are

Figure 1. Distinction between virtual worlds and MMOGs

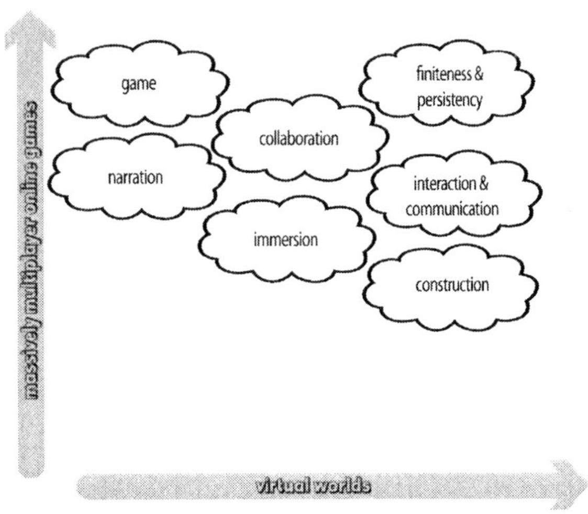

not inevitably games, but games can be a part of a virtual world.

In the following chapter, the didactical components of virtual worlds are systematized and possibilities are offered to design learning environments.

C3-MODEL OF DIDACTICAL COMPONENTS

The conception and development of educational media can be seen as a complex decisional problem (Kerres, 2001). It is important to find the appropriate solution for specific requirements of a learning situation to enshure certain learning processes that lead to learning outcomes. Basic elements of virtual worlds are the representation of persons as artificial identities (avatars), the possibility to communicate, collaborate and interact with each other and with artifacts and to produce user generated content (de Freitas, 2008; Hehl, 2008). Moreover, meta-information for learning, learning content, objects and tasks are activating and supporting learners in their learning process. In the context of virtual worlds, the design of learning scenarios relates to the selection, connection and creation of learning places and objects.

In the following section the basic elements of learning environments will be looked at closer in the context of virtual worlds and they will be related to the C3-model of didactical components (Kerres & de Witt, 2003). The C3-model of didactical components tries to provide a framework for specifying elements of a learning environment and their relative weight. Any learning environment (e.g. face-to-face, e-learning) can be described as consisting of the three components "content", "communication" and "construction":

- A content component that makes learning material available to a learner,
- a communication component that offers interpersonal exchange between learners or learners and tutors and
- a construction component that facilitates and guides individual as well as cooperative learning activities to actively engage on learning tasks with different degrees of complexity (e.g. projects, cases or other assignments).

Learning environments differ in the relative weight of the three components that depends on several dedicatical parameters. How much time should learners spend on activities related to the three components to a large extent depends on the learning objectives. If the learning objectives primarily consist of the acquisition of information and basic knowledge the component "content" is in the foreground and will receive the largest amount of learning time. In "learning communities", the components "communication" and "construction" will receive a larger weight (Kerres & de Witt, 2003).

In the following chapter these components will be looked at closer in the context of virtual worlds.

Figure 2. C3-model of didactical components (© 2003, Kerres & de Witt. Used with permission.)

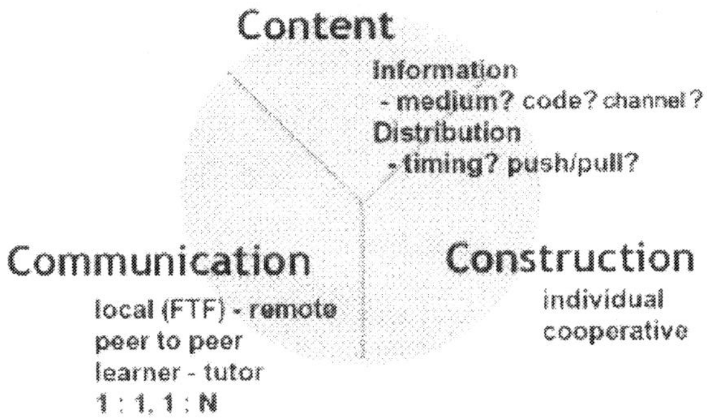

Content

The provision of learning material initiates the necessary cognitive and motivational-emotional processes of the learner. If the knowledge of specific circumstances is a requirement for other communicative or constructive learning activities, the "content" component is of primary relevance (Kerres & de Witt, 2003). The components can be medially implemented in different ways. Virtual worlds are primarily suitable for communication and group forms with (partly) informal character (Hehl, 2008). Besides organised learning environments the user may gain knowledge in a self-directed way with pod casts, presentations or learning paths.

In virtual worlds learners have learning information at disposal in order to be supported in their learning process and obtain relevant information (e.g. tutorials objects with stimulative nature). Assignments, learning objects and educational content have the function of stimulating learners, (e.g. games, 3D-elements). For example, the virtual world of Second Life is reigned by arbitrariness with regard to content and technological freedom, which causes fantasies in the educational context. However, it can also lead to creative contingency with probable phases of disorientation and boredom. Creative chaos is both the weakness and strength of virtual worlds. A balance has to be created between creative variety and paralysing restlessness. Moreover, instead of re-developing the same content again and again, at first the currently available contents should be taken into consideration. For support, wikis and search engines mainly outside Second Life can be used (Gierke & Müller, 2008). On the side of the learners, learning in virtual worlds dot not only contain the hope of finding a copy of traditional teaching-/learning scenarios but also of learning "differently" by immersing into a virtual world. The learners ask for activity, exploration and fun. Virtual worlds offer various possibilities to create a combination of contextual input and playful elements: Instead of building lecture halls and offering lectures creative ideas can be translated which support the activities of the learners, such as role games and explorations for example. With the example of Second Life the following scenarios can be distinguished (Gierke & Müller, 2008 following Horizon Report, 2007):

- lecture (with or without discussion round): demonstration of the syllabus, classical seminar situation with lecturers and virtual presentation techniques
- experiment: learners can try possible solutions and their effects on the object involved
- excursion: visits to other countries or conversion of historical and literary models
- role-play/simulation: managing a virtual company and production of plays
- construction: creating and programming own objects
- consultation/support: support learners during exam preparation

Scenarios can be distinguished between slightly-structured scenarios or heavily-formalised scenarios. If the knowledge of specific circumstances is a requirement for other communicative or constructive learning activities, the content component is of primary relevance. The components can be medially implemented in different ways. Virtual worlds are primarily suitable for communication and group forms with (partly) informal character (Hehl, 2008). Besides organised learning environments the user may gain knowledge in a self-directed way with pod casts, presentations or learning paths.

Communication

For example, the "communication component" seems necessary when knowledge reaches a certain complexity, a deeper understanding of a theoretical framework is required or the knowledge consists of different competing concepts (Kerres & de Witt, 2003). The potential of using virtual worlds in the context of further education lies in the various possibilities of communication and collaboration between teachers and learners and among learners respectively (e.g. role-play, excursion). Depending on the virtual world specific languages (Neuenhausen, 2004), gestures and codes of conduct exist (Götzenbrucker, 2001). Communication demands distinctive communication and social competence, and its implementation is an essential requirement for immersion (see chapter on immersion).

The development and maintenance of a community is of utmost significance (Gierke & Müller, 2008). The use of virtual worlds leads to the constitution of virtual groups and influences the structure and size of personal social networks in the real world. Through the specific communication modality (for example anonymity) relations are expanded into various social groups and cultures. The development of social relationships mostly arises from the virtual world itself because communication and collaboration processes are necessary to reach a certain goal (Götzenbrucker, 2001; Hehl, 2008).

Additionally, being three-dimensional is a specific criterion of virtual worlds. Hehl (2008) highlights the increasing degree of achieved digital interactivity through virtual worlds. This leads to a direct interactive cooperation among people which may cause a feeling of togetherness and a flow-experience despite the distance. In virtual worlds the distance to face-to-face interaction in many relationships is rather small. Most of the time, group communication takes place when duplets and triplets form talking groups, where avatars position themselves in "physical" closeness to the dialogue partner (Götzenbrucker, 2001). Through the reduced distance between learners the willingness to make contact is increased and an easier access to learning takes place due to the well-known classroom atmosphere. However, this may lead to traditional behaviour (Gierke & Müller 2008). The challenge is to design learning tasks which encourage communication and collaboration processes and support the spatial proximity of the avatars.

Construction

The constructive component is the one that facilitates and guides individual as well as cooperative learning activities to actively operate on learning tasks (or assignments) with different degrees of complexity. For example it play an important role when knowledge is to be applied (and not only to be recalled) or it consists of procedures (and not only of declarative knowledge) that require practice (Kerres & de Witt, 2003). For example, in virtual worlds the users have the opportunity to create objects, either individual or cooperative. There are hardly any boundaries to creativity (Gierke & Müller, 2008). The learners can actively participate in the design and learning process by creating their own objects, manipulating interactive applications and by simulating models which would be difficult to exercise or present under real conditions (for example testing a business idea or physical experiments). Although the technique is offering the requirements, the usage of the potential of interaction is essential. The more possibilities for interaction are offered, the stronger the feeling occurs to be present in the virtual world (Neuenhausen, 2004; Rittmann,

2008). The degree of co-designing virtual worlds varies a lot. The open design of Second Life for example is supported by modelling tools and interfaces to other 3D software, which allows the user to generate objects and to insert codes (Rittman, 2008). Thus, it is possible that users work on 3D computer models together in real time and produce media and learning products themselves. On the one side, virtual worlds offer the possibility to experiment without real risks (Hehl, 2008) and therefore allow interaction with venues and people as well as the participation in events which may be refused in the real world and can consequently be compensated. On the other side, the technical requirements for an extensive integration of text designing tools outside textchat and notecards are still missing. That is why, at the moment the usage of virtual worlds is primarily suitable for practise-related tasks and special seminars. Virtual worlds can be designed in a more multifaceted way than learning management systems (LMS). However, in the foreseeable future they are not competitive, as LMS balance the deficit of design possibilities with a simple scalability regarding a greater number of users and the user administration of large teaching/learning environments. A combination of virtual worlds and LMS is already technically possible, as it is about connection and not disconnection of single systems (Gierke & Müller, 2008).

In the following chapter, possibilities are offered to design learning environments in an immersive way.

Immersion

In this chapter the phenomenon of immersion will be looked at. A new quality of immersion in the world which is presented to us and of fading out of the outside world is assigned to virtual worlds. Hereby, our attention is shifted from a (real) world we experience to a world which is real to us for a certain time offering the user what he/she wants. Amongst other things, this virtual world offers distraction, acceptance and friendships. Most of all, immersion is a psychological and perceptive act and is not primarily dependent on staging.

Instructional design of virtual worlds can take this immersive potential into consideration, for example by motivating the user with tasks and avoiding the development of boredom (Rittmann, 2008). For example, a motivating task could be the following: A learner discovers a reproduced Viking village with his Avatar in the virtual (see chapter on content). Rittmann (2008) refers to the phenomenon of the flow-experience following Csikszentmihalyi (2000) and points out the requirement of balancing one's own abilities, needs and feedback.

In a virtual world, optimal feedback to successful acting results in intrinsic motivation and thus the flow-effect (Raschke, 2007). Therefore, computer games make use of action loops with appropriate levels of difficulty and positive feedback to support absent-mindedness. Following Csikszentmihalyi (2000), Rittmann (2008) points out that the flow-experience is a mental state, which one reaches if new tasks have found the right degree between lightness and demand and a human being is in the flow of action and reaction. Thus, absent mindedness occurs through total concentration on the task. Virtual worlds, however, not only offer such absent-minded chains of activities but also provide the discovery of landscapes and the maintenance of social relationships. Thus, visiting a virtual world is not a great flow experience. On the contrary, the sequences in computer games are designed straight and fit smoothly into another. This leads to high concentration, blinding out of other factors, a shortened experience of time spans and a lack of self awareness (Rittmann, 2008). Following Thon (2007) Rittman (2008) describes immersion on four levels: The spatial, ludic, narrative and social level. Virtual worlds hold the characteristics of a "real world" (for example avatars who ask for the way).

Regardless of its size, the virtual world is perceived as such and not as a graphical display with software. The virtual world partly resembles the real world but there are also basic differences. Although virtual worlds are not perceived in a haptic or olfactory way, one can touch things and smell them in a different way.

It is insignificant for the spatial immersion whether it is a photo realistic image or an overbooked comic one. For instructional design Gierke & Müller (2008) conclude that environments that are experienced as authentic allow a higher degree of immersion with avatars. Rittmann (2008) refers to the "Uncanny Valley" effect following Green et al. (2008) and MacDorman (2005) which says that a realistic image may even cause the opposite reaction, as the user constantly looks out for discrepancies and questions the events logically. With regard to the c3-model (see chapter on content) this means that in the graphic design of learning objects (e.g simulation of ecosystems, reproduction of historical personalities) an authentic representation of reality does not always seem to be appropriate.

The design of the room becomes more important with the use of three-dimensionality. By taking the ego-perspective, events can be viewed through the eyes of an avatar and a 360-degree turn of the camera can be undertaken. Thus, the user feels his/her presence in the virtual world and more than before gains the impression of "being there". The view from the ego perspective is not necessarily more immersive all the time. More critical is the ability to manipulate objects and people, the degree to which one can identify with the avatar and the feeling of the user to be part of the world and to be able to move in it without perceiving the medial intermediation. The behaviour of objects in consistence with identified laws of nature is less crucial than the fact that they act and that the user accepts the construction of the virtual room. Avatars allow taking a "picture" of the counterpart. The possibility exists to visualize physical presence and physical feelings (Rittman, 2008). Mostly, this is shown by individual and partly realistic design of the avatars. The communication partners or their avatars respectively are visible and audible where applicable. A visual and auditive combination reinforces the perception of the presence of the interaction partner (Götzenbrucker, 2001). The gesture, style of dressing and appearance of people influence the interaction and communication (Neuenhausen, 2004). Through the social presence a higher degree of immersion in the learning environment is possible than it was with the other variants of E-Learning (The Horizon Report, 2007). With regard to the c3-model (Kerres & de Witt, 2003) it is important to point out that learners should have great scope for individual creativity and interaction (e.g direct manipulability of 3D-models) and diverse possibilities of communication and cooperation.

Regarding the question if immersion is beneficial to the learning process, Gierke & Müller (2008) point out that a stronger emotional involvement with the learning content can be reached through avatars. The learners can take the view of the avatar and experience content in the first person. Through the tight connection with the experiences and emotions of the avatar, these can react to the learner.

The ludic level of immersion is strongly interwoven with the actual design of gameplays and terefore with their goals of the world, avatar development and interaction. The flow experience in virtual worlds is supported by the design of the world, gameplay elements and gratification systems and reinforces itself, by how quicly one learns how to navigate the avatar and how to adjust the interface, etc. to the individual preferences of the user (Rittmann, 2008). It can be assumed that the crossing into the virtual world is perceived consciously (Raschke, 2007). Regardless of the kind of technical interfaces it is not a complete immersion, where no difference between the virtual and the real world occurs (Thiedeke, 2004a). As successful MMORPGs show, this does not seem to be asked from the users, as although the possibility to immerse deeper in form of a classical role play exists, it is hardly ever used (Götzl,

Pfeiffer & Primus 2008). The integration of role-play elements can offer potential for the learning process (see chapter on content). However we have to analyse whether informal „background conversations" should be considered useful or an obstacle.Virtual data gloves do not belong to the day-to-day tools of young computer users. However, immersion does not seem to be dependent on the choice of the input device (Raschke, 2007). Technical perception aids like data gloves, etc. do not force immersion and are not predecessors of physical amalgamation of human being and machine but simply offer hardware-based support of immersion for the user through software products. Thus, a discrepancy between the literary envisaged VR-devices and VR- suits with connection to the central nervous system and the current possibilities to create immersion arises (Rittmann, 2008). Instead of the predicted enforcement of 3D-glasses and data gloves, the game industry (amongst others through their focus on social interaction) allows a high degree of immersion even without complex technique. It might even allow a higher degree of immersion than possible with inconvenient data gloves or similar equipment (Schmidt, 2006). Despite the assumption that the technical interface is not significant, alternatives are developed like for example shutter-glasses which create a 3D experience (Götzl, Pfeiffer & Primus, 2008), with control through physical movements comparable to the Wii or mimic-gesture technologies.

In the real world the fear of false definition judgement and the related negative consequences exists. This fear is comparatively low in computer games, which leads to game situations that are only superficially analysed and problems are solved by "trial and error". However, depending on the degree of immersion, the motivation to make no mistakes can also be high in games (Bopp, 2005), which depends on cost-benefit considerations. If the effort is too high compared with the benefit, even when highly motivated to begin with, one refrains from a detailed analysis of the situation (Bopp, 2005). These examples show, that a greater degree of immersion does not necessarily leads to the improvement of the learning offer.

Various avatars can be created which may have any desired state (for example sex) (Götzenbrucker, 2001). The often strong identification with the avatar induces the immersion (Rittmann, 2008; Schmidt, 2006). Nevertheless, the adult user usually is able to distinguish between him/herself and the avatar (Gremmler, 2008; Rittmann, 2008).

It is about one's own creation, the experimentation of the avatar and trying oneself out. The advantage of half anonymity of the internet compared to real contacts is that at first the strengths of a person are in the foreground and emotions are expressed more strongly, which creates a verbal closeness quickly. The design of avatars can be viewed as an identity encouraging offer and as an active involvement with oneself whilst the virtual world takes place by changing into another role and thus trying out new solution possibilities (Raschke, 2007).

According to Bopp (2005) only little willingness to learn in a game receptively exists. The potential of virtual worlds can be exploited when immersion is not interrupted by obvious learning. However, whether immersion and learning effectively exclude each other still has to be examined systematically. Bopp (2005) advocates the integration of inconspicuous didactical methods to encourage immersion. For example, instead of giving references to tutorials which actively have to be visited by the user, the user is located in a tutorial without being conscious of it. Further "hidden" assistance ("stealth teaching") are information carriers such as posters, notepads or highlighting with light effects or objects through affordance (for example the affordance by a round item to throw it).

Furthermore, the didactical sequencing of individual learning steps should be designed in an increasing level of difficulty. Learned items will be needed again at a later time and can be combined with each other. The single teaching-learning situations are casually built on each other and the challenges are justified in a narrative way. With regard to the didactical components (see chapter on c3-model of didactical components) it has to be taken into consideration that narrative constructs which interweave with an own story appear particularly immersive. In computer games, narration is used to introduce gameplay elements, to explain or to revive scripted scenes and, as a result, increase the feeling of presence. The possibility to immerse into a story and the empathy with the avatars are also given in virtual worlds. Immersion develops when the presented reality of the medium is so convincing that it is forgotten and remains only fictional. Precisely trough narration the virtual world is perceived as a "world". Each event and each object should have a sense. Statically and therefore boring moments can be avoided by life simulations (through non-player characters like for example playing children). Scripted sequences (like for example the overlay of a film) do not disturb immersion as they take place in real time, justify the presence and specific actions respectively whilst other actions (for example chatting) can still take place.

Given elements of the story are combined with elements of the user (own experiences, for example with other users) to form a complex wealth of experiences. The better the user knows the history of this world the more immersive it can function (Rittmann, 2008). Until now, virtual worlds usually have no connecting factors with former worlds.

In the context of social immersion the boundaries between virtual world and real world become blurred. In virtual worlds real social contacts take place and fictional objects are revived through background information and history. Virtual worlds offer various possibilities for communication and interaction with other users and thus the creation of interpersonal contacts of varied intensity (Rittmann, 2008). Thus, the generation of social hubs is relevant. However, in contrast with MMOGs, it is not really implemented effectively in virtual worlds.

Through gestures and spoken emotional expressions in accordance with the design of the virtual world, social processes are supported (see chapter on communication). The virtual representatives are accepted as interaction partners. The acceptance of the virtual counterpart is increased through the outward appearance in form of an avatar and its gestural scope. A peculiarity of virtual worlds is the possibility to combine three-dimensionality with synchronous communication. Nevertheless, the possibility of audio chats is less used than expected. This may be traced back to the danger, that hearing the voices of the dialogue partner and the discussion of real world topics may temporally interrupt immersion (Rittmann, 2008). However, through the integration of non-player characters (NPCs) the immersion is hardly interrupted due to the natural social behaviour (Bopp, 2005). Thiedeke (2004a) raises the question whether NPCs are able to imitate a socially connectable communication partner and which benefit they will bring despite of the communication and cooperation possibilities of multiple users.

MIXED REALITY

In the sense of a "Crosslife" (Gierke & Müller, 2008) or "World Blurring" (Rittmann, 2008) the dividing line between real life and virtual worlds is blurring. A clear distinction is neither possible nor sensible. Through contacts among people in a virtual world, friendships in real life can be extended (see chapter on communication). Thus, meetings take place in the real world to intensify virtual contacts, for example (Götzenbrucker, 2001). The point is not to offer education exclusively in virtual worlds or the real world but to combine them (de Freitas, 2008, Gierke & Müller, 2008). The mistake of thinking that everything has to take place in one closed system has to be avoided (Gierke & Müller, 2008). Also the c3-model is a didactical framework for the design of blended learning arrangements (Kerres & de

Witt, 2003). Within this model, a virtual world can be combined with face-to-face meetings. An additional reflection using other media such as weblogs for example should be offered.

Other possibilities of competence development are awarded to virtual worlds than to computer games which only improve specific courses of action. Amongst other things, virtual worlds support the negotiation of social rulebooks and the differentiation of the own avatars. The question must be raised with regard to which competencies can be attained in the virtual world and how these can be transferred into real life. Another question to be raised is which competences are necessary at all to use virtual worlds (Raschke, 2007). For example, information from real life can be used to solve a virtual problem or emotions in the virtual world are experienced as real (Neuenhausen, 2004). Real world conducts of life are also present in virtual worlds (Raschke, 2007). The virtual reality is a place where one is thinking about the real world (Neuenhausen, 2004). In Second Life, for example the worlds are mixed up by purchases (Hehl, 2008), the purchase of virtual goods (Raschke, 2007) and virtual events which are streamed to the real world or vice versa. Additionally, application programming interfaces allow getting into contact with the outside world (Gierke & Müller, 2008). Sloodle, for example serves as the connecting piece between the learning platform Moodle and the virtual world Second Life. Thus, specific control elements are offered to the user, like a repertoire of gestures typical for teaching, the possibility of saving chat protocols and to enter blog entries into Second Life via a chat line (Gierke & Müller, 2008). Erpenbeck & Sauter (2007) assume a regression regarding the development of competence, as immersion may create emotions and motivation but the learner can also hide behind the identity of the own avatar or create a completely new identity whereby no real social insecurities (dissonances) are created, which however are essential for the development of competence. Accordingly, as many real- decision situations as possible should be initiated, for example by executing role games to create situations that are experienced as critical. Raschke (2007) points out the necessity that users must have the competence to differentiate and reflect upon the different worlds. However, children aged up to approximately four years cannot see this difference. Additionally, some adults also lack the necessary competence. As described beforehand, the technical interfaces between the worlds can be quite different (see chapter on immersion). A trend is currently visible: The relocation of the interfaces into the close environments of the user, as can be seen in the development of games consoles. By making use of image recognition procedures the gestures of the player are directly transferred to the virtual game world. Interaction with the system takes place through motion tracking or wireless devices which recognise position and rotation, which adapt the virtual game and thus the real room. Thus, both virtual as well as real processes overlap in the three-dimensional environment of the player (Gremmler, 2008). Moreover, the interoperability of the avatars is demanded, which means the development of universal avatars, with which one can shift between the different virtual worlds. IBM and Linden Lab have already announced to be working on this development (Gierke & Müller, 2008).

FUTURE RESEARCH DIRECTIONS

Virtual worlds are not undisputed but will gain more importance in the future, as well as all hybrids between virtual worlds and the real world (Hehl, 2008). Regarding the design of learning environments, scenarios have to be tested which connect the real world with the virtual one. Concerning the merger of virtual worlds the requests and developments tend to interoperability (Gierke & Müller, 2008). Despite the current view according to which the kind of technical interface is not in the foreground of immersion (Thiedeke, 2004a), new possibilities of using software supported recognition of hand- and body movements as an alternative to present user interfaces are discussed. Besides the answer to the question of how these developments regarding the technical interfaces will affect the instructional design of virtual learning environments, the consequences of possible interoperability have to be looked at further.

Moreover, clarification is needed regarding the relationship between immersion and learning. Is a higher degree of immersion really accompanied by "better" learning? How immersive shall participants view the virtual world to support their learning process successfully?

For this purpose, the indicators of immersion have to be analysed closer and the relevance of three-dimensionality has to be focused. Assumptions regarding the encouragement of social presence through avatars specifically raise the question of how the spatial-proximity information effects the communication and collaboration processes of learning environments and which challenges for collaborative learning scenarios and the support of the learners are involved. Through the improvement of scalability to a greater number of users, the optimisation of graphics and the improved possibilities of textual design, future development can correct the current weaknesses of virtual worlds regarding the design of learning tasks and fields of application and new learning scenarios can be tried out. However, rather than putting technical criteria into the foreground, it is more important to answer the question concerning which goals are related to the use of virtual worlds in the teaching/learning context and which expectations the users have. The computer game industry integrates the users more and more into the design of computer games. In this free style of structuring the users are supported by "hidden" support offers (Bopp, 2005). However, in contrast with virtual worlds, the scope for co-determination is currently significantly limited. This constraint may be related to the danger of an immersion break due to too much complexity and overhead, so that the degree of immersion in virtual worlds is smaller than in MMOGs. The question therefore concerns how the quantity of co-determination possibilities in the virtual world through the users may effect immersion and the learning processes and how "hidden" support offers can encourage immersion. Rittman (2008) views cultural preconditions as an essential requirement for the acceptance and sustainable usage of virtual worlds. Successful MMOGs are based on the latter regarding content and design. Regarding the development of virtual worlds this assumption should be proven to deduce consequences for the design of future virtual worlds based on these results.

CONCLUSION

The real world is more and more merging with virtual worlds. However, regardless of the kind of technical interface, a conscious differentiation between virtual and real world takes place. From this merger, to the expectations are, on one side, being able to transfer the virtual representatives among different virtual worlds and, on the other side, being able to "transfer" the knowledge gained in the real world to the virtual world and vice versa. As not only existing media didactical concepts and methods should be transferred to virtual worlds and their use should show a benefit, the ubiquitous virtual world offers various possibilities of self-learning and collaborative scenarios. Virtual worlds are not a necessary condition to pursue specific teaching contents, objectives or didactical methods. However they can support and promote specific teaching and learning processes. An essential potential can be seen in the three-dimensionality and the possibilities of interaction, construction and collaboration (see chapter on c3-model of didactical components). According to Thiedeke (2004a) we increasingly live together „in" media and virtualise our existence. Amongst others, this "immersion" is supported by the design of avatars and objects as well as by interaction and communication. Virtual worlds offer various possibilities of communication and interaction with other users and thus the possibility to create interpersonal contacts of varied intensity. The creation of social hubs allows the support of communication processes. A peculiarity of virtual worlds is the possibility to combine three-dimensionality and synchronous communication. The challenge is to initiate events which encourage communication and collaboration processes and support the spatial proximity of the avatars. Virtual worlds gain the potential to be more immersive through the three-dimensionality and the representation of the learner by a virtual representative.

The components content, communication und construction have been systematised in accordance with the C3-model and discussed with regard to the aspect of immersion. On the one side, virtual worlds are ruled by arbitrariness of content and technological freedom which encourages creativity but may lead to disorientation and boredom. On the other side, users can actively be integrated into the design and learning process. However, a deep integration of textual design is missing, which at the moment restricts the fields of application of virtual worlds. Virtual worlds are said to have a new quality of immersion into the world presented to us and of blinding out the surrounding world. Thereby, it is unimportant whether the image is photo realistic or comically exaggerated. It is only important that the user accepts it as the world. The user feels present in the world through three-dimensionality and the possibility to manipulate objects and avatars. The behaviour of the objects in relation to nature laws seems to be less significant than the fact that they do act. Additionally, inconspicuous didactical methods can support immersion. As the virtual world is perceived as a "world" specifically through narration, each event and object should make sense and static moments should be avoided. The combination of given objects with created objects and experiences leads the user to a history of the world, which appears immersive. In conclusion, the question focuses on whether learning is effectively "better" in virtual worlds with a higher degree of immersion.

It has been demonstrated that a virtual world itself does not necessarily lead to improvements in the educational sector. However, the use of virtual worlds can open potentials for distinct innovations. Nevertheless, this needs a dedicated didactical conception of the learning content. According to this perception the innovative technical features themselves are less in the foreground than the question regarding how these features such as cooperative learning may support specific didactical approaches.

REFERENCES

Becker, B. (2004). Zwischen Allmacht und Ohnmacht: Spielräume des "Ich" im Cyberspace. In U. Thiedeke (Ed.), *Soziologie des Cyberspace. Medien, Strukturen und Semantiken* (pp. 170-192). Wiesbaden, Deutschland: VS.

Bopp, M. (2005). Immersive Didaktik. Verdeckte Lernhilfen und Framingprozesse in Computerspielen. In B. Neitzel & R.F. Nohr (Ed.), *Das Spiel mit dem Medium. Partizipation - Immersion – Interaktion* (pp. 170-186). Marburg, Deutschland: Schüren.

Cheal, C. (2007). Second Life: Hype or hyperlearning. *Horizon*, *15*(4), 204–210. doi:10.1108/10748120710836228

Csikszentmihalyi, M. (2000). *Das Flow-Erlebnis. Jenseits von Angst und Langeweile: im Tun aufgehen.* Stuttgart, Deutschland: Klett.

De Freitas, S. (2008). *Serious Virtual Worlds. A scoping study*. SGI.

Erpenbeck, J., & Sauter, W. (2007). *Kompetenzentwicklung im Netz. New Blended Learning mit Web 2.0.* Köln, Deutschland: Wolters Kluwer.

Gierke, C., & Müller, R. (2008). *Unternehmen in Second Life. Wie Sie Virtuelle Welten für Ihr reales Geschäft nutzen können*. Offenbach, Deutschland: GABAL.

Götzenbrucker, G. (2001). *Soziale Netzwerke und Internet-Spielewelten*. Wiesbaden, Deutschland: Westdeutscher Verlag.

Götzl, X., Pfeiffer, A., & Primus, T. (2008). *MMORPGs 360 Grad. Virtuelle Welten & moderne Mediennutzung wissenschaftlich betrachtet*. Neckenmarkt, Deutschland: Edition Nove.

Green, R. D., MacDorman, K. F., Ho, C.-C., & Vasudevan, S. (2008). Sensitivity to the proportions of faces that vary in human likeness. *Computers in Human Behavior, 24*(5), 2456–2474. doi:10.1016/j.chb.2008.02.019

Gremmler, T. (2008). *CyberBionic. Design und Evaluation digitaler Welten*. Heidelberg, Deutschland: Spektrum.

Hehl, W. (2008). *Trends in der Informationstechnologie. Von der Nanotechnologie zu virtuellen Welten*. Zürich, Deutschland: VDF.

Joseph, B. (2007, August). Best practices in using virtual worlds for education. In *Second Life Education Workshop, Part of the Second Life Community Convention,* Chicago.

Kerres, M. (2001). *Multimediale und telemediale Lernumgebungen. Konzeption und Entwicklung*. München, Deutschland: Oldenbourg.

Kerres, M., & de Witt, C. (2003). A didactical framework for the design of blended learning arrangements. *Journal of Educational Media, 28*, 101–114. doi:10.1080/1358165032000165653

MacDorman, K. F. (2005, December). *Mortality salience and the uncanny valley*. Paper presented at the IEEE-RAS International Conference on Humanoid Robots,Tsukuba, Japan.

Müller, A., & Leidl, M. (2007). *Virtuelle (Lern-) Welten. Second Life in der Lehre*. Retrieved January 23, 2009, from http://www.e-teaching.org/didaktik/gestaltung/vr/SL_lehre_langtext_071207_end.pdf

Neuenhausen, B. (2004). *Bildung in der Digitale. Zur Bildungsrelevanz virtueller Welten*. Frankfurt am Main, Deutschland: Peter Lang.

Raschke, M. (2007). *‚Im Computerspiel bin ich der Held.' Wie virtuelle Welten die Identitätsentwicklung von Jugendlichen beeinflussen*. Hamburg, Deutschland: Diplomica.

Rittmann, T. (2008). *MMORPGs als virtuelle Welten. Immersion und Repräsentation*. Boizenburg, Deutschland: Werner Hülsbusch.

Schmidt, F. A. (2006). *Parallel Realitäten*. Sulgen, Deutschland: Niggli.

The Horizon Report. (2007). *The new media consortium*. Retrieved January 23, 2009, from http://www.nmc.org/pdf/2007_Horizon_Report.pdf

Thiedeke, U. (2004a). Wir Kosmopoliten: Einführung in eine Soziologie des Cyberspace. In U. Thiedeke (Ed.), *Soziologie des Cyberspace. Medien, Strukturen und Semantiken* (pp. 15-50). Wiesbaden, Deutschland: VS.

Thiedeke, U. (2004b). Cyberspace: Die Matrix der Erwartungen. In U. Thiedeke (Ed.), *Soziologie des Cyberspace. Medien, Strukturen und Semantiken* (pp. 122-143). Wiesbaden, Deutschland: VS.

Thon, J.-N. (2007). Schauplätze und Ereignisse: Über Erzähltechniken im Computerspiel des 21. Jahrhunderts. In C. Müller, & I. Scheidgen (Eds.), *Mediale Ordnungen: Erzählen, Archivieren, Beschreiben* (pp. 40-55). Marburg, Deutschland: Schüren.

Chapter 19
Principles of Effective Learning Environment Design

Stephen R. Quinton
Curtin University of Technology, Australia

ABSTRACT

New thinking on the design and purpose of learning solutions is needed where the focus is not only on what to learn, but also the strategies and tools that enhance students' capacity to learn and construct knowledge. The vision underpinning this chapter is to extend the notion of advanced learning environments that support learners' to construct and apply knowledge to include the capacity to understand how and why they learn as individuals. Whenever conceptual change occurs as a result of active cognitive processing, higher order thinking emerges, which is further enhanced through discursive interaction with other individuals and groups. A shift in the focus of learning from the passive accumulation of information and knowledge to learning as a life changing experience that is augmented by active, collaborative engagement in the learning process provides direction as to how the complex tasks of learning and creative knowledge construction can be supported in the design of advanced learning environments. The purpose of this chapter is not to argue the need for 'virtual' learning environments – the literature abounds with positive endorsement for such applications. Instead, the strategies and factors that afford learners greater opportunities to engage in rewarding, productive learning experiences are examined with a view to laying down the groundwork and design principles to inform the development of a model for devising educationally effective, multi-modal (face-to-face and online) learning environments.

INTRODUCTION

Whilst many educational institutions throughout the world have introduced online learning as an option for delivering teaching content, little evidence exists of a predominance of innovative solutions that promote pedagogical diversity. Aside from a few notable exceptions, the design of most online learning environments is structured around the traditional instructional delivery model and

DOI: 10.4018/978-1-61520-678-0.ch019

has not taken full advantage of the empowering potential of information and communications technologies (ICT) (Dreher, 2006). Rarely are university students offered the tools to organise their learning activities to suit individual needs and circumstances; collaborative online problem solving activities and group projects seldom inspire rewarding learning experiences; and, seamless collaboration with the wider online community is not consistently encouraged.

At present, many university students use version '1.0' web-based learning management systems that deliver closed, centralised, server-oriented, and distribution-oriented virtual learning environments (VLE). The widespread adoption of VLEs by colleges and universities has led to the dominance of a handful of market leaders that promote the delivery of what is touted as new, advanced modes of learning. The majority however, have opted for little more than an online version of the traditional delivery model and as a consequence, online delivery systems that promote pedagogical diversity are the exception, not the rule. Few online learning systems provide learners with tools to organise themselves; most do not easily permit group learning or support group or problem-based learning; many do not seamlessly integrate with the wider internet and in effect, create 'learning ghettos' (Liber, 2004, pp 137 – 38).

The current reality is that outside the campus intranet, people 'meet' each other in online chat rooms, operate Weblogs, engage in 'virtual' communities, answer questions on 'support' websites (bulletin boards and Wikis), and share resources using highly interactive and intuitive peer-to-peer systems. The Internet continually offers new tools to support such activities, but a discernible mismatch separates what is available on the Internet from what university learning delivery platforms permit. This version '2.0' of the World Wide Web has rapidly evolved to incorporate social, distributed, open, peer-to-peer, and contributive elements that permit multiple layers of communication among people who share interests and resources to dynamically connect and exchange ideas using technologies such as short messaging services (sms), chat, weblogs, wikis, and email. Typically, few of these features are available in leading VLEs. Instead of learning how to create knowledge, learners are confined to receiving information using environments that are devoid of the richness and diversity inherent in face-to-face discourse and interaction.

During collaborative discourse, participants 'build on' the contributions of others. The outcome of such exchange is that each individual re-assesses and reflects on the knowledge they have gained and in the process reconstructs previously held concepts, notions, or ideas. Collaborative learning is achieved if conceptual change is explicitly affirmed and redirected during a sequence of discussions that are guided by the goal of transforming the shared thinking into new concepts and ideas, the supreme prize (ideally) being the emergence of new and creative knowledge. When learning is collaborative, concepts, notions, or ideas are refined or transformed during a collective exchange as transpires during synchronous 'real-time' discussions or over the course of asynchronous activities conducted through sms, email, or bulletin boards.

New design concepts and strategies are required that build on the social use of the web and extend this functionality into the realm of virtual (online networked) learning communities. Active engagement in communities of learning (whether physical or virtual) exposes the learner to the perspectives, ideas, practices, interests, and connections to other knowledge domains that may otherwise not be possible through independent study. In the design approach proposed in this chapter, the learner is encouraged to negotiate pathways (either preset or self-determined) through a multiplicity of contexts whilst simultaneously 'monitored' by community members who provide feedback on the concepts and knowledge generated during the learning process. The capacity for learning and knowledge construction is thus enhanced both individually and collectively.

Today's technologies can assist students to collaborate whilst pursuing individual strategies and approaches to learning as opposed to following the same material as a group under the guidance of a teacher. Technology can also support lecturers to work together to develop and share resource materials and teaching strategies; and technology can be used to enable institutions to collaborate on providing better services to their students. In short, the design concepts and strategies outlined to this point require version 2.0 web functionality and thereby extend the experience to the realm of virtual communities of learning.

THE CORE PRINCIPLES: COLLABORATION, SELF-ORGANISATION, AND ECOLOGICAL SYSTEMS

From a teaching and learning perspective, the primary challenge confronting both lecturer and student is to master new and complex information structures, and to apply the available technologies and essential interpretive skills to participate in virtual learning environments. Within these environments, collaborations among individuals and networks of individuals (groups) are fundamental to the sustained generation of new ideas and to the refinement of accepted ideas through the efficient dissemination and application of knowledge across the networked community.

On the latter point, it should not be assumed that participation in a virtual world (or even the classroom) automatically results in a productive outcome – that is, learning and knowledge. Simply presenting large quantities of information and resources available online may in fact result in distraction and confusion. What is required is akin to that which occurs in nature: coherent bits of information presented so that they self-organise (cognitively) into emergent clusters of new connections in the form of ideas, innovation, and creativity. The difference however, is that the organisation of human thoughts is more complex than self-organisation in nature.

In the natural world, self-organisation is causal, whereas in individuals, cognitive organisation requires an internalised process of pattern recognition in order to form new connections amongst the perceived data and information. The key distinction is that nature is not innately organised, but appears (superficially) to display properties of self-organisation. That is, nature is inherently chaotic, out of which order naturally forms (Gleick, 1987, pp 259 - 262; Sheldrake, 1988, p 113; Rucker, 1988, pp 26 and 113; and Kosko, 1994, pp 21 - 3).

Cognitive self-organisation in learners occurs whenever patterns of connection or relational organisation are either identified or created and then communicated to others. The acts of dialogue, observation, questioning and research result in the retention of information, ideas, and concepts, which in turn gives rise to learning as new information is generated and combined to produce new understandings (Daniel, 1996, p 2; Brown & Thompson, 1997, p 75). The act of creativity is at one moment the process of internalising recognised order, and in the next, of passing the identified order onto the next person as a learned experience. It is in this sense that the (undiscovered) relationships that connect disparate ideas and the nuances of all knowledge domains can lead to the emergence of creative thinking and innovation. In a similar way, the human process of self-organisation also provides an effective means of evaluating (that is, community judged) the depth and quality of the knowledge and expertise that is constantly generated and distributed throughout the broader learning community.

The social element of active engagement in learning communities also poses significant challenges, in particular virtual environments where the relationship between collaboration and learning is crucial. As many experienced educators would know, there are many instances where learning naturally shifts into collaborative discourse involving continual interchange of ideas and views between individuals within a community and between communities, or among individuals and other communities. However, learners may also experience confusion and difficulties in such circumstances. Some communities may confine their focus to the knowledge and skills of a specific profession or others may span several disciplines united by a common purpose (operating for example, as a multi-disciplinary networked partnership). Alternatively, a networked (connected) learning community may be structured as a single organisation or span many organisations. Therefore, support systems and strategies for managing such diverse encounters must be readily available as the need arises. In light of the complexities noted so far, learning environments designed to meet the needs of both individuals and groups require an ecological design approach as derived from networked (natural) systems principles to:

- enable productive social interactions in the virtual world
- identify and provide for the needs of learning communities both in terms of the specific interests at the local level and the connections to broader community networks
- accommodate both individual and group preferences and behaviours
- manage the creation and transfer of knowledge within virtual learning communities, and,
- enable efficient sharing and protection of resources, ideas and the knowledge generated by individual learners and groups participating within and across networked communities.

An emphasis on ecological communities extends the individual's knowledge construction skills to embrace multi-level, interconnected, social learning systems that expose the learner to a broad array of perspectives, practices, interests, and the idiosyncrasies of divergent knowledge domains. The strategies for enhancing learner cognition through connected pathways using ecological or systems design principles are not the only area of relevance to this chapter. Expanding the 'connectedness' (or connectivist) metaphor further, of equal importance to ensuring successful learning is the level of expertise and depth of understanding provided by experts and organisations that participate within a community of learning. For example, consider the Web as comprising a vast number of 'authors' each of whom are members of separate interest groups, many of which embody a large cache of expertise accumulated in both written and tacit form. Given the vastness of the Web, it is relatively easy to locate a niche community with the required expertise or a special interest group with interests that coincide with that of the learner. Once identified, the diversity of input and comments provided by experts who may be situated anywhere throughout the world adds texture to the area of knowledge under examination and thus presents another example of how the Web can be used to enhance the learning process.

Consistent with the notions of connectedness and ecological systems, it is further argued that in order to enhance learning, not only will it be necessary to re-think the purpose of learning environments, but also to devise more advanced and adaptive learning strategies that connect people to people - not people to machines. With this goal in mind, this chapter observes several focal questions as a way of initiating debate on the nature and purpose of learning and associated learning environments in the coming decade. The questions that underpin the main themes of this chapter include:

- what is a creative learning ecology?
- how does learning emerge in ecological learning communities?

- what strategies are needed to enhance learning and creativity in a connected learning ecology?
- how to identify and provide automated support (human and technology assisted) for meeting the needs of networked learning ecologies?

In summary, this chapter examines how the learning experience can be enhanced by applying an alternative perspective on the purpose and design of learning environments where the focus is directed towards the design principles, methods, strategies, and tools that assist students to become creative thinkers and innovative constructors of knowledge. First however, it is important to understand that technology imposes both positive and negative influences on the learning process.

TECHNOLOGY IS TRANSFORMING THE ROLE OF EDUCATION

The rapid acceptance of the Internet, the irrepressible revolution in information distribution, and the increasing sophistication of information and communication technologies (ICT), have converged (self-organised) to create a previously unknown dimension in human communications and expression that directly challenges long-held cultural and institutional boundaries. Moreover, the convergence between computers and communications has created 'virtual' communities and organisations in all fields of endeavour that in part are the result of the abolition of the barriers of time and distance. In the past, these barriers precluded collaboration on a wide range of tasks and activities. Because of these developments, it is now technologically feasible for students and teachers from all over the world to 'meet', collaborate, and exchange views.

In his examination of the current generational uses of information and communication technologies, Candy (2004, p 232) concludes that an unexpected yet fundamental reconceptualisation of the purpose of learning has emerged over recent years. The extent of this shift points to a marked transformation in the learning expectations of young people which is partly attributable to the view that they are the most innovative exploiters of the new mediums, and partly because they will become the next generation of self-directed adult learners. The Millennials (Generation Y or Net Generation, approximate birth years 1977 to 1997) for example, have grown up in a world in which computers, cell phones, and cable television are a normal part of everyday life. They are inundated with information from a multitude of sources, and are capable of using a wide variety of media and devices to communicate, learn, and to be entertained. The most favoured of these sources are those that permit relatively instantaneous, concurrent, communication with multiple people, regardless of geographic boundaries.

The Millennials are also a genuinely interactive generation (Mask, 2002, pp 3 – 4). Virtual chat is used by the current generation to communicate directly with their peers and chat archives attest to the frequent and topical use of the Internet in late night, peer-to-peer conversations that are conducted within the boundaries of their own cultural framework (Carmean and Haefner, 2002, p 5). Today's students not only constantly engage in interactive communications, they expect it. As a result, they are exposed to an unparalleled flow of customs and ideas that may in fact represent a significant step in the development of human cognitive processing.

The available evidence suggests that over the course of the coming decade, technology will exert a major role in breaking down the entrenched barriers instilled by industrial-centric thinking that are not only unsustainable, but will prove inadequate for resolving the educational demands of the twenty-first century. (Tiffin & Rajasingham, 1995, pp 1, 48, 57 and 73; Taylor,

2001, p 1; Taylor, 2002, p 4; Greater Expectations National Panel, 2002 p iii; Frand, 2000, pp 17 and 24; Wenger, 2005, p 10.).

Redefining the boundaries both within and outside the university sector will assure the future relevance of great universities. At each of the local, national, and international levels, it is likely there will be networked groups and organisations made possible through inter-institutional cooperation; a blurring of knowledge boundaries due to the interplay between highly advanced learning environments and instantaneous access to vast repositories of networked resources. As a result, today's educational institutions may one day become 'virtual' communities of learning. Then, as new forms of delivery are devised, the purpose of learning will be tested against the demands of society, the influence of new technologies, and the global economy (Candy, 2004, p 232; Marginson, 2000; Guile, 2003).

THE IMPERATIVE FOR UNIVERSITIES TO PREPARE FOR CHANGE

The full impact of recent technological developments on the way humans interact, how people learn, construct and use knowledge is at present not known. It is known however, that students can be competent in the use a nonlinear electronic form of text (hypertext) that permits multiple interactive authoring and demands high levels of visual literacy. No longer are learners restricted to the linear structure of print and consigned to the tedious task of passively absorbing knowledge. So far, educators have acquired little more than a brief insight into the enormous potential of technology as a productive aid in the learning process (Mott & Granata, 2006, pp 48 – 54).

If the implications of technology-directed change are ignored, especially in relation to learning, then the task of managing an exploding information and knowledge base will soon be insurmountable. As Hill and Hannafin (2001, p 1) observed, while the potential of technology for enhancing teaching and learning may be substantial, it may also be the case that educational practices will be inadequate for preparing graduates to work and learn in an information-centric world. It is also significant that education in general is still described using the language and metaphors of the industrial era, and school organisations continue to reflect the practices and beliefs of the industrial model. A failure to utilise the full power of information technology in most curricula is the result of a mismatch between traditional organisational values and the values ascribed to new technologies (Vrasidas & Glass, 2000, p 58).

In order to manage such unprecedented change, educational institutions should first identify the impact on teaching and learning that will result from the expanding presence of an information-dominated world and then enter into a transitional stage of actively re-examining the design and purpose of their education delivery systems. Otherwise, it is likely that within the coming decade, the skills and thinking abilities currently taught to students will not meet their future needs. To resist change will not benefit students once they graduate. Moreover, a reluctance to incorporate change may result in an education system that is not equipped to provide the thinking skills required in an information society. Only those educational institutions willing to take advantage of the opportunity to master and lead the processes of change will be prepared for the challenges of the future (McCune, 1991, p 3). However attractive such notions may seem at first, the history of introducing technology to teaching and learning provides a timely and valuable lesson. As Thackara (2005, p 158) rightly observes:

Technology fixes for education are an old and discredited story. The delivery of precooked content, by whatever means, is not teaching. Radio, film, television, the videocassette recorder, fax machines, the personal computer, the Internet, and now the mobile phone: It was promised of each of these, in turn, that here was a wonder cure that would transform education for the better. And yet here we are, hundreds of years after the first books were printed, and teachers are still giving lectures, and students still line up to hear them. Why? They do this because the best learning involves embodiment – live experiences and conversation between people: Most people prefer talking to one another to talking to themselves.

Not all educational institutions are resisting the need to embrace change (Ward, 2000, p 26; Salmi, 2000; Gilbert, 2000 and 20032003). There is a growing recognition of several worldwide phenomena: an information explosion of unprecedented magnitude; the rapid proliferation of new advanced technologies; significant changes in work practices; an increasingly fragile natural environment; the growing interdependence of societies; and concerns about changes in established values and institutional practices. As the restrictions of time and space become less relevant, new connections are being electronically forged and the concept of a 'global village' or 'networked community' is becoming a significant influence in learning design. This new reality must be acknowledged.

Just as the origins of the modern university arose from decisive changes that defined the boundaries of how knowledge and learning is derived and delivered, paradoxically these same boundaries are now almost obsolete as the influences of ICT transform that same obsolescence into a new and dynamic vision for the future of learning. If a time could be envisaged when technology is no longer apparent, then the important design issues will be (Thackara, 2005, pp 158 - 59):

- allow much more time for learning than allocated now
- redefine the guidelines that describe how learners, teachers and others relate to one another
- determine how best to design the support systems, platforms and institutions needed to make the first two to happen.

FROM CHAOS TO CREATIVITY: SELF-ORGANISATION AND PROPERTIES OF EMERGENCE

The Internet is not simply a vast network of connected computers. More accurately, it is a protocol for linking many separate computer networks. The actual number of connected computers and networks is impossible to determine. The number of potential links is even more impressive. This enormous complexity is managed by organising machines into a hierarchy of domains, all of which are linked through a system known as Internet Protocol (IP) addresses, a set of unique numbers that is allocated to every computer attached to the system. This numerical address identifies each machine and the various gateways that allow access to the Internet. With the development of information management and file transfer services, the Internet exhibits a capacity for self-organisation and properties of emergence, two clear indicators of complex systems.

The principles of systems theory with its underpinnings of interconnected systems, subsystems and interrelationships among systems illustrate how even the most complex of systems are subject to universal principles of randomness, complexity, chaos, emergent properties, and self-organisation. Such properties are evident in the organisation and structure of information distributed throughout the World Wide Web, or even in human behaviour (including the way we think and learn). The Internet is an example of complexity in practice, displaying many instances of emergent properties (an indicative factor of adaptive complex systems) and self-organisational principles (the natural tendency for order to emerge out of chaos).

A systems theory perspective provides a framework from which to examine and characterise a learning environment, its components, and all its sub-parts. By integrating systems concepts and principles into the design process and by determining how to apply such factors, new ways of thinking, experiencing, exploring, understanding, and describing a learning environment become apparent. The design of learning environments based on a systems perspective should account for a range of factors (Banathy, 1988a, 1991, 1996):

- properties of wholeness and the characteristics that emerge at various systems levels as a result of interaction and synthesis.
- identifying the relationships, interactions, and mutual interdependencies of systems.
- the dynamics of the interactions, relationships, and patterns of connectedness among the components of systems and the changes that manifest over time.
- interpreting and tracking interconnectedness and interdependencies in complex information systems.
- identifying obscure relationships within information systems using complex analysis techniques to derive new insights and meanings.
- managing the difficulties of deriving meaning and the loss of meaning from a surfeit of information.

The application of a systems perspective to learning design assists to determine how the cognitive processes of knowing, thinking, and reasoning can be exploited to facilitate inquiry and generate knowledge (Banathy & Jenlink, 2004, p 49). As signalled by the preceding factors and principles, the identification of relationships within information using enhanced interaction methods provide direction to empower learners to organise, reflect, analyse, and synthesise information to construct new knowledge. What is also alluded to here is the concept of emergent properties.

The term 'properties of emergence' refers to the notion that meaningful order can emerge of its own accord out of complex systems comprised of many interacting parts (Buchanan, 2002, p 198). To put it more simply, emergence occurs in systems where a few simple rules govern the interaction of the component parts. To establish the pre-conditions that give rise to creativity and innovation, several principles of emergent properties assist to design networked learning environments (paraphrased from Lewin, 2001, pp 202 - 3):

1. the source of emergence is the interaction among learners who mutually influence one another. Relationships characterised by mutuality among people, groups and organisations are enabled and encouraged through the provision of access to shared resources and facilities.
2. small changes lead to large effects. Cultivate change through small experiments, problem-solving exercises, and task analysis, while reinforcing the potential for exploring a broad landscape of possibilities without making any judgement as to correctness or wrongness.
3. emergence is certain, but there is no certainty as to what it will arise. Establish conditions conducive to initiating constructive emergence rather than attempting to plan a detailed strategic goal. In other words, evolve outcomes, not design them.
4. a greater diversity of learners engaged in a learning community leads to richer emergent patterns. People of different cultures, expertise, age, personalities, and gender who contribute and interact individually or in teams increase the potential for enhanced creativity.

One notable example of emergent properties originated from the need to source and co-ordinate information for a specific purpose from a large number of networked databases. As a result, individuals and organisations have recognised the need to compile reference indexes specific to their area of interest. In some instances this action has generated the need for information gathering resources out of which has emerged a new whole that has quite literally became more than the sum of the parts. There are now 'virtual' sites that arose not just from one source, but instead through a systematic process of linking information services provided by hundreds or even thousands of web-sites around the world. These sites do not exist in a physical form, they are generated by the Internet in what is often termed 'cyberspace'.

Virtual libraries provide an example of where huge database-managed tables of content are co-ordinated to provide immediate access to servers located anywhere in the world. We are also witness to many attempts to create 'information networks', 'virtual communities', and other co-operative projects. Many researchers for example, now submit their raw data to public databases to allow other interested researchers to access and interpret their results, or to carry out entirely new research. Thus, by combining data from many different sources, it is possible to derive a richer, more diverse knowledge base than if the data were to remain in the hands of individuals.

Other instances of emergent properties exist in technological solutions such as distributed computing where different machines are assigned the task of solving specialised components of much larger and sophisticated problems. From each of these specialised sources it is possible to draw together up-to-date data and compile accurate information about a subject of interest or concern (Bossomaier & Green, 1998, pp 159 - 69). What is now evident is that the technology of the Internet has created an information storage, retrieval, and processing system that display properties characteristic of dynamic systems theory: a multidimensional (non-linear), multi-level, interconnected and interrelated (networked) web of data, information, and knowledge. In essence, the Internet provides an intriguing example of self-organising complexity and connectivity as occurs in practice, which in turn points to the key attributes that influence learning environment design as proposed in this chapter.

CHAOTIC, NETWORKED LEARNING COMMUNITIES

Networked learning communities comprise three key elements: content, coherence, communication. From another perspective, a successful networked learning environment comprises simple rules, a universe of possibilities, and the capacity to adapt (Lewin, 2001, p 216). A self-organising, creative learning community leading to the emergence of new 'thinking' models is dependent upon the establishment of an ecological environment in which the structure adapts and evolves through the dynamic formation of novel, complex relationships and connections. By adopting a chaotic, network approach, both in relation to design and in the means of delivery, paradoxically an ineffective, non-productive community (a stable structure) can be restructured to produce a diversity of perspectives. Such environments are uninspiring and a deterrent to learning.

In this scenario, new sources of contention, dissonance, argument, and innovation are introduced, which undermine the stability imposed over time by a culture of low interaction and ineffective idea generation. Genuine creativity and innovation requires a balance between the natural human tendencies for stability and the dynamic, chaotic participants and elements that challenge the status quo. In this way, change is facilitated and new thinking and new ideas emerge. This balance can be likened to the 'edge of chaos' where spontaneous processes of self-organisation occur and new patterns of 'behaviour' emerge as acts of creativity and innovation. Such complex, adaptive environments thus accommodate every individual schema in many different ways and so increase the likelihood that all learners will experience effective learning, more often.

The acquisition of higher order thinking skills and the meaningful conversion of information into knowledge are not isolated processes as many factors contribute to the establishment of learning environments in which the requisite skills for a knowledge-focussed future can be cultivated. The level of learning effectiveness is also due to (chaotic) group dynamics forming an interactive synergy in which the whole becomes more than the sum of its parts. Given the complexity of the task at hand, how can educators, begin to teach thinking skills to their students? The short answer is to apply a networked ecological model to learning design.

SELF-ORGANISING, ECOLOGICAL LEARNING ENVIRONMENTS

An ecology is defined an open, complex, adaptive system comprised of many dynamically interdependent elements (Brown, 2002, p 13). In nature, all species exist as integral components of an interconnected network of ecosystems and sub-ecosystems displaying systemic properties at all levels (Lewin, 2001). Businesses and corporations also operate in complex networks of interactions, first by forming a community of interest at the local scale, then expanding into wider communities at the national scale, and eventually, broader global communities at the international scale. The rigidly structured, static, linear thinking of the industrial era has evolved into a highly adaptive, dynamic, non-linear, multi-levelled, interconnected network of people, resources, and interests. Unpredictability and chaos operate in an atmosphere of information sharing and knowledge production in which creativity and innovation can and often occurs at a rapid pace. These same principles naturally apply to learning environments where learning is viewed as an open system or ecology of people, groups, resources, activities, supporting tools, and infrastructure. Participants involved in an ecological learning environment share their knowledge and expertise, form groups, and establish projects, each according to their individual interests and personal motivations for contributing resources, sharing ideas, and engaging in communal discourse.

An ecological learning environment assists learners to seek greater value from their learning experiences. The fundamental components are people, places, and ideas connected through a combination of deliberate design and random (chaotic) chance to inspire creative thinking and innovation. Such interactions cultivate awareness and expectations in learners engaged in environments in which human dialogue and activities afford greater opportunities to generate new thinking and ideas. Learning naturally ensues when people interact with emergent ideas and concepts. However, learning is not the only outcome.

Ecological learning design also has the potential to redefine the purpose and goals of education. For this to occur requires a willingness to challenge the assumptions enshrined in our educational ideologies and to examine the purpose and aims of the social and organisational structures that support them. In other words, the nature of power, control, authority, responsibility, and entitlement in learning needs to be transformed into a highly interactive, interconnected, self-organising networked ecosystem of individual learners, teachers, groups, and organisations. As Campos (2004, p 7) explains:

The ecological constructivist perspective suggests that the social environment and the individuals are part of a symbolic ecosystem which is the networked cognitive communication. Configurations of meanings (meanings upon logical structures) are shared and evolve in collaboration across time.

Two factors that make the concept of ecological learning so powerful is diversity and adaptability.

Consider for example, the learning ecology that has formed around the World Wide Web. First, consider that the web is much more than a network of computers, it is a transformative medium that facilitates multiple intelligences (abstract, textual, visual, musical, social, and kinaesthetic), and individual learning styles (Candy, 2004, pp 185 and 305). That is, the Web introduces the potential to match the medium to the specific needs of learners. In short, the Web displays characteristics of an interconnected, ecological learning environment described by Brown (2002) as:

- a collection of interdependent and fluid (virtual) communities of interest
- cross pollinating ideas and knowledge with one another
- constantly evolving and adapting to change and new ideas
- dynamic and self-organising

The Internet also provides an example of how connections can result in new meanings and knowledge. The central premise is that the connections established around unusual 'nodes' of information and activities can support and intensify existing activities. The amplification of learning, knowledge and understanding derived through the conscious extension of a personal network is the epitome of connectivism in that it provides insight into the learning skills and activities that empower learners to create new knowledge. The networked connections are constantly changing (dynamic), responding to interests, experiences, and new understandings, and continually adapted and expanded as more is learned and the volume of accumulated knowledge increases. In essence, a connectivist approach to designing a learning environment presents a model of learning that acknowledges the act of learning involves much more than an individualistic, internalised process.

In light of the foregoing factors (there are many other factors not raised here), it is argued that education in general has been slow to recognise the impact of the Internet and the consequent environmental changes that have transformed what it means to learn. Thus, the untapped value of the Internet for learning is in its capacity to change both the nature and purpose of learning through the power of connectedness. Again, we are reminded that whenever new technologies are employed, the ways people learn inevitably change.

CONTENT, CONTEXT AND CONNECTIONS

In some ways, developing effective teaching content for the online environment goes against the hallmarks of good technical or expository writing taken for granted by many educational designers and curricula writers. The addition of new content does not always connect naturally or logically to existing learning materials. The inherent meaning of the content may change according to need or context application and therefore, its relevance to the expected learning outcomes. If it is assumed that content is fixed and only the connections change then we move to a connectionist theory of learning and enter into the long standing debate between Connectionists and classicists (Stanford University, 1997, p 1). Fodor and Pylyshyn (1988), Fodor and McLaughlin (1990), and Fodor (1997) for example, often dominated in this debate.

On the classical account, strings of symbols represent information in much the same way data is represented in computer memory or on pieces of paper. The connectionist view on the other hand, claims that information is represented non-symbolically by patterns of connections or relationships between networked units. The classical account presents an objectivist (or atomistic) approach to learning design whereas the connectivist position introduces a constructivist, systems theory perspective. The focus of systems thinking is not aimed at applying a building block model, but to the principles of organisation where an object or event is examined in relation to a larger system or whole. Structuring conceptual understanding using a systems approach is known as contextual thinking (Lipman, 1988, p 3).

The concept of connectivism encompasses the integration of the key principles that apply to the theories of chaos, networked systems, complexity, and self-organisation. It is driven by the understanding that decisions are made in response to changing circumstances followed by the assimilation of newly acquired information into the learner's existing cognitive framework. As individuals engage in learning, they are continually exposed to new information. In processing this information, the ability to draw distinctions between important and unimportant information is vital, as is the ability to recognise when new information is out of context and conflicts with existing understandings that are drawn from past decisions and experiences (Siemens, 2004).

By applying connectionist theory principles, learning occurs in instances where individuals encounter unclear or ambiguous activities and projects (either planned or unplanned) that may not be fully resourced. The focus of learning is directed toward discerning the patterns of connected relationships that reside amongst what at first appear to be disparate information sources. In this circumstance, the ability to make connections that inspire learning assumes priority over the learner's experience and understanding. The depth of learning and knowledge gained in the process is directly dependent upon the learner's ability to discern connections between ideas and concepts identified amongst a wide diversity of information and perspectives and their capacity to determine the relevance and accuracy of the acquired knowledge (Siemens, 2006, p 6). We thus begin to identify the design principles that could advantage the construction of effective learning environments.

ENABLERS OF MEANINGFUL LEARNING

If students are to experience meaningful learning in an era of information overload, three convergent factors are essential (Healy, 1991, pp 52 - 3). That is, meaningful learning occurs at the point where developmental readiness, curiosity, and new subject matter converge to create previously unrecognised learning experiences. However, the task of bringing all three factors together to produce creative thinking and learning is not always a straightforward proposition. The successful transition from formal education to coping with the demands of a fast changing future remains largely contingent upon ensuring students are equipped with the 'traditional' skills of critical thinking, rational analysis, problem-solving, research, communication and writing. Equally important, is the need for the skills developed through teamwork, group presentation, negotiation and conflict resolution, the provision and acceptance of feedback, active listening, cross-cultural communication, and finally, time and project management (James, McInnes & Devlin, 2002, p 48). Again, there is an emphasis on the educational significance and value of social networks and collaborative learning.

To complicate matters further, today's students also need to learn much more than the 'know what' (explicit knowledge). Moreover, it is important they experience and understand the 'know how' (tacit knowledge) through personal and active involvement in applying what they have learned. At the interplay between the tacit and the explicit lies deep expertise where the learner is required not just to assimilate the explicit knowledge of a given subject area, but also apply that knowledge by engaging in the practices of the related community of interest (Brown, 2002, p 6).

The Internet is not only an enabler of 'virtual' social networks and learning networks, it also has the capacity (using purpose built tools and systems) to prompt learners to structure, integrate, and interconnect new ideas with pre-existing knowledge and prior experiences facilitated by tools that enable them to rearrange, synthesise and restructure information. This means in effect, that ICT provides a useful aid for teaching the complex tasks of thinking, problem solving, and learning (Candy, 2004, p 230). In the design principles to be synthesised later in this chapter, it is the learner's active identification and creation of relationships amongst data and information that becomes the focus of learning. This is where the inherent connectivity and interactivity of the Web reveals a unique strength in the long history of failed educational technologies.

EMERGENT LEARNING: CONNECTED NETWORKS OF LEARNING

Social networks operate on the relatively simple principle that people, groups, systems, nodes, entities can be connected to create an integrated whole. Changes that occur within any of the components that make up the network generate a ripple effect throughout the entire system. Within an ecological learning environment, learning is focussed on the creation and strategic use of connections and relationships to form new ideas and concepts. Burbules and Callister (1996, p 7) provide a more precise account of what these notions infer by explaining that 'learning' and 'understanding' operate by making connections. They point out that we do not learn information as discrete, isolated facts, but instead integrate new information with prior knowledge. Our best learning they argue, occurs when new information and additional resources are readily connected with multiple nodes of association.

Nodes can be information, ideas, individuals, and communities for example, that become more relevant as the learner is exposed to opportunities for recognising new connections, which in turn lead to cross-pollination of ideas and concepts across learning communities. Thus, a social learning network is a structure within which a coordinated set of resources and activities provide opportunities for learning that empower the learner to create and evolve a range of experiences among people, places, and information. A potentially useful advantage of this design approach is that access to connected information and related media could further prompt students to conceptualise and formulate a non-linear or multidimensional exploration of the presented teaching content (Harris, 2000, pp 36 - 7). In other words, the learner is actively supported to engage in shaping the learning environment to support his or her own motivation for learning. In essence, generating knowledge is what learners do with information resources as they define needs, generate hypotheses, and refine their understanding.

Where individual versus group knowledge is concerned, it is important to recognise that any change in concepts, notions, and ideas derived through networked discourse and argumentation that has become more or less established (stable) during individual or collaborative learning does not automatically indicate evidence of knowledge building (Campos, 2004, p 10). Whereas the resulting outcome may be in the form of knowledge that arises from conceptual changes that have stabilised through group consensus, manifestly unique knowledge that could not be derived by any one individual is the collective result of many interconnected minds.

It is natural to assume that knowledge resides in the minds of individuals, but when tacit knowledge is factored in especially as related to practice, it is quickly realised there is much more to learn than what is already known and understood. Complications arise when considering the broader epistemological topology as a whole in that both tacit and explicit knowledge apply not just to the individual, but also to the social network or 'community of practice'. Much of what is referred to as 'knowing' is made more authentic through active participation in the world and with other people where the focus is directed toward solving practical problems. More specifically, a great deal of an individual's 'knowing' or 'know-how' derives from active participation within a network, much of which is socially constructed, especially in work and social settings. The reasoning just presented reinforces the position that not all knowledge is derived from individuals.

Moreover, the capacity of technologies to facilitate information and knowledge sharing and to seek clarification of the understandings of individuals is a major factor in building on acquired understandings to consolidate deep expertise (Candy, 2004, p 231). Such cognitive activities are increasingly being performed in 'virtual' networked contexts where the co-creation of knowledge is achieved through learning communities. The key concept underpinning such online activity is that through active collaboration on the production, creation, improvement and innovation of knowledge, a community can accomplish much more than the sum of the individual contributions. Campos (2004, p 3), adds further insight to these views:

Knowledge communities that develop within a networked cognitive communication process follow a path in which formal individual structures blend with collectively shared content. Knowledge building represents a collaborative process in which conceptual change and innovation are apparent. Therefore, both conceptual change and innovation are indicators of collaborative learning.

Conceptual change is an intentional and reflective cognitive process leading to higher order thinking, which is the result of the verbal and physical interactions that naturally occur among individuals and groups (Campos, 2004, p 10). In other words, new knowledge emerges when an individual or a group of individuals engages in some form of discourse and interaction with one or more additional participants within an identifiable community of practice. When it is collaborative, concepts, notions and ideas are refined or transformed in a collective exchange as may occur in synchronous 'real-time' discussions or through involvement in asynchronous activities such as the exchange of ideas through a bulletin board. If the shared aim of a community of learners is to leverage knowledge building, then an understanding of how knowledge is distributed across a broader community of learning is offered by Brown (2002, p 7) who explains that during collaborative discourse, participants "build on" the contributions of others. The outcome of this exchange is that participants re-assess and reflect on knowledge and in the process, reconstruct and refine previously held concepts, notions, or ideas. Collaborative learning is achieved if conceptual change is explicitly affirmed and redirected during the sequence of discussions with a view to transforming the shared thinking in new concepts and ideas.

CONNECTIONS, CONCEPTUAL CHANGE, AND KNOWLEDGE CONSTRUCTION

As emphasised in the early part of this chapter, providing access to information without the benefit of equipping students with the skills to convert information into knowledge will prove inadequate for future learning needs. Learners need to reflect on new material, discuss their tentative understandings with others, actively search for additional information in ways that may further illuminate or strengthen their understanding and ultimately build conceptual connections to their existing cognitive framework (Brown & Thompson, 1997, p 75). Megarry (1989, p 50) emphasises the importance of understanding the knowledge building process:

Knowledge is not merely a collection of facts. Although we may be able to memorise isolated undigested facts for short while at least, meaningful learning demands that we internalise the information: we break it down, digest it and locate it in our pre-existing, highly complex web of interconnected knowledge and ideas, building fresh links and restructuring old ones.

As previously noted, concepts may be viewed as nodes in an interconnected or networked system. Representing knowledge as an integrated network of concepts and ideas as opposed to a linear, structured sequence of facts or information affords students the opportunity to discover the relationships and explore the connections in their preferred way. Students are permitted to reconstruct the network (or part of it) so that it aligns more closely with their prior cognitive experiences. While on occasion, there may be a need to impose a more sequential or hierarchical structure to comply with the required learning outcomes, some allowance can be given to providing flexibility in terms of individual learning styles and preferences.

Moreover, a networked structure of concepts permits students to conduct critical interrogations in order to form new conceptual understandings as requisite concepts are mastered. It is technically feasible for example, to provide a networked structure of information and concepts in which predefined sections are connected within a document and/or interconnect across many separate documents. An interesting prospect stems from the possibility that connected information and related media could prompt students to conceptualise and formulate a non-linear or multidimensional exploration of the presented teaching content (Harris, 2000, pp 36 - 7). To illustrate the 'greater than the whole' properties that can emerge from connected, interrelated networks, consider the following account of the connectionist intelligence of bees as described by Bloom (1995, pp 140 - 1):

It is possible for a community of bees to solve problems that could not be tackled by a single bee. An experiment was undertaken where sugar water was placed at the exit of a hive, which over time was moved a few inches, then a few feet, then a few feet more. Each time the bowl was moved, the distance was increased by a precise increment. Initially, the bees followed the movements of the dish but after a few days, the bees would fly from the hive and cluster on a spot where the dish had not been placed – the site where the insects anticipated exactly where the bowl would be placed next. In each instance, their calculations were precisely on target. Even though the brain of a bee is insubstantial – a slender thread of neural fibre barely capable of any process we would regard as intelligence, the bees had worked as a mass brain.

Bloom explains that the strength of a networked intelligence is not dependent on the limited capacities of any one of its many nodes, but is the product of a connected intelligence – the problem solving ability of the network itself. A single bee did not solve the problem of where the bowl would be placed next, but resulted from the interconnected mass of all the bees' brains. A social network solves problems by applying the same principles that underpin the Internet. The connections participants find most useful are strengthened, whereas those connections that prove unproductive are ignored.

It is useful to view the acts of creativity and knowledge construction as cognitive activities in which the abstract combination of previously unrelated mental structures or ideas result in the formation of a new emergent whole. Anyone who has experienced that moment where a new idea arises without apparent prior connection would agree that the resultant outcome is often much more than the mere sum of a collection of unconnected thoughts. However, not only is the effect of the sum of the parts important, but of comparable significance is the notion of the creative process as an expression of the interrelationships that connect the various abstract components. The formation of each new synthesis leads to the emergence of new patterns of relationships with each more complex than the previous, and each extending to higher and higher cognitive levels of a mental hierarchy.

Koestler's view is that contrary to popular beliefs, scientific discoveries do not occur by producing something out of nothing. Instead, researchers combine, relate, and integrate known but previously separate ideas, facts, and associative contexts. The researcher aims to synthesise prior knowledge in a way that adds a new level to the existing knowledge hierarchy. For some, the synthesis of previously unrelated knowledge may result in what is commonly referred to as the 'aha' effect where apparently disparate bits of information suddenly click into place. At this point, we realise new knowledge, and in the process, reach toward higher levels of cognitive understanding (Koestler, 1978, pp 131 - 33).

Consistent with an ecological design approach, the principal factors to note in designing effective learning environments are summarised from the work of Schuur (2003, pp 3 - 7):

- opportunities for ordering and classifying the most important information and knowledge should be offered and made accessible using technologies and mental schemas
- community networks are crucial. Given that a network consists of nodes and connections, learning should focus on strengthening the competences of the individual and on developing connections between individuals.
- although content is important, the focus of design should also be on the development of processes in learning delivery and on managing the complexities of the system
- new learning paradigms should be defined and adopted where learning systems are not restricted to existing learning philosophies and become relevant to a networked society
- learning environments should fulfil the needs of the user. Often a simple resource can be more effective than a well-composed, complete, and complex learning environment.
- evaluation of learning environments must be a continuous iterative process, and
- evaluation of learning environments should focus more on the criteria of the user, than on design, functionality, or cost benefit.

Given the potential for enabling a holistic approach to educational design, the implications for ecological learning systems are profound. Beyond allowing students to proceed through a document by taking prescribed pathways in a linear, regulated pace (the once-heralded attributes of computer-aided instruction), students can instead focus their investigations on questions informed by their own unique interests and experiences. They are empowered to work through and organise materials in ways that make sense to them, developing and comprehending their own heuristics. As new understandings emerge, they discuss their findings with their tutor and/or their fellow peers. This flexible, 'connectivist' approach to inquiry and discussion has many advantages, not the least of which is a capacity to accommodate diverse personal or cultural learning needs. In order to manage complex levels of autonomy and faculty, learners must be experienced in the explicit use of tutorials, guides, indexes, and reading materials designed that provide a basic grasp of what the textual source contains along with the models or heuristics that can be learned and adapted as each student is gradually encouraged to become an autonomous learner.

A SYNTHESIS OF PRINCIPLES FOR STRUCTURING A LEARNING ENVIRONMENT DESIGN MODEL

Part One: Learning Environments as a Catalyst for Learning and Metacognition

The liberating power of ICT extends from its capacity to redefine the learning environment in a manner that allows individual potential to be maximised (Gipson, 1996, p 19). However, technology alone cannot do this. Unless technology is intentionally incorporated with reformed educational practice that acknowledges the primacy of the learner rather than the centrality of the lecturer/teacher, then its use will be limited. This shift in thinking permits the lecturer to become a facilitator of the student's learning as opposed to the repository and provider of knowledge. Moreover, unrestricted access to information and learning materials through technology provides an opportunity for teachers and lecturers to develop and devise learning experiences tuned to individual needs. Most significantly, it affords learners the opportunity to experience both independent and group learning. Thus, the power of technology lies in its capacity to enable individualised learning whilst encouraging participation in collaborative learning environments, a community of learners where learning is the intention, not an incidental outcome. Support for these views is evident in the work of Leidner and Jarvenpaa (1995, p 266) who write:

The effectiveness of information technology in contributing to learning will be a function of how well the technology supports a particular model of learning and the appropriateness of the model to a particular learning approach.

The design of educationally effective learning environments requires the functionally of current delivery systems to be extended to include the enhancement of metacognitive thinking skills acquired through direct 'intelligent' interaction between individual learners and software systems devised for this purpose. For online learners to become skilled in deriving new meanings and understandings, then it follows that software support systems that interact with the investigative/learning process and provide immediate feedback are needed. A parallel requirement is to ensure such tools are readily incorporated into existing learning delivery systems and interoperate with all electronic content and natural language input.

It is feasible for example, to design software support systems that allow learners to make informed decisions about how their learning goals are met by guiding their interactions with 'intelligently' selected and dynamically assembled teaching resources. There are several ways this could be achieved. Using software agents or concept analysis technologies (Dreher, 2006; Dreher & Williams, 2006), key concepts provided through learner input (questions, answers, responses, queries) can be identified and analysed to generate automatic responses such as feedback on progress or additional questions. Learners could also be permitted to request the content display to be dynamically modified to suit their immediate needs by selecting from a range of computer-initiated options generated in response to automated background analyses of their typed input and the selections made during a learning activity. For example, learning resources could be dynamically assembled to generate customised displays based on progress, areas of difficulty, or the need for revision.

In one scenario, learners could make decisions (with varying degrees of guidance) about both content (what to learn) and strategy (how to learn it). They can then employ adaptive, computer-managed, 'intelligent' learning tools to identify and highlight the connections contained within the given information and thus refine their understanding and knowledge. A number of effective strategies can be applied to generate varying degrees of emergent (learning) properties: alert the student to the need for revision and present appropriate alternative material; require the student to repeat a set learning sequence using new materials; dynamically generate quizzes, assignments, or exercises to determine the student's comprehension levels and immediate learning needs; and evaluate students' comprehension levels to provide just-in-time feedback and if required, formal assessment.

The new imperative for today's educationalists is to stay abreast of new technological developments and aspire to excellence in the research and application of ICT to education. This vision can be realised in number of ways (in no set order of importance):

- provide ubiquitous, reliable access to digitised materials and information (learning objects) so that every user – whether learner, researcher, teacher or administrator – is provided access to state-of-the-art technologies that support and enhance their workflow and study activities
- further enhance information retrieval and processing, and multi-mode learning delivery processes by incorporating intelligent machine-to-machine and human to machine dialogue systems, thus freeing the user to apply and benefit from the use of information in more efficient ways
- improve student learning though the provision of autonomous, interactive learning experiences that are supported by dynamically assembled, fully customised learning environments where the focus is on meeting the preferences and needs of each individual
- broaden student access to high quality learning materials and services that facilitate greater choice of access regardless of time, location, and device
- gain greater insight and knowledge on how emerging technologies may underpin innovative teaching, learning, research, and administrative practices
- devise 'intelligent', 'next-generation' technology enhanced learning and research tools (enabling technologies).

The core principles that inform Part One of a model for designing effective learning environments are thus synthesised to include:

- *encourage and support students to negotiate learning pathways through a multiplicity of contexts and domains by applying ecological and connectionist design strategies to dynamically assemble clusters of teaching content and information (also useful for evaluation purposes)*
- *devise and apply intelligent feedback and cognitive support systems that interactively empower learner cognition and respond immediately to learner input through the dynamic assembly of content that is relevant to the specific learning needs of the individual*
- *incorporate 'on-demand' tools for facilitating and managing collaborative encounters whenever the need arises.*

Part Two: Strategies and Design Factors that Afford Increased Learning Opportunities

Whenever individuals and sub-groups focus on the creation and strategic use of connections and relationships to form new ideas and concepts, any changes that occur within known components have the potential to inspire learning and knowledge generation across the entire system. The likelihood that a new concept will be made evident to other individuals within the network is dependent upon how well it is linked to supporting information and other resources. Thus, a networked community can be described as a decentralised structure within which coordinated sets of resources and activities assist participants to create and evolve a range of experiences among people, places, and information. In other words, the members who make up the network are afforded an opportunity to engage in shaping the discussions and interactions that directly support his or her incentive for involvement.

Networked learning communities operate on the relatively simple principle that individuals, groups, information, resources, and ideas are interrelated in a myriad of ways to create a highly productive and innovative whole. As each individual and group is exposed to the flow of information that occurs throughout the network, the relevance and depth of understanding of the available resources and related activities expands and leads to increased opportunities for identification and connection of ideas and concepts that emerge from the interactions and discourse that occur throughout a learning community.

To be successful however, learning activities (whether face-to-face or online) require meaningfulness and collaboration. However, the dynamics of networked learning environments differ fundamentally from the traditional classroom and distance education models in that their design should also encompass ecological and connectivist principles whilst displaying properties characteristic of adaptive, interactive, evolving systems (chaotic). In order to provide for the social, biological, and environmental aspects of human experiences that are critical to establishing effective learning, educational environment design should be composed of three key components:

- a means of organising learner input and experience
- a mechanism for applying that experience into context, and
- a means of empowering learners to create knowledge and to share the experiences of other individuals or groups.

Online games provide unique insights into learning environment design as they faithfully illustrate the potential of a networked learning community and the ecological, chaotic principles that assist to realise that potential. Albeit informal, learning in a game context occurs in a highly social, collaborative way. Teams and groups are constantly formed and reformed to ensure the needs and desires of the entire community are always met. A community of peers and advisors is readily available to assist both new and experienced players as needed and to undertake research and development to ensure continual improvement to the game and the available resource base. All players are actively involved in many aspects of the game community and although not all contribute equally, innovation is distributed in a parallel, decentralised process resulting in a bottom-up, self-organising collaborative system. Games environments therefore, are self-organising and self-sustaining displaying properties of emergence in a many creative ways. For higher learning institutions, the advantage of online games communities is that the same social ecology principles that encourage networked collaboration and interaction in real-world communities of practice can be applied as a proven model for online learning environment design.

Pivec and Dziabenko (2004) conclude that for the purposes of learning, the new forms of interactive content developed for electronic games hold considerable promise. They emphasise that already the game-based learning model has been successfully adapted to formal education, in particular, in military, medicine, and training applications. They argue that whenever students engage in learning environments modelled on proven game theory principles, they learn to understand and combine different points of view in a wide variety of unexpected ways: understanding individual/corporate interests versus the interests of teams and societies; discerning their own points of view whilst remaining aware of the perspectives and opinions of others; applying not just singular factors, but also integrate multiple aspects to resolving problems; and knowing how to turn confrontation into cooperation. There are many aspects of electronic game design that benefit the learning process. For example, learners can:

- be encouraged to combine knowledge from different subject/discipline areas
- choose from a number of given solutions or make decisions at critical decision points
- test how the outcome of the game changes based on their decisions and actions, and
- contact other team members to discuss and negotiate subsequent steps, thus improving social skills.

In citing the work of other researchers, Pivec and Dziabenko (2004, p 15) highlight the increasing demand for greater interactivity to be built into learning materials. In their view, there is a clear need to support and facilitate the learning process by offering a variety of different knowledge presentations and to create opportunities to apply that knowledge within the virtual world. To achieve this goal, they advocate the need for complex levels of interactivity to stimulate learner engagement, and to apply "different interactivity concepts such as object, linear, construct or hyperlinked interactivity, non-immersive contextual interactivity and immersive virtual interactivity".

The provision of advanced learning environments (physical and virtual) that cultivate sustainable virtual learning communities presents an effective strategy for facilitating mutual learning and information exchange among teachers, practitioners (experts), academics, administrators, and researchers. Moreover, the networked learning community model as described in this chapter provides a fertile platform from which to theorise the principles that support the introduction of new strategies to enhance learning capability. The value of such a foundation is most evident in its potential to explain how to exploit the depth of learning that can be derived from the interplay of individual and group activities. Where social change is concerned, the question to resolve is how to engage individuals and groups in communal discourse and mutually co-operative activities in which experts and organisations define, capture, and facilitate the transfer of deep learning capability, creative knowledge construction, and specialist expertise to other individuals and groups.

The concepts of learning communities and social networks have the capacity to transform online learning design and the way research, debate and work is conducted in universities. It also introduces an opportunity to inform the transition from a centralised, institution-based education system that is dependent on a top-down structure and rigid standards to a decentralised, bottom-up grassroots system for generating creative thinking and resource sharing based on informal, ad hoc standards. The essential factors to observe are that the design and structure of a networked learning environment should not be limited to technological application and interface design for the human participants. Nor should it be confined to the provision of curricula and learning materials.

The core principles that inform Part Two of a model for designing effective learning environments are thus synthesised to include:

- *devise adaptive / interactive strategies that connect people to people and information, not people to machines*
- *apply a bottom-up design approach to empower and motivate learners to assume responsibility for managing and participating in the learning environment*
- *facilitate active engagement in the learning process using strategies aimed at fostering both independent and collaborative learning*
- *encourage experts and organisations to engage in collaborative knowledge production and facilitation of understanding*

– in effect, a connected network of mentors / interest / practice.

CONCLUSION: THE CHALLENGE BEFORE US

The task of bridging the transition from 'traditional' learning to individualised, human or electronically facilitated learning is fraught with difficulties. As implied, success in meeting the future needs of learners requires radically new teaching methods and strategies. Any attempt to accommodate the skills and preferences of current generation computer 'literate' students (Millennials) will inevitably compel education designers to think entirely 'outside the box' and consider design strategies that are in line with students' expectations and demands. Such strategies might feasibly include the provision of:

- user defined and dynamically generated teaching material that is relative to the current context
- 'intelligent' search and cognition support tools capable of interpreting meaningful keywords and interacting with learners
- the ability for learners to annotate and record ideas at will and to receive constructive responses
- automatic display of learning and assessment activities, and immediate provision of feedback tailored to students' performance and learning needs
- traditional print-based libraries to become an integral component of a vast network of digitised information resources.

Thus, assuming such innovations are viable, the nature and function of the learning environment is poised on the verge of a dramatic transformation, in particular with regard to the application of distributed computing and communications systems, advanced learning systems, sophisticated adaptive (ecological) design strategies, and universal access to high quality learning resources irrespective of device, location, and time.

Proficiency in the application of higher order cognitive competencies to the creative construction of knowledge extends well beyond the transmission of prescribed knowledge and the application of traditional problem-solving skills. This in turn raises the many latent and complex problems of how to assist learners to structure knowledge and to identify the key relationships and properties that connect predefined knowledge to unfamiliar teaching content while taking into account contextual relevance, innate cultural biases, and the need to produce innovative, creative solutions. Resolving such complex issues requires learners to model the conceptual structure of a targeted knowledge domain. Such cognitive models can be supported through the provision of tailored navigational strategies using 'intelligent' software systems to manage and enhance their knowledge construction skills through the strategic exploitation of digitised teaching resources and the dynamic selection and contextualisation of teaching materials.

A major challenge facing educationalists is not just to design and deliver innovative learning solutions, but also to devise learning design methodologies that employ emerging technologies to support the refinement of knowledge creation skills such as analysis, problem-solving, conceptual thinking, and metacognition (which is dependent on and thus further complicated by tacit, experiential knowledge). Over the coming decade, all these skills will be highly valued by individuals, organisations, and society in general. With these outcomes in mind, the ideal learning environment should assist learners to derive answers to the broad level 'meta-questions' of: how do I know what I need to learn?; how do I get there?; how am I progressing?; are my goals still relevant?; what are the best learning models for me?; and, what are the effects of social change, culture, and market needs on my personal learning goals?

Given the tenor of the preceding views, learning in the immediate future should demonstrate a clear pedagogical and technological capacity to interweave all known aspects of the learning process within a loosely structured (flexible) environment where the focus is on the needs and preferences of the individual. In other words, addressing the quality and effectiveness of learning are not the only factors to consider. Future learning environments, regardless of the delivery mode, should facilitate support for the divergent needs of current and past generations, from pre-school through to senior citizens. These needs apply to the distinctive attributes of; technology use and skills; personal influences, needs and aspirations; values, perceptions and attitudes; and, current and future concerns. Emphasis should also be given to identifying and allowing for variations in learner behaviours, inter-personal communication skills, preferred learning strategies, and intelligence type relative to all generations, interests, and modes of learning. In essence, the individualisation of learning requires an evolving research programme of design, experimentation and development augmented by qualitatively and quantitatively distinct modes of support and resources.

Ultimately, the goal of designing effective learning environments is to support the lifelong learning needs and personal development of all individuals through the provision of dynamically facilitated and/or self-directed environments, characterised by flexible, ubiquitous, and/or mobile delivery at any time and to any place. A systemic focus on flexible, individual learning redirects the focus of research towards the creation of new methods of learning while recognising the need for learners to develop knowledge skills that demand entirely new perspectives on the purpose of learning. For example, 'just-in-time', 'incremental', and 'on-the-fly' learning provide three access methods that are well suited to the preceding design approaches and offer the advantage of being readily transferable to many environments (thus raising the possibility of providing professional development to companies, governments, and organisations).

Whilst formal education is useful for transferring specific skills and competencies for the purpose of gaining qualifications, the evidence is mounting that it is failing to encourage the higher order analysis, problem solving and knowledge construction skills (metacognitive thinking) required for the twenty-first century. As currently practised, education is inherently counterproductive to creative thinking.

Education not only has the capacity to stifle creativity and innovation. Unmotivated teachers, irrelevant curriculum, substandard learning environments, and uncomfortable conditions all contribute to unsatisfactory learning outcomes. Despite such limitations, many of us would recall that special teacher who was able to connect with our unique learning needs and styles in ways that changed our personal learning experience from a tedious, unrewarding chore to something that was intrinsically fulfilling and life changing. With the 'right' teacher, in the 'right' learning environment, using the 'right' resources, individual learners can be encouraged, motivated, and inspired to be highly creative and innovative.

Once identified, the 'right' combination can be incorporated to construct dynamic, 'intelligently interactive' learning environments that respond as and when required by the learner. Only then (I believe) will it be possible to inculcate the cognitive support tools and thinking strategies that will enable learners to adopt a creative mindset. Whilst it may be countered that creativity can never be taught, at the very least 'creative thinkers' can be better equipped with the cognitive tools that assist to derive elegant solutions to complex problems. This chapter is intended to encourage such direction.

The current line of reasoning represents the core of my philosophy on learning design. The right educational approach holds the potential to add considerable learning value to the individual regardless of whether it is applied to the K-12, high school, college or the university sector. The value I refer to is greater than the sum total of all known and measurable aspects of the learning process in that it inspires creativity regardless of age, interest, profession, and educational level.

Thus, a more inclusive approach to articulating what is meant by 'learning' is crucial to ensuring successful participation in a world that is increasingly focussed on innovative knowledge. Today's young people exercise their creative imagination in ways 'undreamt' of a few ago. They also want (and demand) continuous education and ready access to 'always-on' information and knowledge. These expectations can only be satisfied through advanced educational practices that are guided by revolutionary design models. Equally critical is continued research to determine the needs, preferences, and propensities of disaffected ethnic groups, disabled people, the mature aged, and senior citizens.

Taken as a whole, it is conceivable that education as we have known it over the past century is poised on the verge of entering into new realms of possibilities that will transform accepted views on the role and purpose of learning. The emergent power of the web and related technologies makes it both desirable and viable to not just access and manage far more information than previously thought possible, but also to ensure learning effectiveness will remain the primary goal. Again, the reader is reminded that regardless of the promised potential, we should not lose sight of the fact that ready access to information does not always equate to being educated, in particular when employing asynchronous and computer-mediated 'distance' communication modes. As noted several times, it is not enough to deliver information and assume learning will result. Moreover, the technological solutions proposed in the preceding pages are intended to support the learner's cognitive processes and not in any way do the work for them. This qualification raises a timely warning to consider the question of how we can ensure technology supports exploration and learning.

In practice, the strategies required for constructing effective learning environments are highly complex and diverse requiring an ecological, systems-based design approach. Then, as connectivist principles are applied, learners can be empowered and supported to participate in learning communities where an 'edge of chaos' strategy inspires all participants to be innovative thinkers and creative constructors of knowledge.

REFERENCES

Banathy, B. H. (1988a). Systems inquiry in education. *Systems Practice*, *1*(2), 193–211. doi:10.1007/BF01059858

Banathy, B. H. (1991). *Systems design of education*. Englewood Cliffs, NJ: Educational Technology.

Banathy, B. H. (1996). *Designing social systems in a changing world*. New York: Plenum Press.

Banathy, B. H., & Jenlink, P. M. (2004). Systems inquiry and its application in education. In D. H. Jonassen (Ed.), *Handbook of Research on Educational Communications and Technology (2nd ed.)*. Mahwah, N.J.: Lawrence Erlbaum Associates, Inc.

Bloom, H. (1995). *The Lucifer principle: A scientific expedition into the forces of history*. St. Leonards, NSW, Australia: Allen and Unwin.

Bossomaier, T., & Green, D. (1998). *Patterns in the sand: Computers, complexity and life*. St. Leonards, NSW, Australia: Allen and Unwin.

Brown, A., & Thompson, H. (1997). Course design for the WWW - Keeping online students onside. In *Proceedings of the 14th Annual ASCILITE conference* (pp 74 – 81). Perth, Western Australia: Academic Computing Services, Curtin University of Technology.

Brown, J. S. (2002). Growing up digital: How the Web changes work, education, and the ways people learn. *United States Distance Learning Association*. Retrieved January 2008, from http://www.usdla.org/html/journal/FEB02_Issue/article01.html

Buchanan, M. (2002). *Small world: Uncovering nature's hidden networks*. London: Weidenfeld & Nicolson.

Burbules, N., & Callister, T. A. (1996). Knowledge at the crossroads: Some alternative futures of hypertext learning environments. *Educational Theory*.

Campos, M. (2004, April). A constructivist method for the analysis of networked cognitive communication and the assessment of collaborative learning and knowledge-building. *Journal of Asynchronous Learning Networks*, *8*(2).

Candy, P. (2004 August). *Linking thinking: Self-directed learning in the digital age*. Report funded under the Research Fellowship Scheme of the Department of Education, Science and Training.

Carmean, C., & Haefner, J. (2002, November/December). Mind over matter: Transforming course management systems into effective learning environments. *EDUCAUSE Review*, ▪▪▪, 5.

Daniel, J. S. (1996). *Mega-universities and knowledge media: Technology strategies for higher education*. London: Kogan Page.

Dreher, H. (2006). *Interactive On-line Formative Evaluation of Student Assignments*. Paper presented at InSITE 2006, June 25-28, Greater Manchester, England. Retrieved October 2007, from http://2006.informingscience.org/

Dreher, H., & Williams, R. (2006). Assisted query formulation using normalised word vector and dynamic ontological filtering: Flexible query answering systems. In *Proceedings of 7th International Conference, FQAS 2006*, Milan, Italy (pp. 282 –294).

Fodor, J. (1997). Connectionism and the problem of systematicity: Why Smolensky's solution still doesn't work. *Cognition*, *62*, 109–119. doi:10.1016/S0010-0277(96)00780-9

Fodor, J., & McLaughlin, B. (1990). Connectionism and the problem of systematicity: Why Smolensky's solution doesn't work. *Cognition*, *35*, 183–204. doi:10.1016/0010-0277(90)90014-B

Fodor, J., & Pylyshyn, Z. (1988). Connectionism and cognitive architecture: A critical analysis. *Cognition*, *28*, 3–71. doi:10.1016/0010-0277(88)90031-5

Frand, J. L. (2000, September/October). Information-Age mindset: The changes in students and implications for higher education. *EDUCAUSE Review*, ▪▪▪, 17–24.

Gilbert, S. (2000, February 14). A new vision worth working toward - connected education and collaborative change. Retrieved January 2008, from http://www.tltgroup.org/gilbert/NewVwwt2000--2-14-00.htm

Gilbert, S. (2003, March 4). Why Bother? *Teaching Learning and Technology group*. Retrieved January 2008, from http://www.tltgroup.org/gilbert/WhyBotherArticle.pdf

Gipson, S. (1996). *Feral, Facsimile of Facilitated? Technology Serving Teaching and Learning.* Tridos School Village, Chiang Mai, Thailand: Learning and Teaching: Implications for Gifted and Talented Students.

Gleick, J. (1987). *Chaos.* London: William Heinemann Ltd.

Greater Expectations National Panel. (2002). Greater expectations: A new vision for learning as a nation goes to college. *The Association of American Colleges and Universities.* Retrieved June 2007, from http://www.greaterexpectations.org/

Guile, D. (2003). From 'Credentialism' to the 'Practice of Learning': reconceptualising learning for the knowledge economy. *Policy Futures in Education, 1*(1), 83–105. doi:10.2304/pfie.2003.1.1.10

Harris, D. (2000). Knowledge and networks. In T. Evans & D. Nation (Eds.), *Changing University Teaching: Reflections on Creating Educational Technologies* (pp. 36 – 7). London: Kogan Page.

Healy, J. M. (1991). Endangered minds. In D. Dickinson (Ed.), *Creating the Future: Perspectives on Educational Change* (pp. 52 – 8). Aston Clinton, UK: Accelerated Learning Systems Limited.

Hill, J. R., & Hannafin, M. J. (2001). Teaching and learning in digital environments: The resurgence of resource-based learning. *Educational Technology Research and Development, 49*(3). doi:10.1007/BF02504914

James, R., Mcinnis, C., & Devlin, M. (2002). Assessing learning in Australian universities: Ideas, strategies and resources for quality in student assessment. *Centre for the Study for Higher Education for the Australian Universities Teaching Committee.* Retrieved January 2008, from http://www.cshe.unimelb.edu.au/assessinglearning/docs/Online.pdf

Koestler, A. (1978). *Janus – A summing up.* Tiptree, UK: The Anchor Press Ltd.

Kosko, B. (1994). *Fuzzy Thinking - A New Science of Fuzzy Logic.* Hammersmith, London, UK: Harper Collins.

Leidner, D. E., & Jarvenpaa, S. L. (1995, September). The use of information technology to enhance management school education: A theoretical view. *MIS Quarterly, 19*(3), 265–292. doi:10.2307/249596

Lewin, R. (2001). *Complexity: Life at the edge of chaos.* Guernsey, Channel Islands: The Guernsey Press.

Liber, O. (2004). Cybernetics. e-Learning and the Education System. *International Journal of Learning Technology, 1*(1), 127–140. doi:10.1504/IJLT.2004.003686

Lipman, M. (1988). Critical thinking: What can it be? *Resource Publication,* 1(1).

Marginson, S. (2000, May). Rethinking academic work in the global era. *Journal of Higher Education Policy and Management, 22*(1), 23–35. doi:10.1080/713678133

Mask, T. (2002). *Are millennials smarter?* Retrieved November 2008, from http://www.citeulike.org/user/smbrower/author/Mask:T

McCune, S. D. (1991). Restructuring education. In D. Dickinson (Ed.), *Creating the future: Perspectives on educational change* (pp. 162-182). Aston Clinton, UK: Accelerated Learning Systems Limited.

Megarry, J. (1989). Hypertext and compact discs: The challenge of multimedia learning. In C. Bell, J. Davies & R. Winders (Eds.), *Promoting Learning: Aspects of Educational and Training Technology XXII* (pp. 50). London, UK: Kogan Page.

Mott, J. D., & Granata, G. (2006). The value of teaching and learning technology: Beyond ROI. *EDUCAUSE Quarterly, 29*(2), 48–54.

Pivec, M., & Dziabenko, O. (2004). Game-based learning in universities and lifelong learning - UniGame: Social Skills and Knowledge Training, Game Concept 1. *Journal of Universal Computer Science, 10*(1).

Rucker, R. (1988). *Mind tools: The mathematics of information*. London: Penguin Books.

Salmi, J. (2000 June). Tertiary education in the twenty-first century: Challenges and opportunities. *World Bank's Tertiary Education Thematic Group*. Retrieved March 2008, from http://wbln0018.worldbank.org/LAC/lacinfoclient.nsf/0/2d9645fd1eaab499852569ed005ccbc3/$FILE/62.pdf

Schuur, K. (2003). *A holistic vision of the future of eLearning*. Paper presented to a seminar series on Exploring Models and Partnerships for eLearning in SMEs. Retrieved March 2006, from http://www.theknownet.com/ict_smes_seminars/papers/Schuur.html

Sheldrake, R. (1988). *The presence of the past*. London, UK: William Collins Sons and Co.

Siemens, G. (2004). *Connectivism: A learning theory for the digital age*. Retrieved February 2008, from http://www.elearnspace.org/Articles/connectivism.htm

Siemens, G. (2006). Connectivism: Learning and knowledge today. In *Education.au Global summit 2006: Technology connected futures*. Retrieved February 2008, from http://www.educationau.edu.au/jahia/webdav/site/myjahiasite/shared/globalsummit/gs2006_siemens.pdf

Stanford University Metaphysics Research Lab. (1997). *The Stanford encyclopedia of philosophy: Connectionism*. Retrieved October 2007, from http://plato.stanford.edu/entries/connectionism/#3

Taylor, J. C. (2001 June). Fifth Generation Distance Education. Higher Education Series Report No. 40. *DETYA, Higher Education Division.*

Taylor, J. C. (2002). *Automating e-Learning: The Higher Education Revolution*. Paper submitted to the Australian Government Department of Education, Employment and Workplace Relations report 'Our Universities Backing Australia's Future Higher Education Review Process.' Retrieved February 2008 from http://www.backingaustraliasfuture.gov.au/submissions/issues_sub/pdf/i43_3.pdf

Thackara, J. (2005). *In the bubble: Designing in a complex world*. Cambridge, MA: MIT Press.

Tiffin, J., & Rajasingham, L. (1995). *In search of the virtual class - Education in an Information Society*. London, UK: Routledge.

Vrasidas, C., & Glass, G. V. (2000). *Distance education and distributed learning*. Charlotte, NC: Information Age Publishing.

Ward, D. (2000, January/February). Catching the waves of change in American higher education. *Educause Review*. Retrieved January 2008, from http://www.educause.edu/pub/er/erm00/pp022031.pdf

Wenger, E. (2005). *Learning for a Small Planet – A Research Agenda, Version 2.0 (revised September 2006)*. Retrieved November 2007, from http://ewenger.com/research/LSPfoundingdoc.doc

Chapter 20
Lecturing Tomorrow:
Virtual Classrooms, User Centered Requirements and Evaluative Methods

Thomas Czerwionka
Hamburg University of Technology, Germany

Michael Klebl
FernUniversität in Hagen / University of Hagen, Germany

Claudia Schrader
FernUniversität in Hagen / University of Hagen, Germany

ABSTRACT

This chapter presents a survey methodology addressing learners' requirements, their expectations and experiences regarding challenges in the implementation process of new educational technology in educational institutions. The presented methodology was devised and applied during the pilot use of a web conferencing system (in its educational form as a virtual classroom) in distance education, and combines the evaluation of usability, acceptance and expected benefits in order to generate statements and to substantiate decisions on educational technology at an early stage of its institutional introduction. The methodical procedure, survey instruments and results from its exemplary exertion are described. The overall objective of this chapter is to prove the appropriateness of this multi-perspective and user centered approach towards the examination of utility, resulting in a pragmatic and transferable tool for the evaluation of the three named factors.

INTRODUCTION

There is no question that information and communication technologies as well as multimedia are a growing part of today's higher education, especially in distance education. Traditionally focused on asynchronous communication based on printed material or on online tools, the possibilities to interact with tutors or peers in distance education are limited, since the people involved in teaching and learning are usually located far from each other. In distance education, learning instructions are given for the most part asynchronously by letter post or through the internet. This allows for the main advantages of distance education, i.e. the learners' independence in space and time, but provides for several problems

DOI: 10.4018/978-1-61520-678-0.ch020

for learners that are characteristic for distance education, like isolation, inactivity, high dropout rates due to frustration and the lack of motivation to continue studying. Based on the emergence, the development and the widespread use of new communication and collaboration technologies, leading up to applications and services of Web 2.0, it is possible to address these problems and develop and implement more interactive virtual learning environments. These educational settings for distance education include features oriented at conventional pedagogy, such as online assessment, user feedback or learning communities, formerly attributed to conventional education only.

Along with the diffusion of applications and services of Web 2.0, complemented by mobile and ubiquitous computing, synchronous online collaboration becomes an application of computer-mediated interaction ready for everyday use and available for (almost) everybody. Virtual worlds that enable the interaction of users controlling avatars in three-dimensional environments, like common massively multiplayer online games or Second Life, are quite inventive applications and undoubtedly promising for educational use. However, along with these prominent and futuristic technologies, synchronous online collaboration using advanced web conferencing systems develops from invention to innovation and diffusion. This means that synchronous communication and collaboration via the internet is steadily spreading in the workplace as well as in private use and is being increasingly implemented in education – not only in projects of design and development, but meanwhile also for regular and widespread use in educational settings.

On that basis, in this chapter we chose web conferencing systems in their educational form as virtual classrooms as an exemplar for considerations on user centered requirements and evaluative methods in the process of implementation of new educational technologies. In order to examine user centered requirements, we devised a pragmatic and transferable tool for evaluating expectations, needs and experiences of users at an early implementation stage of a new and emerging educational technology. The overall objective of this chapter is to prove the appropriateness of this survey methodology combining the evaluation of usability, acceptance and expected benefits during the pilot use of a new educational technology. In this context, the main research question of this chapter focuses on a learner-driven view with the intention of examining what features of new technology in educational settings provide real advantages, and which features may simply add to the complexity of interaction, thus distracting attention and cognitive capabilities. The survey methodology presented here is intended to generate statements and to substantiate decisions on new educational technology in an early stage of its institutional introduction and should allow for a transfer to other areas of technology enhanced learning.

To address the described purpose of this chapter, Section 2 will start with a brief overview detailing functions, main characteristics and possible educational scenarios of implementing virtual classrooms in distance education and responding to the question of why virtual classrooms should be implemented, using this as a paradigm for the diffusion of new educational technology in educational institutions. After defining the concept of the virtual classroom in education and describing opportunities of implementing virtual classrooms, the impact of three different but interrelated learner-based variables of usability, acceptance, and expected educational benefits on the effectiveness of virtual classrooms in distance education are explained in this section. Section 3 will explicate the survey methodology itself. The report on a survey during the pilot use of a web conference system at the FernUniversität in Hagen illustrates and substantiates the description of the methodical procedure and the survey instruments. For completeness, the results of this exemplary study investigating promising and critical aspects of usability, acceptance and expected benefits are presented. Concluding the chapter in Section 4, results as well as the appropriateness of the survey methodology combining the evaluation of usability, acceptance and expected benefits at an early implementation stage are discussed. In this context, viewpoints are also presented concerning aspects that should be especially considered in future technology enhanced learning.

VIRTUAL CLASSROOMS: FOUNDATIONS

The theoretical part of this chapter will introduce and discuss potential reasons for developing, implementing and using web conferencing systems in their educational function as virtual classrooms. Different design approaches for using them in distance education are presented in the next section. The importance of taking learners' requirements into account while designing effective virtual classrooms with interactive design characteristics is described in the last section of this theoretical part.

Functions, Characteristics and Potential Reasons for Using Virtual Classrooms in Distance Education

The shortest but also the most distinctive definition of the virtual classroom function for education is a virtual environment allowing a group of teachers and learners to meet and interact in real time over the internet by a set of communication features such as voice, video webcam and chat; presentation features for collaboration like a whiteboard, a presentation screen for slideshows and also polling for presenting and exchanging information (Chapman & Wiessner, 2008). In summary, some of the typical characteristics of virtual classrooms include (but not limited to): They are computer and internet-based, user-controlled and interactive, and communication and collaboration-based.

Based on the stated problems of distance teaching universities, virtual classrooms are considered in distance education: Current research has demonstrated few measurable differences between the conventional asynchronous distance and traditional educational settings. Some learners have migrated back to the classroom so that they can be with 'live' people (Guernsey, 1998). Thus, concerning the function of synchronous communication and collaboration, the educational purpose of virtual classrooms could be to stimulate the interaction between teachers and learners as well as amongst the group of learners in distance education. virtual classrooms could bridge a gap between teachers and learners and allow personal interaction which is not given in conventional distance teaching and in asynchronous virtual learning. Learners have the possibility to learn cooperatively with others to solve learning problems and work on authentic tasks (Scott, Castañeda, Quick, & Linney, 2008). This could help learners to understand that effective learning is a social, collaborative process. It may decrease the feeling of loneliness and provide an environment for successful study. Using tools like a whiteboard or presentation screen, learning could be made public. Information, materials and drafts could be presented and discussed; learners can share knowledge, have the opportunity to learn from all others and receive input from multiple perspectives in real time. It could be argued that the depth of learners' engagement with learning content seems to be greater when they must communicate their thoughts online both to the teacher and to other learners (Adesope, Adesope, & Ojeme, 2008; Chapman & Wiessner, 2008). Resulting in deeper learning activities, learners could generate relevant knowledge more professionally. Finally, the last reason for implementing virtual classrooms in distance education is that using new technologies also enhances technology learning: Nowadays, people get overwhelmed with the need to learn and use (internet) technology for communication and collaboration. To sum up, there is no doubt about the role of virtual classrooms as a new kind of communication and collaboration technology for an effective and efficient teaching and learning process. Implementing virtual classrooms could make distance education available and comfortable for a larger number of people. Moreover, learners could apply skills and competencies by interacting with technology, learning material and other people.

Thus, advanced web conferencing systems facilitate new forms of synchronous online learning in distance education and are currently gaining more popularity in distance teaching universities, in order to increase motivation, communication, collaboration and also the quality of the learning experience (Martin, 2005). A significant change for teaching and learning in distance teaching universities is thus implied: The asynchronous scenarios are complemented by synchronous settings. The main advantage of distance education – independence of time – is restricted for the expected benefits of traditional educational, i.e. synchronous interaction, such as social presence, spontaneity, and shared context. Generally, the introduction of new technologies like web conferencing systems causes a significant change for educational institutions. However, not only educational institutions but also individual people in the roles of learners are challenged by the use of the new and advanced tools. A new technology provides new features and applications that are not necessarily common to the users. Even if new functions connect to familiar tools, such as a web conferencing system that enhances well-known situations of telephone calls and internet relay chat, the effects of new tools unfold rather slowly since the application and beneficial use of new functions like a shared whiteboard have to be discovered and developed.

Teaching and Learning Scenarios of Virtual Classrooms in Distance Education

To support synchronous teaching and learning in distance education by using virtual classrooms, their mentioned variety of features and functions includes diverse opportunities to be implemented in quite typical educational settings. Common and well-known patterns of interaction between all participants are transferred to virtual space, enabling synchronous communication and fostering collaboration independent of space. Based on the current use of virtual classrooms at the FernUniversität in Hagen, only few educational scenarios will be presented:

- *Online lecture*: Using virtual classrooms for online lectures gives a wider audience the possibility to view the lecture independently of space. Here, a lecturer presents a particular subject online. Learners normally follow the lecture from their desktop at home or at work (Chung, 2004). Especially the cited features for presentation, such as slideshow and whiteboard, are important to support the oral lecture. However, both video conferencing as well as features for feedback like status signals and polls are of high importance for online lectures. Furthermore, they allow communicating via text chat, enhancing the quality of feedback to the lecturer during the speech. The function of recording sessions is useful for reviewing them.
- *Online seminar*: In seminars, learners adopt an active role in the process of teaching and learning. Alone or in groups, they contribute in discussions, with seminar papers or presentations, for reviews, in case studies, in experiments or by solving given problems (Graham & Misanchuk, 2004). The interaction in an online seminar can be as manifold as learning in the ordinary

classroom. Often, synchronous online sessions are combined with the use of virtual learning environments like virtual classrooms for asynchronous learning. Then, periods of asynchronous collaboration alternate with synchronous sessions focusing mainly on communication. Sessions with virtual classrooms may serve for the coordination of activities, e.g. the formation of groups and the assignment of tasks, as well as for presentation and discussion, e.g. the presentation of results by different work groups. The possibility to open virtual classrooms for meetings of learning groups independently of the tutor's presence also deserves mention here.

- *Online colloquium, online office hours*: When learners in distance education have specific concerns for which they need to consult lecturers, they have to use communication technology (Wallace & Wallace, 2001). Here, virtual classrooms primarily offer video in addition to telephone and text chat or e-mail. Therefore, virtual classrooms may be used for tutoring and mentoring one-to-one, e.g. for consultation on assignments, assessments and thesis writing. The open invitation to the participants in a course may result in an online colloquium on specific topics of the course, e.g. during the preparation of an exam.
- *Online autonomous learning group*: Since distance education relies much on self-regulated learning, autonomous learning groups are of particular importance for academic achievement. In order to foster distributed learning groups, virtual classrooms can be opened for autonomous purposes by enrolled learners and serve as a meeting point for students who want to learn cooperatively (Scott et al., 2008). For this intention, individual students representing a group of learners are granted the administrative rights for session planning and time management.

In summary, based on the described functions as well as the presented variety of opportunities of implementing virtual classrooms in diverse educational settings, there seems to be a lot of potential reasons for using virtual classrooms in distance education. However, the numbers of studies reporting on implementation of virtual classrooms in various (higher) distance education settings are rather limited. Moreover, no clear conclusion has yet been reached concerning the learners' requirements, expectations and experiences in using virtual classrooms. In our opinion, in order to design a user-friendly adoption of virtual classrooms for learning purposes in educational settings, the viewpoint of learners has to be taken into account. This aspect is discussed in the following section.

Learners' Expectations, Needs and Experiences

Relying on learners' expectations, needs and experiences concerning virtual classrooms is important, because it cannot be automatically assumed that only by implementing a new educational technology with its variety of features in different educational settings will it be expected and experienced as an effective tool by learners. We argue that for virtual classrooms to reach their potential in positively stimulating learners in distance education, it is imperative that learners perceive the virtual classroom as an effective tool. In a learner-driven view, the utility of a new educational technology is influenced by three different but interrelated criteria: by the virtual classroom as a teaching and learning tool itself in the form of the perceived intrinsic or objective experienced usability, by the viewpoint of learners in the form of the acceptability of using virtual classrooms and, based on the interrelation between users and the virtual classroom, by the needs in the form of expected benefits of virtual classroom features. We suggest a multi-perspective approach towards the examination of user centered requirements based on the combination of these three criteria that form the basis for the evaluation methodology presented in this chapter:

The *perceived usability* of a new educational technology, conceived by learners as a combination of technical as well as affective aspects, gives an account of its appropriateness for the intended use in learning scenarios (Hassenzahl, 2001). According to the research in the field of technology acceptance, technical system aspects have served as the basis for a number of questionnaires in software evaluation (e.g. Gediga & Hamborg, 1999; Kirakowski, 1996; Prümper, 1997). In contrast, more recent approaches also take affective elements into account, realizing that affective aspects like fun, fascination and enjoyment also appear to contribute to users' overall satisfaction with a tool, and motivate them to work with and thereby have an impact on the perceived usability of technology (Hassenzahl, Burmester, & Koller, 2003). Thus, these current studies shed light on the interrelation between technical and affective perspectives. A technically deficient system will not receive good evaluations regarding its ability to fulfill a task despite a high fun factor; conversely, a technically effective system that gives its user no satisfaction will also be judged as inadequate, true to the motto: 'If it doesn't feel right, who cares if it works?' (Hassenzahl & Hofvenschiöld, 2003, p. 135). According to this, Hassenzahl (2004) preferred the following four dimensions concerning the usability of software:

- *Pragmatic quality:* Pragmatic quality describes the ability of a product to satisfy the need to meet a goal by providing useful and usable functions.
- *Hedonic quality – Stimulation*: The quality of stimulation is the ability of a product to satisfy the need for improving one's own knowledge and skills. Products can support personal development by being stimulating – for example, through novel, interesting functionalities and possibilities for interaction.
- *Hedonic quality – Identity*: The quality of identity is the ability of a product to communicate messages to relevant others that promote self-worth. People express themselves through objects. They wish to be seen in a particular way by others. A product can support this by communicating a particular identity and, for example, being professional, 'cool', or modern.
- *Attractiveness*: The quality of attractiveness describes an overall positive or negative evaluation of the product.

In conclusion, concentrating only on system qualities in the implementation phase of new educational technologies in educational institutions seems to be counterproductive. In educational processes, first and foremost, software applications should inspire and motivate. Secondly, the intensity of use on the part of learners is hard to predict reliably, so exhaustive mastery of the technical software characteristics cannot be guaranteed. And thirdly, in the implementation phase a global first impression is more important than the evaluation of technical system characteristics, which is intended for the process of software development (Wandke, 2004). Based on this, it seems to be important to account for affective elements rather than for technical or performance related perspectives in order to examine the perceived usability.

With respect to the shown perceived usability, the disposition to use a tool for learning can be determined by modeling learners' *acceptance* of a new technology as well. Understanding why learners accept technology for educational purpose has been one of the most challenging issues in the research field of new technologies (Swanson, 1988) and also in this part of study. Acceptance, normally seen as 'the behavioral acceptance to use new technologies for different tasks' (Simon, 2001), is a learner characteristic and, at least partly, subjective. Explaining the acceptance as well as the factors that influence it, the technology acceptance model (TAM) introduced by Davis (1989) and expanded by Venkatesh (2000) and Venkatesh and Davis (2000) is specifically tailored for explanations of learner acceptance of new technology tools. Applying the TAM to this new context of virtual classrooms, the second main issue is to ask what factors determine learners' acceptance of virtual classrooms. The TAM attempts to derive and predict the importance of personal as well as contextual key factors of learners' acceptance. Based on the theory of reasoned action (Ajzen & Fishbein, 1980), behavioral acceptance in the form of actual use (AU) is determined by the behavioral intention to use (BIU) technologies like virtual classrooms, which is viewed as being jointly affected by the two factors of 'perceived usefulness' (PU) and 'perceived ease of use' (PEOU) (e.g., Agarwal & Prasad, 1999; Venkatesh, 2000). PU is defined as 'the prospective user's subjective probability that using a specific application system will increase his or her [...] performance within an organizational context' (Davis, Bagozzi, & Warshaw, 1989, p. 985), while the PEOU refers to 'the degree to which the prospective user expects the target system to be free of effort' (Davis et al., 1989, p. 985). Furthermore the TAM identifies and takes into account the impact of external factors such as system design characteristics, task and user characteristics and attitudes as well as learners' previous experiences of using virtual classrooms. Integrating all these factors that influence the willingness to adopt and may facilitate (further) use of virtual classrooms makes an extensive view on acceptance possible. Based on research in this field, many studies propose a view in which the acceptance by learners is positively related to the degree of adoption and further utilization of new technologies (e.g., Venkatesh & Davis, 2000; Park, 2008). Basing ourselves on the assumption of learners' acceptance, it can be argued that a high degree of acceptance has positive effects on the effectiveness of virtual classrooms in distance education. In summary, regarding utilizing a new educational technology to an acceptable degree, it is important to examine the use and the technology's adoption from the learners' perspective.

Examining *expected benefits* draws the attention from single features of a specific product that is introduced and tested to more general principles that a new technology employs. In addition to perceived usability und acceptance, the interrelation between users' needs and the general functionality that technical systems provide can be determined in terms of expected benefits. They become indicators for users' needs, beyond the particular use in the test scenario. In the development, design and implementation of a new technology, there is a general relation between tasks, requirements, functions and benefits (Diaper, 2004). People use technical tools in order to perform tasks. However, users normally are oblivious to the relation of single requirements and emerging benefits (Goguen, 1996). Rather, they observe specific and outstanding features of a tool that thus are subject to evaluation. For instance, users' may well experience the benefit of a shared whiteboard for synchronous online learning. But they normally are not aware of the origins of this benefit. They perceive a feature as useful or useable, without reflecting on the purpose of use of this feature, e.g. not deliberating on the effort to share ideas with a shared whiteboard in comparison to sharing ideas without a shared whiteboard or by means of other tools. Nevertheless, in the comparison of different equivalent tools for a specific purpose, expected benefits become more relevant than perceived usability of single product features. When people have to decide between different alternatives, e.g. in purchase decisions or in procurement processes, they consider attributes that are common to all competing products as well as trade-offs between attributes. A common method to measure the needs for distinctive features and to model the effects of trade-offs concerning expected benefit is conjoint analysis. Different types of data collection and different models of data analysis share the basic ideas of conjoint analysis, which is a prevalent technique in market research (Green, Krieger, & Wind, 2003). According to the notion of conjoint analysis, people decide between alternatives based on the implicit valuation of several attributes that distinguish these options. If people are requested to choose between a controlled set of alternatives that are described by common attributes, these implicit valuations of different attributes can be determined from their choice. As a result, the importance of a feature for the overall preference can be estimated (Green et al., 2003). On that basis, we account for expected benefits by estimating the valuation of features and feature groups. These indicators for more general users' needs may inform the decisions on the implementation of new educational technology. They deserve particular attention, in order to foster adoption of new educational technology, to provide for accordance to educational aims and to facilitate participation in the organization of educational practice.

Given these different but interrelated perspectives on the use and utility of new educational technology, the effectiveness of technology that is introduced in educational institutions is considered to depend on its usability, primarily represented by affective aspects, on learners' acceptability of its use and on learners' expected benefits from its features. To sum up the theoretical part, using virtual classrooms as a paradigm for the diffusion of new educational technology in educational institutions, the main research questions for the survey methodology presented in this chapter based on the viewpoint of learners can be formulated as follows:

1. Based on the usability of virtual classrooms, what are learners' perceptions of affective elements as important usability factors after using the virtual classroom in different educational settings?
2. Based on the learners' perspective, what is the impact of using virtual classrooms on acceptance in (higher) distance education? What factors directly and indirectly determine learners' intention to use virtual classrooms?
3. Based on the expected benefits as a criterion for users' needs, how relevant are the functionality and the interface of virtual classrooms for teaching and learning? What features seem to be effective before and after using virtual classrooms in different educational settings? What features provide real advantages, make it attractive and engaging and which features may simply add to the complexity of interaction, thus distracting attention and cognitive capabilities?

AN EXEMPLARY STUDY: USABILITY, ACCEPTANCE AND EXPECTED BENEFITS

In order to investigate the research questions mentioned, an exemplary study was conducted concerning the introduction of virtual classrooms at the FernUniversität in Hagen. More often than not, current research for evaluating new technologies is focused on just one specific educational issue, e.g. concerning learners' satisfaction with tools and settings or mastery of specific content. In contrast, the general objective of the presented methodology is to gain insight into the interrelation between learners and specific tools, into the needs and the expected benefits concerning features and into the effectiveness of new tools in their ability to facilitate learning during pilot use. The following first section gives a short account of evaluation methodology including participants, object of evaluation, procedure as well as the evaluation instruments. Subsequently, the main results are reported in Section 3, which generates statements and substantiates decisions for a specific field of implementation, e.g. a single educational institution beyond pilot use during implementation.

Participants

Seventy-eight students, studying at FernUniversität in Hagen, Germany, participated in the study. The age of the participants ranged from 25 to 50 years, with two majorities between 26 and 30 years (25.6%) and between 36 and 40 years (25.6%). A total of 20.5% of the participants were between 31 and 35 years and finally 14.1% between 36 and 40 years old. The ratio of women to men was 2:1 (65.4% female, 34.6% male). Most of the students were enrolled at the Faculty for Social and Cultural Science (73.1%), a smaller quantity at the Faculty of Mathematics and Computer Science (15.4%) and the Faculty of Economics (11.5%). All participants reported mainly 'good' or 'very good' proficiency in the use of internet-based communication technology like chat, internet or e-mail ($4.04 \leq M \leq 4.68$; $0.55 \leq SD \leq 0.95$ on a scale from 1 'very low' to 5 'very good'), but less experience with web conferencing systems in their educational form as virtual classrooms ($2.63 \leq M \leq 2.91$; $0.94 \leq SD \leq 1.13$). Especially with virtual classrooms, most of the participants had no experience (91.1%). However, they were generally disposed to use virtual classrooms for their study ($4.34 < M < 4.75$; $0.46 \leq SD \leq 0.64$ on a scale from 1 'skeptical' to 5 'open-minded').

Adobe Connect as an Object of Evaluation and Its Implementation in Distance Education

The study was conducted during the 2007/2008 winter semester accompanying the pilot use of Adobe Acrobat Connect Professional (short: Adobe Connect) at the FernUniversität in Hagen. Adobe Connect is a web conferencing tool that allows transmitting voice and video. This tool offers quite a number of functions for communication, presentation and collaboration, such as text chat, shared whiteboard, application sharing, voting tools, file exchange as well as the facility to record and replay sessions. It can be stated that this specific tool employs and represents various principles of online collaboration that can be utilized in synchronous distance learning scenarios. After a preliminary review of different web conferencing systems, Adobe Connect was chosen for the pilot study for that reason. Hence, for our study, Adobe Connect was considered from two perspectives: On the one hand, Adobe Connect serves as a model of (usually competing) web conferencing systems for the evaluation in test scenarios in order to facilitate decisions on appropriateness, acceptance and accordance to educational aims of diverse functions and features. On the other hand, Adobe Connect is a candidate for the long term and institution-wide implementation, competing with other web conferencing systems.

In order to provide practical experience with this new educational technology in real life educational settings, exemplary educational scenarios for synchronous online learning serve as test scenarios for the evaluation in question. These courses include the various typical settings in teaching and learning that have been described above: online lectures, online seminars, online colloquiums and online office hours, and finally, online autonomous learning groups. The field for the evaluation of Adobe Connect during its implementation does not resemble the ideal situation of a laboratory environment. On the contrary, both users and researchers gain practical experience with new tools for teaching and learning in educational situations rich in contextual influences. Here, a framework of authentic educational situations starts the evaluation of the educational technology in question.

Procedure

All students participating in at least one of the educational forms of synchronous online learning based on Adobe Connect were asked to complete two online questionnaires, one before the first session with the web conferencing system started, the second after finishing live online learning sessions. A total of 78 students took part in the survey: 56 (71.8%) completed the first questionnaire, 45 (57.7%) the second (with an overlapping amount of 23 students/ 29.5% who filled out both questionnaires). In the following, our data analyses regarding usability and acceptance refer to the students who finished only the second questionnaire. Concerning expected benefits, the conjoint analysis examined both groups (before and after) separately. Here, only the examination of differences between both measuring times refers to paired samples of students who completed both questionnaires when they took part in the sessions.

Evaluation Instruments

The online questionnaires merged three approved instruments for the evaluation of new technology that examine *usability*, *acceptance* and *expected benefits*. Furthermore, for an evaluation of the online courses, the scales of the 'Trierer Inventar zur Lehrevaluation – modular' ('Trier Inventory for the Evaluation of Teaching – modular', TRIL-MOD; Gollwitzer, Kranz, & Vogel 2006) were added. In the following, we give a short description of the conception of the survey by the specification of instruments.

For evaluating the *usability* of Adobe Connect, the questionnaire was based on the original 'AttrakDiff2' instrument from Hassenzahl (2004). It consists of a semantic differential of 28 items on a bipolar seven-stage rating scale. This instrument measures so-called pragmatic and hedonic qualities as well as the attractiveness of an interactive product (see above). For the evaluation in this study, from among all 28 AttrakDiff-items, one of each pair of item specifications was selected and put in the form of a declarative sentence, for which a 5-point Likert scale measured the subject's level of agreement (from 'I strongly disagree' to 'I strongly agree'). Because of the modifications, the reliability coefficients for the scales with the new item formulations and the discriminative power coefficients of the items were tested. These tests showed a high level of reliability for all scales with most marginal possibilities of heightening, whereby the internal consistency of the scales was demonstrated. The scales were composed of the following items:

- Scale *Pragmatic quality*: 'I experience Adobe Connect as human/ simple/ practical/ intricate/ incalculable/ clear/ fractious' (Cronbach's $\alpha = .86$).
- Scale *Hedonic quality – Stimulation*: 'I experience Adobe Connect as inventive/ creative/ bold/ innovative/ absorbing/ challenging/ conventional' (Cronbach's $\alpha = .83$).
- Scale *Hedonic quality – Identity*: 'I experience Adobe Connect as isolating/ professional/ inelegant/ substandard/ incorporating/ presentable/ a tool that brings me closer to people' (Cronbach's $\alpha = .84$).
- Scale *Attractiveness*: 'I experience Adobe Connect as unpleasant/ ugly/ friendly/ inviting/ good/ appealing/ motivating' (Cronbach's $\alpha = .91$).

In order to assess the learners' *acceptance*, the designed instrument applies former measurement scales based on the originals put forward by Davis (1989) and which were obtained from prior studies (Venkatesh, 2000; Landry, Rodger, & Hartman 2006; Jung, Loria, Mostaghel, & Saha, 2008; Park, 2008).

- According to the theoretical model, the *behavioral intention to use* Adobe Connect is measured by the following item: 'I plan to use Adobe Connect in the future'. The item was followed by a 5-point Likert-scale ranging from 'strongly disagree' to 'strongly agree'.

- The *perceived ease of use* as a level of the learners' agreement is measured by the following statements: 1) 'Adobe Connect as virtual classroom is easy for me to use', 2) 'The handling of Adobe Connect does not demand any efforts', 3) 'The handling of Adobe Connect is clear and comprehensible'. Items were followed by the same 5-point Likert-scale (Cronbach's $\alpha = .83$).
- *Perceived usefulness* measures the level of learners' agreement with the following items: 1) 'My learning performance is enhanced when using Adobe Connect', 2) 'The effectiveness of my activities for study is enhanced', 3) 'In my opinion, Adobe Connect is useful for my activities in study'. Again, a 5-point Likert-scale was used (Cronbach's $\alpha = .88$).
- *Behavioral acceptance* in the form of the actual use of Adobe Connect was measured by the following question: 'In addition to the attended class, how many hours per week did you personally use Adobe Connect?' The learners are asked to answer with a number for the question.
- Beyond, *external factors* like the use and experiences with Adobe Connect as well as other communication and collaboration technologies could have an impact on learners' acceptance. Therefore, other technology use was measured by learners' usage frequency of seven other technologies: 1) tools for presentation (e.g. PowerPoint), 2) audio conferencing, 3) video conferencing, 4) email, 5) chat, 6) groupware or collaborative software (e.g. other web conferencing systems) and 7) internet. Learners responded using a 5-point Likert-scale from 'very bad' to 'very good' (Cronbach's $\alpha = .86$).

For the evaluation of *expected benefits* we designed a full profile conjoint analysis. For this part of the questionnaire, students were asked to compare several fictional web conferencing tools, which were described by four attributes, and to rank them according to their suitability for widespread use in different educational settings. For all four attributes (i.e. feature groups) we devised three levels (i.e. features) assuming discrete preferences for all attributes (partworth model; Green et al., 2003). The details are given in Table 4. In a fractional factorial design that is based on orthogonal arrays (Hauser & Rao, 2003), nine fictional web conferencing tools were selected from 81 (3^4) possible combinations of three alternative features within four feature groups. These tools were presented to the students in both surveys, i.e. before and after they participated in synchronous online learning settings. Table 1 shows an exemplary description of two out of nine tools, which were labeled meaninglessly with the international radiotelephony spelling alphabet.

Results

The study provided empirical evidence to prove that a virtual classroom can be an effective tool in (higher) distance education. The analysis reveals positive indications that the idea of web

Table 1. Description of two out of nine alternative tools in the full profile conjoint analysis

Charlie	Delta
Audio and video conferencing for all participants	Simple and robust voice transmission
Presentation of various file formats	Presentation of various file formats
Sessions or rooms for subgroups	Simple polls and tests
Integration in an online course management system	Recording of sessions

Table 2. Evaluation of usability dimensions (range: min. = 1 to max. = 5)

Scale	M	SD
Pragmatic quality	3.92	0.73
Hedonic quality – Stimulation	3.73	0.69
Hedonic quality – Identity	4.15	0.61
Attractiveness	4.23	0.62

conferencing systems could substantially contribute to the attempts of providing new technical design solutions for effective communication and collaboration in distance education as well as in preparation to face the challenges of future working environments. Generally, the students demonstrated high positive attitudes towards the idea of using a virtual classroom and were enthusiastic about its implementation in current educational settings.

In terms of usability, a descriptive analysis firstly shows that students rate Adobe Connect positively across all measured usability dimensions (see Table 2). A comparison of the results of different user groups (male/female students, students with/without experience with web conferencing systems) entails an identical rank order of the usability scales in these groups. In addition, t-tests show no significant mean differences between the cited groups.

With regard to relationships between usability scales as well as between usability and other criteria covered by our study, the following results are noteworthy. In addition to the high correlation between the scales Identity and Attractiveness ($r = .88$, $p = .000$), there are also significant correlations between students' overall opinion of the software and aspects of acceptance: The scales for relevance and for the intention to use correlate at a medium level with the scale Attractiveness (both $r = .54$, both $p = .000$). Considering the acceptance, among the students two subsets can be described with significant correlation regarding the usability quality of stimulation: The scales for the perceived usefulness and relevance correlate at a medium with the scale Stimulation ($r = .51/.50$, both $p = .001$). As the rating scales for the course, the usability scale Stimulation is aimed at the improvement of students' skills and knowledge. Nevertheless, all correlations between the scales for the course and the usability scale are small or very small ($r < .50$).

Concerning the purpose to test the learners' acceptance of virtual classrooms, all described scales along with their respective means and standard deviations were analyzed. As shown in Table 3, the mean lies between M = 3.36 and 4.53, which is more than the middle of the 5-point scale. Also, the standard deviation in each case is relatively low, ranging between SD = 0.58 and 1.09. Moreover, based on the main issue of acceptance, the means of all scale-based associations of items such as the perceived ease of use (PEOU; M = 4.03, SD = 0.83), the perceived usefulness (PU; M = 4.31, SD = 0.69), the behavioral intention to use (M = 4.53, SD = 0.58) as well as the actual use (M = 3.36, SD = 1.09) demonstrate high levels of learners' acceptance for using virtual classrooms. Furthermore, the second objective of the acceptance-part of the study was to investigate which of the assumed factors determine the acceptance of learners and thus test the technology acceptance theory in a new context. In order to test whether there is a relationship between the variables, Pearson's correlation coefficient analysis for normal distributed data as well as Spearman's correlation coefficient analysis were conducted. Firstly, there is a positive relationship between

Table 3. Mean scores and standard deviations for acceptance scales

Scales	M	SD
Perceived Ease of Use	4.03	0.83
Perceived Usefulness	4.31	0.69
Behavioral Intention to Use	4.53	0.58
Actual Use	3.36	1.09
External Factors: Experiences With Other Media	3.60	0.71

the two independent variables PEOU and PU and their dependent variable behavioral intention to use (PU: r = .78, p = .001; PEOU: r = .32, p = .030). Both PU as well as PEOU are significant predictors of the intention to use virtual classrooms. But even though both factors are significantly related to the intention to use, the analysis also reveals a much stronger impact of perceived usefulness on the behavioral intention to use as compared to perceived ease of use. Testing it in a regression analysis, this regression model shows that the relationships between the variables are significant (F-ratio = 25.26, p = .000), but it also just explains 54.6% of the variance in behavioral intention. This means that approximately 46.4% of the variation is explained by other factors that have not been investigated. Furthermore, looking at the PU as well as the PEOU, PU seems to be the strongest factor supporting the intention to use (Beta = .70, t = 6.31, p = .001). This corresponds to what has been found in previous research based on the technology acceptance model. A possible reason for why perceived ease of use to a lesser extent impacts on the attitude towards using a system as compared to perceived usefulness is that perceived ease of use might be a predictor of perceived usefulness impacting directly on that variable. This has been proposed in previous research and thus was tested. The correlation coefficients among PU and PEOU are low but positive (r = .36, p = .013) in this investigation. Also, external factors in the form of the measured experiences with other technologies is significantly correlated with perceived ease of use (r = .50, p = .013), suggesting that these two variables are related to each other. Finally, as suggested in the technology acceptance model, the behavioral intention to use also has a positive effect on learners' actual use. Results demonstrate a low relationship between both (r = .46, p = .001).

A full profile conjoint analysis serves to determine users' needs concerning distinctive principles, features and applications of tools for synchronous online learning, irrespective of the perceived ease of use of a specific web conferencing tool. According to the model assumption of conjoint analysis, the valuations of single attributes add up to the valuation of each single product. In the first step of data analysis, we used ordinary least squares (OLS) regression to estimate the valuations of the single attributes per person. The analysis by ordinary least squares is considered as an adequate approximation for conjoint analysis in common research practice (Hauser & Rao, 2003). In a second step, the arithmetic averages of these valuations for all participants serve as the value for the representative valuation of a single feature.

The next steps ask for the partworth of each attribute, i.e. the relevance of each feature group for the overall preference. This estimation is based on the following model assumption: An attribute with high variance for the valuation of its levels is of higher importance for the overall preference than attributes with rather consistent valuations (Backhaus, Erichson, Plinke, & Weiber, 2005). In the third step, for each person the ratio between the range of values for the valuation of single levels for an attribute (i.e. three features within a feature group) and the sum of the range of values for valuation of each attribute (i.e. all feature groups) is calculated. In a forth step, the arithmetic averages of these partworth values serve as the value for the representative valuation of a feature group.

The pre-post design of the study motivates a dependent t-test or a Wilcoxon signed-rank test for paired samples. For the study presented here we found only few differences between the valuations before and after synchronous learning sessions (see Table 4). Regarding the expected benefits we want to draw attention to the following results:

- For both measuring times the partworth value of communication features exceeds the valuation of other feature groups considerably.
- Within the communication features, audio and video conferencing for all participants is the most distinctive feature, hence of highest expected benefit.
- For the presentation features, participants clearly prefer pointer and notes for the presentation of slides. From this expected benefit a need for additional orientation during a presentation can be stated.
- For collaboration, the possibility to open sessions for subgroups is of high importance. However, there is a significant difference for the importance of simple polls and tests. They are rated more important after the synchronous learning sessions. Probably a good use of these tools led to a change in the valuation by the students.
- Amongst the features for organization, the facility to record sessions attains the highest valuation. Features of access are of lesser importance.

CONCLUSION

In order to analyze students' expectations, needs and experiences regarding the implementation of a new educational technology in an established educational setting, we devised a pragmatic and specific evaluation of usability, acceptance and expected benefits. We explicated the methodology that we already employed for a survey concerning the implementation of a web conferencing tool for synchronous online learning in a distance teaching university via the specification of instruments, theoretical backgrounds and data analysis.

In the following, after a discussion of the evaluation results presented in the last section, we give a description of how the research methodology met the requirements between considerations concerning objects as well as objectives of the evaluation and conditions in the field of research. Some prospects on how future advancements in technology enhanced learning could give more attention to appropriateness, acceptance and accordance to educational aims are included in this part.

Outcomes and Their Applicability

The overall results described in the previous section confirmed students' high positive attitudes towards the idea of using a virtual classroom in distance education. This insight furthered the process of implementation and diffusion of web conference systems within the FernUniversität in Hagen. Students' expectations, needs and experiences regarding virtual classrooms served as an important justification for further investment and involvement aiming at the widespread use of web conference systems within distance education. The outcomes concerning the different criteria in the evaluation resulted in further adjustments in the implementation process.

The results regarding *usability* lead to the interpretation that the virtual classroom appeals to different user groups in the same way. This is an

Table 4. Estimated partworth values for features and feature groups in the full profile conjoint analysis

Attributes, i.e. feature groups **Levels of attributes, i.e. features**	**Estimated partworth value before participation**	**Estimated partworth value after participation**	**Significance for differences***
Communication features	*51.20%*	*48.97%*	
Simple and robust voice transmission	-1.14	-1.27	
Audio and video conferencing for all participants	2.13	2.05	
Requests to speak, list of speakers and forwarding of the right to speak	-0.99	-0.78	
Presentation features	*12.35%*	*16.40%*	
Presentation of slides	-0.29	-0.60	
Presentation of slides with pointer and notes	0.13	0.34	
Presentation of various file formats	0.16	0.27	
Collaboration features	17.99%	14.82%	
Sessions or rooms for subgroups	0.55	0.38	
Simple polls and tests	-0.41	0.08	$p < 0.050$
Application sharing	-0.14	-0.46	
Organization features	*18.46%*	*19.80%*	
Simple self-registration as a guest	-0.12	-0.42	
Integration in an online course management system	-0.14	-0.39	
Recording of sessions	0.26	0.80	
*) Wilcoxon signed-rank test for paired samples			

advantage in the long-term widespread deployment of the system, since in the design of different courses, the preferences or objections from particular groups need to be taken into account to a much lesser extent than is usually expected. This justified the general use of one web conference system for different educational scenarios.

It seems likely that students' ratings for diverse (and not only usability) aspects might worsen slightly with a longer period of use, without this necessarily representing a 'worse' place for the software in teaching. Decreasing ratings can instead reflect a normal reduction in the novelty value of the virtual classroom. Precipitant changes in course conception are not necessary on this account.

Students clearly distinguish between the total contribution of the course to their learning process and the role specifically ascribed to the Adobe Connect tool. On the level of a single course, Adobe Connect is seen as one element among others which can contribute to a positive opinion regarding this specific course. In contrast, students have a high opinion of the potential for Adobe Connect particularly with regard to their entire range of studies. Despite possibly lower ratings in certain individual courses, this indicates a recommendation for the long-term introduction of the system.

The presented study investigated the issue of students' *acceptance* as well as the factors of acceptance of virtual classrooms for distance education. Altogether the results of this study suggest the acceptance of virtual classrooms to use. Above all, students' intention to use virtual classrooms is determined by the perceived usefulness. If students do not perceive the tool to be useful, the efforts might not show the results expected. Thus, lecturers need to communicate benefits of using virtual classrooms to the students. This insight was taken as guideline for the introduction of the web conference systems in educational scenarios.

Furthermore, the results confirm the impact of the perceived ease of use on the perceived usefulness. Students perceive a system as more useful if less difficulty in using it is experienced. Even though the factors of perceived ease of use and perceived use of virtual classrooms seem to be significant predictors of students' intention to use virtual classrooms, results show that the intention to use is also caused by other factors (e.g. personal factors such as age, background, a possible social influence or perceptions of risk). Moreover, there is a positive and direct impact of students' willingness to use on the actual use. The predicted relationship is also low, meaning that even though students might have a positive intention to use, they might still end up not using it. Here, the need for further encouragement to use the web conference system was determined for the introduction process.

A simple conclusion can be drawn from the result that communication features are of high importance for the *expected benefits* of virtual classrooms, with audio and video conferencing as the most distinctive feature: Undoubtedly, audio and video conferencing is the core functionality of web conferencing in synchronous online learning. Especially the transmission of video adds to synchronous communication via voice or text chat. Hence, development, design and implementation have to focus on this core functionality. Or more generally: It can be stated that a focus on core functionalities in educational technology is valued by the students. In the process of implementation, this insight resulted in a commitment towards web conference systems with high functionality in audio and video conferencing, while dismissing the suggested use of audio conferencing systems.

The high valuation of the facility to record and replay sessions can be interpreted in relation to an initial issue discussed above. With the introduction of web conferencing systems in distance teaching, the independence of time for individual learning is given up for the benefits of synchronous interaction. Here, the recording facility seemingly offers a means to bridge this contradiction, since synchronous sessions can be used asynchronously as well. Compared to this, the low rating for the integration in an online course management system prompted the reduction of efforts invested here.

Appropriateness of the Survey Methodology

The experience during the realization of the surveys demonstrated the pertinence of the suggested methodology to the objectives of the evaluation as well as to the basic conditions in the field. Approved instruments that are merged in the questionnaires and common methods of data evaluation provide for the quality criteria in research. The use of online questionnaires is well accepted in the research field and especially suited for a setting in distance education. The questionnaires allow for the integration of specific evaluation instruments for different facets of implementation, and with the full profile conjoint analysis they offer a way of data collection dissimilar from rating scales – a variation which can motivate seriousness and completion.

With reference to quality criteria, our methodology generates statements and substantiates decisions for a specific field of implementation, i.e. a single distance learning institution. Given these general aims of the evaluation, informative results for the process of implementation can be drawn from the pilot use, where only a small number of test persons participate in test scenarios and the survey. Here, one major limitation of our approach has to be mentioned: The methodology we presented in this chapter serves as a diagnostic instrument, not as a methodology for empirical research. However, given the latter intention, we consider the methodology as a pragmatic tool for evaluating expectations, needs and experiences of users when utilizing new and emerging educational technology. Since the theoretical and empirical foundations are well known and accepted in the field of user centered requirements evaluation, the methodology should allow for a transfer to others fields of technology enhanced learning, where implementation and diffusion of new technology in educational institutions is of concern. Of course, this approach focuses on utility as it is perceived by only one group of stakeholders, i.e. the students, in the process of implementation and diffusion. Other criteria, like technical and fiscal determinants, different views of stakeholders or cognitive factors, are not in the scope of this methodology.

In summary, all results show that the holistic approach illustrated in the evaluation method described here allows conclusions to be drawn that support a meaningful implementation of a new technology in educational processes. The pre-post design supports a differentiated examination of usability, acceptance and expected benefits. While usability undoubtedly has to be examined after practical use, two questionnaires enable to survey the factors that influence acceptance split on two measurement times. This enables the validation of a process model for technology acceptance regarding the intentions to use a new tool that are independent of practical experience with the tool compared to those factors that are dependent of insights acquired during practical use. However, there are only few alterations of attitudes before and after the practical use of a virtual classroom. This result provides an argument for the reliability of initial ratings of new principles, features and applications of educational technology. A rather short period of practical experience with the tool in real educational settings did not have measurable impact on the attitudes.

Nevertheless, expected benefits may change notably, as we have already stated for the use of simple polls and tests in synchronous learning sessions. Good use in educational settings may alter the expected benefit of certain features. This conclusion is confirmed by the above-mentioned predicted low relationship between students' willingness to use and their actual use, which could indicate that students would like to use virtual classrooms more but do not have the option, as the lecturer might not fully utilize its potential in the course. For this limitation of the methodology presented in this chapter, further research should investigate especially the long term effects of the efficient application of certain technologies in educational settings, as well as the consequences of inadequate use.

REFERENCES

Adesope, T., Adesope, O., & Ojeme, C. (2008). *Traditional and online forms of education: Proposing a common ground.* Paper presented at the E-Learn 2008, World Conference on E-Learning in Corporate, Government, Healthcare, & Higher Education of the Association for the Advancement of Computing in Education, Las Vegas, NV, USA.

Agarwal, R., & Prasad, J. (1999). Are individual differences germane to the acceptance of new information technologies? *Decision Sciences*, *30*, 361–391. doi:10.1111/j.1540-5915.1999.tb01614.x

Ajzen, I., & Fishbein, M. (1980). *Understanding attitudes and predicting social behavior.* Englewood Cliffs, NJ: Prentice-Hall.

Backhaus, K., Erichson, B., Plinke, W., & Weiber, R. (2005). *Multivariate Analysemethoden. Eine anwendungsorientierte Einführung [Multivariate analysis methods. an application-oriented introduction] (11th ed.)*. New York: Springer.

Chapman, D., & Wiessner, C. (2008). *Exploring engaged learning as a tool for evaluating Web conferencing.* Paper presented at the E-Learn 2008, World Conference on E-Learning in Corporate, Government, Healthcare, & Higher Education of the Association for the Advancement of Computing in Education, Las Vegas, NV, USA.

Chung, Q. B. (2004). *The sage on the stage in the digital age: In support of digital lecture higher e-learning.* Paper presented at the Proceedings of the 3rd European Conference on E-Learning, Paris, France.

Davis, F. D. (1989). Perceived usefulness, perceived ease of use and user acceptance of information technology. *MIS Quarterly, 13*(3), 318–340. doi:10.2307/249008

Davis, F. D., Bagozzi, R., & Warshaw, P. (1989). User acceptance of computer technology: A comparison of two theoretical models. *Management Science, 35*(8), 982–1003. doi:10.1287/mnsc.35.8.982

Diaper, D. (2004). Understanding task analysis for human-computer interaction. In N. Stanton (Ed.), *The Handbook of Task Analysis for Human-Computer Interaction* (pp. 5-48). Mahwah, NJ: Erlbaum.

Gediga, G., & Hamborg, K.-C. (1999). IsoMetrics: Ein Verfahren zur Evaluation von Software nach ISO 9241/10 [IsoMetrics: A Technique for Evaluation of Software in accordance to ISO 9241/10]. In H. Holling & G. Gediga (Eds.), *Evaluationsforschung [Evaluation Research]* (pp. 195-234). Göttingen, Germany: Hogrefe.

Goguen, J. A. (1996). *Formality and informality in requirements engineering.* Paper presented at the Proceedings of the 2nd International Conference on Requirements Engineering (ICRE '96), Colorado Springs, CO, USA.

Gollwitzer, M., Kranz, D., & Vogel, E. (2006). Die Validität studentischer Lehrveranstaltungsevaluationen und ihre Nützlichkeit für die Verbesserung der Hochschullehre: Neuere Befunde zu den Gütekriterien des 'Trierer Inventars zur Lehrevaluation' (TRIL) [The validity of students' course evaluation and its benefit for the improvement of academic teaching: New results on quality factors of the 'Trierer Inventory for the Evaluation of Teaching' (TRIL)]. In G. Krampen & H. Zayer (Eds.), *Didaktik und Evaluation in der Psychologie [Didactics and Evaluation in Psychology]* (pp. 90-104). Göttingen, Germany: Hogrefe.

Graham, C. R., & Misanchuk, M. (2004). Computer-mediated learning groups: Benefits and challenges to using groupwork in online learning environments. In T.S. Roberts (Ed.), *Online collaborative learning: Theory and practice* (pp. 181-202). Hershey, PA: Idea Group Inc (IGI).

Green, P. E., Krieger, A. M., & Wind, Y. (2003). Marketing research and modeling: Progress and prospects. In Y. Wind & P. E. Green (Eds.), *Marketing Research and Modeling: Progress and Prospects: A Tribute to Paul E. Green (1st ed.)* (pp. 117-140). Berlin, Germany: Springer US.

Guernsey, L. (1998). Colleges debate the wisdom of having on-campus students enroll in online-line classes. *The Chronicle of Higher Education.* Retrieved January 10, 2009, from http://chronicle.com/che-data/articles.dir/art-44.dir/issue-29.dir/29a02901.htm

Hassenzahl, M. (2001). The effect of perceived hedonic quality on product appealingness. *International Journal of Human-Computer Interaction, 13*(4), 481–499. doi:10.1207/S15327590IJHC1304_07

Hassenzahl, M. (2004). Mit dem AttrakDiff die Attraktivität interaktiver Produkte messen [Measuring the Attractiveness of Interactive Products with AttrakDiff]. In M. Hassenzahl & M. Peissner (Eds.), *Usability Professionals 2004* (pp. 96-100). Stuttgart, Germany: German Chapter of the Usability Professionals Association.

Hassenzahl, M., Burmester, M., & Koller, F. (2003). AttrakDiff: Ein Fragebogen zur Messung wahrgenommener hedonischer und pragmatischer Qualität [AttrakDiff: A Questionnaire for the Measurement of Perceived Hedonic and Pragmatic Quality]. In G. Szwillus & J. Ziegler (Eds.), *Mensch & Computer 2003: Interaktion in Bewegung [Human & Computer 2003: Interaction on the Move]* (pp. 187-196). Stuttgart, Germany: Teubner.

Hassenzahl, M., & Hofvenschiöld, E. (2003). 'If it doesn't feel right, who cares if it works?' oder: Muss Software mehr als nur gebrauchstauglich sein? ['If it doesn't feel right, who cares if it works?' or: Does Software have to be more than Useful?] In M. Peissner (Ed.), *Usability Professionals 2003* (pp. 135-139). Stuttgart, Germany: German Chapter of the Usability Professionals Association.

Hauser, J. R., & Rao, V. R. (2003). Conjoint analysis, related modeling, and applications. In Y. Wind & P. E. Green (Eds.), *Marketing Research and Modeling: Progress and Prospects: A Tribute to Paul E. Green (1st ed.)* (pp. 141-168). Berlin, Germany: Springer US.

Jung, M.-L., Loria, K., Mostaghel, R., & Saha, P. (2008). E-Learning: Investigating university student's acceptance of technology. *European Journal of Open, Distance and E-Learning*. Retrieved January 10, 2009, from http://www.eurodl.org/materials/contrib/2008/Jung_Loria_Mostaghel_Saha.htm

Kirakowski, J. (1996). The software usability measurement inventory: Background and usage. In P. W. Jordan (Ed.), *Usability evaluation in industry* (pp. 169-177). London: Taylor & Francis.

Landry, B. J. L., Rodger, G., & Hartman, S. (2006). Measuring student perceptions of blackboard using the technology acceptance model. *Decision Sciences Journal of Innovative Education, 4*(1), 87–99.

Martin, M. (2005). Seeing is believing: the role of videoconferencing in distance learning. *British Journal of Educational Technology, 36*(3), 397–405. doi:10.1111/j.1467-8535.2005.00471.x

Park, N. (2008). *User acceptance of e-learning in higher education: An application of technology acceptance model*. Paper presented at the annual meeting of the International Communication Association, Sheraton New York, New York City, NY. Retrieved January 10, 2009, from http://www.allacademic.com/meta/p14794_index.html

Prümper, J. (1997). Der Benutzungsfragebogen ISONORM 9241/10: Ergebnisse zur Reliabilität und Validität [The usability questionnaire ISONORM 9241/10: Results on reliability and validity]. In R. Liskowsky (Ed.), *Usability Engineering. Integration von Mensch-Computer-Interaktion und Software-Entwicklung [Usability Engineering. Integration of Human-Computer Interaction and Software Engineering]* (pp. 253-262). Stuttgart, Germany: Teubner.

Scott, P., Castañeda, L., Quick, K., & Linney, J. (2008). Synchronous symmetrical support: A naturalistic study of live online peer-to-peer learning via software videoconferencing. *Interactive Learning Environments, 16*(1), 1–16. doi:10.1080/10494820701772645

Simon, B. (2001). *E-Learning an Hochschulen. Gestaltungsräume und Erfolgsfaktoren von Wissensmedien [E-Learning in Academics. Design Scope and Success Factors of Knowledge Media]*. Köln, Germany: Josef Eul Verlag.

Swanson, E. B. (1988). *Information system implementation: Bridging the gap between design and utilization*. Homewood, IL: Irwin.

Venkatesh, V. (2000). Determinants of perceived ease of use: Integrating perceived behavioral control, computer anxiety and enjoyment into the technology acceptance model. *Information Systems Research, 11*, 342–365. doi:10.1287/isre.11.4.342.11872

Venkatesh, V., & Davis, F. D. (2000). A theoretical extension of the technology acceptance model: Four longitudinal field studies. *Management Science, 46*(2), 186–204. doi:10.1287/mnsc.46.2.186.11926

Wallace, F. L., & Wallace, S. R. (2001). Electronic office hours. A component of distance learning. *Computers & Education, 37*(3-4), 195–209. doi:10.1016/S0360-1315(01)00046-X

Wandke, H. (2004). Usability-Testing. In R. Mangold, P. Vorderer & G. Bente (Eds.), *Lehrbuch der Medienpsychologie [Textbook of Media Psychology]* (pp. 325-354). Göttingen: Hogrefe.

Chapter 21
Virtual Experiments in University Education

Rob J.M. Hartog
Wageningen University, The Netherlands

Hylke van der Schaaf
Wageningen University, The Netherlands

Adrie J.M. Beulens
Wageningen University, The Netherlands

Johannes Tramper
Wageningen University, The Netherlands

ABSTRACT

A university curriculum in natural and engineering sciences should provide students enough time and adequate facilities to design and carry out experiments and to analyze and interpret experimental results. However, laboratory facilities require considerable investments, and the experiments themselves can also be very expensive. Furthermore, in many universities, scheduling laboratory practice can be quite constrained. It is often difficult to realize learning scenarios in which experimentation is an integral component. Finally, alignment of actual laboratory classes and assessment is seldom satisfactory. This chapter discusses potential benefits of and limitations to virtual experiment environments or virtual laboratories in university education. In addition, we aim to identify feasible objectives for faculty-based projects on design, realization and use of virtual experiments in university education.

INTRODUCTION

Active learning and inquiry are generally promoted as important modes of learning (Bransford, Brown et al., 2003). In particular, there is a huge body of literature on inquiry and the 'nature of science' in secondary education (see for instance Bybee, 2002; Clough, 2002; Flick & Lederman, 2006; Jong, 2006; Linn, Davis et al., 2004; Linn, Lee et al., 2006; Lunetta, Hofstein et al., 2007; Reiser, Smith et al., 2001; Schwartz, Lederman et al., 2004; Slotta, 2004). Major elements of inquiry are scientifically-oriented questioning, prioritizing evidence, using evidence for explanations, connecting explanations to scientific knowledge, communication and justi-

DOI: 10.4018/978-1-61520-678-0.ch021

fication. Thus, inquiry is much more than 'hands-on' activity (Bybee, 2004; Clough, 2002). Bybee (2004) notes that in many educational discussions on inquiry in science classrooms the relationship between educational objectives and means and methods to achieve these objectives is confused. Several authors show that such confusion can also be found in much of the literature on general learning objectives of BSc/undergraduate laboratory classes in natural and engineering university curricula (Feisel & Rosa, 2005; Kirschner & Meester, 1988). Articulating goals into objectives and requirements for laboratory classes appears to be difficult. We largely attribute this to the gap between objectives that faculty wants to achieve and the actual feasibility of objectives given the practical constraints of traditional means and methods. Literature on desired learning objectives of laboratory practice in higher education is mostly in keeping with the characteristics of inquiry (see for instance Buntine, Read et al., 2007; Diederen, Gruppen et al., 2006; Domin, 1999a, 1999b; Johnstone & Al-Shuaili, 2001; Perreault, Litt et al., 2006). At the same time, specifically in university education, the components of inquiry are strongly orientated towards the curriculum's particular knowledge domain and particularly to knowledge of specific equipment, methods and materials (see for instance Ana R. Linde, 2006; Brown, 2006; Buntine, Read et al., 2007; Tânia M. F. Günther, 2003).

Laboratory classes in BSc/undergraduate curricula are often criticized. In particular, reviews suggest that these classes are often inefficient and isolated and incorporate the wrong tasks (Hawkes, 2004; Kirschner & Huisman, 1998; Kirschner & Meester, 1988). If students are not engaged in an integrated learning experience that incorporates all major components of inquiry, and if experimentation is detached from other scientific activities, students are unlikely to acquire an adequate image of the nature of science (see for instance Alberts, 2005). However, achieving integrated learning experiences in laboratory classes in BSc/undergraduate curricula poses big challenges for many universities. First, laboratories require considerable investments. Second, even when adequate laboratory facilities are available, limited laboratory capacity, limited instructor capacity and curricular constraints tend to create difficult scheduling problems. Additionally, experiments may require long lead-times, expensive materials and safety measures.

In many countries, laboratory facilities and subject matter expertise are scarce. For many prospective students in these countries, distance learning may be a good opportunity to receive higher education. However, the question remains: how can distance learning can go hand in hand with the need to enable and support students in developing experimental competencies?

Advances in information and communication technology (ICT) and wide spread awareness of computer games and sophisticated virtual reality environments for training, such as flight simulators, seem to promise at least partial solutions for these curricular problems. In addition, learning management facilities in most universities provide already direct access to digital learning materials. Most of these learning materials are presentational, but some of these materials enable students to carry out 'virtual experiments'.

Another relevant development of the last decade is the integration of ICT into many scientific disciplines. In fact, much of the experimental work in many natural and engineering sciences would now be impossible without ICT. Management and retrieval of a wide variety of data and data types is often an integral aspect of experimental work. In carrying out an experiment, the experimenter often controls experimental conditions by computer and the computer presents experimental results. In these experimental settings, the gap between a reality presented by a virtual experiment environment and a real experiment environment can be relatively small. For instance, a virtual control panel for a chemical reactor (Cartier, 2007) is not so different from a real control panel (see

Figure 1). Often, the learning experience of the student would not be different if the screen views presented by the computer came from a virtual phenomenon instead of coming from a real phenomenon. Another example is virtual microscopy (Araujo-Jorge, Cardona et al., 2004; Dee, Donnelly et al., 2007; Glatz-Krieger, Spornitz et al., 2006; Krippendorf & Lough, 2005; Lee, 2005; Stewart, Bevans-Wilkins et al., 2008; Weinstein, Descour et al., 2005). In much research, for instance in biology, the main user interface component of a microscope is now a computer screen (see Figure 4). Yet another development is the increased importance of computer simulation models in research activities in many disciplines. Because researchers are becoming more familiar with such developments, the step towards educational use of virtual experiment environments is likely to become easier. Finally, the advance of ICT over the last decades has reduced the costs of developing relatively simple educational virtual experiment environments.

These developments have given rise to research aimed at determining the educational effectiveness of specific aspects of such virtual experiment environments (see for instance Trindade, Fiolhais et al., 2002; Zacharia, Olympiou et al., 2008) and to projects primarily aimed at delivering and using virtual experiment environments and relating this use to specific learning objectives (Aegerter-Wilmsen, Bisseling et al., 2003; Busstra, Hartog et al., 2007; Diederen, Gruppen et al., 2006; El-Sayed S. Aziz, 2009; Hernández-Morales, Reyes-González et al., 2005; Holzinger, Emberger et al., 2008; Huang & Huang, 2003; Javier González-Cruz, 2003; Limniou, Papadopoulos et al., 2007; Liu, Amagai et al., 2001; Mzoughi, Herring et al., 2007; Raineri, 2001; Ramasundaram, Grunwald et al., 2005; Ribando, Richards et al., 2004; Schaaf, Vermue et al., 2003b; Sessink, Beeftink et al., 2006; Shin, Yoon et al., 2002; Sime & Kemp, 2008; Stone, 2007).

We characterize these projects as 'faculty-based'. The initial frame of reference for a faculty-based project is its direct educational context. When the abovementioned articles were published, most of the projects mentioned were not yet in a stage in which the scale of use in itself was the most important factor for sustainability. For this reason, we regard such efforts as 'pilot' or 'bootstrapping' projects. In projects like these, faculty searches for a feasible match between

Figure 1. The control panel for a virtual chemical reactor as shown in the picture is not very different from the control panel of a real chemical reactor

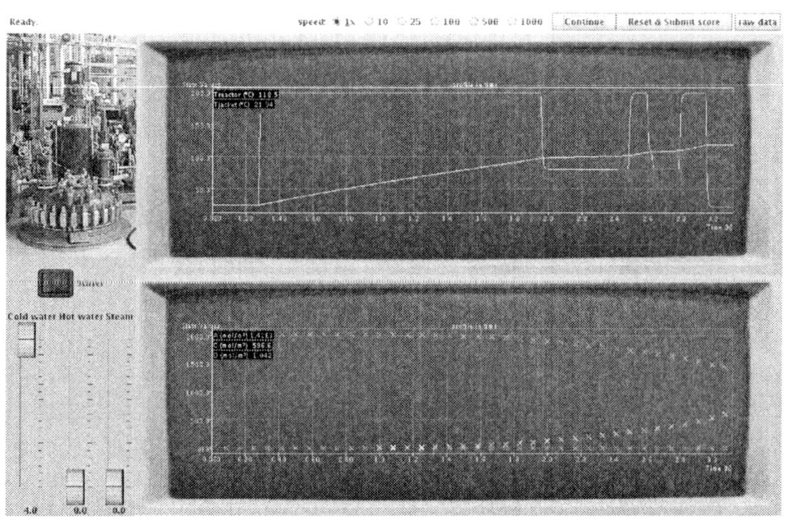

Figure 4. Screen dump of a virtual fluorescence microscope in Cell Biology: a VEE that enables students to investigate the relation between a DNA sequence and the function of the corresponding protein

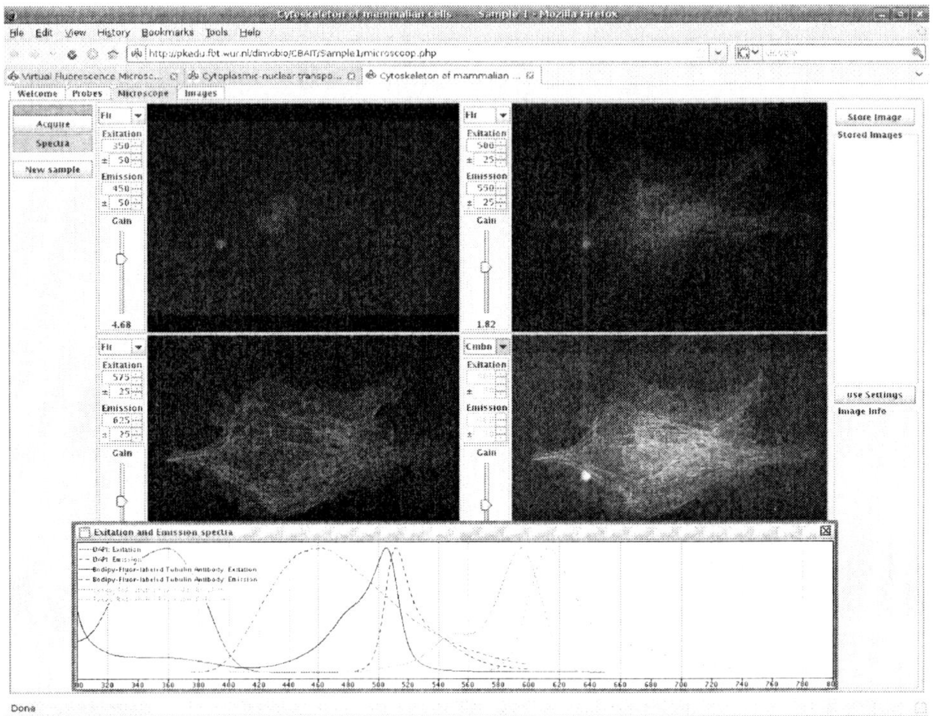

opportunities offered by new information technology and needs recognized by faculty. This is not a straightforward task. A comparative literature overview of real, virtual and remote experiment environments (Ma & Nickerson, 2006) reveals an unresolved debate on the feasibility of learning objectives in the different types of environment.

In this chapter, we aim to identify design requirements and feasible objectives for faculty-based projects on design, realization and use of educational virtual experiment environments in university curricula. From this point on, we will use the term 'Virtual Experiment Environment (VEE) to refer to any educational resource that enables students to design and/or to carry out virtual experiments and/or to process data, and to analyze and interpret results. It may be worth noting that within a number of scientific disciplines, for instance in biology, such environments are often coined as 'dry labs' as opposed to real laboratories, which are referred to as 'wet labs'. Other terms found in the literature are 'in silico' experiments as opposed to 'in vivo' and 'in vitro' experiments.

BACKGROUND

Widespread use of web-based virtual realities, computer simulations and computer games are making faculty increasingly aware of the possibilities of ICT for 'virtual laboratory practice' or 'virtual experiment practice'. For a university professor who wants to link theory and practice in a specific course using a VEE, a first step would seem to search the web for VEEs that would match the course's learning objectives. There are a range of learning object repositories, broker sites, portals and a number of websites that link to web-based educational resources or learning objects.

Examples are Ariadne, the BEN portal, CLOE, EDNA, GLOBE, iLumina, LORNET, MERLOT, NIME, OCWconsortium, Score, SMETE digital library, WikiMedia. (Ariadne-Foundation, 2007; Desire2learn, 2005; Education.au, 2008; GLOBE, 2008; LORNET, 2007; MERLOT, 2007; NIME, 2008; NSDL, 2005, 2008; OCWconsortium, 2007; SMETE-Open-Federation, 2003; SREB, 2006; WikimediaFoundation, 2008). These sites provide access to a variety of presentational and interactive educational resources. Many of the latter enable the student to prepare virtual experiments and/or to do virtual experiments. Moreover, interactive resources often support the student in processing, analyzing and interpreting experimental results. Many of these resources are Java, Flash or Shockwave applets or applications based on web-server technology. Interesting examples can also be found at (Christian, 2008; CUBoulder, 2008; Fendt, 2008; Huang, 2008; JHU, 2000).

Two Large-Scale Projects

In this subsection, we will briefly describe the Virtual Courseware project and the PhET project. Both have produced sets of interactive learning objects that hundreds of thousands of students have used.

The Virtual Courseware Project

Desharnais and Limson (2007) describe the Virtual Courseware project at California State University (CSU) and its history starting in 1988 when the NeXT computers for higher education were introduced. In successive years, CSU developed a variety of NeXTSTEP applications for science classes supported by major grants from the National Science Foundation (NSF) and matching CSU funds. When the web came into being one of these NeXTSTEP applications was redesigned as the Virtual FlyLab. This Virtual FlyLab enabled virtual genetic crosses and has been used by more than 665 thousand students since its introduction. Shortly thereafter, the Virtual Earthquake became available and more than 1.5 million certificates of completion have been issued to students. A commercial website started to make a series of 12 biology simulations available for college and high school students. Up to now, more than 500 thousand of these applet subscriptions have been purchased.

Desharnais and Limson (2007) describe ten current design principles for virtual courseware. We have transformed these principles into the following 'soft' requirements. The virtual courseware should

1. be aligned to available learning standards or objectives;
2. be web-based and easily accessible;
3. be interactive, intuitive and inquiry-based;
4. reinforce scientific methodology and critical thinking;
5. be open-ended with linear demonstration tours;
6. include simulated random experimental error;
7. enable recording and saving of experimental results;
8. incorporate assessment tools;
9. be customizable by instructors;
10. include on-line help and instructor documentation.

Below we will discuss these requirements in the context of initiating educational virtual experiment efforts in university education.

The PhET Project

A project that delivered about 80 educational computer simulations, which fall within our VEE definition, is the PhET project (CUBoulder, 2008). The following categories of desirable elements are common features of PhET simulations (Wieman, Adams et al., 2008).

- familiar elements (faucets, speakers et cetera).
- Visible representations of the invisible (e.g. 'showing' molecules).
- Multiple representations (e.g. density changes in a graph and in an animation).
- Multiple direct manipulable variables (e.g. with sliders).
- Instruments for quantitative measurements (measuring tape, clock, pressure meter).
- Animated graphics.

A final feature, which cannot so easily be presented in terms of desired elements, is "Distortion and simplification of reality to enhance educational effectiveness." In the same vein as with the Virtual Courseware, we might regard the common features of the PhET simulations as 'soft' requirements. Three other PhET requirements aim to make the simulations engaging. First, the user must have direct control in a dynamic visual environment. Second, challenges must be balanced (not too hard, not too easy), and finally, visual complexity must be balanced (arousing curiosity, but not overwhelming).

FACULTY-BASED DESIGN OF A VEE

Currently, we estimate the overall number of available VEE type resources for university education to be about a few thousand for all disciplines. For a specific course in a specific research discipline, it is often relatively difficult to find a VEE that fits one of the pertinent learning objectives. That said, the advance of web technology makes it increasingly attractive for faculty to invest efforts in small faculty-based projects on design and realization of a VEEs.

In the last decade, Wageningen University (WU) has invested considerably in the design, realization, implementation, use and evaluation of digital learning materials. Many of these learning materials are VEEs that extend or complement in some way the educational possibilities of existing laboratory classes, lectures and project-based learning scenarios. Experience in these faculty-based projects has taught us that formulating the design goal, articulating the goal into learning objectives and other requirements and defining corresponding assessments requires considerable effort. Formulating design requirements for VEEs is quite different from formulating design requirements for 'wet' laboratory classes. Every university professor in natural and engineering sciences knows and understands the constraints imposed by budgets and facilities on laboratory practice. In contrast, it can be a challenge for this same group to grasp budgets and constraints related to virtual laboratory practice. An important aspect of this challenge is assessing the feasibility of satisfying different sets of requirements given practical constraints of limited budget, time, available technology and infrastructure. It should be noted that these are well known issues in the literature on requirements engineering (see for instance Gilb, 1997; Sommerville, 2007).

Opportunities Provided by VEEs

Along some dimensions, virtual laboratory practice is much less constrained than real laboratory practice. For instance, VEEs allows students to carry out experiments that would otherwise be too dangerous (Cartier, 2007), would be too expensive or would take too much time (Sessink, Beeftink et al., 2006). In addition, students can access a VEE from any location that provides access to the web, while real laboratory practice is often restricted to the use of devices and materials, the availability of which is largely determined by the department's research activities. Moreover, for practical purposes, the capacity of the VEE may be regarded as unlimited. In short, the problem of scheduling VEE activities is almost unconstrained with respect to time, place and capacity. Finally, developments in web technology enable ways of collaboration and communication in VEEs that cannot easily be realized in real labs.

Shortcomings of VEEs

Along other dimensions, VEE practice is more constrained than practice in a real environment. For instance, it is often mentioned is that virtual laboratory practice does not yet enable students to practice psycho-motoric skills such as pipeting or handling glassware. More importantly, VEEs do not provide students with experiences that are needed to construct certain essential tacit knowledge. Kirschner and Huisman (1998) argue that this tacit knowledge is the most essential reason for providing 'wet laboratory' experience in many university curricula.

Learning to Handle Rapidly Changing Web Technology and Costs

Finally, constraints in the design space for a VEE are fuzzy and change quite rapidly over time. In addition, the actual design space for a specific VEE will depend on the available budget that can be invested. While this also holds true for real laboratory facilities, the rate of change of the costs of new possibilities is very different. Given a certain budget, VEE designers must learn to handle rapidly decreasing costs of available technology and a corresponding rapid expansion of the design space.

Examples of Faculty-Based Virtual Experiment Environments

Definitions of project goals and objectives are based on a match between means and ends. For faculty to be able to define the goal and objectives in the design of a VEE, they must have some grasp of the possibilities and limitations of VEEs. To provide some feeling for the design space of faculty-based VEEs, we now present a set of VEEs that we have realized and that have been in use for a number of years.

Cell Growth Virtual Experiments

An important part of the biotechnology curriculum at WU is learning how to design experiments to find values for certain model parameters. In particular, students have to become familiar with models related to microbial cell growth. When students learn how to design experiments it is important that they can carry out their experiments to see if these yield useful data. Cell-growth experiments usually take a long time to execute, so it is not always feasible to let students design and do many of these experiments.

The virtual cell-growth experiments lab was created to allow biotechnology students to design and carry out as many cell growth experiments as they like (Sessink, 2005). In this VEE (see Figure 2), students have to determine several organism-specific parameters for a common growth model. To begin, they already know the growth model on a theoretical basis and they know what equations the model consists of. However, they do not yet grasp what this means in practice. Each student determines the parameters for a different micro-organism. As such, students can design and execute growth experiments with 'their' micro-organism. They can choose to do batch or continuous experiments and can freely select the starting conditions for the experiment. They also have to decide at what times they want to take samples to determine the amount of biomass and glucose (higher accuracy implies higher costs). The VEE simulates random experimental error, which the student has to take into account when designing the experiment. From the data, the student can calculate the growth parameters for their micro-organism. During the setup and execution of an experiment, the student can ask for

Figure 2. The virtual microbiology laboratory enables students to design and carry out experiments to determine cell growth parameters

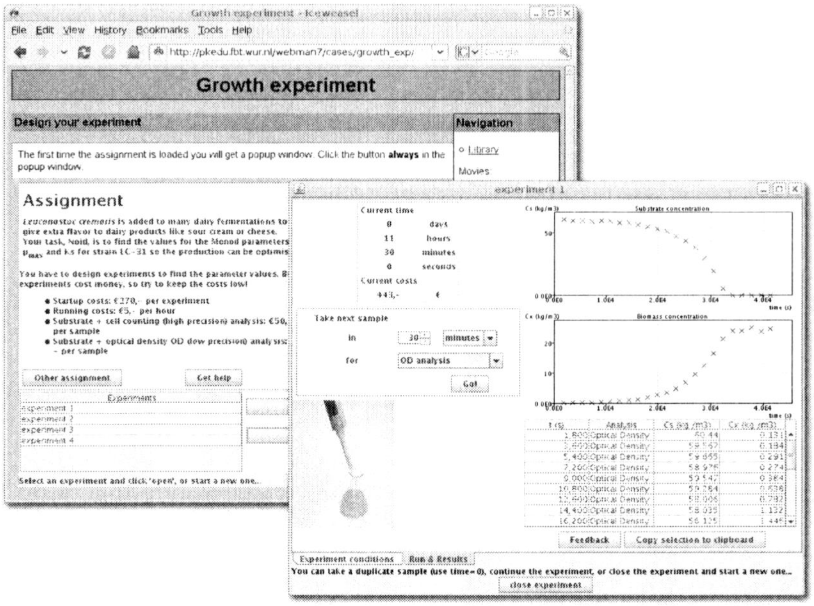

feedback on his experiment. The VEE also keeps track of the virtual costs the student accrues with his experiments.

Downstream Process Designer

The downstream process design environment designer (DSPD see figure 3) (Schaaf, Vermue et al., 2003a; Schaaf, Vermue et al., 2003b) enables the student to design and simulate an industrial protein purification process. The protein must be recovered from a watery mixture of micro-organisms, left-over nutrients and the desired product. The downstream process separates the desired product from the rest of the reactor contents. Design of a downstream process implies selecting and connecting unit-operations, such as centrifuges and filtration units, and setting control parameters such that specific requirements, for instance with respect to yield, purity and total investment costs, are satisfied.

In the biotechnology curriculum, students have to learn the features of commonly used unit-operations and how they function. The students also have to learn to design a downstream process using those unit-operations. The DSPD presents the student with a reactor with content and allows the student to select unit-operations, change the unit-operation order and alter the most important settings of each unit-operation. After each action, the student can ask the DSPD to simulate what happens to the different substances in the reaction mixture in each of the unit-operations and to calculate several performance indicators for the overall process. The student is free to try out different combinations of unit-operations, different orders of unit-operations, and different settings.

The DSPD contains a mathematical model for each unit-operation that calculates the out-flow of a unit based on the settings selected by the student and on the in-flow, which is the out-flow of the previous unit. The number of different orderings and settings is nearly infinite. Each unit-operation can signal potential malfunctioning due to inconsistent combinations of units and parameter settings.

Figure 3. Screen dump of a small part of a downstream process design environment

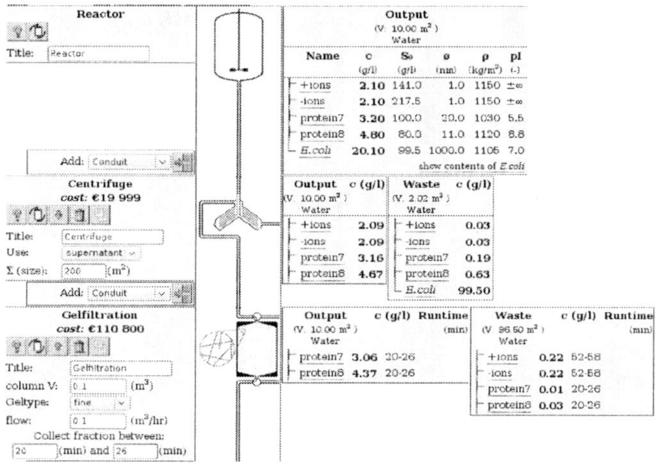

The DSPD is embedded into a set of digital cases about downstream process design. In each case, the student receives an assignment to design a downstream process that satisfies a specific set of authentic design requirements. These are, for instance, requirements with respect to purity of the product, cost and produced waste. After completing his design, the student is confronted with a change in the upstream process. This results in a different composition of the reactor content. To accommodate the reactor content's new composition, the student has to adjust or redesign the downstream process. At the end of each case, a student can access designs of other students who scored best on certain design requirements, such as the design with the highest purity or the lowest cost. This stimulates students to reflect on their own design and to invest additional efforts in improving it.

The Simple Cloning Lab (SCL)

The SCL (Hartog, Schaaf et al., 2003; Verver & Bisseling, 1997) is a website based on an internal model consisting of a number of tree structures. In this model, five 'virtual students' are each doing a cloning experiment. They have to clone DNA fragments into a bacterium and analyze a number of the resulting clones with various techniques. In general, a node in a tree structure represents one of the many situations at which a student can arrive. Most of these situations are the result of a typical mistake or a typical sequence of mistakes that a student can make. The role of the real student is to supervise the virtual students. Each node branches into a set of possible recommendations to the virtual student. The real student has to inspect the virtual students' intermediate and final results and their lab journals. Next, the real student can select a specific recommendation. This essentially implies following a hyperlink to a previous or next node. The VEE includes a web-based manual and a set of three-minute instructional movies on procedures. By advising the virtual students, the real student becomes acquainted with almost every elementary thing that can go wrong in the real lab.

The SCL has several important characteristics. First, in a few days any university teacher can master the web technology tools that are needed to build a website such as the SCL. Second, the SCL beautifully illustrates that learning materials like this capture much of an experienced teacher's so-called pedagogical content knowledge (PCK) (see for instance Abell, 2008; Shulman, 1987). Third, the underlying model is not a computational model but a data model. In this respect, the SCL is comparable to Interactive Screen Experiments (ISE) (see Kirstein & Nordmeier, 2007; Lambourne, 2007). In principle, an ISE is a virtual experiment the screen views of which are real images of real states of equipment or real states of a system. A student can interact with these images. Depending on the choices made by the student the next image or videoclip appears. Virtual microscopes are probably the simplest ISEs.

An Example of a Virtual Device: The Virtual Microscope

Practical work is also intended to enable the student to learn how to handle laboratory equipment. Virtual equipment might be suitable for this purpose (Neumann & Welzel, 2007; Waller & Foster, 2000). An example of a context in which training with virtual equipment makes sense because of limited availability of expensive real equipment and because of long experiment times is fluorescence microscopy in cell biology. In such an experiment, the DNA sequence for a fluorescent marker is connected to the DNA sequence for a protein of which we want to find out the function. A fluorescent microscope is then used to locate this marked protein (see Figure 4). The student has to set the wavelengths of the different light filters for the different imaging channels of the microscope. It is not realistic to have many students do this type of experiments in a wet lab practical because such a practical would take weeks and because of the limited availability of a fluorescent microscope. In a VEE, students can design a DNA construct and use the virtual microscope to study the effect of the construct in the cell. In this way, they learn the possibilities and limitations of the fluorescence microscope as well as how to handle such a microscope. Like a real fluorescent microscope, a virtual fluorescence microscope produces images on a computer screen and most of its settings can also be changed on the computer screen. Consequently, operating and using a real microscope is not so different from operating and using a virtual microscope (Dee, Donnelly et al., 2007; Krippendorf & Lough, 2005; Lee, 2005). It is important to note that the cell images are real images; it is just the relationship between parameter settings and images that is virtual.

Other VEEs Based on Qualitative Models

Over the years, a range of other VEEs have been realized that are partly or completely based on qualitative models. All of these VEEs are still in use (Aegerter-Wilmsen, Bisseling et al., 2003; Aegerter-Wilmsen, Coppens et al., 2005; Aegerter-Wilmsen, Janssen et al., 2005; Aegerter-Wilmsen, Janssen et al., 2006; Busstra, Hartog et al., 2007; Diederen, Gruppen et al., 2006; Wilmsen, Bisseling et al., 2002). One design pattern used in these VEEs requires the student to select a method, materials or object types, operations or equipment and experimental steps (Busstra, Hartog et al., 2007). The student then has to select an ordering of the experimental steps that makes sense. The sets of methods, materials, object types, operations, devices and experimental steps span a design space for the student's experiment. Within the design space, a set of constraints determines what complete experiments are possible. Some of these VEEs support the student in learning to build models in specific knowledge domains and to mentally construct concepts that are important in these domains.

HIGHLIGHTING MAIN GENERIC REQUIREMENTS

PhET simulations versus Virtual Courseware

Although the descriptions of the PhET simulations in (Wieman, Adams et al., 2008; Wieman & Perkins, 2006) are less explicit about the requirements (1) to (10) given for Virtual Courseware, we conclude from a trial of several PhET simulations that these simulations satisfy the Virtual Courseware requirements (2), (3) and (5).

Apart from a difference in focus (biology versus physics), the most important differences between the Virtual Courseware products and the PhET products are the following:

First, the Virtual Courseware products involve more goal-directedness in (1) and (8) and guidance in (4), (5) and (10) than the PhET simulations. In this respect, it is remarkable that both PhET articles mentioned above do not present the PhET simulations as 'inquiry-based'. Note however, that the difference is mainly a matter of degree of guidance and the form of guidance. The PhET simulations incorporate a good amount of hidden guidance in terms of simplified representations, limited sets of controllable variables and parameters, and limited value ranges. Second, the PhET simulations require visible representations and animated graphics, while these are much less emphasized in the description of Virtual Courseware.

Faculty-Based VEEs versus PhET Simulations and Virtual Courseware

Important differences between the faculty-based VEEs and the Virtual Courseware and PhET simulations are clearly influenced by funding: the former are only financed by the university while the latter two are far beyond the 'bootstrapping stage' and have been able to raise funds from a range of other organizations. External funding is likely to correspond directly to usefulness outside the direct faculty context. Moreover, funding by an organization such as the NSF is likely to reflect national standards. These conditions will act as constraints on the selection of topics and learning objectives within the subject matter, such as physics and biology for PhET and Virtual Courseware. In particular, the selection of topics and learning objectives largely fits a target population that would be classified as upper secondary education in Europe. In contrast to this, the learning objectives of faculty-based VEEs, such as the examples described above and the examples listed in the introduction, are usually from a much more specialized research field.

A second important difference with the Virtual Courseware project is that no standard learning objectives exist for faculty-based VEE-oriented projects. Rather, the possibility to realize a certain VEE may allow learning objectives to be achieved that faculty find important, but that are not yet supported in the curriculum. These learning objectives are likely to be related to faculty's research focus.

Adopting Virtual Courseware Requirements and PhET Features for VEEs

Apart from these differences, the requirements (2) to (8) of the Virtual Courseware project de facto also apply to our projects. We propose to adopt these requirements for faculty-based VEE development. However, the requirements have not yet been operationally defined. This implies that we do not yet have a procedure for determining if the requirements are satisfied. This especially holds true for requirements stating that the materials should be 'intuitive' and 'inquiry-based'. These requirements will still raise questions such as: "intuitive for whom?" and "how much guidance is compliant with the term 'inquiry-based'?"

As to Virtual Courseware requirement (9) 'customizability', it depends a little on how this is defined. All professors who use our materials believe it to be important that they can easily correct textual or numerical errors or errors in formulas – if there are any. We agree that the materials should enable this.

A requirement in the Virtual Courseware project that we did not adopt in our faculty-based VEEs is requirement (10) to incorporate on-line help and instructor manuals. Research based on interviews with students using PhET simulations provides evidence that we should avoid the need for help (Adams, Reid et al., 2008). In addition, we believe that most faculty just do not have the time to read additional information. Initial experience with faculty in other universities who use our material in their courses, seems to confirm this. Faculty would like a system that speaks for itself. This is indeed what the PhET simulations do.

In addition to the general direction given by the adopted Virtual Courseware requirements we propose to adopt the first six PhET features as well. We believe that, from a technical viewpoint, realizing these features becomes more and more within reach of faculty-based projects. Nevertheless, anyone who compares our materials with PhET materials will regard most of our materials as strikingly different from the PhET materials. This partly has to do with budgetary limitations but also with the PhET philosophy of 'distortion and simplification of reality'. However, because a discussion of the way in which PhET simulations distort reality, requires us to describe many of the PhET simulations and discuss decisions made by the PhET team, we consider this topic beyond the scope of this chapter.

Categories of Learning Objectives That Are Feasible in Faculty-Based VEEs

Most of the faculty-based VEEs that are currently being used support students in acquiring design competencies within a specific disciplinary context such as designing an industrial protein purification process or an experiment to estimate cell growth parameters. In addition, these VEEs support students in acquiring practical knowledge of unit operations, devices, equipment and methods, and, in particular, knowledge of the interfaces of these entities. Moreover, students mostly gain an initial understanding of the concepts that are basic to these entities. Finally, the SCL and the VEE for Food Chemistry even more so, also aim at making students aware of the benefits of planning their experimental work.

These learning objectives had not been realized with real laboratory facilities. At the same time, they prove to match well with technically simple possibilities of web technology. We relate this to the larger degree of freedom that can be realized in virtual environments in comparison to what is possible in real laboratory environments.

DIRECTIONS FOR FUTURE RESEARCH

Aligning Objectives, Activities and Assessment

Learning goals, objectives, learning environments, learning activities and assessment should all be aligned (Anderson & Krathwohl, 2001; Anderson, 2007; Biggs, 1999; Bransford, Brown et al., 2003; Joosten-tenBrinke, Bruggen et al., 2005; Linn, Davis et al., 2004). For any specific VEE, meaningful assessment is also important in order to generate confidence in its usefulness among faculty beyond the VEE's source of origin (Mayo, 2009). One type of assessment is performance assessment. Performance assessment is assessing if the student demonstrates competent behavior. VEEs that are used to acquire a certain level of design competence in a specific engineering context provide a natural basis for logging and analyzing the student's behavior and thus for performance assessment. In fact, each interaction used in the VEEs that we have discussed can be mapped onto one or more of the interactions in the QTI 2.0 definition (IMS, 2005) for question and test interoperability.

A problem in analyzing the student behavior logs is that the student's competence is not the only factor that determines the student's behavior. For instance, two students may each make a different, but correct, choice at any point. However, the choice of one student may be a lucky choice while the choice of the other student may bring this student into a 'difficult part' of the design space. Moreover, a little error of one student might bring this student in a difficult situation while a comparable error of the other does not. While this is a problem in many authentic performance assessment environments, semi-authentic design environments, such as the downstream processing environment, may provide opportunities to distinguish 'bad luck' components from actual design competence.

A more ambitious option is to aim at assessment of mental models. Jonassen and Cho (2008) propose to offer graphical tools for concept mapping and for the design of basic computer simulation models (such as Stella ™) to students in order to enable them to externalize their mental models and to provide a basis for purposeful interaction and assessment.

From Built-in Guidance to Knowledge Management

Guidance implies learning goals, learning objectives and knowledge of the students' knowledge. Insofar the VEE and the experiments within the VEE are intended to support achievement of specific learning goals and objectives, a certain degree of student guidance is often advised. It should be noted though that the degree of student guidance is a topic of debate in the literature (Hmelo-Silver, Duncan et al., 2006; Holzinger, Kickmeier-Rust et al., 2009; Kirschner, Sweller et al., 2006). One question is about finding a suitable balance between inquiry and direct instruction or guidance (Jong, 2006). However, in this section we want to focus on the question if guidance should be embedded in the VEE.

Embedded or built-in guidance (for instance feedback on the student's actions) assumes built-in assumptions of the student's state of knowledge. The more knowledge the VEE implicitly or explicitly requires, the smaller the population will be that can make effective use of this VEE unless the gap between assumed prior knowledge and actual prior knowledge is bridged. Bridging this gap is usually the role of the teacher. Instead of an approach based on built-in guidance that works only for a small homogeneous student population based on thorough research of the prior knowledge of the students in this population, a knowledge management approach is more generic. Such an approach may be based on automated recording of interactions between instructors and students. Whenever a student arrives in a situation in the VEE where (s)he needs guidance, the VEE should be able to contact an on-line instructor and ask for assistance or to link the student to a relevant 'piece of knowledge' that is based on or just identical with an earlier recorded interaction. Such an approach would be an extension of the 'active documents' paradigm (Heinrich & Maurer, 2000; Maurer, 2003). The concept of active documents enables identification and reuse of the users' relevant on-line interactions that have been initiated earlier in connection to a specific issue in a specific document. If applied to a VEE, such an approach would also make use of the state of the VEE from which the student asked for assistance. In addition, the knowledge management system might also make use of the student's history within the VEE.

The Advent of Computer Games and Immersive Interfaces

Finally, it is likely that technology of computer games becomes available for educational purposes and that human computer interfaces (see for instance Nintendo, 2008) will become increasingly advanced. Also, technology like The Cave™ that allows users to feel physically 'inside' a virtual reality will become more widely available and a growing number of educators has had a glimpse of its possibilities in educational context (Gallus Jr, Cervato et al., 2006; Limniou, Roberts et al., 2008). Thus, it should become within reach to incorporate such technology into VEEs and to integrate psycho-motoric skills in the student's learning experience. In addition, more advanced interfaces may enable the student to feel that (s) he is participating in a realistic experience. In comparing virtual, remote and real laboratories, Ma and Nickerson (2006) suggest that feeling of 'presence' may be one of the most essential dimensions that impact learning in one of these environments. They also note that differences between environments along this dimension are becoming smaller. Dede (2009) describes how 'immersive' interfaces can enhance education. In particular, immersive interfaces enable the student to shift between egocentric frames of reference (supporting concrete learning) and exocentric frames of reference (supporting abstract learning). In addition, 'immersed' students may learn to behave like scientists, working with other 'virtual' scientists in an environment that is a bit like 'second life' (LindenLab, 2005), but the design of which is based on the 'situated learning model'. Initial research suggests that knowledge learned in such an environment seems to be easier to apply in the real world, than knowledge learned in more traditional educational settings (Dede, 2009).

CONCLUSION

VEEs imply a huge potential for stimulating student activity in university education, enabling inquiry mode learning, and providing learning experiences that are better integrated in the curriculum than traditional laboratory classes. Currently, most faculty's primary interest in investing in VEEs does not stem from an intention to replace laboratory classes. Rather, they see a VEE as a complement to laboratory classes and other learning scenarios, such as lectures, group discussions and problem-based learning. In short, faculty hope that VEEs will provide more integrated learning experiences for their students.

Design, development, implementation and use of VEEs in higher education requires deep involvement of faculty. Formulating a feasible match of opportunities provided by web technology and needs of students and faculty in terms of requirements and learning objectives can consume considerable project resources. Such efforts can be reduced by adopting requirements and learning objectives formulated in other projects. Faculty-based projects can very well adopt most of desired features and the requirements that have proven their value in the PhET initiative and the Virtual Courseware initiative. Adopting learning objectives from the PhET or Virtual Courseware initiatives is less straightforward. A review of our own projects and literature on other faculty-based VEE-oriented projects in natural and engineering sciences shows that the resulting VEEs support students primarily in acquiring both conceptual and practical knowledge of equipment and methods as well as design competencies within the direct context defined by the VEE. In our view, these categories of objectives make sense and prove to be feasible in faculty-based projects. Carrying out design tasks, such as the design of experiments, the design of models or the design of industrial processes, is not yet an important part of many BSc/undergraduate curricula. We expect that there is a considerable hidden demand for VEEs that support students in learning such tasks. Focusing on this demand seems to be a good strategy for faculty-based projects.

We noted that finding a good balance between guidance and inquiry is a topic of debate in the literature. This might be one reason not to embed much guidance in the learning material but to regard guidance initially as a task for the teacher. A second reason why faculty should be wary of embedding much guidance into a VEE is that guidance has to rely on assumptions about the prior knowledge of the students. Unless every student in the target population has the same background it is unlikely that faculty can make accurate assumptions about the prior knowledge of each student. This becomes particularly relevant when one takes into account the global demand for higher education. The student population of many universities often consists of several or even many nationalities. Moreover, advances in web technology enable universities to provide new ways of distance learning in response to this global demand. However, most faculty will have difficulty to make correct assumptions about the prior knowledge of students from all over the world. Instead, a knowledge management approach that uses on-line interactions between teachers and students in order to generate guidance should be further developed. Research along this line would primarily aim at enhancement of infrastructural services. Such research would be relatively difficult to carry out within faculty-based projects.

Because the costs per student of a VEE are almost inversely proportional to the number of student users, faculty-based projects aiming to develop such VEEs are particularly interesting for large-enrollment courses. These might be on-campus or off-campus (i.e. distance learning) learning scenario's.

For other higher education contexts it is still difficult to find sustainable business models for VEE type learning environments and educational computer simulations (Wieman & Perkins, 2006). This problem has also been observed for instance for computer games with academic content (Mayo, 2009).

REFERENCES

Abell, S. K. (2008). Twenty years later: Does pedagogical content knowledge remain a useful idea? *International Journal of Science Education, 30*(10), 1405–1416. doi:10.1080/09500690802187041

Adams, W., Reid, S., LeMaster, R., McKagan, S., Perkins, K., & Dubson, M. (2008). A study of educational simulations part ii – interface design. *Journal of Interactive Learning Research, 19*(4), 551–577.

Aegerter-Wilmsen, T., Bisseling, T., & Hartog, R. (2003). Web based learning support for experimental design in molecular biology: A top-down approach. *Journal of Interactive Learning Research, 14*(3), 301–314.

Aegerter-Wilmsen, T., Coppens, M., Janssen, F. J. J. M., Hartog, R., & Bisseling, T. (2005). Digital learning material for student-directed model building in molecular biology. *Biochemistry and Molecular Biology Education, 33*, 325–329. doi:10.1002/bmb.2005.49403305325

Aegerter-Wilmsen, T., Janssen, F., Hartog, R., & Bisseling, T. (2005). Digital learning material for model building in molecular biology. *Journal of Science Education and Technology, 14*(1), 123–134. doi:10.1007/s10956-005-2740-3

Aegerter-Wilmsen, T., Janssen, F., Kettenis, D., Sessink, O., Hartog, R., & Bisseling, T. (2006). Introducing molecular life science students to model building using computer simulations. *Journal of Computers in Mathematics and Science Teaching, 25*(2), 101–122.

Alberts, B. (2005). A wakeup call for science faculty. *Cell, 123*(5), 739–741. doi:10.1016/j.cell.2005.11.014

Anderson, L. W., & Krathwohl, D. R. (2001). *A taxonomy for learning, teaching and assessing: A revision of bloom's taxonomy of educational objectives*. New York: Longman.

Anderson, T. R. (2007). Bridging the educational research-teaching practice gap: The power of assessment. *Biochemistry and Molecular Biology Education, 35*(6), 471–477. doi:10.1002/bmb.20135

Araujo-Jorge, T. C., Cardona, T. S., Mendes, C. L. S., Henriques-Pons, A., Meirelles, R. M. S., & Coutinho, C. M. L. M. (2004). Microscopy images as interactive tools in cell modeling and cell biology education. *Cell Biology Education, 3*, 99–110. doi:10.1187/cbe.03-08-0010

Ariadne-Foundation. (2007). *Ariadne*. Retrieved April 9, 2009, from http://www.ariadne-eu.org/

Biggs, J. B. (1999). *Teaching for quality learning at university*. Buckingham, UK: Open University Press.

Bransford, J. D., Brown, A. L., & Cocking, R. R. (2003). *How people learn: Brain, mind, experience, and school. Expanded edition.* Washington DC: National Academy Press.

Brown, L. R. (2006). Teaching technical and professional skills using a laboratory exercise: A comparison of two methods of plasmid preparation. *Biochemistry and Molecular Biology Education, 34*(3), 194–198. doi:10.1002/bmb.2006.49403403194

Buntine, M. A., Read, J. R., Barrie, S. C., Bucat, R. B., Crisp, G. T., & George, A. V. (2007). Advancing chemistry by enhancing learning in the laboratory (acell): A model for providing professional and personal development and facilitating improved student laboratory learning outcomes. *Chemistry Education Research and Practice, 8*(2), 232–254.

Busstra, M. C., Hartog, R., Kersten, S., & Műller, M. (2007, March). Design guidelines for the development of digital nutrigenomics learning material for heterogeneous target groups. *Advances in Physiology Education, 31*, 67–75. doi:10.1152/advan.00090.2006

Bybee, R. (Ed.). (2002). *Learning science and the science of learning*. Arlington, VA: NSTA Press.

Bybee, R. (2004). Scientific inquiry and science teaching. In *Scientific inquiry and nature of science* (pp. 1-14).

Cartier, J. (2007). *Chemical reactors and fermentors: Simulation and modeling*. Lausanne, Switzerland: Ecole Polytechnique Federale de Lausanne.

Christian, W. (2008). Physlets®. Retrieved January 15, 2009, from http://webphysics.davidson.edu/Applets/Applets.html

Clough, M. P. (2002). Using the laboratory to enhance student learning. In R. W. Bybee (Ed.), *Learning science and the science of learning: Science educators' essay collection* (pp. 85 - 96). Arlington VA: NSTA Press.

CUBoulder. (2008). PhET. Retrieved January 15, 2009, from http://phet.colorado.edu/

Dede, C. (2009). Immersive interfaces for engagement and learning. *Science, 323*(5910), 66–69. doi:10.1126/science.1167311

Dee, F., Donnelly, A., Radio, S., Leaven, T., Zaleski, M., & Kreiter, C. (2007). Utility of 2D and 3D virtual microscopy in cervical cytology education and testing. *Acta Cytologica, 51*(4), 523–529.

Desharnais, R. A., & Limson, M. (2007). Designing and implementing virtual courseware to promote inquiry-based learning. *MERLOT Journal of Online Learning and Teaching, 3*, 30–39.

Desire2learn. (2005). CLOE: Cooperative learning object exchange. Retrieved January 15, 2009, from http://cloe.desire2learn.com/

Diederen, J., Gruppen, H., Hartog, R., & Voragen, A. G. J. (2006). Design and evaluation of digital assignments on research experiments within food chemistry. *Journal of Science Education and Technology, 15*(3,4), 227 - 246.

Domin, D. S. (1999a). A content analysis of general chemistry laboratory manuals for evidence of higher-order cognitive tasks. *Journal of Chemical Education*, *76*(1), 109–111.

Domin, D. S. (1999b). A review of laboratory instruction styles. *Journal of Chemical Education*, *76*(4), 543–547.

Education.au. (2008). *Edna: Australia's free online network for educators*. Retrieved April 9, 2009, from http://www.edna.edu.au/edna/go

El-Sayed, S., Aziz, S. K., & Chassapis, C. (2009). Content-rich interactive online laboratory systems. *Computer Applications in Engineering Education*, *17*(1), 61–79. doi:10.1002/cae.20210

Feisel, L. D., & Rosa, A. J. (2005). The role of the laboratory in undergraduate engineering education. *Journal of Engineering Education*, *94*(1), 121–130.

Fendt, W. (2008). *Java applets on physics*. Retrieved April 9 2009, from http://www.walter-fendt.de/ph14e/

Flick, L. B., & Lederman, N. G. (2006). *Scientific inquiry and nature of science: Implications for teaching, learning, and teacher education*. New York: Springer.

Gallus, W. A. Jr, Cervato, C., Cruz-Neira, C., & Faidley, G. (2006). A virtual tornadic thunderstorm enabling students to construct knowledge about storm dynamics through data collection and analysis. *Advances in Geosciences*, *8*, 27–32.

Gilb, T. (1997). Towards the engineering of requirements. *Requirements Engineering*, *2*(3), 165–169. doi:10.1007/BF02802774

Glatz-Krieger, K., Spornitz, U., Spatz, A., Mihatsch, M., & Glatz, D. (2006). Factors to keep in mind when introducing virtual microscopy. *Virchows Archiv*, *448*(3), 248–255. doi:10.1007/s00428-005-0112-2

GLOBE. (2008). *Global learning objects brokered exchange*. Retrieved June 24, 2008, from http://www.globe-info.org/

Gonzalez-Cruz, J., Rodriguez-Sotres, R., & Rodriguez-Penagos, M. (2003). On the convenience of using a computer simulation to teach enzyme kinetics to undergraduate students with biological chemistry-related curricula. *Biochemistry and Molecular Biology Education*, *31*(2), 93–101. doi:10.1002/bmb.2003.494031020193

Günther, T. M. F., da Silva, F. C. M., & Günther, A. R. (2003). Titrant standardizations: A research-oriented laboratory practice. *Biochemistry and Molecular Biology Education*, *31*(2), 123–126. doi:10.1002/bmb.2003.494031020201

Hartog, R., Schaaf, H. V. D., & Verver, J. (2003). Elearning. *Agro Informatica*, *16*(4), 9–11.

Hawkes, S. J. (2004). Chemistry is not a laboratory science. *Journal of Chemical Education*, *81*(9), 1257.

Heinrich, E., & Maurer, H. (2000). Active documents: Concept, implementation and applications. *Journal of Universal Computer Science*, *6*(12), 1197–1202.

Hernández-Morales, B., Reyes-González, A., Barrera-Godínez, J. A., & Ingalls-Cruz, A. (2005). *A virtual laboratory for teaching transport phenomena*. Paper presented at the World Conference on Educational Multimedia, Hypermedia and Telecommunications 2005, Montreal, Canada.

Hmelo-Silver, C. E., Duncan, R. G., & Chinn, C. A. (2006). Scaffolding and achievement in problem-based and inquiry learning: A response to Kirschner, Sweller, and Clark. *Educational Psychologist*, *42*(2), 99–107.

Holzinger, A., Emberger, W., Wassertheurer, S., & Neal, L. (2008). Design, development and evaluation of online interactive simulation software for learning human genetics. *Elektrotechnik und Informationstechnik, 125*(5), 190–196. doi:10.1007/s00502-008-0537-9

Holzinger, A., Kickmeier-Rust, M. D., Wassertheurer, S., & Hessinger, M. (2009). Learning performance with interactive simulations in medical education: Lessons learned from results of learning complex physiological models with the haemodynamics simulator. *Computers & Education, 52*(2), 292–301. doi:10.1016/j.compedu.2008.08.008

Huang, C. (2008). Virtual labs interactive media Stanford University. Retrieved January 17, 2009, from http://virtuallabs.stanford.edu

Huang, C., & Huang, H. K. (2003). Interactive instruction of cellular physiology for remote learning. *Cellular and Molecular Biology, 49*(8), 1377–1384.

IMS. (2005). *Question and test interoperability*. Retrieved April 9, 2009, 2006, from http://www.imsglobal.org/question/index.html#version2.0

JHU. (2000). *Virtual laboratories*. Retrieved January 17, 2009, from http://www.jhu.edu/virtlab/virtual-laboratory/

Johnstone, A. H., & Al-Shuaili, A. (2001). Learning in the laboratory; some thoughts from the literature. *University Chemistry Education, 5*, 42–50.

Jonassen, D., & Cho, Y. H. (2008). Externalizing mental models with mindtools. In *Understanding models for learning and instruction* (pp. 145-159).

Jong, T. d. (2006). Computer simulations: Technological advances in inquiry learning. *Science, 312*(5773), 532–533. doi:10.1126/science.1127750

Joosten-Brinke, D., Bruggen, J. v., Hermans, H., Burgers, J., Giesbers, B., Koper, R., et al. (2005). Modeling assessment for re-use of traditional and new types of assessment. *Computers in Human Behavior*.

Kirschner, P. A., & Huisman, W. (1998). Dry laboratories in science education. *International Journal of Science Education, 20*(6), 655–682. doi:10.1080/0950069980200605

Kirschner, P. A., & Meester, M. A. M. (1988). The laboratory in higher science education: Problems, premises and objectives. *Higher Education, 17*, 81–98. doi:10.1007/BF00130901

Kirschner, P. A., Sweller, J., & Clark, R. E. (2006). Why minimal guidance during instruction does not work: An analysis of the failure of constructivist, discovery, problem-based, experiential, and inquiry-based teaching. *Educational Psychologist, 41*(2), 75–86. doi:10.1207/s15326985ep4102_1

Kirstein, J., & Nordmeier, V. (2007). Multimedia representation of experiments in physics. *European Journal of Physics, 28*(3), 115–126. doi:10.1088/0143-0807/28/3/S11

Krippendorf, B. B., & Lough, J. (2005). Complete and rapid switch from light microscopy to virtual microscopy for teaching medical histology. *Anatomical Record. Part B, New Anatomist, 285B*(1), 19–25. doi:10.1002/ar.b.20066

Lambourne, R. (2007). Laboratory-based teaching and the physics innovations centre for excellence in teaching and learning. *European Journal of Physics, 28*(3), 29–36. doi:10.1088/0143-0807/28/3/S03

Lee, S. (2005). Virtual microscopy:Applications to hematology. *Laboratory Hematology, 11*(1), 38–45. doi:10.1532/LH96.04059

Limniou, M., Papadopoulos, N., Giannakoudakis, A., Roberts, D., & Otto, O. (2007). The integration of a viscosity simulator in a chemistry laboratory. *Chemistry Education Research and Practice*, *8*(2), 220–231.

Limniou, M., Roberts, D., & Papadopoulos, N. (2008). Full immersive virtual environment CAVE™ in chemistry education. *Computers & Education*, *51*(2), 584–593. doi:10.1016/j.compedu.2007.06.014

Linde, A. R., & Garcia-Vazquez, E. (2006). A simple assay to quantify metallothionein helps to learn about bioindicators and environmental health. *Biochemistry and Molecular Biology Education*, *34*(5), 360–363. doi:10.1002/bmb.2006.494034052653

LindenLab. (2005). *Second life*. Retrieved January 16, 2009, from http://secondlife.com

Linn, M. C., Davis, E. A., & Bell, P. (2004). Inquiry and technology. In M. C. Linn, E. A. Davis & P. Bell (Eds.), *Internet environments for science education* (pp. 3 - 27). Mahwah, NJ: L. Erlbaum Associates.

Linn, M. C., Lee, H.-S., Tinker, R., Husic, F., & Chiu, J. L. (2006). Inquiry learning: Teaching and assessing knowledge integration in science. *Science*, *313*(5790), 1049–1050. doi:10.1126/science.1131408

Liu, D., Amagai, S., & Cordon, A. (2001). Development and evaluation of virtual labs and other interactive learning tools. *Biochemistry and Molecular Biology Education*, *29*, 163–164.

LORNET. (2007). *LORNET*. Retrieved February 5, 2009, from http://www.lornet.org/

Lunetta, V. N., Hofstein, A., & Clough, M. P. (2007). Learning and teaching in the school science laboratory: An analysis of research, theory, and practice. In *Handbook of research on science education* (pp. 393-441).

Ma, J., & Nickerson, J. V. (2006). Hands-on, simulated, and remote laboratories: A comparative literature review. [CSUR]. *ACM Computing Surveys*, *38*(3). doi:10.1145/1132960.1132961

Maurer, H. (2003). Important aspect of knowledge management. In *Important aspect of knowledge management* (pp. 245 - 254).

Mayo, M. J. (2009). Video games: A route to large-scale stem education? *Science*, *323*(5910), 79–82. doi:10.1126/science.1166900

MERLOT. (2007). *Multimedia educational resource for learning and online teaching*. Retrieved April 9, 2009, from http://www.merlot.org/merlot/index.htm

Mzoughi, T., Herring, S. D., Foley, J. T., Morris, M. J., & Gilbert, P. J. (2007). Webtop: A 3D interactive system for teaching and learning optics. *Computers & Education*, *49*(1), 110–129. doi:10.1016/j.compedu.2005.06.008

Neumann, K., & Welzel, M. (2007). A new labwork course for physics students: Devices, methods and research projects. *European Journal of Physics*, *28*(3), 61–69. doi:10.1088/0143-0807/28/3/S06

NIME. (2008). *National institute for multimedia education*. Retrieved February 5, 2009, from http://www.nime.ac.jp/en/

Nintendo. (2008). *Wii*. Retrieved April 9, 2009, from http://www.nintendo.com/wii

NSDL. (2005). *Ilumina educational resources for science and mathematics*. Retrieved April 9, 2009, from http://www.ilumina-dlib.org/

NSDL. (2008). *The BEN portal*. Retrieved April 9, 2009, from http://www.biosciednet.org/portal/

OCWconsortium. (2007). *Open courseware consortium*. Retrieved April 9, 2009, from http://www.ocwconsortium.org/

Perreault, E. J., Litt, M., & Saterbak, A. (2006). Educational methods and best practices in BME laboratories. *Annals of Biomedical Engineering*, *34*(2), 209–216. doi:10.1007/s10439-005-9030-3

Raineri, D. (2001). Virtual laboratories enhance traditional undergraduate biology laboratories. *Biochemistry and Molecular Biology Education*, *29*, 160–162.

Ramasundaram, V., Grunwald, S., Mangeot, A., Comerford, N. B., & Bliss, C. M. (2005). Development of an environmental virtual field laboratory. *Computers & Education*, *45*(1), 21–34. doi:10.1016/j.compedu.2004.03.002

Reiser, B. J., Smith, B. K., Tabak, I., Steinmuller, F., Sandoval, W. A., & Leone, A. J. (2001). Bguile: Strategic and conceptual scaffolds for scientific inquiry in biology classrooms. In *Cognition and instruction: Twenty-five years of progress* (pp. 263 - 305). Mahwah, NJ: L. Erlbaum Associates.

Ribando, R. J., Richards, L. G., & O'Leary, G. W. (2004). A 'hands-on' approach to teaching undergraduate heat transfer. In *Symposium on Mechanical Engineering Education (ASME IMECE '04)*, Anaheim, CA.

Schaaf, H. d., Vermue, M., & Tramper, J. (2003a). *Downstream process design.* Retrieved April 9, 2009, from http://pkedu.fbt.wur.nl/demos/design.html

Schaaf, H. d., Vermue, M., Tramper, J., & Hartog, R. (2003b). A design environment for downstream processes for bioprocess-engineering students. *European Journal of Engineering Education*, *28*(4), 507–521. doi:10.1080/0304379032000101863

Schwartz, R. S., Lederman, N. G., & Crawford, B. A. (2004). Developing views of nature of science in an authentic context: An explicit approach to bridging the gap between nature of science and scientific inquiry. *Science Education*, *88*(4), 610–645. doi:10.1002/sce.10128

Sessink, O. (2005). *Cell growth experiments.* Retrieved April 9, 2009, from http://pkedu.fbt.wur.nl/demos/growth.html

Sessink, O., Beeftink, R., Tramper, J., & Hartog, R. (2006). Virtual parameter-estimation experiments in bioprocess-engineering education. *Bioprocess and Biosystems Engineering*, *28*, 379–386. doi:10.1007/s00449-005-0042-z

Shin, D., Yoon, E. S., Lee, K. Y., & Lee, E. S. (2002). A web-based, interactive virtual laboratory system for unit operations and process systems engineering education: Issues, design and implementation. *Computers & Chemical Engineering*, *26*(2), 319–330. doi:10.1016/S0098-1354(01)00749-9

Shulman, L. (1987). Knowledge and teaching: Foundations of the new reform. *Harvard Educational Review*, *57*, 1–22.

Sime, J.-A., & Kemp, B. (2008). A 3D multi-user virtual laboratory: Is successful implementation enough? In *Proceedings of world conference on educational multimedia, hypermedia and telecommunications* (pp. 3539-3547). Chesapeake, VA: AACE.

Slotta, J. D. (2004). The web-based inquiry science environment (wise): Scaffolding knowledge integration in the science classroom. In M. C. Linn, E. A. Davis & P. Bell (Eds.), *Internet environments for science education* (pp. 203 - 231). Mahwah NJ: L. Erlbaum Associates.

SMETE-Open-Federation. (2003). *SMETE digital library*. Retrieved January 15, 2009, from http://www.smete.org

Sommerville, I. (2007). *Software engineering* (8th ed.): Pearson Education.

SREB. (2006). SCORE sharable content object repositories for education. Retrieved juli 31 2007

Stewart, J., Bevans-Wilkins, K., Bhattacharya, A., Ye, C., Miyazaki, K., & Kurtycz, D. F. I. (2008). Virtual microscopy: An educator's tool for the enhancement of cytotechnology students' locator skills. *Diagnostic Cytopathology*, *36*(6), 363–368. doi:10.1002/dc.20821

Stone, D. C. (2007). Teaching chromatography using virtual laboratory exercises. *Journal of Chemical Education*, *84*(9), 1488–1496.

Trindade, J., Fiolhais, C., & Almeida, L. (2002). Science learning in virtual environments: A descriptive study. *British Journal of Educational Technology*, *33*(4), 471–488. doi:10.1111/1467-8535.00283

Verver, J., & Bisseling, T. (1997). *Simple cloning lab*. Retrieved January 15, 2009, from http://fbt.wur.nl/bmt1/

Waller, J. C., & Foster, N. (2000). Training via the web: A virtual instrument. *Computers & Education*, *35*, 161–167. doi:10.1016/S0360-1315(00)00023-3

Weinstein, R. S., Descour, M. R., Liang, C., Richter, L., Russum, W. C., Goodall, J. F., et al. (2005). Reinvention of light microscopy: Array microscopy and ultrarapidly scanned virtual slides for diagnostic pathology and medical education. In J. Gu & R. W. Ogilvie (Eds.), *Virtual microscopy and virtual slides in teaching: Diagnosis and research* (pp. 9–35). Philadelphia, PA: CRC Press.

Wieman, C. E., Adams, W. K., & Perkins, K. K. (2008). PhET: Simulations that enhance learning. *Science*, *322*, 682–683. doi:10.1126/science.1161948

Wieman, C. E., & Perkins, K. K. (2006). A powerful tool for teaching science. *Nature Physics*, *2*(may).

WikimediaFoundation. (2008). *Wikimedia*. Retrieved April 9, 2009.

Wilmsen, T., Bisseling, T., & Hartog, R. (2002). Web based learning support for experimental design in molecular biology. In P. Barker & S. Rebelsky (Eds.), *Proceedings of Ed-media 2002*, Denver (pp. 2063-2068).

Zacharia, Z. C., Olympiou, G., & Papaevripidou, M. (2008). Effects of experimenting with physical and virtual manipulatives on students' conceptual understanding in heat and temperature. *Journal of Research in Science Teaching*, *45*(9), 1021–1035. doi:10.1002/tea.20260

Chapter 22
Virtual Learning Environment (ClassSim) Examined Under the Frame of Andragogy

Lisa Carrington
University of Wollongong, Australia

Lisa Kervin
University of Wollongong, Australia

Brian Ferry
University of Wollongong, Australia

ABSTRACT

ClassSim, an online simulation, was developed to support existing teacher education programs by providing pre-service teachers with access to additional classroom experience. This research reports on how pre-service teachers make use of the virtual learning environment to link knowledge from university coursework with field experiences and through this, we are able to examine affordances the virtual environment offers pre-service teacher learning. Andragogy provides a theoretical framework to review and make assumptions about the nature of learning for the participants. A comparative case study approach allows for in-depth comparison of two cohorts of pre-service teachers (first and final year) as they interact with the ClassSim environment.

INTRODUCTION

The ClassSim learning environment was conceptualised by Ferry, Kervin, Cambourne, Turbill, Hedberg, and Jonassen and was developed with the support of a large grant from the Australian Research Council. It was anticipated that the software would support existing teacher education programs by providing additional classroom experience through a virtual environment. This chapter looks to explore first and final year pre-service teachers' engagement with ClassSim though the lens of the assumptions of Andragogy as the nature of their learning is examined.

DOI: 10.4018/978-1-61520-678-0.ch022

BACKGROUND

Achieving balance between the theoretical and practical components of teacher education is a challenge currently facing those involved in the design, delivery and accreditation of teacher education (MACQT, 1998; Educational Training Committee, 2005). An unmistakeable gap is claimed between what teachers are taught during their university studies and what they are expected to do at the 'chalk-face' in their professional career (Cole & Knowles, 2009). The Ramsey (2000) review of teacher education in New South Wales, Australia highlighted that pre-service teachers do not understand how classroom practice produces effective student learning, and Kervin and Turbill (2003) found that many beginning teachers find it difficult to adjust to classroom life because they are often unable to retrieve important theoretical knowledge when they need it. Therefore it seems reasonable to suggest that teacher education should have stronger links between field experience and theoretical studies.

There is a considerable body of literature supporting the claim that there is a need to integrate these aspects of pre-service teacher education to address the perceived irrelevance of theory to students (for example Brady, Seagal, Bamford, & Deer, 1998; Darling-Hammond, 1999; Lanier & Little, 1986; Sorin, 2004), thus enabling pre-service teachers to gain a better understanding of the theory/practice nexus (MACQT, 1998). An early integration of field experiences would enable pre-service teachers to gain a better understanding of the theory/practice nexus (MACQT, 1998). Further, a philosophy of reflective practice will help pre-service teachers articulate the theory to practice relationship (Brady, Seagal, Bamford, & Deer, 1998).

Herrington and Oliver (2000) have suggested that educators need to look for ways to create authentic environments that allow learners to develop integrated knowledge that is retrievable in real life settings in addition to tradition field experiences. Modern technologies, such as simulations, have the potential to provide pre-service teachers with a safe authentic environment in which to explore possibilities and experiment with decision-making opportunities while drawing upon their theoretical and practical knowledge before entering a classroom. Researchers such as Reigeluth and Schwartz (1989) and Breuer and Kummer (1990) argue that a virtual environment such as a simulation enables learners to master cognitive processing skills by allowing them to apply the theory of their training within a realistic environment. Therefore the skills that are acquired during the use of a simulation can transfer to real life situations. Further, Gatto (1993:154) contends that "students who use simulations, manipulate variables and so on would be better prepared to perform in real situations than those students who rely on other instructional media, such as text, which can only provide information and hints on how to do something". Thus, simulations have the potential to enhance the connections made between theory and what this might look like in practical situations. Furthermore it can be argued that learners who use simulations in their training may be better equipped to transfer the knowledge and skills they acquired during their education to a real life scenario.

Virtual Learning Environment

ClassSim (Faculty of Education, 2005, University of Wollongong) enables the user to assume the role of a teacher in a virtual classroom. Throughout the running time of the simulation the user is required to make decisions about the structure and sequence of a teaching block, classroom management and respond to individual students. A number of design features have been included: the incorporation of targeted students, an embedded reflective tool called the 'Thinking Space', support materials and decision-making opportunities.

The targeted students were designed to represent the more challenging students teachers are often faced with in the classroom, while also being representative of the range of needs and abilities of students within a typical classroom. 'Student Updates' are available throughout the simulation, usually during and after a behaviour management incident or a significant teaching moment. Figure 1 shows an example of a student update, designed to provide feedback on the how the approach taken by the user has impacted upon a particular targeted student.

The embedded cognitive tool, the 'Thinking Space', provides a framework in which the user can reflect upon issues within the virtual classroom, articulate their rationale at decision points, begin to identify underlying influences that affect their use of the virtual learning environment, and keep a record of their professional learning. Key questions and prompts are provided to help users to articulate, justify and reflect on the decisions they make. Figure 2 presents the 'Thinking Space' tool.

Support materials are available at differing times, dealing with a wide range of topics referred to throughout the simulation. Summaries include links to websites, textbooks and other literature. The summaries include information about a number of teaching strategies, classroom management techniques and professional terminology used throughout the simulation. The support materials were incorporated into the design of the virtual learning environment to inform and support the pre-service teachers in making connections between the 'theory' and the practice of teaching as they make decisions within the simulation. Figure 3 provides an example of support material found within ClassSim.

Throughout the running time of ClassSim the user encounters a number of decision-making opportunities. These are concerned with classroom management, student behaviour, and teaching and learning decisions. When this occurs the user is asked to select from various options in order to

Figure 1. 'Student Update' of Harley (© 2009 Faculty of Education, University of Wollongong. Used with permission)

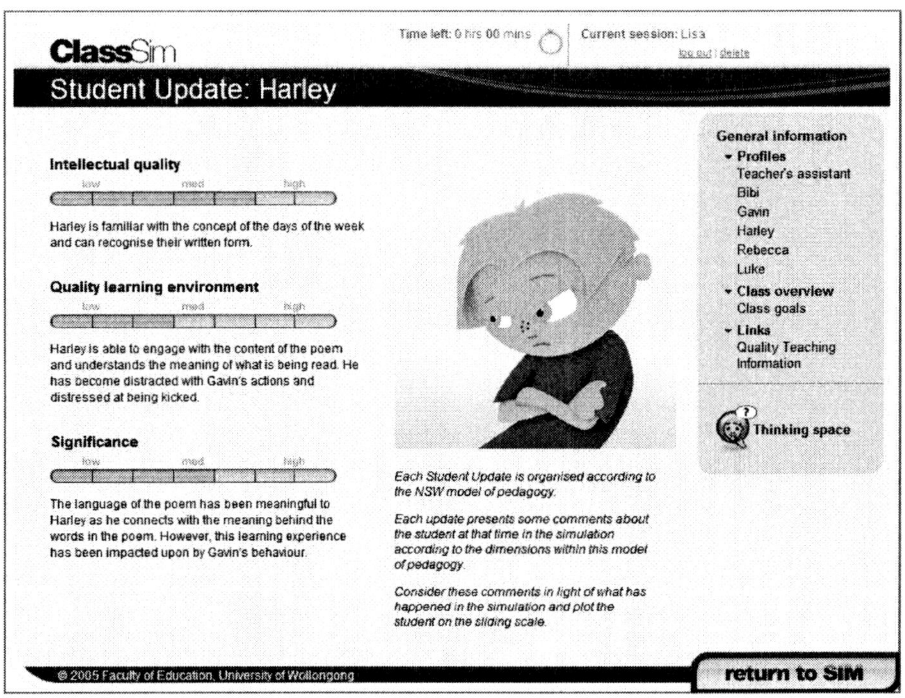

Figure 2. 'Thinking Space' (© 2009 Faculty of Education, University of Wollongong. Used with permission)

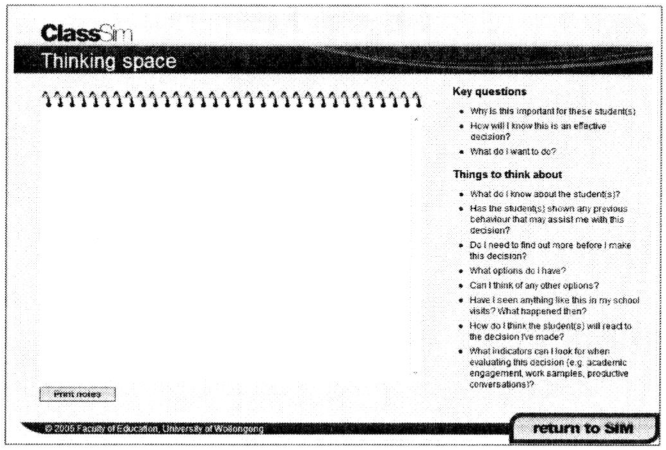

proceed. Overall, this virtual learning environment has the typical advantages of simulations such as the ability to allow users to slow down or accelerate classroom events, revisit and reflect on critical decision points and replay events in the light of new understandings.

Andragogy as the Theoretical Framework to Examine Pre-Service Teacher Learning

Andragogy has been defined as the "art and science of helping adults learn" (Knowles, 1990:54), and thus works to professionally guide adult learners with the ultimate aim being to facilitate change in an adult person (Knowles, Holton, and Swanson, 1998:60). Overall, andragogy is "a way of thinking about working with adult learners" (Merriam & Brockett, 1997:135). Further, andragogy has "exercised a significant influence on the practice of adult education" (Pratt, 1988:160) and it is claimed to be the "best-known theory of adult learning" (Merriam & Caffarella, 1991:249), as it is "synonymous with the education of adults" (Pratt, 1988:160). For the past 40 years, andragogy has become a dominant adult education framework. It has been described as "the preeminent and persistent practice-based, instructional method" (Rachal, 2002:211), a "guiding principle on how best to educate adults" (Beder & Carrea, 1998:75), and, a "set of guidelines for effective instruction of adults" (Feuer & Gerber, 1988:35).

The purpose of this inquiry was to investigate how pre-service teachers make use of a virtual learning environment provided by an online simulation to link knowledge from university coursework with field experiences. Therefore Andragogy provided a framework in which the learning of the pre-service teacher participants can be reviewed and assumptions about their learning drawn. Adult learning is influenced by the five main assumptions of Andragogy, which are interrelated. These include:

- Self-Concept: As a person matures, he or she moves from dependency to self-directness.
- Experience: Adults draw upon their experiences to aid their learning.
- Readiness: The learning readiness of adults is closely related to the development tasks of his or her social roles.
- Orientation: As a person learns new knowledge, he or she wants to apply it

Figure 3. Summary of parent helpers in the classroom (© 2009 Faculty of Education, University of Wollongong. Used with permission)

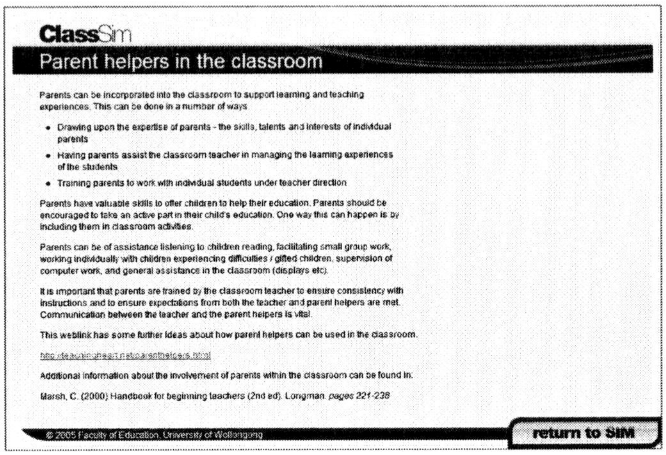

immediately in problem solving. Thus an adult is more problem centered than centered in learning (Knowles, 1980:44-45).

- Motivation (Later added): As a person matures, he or she receives their motivation to learn from internal factors (Knowles, 1984:9-12).

These five main assumptions are interrelated and work together to account for how and why an adult learner acquires new information. Figure 4 represents these connections.

In this inquiry, the five assumptions of Andragogy work together to explain the learning of the pre-service teachers and how this learning relates to their engagement with the virtual learning environment provided by ClassSim, their university coursework, field experiences, previous experiences, and other factors that may influence their learning (see Figure 5).

Overview of Inquiry's Methodology

A comparative case study approach was adopted for the research, utilising semi-structured interviews, observations and the collection and analysis of artefacts as data collection procedures. This design enabled the researchers to focus upon and compare two groups of pre-service teachers (first and final year students) enrolled in one Australian university, whilst taking into consideration the contextual conditions (such as the participants' field experiences).

Data collection began with the use of a demographic survey of all 187 students enrolled in the first year and 150 students enrolled in the final year of a teacher education undergraduate degree to enable purposive selection of the participants. Observations of the focus pre-service teacher participants were collected as they engaged with the software and interacted with their peers. Artefacts ('Thinking Space' entries) and semi-structured interviews occurred subsequent to interaction with ClassSim. The participants continued with their usual university coursework and field experiences, during which the researchers collected the participant reflections and conducted further semi-structured interviews. The first year pre-service teacher data was collected during the first semester of the first year, while the final year pre-service teacher data was collected during the final semester of their degree.

The data were coded (open and axial) and categorised according to emerging themes within data.

Figure 4. Assumptions of andragogy

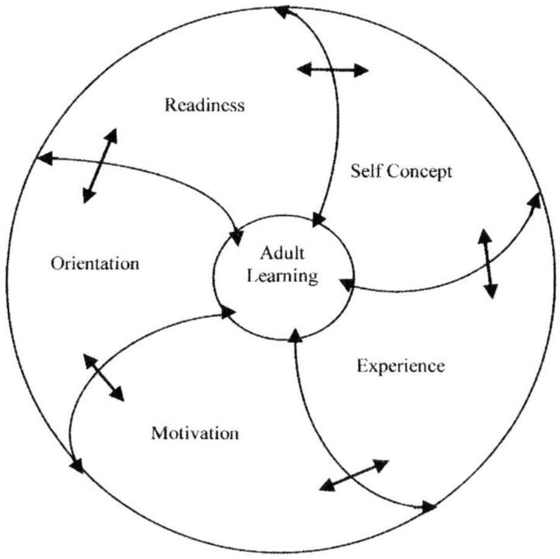

Figure 5. Pre-service teacher learning in relation to andragogy

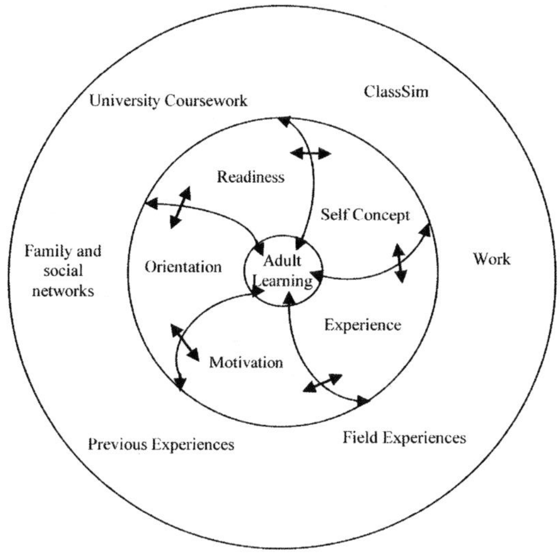

Open coding was used to identify broad concepts such as: purpose, reflection, theory to practice connections, and design. This was followed by axial coding to explore patterns and converging trends in the data leading to possible themes including: readiness, orientation, motivation, experience and self concept. Andragogy provided a lens to compare and contrast the two case studies (first and final year pre-service teachers).

THE ASSUMPTIONS OF ANDRAGOGY EXAMINED IN CONNECTION WITH EXAMPLES OF PRE-SERVICE TEACHER LEARNING

In this inquiry, the five assumptions of Andragogy ('Readiness', 'Orientation', 'Motivation', 'Experience', and 'Self Concept') work together to explain the learning of the pre-service teachers and how this learning relates to their engagement with the virtual learning environment provided by the ClassSim, their university coursework, field experiences, previous experiences, and other factors that may influence their learning. These assumptions while already introduced, will be described and discussed further with sub-themes that emerged from data analysis.

Readiness

"Adult's become ready to learn those things they need to know and be able to do in order to cope effectively with their real-life situations" (Knowles, Holton & Swanson, 1998:67). A critical implication of this assumption is the importance of timing. Knowles, Holton, and Swanson (1998) state that the timing of learning experiences need to coincide with developmental tasks. Merriam and Caffarella (1999:330) explain that an individual's personal development into readiness "is both inherent in and an outcome of the process" of learning. Thus, an adult's readiness to learn is a developmental process which depends on the individuals' exposure to real-life situations which force them to act and learn. 'Readiness' was identified in the data from both cases in a number of ways including purpose, value to learning, changing role, and timing.

Purpose

The findings of this inquiry reveal that the majority of first year pre-service teachers found ClassSim to be an important tool in preparing them for their first field experience. This finding was reinforced by the findings of the final year pre-service teachers who suggested that ClassSim was an unnecessary tool in preparing them for their final field experience and that the ClassSim was probably more suitable for first year pre-service teachers as a possible introduction to the practicalities of a classroom. This may be due to the fact that the first year pre-service teachers had little to no experience working in a classroom and their engagement with ClassSim provided them opportunity to take on the role of a teacher for the first time, thereby somewhat preparing them for their impending first field experience. In contrast the final year pre-service teachers have been on two full field experiences and have had a number of occasional visits to schools throughout their degree, and thus felt prepared to undertake their role as student-teacher during their final field experience.

As the first year pre-service teachers identified themselves as having little to no experience working with children in a classroom, they utilised their engagement with ClassSim to experiment with decision making opportunities and the consequences of these decisions. "I think it has been really helpful, definitely, before we go out into schools. Particularly with people like me who hadn't been dealing with the kids as much as other people might have in classrooms" (I_Michael_24/07). It also appears as though some of the final year pre-service teacher's were reminded of the consequences of decisions made whilst engaging with ClassSim. Thus the findings suggest that ClassSim was a valuable tool in preparing the first year pre-service teachers for the decisions they may be faced within a 'real' classroom and as a reminder to final year pre-service teachers of the consequences a decision made. Therefore the data indicates that the decision making opportunities of ClassSim played an important role in the first and final year pre-service teachers' preparation for their impending field experiences.

Value to Learning

The findings of the first year pre-service teachers suggest that access to the virtual learning environment's support material enabled them to make valuable links to their coursework and associated readings. The findings indicate that terminology such as 'literacy block' was one example of this, where a first year pre-service teacher was able to better understand what a 'literacy block' is and how it might look in a Kindergarten class through her engagement with the scenarios presented and access to the summary material. This was reinforced by interview data collected from a final year pre-service teacher who suggested a first year pre-service teacher would have been able to make valuable connections between a subject focusing on 'language and literacy' for primary aged children and ClassSim as a virtual practical example with supportive literature. "I wouldn't know how to do it [design a teaching block] at the moment but with the ClassSim and the tutorials and the lectures that we're doing at the moment I will develop the skills to do so" (I_Daniel_20/03). Therefore the findings indicate that the support material available throughout the virtual learning environment enabled the users to make valuable connections to their current and past subject content via the scenarios presented and the additional support material available.

In contrast, the final year pre-service teachers were unable to make valuable connections between their university coursework and their engagement with ClassSim. This may be due to the knowledge they have accumulated throughout their degree and the quality of their previous field experiences. This knowledge and experience may be too advanced to make any valuable connections. This is not to suggest that they did not make any connections, rather it is the value of these connections that are in question with regards to the stage of learning the final year pre-service teachers are at and/or the development of their professional identity.

Furthermore, the findings indicate that some of the final year pre-service teachers did find their engagement with ClassSim to be valuable to their learning. This came in the form of ideas for their future lesson plans. The final year pre-service teachers may have identified this as being beneficial as they were in their final year of their degree and the prospect of teaching their own class seems a more tangible experience. "It gave me great ideas for doing things. I thought that was the most valuable part of the whole experience... It's good for professional development. Because you have to share ideas, you have to pitch other people's things" (I_Isabella_20/08). Thus, it was found that the lesson ideas were more advantageous to their present learning needs and future careers as teachers. Overall, the findings suggest that the episodes (or lessons) presented in ClassSim were valuable resources for the final year pre-service teachers.

Changing Role

The first year pre-service teachers were in the initial stages of progressing from the role of a student to that of a teacher. It appears as though this was due to the first year pre-service teachers' lack of experience in the role of a teacher, and more importantly their previous role as a student for the entirety of their education (as the majority of the first year participants have proceeded on to tertiary studies straight from high school). Thus, moving from the role of a student to that of a teacher is an important step in the development of a professional identity. "I thought it [ClassSim] was really good because I'd never been in like a classroom situation when I'd been a teacher so it's just like a different angle" (I_Rachael_29/03). The lack of evidence suggesting that the final year pre-service teachers were progressing from a student to a teacher emphasises this point, as the final year pre-service teachers have had some experience as a teacher whilst of field experience and have begun developing their professional identity. Overall, the first year pre-service teachers indicated that engaging with ClassSim enabled them to experience the role of a teacher for the first time and thus assisting them to better understand the role of a teacher.

Timing

The findings indicate that although both the first and the final year pre-service teachers' engagement with ClassSim coincided with their stage of learning and induced their learning in particular areas, these were quite different in nature. The findings of the first year pre-service teachers reveals that they utilised their engagement with ClassSim to gain a glimpse into the workings of a classroom and thus were induced to learn more about the role of a teacher in regards to decision making and interacting with children. In contrast, the final year pre-service teachers were induced to learn about aspects of the role of a teacher in more depth. For example, one final year participant was encouraged to learn more about the emotional affect of her decisions upon her students, whereas a first year participant was induced to learn more about interacting with children. This may be because the first year pre-service teachers have limited knowledge about the practicalities of a classroom and thus are at a less advantaged stage of their learning. Therefore many of the first year pre-service teachers may have utilised a more exploratory approach when engaging with the virtual learning environment, whereas the majority of the final year participants appeared to have adopted a more in-depth approach.

Orientation

'Orientation' assumes an adult learner is task or problem-orientated in their learning. Thus, as an adult learns new knowledge, he or she wants to apply it immediately through problem solving. 'Orientation' was identified in the data of both cases and will be discussed according to the relevant scenarios presented in ClassSim and the participants' identification of their need for new knowledge.

Relevant Scenarios

The findings suggest that both the first and final year pre-service teachers were able to make connections between what they were learning in ClassSim and how it applies to their future career as a teacher. The first year pre-service teachers found their engagement with the virtual learning environment to present them with relevant, real-life examples of a classroom. They made comment that ClassSim prepared them for the amount of interruptions a teacher might face during a typical day thus reinforcing their understanding of time management. They also indicated ClassSim provided them with a tangible scaffold on how a teaching block might be structured. Overall, the first year pre-service teachers explained that ClassSim was a relevant learning tool as it enabled them to gain insight about the role of a teacher and the scenarios they may encounter. In regards to the findings of the final year pre-service teachers, some of the participants found ClassSim to be a good representation of a 'real' classroom. They made comment on the use of authentic resources – specifically images and work samples for the virtual children, comparing them to work samples seen on field experience.

Although both cohorts of participants found the ClassSim to present relevant and real-life scenarios, their comments are quite different. It appears as though the first year pre-service teachers may have identified similarities on a more superficial level, looking at the overall role of a teacher, the final year pre-service teachers have identified similarities on a deeper level, focusing upon the role of a teacher in regards to understanding individual children's needs and the teaching resources used on a day-to-day basis. This can be attributed to their developmental stage. The first year pre-service teachers are still in their initial stages of understanding teaching and developing a professional identity, and thus used ClassSim to gain a 'big picture' understanding of their future career. Alternatively, the final year pre-service teachers have had two and a half years of field experiences and university coursework, and thus have had more time to gain understanding of the role of a teacher and develop a professional identity. Therefore, it appears as though their use of the ClassSim was to improve upon their previous understandings and delve deeper into the practicalities of a classroom.

Need for New Knowledge

The findings of both cohorts of participants indicate that engagement with the virtual learning environment enabled the pre-service teachers to identify areas of their learning that need further development. The first year participants suggested that they needed to gain a better understanding of the role of a teacher. "I gained knowledge of how little I knew and it just made me aware of the facets of teaching… more than anything, it was just sort of a real shock at the time about how holistic you're teaching has to be rather than just education based" (I_Kellie_23/07). Another finding from the first year pre-service teachers was that they felt unprepared to make a number of decisions within the virtual classroom. This may be due to their lack of experience and knowledge about teaching and the role of a teacher. As these participants are first year university students, it was expected that they have limited knowledge and experience in these areas. Thus, it appears that engagement with ClassSim served as an introductory tool for new pre-service teachers to gain a 'big picture' look at a classroom and the teacher's role within it, and subsequently identify areas of their learning that they feel is important to their immediate and future learning needs.

The final year pre-service teachers also identified areas in their learning that require development as a result of engaging with ClassSim.

These areas were predominately concerned with the integration students with specific needs. For example, "I don't have any experience working with children with a second language in any capacity even when I was at school. I think for me that was a really big highlight. You know how do I deal with this? If I've got a child in the class that can't speak the language or parents can't speak the language how do I make it relevant for them?" (I_Marc_13/11). This suggests that these final year pre-service teachers have had limited experience working with individual children during their field experience, possibly due to the school contexts within the area, and ClassSim has encouraged them to consider these students as possible students in their future classrooms. Another interpretation of the findings may be that the final year pre-service teachers feel confident in their ability to undertake the role of a teacher during a teaching block, and have used their engagement with ClassSim to look more closely at the needs of individual students and how they can best cater for them. Overall, the findings indicate that through their engagement with ClassSim the pre-service teachers were able to identify areas of their learning that need further development before they are enter their career as a teacher.

Motivation

Knowles (1984) suggests that as a person matures, he or she receives their motivation to learn from internal factors. For the purpose of this inquiry the 'motivation' will be discussed according to four factors; success, volition, value, and enjoyment in relation to the participants' engagement with ClassSim.

Success

The findings indicate that both the first and final year pre-service teachers were able to gain a sense of success whilst engaging with the virtual learning environment. This came in the form of internal motivations. One of the internal motivators of ClassSim came in the form of the user achieving an unknown or pre-defined purpose, such as better understanding the role of a teacher or gaining pedagogical content knowledge. A number of the first year pre-service teachers identified a sense of accomplishment at gaining a better understanding if the role of a teacher and better understanding of the decisions they will be required to make as a teacher. This suggests that the first year pre-service teachers found engagement with ClassSim to be a successful experience as it provided them with their first practical experience in a classroom and knowledge about the role of a teacher.

Another internal motivator of the virtual learning environment can be seen in the design of the ClassSim where the user gains a sense of job satisfaction. This occurs after a decision making opportunity where the lesson progression is directed by the decisions made by the user. In addition the user can access 'Student Updates' and check the progression of the targeted children in relation to their decision. The findings indicate that both cohorts of participants found this to be a useful tool in assessing their success. The participants indicated that the 'Student Updates' provided them with a concrete means of gauging their success and in the creation of a two hour teaching block and meeting the needs of their virtual students. "The sequencing activity … proves to be a good choice as it meets the needs of all students and their behaviour at this point is maintained at a medium level" (TS_Mia_18/08). Thus, it appears that the 'Student Updates' were important tools in the users' ability to assess their success in regards to student engagement and lesson progression. It may be important to note, that although the design of ClassSim includes a countdown of time, the findings indicate that this function did not contribute to the users' sense of accomplishment.

Volition

Through the design of the virtual learning environment, the users were empowered to make decisions that can affect their virtual classroom. Thus, it appears that this ability to make decisions was a key motivator in their engagement with ClassSim. A number of the first year pre-service teachers commented on their limited authority to make decisions whilst on field experience, and that their experience thus far has been restricted to merely observing the teacher and students. However, through their engagement with ClassSim they were able to assume the role of a teacher for the first time and make a number of decisions. "We are there [on field experience] going along for the ride, but it is someone else's journey and somebody else's decision-making, whereas in the sim we are making the decisions" (I_Jasmine_29/03). The findings indicate that the ability to make decision and experience the consequences of these decisions was an important aspect of engaging with ClassSim for the first year pre-service teachers. The decision making opportunities presented in the virtual learning environment was identified by a couple of final year participants as an important feature of their use of ClassSim. They suggested that although their previous field experiences gave them the opportunity to make decisions within a 'real' class, they were previously prohibited from organising the structure of the own 'literacy block'. However, through their engagement with ClassSim they were free design the sequence and structure of their own 'literacy block'. Thus, it appears that the decision making opportunities of ClassSim empowered the user to take control of their own class.

Although some of the final year pre-service teachers found ClassSim to be an empowering experience in regards to the design of their own teaching block, many of the final year participants found their engagement with ClassSim to be too restrictive in terms of decision making opportunities. "I had to do one thing or the other it was like, 'well you're going to have to pick one of the options', so I chose the one I'd more likely do. But there was one I thing I wrote down in my thinking space where I just went 'I'd choose neither'" (I_Ross_22/08). The findings suggest that the number of options available at each decision making opportunity was too limiting for the final year pre-service teachers to feel a sense of ownership of their virtual class. This may indicate that a number of the final year pre-service teachers believed that the ClassSim did not cater to their preferred choice at decision making opportunities, and thus was unsupportive of their level of knowledge and skills. However, the final year participants did allude to the fact that they utilised their 'Thinking Space' to suggest alternative options at most decision making opportunities. Therefore the 'Thinking Space' appeared to enable them to gain a sense of empowerment in voicing their opinion, even though this reflection did not alter the overall progress of the lesson and management of the class. Overall, it appears as though the decision making opportunities of ClassSim did not allow most final year pre-service teacher to gain a sense of ownership of their virtual class.

Value

The findings of this inquiry suggest that the majority of first year pre-service teachers found the virtual learning environment provided by ClassSim to be an important tool in preparing them for their first field experience (as discussed under the assumption of 'readiness' - purpose), and as a tool to make valuable connections between theory and practice (also discussed under the assumption of 'readiness' - value to learning). The first year pre-service teachers suggested that their engagement with ClassSim was valuable as it enabled them to better understand teaching strategies such as questioning and it gave them the opportunity to repeat lessons, unlike in a 'real' classroom situation. This indicates that the first year pre-service teachers found the scenarios presented in Class-

Sim, along with the relevant support material, to be valuable in better understanding teaching terminology and strategies, thereby enhancing their learning. It also suggests that they found the ClassSim to be a safe environment in which they can direct their lessons without fear of adversely affecting 'real' children through poorly made decisions. The final year pre-service teachers also found the virtual learning environment provided by ClassSim to be a valuable tool in practicing their teaching techniques and as a tool to make valuable connections between theory and practice. One participant commented on the obvious links between the university lectures she has attended and the knowledge found in the support material. "It just helps to see what you're being taught in the lectures" (I_Lauren_22/08). However most suggested that the first year pre-service teacher may find the experience more beneficial in regards to their learning, as first year pre-service teachers may be able to use the experience to gain a 'big picture' understanding of a classroom and make links to their first year subject matter. Therefore, it appears as though most participants found their engagement with ClassSim to be somewhat valuable to their learning.

Enjoyment

The findings indicate that the first and final year pre-service teachers found enjoyment in engaging with the virtual learning environment. This was often linked to the belief that ClassSim was a safe environment in which they were free to take chances with their decision making opportunities, some even likening the virtual learning environment to a game. The use of the phrase 'game' suggests that the participants enjoyed playing with the virtual characters within the virtual scenarios. Thus it appears that engagement with ClassSim was a pleasurable and enjoyable experience.

Although some final year pre-service teacher found enjoyment in their engagement with the virtual learning environment, others suggested that this game like resemblance created feelings that there were only 'right' and 'wrong' answers/decisions, thus detracting from their enjoyment.

"I feel like I was playing a game when I play it because there still seems to be a right and wrong answer and I don't think that's right... to see what you thought was the right decision" (I_Isabella_12/11). Thus, it appears that some participants may have associated their engagement with ClassSim with an exam or test of their competencies, thereby distracting from their enjoyment.

Experience

Argote, McEvily, and Reagans (2003) point to experience as an important factor in one's ability to create, retain and transfer knowledge. Knowles (1980) suggests that adults possess a reservoir of experiences that affect how they perceive the world. Thus, adult learners enter an educational setting with both a different quality and greater volume of life experiences than children. However it is important to note that, "while all learning begins with experience, this is not experience for which the learners already have a solution or response" (Jarvis, 1992:15). Knowles, Holton, and Swanson (1998) also note that even though adult learners bring with them greater experiences, these experiences can have potentially negative effects. They explain that adult learners "tend to develop mental habits, biases, and presuppositions that tend to cause us to close our minds to new ideas, fresh perceptions, and alternative ways of thinking" (Knowles, Holton, & Swanson, 1998:66). The assumption of 'experience' will be discussed according to the how each case of participants used their previous knowledge and experience when making decisions and reflection.

Previous Knowledge and Experience

The findings indicate that both cohorts of participants were able to draw upon their previous experiences and knowledge to aid their learning.

The findings suggest that most of the first year pre-service teachers were able to draw upon their experience working with ClassSim when on their first field experience. These include the basic structure of a 'literacy block', the use of modelled, guided and independent teaching strategies in lessons, time management, bathroom breaks, and behaviour management techniques. The findings indicate that while on field experience the only identified knowledge and experience drawn upon was their engagement with ClassSim. This may be because ClassSim was the first classroom experience most of the first year pre-service teachers had before their field experience. An important finding was that none of the first year pre-service teachers identified themselves as drawing upon their university studies while of field experience. This may indicate that they have yet to make strong connections between the theory of teaching (university coursework) and the practice of teaching (field experiences and ClassSim). Therefore it appears as though the first year pre-service teachers found their engagement with ClassSim to prepare them for their first field experience and the practicalities of a classroom.

Through their use of ClassSim the final year pre-service teachers are presented with scenarios which tap into their previous experiences and knowledge base. The findings indicate that all of the final year pre-service teacher participants were able identify when and where they drew their knowledge and experience from when faced with a decision making opportunity within the virtual learning environment. The findings suggest that all of the final year pre-service teachers were able to draw upon their previous field experiences whilst engaging with ClassSim, and some were able to identify when they drew upon their university knowledge when using the virtual learning environment. This indicates that not only did they find ClassSim to be similar to their field experiences, they also were able to make connections between their university acquired knowledge and the practice of teaching. This may be because the final year pre-service teachers have made a number of strong connections between the theory of teaching (university coursework) and the practice of teaching (field experiences and ClassSim). This understanding of the interrelatedness of theory and practice also suggests that these final year participants have a better developed professional identity. Therefore it appears that the final year pre-service teachers were able to identify when and where they drew their knowledge and experience from when faced with a teacher/classroom related task/problem, whilst building stronger connections between their university coursework and the practicalities of a classroom.

Reflection

The findings indicate that the majority of the first year students did not reflect upon their habits, bias, and assumptions in their 'Thinking Space' or in their field experience reflections, rather some identified their assumptions and often assessed these assumptions during interviews with the researcher. Most of these assumptions were based upon the engagement of their students. Comments were made regarding the inner thoughts of the virtual students, the differing student needs, questioning of students, and the assumption of a 'good' and 'bad' student. The findings indicate that through the use of the 'Student profiles' and 'Student Updates' the first year pre-service teachers were able to understand that each student is unique is their needs as a learner and thus, as a teacher they must cater to these needs. These tools also provided the first year pre-service teachers with a better understanding of the engagement of students, whether or not they appear to be engaged on a superficial level. These assumptions may be due to the participants' limited experience in working with children in the context of a classroom. Thus, it appears as though many of the first year pre-service teachers had a number of assumptions about students which were reassessed as a result of their engagement with ClassSim.

The findings indicate that the majority of the final year pre-service teachers used their 'Thinking Space' to reflect upon their decision making processes and record their professional learning. "I used the 'Thinking Space' to keep my notes. You can write down stuff you come across, which is good for learning, you know re-visiting something you learnt and better understanding it" (I_Lauren_16/11). Most final year participants reflected upon the possible consequences of each decision thus making a more informed decision. This technique of assessing each decision based upon possible consequences may be due to their previous field experiences or their university based knowledge. Another participant suggested that that by storing information she previously learnt during her studies in her 'Thinking Space' and re-visiting this information at a later date enabled her to better understand the information, thus enhancing her learning. This may suggest that this final year participant feels the need to refresh her understanding of concepts and strategies. It could also indicate that by re-examining her reflections she is engaging in *reflection on the reflection-in-action* (Schön, 1987) in order to gain a better understanding of her learning. Overall, it appears as though the ClassSim's 'Thinking Space' was an important tool in the learning of both first and final year pre-service teachers.

Self Concept

Knowles, Holton, and Swanson (1998:65) state that "adults have a self-concept of being responsible for their own decisions, for their own lives". It is believed that "adults want to be the origin of their own learning and will resist learning activities they believe are an attack on their competence" (Speck, 1996:36). Thus, the adult learner needs to have some control over the what, who, how, why, when, and where of their learning. Knowles, Holton and Swanson (1998:65) suggest that adult learning situations should take steps to "create learning experiences in which adults are helped to make the transition from dependant to self-directed learners". 'Self concept' will be discussed in terms of structure and support of learning experiences, reflection, and professional identity.

Structure and Support and Learning Experiences

The findings reveal that the first year participants utilised the virtual learning environment's branching opportunities to follow areas of interest and gain access to multiple forms of support material, thereby following a path of learning that most appropriately suits their needs. The findings indicate that the virtual learning environment's support material was referred by the first year participants to make more informed decisions and supplement their learning experiences by introducing unfamiliar terminology and to clarify understandings. "It helped you to link theory to practice using things like the summaries and understanding the theory and the background ideas. With the notes you see the theory behind it but then with the actual ClassSim you see how it was applied and how it worked" (I_Jasmine_25/07). This may be due to the stage of learning they were at. As they are in the beginning weeks of their university studies, it is understandable that they have limited knowledge of teaching terminology and techniques. Thus, ClassSim enabled the first year pre-service teachers to engage with classroom based scenarios and the relevant sources of information thus providing support and structure for those who need it.

In contrast, the findings suggest that the final year pre-service teachers did not make use of the support material available as they were confident in their knowledge and understanding of teaching terminology and strategies presented within the virtual learning environment. Thus, it appears as though the final year pre-service teachers have made strong connections between their university coursework and field experiences, and are able to apply their knowledge and experiences to their engagement with ClassSim without the addition aid of the support material. Therefore the final year pre-service teachers utilised the virtual learning environment's branching opportunities to skip sections already understood thus following a path of learning that most appropriately reflects their needs.

Professional Identity

A major finding of the first year data was that engagement with the virtual learning environment enabled many of the first year participants to begin their transition from the mindset of a student to that of a teacher. A number of first year pre-service teachers made comment suggesting that their engagement with ClassSim helped them to better understand the role of a teacher. "It was a lot of fun. It was a really good experience, because I actually got to see that I could actually teach, I wasn't just thinking that I might" (I_Serena_23/03). This may be because their engagement with ClassSim was the first time they had assumed the role of a teacher in a classroom. Therefore the findings indicate that the first year participants' engagement with ClassSim was a notable experience which initiated the development of their professional identity (the belief that they are teachers).

The findings suggest that engagement with ClassSim enabled both the first and final year pre-service teachers to develop and articulate their personal teaching philosophy. The first and final year pre-service teachers used their 'Thinking Space' reflect upon the role of a teacher in connection with their own teaching philosophy. In addition, the participant interviews enabled them to identify and articulate their teaching philosophy. They were able to identify various teaching and learning decisions, classroom management decisions, and behaviour management decisions that they were passionate for or against. "A teacher should praise students as much as possible as it allows them to feel a sense of worth within the classroom... By the teacher praising the students she is rewarding their efforts within the classroom. This is essential, as each student needs to be acknowledged in some way for contributing to class discussion" (TS_Ross_21/08). Overall, the findings indicate that through engagement with the virtual learning environment and other experiences, many of the first and final year pre-service teachers were able identify and articulate their emerging teaching philosophy thus developing their own professional identity.

Another finding is that some of the final year pre-service teachers were able to make connections between their university coursework and their field experience (as previously discussed) via engagement with the virtual learning environment, thereby supporting their professional identity.

FUTURE RESEARCH DIRECTIONS

The research team are currently exploring three future directions. First we conducted a pilot study with first-time (neophyte) parents who had recently enrolled their children at a local school. We found that their experience in using ClassSim appeared to provide them some insights into the work of their child's teacher. Later in the year we will follow up this group and interview teachers and the parents who used ClassSim to find out if the virtual experience with ClassSim had developed common understandings that were of benefit to these stakeholders. The outcome of this pilot study will be used to inform a larger study across a number of schools as an online environment, such as ClassSim, may provide neophyte parents an insight into how schools work and relieve some of the anxiety they feel as first-time parents of school-aged children.

Second, we have begun process of developing a simulated learning environment that can be used to instruct researchers in ethical research practices. This is in response to suggested changes in practices in research training in Australia. At this stage a series of illustrative cases have been created and these will form the basis of the virtual learning environment.

Third, the authors have recently presented a panel presentation at a large international conference with a group of international collaborators from Korea and the USA. Each of these collaborators have been addressing similar problems using a variety of strategies such as second life environments and online simulations that are programmed to respond according evidence-based learner profiles and evidence-based research on classroom management and learning styles. This group of researchers are applying for funding to conduct an international workshop whose goal is to develop a design concept that combines our work into a simulated learning environment that can be used internationally. If successful funding is forthcoming we will develop and test this virtual learning environment in USA, Australia and Korea. Our preliminary discussions have focused on the use of avatars and social networking to create an even more engaging virtual learning environment.

CONCLUSION

In conclusion, the five assumptions of Andragogy ('Readiness', 'Orientation', 'Motivation', 'Experience', and 'Self Concept') work together to explain the learning of the pre-service teachers and how this learning relates to their engagement with the virtual learning environment provided by the ClassSim, their university coursework, field experiences, previous experiences, and other factors that may influence their learning. Findings from this inquiry have established that engagement with ClassSim played an important role in preparing the pre-service teachers for their field experience, as it enabled them to explore the practicalities of a classroom before entering a 'real' classroom. In addition, the pre-service teachers were able to experiment with decision making opportunities and as a result became more confident to make similar decisions in a 'real' classroom. Analysis of the assumption of 'Readiness', revealed that ClassSim provided the pre-service teachers with a practice ground in which they were able to learn the things they need to know and be able to do in order to cope effectively with a real-life situation.

The simulation pathway is determined by the users' interaction with decision making opportunities; which are based upon 'real-life' scenarios. Thus, upon reflection of the assumption 'Orientation', ClassSim provided the pre-service teacher with a task/problem orientated learning environment which enabled them to apply their knowledge immediately through problem solving.

The design of ClassSim also catered for user motivation. This is evident in the inquiry's findings regarding success (via 'Student Updates'), volition (through the decision making capabilities of ClassSim), value (through the use of ClassSim support material and the user's prior knowledge and understandings), and enjoyment (game - safe environment to practice decision making).

According to the assumption of 'Experience', adult learners enter an educational setting with both a different quality and greater volume of life experiences than children. Through engagement with ClassSim the pre-service teachers are presented with scenarios which tap into their previous experiences and knowledge base. Furthermore, the design of ClassSim enables the user to address their previous knowledge base in a critical manner and to reflect upon their decision making processes and record their professional learning, via the 'Thinking Space'. Through the use of the 'Thinking Space' the pre-service teachers were also able to identify and articulate their emerging teaching philosophy thus developing their own professional identity.

Overall, it appears that simulations offer significant potential as effective learning tools for adult learners. Examining the interaction patterns of two cohorts of preservice teachers through the theoretical frame of Andragogy has enabled the affordances of simulation to be examined. A carefully designed learning environment, coupled with knowledge of the potential users and their professional situations, supports learners to make meaningful connections between the field and theory.

REFERENCES

Argote, L., McEvily, B., & Reagans, R. (2003). Managing knowledge in organizations: An integrative framework and review of emerging themes. *Management Science*, *49*, 571–582. doi:10.1287/mnsc.49.4.571.14424

Beder, H., & Carrea, N. (1988). The effects of andragogical teacher training on adult students' attendance and evaluation of their teachers. *Adult Education Quarterly*, *38*(2), 75–87. doi:10.1177/0001848188038002002

Brady, L., Segal, G., Bamford, A., & Deer, C. (1998). *Student perceptions of the theory/practice nexus in teacher education: a longitudinal study.* A paper presented at the Australian Association for Research in Education (AARE), Adelaide, Australia.

Breuer, K., & Kummer, R. (1990). Cognitive effects from process learning with computer-based simulations. *Computers in Human Behavior*, *6*, 69–81. doi:10.1016/0747-5632(90)90031-B

Cole, A. L., & Knowles, J. G. (2000). *Researching Teaching: Exploring Teacher Develoment Through Reflective Inquiry*. Boston: Allyn and Bacon.

Darling-Hammond, L. (1999). *Reshaping teaching policy, preparation, and practice: Influences of the National Board for Professional Teaching Standards.* Washington, DC: American Association of Colleges for Teacher Education.

Educational Training Committee. (2005). *Report on the inquiry into the suitability of pre-service teacher training in Victoria.* Presented in Melbourne, Parliament of Victoria.

Ferry, B., Kervin, L., Cambourne, B., Turbill, J., Hedberg, J., & Jonassen, D. (2005). Incorporating real experience into the development of a classroom-based simulation. *Journal of Learning Design*, *1*(1), 22–32.

Feuer, D., & Gerber, B. (1988). Uh-oh: Second thoughts about adult learning theory. *Training (New York, N.Y.)*, *25*(12), 31–39.

Gatto, D. (1993). The use of interactive computer simulations in training. *Australian Journal of Educational Technology*, *9*(2), 144–156.

Herrington, J., & Oliver, R. (2000). An instructional design framework for authentic learning environments. *Educational Technology Research and Development*, *48*(3), 23–48. doi:10.1007/BF02319856

Jarvis, P. (1992). *Paradoxes of learning: On becoming an individual in society.* San Francisco: Jossey Bass.

Kervin, L., & Turbill, J. (2003). Teaching as a craft: Making links between pre-service training and classroom practice. *English Teaching: Practice and Critique*, *2*(3), 22–34.

Knowles, M. (1970). *The modern practice of adult education: Andragogy versus pedagogy.* New York: Association Press.

Knowles, M. (1980). *The modern practice of adult education: From andragogy to pedagogy*. Englewood Cliffs, NJ: Cambridge Adult Education.

Knowles, M. (1984). *Andragogy in action: Applying modern principles of adult education.* San Francisco: Jossey-Bass.

Knowles, M., Holton, E., III, & Swanson, R. (1998). *The adult learner.* Houston, TX: Gulf Publishing.

Lanier, J. E., & Little, J. W. (1986). Research on teacher education. In M.C. Wittrock (Ed.), *Handbook of Research on Teaching* (pp. 527-569). New York: Macmillan.

Merriam, S. B., & Brockett, R. (1997). *The profession and practice of adult education: An introduction.* San Francisco: Jossey-Bass Publishers.

Merriam, S. B., & Caffarella, R. S. (1991). *Learning in adulthood: A comprehensive guide.* San Francisco: Jossey-Bass Publishers.

Merriam, S. B., & Caffarella, R. S. (1999). *Learning in adulthood: A comprehensive guide.* San Francisco: Jossey Bass.

Pratt, D. D. (1998). Andragogy as a relational construct. *Adult Education Quarterly, 32*(3), 160–181.

Rachal, J. R. (2002). Andragogy's detectives: A critique of the present and a proposal for the future. *Adult Education Quarterly, 53*(3), 210–227. doi:10.1177/0741713602052003004

Reigeluth, C. M., & Schwartz, E. (1989). An instructional theory in the design of computer-based simulations. *Journal of Computer-Based Instruction, 16*(1), 1–10.

Sorin, R. (2004). Webfolio: An online learning community to help link university studies and classroom practice in preservice teacher education. *Australasian Journal of Educational Technology, 20*(1), 101–113.

Chapter 23
Supporting the Comprehension of Complex Systems with Video Narratives

Weiqin Chen
University of Bergen, Norway

Nils Magnus Djupvik
Mindlab AS, Norway

ABSTRACT

Complex systems are difficult to understand, and without extended training and experience, people tend to misperceive these systems. Although current simulation tools illustrate what is happening in complex systems, they lack the means to represent the narrative aspects of the exhibited behaviours, in order to provide an account for the behaviours. The goal of this research is to provide visualizations of complex dynamic system behaviours with multimedia, focusing on video narratives, and to study the implications and added values of the video clips. The target users are primarily university students in System Dynamics. The method could also be of value both to lower level school students as well as to policy makers and general population who must deal with challenging complex problems. A pilot study was conducted and the findings confirmed our prior expectations; namely, that providing the users with video clips facilitates their learning process.

INTRODUCTION

The world we live in is dynamic and complex. The complexity lies in interconnected components whose behaviour is not explained exclusively by their properties. Rather, the behaviour *emerges* from the interconnectedness of these components (Bar-Yam, 1997; Sabelli, 2006). According to the *Journal of Advanced Complex Systems*, a complex system is a system comprised of a (usually large) number of (usually strongly) interacting entities, processes, or agents, the understanding of which requires the development, or the use of, new scientific tools, nonlinear models, out-of equilibrium descriptions and computer simulations. For example, the housing prices might be influenced by the expenses of building new houses, the prices of land, the number of jobs, the availability of workers, and the number of new houses which are built. These factors interact with each other and the interactions contribute to

DOI: 10.4018/978-1-61520-678-0.ch023

the fluctuations of the housing prices. In fact examples of complex systems can be found in a wide variety of domains including climate, ecological networks, insect colonies, neural networks in the brain that produce intelligence and consciousness, social networks comprised of transportation, utilities, and telecommunication systems, as well as economies.

Understanding and reasoning about complex systems places a huge burden on working memory resources and is often counterintuitive or conflicts with commonly held beliefs (Casti, 1994; Feltovich, Coulson, & Spiro, 2001; Hmelo-Silver & Azevedo, 2006; Narayanan & Hegarty, 1998; Wilensky & Resnick, 1999). Computer simulations allow formal and experimental investigation of various complex systems. For example, simulations are designed to model the spread of infectious disease on social networks. Users can use the simulation to explore the effects of complex pharmaceutical interventions and non-pharmaceutical interventions on the spread of the disease (Barrett, Bisset, Eubank, Feng, & Marathe, 2008). Computer simulations are also used to model climate changes and interpret the changes in the past and predict the future (Hansen et al., 2007; West & Dowlatabadi, 1999). In Artificial life simulations are used to study the phenomena of living systems to understand the complex information processing that defines such systems (Bedau, 2003; Langton, 1995). In most of these simulations data visualization with charts and graphs is one of the most important aspects. Users can explore the simulations by manipulating parameters and observe the changes in the data visualization. However, it is not common to include videos in the visualization of simulations.

The current best understandings and analytical tools in the physical and social sciences (informed by complex systems) are continuing to expand beyond the reach of the working knowledge of professionals, policy makers, and citizens, who must deal with challenging social and global problems in the 21P^stP century (Jacobson & Wilensky, 2006). Learning scientists have identified opportunities to help address the these challenges, calling for, among others, a systematic study focusing on what types of scaffolds or other learning aids are needed to support the understanding of complex systems (Sabelli, 2006). This involves both formal and informal learning as well as lifelong learning. The key issue is the teaching and learning of complex system knowledge and understanding of system thinking.

The development of advanced technology has resulted in interactive learning environments, including simulations, multimedia and other web-based learning environments, that may facilitate the understanding of complex systems. Simulation provides more experiential, explorative, and inquiry-based learning opportunities and has been widely used in various educational contexts from natural science to social study, from elementary school to high education, and from classroom to informal and lifelong learning. Studies have shown that simulation-based learning can be highly motivating and engaging and leading to deeper understanding of content and development of higher order thinking skills (Gredler, 2004; Hmelo & Day, 1999; Lee, 1999; Swaak & de Jong, 2001a; Veenman, Prins, & Elshout, 2002). Researchers have also studied learning mechanisms and reasoning skills that must be deployed to support learning about complex systems. For example, de Jong and colleagues (de Jong et al., 2005) identified and listed key factors necessary for effective discovery-based learning environments, to foster learning about particular complex systems, including generic knowledge about models, domain knowledge, general skills and scientific reasoning skills.

Visualization techniques have been adopted to support the uses of multiple representations of abstract concepts (Mayer, 2001). Multimedia learning theory focuses on how people integrate verbal and visual information in their learning processes. Video as a form of media have been widely used in learning in various disciplines such as nursing (Green et al., 2003; Smith-Stoner & Willer, 2003; Smith, 1991), medicine (Gandsas, McIntire, Palli, & Park, 2002), social work (Robin, Reardon, & Strand, 2001), economics (Hashmi & Guvenli, 2001), and engineering (Foertsch, Moses, Strikwerda, & Litzkow, 2002). In teacher education video case studies of exemplary teaching practices were used to outline the narratives and allow for close examinations of interactions, thus help students to develop knowledge and understandings of the relationships that exist between curriculum, teaching and learning, assessment and reporting (Brophy, 2004; Hollingworth, 2006; Risko, 1991).

System dynamics is a methodology for analysing and understanding how dynamically complex systems behave through modelling, simulation and analysis (Sterman, 2000). Interacting with system dynamics simulations may help in understanding causal relationships between components, and in revealing mistaken assumptions about the model. However, a problem with system dynamic simulation models, built with simulation software, is that they are often quite complex. Although these models show the behaviour of the system, the account of the behaviour is embedded in the structure of the models and the user has to perform the analysis manually, which is a highly challenging task and usually difficult for an untrained user. Although simulations supported by video and media has been widely used in education in some disciplines (Wissick, Gardner, & Langone, 1999; Wissick, Lloyd, & Kinzie, 1992), it is not common to use videos in system dynamics simulations although videos may help to make the models more transparent and are especially beneficial for novice or less-motivated learners (Alessi, 2000).

Inspired by previous research on using videos in education and pedagogical scaffolding for learning complex systems, our research aims to address the challenge of understanding complex system behaviours and study how video clips in system dynamics simulation can support the comprehension of the models behind complex dynamic systems. More specifically, we tried to shed some light on the following research questions:

1. How should video clips be integrated in a simulation to represent behaviour of system dynamic models?
2. How does the use of video clips support its users' comprehension of complex systems?

The intended users in our research include students (with and without knowledge about system dynamics) as well as general population who are interested in understanding the behaviour of complex systems.

In order to address these research questions, we adopted design research methodology (Hevner, March, Park, & Ram, 2004). We first developed a prototype of the Simulation Visualization Lab (SVL), based on theories of system dynamics and multimedia learning. Then we conducted a pilot study to study how users use the system, to receive feedback on the design, and to understand the added value of the video clips. Currently, we are improving the prototype, based on the feedback, and are planning another round of formative evaluation.

This chapter is organized as follows. We begin by introducing the VOCS project, of which the research in this paper is a part. This is followed by discussion of some specific research areas into which the work presented in this paper falls. We then present the design, development and evaluation of the SVL. Finally, we discuss the research in terms of the research questions and conclude the paper by identifying some future research directions.

BACKGROUND: THE VOCS PROJECT

The research presented in this paper is a part of the VOCS project (Visualization of Complex Sys-

Figure 1. Quito Model (stock and flow diagram)

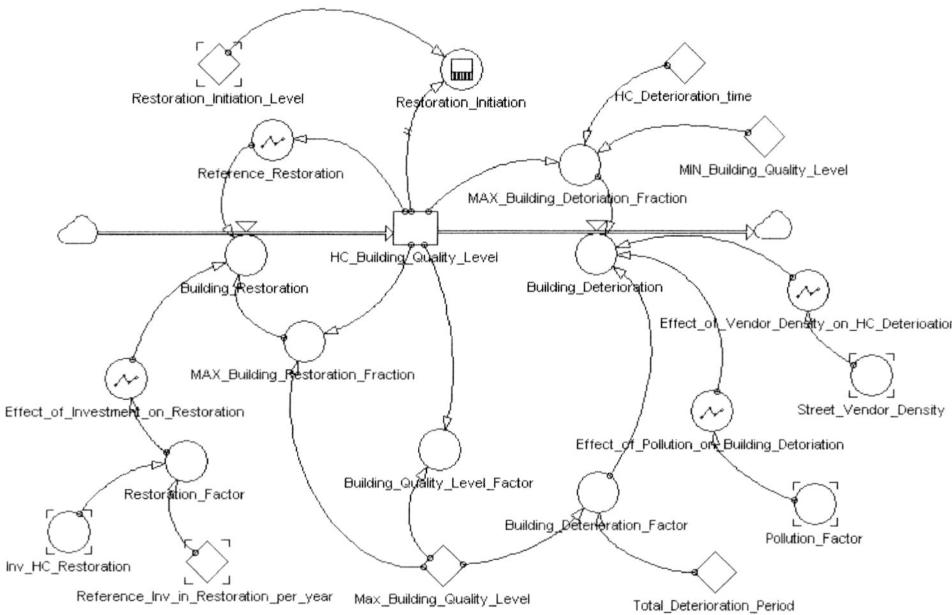

tems). This project aims at providing visualizations of system dynamics models, so that users without knowledge of system dynamics can understand and make decisions, based on the models. One of the models is of the historical centre in Quito, the capitol of Ecuador. The intention behind the Quito model was to create a heritage management tool that could be used for planning and management. This model can also be used as a tool for planners to present policies to citizens, or as a learning tool for understanding the complex process of managing a city.

The Quito simulation model was built with simulation software Powersim Studio™ by experts in system dynamics. The model consists of 245 variables, which are divided into 8 sectors (Figure 1):

- *Population* depicts issues related to population.
- *Formal Employment* deals with the business infrastructure and related job issues.
- *Informal Employment* is the sector that deals with issues related to the number of street vendors located in the historic centre.
- *Tourism* describes the development of the tourism activity within Quito, and consequently, of the historic centre.
- *Environment* portrays the pollution aspects of the city, mainly related to air pollution.
- *Government* is the sector which accounts for the local authorities' income, investments and expenses.
- *Historic Centre* presents the development of the historic buildings' infrastructure quality.
- *Crime* handles the change in the offences committed.

The purpose of the Quito simulation model is to represent all of the challenges of managing a city of mixed use: a city for locals, tourists, different social groups, commerce and housing. The focus is on a selection of key issues that are frequently listed as problem areas for the historic centre of Quito and as subjects of planning and future regulations. Since the buildings in the historic centre have major impact on tourism, the preservation of the historic centre has been an important objective for cultural, as well as economic, reasons (Skartveit, Goodnow, & Viste, 2003). The quality of the buildings of the historic centre is affected by various factors, such as air pollution (mostly from traffic), unorganized street sellers, and how much money the government is spending on building maintenance and renovation.

The aim of the research presented in this chapter is to create an environment that helps users to understand the Quito simulation model by using visualizations (focusing on video narratives) to represent behaviours of the model. No knowledge about system dynamics should be needed to use this environment. Visualizations are to make the model easier to understand and to be more accurately perceived.

RELATED RESEARCH AREAS

The research methodology that we have adopted is design science research. Design research involves the analysis of the use and performance of designed artifacts to understand, explain and, very frequently, to improve on the behaviour of aspects of Information Systems. Design science research seeks to create innovations "through which the analysis, design, implementation, management and use of information systems can be effectively and efficiently accomplished" (Hevner, March, Park, & Ram, 2004). A general design science methodology includes cycles of identification of needs, development and evaluation. In addition, a final conclusion phase can be added (Gregg, Kulkarni, & Vinze, 2001). In this project, iterations of requirement analysis, development and evaluations have been conducted.

System Dynamics

System dynamics offers an analysis of the behaviour of the system under investigation. This analysis allows users to link the observed behaviour to the underlying structure of the system (Sterman, 2000). Causal relationships are uncovered during the analysis and connected in a conceptual causal loop diagram. The causal loop diagram then defines the basic structure of the system and how the different components of the system are connected. Stock and flow diagram shows the causal relationship of the levels, rates, and constants in a system (Figure 1). In contrast to causal loop diagram which does not distinguish rate from level and constant, stock and flow diagram distinguish the three variables. Sometimes it also distinguishes what kind of flow is moving in the diagram in the link. One of the main drawbacks with stock and flow diagrams is that there is no embedded visualization that relates model structure with model behaviour.

The most central concepts for analysis are feedbacks, delays and nonlinearities. Feedback refers to the phenomenon that an effect may affect its cause – so that another, perhaps stronger or weaker, effect is achieved the next time around. All dynamics in systems arise from the interaction of two types of feedback loops: Positive loops, also called reinforcing loops, and negative loops, also called balancing loops (Sterman, 2000). A positive feedback loop tends to reinforce, or amplify, whatever is happening in the system. For example, population increases itself through births. As the population increases, the number of births also increases. The city can, however, only support a certain number of people. Negative loops counteract and oppose change; for example, as the population density increases and the city reaches its carrying capacity, the population growth decreases. If this capacity is reached, the population will start to fall. The feedbacks do not always appear immediately. It takes time for the decisions to affect the state of a system. A delay is a process whose output lags behind its input in some fashion (Sterman, 2000). Nonlinearity refers to a relationship between a cause and an effect that is not linear. Population growth is an example of nonlinearity. The population will grow slowly in the beginning, when the population is low, but as the population grows, it will grow faster and faster (exponential growth) until it reaches the carrying capacity. The delay in the negative feedback loop may cause the system to overshoot and oscillate around the carrying capacity level.

Computer simulation models help users to learn about dynamic complexity, understand the sources of policy resistance, and design more effective policies (Sterman, 2000). In order to create a simulation based on the causal loop diagram, simulation software is needed to build a simulation model. A variety of tools exist today for creating simulation of dynamic systems, for example Powersim Studio™, Vensim® and AnyLogic™.

In the Powersim Studio™ software, the underlying structure of a complex system is represented in the model (Figure 1). The model shows only the structure and gives the user no information about the behaviour of the system. The simulation software and the theory of system dynamics together provide the means to simulate the behaviour of a system, but a user needs both knowledge about system dynamics and the simulation software, to be able to understand the connection between model structure and behaviour (Richardson, 1996). According to Richardson (1996), one of the future challenges in the field of system dynamic is to develop software support for understanding model behaviours. Although in recent years researchers have made a substantial effort in simplifying dynamic simulators and improving interfaces to facilitate model behaviour understanding, the overall results are rather mixed and users still have difficulties in understanding and managing dynamic systems (Bois, 2002; Howie, Sy, Ford, & Vicente, 2000; Jensen & Brehmer, 2003).

Multimedia Learning

In order to support the understanding of model behaviours, the information included in the model should be presented in a manner that makes it easy to understand (Sterman, 1994). According to Mayer (Mayer, 1997), multimedia learning occurs when learners receive information presented in more than one mode, such as in pictures and words. He argued that the design of multimedia instructional materials should be based on a theory of multimedia learning, with a particular focus on how people integrate verbal and visual information in their learning processes.

The theory of multimedia learning does not see the learner as a knowledge acquirer, but more as a knowledge constructor (Mayer, 1997). The learner actively selects and connects pieces of visual and verbal knowledge. According to Mayer's (Mayer, 1997) generative theory, meaningful learning occurs "when learners select relevant information from what is presented, organize the pieces of information into a coherent mental representation, and integrate the newly constructed representation with others".

Split-attention occurs when information, which is difficult to understand in isolation, is presented by multiple sources at the same time and must be mentally integrated to achieve understanding. When the sources of information are separated in space or time, they must be related and mentally integrated by the learner. The searching and matching of related information requires working memory learning (Kalyuga, Chandler, & Sweller, 1999). An experiment performed by Mayer (Mayer, 1997) revealed that students presented with animation-with-narration produced approximately 50% more creative solutions on problem-solving questions than did students presented with animation-with-text.

Multimedia learning theory has guided the design of the components in the SVL user interface. For example, visualizations (videos and images) are presented in correspondence with the simulations and the video-links are presented with supporting titles.

THE SIMULATION VISUALIZATION LAB (SVL)

This section describes the design and development process of the SVL. Some technical details are also provided.

Identifying Requirements

The Simulation Visualization Lab (SVL) was developed to provide users with rich information about the system, enhance their understanding of the models, and thus facilitate and improve their decision-making. The SVL can also be used in system dynamics teaching and learning. The initial requirements for the SVL include:

- Run the Quito model
- Manipulate and retrieve model variables
- Visualize chosen model variables through videos and other visualization media.

As SVL needed to be able to run the Quito model, the first task was to make the SVL communicate with the model. Because the Quito model is a Powersim model, SVL needed to communicate with the Powersim Studio™ software. The second task was to implement the logical mapping between the different variables, the video and other type of visualizations. The third task was to implement a user interface that presents these visualizations to users.

System Design and Development

The design and development is an iterative process. In addition to unit testing (Beck, 2002), the prototypes are regularly tested by potential users. Feedback is collected to guide the improvement on the design of the prototype.

The SVL Architecture

SVL consists of three main components: The SVL Client, the Powersim Web service and the SVL Server (Figure 2). The basis of SVL is the simulation model, which is built from the city of Quito. The causal relationships between the variables in the model generate the dynamics in the simulation. The Simulation Visualization Lab retrieves data from the simulation model (Powersim simulator in Figure 2) and generates suitable visualizations for user interface (SVL Client in Figure 2). The users may communicate with the simulation and manipulate the model's variables through the SVL Client.

Figure 2. SVL system architecture

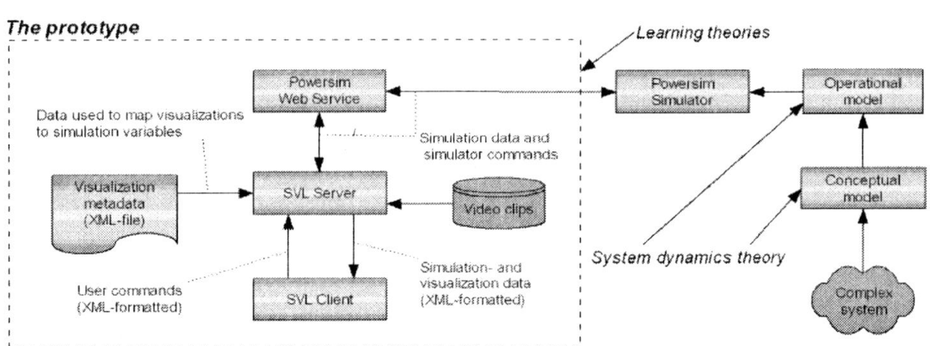

The SVL User Interface

In the simulation, the user takes the role of the decision-maker in the city of Quito. The decisions are made by manipulating the sliders in the control panel (Figure 3). The control panel provides the user with buttons to start and stop the simulation, and a set of sliders to set budgets for variables such as "Law enforcement" and "Garbage clearing". The states of the 245 variables in the Quito model are affected by the setting of the budget. The simulation may be paused by the user at any time.

In the middle part of the interface is a map of the central part of the city of Quito. The map contains animated squares representing the number of tourists and street vendors in the city centre. The simulation time is represented through a timeline and a label showing current year in the upper part of the interface.

When the user starts the simulation by pressing the play-button, the squares in the map start animating and, as time progresses, the curves begin to be drawn. The influences of the budget on the model variables can be identified by observing the growth of the curves and the changes in the map. The big curves on the left are curves with video-links (Figure 3). Each curve represents a variable and contains links to video clips representing the different states of that variable. All video-curves start with one video-link illustrating the initial state of the variable in the first simulation year. New video-links automatically appear as the state of the variable changes in the course of the simulation. This is implemented by an algorithm that chooses the most suitable clip from a set of video clips that can be visualized at each state. Each video clip is annotated with states of associated variables. When the user clicks on a video-link, a video clip representing the current state of that variable appears on the screen. For example, if the pollution reaches a certain level, a video clip of a taxi driver who complains about smog during rush hour is shown. Each video-link has a title attached to it, describing the topic of the video-clip.

The video clips show short interviews (20-30 seconds) of people from Quito. Various population

Figure 3. Screenshot of the SVL user interface

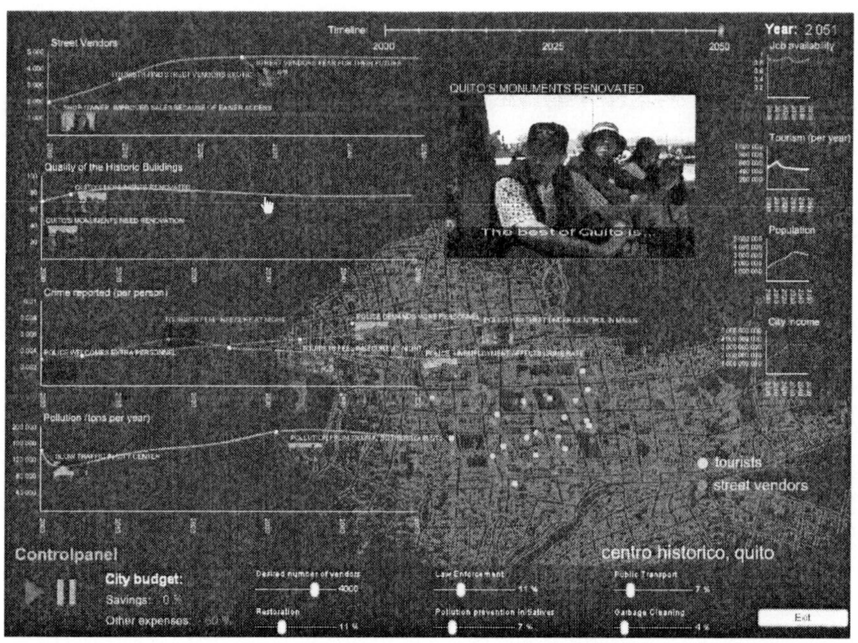

groups are represented in the videos; the police, street vendors, taxi drivers, pedestrians, shop owners, tourists etc. Most of the people in the videos speak Spanish, therefore the video clips are provided with subtitles. All of the curves and sliders are provided with tooltips that give the user a simple description of the variable to which the slider or curve is connected.

Implementation Details

This section presents some implementation details of the main components of SVL, including the communication between SVL server and client and the mapping between model variables and visualizations.

UThe SVL Server-Client Communication

The SVL client is the user interface to SVL. It is responsible for two main tasks:

1) interpreting the simulation data and visualization data supplied by the SVL server (The client uses the data provided by the server to build the graphical user interface);
2) allowing users to interact with the simulation model by changing the budgets. These actions are passed on to SVL server.

The SVL Server is responsible for:

1) creating and managing multiple simulation sessions (SVL allows multiple clients to connect to server simultaneously);
2) running simulation models;
3) selecting suitable visualizations (video clips and images) for representing the variables specified and generating visualization data for the client;
4) providing the SVL Client with simulation and visualization data.

When the user provides the client with a server address and a port number and presses the connect-button, the SimulationClient class establishes a connection to the SVL server (Figure 4). This class is responsible for all communication with the server through an XMLSocket object provided by the Macromedia Flash ActionScript API. Through the XMLSocket object, the client is able to maintain a permanent connection to the server. The connection provided may send and retrieve data formatted as plain text or XML.

There are three types of data that are sent between the SVL Client and the Server:

- Simulation data: The name of the model, the current simulation time and whether the simulation is playing or not.

Figure 4. Server-client communication

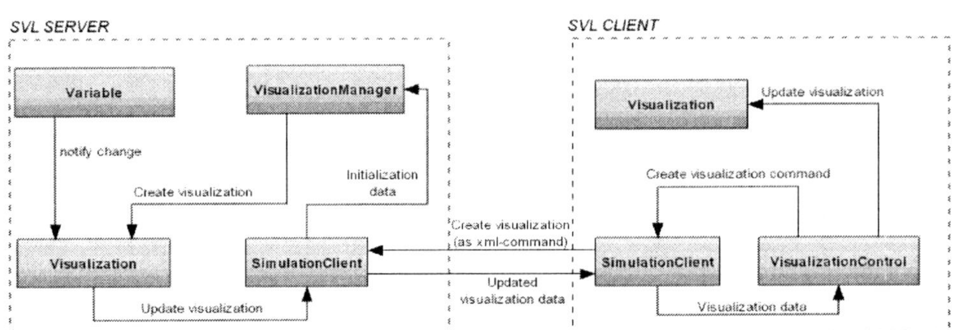

- Visualization data: Data used by SVL Client to create and update the visualizations (e.g. videos and curves).
- Server commands: The Client executes commands on the server by sending command objects (formatted as xml) to the server.

Some user actions, such as selecting a video-link and enlarging the video do not require a server command. In order to support logging of all actions, the server is notified through XML messages when these actions are performed.

The Client can be implemented in almost any language, as all communication is XML-based. Macromedia Flash was chosen because it facilitates rapid development of graphically rich user interfaces, and has particular support for working with photos, videos and animations.

Mapping Between Model Variables and Visualizations

Metadata is used to map actual visualizations (video clips and images) to model variable states. The name attribute contains a reference to a filename or an URL. This could, for instance, be an image file or a video file. The metadata may vary between the different types of visualizations. Video visualizations contain more metadata than do image visualizations. In addition to the name of the actual video file or image file, the video also contains a title and a description of the video.

All actual visualizations are connected to at least one state of a variable, but may, however, be used by multiple variables at multiple states. For instance, a video or image illustrating a clean street may also be used to illustrate an empty street.

In order to find an appropriate video or image for the current state, an algorithm that can find the closest available visualization was created. A *findClosestElement* method is developed to find the visualization whose state is the closest to the current state of the variable. When, for instance, a variable state is updated, it checks the metadata to see if another video is mapped to a state closer to the current variable state.

System Evaluation

Even though the simulation model is a significant basis for SVL, the purpose of the pilot study is not to assess the quality of the model, but to investigate whether SVL, especially through the addition of video clips, can enhance the users' understanding of the simulation model. In addition, through the study, we hope to identify possible improvements for SVL. The data were collected from two separate tests. The first was an online test where users (identified by IP addresses) visited a webpage where they could try out SVL. The other was a lab test conducted with eight first year university students, who tested SVL and answered questions.

The Online Test

The purpose of the online test was mainly to collect quantitative data, in order to uncover what features the users used, which actions they performed, and the frequency of these actions. SVL was set up on a server allowing all online users to connect and test out the system. No restrictions were made as to how many times each user could run. The online test last for three months.

We recruited participants by sending out emails with the link to SVL to a number of mailing lists. The majority of the online users were interested in simulation in general without knowledge about system dynamics. The SVL Server logs all activities during the simulation sessions conducted by online users. The log contains all data about the visualizations of the variables and the user's actions, including slider usage, pausing of the simulation and videos watched. The user's IP-address and username were stored, in order to distinguish unique sessions.

Unique Sessions and Simulation Time

We identified 80 unique sessions (each session represents a play of the simulation). It is, however, difficult to figure out exactly how many unique users played the simulation, even though the names of the users and their IP-addresses were logged. Several users may have shared an IP-address and one user may have connected from several machines with different IP-addresses. 42 out of the 80 sessions were created from unique IP-addresses. If we assume each unique IP-address is associated with one unique user, then each user played two sessions on average.

To play the entire simulation without pausing takes about 14 minutes. The log shows that 35% of the sessions were finished. The average number of simulation years played was 27.10 (the whole simulation runs 50 years).

Variable and Video Usage

One interesting aspect that was analyzed was the kind of videos and variables on which the users focused. As all videos are connected to a variable, this could be analyzed by looking at what kind of video the users watched the most.

Table 1 shows the percentage of videos watched. These videos represent different variables including street vendors, quality of historical buildings, crime reported, and pollution. Table 2 shows the average usages (how many times) the budget variables in each session. These variables are controlled by the sliders in the user interface (lower part in Figure 3). The most popular budget variable was "Law enforcement". One potential explanation could be that the connection between the variables "Law enforcement" and "Crime reported" is found by most users. According to de Jong and van Joolingen (1998), people tend to look for information that confirms their hypotheses. Since it is common knowledge that funding law enforcement is one way to reduce crime, the users may be trying to prove this, more than testing alternative hypotheses. Another explanation could be that the "Law enforcement" is one of the budget variables that are most sensitive to changes. A small change in this variable could have major immediate impact on the other variables. This sensitivity could have led the user to frequently experiment with this variable.

In the budget variables, "Garbage clearing" was rarely used. One explanation could be that, unlike "Law enforcement", the "Garbage Clearing" variable had no profound relation with other variables. The videos provide useful information about the budget variables, but only one of the videos available provides explicit information about the garbage in the streets. The lack of direct access to domain knowledge could be a reason that "Garbage clearing" was seldom used (de Jong & van Joolingen, 1998).

The Lab Test

In order to understand the effect of the video clips in SVL, we conducted a lab test. Eight first year

Table 1. Video usage

	Videolinks shown	Videolinks watched	Watched percentage
Street vendors	157,00	49,00	15,95%
Quality of historic buildings	158,00	42,00	13,73%
Crime reported	163,00	56,00	15,48%
Pollution	208,00	56,00	14,37%

Table 2. Budget variable usage (average use per session)

Desired number of vendors	2,13
Law enforcement	2,95
Public transportation	2,45
Restoration	2,21
Pollution prevention initiatives	2,18
Garbage clearing	1,25

university students with major in information science participated in the lab test. All participants have taken one semester system dynamics course where they learned the basic knowledge of system dynamics (feedbacks, delays and nonlinearities) and simulation models. The simulation they learned included only the diagrams without any visualization (e.g. charts, graphs and videos). In the test they were not given any particular task to solve, or any specific goal, but were encouraged to try to use SVL to learn about Quito and the issues with which the city is struggling. The participants took the role of the decision-makers. They learned about the system by making decisions and observing how the decisions affect different aspects of Quito city. They were asked to keep the following two questions in mind while trying out SVL:

- What are the main challenges of the city and how are these challenges experienced by different population groups?
- The simulation model presents different elements of the city: Street vendors, pollution, crimes reported etc. How do the elements affect each other? (Find the causal relationships).

Data were collected by using the following methods:

- *Observations:* During the lab test, we observed the participants using SVL and took notes. Remote control software was installed on the participant's computer so that their keyboard and mouse movements were also captured.
- *Logs:* All the simulation sessions were logged for later analyses. The simulation server tracks and logs all user actions and messages sent between the clients and the server, error messages, important user actions such as video selections and manipulation of the sliders, etc. These logs are used to evaluate the interface and to identify problems the participants may have had during the test.
- *Interviews:* Participants were interviewed after they had tested out SVL. The goal of the interview was to compare results and to validate the findings from the observations. More specifically, we intended to capture, in greater detail, the participants' experience from using SVL and to assess their view of the multimedia information in the system, particularly the perceived value of the video clips. Audio recordings were made during the interviews. The interviews were semi-structured and the questions included the following three aspects:
  - The quality of the user interface, including general intuitiveness of the interface, the design of different interface elements (frequency of use, intuitiveness, size, and colors), satisfying features and missing features, and the information provided.

- The importance of the videos, including thoughts about SVL as a learning tool (pros and cons), thoughts about how the video clips are used in SVL, information provided by the video clips, and how the video clips affected the participant's actions.
- Domain knowledge, including the main challenges for the city, e.g. the street vendors (opinions and concerns), pollution (what causes pollution in Quito?), the historical centre (importance of the historic centre), crime (causes, consequences), and their effects on other aspects of Quito city.

User Interface

Most participants thought that the user interface in SVL was easier and more flexible than the user interface in the Powersim software -- SVL separates the interface from the simulation model and hides the very complex model from the users, and it also provides users with more flexibility in controlling model variables. Six out of eight participants recognized the video links without assistance. The tooltips were found useful. It was also reported that additional information explaining the elements in the interface would have been helpful.

Some participants reported that the interface was a bit overwhelming, with too many information elements. Because the interface presents much simultaneous information, some of the participants experienced split-attention effects (Mayer, 1997). For example, some responded that it was easy to miss new video clips if the simulation was running while the sliders were manipulated, and suggested that the sliders could be deactivated while the simulation is playing.

One of the issues that were considered during the design and development of SVL was the amount of system control that should be implemented in the user interface. In the interface of SVL, the amount of system control is minimized (Swaak & de Jong, 2001b). The participants had different opinions on this matter. The observations revealed that some participants paused the simulation before changing the sliders (18 out of 21 sessions were paused), and observed the simulation for some time before making new decisions. This is important, in order to learn about the system. However, this kind of behaviour cannot be expected from people who do not have a good understanding of system dynamics. The finding from the online test, where only 18 out of 80 sessions were paused, confirmed this argument. Therefore, the amount of system control should be increased for users without knowledge of system dynamics.

The Usage and Effect of Video Clips

Table 3 shows the percentage of videos watched in the lab test. Table 4 shows the average usages (how many times) the budget variables in each session. As in the online test, "Law enforcement" was again the most popular budget variable. More details on the summary of video usage can be found in Table 5.

On average, each participant watched nine video clips. Six out of eight participants thought the video clips were helpful in finding the causal relationships and they used the information from the video for their making decisions.

It was reported that the videos made it easier to "*combine things together*" and to find connections between different "parts" of the system. This indicates that they were able to build their mental model by integrating representations (Mayer, 1997). Some reference levels of the variables (e.g. crime) can be difficult to deduce without specific domain knowledge. The videos (and the titles) were reported to be helpful for the participants and gave them a clue whether the level was high or low. When asked if he gathered any information from the videos, one of the participants responded:

Table 3. Video usage

	Videolinks shown	Videolinks watched	Watched percentage
Street vendors	46,00	27,00	58,69%
Quality of historic buildings	48,00	27,00	56,25%
Crime reported	69,00	31,00	44,92%
Pollution	59,00	23,00	38,98%

Table 4. Budget variable usage (average use per session)

Desired number of vendors	5,52
Law enforcement	6,38
Public transportation	5,43
Restoration	5,90
Pollution prevention initiatives	5,86
Garbage clearing	5,52

Yes, for instance, I was trying to keep the crime reports stable, because I think that the main issue for tourists is to have a safe place to go. And then when I realized that the starting level was normal level of crime in the streets, because of the video I'd seen, I figured that that was the right level for the quantity of policemen in the streets, so I could go ahead with other variables to track.

Several participants emphasized the importance of the video clips in providing feedback during the simulation:

When the tourists say the bad part of Quito is the pollution ... and then you see that your curve is going up... You see, this is like the feedback I was talking about. And then I say Oh, gee, I need to increase my budget in pollution prevention and decrease it [the pollution] a little bit because it is too much pollution.

Apparently the feedback from the video-links made the participant aware of the high pollution. Some reported that the feedback helped them to evaluate their decisions and figure out if their choices were good or not. Most participants (6 out of 8) responded that they based their decisions on the information provided by the videos:

Yes, the opinion of the tourists on pollution. The shop owner feels that without ambulant sellers, the business improved. The police talking about the increase of crime was not so useful, because I noticed before that the employment was decreasing, so I understand that something was wrong and could not be solved by the police, so I increased the number of vendors in the street just to stop that.

One of the main intentions behind the implantation of the video-links on the curve was to help the users connect the video clips to states in time. The interviews and the observations revealed that most participants (7 out of 8) understood that the videos were connected to states in time without any explanation provided. One of the participants commented on the video-links:

The interesting thing is I think you link it to certain points in time, for example "police welcomes extra

Table 5. Video usage summary (Lab test)

ID	Videos watched (average)	Recognized the connection between videos and states	Recognized the links without support	Thought the video-clips were helpful	Impact of videos	Used information from the videos
1	6,5	Yes	Yes	No	Did not find the videos any helpful. Thinks the videos were not informative.	No. Thinks the titles gave her enough information
2	13,5	Yes	Yes	Yes	Thinks that getting direct feedback from people makes her care more about their situation.	Yes
3	9	Yes	Yes	Yes	Thinks the information from the videos are easier to remember	Yes
4	4	Yes	No	Yes	The feedback from the videos helped evaluating the decisions	Yes
5	13	Yes	No	No	Did not watch the videos during the simulation, but looked at some videos when instructed after the simulation	No
6	12	Yes	Yes	Yes	Videos drew attention and made her care more.	Yes
7	10	Yes	Yes	Yes	Thinks that the videos made it more "lively" and that they helped finding causal relationships.	Yes. But thought the titles gave him enough information
8	6	No	No	Yes	Thinks the videos were helpful when making decisions.	Yes

personnel" or "police has theft under control in malls" – that tells me a lot! And it's obviously not by accident that it's appearing now and not before. So you give me more information than if you would provide only by television or in other mechanisms. You tell me something about interpretation of what's going on.

Several participants expressed how the videos showing actual people living in Quito made the experience more real (Skartveit, 2008). They liked meeting and receiving feedback from real people. For example, the video showing the shop owner being interviewed while customers were coming in and out of the shop made the participants become more aware of the real situation of the shop owner. Several commented on how the video clips showing real people made them care more and think more about the consequences, before making decisions. One of participants commented on the videos showing real people:

If I just deal with virtual interface, say, I'm playing a game, I don't need to take so much care. But if you get direct contact with the people, you know, they are really struggling in their situation, so you should take more care in what you are doing. It has consequences.

The participants' mental models (Gentner, 2002; Sterman, 2000) do not always correlate with the causal relationships in the model. One of the participants thought that reducing the number of street vendors on the streets causes the job availability to increase. This does not coincide with the simulation model. If the street vendors are removed from the streets they are relocated to malls. This information is, however, only available in the video clips. By watching the video, some participants were able to identify the mismatch between their mental model and the simulation model.

During the interviews, several responded that the videos made the simulation more fun. This could explain why 35% of the users participating in the online test played the entire game. It is possible that they wanted to stay in the simulation to see what happened and what videos would appear.

Some of the participants talked about how videos could better capture the user's attention. Several mentioned how some videos made a bigger impression than others. *"For example the policeman, he didn't impact me that much. But the woman ...[laughs] there was a big impression. And the shoe seller also was a good impression. There are some videos that I remember more than others."* This participant explained that the video of the woman (a street vendor) almost made her cry.

However, not all students thought the videos were helpful. Two out of eight reported that they did not use any information from the videos. One thought the videos would have been more helpful if they were captured in a controlled environment with less distracting elements. She also thought the information from the videos were less accurate than information presented as text.

CONCLUSION AND FUTURE RESEARCH

In this paper, we present the development and evaluation of the Simulation Visualization Lab. SVL aims to help users understand the structure of Quito model and make decisions by visualizing the behaviour of the models using video narratives. The system was evaluated in a pilot study which consisted of two tests. The first test was an online test where users could visit a webpage and try out SVL Client. The other was a lab test conducted in a computer lab, where eight first year university students participated and answered questions about their experience using the system. The target users are primarily university students in System Dynamics. The method could also be of value both to lower level school students as well as to policy makers and citizens who must deal with challenging complex problems.

Technically, the Simulation Visualization Lab fulfils the specified requirements of being able to run the model, to make changes to model variables and to visualize model variables with video clips and other visualization media. While we did not measure the learning effect of the video clips in the pilot study, the interviews and the observations clearly indicate that the videos added value to the users' comprehension of the system. The findings from the pilot study confirm our prior expectations; namely, that providing the users with video clips may be able to facilitate the understanding of complex dynamic behaviours and the learning of complex system knowledge. However, further research is needed to study the system in more authentic situations with different potential user groups (e.g. citizens, policy makers, students) and provide evidence on whether the video narratives are in fact effective for understanding the complex system represented by the Quito model.

Several ideas and suggestions for future work were revealed during the development and the evaluation of the system:

- ***Improving monitoring support.*** Two of the key activities in educational simulations are designing and monitoring decisions (Veermans & van Joolingen, 1998). The lab test revealed that it was difficult for the participants to monitor their decisions in SVL. Most participants did not remember what kind of decisions they made, and at which time they were made. In order for users to monitor and evaluate their decisions, the decisions should be reported in SVL. They could be presented in the curves with a line indicating the point in time at which the decisions had been made. In order to make it easier for the users to track decisions over time, it may be beneficial to use graphical representations of the decisions.

- ***Adaptable user interface.*** Due to the complexity of the user interface, an adaptable user interface, which can provide different information based on different experience levels of the users, is suggested. One implementation could be to create several predefined interfaces, with one user interface per skill level in system dynamics. When the user logs into the system, s/he could choose a skill-level from a list. If the user specifies "novice" s/he will be presented with a simpler interface than if s/he specifies "advanced" or "expert". A more advanced solution would be to make the system adapt dynamically to the user's level. The system would then need to have a module for modelling users (Sleeman & Brown, 1982), which analyzes the user's behaviour and evaluates his/her skill-level based on the interactions between the user and the system. The user model will make the system able to adapt dynamically to each individual user. If, for instance, the user makes some obvious novice mistakes, the system will lower the complexity and provide more help. The degree of system control (Swaak & de Jong, 2001b) will then depend on the user's skill level.
- ***Dynamic analysis of the model.*** The current version of SVL selects video clips based only on the current state of a variable. A useful improvement could be to include an analysis of the structure of the model (Chen & Frotjord, 2006). By analyzing the model, in addition to observing the behaviours, the videos could present a more precise and detailed explanation about what is actually happening in the dynamic system. In the Quito model, this would, for instance, make it possible to explain why the tourists are leaving Quito.

The increasing complexity of the world calls for effective methods to support the understanding of complex systems and building complex system thinking skills. The results from learning sciences research can help address these challenges by providing theoretical understanding of the learning process from cognitive to metacognitive level and empirical base for when, how and why to scaffold learning about complex system (Hmelo-Silver & Azevedo, 2006). In our research, the multimedia learning theory has provided us guidelines when developing the system. Not much research has been conducted on using videos as narratives to represent system dynamics models in simulation, and the research presented in this chapter can thus be considered to be the first step in this direction.

ACKNOWLEDGMENT

The authors would like to thank all participants in the VOCS projects and the anonymous reviewers for their constructive comments.

REFERENCES

Alessi, S. (2000). Designing educational support in system-dynamics-based interactive learning environments. *Simulation & Gaming, 31*, 178–196. doi:10.1177/104687810003100205

Bar-Yam, Y. (1997). *Dynamics of complex systems*. Reading, MA: Addison-Wesley.

Barrett, C. L., Bisset, K. R., Eubank, S. G., Feng, X., & Marathe, M. V. (2008). EpiSimdemics: an efficient algorithm for simulating the spread of infectious disease over large realistic social networks. In *Proc. of the ACM/IEEE Conference on Supercomputing* (pp. 1-12). Piscataway, NJ: IEEE Press.

Beck, K. (2002). *Test-driven development: By example*: Addison-Wesley.

Bedau, M. A. (2003). Artificial life: organization, adaptation and complexity from the bottom up. *Trends in Cognitive Sciences*, *7*(11), 505–512. doi:10.1016/j.tics.2003.09.012

Bois, J. R. (2002). *Decisions within complex systems: an experimental approach using the STRATEGEM-2 computer game.* Unpublished Doctoral thesis, State University of New York, Albany.

Brophy, J. (Ed.). (2004). *Using video in teacher education*: Elsevier.

Casti, J. L. (1994). *Complexification: Explaining a paradoxical world through the science of surprise*. New York: HarperCollins.

Chen, W., & Frotjord, L. (2006). Scaffolding the comprehension of complex systems with explanation. In Kinshuk, R. Koper, P. Kommers, P. Kirschner, D. Sampson & W. Didderen (Eds.), *The Sixth IEEE Int. Conf. on Advanced Learning Technologies* (pp. 869-871). Kerkrade, The Netherlands: IEEE Computer Society.

de Jong, T., Beishuizen, J., Hulshof, C., Prins, F., van Rijn, H., & van Somersen, M. (2005). Determinants of discovery learning in a complex simulation learning environment. In P. Gardenfors & P. Johansson (Eds.), *Cognition, education, and communication technology* (pp. 257-283). Mahwah, NJ: Lawrence Erlbaum Associates, Inc.

de Jong, T., & van Joolingen, W. R. (1998). Scientific discovery learning with computer simulations of conceptual domains. *Review of Educational Research*, *68*, 179–201.

Feltovich, P. J., Coulson, R. L., & Spiro, R. J. (2001). Learners' (mis)understanding of important and difficult concepts. In K. D. Forbus & P. J. Feltovich (Eds.), *Smart machines in education: The coming revolution in educational technology* (pp. 349-375). Menlo Park: CA: AAAI/MIT Press.

Foertsch, J., Moses, G., Strikwerda, J., & Litzkow, M. (2002). Reversing the lecture/homework paradigm using eTEACH web-based streaming video software. *Journal of Engineering Education*, *91*, 267–275.

Gandsas, A., McIntire, K., Palli, G., & Park, A. (2002). Live streaming video for medical education: a laboratory model. *Journal of Laparoendoscopic & Advanced Surgical Techniques. Part A.*, *12*, 377–382. doi:10.1089/109264202320884135

Gentner, D. (2002). Mental models, Psychology of. In N. J. Smelser & P. B. Bates (Eds.), *International encyclopedia of the social and behavioral sciences* (pp. 9683-9687). Amsterdam: Elsevier Science.

Gredler, M. E. (2004). Games and simulations and their relationships to learning. In D. H. Jonassen (Ed.), *Handbook of research on educational communications and technology* (2nd ed., pp. 571-581). Mahwah, NJ: Lawrence Erlbaum.

Green, S., Voegeli, D., Harrison, M., Phillips, J., Knowles, J., & Weaver, M. (2003). Evaluating the use of streaming video to support student learning in a first-year life sciences course for student nurses. *Nurse Education Today*, *23*, 255–261. doi:10.1016/S0260-6917(03)00014-5

Gregg, D., Kulkarni, U., & Vinze, A. (2001). Understanding the philosophical underpinnings of software engineering research in information systems. *Information Systems Frontiers*, *3*(1), 169–183. doi:10.1023/A:1011491322406

Hansen, J., Sato, M., Ruedy, R., Kharecha, P., Lacis, A., & Miller, R. (2007). Climate simulations for 1880-2003 with GISS modelE. *Climate Dynamics*, *29*, 661–696. doi:10.1007/s00382-007-0255-8

Hashmi, M., & Guvenli, T. (2001). Multimedia content on the web: problems and prospects. *Managerial Finance*, *27*, 34–41. doi:10.1108/03074350110767277

Hevner, A. R., March, S. T., Park, J., & Ram, S. (2004). Design science in information systems research. *MIS Quarterly*, *28*(1), 75–105.

Hmelo, C., & Day, R. (1999). Contextualized questioning to scaffold learning from simulations. *Computers & Education*, *32*(2), 151–164. doi:10.1016/S0360-1315(98)00062-1

Hmelo-Silver, C., & Azevedo, R. (2006). Understanding complex systems: Some core challenges. *Journal of the Learning Sciences*, *15*(1), 53–62. doi:10.1207/s15327809jls1501_7

Hollingworth, H. (2006). Learning about teaching – using video. *Professional Educator*, *5*(2), 30–34.

Howie, E., Sy, S., Ford, L., & Vicente, K. J. (2000). Human - computer interface design can reduce misperceptions of feedback. *System Dynamics Review*, *16*(3), 151–171. doi:10.1002/1099-1727(200023)16:3<151::AID-SDR191>3.0.CO;2-0

Jacobson, M., & Wilensky, U. (2006). Complex systems in education: Scientific and educational importance and implications for the learning sciences. *Journal of the Learning Sciences*, *15*(1), 11–34. doi:10.1207/s15327809jls1501_4

Jensen, E., & Brehmer, B. (2003). Understanding and control of a simple dynamic system. *System Dynamics Review*, *19*(2), 119–138. doi:10.1002/sdr.267

Kalyuga, S., Chandler, P., & Sweller, J. (1999). Managing split-attention and redundancy in multimedia instruction. *Applied Cognitive Psychology*, *13*, 351–371. doi:10.1002/(SICI)1099-0720(199908)13:4<351::AID-ACP589>3.0.CO;2-6

Langton, C. (Ed.). (1995). *Artificial life*. Cambridge, MA: MIT.

Lee, J. (1999). Effectiveness of computer-based instructional simulation: A meta analysis. *International Journal of Instructional Media*, *26*(1), 71–85.

Mayer, R. E. (1997). Multimedia learning: Are we asking the right questions? *Educational Psychologist*, *32*(1), 1–19. doi:10.1207/s15326985ep3201_1

Mayer, R. E. (2001). *Multimedia learning*. New York: Cambridge University Press.

Narayanan, N. H., & Hegarty, M. (1998). On designing comprehensible interactive hypermedia manuals. *International Journal of Human-Computer Studies*, *48*, 267–301. doi:10.1006/ijhc.1997.0169

Richardson, G. P. (1996). Problems for the Future of System Dynamics. *System Dynamics Review*, *12*(2). doi:10.1002/(SICI)1099-1727(199622)12:2<141::AID-SDR101>3.0.CO;2-O

Risko, V. (1991). Videodisc-based case methodology: A design for enhancing preservice teachers' problem-solving abilities. In B. Hayes & K. Camperell (Eds.), *Developing lifelong readers: Policies, procedures, and programs* (Vol. 11, pp. 121-136). Utah State University: American Reading Forum.

Robin, S., Reardon, R., & Strand, B. (2001). A video streaming pilot project: applications in social work training and education. *Journal of Technology in Human Services, 18*, 133–143. doi:10.1300/J017v18n03_09

Sabelli, N. (2006). Complexity, technology, science, and education. *Journal of the Learning Sciences, 15*(1), 5–9. doi:10.1207/s15327809jls1501_3

Skartveit, H.-L. (2008). *Representing the real: Documentary, simulation and play.* Unpublished PhD Dissertation, University of Bergen, Bergen.

Skartveit, H.-L., Goodnow, K., & Viste, M. (2003, June). *Visualized system dynamics models as information and planning tools.* Paper presented at the Informing Science + Information Technology Education Joint Conference, Pori, Finland.

Sleeman, D. H., & Brown, J. S. (Eds.). (1982). *Intelligent tutoring systems*. New York: Academic Press.

Smith, S. (1991). Experiential learning. In S. Pendelton & A. Myles (Eds.), *Curriculum planning in nursing education*. London: Edward Arnold.

Smith-Stoner, M., & Willer, A. (2003). Video streaming in nursing education: bringing life to online education. *Nurse Educator, 28*, 66–70. doi:10.1097/00006223-200303000-00007

Sterman, J. (1994). Learning in and about complex systems. *System Dynamics Review, 10*(2-3), 291–330. doi:10.1002/sdr.4260100214

Sterman, J. (2000). *Business dynamics: Systems thinking and modelling for a complex world*. New York: Irwin/McGraw-Hill.

Swaak, J., & de Jong, T. (2001a). Discovery simulations and the assessment of intuitive knowledge. *Journal of Computer Assisted Learning, 17*, 284–294. doi:10.1046/j.0266-4909.2001.00183.x

Swaak, J., & de Jong, T. (2001b). Learner vs. system control in using online support for simulation-based discovery learning. *Learning Environments Research, 4*, 217–241. doi:10.1023/A:1014434804876

Veenman, M. V. J., Prins, F. J., & Elshout, J. J. (2002). Initial inductive learning in a complex computer simulated environment: The role of metacognitive skills and intellectual ability. *Computers in Human Behavior, 18*(3), 327–341. doi:10.1016/S0747-5632(01)00038-3

Veermans, K., & van Joolingen, W. R. (1998). Using induction to generate feedback in simulation based discovery learning environments. In B. P. Goettl, H. M. Halff, C. L. Redfield & V. J. Shute (Eds.), *Lecture Notes in Computer Science, Proceedings of the 4th International Conference on Intelligent Tutoring Systems.* (Vol. 1452, pp. 196-205). London: Springer-Verlag.

West, J. J., & Dowlatabadi, H. (1999). On assessing the economic impacts of sea-level rise on developed coasts. In T. E. Downing, A. A. Olsthoorn & R. S. J. Tol (Eds.), *Climate changes and risk* (pp. 205-220). New York: Routledge.

Wilensky, U., & Resnick, M. (1999). Thinking in levels: A dynamic system approach to making sense of the world. *Journal of Science Education and Technology, 8*, 3–19. doi:10.1023/A:1009421303064

Wissick, C. A., Gardner, J. E., & Langone, J. (1999). Video-based simulations: Considerations for teaching students with developmental disabilities. *Career Development for Exceptional Individuals, 22*(2), 233–249. doi:10.1177/088572889902200206

Wissick, C. A., Lloyd, J. W., & Kinzie, M. B. (1992). The effects of community training using a videodisc-based simulation. *Journal of Special Education Technology, 11*, 207–222.

Chapter 24
Physical Education 2.0

Rolf Kretschmann
University of Stuttgart, Germany

ABSTRACT

Thinking of subjects at school and integrating digital media and technology, one might not think of looking at physical education first. But the pedagogical potentials of digital media integrated in physical education can easily be outlined. Therefore, the concept of Physical Education 2.0 is developed that posits a framework for designing pedagogical scenarios after informing about the old-fashioned Physical Education 1.0, technical devices, software and internet offers, and categorizing pedagogical scenarios by literature review. The imagination of future pedagogical scenarios leads to a deeper awareness of possible physical education developments. Moreover, implementation premises for Physical Education 2.0 in different areas are displayed. Furthermore, future research directions in this special research field with almost tabula rasa character are given. Shortly, the aim of the paper is to give an introduction and overview of the wide scope of digital media within physical education.

INTRODUCTION

Scanning through subjects at school, while searching for fruitful and sensible application and implementation of digital media, one might not turn to look at physical education at first pick. Physical education is usually understood as a school subject that contains exercise content and takes place in the gymnasium, instructed by a former athlete or trainer from the field of sports, the so called physical education teacher. Students have to improve their fitness skills and learn various techniques of certain sports. The learning process is connected with sweat in the truest sense of the word. Due to this common connotation associated with human movement and physical activity, and actually doing sports and exercise, the notion of a pedagogical benefit of digital media (or media at all) comes not into mind at first sight. Hence, the human body is seen as main media in physical education. Media

DOI: 10.4018/978-1-61520-678-0.ch024

and informational technologies are not connected with physical education in the common sense. Two strands of argumentation can be identified to be the reason of the missing interlinking.

Media and informational technologies appear as a threat to children and adolescents in mass media. "Fat, stupid and lazy" kids were proclaimed as the most probable product of media consumption. Several surveys back up this discussion in the mass media (e.g. Common Sense Media, 2008; Marshall, Biddle, Gorely, Cameron, & Murdey, 2004; Mössle, Kleimann, & Rehbein, 2007, 2009). Therefore, media and technology in general are not connected to a healthy life style and a huge amount of physical activity either. Physical education seems to serve as an opposite construct against media consumption, wherein students can compensate their lack of physical activity of their daily life (Morgan, Beighle, & Pangrazi, 2007). Though media is seen to somehow block the intention of bringing students back to physical activity, physical education should focus on exercise and movement itself, being the subject in school predestined for this intention. In this argument, media within physical education is held as a foreign object, which is contrary to the physical activity tasks and attitude. This is the first reason.

The second reason lies in the perceived importance of physical education in comparison to other school subjects. Physical education is not a major subject (Lai & Wong, 2006). Throughout the big international comparative studies concerning educational outcomes, physical education is not considered. Neither the well known and famous PISA (Program for International Student Assessment) (Organisation for Economic Co-Operation and Development: OECD, 2006a, 2006b) nor PIRLS (Progress in International Reading Literacy Study) (Mullis, Martin, Kennedy, & Foy, 2007) and TIMSS (Trends in Mathematics and Science Study) (Mullis, Martin, Gonzales, & Chrostowski, 2004a; Mullis et al., 2004b) put physical education into focus. Similar to art or music, physical education belongs to the minor subjects at school (Lai & Wong, 2006). In addition, media studies in the field of school research have not taken any interest in physical education at all. For instance, the international study SITES (Second Informational Technology in Education Study) (Law, Pelgrum, & Plomp, 2008) is more concerned with school subjects from the domain of natural sciences, mathematics, and language acquisition. Due to the missing presence in the research field of ICT (Information and Communication Technology), and therefore not being subject of research in important international studies, physical education consequently lacks of importance and reputation, when it comes to terms of media use and implementation.

Nonetheless, physical education immanently offers a lot of possibilities for the use of digital media, just as well as other school subjects do. Physical education has the task to develop 21st century skills like media and computer literacy (Buckingham, 2003; Mohnsen, 1999), as each school subject intends. Though integrating technology into schools is important for the development of those skills, technology has to be integrated into physical education as well (Mitchell, McKethan, & Mohnsen, 2004). Thus, the great question arises, how technology can be embedded into physical education. The forthcoming answer may hopefully produce a notion of a sensible pedagogical connection between the two worlds of sports and technology usage within school.

For the revealing of the pedagogical potentials of the use of digital media in physical education, the first step is to describe old-fashioned and obsolete physical education, which may be called Physical Education 1.0. The second step is to enlighten the concept of Physical Education 2.0 by giving a brief overview of useful technical devices, software and internet offers, which can easily be embedded in pedagogically sensible scenarios by the physical educator. Therefore, exemplary and categorical examples of these pedagogical scenarios are posited, including a framework for a didactical design for generating further implementations of digital media in physical education. The third step is to imagine future pedagogical scenarios through describing hypothetical physical education development. The fourth and last step is to depict implementation areas, wherein the terms and conditions of a straightened usage of digital media can be boosted, including gymnasium development, curriculum development, and teacher education development. Finally, future prospects are given, that try to anticipate further (research) development of physical education integrating digital media, stating the wide scope for development within this specific subject.

Hence, the aim of the paper is to give an introduction and overview of the wide field of integrating digital media into physical education, that is still in need to be explored, supported, and developed further.

BACKGROUND

Consulting the benchmarking (English written, international) educational text books used within the academic studies of sport science and physical education teacher education (e.g. Graham. Holt/ Hale, & Parker, 2007; Kirk, Macdonald, & O'Sullivan, 2006; Lumpkin, 2007; Siedentop, 2008; Siedentop, Hastie, & van der Mars, 2004), one cannot put away the fact that the use of digital media within physical education is even more than underrepresented. Actually, there is no clue for a connection of digital media and physical education at all. Therefore, the sensible use of digital media within physical education has not played a significant role within in the academic discourse at first sight. Nonetheless, literature review states a few monographs that try to establish a relationship between digital media and physical education (Mitchell & McKethan, 2003; Mitchell, McKethan, & Mohnsen, 2004; Mohnsen, 1999; 2008).

However, physical education research was occupied with the technology theme since the upcoming turning of the century (David, Bouthier, Marsenach, & Durey, 1999; Mohnsen, 1999). Literature review can state a few articles on the topic of technology connected to the area of physical education, physical education teacher education, and higher education.

With reference to physical education teacher education, a group of papers focus on perception, attitude, technology competence, and use of technology of physical education teachers (Ince, Goodway, Ward, & Lee, 2006; Thomas & Stratton, 2006; Yaman, 2008; Yaman, 2007b, 2009). On the other hand, only two papers deal with the student's view. Yaman (2007a) surveys the perceptions of physical education students towards the internet, while Gubacs (2004) describes the student's view within a project-based learning scenario integrating technology.

Within the field of higher education, Bennett and Green (2001) examine sport science students learning outcomes in an online environment, but cover only theoretical classroom courses. So do Nichols and Levy (2009); the authors discuss e-learning courses for college student-athletes.

Only a few papers focus mainly on physical education teacher education. While Tearle and Golder (2008) examine physical education teacher education in the United Kingdom, Fiorentino and Castelli (2005) tend to inform physical education teachers of digital video editing and producing. Schell (2004) is concerned with giving physical education teacher education students the right advice for their instructions in technology involved settings. Bredel, Fischer, and Thienes (2005) describe selected didactical arrangements containing digital media within physical education teacher education.

Regarding coach education, Stewart (2006) informs about a concept of integrating online education in traditional coach education. Leser, Uhlig, and Uhlig (2008) present a blended learning concept using an online tool for soccer coach education, while Keller (2008) provides a blended learning concept for physical education teacher education for track and field.

According to curriculum, several papers standardize technology use in physical education, mostly trying to combine the NASPE (National Association for Sport & Physical Education) standards for physical education (NASPE, 2004) with technology use (Mitchell, 2001; Mitchell, 2006; Mohnsen, 2005a, 2005b, 2005c).

Concerning internet offers, Pennington and Graham (2002), and Pennington, Wilkinson, and Vance (2004) analyze the postings by physical education teachers of the mailing list NASPE-L, which is the official mailing list by NASPE. Elliot, Stanec, McCollum, and Stanley (2007) inform about which internet resources are of relevance for physical education teachers and how they can use them. Sturm (2008) describes open learning online resources from the field of human movement and training, while Danisch, Müller, and Schwier (2006) illustrate the development of an online environment for the didactics of sport games.

Computer game studies can be found at Hebbel-Seeger (2008b), who states the benefit of sailing simulation software for the progress of real skill development in sailing. While Kretschmann (2008a) focus on a competence model in general, Hayes and Silberman (2007) provide the use of video games in physical education. Trout and Zamora (2005) give an example of using the game "Dance Dance Revolution" (Konami) in physical education class.

Strategy documents were developed and discussed by Baca, Hanke, Hebbel-Seeger, Igel, Vohle, and Wiemeyer (2007), Borkenhagen, Igel, Mester, Olivier, Platen, Wiemeyer, and Zschorlich (2006), and Hebbel-Seeger (2008a). These papers provide a strategy for the broadening of digital media use within the field of sports and sport science.

Finally, articles directly referring on physical education and integrated technologies can be found. Though Ladda, Keating, Adams, and Toscano (2004) proclaim to give an overview of the use of technology in physical education, including the use of heart rate monitors, pedometers and software offers, other authors focus on specific technology use in physical education. PDAs (Personal Digital Assistant) (DerVanik, 2005; McCaughtry & Dillon, 2008; Wegis & van der Mars, 2006) and pedometers (Cagle 2004; Dunn & Tannehill, 2005; McCaughtry, Oliver, Dillon, & Martin, 2008) are covered most frequently. Dober (2003, 2004), and Thienes, Fischer, and Bredel (2005) give an overview of digital media for and within physical education, but only from the national German perspective.

In addition, some authors focus on special topics. Butler (2004) is dealing with interactive whiteboards in comparison with chalk and blackboard. Dober (2006) shows a way of integrating laptops into physical education class. Fischer, Thienes, and Bredel (2005) evaluated CD-ROMs for physical education and physical education teacher education. Hastie and Sinelnikov (2007) outline the use of web-based portfolios in physical education. Woods, Karp, Shimon, and Jensen (2004) describe the pedagogical use of web-quests in physical education.

In conclusion, literature review does not show a tabula rasa, but only little research done in the field of physical education and technology. Due to the importance of 21st century skills for today's students, the mission is to bring the relatively small strand of digital media and physical education into the main stream academic discourse and educational textbooks. At least one German edited educational text book contains a chapter about new media within physical education (Danisch & Friedrich, 2007): Handbuch Sportdidaktik (engl. Handbook of Sport Didactics) (Lange & Sinning, 2007).

PHYSICAL EDUCATION 2.0: ASPECTS, ELEMENTS, PREMISES

To make a sensible linking of digital media and physical education clearer, it is necessary to draw an image of an old-fashioned physical education. This image is usually being associated by the common body of current adults, which were inevitably socialized by physical education during their school days. Based on that image of Physical Education 1.0, the concept of Physical Education 2.0 can be grounded, whereas its elements, premises, and practical examples will be described next.

The term of Physical Education 2.0 refers to the term "Web 2.0" (O'Reilly, 2005) in two ways. First, there is the shift from the consuming attitude of Web 1.0 to Web 2.0 with user generated content and social networking. This shift mirrors the shift from teacher centered teaching methods of the old-fashioned Physical Education 1.0 concept to Physical Education 2.0 with various teaching methods and a changed teacher role. Second, the appendix 2.0 means an upgrade and further development of a conceptual framework compared to the appendix 1.0. Accordingly, Physical Education 2.0 is the product of further development integration media and technologies, whereas Physical Education 1.0 stands for an obsolete version of physical education concepts without technology.

Physical Education 1.0

Physical education is normally associated with exercise, heading towards certain motor skills and their training. A kind of "drill instructor", supposed to be the physical education teacher, manages the instructions. He or she is standing in front of the class most of the time, giving personal advice where it is needed. Students are supposed to be held "in motion" and physically active for (almost) the whole session. Media in usage are the teacher himself and his or her voice.

The teacher role is iced to a solid instructional one. The physical educator is giving orders which the students have to fulfill. He or she gives the orders in a verbal manner, using intonation and strength of the human voice. On occasion, the exercising is interrupted by technique demonstrations by the teacher himself or herself (e.g. Basketball layup). Students are supposed to draw an own cognitive image of the specific movement, learning by imitation (Nixon & Locke, 1973). The next step is to practice the demonstrated technique over and over. Every now and then the teacher gives advice and hints to some students, who have problems at performing the technique in question. At the end of a lesson a sports game has to be played (e.g. Basketball). In this case the teacher serves as referee and trainer for all participating students.

Like this or something like that, physical education is described and remembered by most people. We all are socialized by physical education (or physical training scenarios) and have made up an individual opinion and attitude towards it. Mostly, one can remember sweating while exercising and learning certain sport techniques. Shortly, this obsolete concept of "Physical Education 1.0" uses the same methods of teaching, orders and organization every lesson throughout the school year. The paradigm of an instructional design theory for physical educators (Vickers, 1990) being a drill instructor is obvious. No media is used at all; the human body is just enough.

In better physical education classes the Physical Education 1.0 setting is sometimes supported by drawn images of the correct technique of a certain sport or a video of an exemplarily good game play. Sometimes students are recorded on video tape and are given instant video feedback according to their motor skills and motor behavior (Hamlin, 2005). For instance, Roberts and Brown (2008) use instructional videos in aquatic education. The latter might be titled as "Physical Education 1.5", if a digital camera is used and the videos are stored and distributed on digital media as well.

Mostly, disregarding and disrespect towards digital media in physical education or even media in general are flanking the Physical Education 1.0 position. This might be accompanied by prejudices of digital media causing "fat, stupid and lazy" children. One might even hear supporters of the concept of Physical Education 1.0 among physical education teachers, being afraid of being replaced by digital media.

Although there is serious development in teaching methods and styles (e.g. Byra, 2006; Kirk & McPhail, 2002), media usage is definitely a minority phenomenon. Cooperative Learning, constructivist approaches including situated learning, TGfU (Teaching Games for Understanding), etc., are not linked to digital media, when it comes to the discussion of good physical education. However, a good physical education can be without digital media, but a modern one includes digital media, which is preparing students for the 21st century (Mohnsen, 1999).

Physical Education 2.0

In the following section technical devices, specific software and internet offers are described, building the basis of possible digital media being used in specific pedagogical scenarios in physical education. Furthermore, a didactical framework for the implementation of digital media in physical education will be developed, which can be used by physical educators to form pedagogical scenarios integrating digital media.

Technical Devices/ Hardware

Mohnsen (2008) lists a huge amount of technological items that have the inner potential of a use in physical education. For technical devices the following selected components can be listed:

- Computers and laptops: The main advantage of laptops compared to desktop computers is portability. Laptops can be used anywhere in the gymnasium, even without a power socket, at least for the maximum battery run duration.
- LCD projectors, digital video and digital photo cameras: Portable LCD projectors can be used to display content of a laptop or digital video and digital photo cameras. The latter ones mostly include the feature of recording a large amount of time on a digital storage. The disadvantage of LCD projectors is the need for a power socket and a projection screen. Usually they are very rare at common schools, especially for gymnasium application. Of course, digital cameras can be connected to normal TVs. The exclusive usage of digital cameras allows only a few students to watch recorded (movement) performances due to the small size of the LCD screens manufactured into these devices.
- Audio equipment (MP3-players, HiFi racks): Rhythm and dance education within physical education classes are usually supported by audio equipment.
- Heart monitors: Heart monitors are used to maintain the heart rate in a certain heart rate zone. The heart rate is measured by a chest strap which gives the student instant feedback about his or her heart rate while exercising.
- Pedometers: Pedometers are counting steps over a certain amount of time. Steps can be a measure for the physical activity level.
- Handhelds (mobile phones, PDAs, GPS devices): Software applications can be installed on handhelds which can be used for the assessment of human movement performance, for instance (e.g. movement diaries, game statistics, exercise results). GPS devices can be used for orienteering races.
- Video game consoles (Playstation, Sony Computer Entertainment; Eye Toy, Sony Computer Entertainment; Wii, Nintendo),

dance mats (Dance Dance Revolution, Konami), and Gamebike (Cateye): Video game consoles provide several user interfaces that involve human movement as a method for playing a virtual game character. These so called exergames increase the physical activity level while playing video games. Dance mats are a specific kind of these interfaces: a digital mat is used as game pad, whereas the player has to perform dance moves on the mat which are measured by the mat itself and transformed into digital game play. The Gamebike (Konami) is an interactive video-based exercise bicycle. The exercise bicycle is connected to a gaming console, whereas the biker has to solve different tasks and levels on a virtual track.

- Makoto Fitness Arena (Makoto): The Makoto Fitness Arena (Makoto) is a standalone device that requires the user to react to sounds and lights. The user is placed in the center of the device, which consists of three corner poles. The user has to tap randomly litting lights on each of the poles as fast as possible.

Technical devices as listed above should and can truly be considered to be used within physical education. Linking technical devices with physical education could be held as the initial starting point for getting over the concept of Physical Education 1.0. Though it seems that most physical educators and sport pedagogues do not know of technical devices meant to be used in physical activity contexts, enlightment in the sense of generating and improving knowledge about the existence of these devices is the key for fostering up-to-date thinking in terms of modern physical education (Mitchell et al., 2004; Mohnsen, 1999).

Software and Internet

After gathering knowledge about technical devices to be considered within physical education, the next step will be taking a closer look at software and internet offers in the field of sport to forward the development of the Physical Education 2.0 concept.

Software

Though it is possible to identify the benchmarking international educational textbooks in the area of sport science and physical education pedagogy, this procedure can't be replicated for the field of sport software. Educational sport software is produced by national or regional developers and is normally very hard to access from other countries or regions. Due to this kind of circumstances, mainly national examples from Germany and a few international accessible examples will be given.

The following list can be posited to represent software offers exemplarily:

- „Fußball/ Schwimmen/ Volleyball – Bausteine für einen sicheren und attraktiven Unterricht" (Friedrich, 2004; Bredel, 2003; Fischer, 2005) (engl. "Soccer/ Swimming/ Volleyball – Building blocks for a secure and attractive education") (three CDs/ DVDs developed by the Department of Sport and Sport Science at the University of Dortmund, Germany, and the Department of Sport Science at the University of Giessen, Germany)
- "Basketball Elements" (Richter, 2007)
- "Simi Scout" (SIMI Reality Motion Systems) (Scouting and game play analysis software)
- "Simi Motion" (SIMI Reality Motion Systems) (3D analysis of human movement)

- Playbook series for basketball, American football, soccer, water polo, volleyball, and hockey (Jes-Soft) (playbook software)
- Digital sports-games (computer and video games: e.g. NBA Live, Electronic Arts; FIFA, Electronic Arts, etc.)

There are three kinds of sports software to differentiate. First, there is educational software that is supposed to be used in educational contexts as physical education or physical education teacher education (e.g. "Fußball/ Schwimmen/ Volleyball – Bausteine für einen sicheren und attraktiven Unterricht", Friedrich, 2004; Bredel, 2003; Fischer, 2005). This software normally includes videos of the specific sport techniques and/ or game tactics, including theoretical information based on the academic knowledge of sport science. Methods, drills and hints for teaching classes are also embedded. Beginners should use the information to boost their learning process.

Second, there is software that is meant to be used in the field of professional sports, either to analyze game play (e.g. Simi Scout, SIMI Reality Motion Systems) or to analyze human movement itself (e.g. Simi Motion, SIMI Reality Motion Systems). Coaches, exercise scientists, and sport scientists (and also students of sport science) are usually aware of dealing with these contents and constraints.

Third, there is commercial gaming software that does not intend to educate, but to entertain. The approach of Digital Game-Based Learning (Prensky, 2001) tries to use the motivational and immersive power of video games in educational affairs. For digital sports-games, Hayes and Silberman (2007), Hebbel-Seeger (2008b), Kretschmann (2008a), and Trout & Zamora (2005) tried to employ those games for pedagogical learning outcomes.

Internet

The world-wide-web provides almost endless information about almost everything. Though there is no international database which includes internet resources addressed to physical educators, the procedure will be equal to the one of the software section. Thus, present national offers are followed by a few international ones. Treadwell (2001) listed and commented internet sites for educational purposes, including some for physical education teachers. A list of English spoken websites, relevant to physical education teachers, can be found at Elliot et al. (2007).

The following list can be posited, representing internet offers exemplarily:

- www.sportpaedagogik-online.de (engl. "sport pedagogy online") (offer for physical education teachers for planning physical education)
- www.spingate.de (table tennis) (developed by the German Sport University Cologne)
- www.5min.com (video archive covering training in selected sports)
- Wikipedia Sports Portal (in different languages) (information about certain sports and sport in general, and materials for sport education)
- www.youtube.com (archive of sport events, sports culture, e.g. the Philippine folkdance tinikling).

Regarding the internet offers, one can differentiate between two different kinds of offers. On the one hand, educational use is intended and proclaimed (e.g. www.sportpaedagogik-online.de). On the other hand, informing about a certain sport or sport phenomenon is intended. In this case, the offer (e.g. Wikipedia) addresses to a specific community (e.g. gamers, surfers, etc.) or social group that is not necessarily related to physical education. Nonetheless, these materials can easily be embedded in pedagogical scenarios to support learning processes within physical education.

Indubitable, both lists could be drawn much longer, but an (international) compendium that includes all software and internet offers for sports and physical education is still missing. The intention is just to give a brief overview. The amount of internet offers is still increasing, whereas physical educators should be observant.

Learning management systems (LMS) (e.g. Moodle, Blackboard, etc.) can be an option either, that unify both software and internet offers by providing a platform that can be formed and filled up with educational content by the physical educator, since the technical infrastructure is available and media literacy is of an adequate level.

Pedagogical Scenarios: Present

Literature review (Bennett & Green, 2001; Bredel et al., 2005; Butler, 2004; Cagle 2004; Danisch, 2008; Danisch et al., 2006; DerVanik, 2005; Dober, 2003, 2004, 2006; Dunn & Tannehill, 2005; Elliot et al., 2007; Fischer et al., 2005; Hebbel-Seeger, 2007; McCaughtry & Dillon, 2008; McCaughtry et al., 2008; Mitchell & McKethan, 2003; Mitchell et al., 2004; Mohnsen, 2008; Stewart, 2006; Thienes et al., 2005; Wegis & van der Mars, 2006) allows identifying four main pedagogical scenarios integrating digital media within physical education: Homework and theory, informational input (plenum) (LCD projector and laptop), learning stations (with one or several stations integrating digital media), and feedback.

Homework and Theory

Learning within physical education class does not only take place during face-to-face lessons. Students are demanded to prepare forthcoming lessons and rework passed sessions (Bennett & Green, 2001). In these cases digital media can support the preparation or reworking (Danisch et al., 2006; Stewart, 2006). For example, students can use a CD/ DVD (e.g. "Basketball Elements", Richter, 2007) to prepare a specific sports technique (e.g. set shot in Basketball) that is planned to be tackled in the next lesson. So they can start at a higher level in the (motor) learning process, because they have already gained knowledge about a certain technique (Bredel et al., 2005; Thienes et al., 2005). This prevents students from being overstrained in face-to-face lessons by trying to manage motor control and motor knowledge simultaneously.

Knowledge about rules, tactics, and game play can be acquired by students on their own, as homework for instance (Mitchell et al., 2004). The physical educator can also use podcasts, that can include both knowledge and theory, and technique and game play videos (Danisch, 2008; Hebbel-Seeger, 2007).

Therefore, internet offers can be employed for preparation for or reworking of a physical education lesson (Dober, 2003, 2004; Elliot et al., 2007).

Web-based portfolios, wherein students can arrange their learning and exercise achievements, can also be used as a homework task (Hastie & Sinelnikov, 2007). In this case the students with the best portfolio designs or results might be given prizes. This can lift motivation towards engaging in digital media.

Moreover, web-quests can be a sensible activity for homework (Woods et al., 2004). For instance, students can inform themselves about the history of Basketball (e.g. rules, founder, international development, etc.), working on sensible tasks in a playful setting. But the preparation of a web-quest takes time and has to be done carefully, though it is a serious damage to the educational process if links are broken or a URL is badly misspelled (Zheng, Perez, Williamson, & Flygare, 2008).

Outsourcing theoretical contents gives physical educators more time for physical activity contents and actual movement within the lessons. However, the main advantage of this scenario is that students can adapt their own learning tempo according to the software or internet offer.

Informational Input

Using an LCD projector that is connected to a laptop gives the physical educator the opportunity to provide information to all students at the same time

(Bredel et al., 2005; Fischer et al., 2005; Thienes et al., 2005). Content is provided digitally on the laptop (e.g. software, videos, and internet offers if W-LAN is available). For example, the teacher can employ embedded videos of educational software (e.g. "Volleyball – Bausteine für einen sicheren und attraktiven Unterricht", Fischer, 2005) to show the students the "right" technique from different angles using slow-motion and freezing in addition (Mohnsen, 2008). The teacher could also display specific tactical behaviors (e.g. offensive plays in volleyball), that is provided by animations within the software. Innovative technology like interactive whiteboards can also be used to provide information and support the interactive discussion process with the students about the provided information (Butler, 2004).

The advantage of this scenario is that all students can be reached at the same time and can benefit from the same educational software (or offer). The disadvantage of this scenario lies in the reduction of actual time of physical activity and movement within a lesson. Therefore, the theoretical input must not last too long; otherwise the time for putting theory into praxis might be too short.

Learning Stations

Within arranged learning stations one or more station(s) can consist of a digital media offer (Dober, 2006). For example, one station stages a laptop including specific software (e.g. "Basketball Elements", Richter, 2007) for analyzing videos for the smash), whereas the other stations provide well known drills for practicing a technique (Bredel et al., 2005; Dober, 2004; Thienes et al., 2005). Normally, groups of students pass through each station while working at each station for a given time period. Thus, working together in groups encourages cooperative learning (Johnson, Johnson, & Holubec (1990).

Mobile podcast devices for video content (either web streaming or memory card storage) can also be part of a station. The handheld can display videos of the right sport technique, giving students advice in terms of demonstration (Danisch, 2008; Hebbel-Seeger, 2007).

The critical thing about the arrangement of learning circles is the selection and order of each station, duo to each student group has to pass through all stations. Each station has to be a possible and sensible starting and ending point of a loop (Schmoll, 2007).

Feedback

In this scenario digital media is used to give students instant feedback relating to their motor skills. A laptop, a LCD beamer, a digital video camera, and video delay software (e.g. "Simi VidBack", SIMI Reality Motion Systems) are needed. For example, pairs of students perform an exercise relating to a specific technique (e.g. digging in volleyball). While exercising the digital video camera records the performance. The camera is connected to the laptop whereas the video delay software is running. The software delays the playing of the recorded performance by 60 seconds. The laptop screen is duplicated via the LCD projector, so the students get a bigger screen view of their recorded performance. After having exercised 60 seconds, the exercising

Figure 1. Learning stations

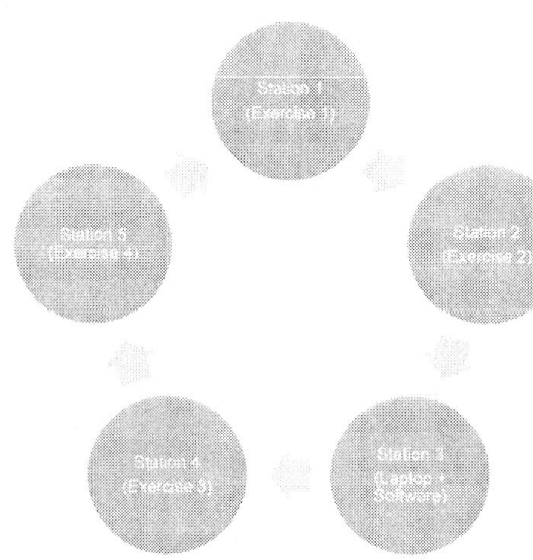

student pair moves on to the projection screen and the students give instant feedback to each other relating to motor skill development. In the mean time the next student pair is exercising and being recorded (Bredel et al., 2005).

Students are required to have a certain knowledge and skill level, so that the feedback becomes sensible feedback. Furthermore, students have to be aware of the critical issues of the technique in question and need to be used to be recorded on video, including watching themselves and other students on video.

In a different case, students can be recorded on video tape, whereas the video is digitalized and edited by the physical educator (Fiorentino & Castelli, 2005). The benefit lies in the edited content. Certain sections of the whole recording can be cut out and reunited to a new sequence. This sequence may contain typical errors of a student, performing a sports game. Hints can be added in a digital text document by the physical educator. Finally, the videos and hints can be given to the student via CD/ DVD or USB memory stick. The difference to Physical Education 1.5 lies in the post-editing of the video material and the distribution on digital media.

In another case, PDAs (McCaughtry & Dillon, 2008; DerVanik, 2005; Wegis & van der Mars, 2006) and pedometers (Cagle 2004; Dunn & Tannehill, 2005; McCaughtry et al., 2008) can be embedded in a feedback scenario. PDAs can be used by the teacher or by the student to assess exercise data or game performance (Wegis & van der Mars, 2006).

Didactical Design

Forming pedagogical scenarios integrating digital media in physical education to fulfill the concept of Physical Education 2.0 is not easy. The following figure intends to illustrate issues to be recognized while generating pedagogical scenarios within this field.

Regarding the setting, learning theory (e.g. constructivism, situated learning), learning target(s) (e.g. motor skill development, social awareness), curriculum (e.g. national standards), and individual school resources (e.g. availability of technical devices, money) have to be considered.

Regarding lessons, planning, analyzation, and realization in connection and involvement of the relevant persons (teacher and/ or student), technical devices, software and internet offers (technology) have to be integrated in a coherent comprehensive manner.

Pedagogical Scenarios: Future

Utopias and science fiction imaginations of the future are recommended by mass media and therefore part of our daily life. However, researchers and serious writers tried (and still try) to imagine the future. For instance, Beare (2001) was trying to reinvent school, while Horx (2006) describes potential school development within the future society.

Figure 2. Feedback scenario (adapted from Bredel et al., 2005)

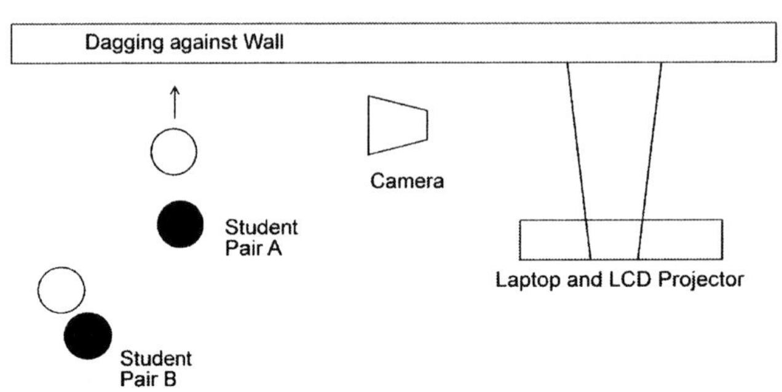

Figure 3. Framework for the use of digital media in physical education (adapted from Kretschmann, 2008b)

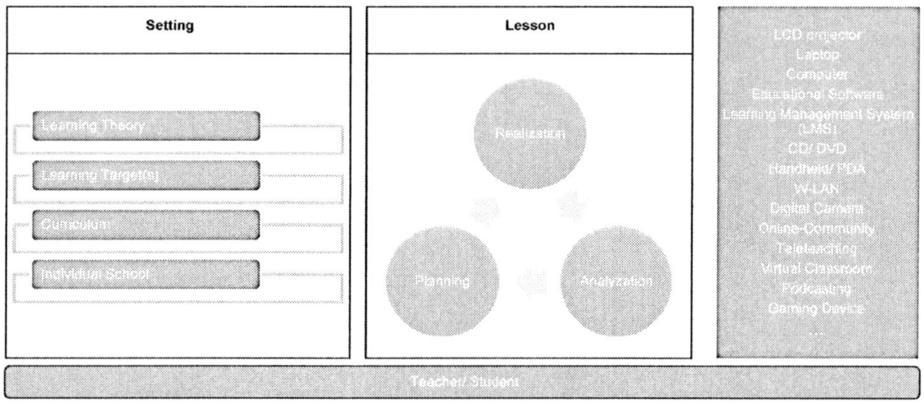

Having displayed pedagogical scenarios of the present, including a didactical design model, one might turn to the future of sports and physical education. Due to the theoretical concept of future research and imagination being a serious and fruitful business, one might employ our imagination to draw alternative images of the future (Bell, 1996). Mohnsen (2008) gives a brief description of future physical education in the year 2015, when digital media (devices, software and internet offers) are accessible for students 24 hours a day, seven days a week. They participate daily in physical activities on their own by using the devices. Thus a blended learning concept is established, whereas students are to learn virtually in online courses. Students do not need to attend physically all the time. Physical education is no longer a physical attendance based subject.

In any case, how will physical education look like in the far future? The following hypothetical scenarios try to outline possible physical education development. The intention is to establish awareness for future physical education development and technology. This awareness might serve as a basis for reflection upon physical education itself.

Face-to-Face and Distance Education

Following the future scenario of Mohnsen (2008), physical education only uses sporadic face-to-face lessons. In these lessons the teacher only gives feedback to the students about their motor development and achievements. The whole class obligatory meets at the beginning and the end of the school year. At the beginning of the school year, learning goals of the curriculum are introduced and discussed. At the end of the school year the students are assessed using some motor tests for grading. Devices as heart rate monitors, pedometers, and accelerometers are accessible for all students, so students practice and train on their own. Thus, students can documents their achievements electronically using a virtual learning online environment. The virtual learning online environment allows communication with other students through portable devices (PDA, smart phone), so students can support each other during the learning process. If necessary, students can contact selected physical education teachers and talk with them via video conferencing in real time to be given immediate feedback (e.g. heart rate monitor results: Wills, 2006).

Theoretical content of the sub disciplines of sport science (e.g. sport psychological interventions) and of certain topics of the curriculum (e.g. theory of basketball and its techniques) can be learned online. An expert software system with online lectures and tests informs the students and gives advice to their current fitness and training conditions. Technology assisted self learning with few attendance education at school is the major approach to physical education, containing a strong aspect of responsibility of the individual.

Teacher Role

In this scenario the teacher role has finally shifted from instructor to advisor (Hartnell-Young, 2003; Scrimshaw, 1997). Students try to solve their problems on their own. The consuming mentality has changed to a self learning one. Students even choose their individual learning goals (e.g. fitness development, improving tactical skills). The curriculum offers various options for the students, so students can choose the ones that individually fit best. Due to the amount of possible curriculum content options, the teacher is only accessible for students when they need advice. Therefore, students can date the teacher, so they can talk via video conference or even face to face, in case the teacher decides that the problem needs to be discussed physically attendant. The teacher is something like a mentor to the student, who helps if he or she is needed. Teachers do not need to demonstrate sport techniques anymore, because students can get this content from virtual learning environments. Furthermore, teachers do not have to organize face-to-face lessons or teams for sport games. Students have to do this by themselves. Only if students ask for support by the teacher, when they meet to play a sports game (e.g. Basketball), for instance, the teacher comes over as a "watcher". If he or she is asked to give hints for better game play he or she will help out.

If there is any problem with software or devices, technical stuff is responsible for this and will be contacted by the students. However, the teacher has to be familiar with the devices and software, but he or she has to be a pedagogical expert, not a technical one.

E-Sports

The E-Sports community has already established an international league and competition system, wherein "professional" gamers compete against each other, playing commercial computer games. E-Sports is "an area of sport activities in which people develop and train mental or physical abilities in the use of information and communication technologies" (Wagner, 2006, p. 439).

Following this wide E-Sports definition two different scenarios are possible. First, video and computer games, with "traditional" user interfaces (keyboard and gamepad) will gain real sports status and will be held as a sport among physical sports (e.g. basketball). Therefore, gaming is part of physical education, though not in the gymnasium, but in normal classrooms, wherein special gaming computers and devices are accessible for students. All kinds of computer game genres are relevant for physical education (e.g. shooters, digital sports-games, simulations, etc.). Students do not need to change clothes for that part of physical education. They can attend in regular daily clothes. Real exercise has not vanished, but is only one part among E-Sports and informal leisure sports outside school. In this case it is also plausible that commercial digital sports-games are used to assist motor learning for certain sports (Hayes & Silberman, 2007; Hebbel-Seeger, 2008b; Kretschmann, 2008a).

Secondly, physical education is enhanced through video and computer games, which are commercially produced for the use within physical education. Following the usage of dance mats (Dance Dance Revolution, Konami) and Wii (Nintendo), the so called exergames (games that provide exercise by different user interfaces) (Chamberlin & Gallagher, 2008) will be employed to assist motor learning. The technology for movement measuring will be that good, that fine motor activities can be measured and used as input for the digital game play. Therefore, the whole body comes in, while both gross and fine motor skills are trained throughout the gaming experience (Kretschmann, 2008a). Some lessons will be held as distance education, wherein students meet at a certain time to compete virtually against each other. In this case every student has got the needed equipment at home, including enough space for spatial movement.

Abolition of Physical Education

In this scenario physical education has vanished from the canon of school subjects (Vertinsky, McKay, & Petrina, 2004). This may appear as a dystopia from the sport pedagogue's point of view. Actually, this scenario is a utopia, because future society and students have gathered an awareness of a healthy lifestyle; and this lifestyle contains physical activity, of course. Gymnasiums at school still exist, but they are only used for sport events like school team competitions. Several sport competence centers exist, where students are allowed to participate in various motor activities for free. Striking refunds, gratification and prizes are given to those students, who are notably healthy according to motor testing and examination. The sport competence centers also provide serious information about sport science theory, working closely together with sport science departments at universities.

In an alternative version of this scenario there are no sport centers at all. Students and the whole population have to train themselves at home on their own. Only rich people can employ a fitness coach for advice. Due to urbanization, only few gymnasiums exist, which are owned by private clubs or fitness centers. Of course, students have to pay money to participate in the gymnasium offers. The fitness market has reacted and created training devices for home usage. Thus, this is the way students train themselves. The manufactured training devices include expert system software, which has actually replaced the physical educator or trainer.

Actuating Elements, Cyborg, and Motor Program

In this scenario one can differentiate between three kinds of treatment in the motor learning process. They are subsumed according to their approach of enhancing the natural human body with technology.

The first case is placed in the area of sports technology, equipment, and clothing. Among sports goods one might find clothing that is enhanced by actuating elements. These so called actuating elements react according to a biophysical signal. This signal might be sweat, and the reaction might be starting a cooling system embedded in a running jacket. Thinking further, the signal might be muscle tone, and the reaction might be muscle stimulation. Or the signal might be some visual input (e.g. an integrated camera and microprocessor to analyze environmental data) or spatial data (e.g. accelerometer data, GPS data), and the reaction might still be muscle stimulation. Hence, this technological enhancement could make sure that the right muscles contract at the right time during the performance of a certain sport technique movement. Imagine doing a somersault in the air, whereas sensors measure height, angles, and speed, activating actuating elements, which cause the right muscle stimulation at the right time to support the adequate performance of the somersault in the air. Following, learning of all sport techniques can be enhanced by such a technology.

The second case is based on the so called "Cyborg Project" by Warwick (2002). An electrode array (a specialized manufactured microchip) was implanted into Warwick's arm. A simulation of a complex neural system made him able to control a robot arm, just using his own arm with the implanted chip. Thus, the robot arm could mimic Warwick's own arm. Following this approach, the next step could be the construction of a robotic armor. The armor could serve as strengthener of physical energy and power skills of the human body. Imagine a robot armor that can lift a multiple of one's own body weight, and can run faster and jump higher than normal human beings. The development of that technology would change our regards towards competitive elite sports and to physical education as well. Ethical considerations and constraints are strongly involved, too.

The third case is known from science fiction, specifically the movie "The Matrix" (Silver, Wachowski, & Wachowski, 1999). Within the movie a computer program is used to "update" the mindset of a certain person with knowledge and motor skills (e.g. martial arts skills). Imagine an interface to one's brain (e.g. microchip) that can be used as an interface to put new motor programs into your brain. After the procedure one is capable of performing every human movement and sport technique one might think of (e.g. basketball skills). The effectiveness of this special kind of motor learning and control would only be limited to one's individual body constitutions. Thus, this method would revolutionize traditional treatments to establish or modify motor programs (Schmidt, 1980).

Implementation Areas

The implementation process of digital media does not fulfill itself (Dober 2004; Hebbel-Seeger, 2007). Lifting Physical Education 1.0 and 1.5 to Physical Education 2.0 takes time and needs various starting points. Implementation has to begin simultaneously at the lots of gymnasium, curriculum, and teacher education to build the premises for the concept of Physical education 2.0.

The German strategy documents (Baca et al., 2008; Borkenhagen et al., 2006) proclaim strategies for universities and sport science in general. They do not specifically focus on physical education, but some claims foreshadow possible physical education development.

Gymnasium Development

The future gymnasium needs to shift from technology isolated buildings to the integration of W-LAN, LCD projectors, computers, handhelds for every student, and adequate number of power sockets, etc., including separated media rooms with doorways to the gymnasium. Especially, buildings under construction or gymnasiums needing renovation are objects of interest. Hence, the initializing process for the development of a technology friendly gymnasium for future physical education can start. Problems are considered in places, to where certain physical education content is outsourced; that is true to the cases of swimming, track and field, stadium and outdoor sports (e.g. American football, skiing, etc.). Using technology in a swimming hall might come to be an impossible task. Track and field, stadium sports and skiing lack of a power socket in the outdoor environment. In addition, weather can be a concern, whereas laptops and PDAs should be waterproof.

Surely, budget restraints are the most blocking force in this case (Gillard, Bailey, & Nolan, 2008). Nonetheless, development should focus on building the needed infrastructure (Borkenhagen et al., 2006; Holzrichter, 2001).

Curriculum Development

Technology needs to be embedded into the physical education curriculum and standards. Combining or fusing national standards (e.g. NASPE, 2004) with technology standards into another publication, as Mitchell (2001), Mitchell (2006), and Mohnsen (2005a, 2005b, 2005c) do, is not enough. In this case a second standard is created, that will certainly compete with the original standard. The primary standard needs to integrate digital media and its sensible use, so that a secondary document is not needed. Physical education can provide and develop media and computer literacy of students just like other school subjects are supposed to. Thus, the upcoming editions of national (or even international) standards for physical education should integrate technology as a natural element.

Teacher Education Development

Digital media needs to be integrated into physical teacher education at universities, and in further and higher education in general. Mitchell and McKethan (2003) give examples of this integration, while Reinmann (2005) claims for integrating digital media in teacher education in general, promoting a blended learning concept using learning management systems (LMS). The latter can easily be adopted for physical education teacher education (Bennet & Green, 2001; Danisch et al., 2006; Keller, 2008; Stewart, 2006). Students should gather early experience with the use of digital media within the field of sport and physical education. Furthermore, students should engage in digital media from the very beginning of their student career at university.

Baca et al. (2007), and Borkenhagen et al. (2006) promote severe production of content for higher education in the field of sport science. This includes and will hopefully generate content for physical education teacher education, too. In addition, Samson, Igel, and Meiers (2006) surveyed professors of sport science departments at university. Surveys like this might help to create an awareness of digital media and its value and importance (Borkenhagen et al., 2006).

FUTURE RESEARCH DIRECTION

Due to 21st century skills and up-to-date-education (Mohnsen, 1999), the dosage of digital media is the key of a sensible, well reasoned and sophisticated Physical Education 2.0, which is embedded and developed using the posited framework. The question of the "right" proportion of media and movement in a blended learning concept cannot be answered yet (Dober, 2004; Nichols & Levy, 2009).

At present, research and academic discourse lacks in several categories (according to Kretschmann, 2008b):

- Curriculum Development: Scanning through national (and available English written) curricula of physical education, digital media is highly underrepresented and needs to be significantly anchored therein.
- Media Database: An (international) database with commentaries to media offers and evaluated usage documentary is still missing.
- Documentation of Digital Media Use: Scanning through literature leads to marginally few reports of a sensible and elaborated digital media use within physical education. In-depth descriptions for digital media use scenarios are highly recommended.
- Empirical Findings: Research crucially lacks of empirical findings integrating digital media within physical education. There is still much work to do, creating the empirical background for the practical use and benefit of technology in physical education.
- Gymnasium Resources: The relationship between technology and gymnasiums still seems to be held as an alienated relationship. Technology in the gymnasium seems to be a foreign object.
- Dissemination of E-Learning Projects within Sport Science: sport scientific projects (e.g. "eBuT", http://www.bewegung-und-training.de) are not put into any context of practical use within physical education. Although this step would be manageable, it is not taken so far.
- (Further) Teacher Education: Digital media needs to be integrated into physical education teacher education and

physical education teacher further education. Although there are selective offers, an elaborated curricula concept lets waiting for it.

- Implementation Strategies: Strategies for the implementation process of digital media into physical education are still missing. Successful and sustainable implementation guidelines and serious advice for a (national) school system and individual schools can't be found.

For the future towards the next upgrade to Physical Education 3.0 one might consider video cube walls technology, that allows to (inter)act in a cube, whose walls consist of screens (scenarios of virtual reality) or electronic devices like ski goggles, that fade in track information (scenarios of augmented reality) (Haggerty, 1997). But in comparison to the outlined future pedagogical scenarios above, this sounds old-fashioned somehow. Hence, the imagination of the future of physical education lets current innovative technologies appear as obsolete and boring, even before they are actually developed further. This is one of the outcomes of drawing possible futures (Bell, 1996). The prize to pay for enlightment and awareness is anticlimax. Nonetheless, future is still to come and it is not set up at the moment.

Further research and discussion might turn to the everlasting theme of surplus value of technology within physical education: what is exactly the benefit of digital media within physical education? For students, teachers, and the society, different answers might be given. Experimental study designs will be needed to research this field. However, recent research inclines an overestimation of multimedia (Wiemeyer, 2003) and motivational increase (Fischer et al., 2005). Anyhow, physical education research is still in need to tackle this question in an elaborated (empirical) way.

CONCLUSION

Finally, the subject of physical education which is apparently little associated with technology, has become a subject of interest for pedagogues associated with media and technology. From the beginning at Physical Education 1.0 (and 1.5) the brief overview of technical devices, software and internet offers lead to the use of such media within physical education class, forwarding the concept of Physical Education 2.0. Different kinds of pedagogical scenarios could have been developed and enhanced by striking examples, leading in a framework that illustrates the areas to be considered while planning digital media use in physical education. During this positing, imaginations of future physical education lead to a deeper awareness of physical education development according to technology. But to implement the concept of Physical Education 2.0 premises in gymnasium development, curriculum development, and teacher education development are still to be fostered.

Obviously, the field of academic research within the intersection of digital media and physical education is almost a tabula rasa that needs to be explored by researches, teachers, students, parents, politicians, and any other interested group of persons.

Hopefully, the aim of the paper to give an overview of the scope of digital media within physical education is achieved. To give an interested reader, who does not necessarily have to come from the field of sport science and physical education, a glimpse of the pedagogical potentials digital media have within the world of physical education, might be a way to intrude into the academic discourse within sport science by employing "outsiders" to take part in and develop further a field that is still up to grow bigger.

REFERENCES

Baca, A., Hanke, U., Hebbel-Seeger, A., Igel, C., Vohle, F., & Wiemeyer, J. (2007). Kommentierung des Strategiepapiers, Zum breiten Einsatz der Neuen Medien in der Sportwissenschaft‘ durch den ad-hoc-Ausschuss, Digitale Medien‘ der Deutschen Vereinigung für Sportwissenschaft. *Leipziger Sportwissenschaftliche Beiträge*, *48*(2), 132–136.

Beare, H. (2001). *Creating the future school (Student Outcomes and the Reform of Education)*. London: Routledge Falmer.

Bell, W. (1996). What do we mean by future studies? In R. A. Slaughter (Ed.), *New Thinking for a New Millennium* (pp. 3-25). London: Routledge.

Bennett, G., & Green, F. P. (2001). Student Learning in the Online Environment: No significant Difference? *Quest*, *53*(1), 1–13.

Borkenhagen, F., Igel, C., Mester, J., Olivier, N., Platen, P., Wiemeyer, J., & Zschorlich, V. (2006). Strategiepapier: Zum Einsatz der neuen Medien in der Sportwissenschaft. Hochschulpolitische Empfehlungen und fachwissenschaftliche Programmatik. *Leipziger Sportwissenschaftliche Beiträge*, *47*(2), 126–146.

Bredel, F. J. (2003). *Schwimmen. Bausteine für einen sicheren und attraktiven Unterricht*. Münster, Germany: Gemeindeunfallversicherungsverband Westfalen-Lippe.

Bredel, F. J., Fischer, U., & Thienes, G. (2005). Beispiele zum Einsatz digitaler Medien in der fachpraktischen Universitätsausbildung und im Sportunterricht. *Sportunterricht*, *54*(1), 17 21.

Buckingham, D. (2003). *Media education: Literacy, learning and contemporary culture*. Cambridge, UK: Polity Press.

Butler, L. L. (2004). Chalk, what chalk? [JOPERD]. *Journal of Physical Education, Recreation & Dance*, *75*(9), 12.

Byra, M. (2006). Teaching styles and inclusive pedagogies. In D. Kirk, D. Macdonald & M. O'Sullivan (Eds.), *The Handbook of Physical Education* (pp. 449-466). London: Sage.

Cagle, B. (2004). Stepping up with pedometers. *Strategies: A Journal for Physical and Sport Educators*, *17*(3), 27-28.

Chamberlin, B., & Gallagher, R. (2008). *Exergames. Using video games to promote physical activity*. Paper presented at the Children, Youth and Families At Risk (CYFAR) Conference, San Antonio, TX. Retrieved April 10, 2009, from http://www.cyfernet.org/cyfar08/research/chamberlin/chamberlin-research1.pdf

Common Sense Media. (2008). Media + Child and Adolescent Health: A Systematic Review. *Common Sense Media.*

Danisch, M. (2008). *Das Web 2.0 in der Sportwissenschaft*. Invited paper presented at a meeting of the Multimedia Initiative Hessen, Wiesbaden.

Danisch, M., & Friedrich, G. (2007). Neue Medien im Sportunterricht. In H. Lange & S. Sinning (Eds.), *Handbuch Sportdidaktik* (pp. 319-329). Balingen, Germany: Spitta.

Danisch, M., Müller, L., & Schwier, J. (2006). eLearning in der Sportspielvermittlung. Entwicklung von multimedialer Lernsoftware für die Optimierung von Sportspiel-Techniken und Aufbau eines sportwissenschaftlichen Webportals "Sportspiele." . *Spectrum der Sportwissenschaften*, *18*(1), 23–39.

David, B., Bouthier, D., Marsenach, J., & Durey, A. (1999). French research into the didactics and technology of physical activities and sports: An expanding new field. *Instructional Science*, *27*, 147–163.

Dober, R. (2003). Sportpädagogik und Sportpraxis im Internet. www.sportunterricht.de – Ein Mitmachprojekt für alle, die sich für Lehren und Lernen im Sport interessieren. *SportPraxis, 44*(5), 33-35.

Dober, R. (2004). Neue Medien im Sportunterricht. Ideen und Anregungen zum Computereinsatz beim Lehren und Lernen im Sport. In E. Christmann, E. Emrich & J. Flatau (Eds.), *Schule und Sport* (pp. 281-288). Schorndorf, Germany: Hofmann.

Dober, R. (2006). Mit dem Notebook in die Turnhalle. *L.A. Multimedia, 3*(1), 18–19.

Dunn, L., & Tannehill, D. (2005). Using pedometers to promote physical activity in secondary physical education. *Strategies: A Journal for Physical and Sport Educators, 19*(1), 19-25.

Elliott, S., Stanec, A. S., McCollum, S., & Stanley, M. A. (2007). Uses of the Internet by health and physical education teachers. *Strategies: A Journal for Physical and Sport Educators, 20*(5), 19-27.

Ficher, U. (2005). *Volleyball. Bausteine für einen sicheren und attraktiven Unterricht.* Münster, Germany: Gemeindeunfallversicherungsverband Westfalen-Lippe.

Fiorentino, L. H., & Castelli, D. (2005). Creating a virtual gymnasium. [JOPERD]. *Journal of Physical Education, Recreation & Dance, 76*(4), 16.

Fischer, U., Thienes, G., & Bredel, F. J. (2005). CD-ROMs für den Sportunterricht und die Sportlehrerausbildung - ausgewählte Evaluationsergebnisse. *Sportunterricht, 54*(1), 11–16.

Friedrich, G. (2004). *Fußball. Bausteine für einen sicheren und attraktiven Unterricht.* Münster, Germany: Gemeindeunfallversicherungsverband Westfalen-Lippe.

Gillard, S., Bailey, D., & Nolan, E. (2008). Ten reasons for IT educators to be early adopters of IT innovations. *Journal of Information Technology Education, 7*, 21–33.

Graham, G. M. Holt/ Hale, S. A., & Parker, M. A. (2007). *Children moving. a reflective approach to teaching physical education (8th ed.).* New York, NY: McGraw-Hill.

Gubacs, K. (2004). Project-based learning: A student-centered approach to integrating technology into physical education teacher education. [JOPERD]. *Journal of Physical Education, Recreation & Dance, 75*(7), 33.

Hamlin, B. (2005). Motor competency and video analysis. *Teaching Elementary Physical Education, 16*(5), 8–13.

Hartnell-Young, E. (2003). From facilitator to knowledge-builder: A new role for the teacher of the future. In C. Dowling & K.-W. Lai (Eds), *Information and Communication Technology and the Teacher of the Future* (pp. 159-164). Boston, MA: Kluwer Academic Publishers.

Hastie, P. A., & Sinelnikov, O. A. (2007). The use of web-based portfolios in college physical education activity courses. *Physical Educator, 64*(1), 21–28.

Hebbel-Seeger, A. (2007). Blended Learning in Theorie-Praxis-Veranstaltungen: Beispiele für den Einsatz von computergestützen Lehr- und Lernanwendungen. In V. Scheid (Ed.), *Sport und Bewegung vermitteln* (Schriften der Deutschen Vereinigung für Sportwissenschaft, No. 165, pp. 185-187). Hamburg: Czwalina.

Hebbel-Seeger, A. (2008a). Hochschuldidaktik im Zeitalter digitaler Medien: Erfolg und Nachhaltigkeit setzen auf den "shift from technology to use". *Ze-phir, 14*(2), 19–22.

Hebbel-Seeger, A. (2008b). Videospiel und Sportpraxis – (K)ein Widerspruch. *Zeitschrift für e-learning, 4*(3), 9-20.

Holzrichter, D. (2001). Gymnasium makeovers. *Athletic Business, 25*(1), 59-60, 62-65.

Horx, M. (2006). *Wie wir leben werden. Unsere Zukunft beginnt jetzt* (3rd rev. ed.). Frankfurt/Main: Campus.

Ince, M. L., Goodway, J. D., Ward, P., & Lee, M.-A. (2006). The effects of professional development on technological competency and the attitudes urban physical education teachers have toward using technology. *Journal of Teaching in Physical Education, 25*(4), 428–440.

Johnson, D. W., Johnson, R. T., & Holubec, E. J. (1990). *Circles of learning: Cooperation in the classroom*. Edina, MN: Interaction Book Co.

Keller, I. (2008). Blended Learning in der methodisch-didaktischen SportlehrerInnenausbildung am Beispiel Leichtathletik. *Zeitschrift für e-learning, 4*(3), 33-44.

Kirk, D., Macdonald, D., & O'Sullivan, M. (Eds.). (2006). *The handbook of physical education*. London: SAGE.

Kirk, D., & McPhail, A. (2002). Teaching games for understanding and situated learning: Rethinking the Bunker-Thorpe model. *Journal of Teaching in Physical Education, 21*, 177–192.

Kretschmann, R. (2008a). Development of Competencies by Playing Digital Sports-Games?! In T. Conolly & M. Stansfield (Eds.), *Proceedings of the 2nd European Conference on Games-Based Learning* (pp. 243-250). Reading, MA: Academic Publishing Limited.

Kretschmann, R. (2008b). *Einsatzmöglichkeiten und Entwicklungsszenarien digitaler Medien im Schulsport*. Paper presented at the Annual Conference of the Sektion Sportpädagogik (eng. Division Sport Pedagogy) of the Deutsche Vereinigung für Sportwissenschaft (engl. German Association of Sport Science), German Sport University, Cologne.

Ladda, S., Keating, T., Adams, D., & Toscano, L. (2004). Including technology in instructional programs. [JOPERD]. *Journal of Physical Education, Recreation & Dance, 75*(4), 12.

Lai, Y. C., & Wong, T. W. (2006). The cluster model for conducting Learning Study for minor subjects in schools. In P. L. Jeffrey (Ed.), *Proceedings of the Australian Association for Research in Education (AARE) Annual Conference 2006*. Adelaide, Australia: AARE.

Lange, H., & Sinning, S. (Eds.). (2007). *Handbuch Sportdidaktik*. Balingen, Germany: Spitta.

Leser, R., Uhlig, M., & Uhlig, J. (2008). T-A-P – Eine E-Learning-Anwendung aus der Fußballpraxis. *Zeitschrift für e-learning, 4*(3), 21-32.

Lumpkin, A. (2007). *Introduction to physical education, exercise science, and sport studies* (7th ed.). New York: McGraw-Hill.

Marshall, S. J., Biddle, S. J. H., Gorely, T., Cameron, N., & Murdey, I. (2004). Relationships between media use, body fatness and physical activity in children and youth: a meta-analysis. *International Journal of Obesity, 28*, 1238–1246. doi:10.1038/sj.ijo.0802706

McCaughtry, N., & Dillon, S. R. (2008). Learning to Use PDAs to enhance teaching: The perspectives of preservice physical educators. *Journal of Technology and Teacher Education, 16*(4), 483–508.

Mitchell, M., & McKethan, R. (2003). *Integrating technology and pedagogy in physical education teacher education*. Cerritos, CA: Bonnie's Fitware Inc.

Mitchell, M., McKethan, R., & Mohnsen, B. (2004). *Integrating technology and physical education*. Cerritos, CA: Bonnie's Fitware Inc.

Mitchell, M. S. (2001). Using technology in elementary physical education. *Strategies: A Journal for Physical and Sport Educators, 14*(6), 28-31.

Mitchell, S. (2006). Unpacking the standards. [JOPERD]. *Journal of Physical Education, Recreation & Dance*, *77*(2), 20–24.

Mohnsen, B. (1999). *The new leadership paradigm for physical education. What we really need to lead*. Reston, VA: NASPE Publications.

Mohnsen, B. (2005a). Addressing technology standards: What is the role of the physical educator? [JOPERD]. *Journal of Physical Education, Recreation & Dance*, *76*(7), 48.

Mohnsen, B. (2005b). Integrating the NETSS into physical education. *Learning and Leading with Technology*, *32*(6), 20–21.

Mohnsen, B. (2005c). Notebooks, handhelds, and software in physical education (Grades 5-8). *Teaching Elementary Physical Education*, *16*(5), 18–21.

Mohnsen, B. (2008). *Using technology in physical education (6th ed.)*. Cerritos, CA: Bonnie's Fitware Inc.

Morgan, C. F., Beighle, A., & Pangrazi, R. P. (2007). What are the contributory and compensatory relationships between physical education and physical activity in children? *Research Quarterly for Exercise and Sport*, *78*(5), 407–412.

Mössle, T. Kleimann; M., & Rehbein, F. (2007). *Bildschirmmedien im Alltag von Kindern und Jugendlichen: Problematische Mediennutzungsmuster und ihr Zusammenhang mit Schulleistungen und Aggressivität* (Interdisziplinäre Beiträge zur kriminologischen Forschung, 33). Baden-Baden, Germany: Nomos.

Mullis, I. V. S., Martin, M. O., Gonzales, E. J., & Chrostowski, S. J. (2004a). *TIMSS 2003. International Mathematics Report. Findings From IEA's Trends in International Mathematics and Science Study at the Fourth and Eighth Grades*. Chestnut Hill, MA: Boston College.

Mullis, I. V. S., Martin, M. O., Gonzales, E. J., & Chrostowski, S. J. (2004b). *TIMSS 2003. International Science Report Findings From IEA's Trends in International Mathematics and Science Study at the Fourth and Eighth Grades*. Chestnut Hill, MA: Boston College.

Mullis, I. V. S., Martin, M. O., Kennedy, A. M., & Foy, P. (2007). *PIRLS 2006. International Report: IEA's Progress in International Reading Literacy Study in Primary School on 40 countries*. Chestnut Hill, MA: Boston College.

National Association for Sport and Physical Education (NASPE). (2004). *Moving into the future. National standards for physical education (2nd ed.)*. Reston, VA: McGraw-Hill.

Nichols, A. J., & Levy, Y. (2009). Empirical assessment of college student-athletes' persistence in e-learning courses: A case study of a U.S. National Association of Intercollegiate Athletics (NAIA) institution. *The Internet and Higher Education*, *12*(1), 14–25. doi:10.1016/j.iheduc.2008.10.003

Nixon, J. E., & Locke, L. (1973). Research in teaching in physical education. In R. M. W. Travers (Ed.), *Second handbook of research on teaching* (pp. 1210-1242). Chicago, IL: Rand McNally.

O'Reilly, T. (2005). *What is Web 2.0? Design patterns and business models for the next generation of software*. Retrieved April 10, 2009, from http://www.oreillynet.com/pub/a/oreilly/tim/news/2005/09/30/what-is-web-20.html

Pennington, T., & Graham, G. (2002). Exploring the influence of a physical education listserv on K-12 physical educators. *Journal of Technology and Teacher Education*, *10*(3), 383–405.

Pennington, T., Wilkinson, C., & Vance, J. (2004). Physical educators online: What is on the minds of teachers in the trenches? *Physical Educator, 61*(1), 45–56.

Prensky, M. (2001). *Digital game-based learning.* London: McGraw Hill.

Reinmann, G. (2005). *Blended Learning in der Lehrerbildung. Grundlagen für die Konzeption innovativer Lernumgebungen.* Lengerich, Germany: Pabst.

Richter, T. (2007). *Basketball Elements* [Computer Software]. Schorndorf, Germany: Hofmann.

Roberts, T., & Brown, L. (2008). Learn more in less time: fundamental aquatic skill acquisition via video technology. *Strategies: A Journal for Physical and Sport Educators, 21*(4), 29-31.

Samson, T., Igel, C., & Meiers, R. (2006). An empirical analysis of the utilization of new media in sports science. *International Journal of Computer Science in Sports, 2*(5), 86–89.

Schell, L. A. (2004). Teaching learning styles with technology. [JOPERD]. *Journal of Physical Education, Recreation & Dance, 75*(1), 14.

Schmidt, R. A. (1980). Past and future issues in motor programming. *Research Quarterly, 51*(1), 122–140.

Schmoll, L. (2007). *Lernen an Stationen im Sportunterricht. Sechs Lernen an Stationen mit Kopiervorlagen für den Sportunterricht in der Sekundarstufe I und II.* Baltmannsweiler, Germany: Schneider Hohengehren.

Scrimshaw, P. (1997). Computers and the teacher's role. In B. Somekh & N. Davis (Eds.), *Using Information Technology Effectively in Teaching and Learning. Studies in pre-service and in-service teacher education* (pp. 99-112). London: Routledge.

Siedentop, D. (2008). *Introduction to Physical Education, Fitness, and Sport* (7th ed.). Boston, MA: McGraw-Hill.

Siedentop, D., Hastie, P. A., & van der Mars, H. (2004). *Complete Guide to Sport Education.* Champaign, IL: Human Kinetics.

Silver, J. (Producer), Wachowski, A., & Wachowski, L. (Directors). (1999). *The Matrix* [Motion picture]. Hollywood: Warner Bros. Pictures.

Stewart, C. (2006). Coach education online: The Montana model. [JOPERD]. *Journal of Physical Education, Recreation & Dance, 77*(4), 34–36.

Sturm, R. (2008). Offene Lernressourcen in Sport und Sportwissenschaft – Hochschulübergreifende E-Learning-Angebote am Beispiel des Bildungsnetzwerkes ‚Bewegung und Training'. *Zeitschrift für e-learning, 4*(3), 45-55

Tearle, P., & Golder, G. (2008). The use of ICT in the teaching and learning of physical education in compulsory education: how do we prepare the workforce of the future? *European Journal of Teacher Education, 31*(1), 55–72. doi:10.1080/02619760701845016

Thienes, G., Fischer, U., & Bredel, F. J. (2005). Digitale Medien im und für den Sportunterricht. *Sportunterricht, 54*(1), 6–10.

Thomas, A., & Stratton, G. (2006). What we are really doing with ICT in physical education: A national audit of equipment, use, teacher attitudes, support, and training. *The British Journal of Educational Psychology, 37*(4), 617–632.

Treadwell, M. (2001). *1001 Best Internet Sites for Educators* (2nd ed.). Arlington Heights, IL: SkyLight Professional Development.

Trout, J., & Zamora, K. (2005). Using Dance Dance Revolution in Physical Education. *Teaching Elementary Physical Education, 16*(5), 22–25.

Vertinsky, P., McKay, S., & Petrina, S. (2004). In P. Vertinsky & S. McKay (Eds.), *Disciplining Bodies in the Gymnasium. Memory, Monument, Modernism*. London: Routledge.

Vickers, J. N. (1990). *Instructional Design for Teaching Physical Activities: A Knowledge Structures Approach*. Champaign, IL: Human Kinetics Publishers.

Wagner, M. (2006). On the scientific relevance of eSports. In H. R. Arabnia (Ed.), *Proceedings of the 2006 International Conference on Internet Computing and Conference on Computer Game Development* (pp. 437-440). Las Vegas, NV: CSREA Press.

Warwick, K. (2002). *I, Cyborg*. London: Century.

Wegis, H., & van der Mars, H. (2006). Integrating assessment and instruction: Easing the process with PDAs. [JOPERD]. *Journal of Physical Education, Recreation & Dance*, *77*(1), 27–34.

Wiemeyer, J. (2003). Learning with multimedia - more promise than practice? *International Journal of Computer Science in Sport*, *2*(1), 102–116.

Wills, E. (2006). Let's get virtual. *Teacher Magazine*, *17*(6), 9–10.

Woods, M. L., Karp, G. G., Shimon, J. M., & Jensen, K. (2004). Using Webquests to create online learning opportunities in physical education. [JOPERD]. *Journal of Physical Education, Recreation & Dance*, *75*(8), 41.

Yaman, C. (2008). The abilities of physical education teachers in educational technologies and multimedia. *The Turkish Online Journal of Educational Technology*, 7(2), 20-31. Retrieved April 10, 2009, from http://www.tojet.net/results.asp?volume=7&issue=2&year=2008

Yaman, M. (2007a). The attitudes of the physical education students towards internet. *The Turkish Online Journal of Educational Technology*, 6(4), 79-87. Retrieved April 10, 2009, from http://www.tojet.net/results.asp?volume=6&issue=3&year=2007

Yaman, M. (2007b). The competence of physical education teachers in computer use. *The Turkish Online Journal of Educational Technology, 6*(4), 46-55. Retrieved April 10, 2009, from http://www.tojet.net/results.asp?volume=6&issue=4&year=2007

Yaman, M. (2009). Perceptions of students on the applications of distance education in physical education lessons. *The Turkish Online Journal of Educational Technology, 8*(1), 65-72. Retrieved April 10, 2009, from http://www.tojet.net/results.asp?volume=8&issue=1&year=2009

Zheng, R., Perez, J., & Williamson, J, &; Flygare, J. (2008). WebQuests as perceived by teachers: Implications for online teaching and learning. *Journal of Computer Assisted Learning*, *24*(4), 295–304. doi:10.1111/j.1365-2729.2007.00261.x

Compilation of References

Abell, S. K. (2008). Twenty years later: Does pedagogical content knowledge remain a useful idea? *International Journal of Science Education*, *30*(10), 1405–1416. doi:10.1080/09500690802187041

Active Words Inc. (2008). Active Words. Retrieved September 18, 2008, from http://www.activeworlds.com

Adams, C. (2006). PowerPoint, habits of mind, and classroom culture. *Journal of Curriculum Studies*, *38*(4), 389–411. doi:10.1080/00220270600579141

Adams, C. (2008). PowerPoint's pedagogy. *Phenomenology and Practice*, *2*(1), 63–79.

Adams, C. (in press). The poetics of PowerPoint. *Explorations in Media Ecology*, *7*(4), 43-58.

Adams, W., Reid, S., LeMaster, R., McKagan, S., Perkins, K., & Dubson, M. (2008). A study of educational simulations part ii – interface design. *Journal of Interactive Learning Research*, *19*(4), 551–577.

Adesope, T., Adesope, O., & Ojeme, C. (2008). *Traditional and online forms of education: Proposing a common ground.* Paper presented at the E-Learn 2008, World Conference on E-Learning in Corporate, Government, Healthcare, & Higher Education of the Association for the Advancement of Computing in Education, Las Vegas, NV, USA.

Aegerter-Wilmsen, T., Bisseling, T., & Hartog, R. (2003). Web based learning support for experimental design in molecular biology: A top-down approach. *Journal of Interactive Learning Research*, *14*(3), 301–314.

Aegerter-Wilmsen, T., Coppens, M., Janssen, F. J. J. M., Hartog, R., & Bisseling, T. (2005). Digital learning material for student-directed model building in molecular biology. *Biochemistry and Molecular Biology Education*, *33*, 325–329. doi:10.1002/bmb.2005.49403305325

Aegerter-Wilmsen, T., Janssen, F., Hartog, R., & Bisseling, T. (2005). Digital learning material for model building in molecular biology. *Journal of Science Education and Technology*, *14*(1), 123–134. doi:10.1007/s10956-005-2740-3

Aegerter-Wilmsen, T., Janssen, F., Kettenis, D., Sessink, O., Hartog, R., & Bisseling, T. (2006). Introducing molecular life science students to model building using computer simulations. *Journal of Computers in Mathematics and Science Teaching*, *25*(2), 101–122.

Agarwal, R., & Prasad, J. (1999). Are individual differences germane to the acceptance of new information technologies? *Decision Sciences*, *30*, 361–391. doi:10.1111/j.1540-5915.1999.tb01614.x

Ajzen, I., & Fishbein, M. (1980). *Understanding attitudes and predicting social behavior.* Englewood Cliffs, NJ: Prentice-Hall.

Ala-Mutka, K., Bacigalupo, M., Kluzer, S., Pascu, C., Punie, Y., & Redecker, C. (2009). Review of Learning 2.0 Practices. In IPTS technical report prepared for publication. Seville, Spain: IPTS. Retrieved April 18, 2009 from http://ipts.jrc.ec.europa.eu/publications/pub.cfm?id=2139

Alavi, M. (1994). Computer-mediated collaborative learning: An empirical evaluation. *MIS Quarterly*, *18*(2), 159–174. doi:10.2307/249763

Albert, D., & Lukas, J. (Eds.). (1999). *Knowledge spaces: Theories, empirical research, and applications*. Mahwah, NJ: Lawrence Erlbaum Associates.

Alberts, B. (2005). A wakeup call for science faculty. *Cell, 123*(5), 739–741. doi:10.1016/j.cell.2005.11.014

Alessi, S. (2000). Designing educational support in system-dynamics-based interactive learning environments. *Simulation & Gaming, 31*, 178–196. doi:10.1177/104687810003100205

Alessi, S., & Trollip, S. (2001). *Third edition multimedia for learning: Methods and development*. Needham Heights, MA: Pearson Education.

Aljanazrah, A. M., & Bader, H. J. (2006). Chemielehrerfortbildung durch E-Learning und Labortag – Entwicklung, Erprobung und erste Erfahrungen. *CHEMKON, 13*(2), 69. doi:10.1002/ckon.200610040

Allemann-Ghionda, C. (2008). Vom Postulat zur bildungspolitischen und didaktischen Umsetzung? In L. Rosen & S. Farrokhzad (Eds.), *Macht – Kultur – Bildung* (pp. 147-163). Münster, Germany: Waxmann Verlag.

Ally, M. (2004). Foundations of educational theory for online learning. In T. Anderson & F. Elloumi (Eds.), *Theory and practice of online learning* (pp. 3-31). Athabasca: Athabasca University.

Ally, M. (Ed.). (2009). *Mobile learning. Transforming the delivery of education and training*. Edmonton: AU Press (Athabasca University). Retrieved May, 2009, from http://www.aupress.ca/index.php/books/120155

Amnesty International. (1995). *Unterrichtspraxis Menschenrechte. Folter und Gewalt*. Solothurn, Switzerland: Amnesty International.

Anderson, C. A., & Bushman, B. J. (2001). Effects of violent video games on aggressive behavior, aggressive cognition, aggressive affect, physiological arousal, and prosocial behavior: A meta-analytic review of the scientific literature. *Psychological Science, 12*, 353–359. doi:10.1111/1467-9280.00366

Anderson, J. Q., & Rainie, L. (2008). The future of Internet III. *Pew Internet & American Life Project*. Retrieved May 1, 2009, from http://www.pewinternet.org/~/media//Files/Reports/2008/PIP_FutureInternet3.pdf.pdf

Anderson, L. W. (Ed.). Krathwohl, D.R. (Ed.), Airasian, P.W., Cruikshank, K.A., Mayer, R.E., Pintrich, P.R., Raths, J., & Wittrock, M.C. (2001). *A taxonomy for learning, teaching, and assessing: A revision of Bloom's Taxonomy of Educational Objectives* (Complete edition). New York: Longman.

Anderson, L. W., & Krathwohl, D. R. (2001). *A taxonomy for learning, teaching and assessing: A revision of bloom's taxonomy of educational objectives*. New York: Longman.

Anderson, P. (2007, February). What is Web 2.0? Ideas, technologies and implications for education. *JISC Technology and Standards Watch*. Retrieved December 9, 2008 from http://www.jisc.ac.uk/media/documents/techwatch/tsw0701b.pdf

Anderson, T. R. (2007). Bridging the educational research-teaching practice gap: The power of assessment. *Biochemistry and Molecular Biology Education, 35*(6), 471–477. doi:10.1002/bmb.20135

Annetta, L. A., & Murray, M. R. (2006). Serious games: Incorporating video games in the classroom. *EDUCAUSE Review, 3*, 16–22.

Araujo-Jorge, T. C., Cardona, T. S., Mendes, C. L. S., Henriques-Pons, A., Meirelles, R. M. S., & Coutinho, C. M. L. M. (2004). Microscopy images as interactive tools in cell modeling and cell biology education. *Cell Biology Education, 3*, 99–110. doi:10.1187/cbe.03-08-0010

Argote, L., McEvily, B., & Reagans, R. (2003). Managing knowledge in organizations: An integrative framework and review of emerging themes. *Management Science, 49*, 571–582. doi:10.1287/mnsc.49.4.571.14424

Ariadne-Foundation. (2007). *Ariadne*. Retrieved April 9, 2009, from http://www.ariadne-eu.org/

Atkins, D., Seely Brown, J., & Hammond, A. L. (2007). *A review of the Open Educational Resource movement: achievements, challenges and new opportunities, report to the William and Flora Hewlett*

Foundation. Retrieved May 2, 2009, from http://www.hewlett.org/NR/rdonlyres/5D2E3386-3974-4314-8F67-5C2F22EC4F9B/0/AReviewoftheOpenEducationalResourcesOERMovement_BlogLink.pdf

Ausubel, D. P. (1968). *Educational psychology: A cognitive view.* New York: Holt, Rinehart & Winston.

Avgeriou, P., Papasalouros, A., Retalis, S., & Skordalakis, M. (2003). Towards a Pattern Language for Learning Management Systems. *Educational Technology & Society, 6*(2), 11–24.

Baca, A., Hanke, U., Hebbel-Seeger, A., Igel, C., Vohle, F., & Wiemeyer, J. (2007). Kommentierung des Strategiepapiers, Zum breiten Einsatz der Neuen Medien in der Sportwissenschaft' durch den ad-hoc-Ausschuss, Digitale Medien' der Deutschen Vereinigung für Sportwissenschaft. *Leipziger Sportwissenschaftliche Beiträge, 48*(2), 132–136.

Backhaus, K., Erichson, B., Plinke, W., & Weiber, R. (2005). *Multivariate Analysemethoden. Eine anwendungsorientierte Einführung [Multivariate analysis methods. an application-oriented introduction] (11th ed.).* New York: Springer.

Baddeley, A. (1998). Working memory. *Comptes Rendus de l'Académie des Sciences. Série III, Sciences de la Vie, 321*(2-3), 167–173. doi:10.1016/S0764-4469(97)89817-4

Baecker, D. (2007). *Studien zur nächsten Gesellschaft.* Frankfurt, Germany: Suhrkamp.

Banathy, B. H. (1988a). Systems inquiry in education. *Systems Practice, 1*(2), 193–211. doi:10.1007/BF01059858

Banathy, B. H. (1991). *Systems design of education.* Englewood Cliffs, NJ: Educational Technology.

Banathy, B. H. (1996). *Designing social systems in a changing world.* New York: Plenum Press.

Banathy, B. H., & Jenlink, P. M. (2004). Systems inquiry and its application in education. In D. H. Jonassen (Ed.), *Handbook of Research on Educational Communications and Technology (2nd ed.).* Mahwah, N.J.: Lawrence Erlbaum Associates, Inc.

Bandura, A. (1977). Self-efficacy: Toward a unifying theory of behavioral change. *Psychological Review, 84*(2), 191–215. doi:10.1037/0033-295X.84.2.191

Bandura, A. (1997). *Self-efficacy: The exercise of control.* New York: W.H. Freeman.

Barab, S. A., Squire, K. D., & Dueber, W. (2000). A co-evolutionary model for supporting the emergence of authenticity. *Educational Technology Research and Development, 48*(2), 37–62. doi:10.1007/BF02313400

barcamp.org. (2008). *The rules of BarCamp.* Retrieved February 6, 2009, from http://barcamp.org/TheRulesOfBarCamp

Barrett, C. L., Bisset, K. R., Eubank, S. G., Feng, X., & Marathe, M. V. (2008). EpiSimdemics: an efficient algorithm for simulating the spread of infectious disease over large realistic social networks. In *Proc. of the ACM/IEEE Conference on Supercomputing* (pp. 1-12). Piscataway, NJ: IEEE Press.

Barry, C., & Lang, M. (2001). A survey of multimedia and Web development techniques and methodology usage. *IEEE MultiMedia, 8*(3), 52–60. doi:10.1109/93.917971

Bar-Yam, Y. (1997). *Dynamics of complex systems.* Reading, MA: Addison-Wesley.

Bates, A. (2000). *Managing technological change; Strategies for colleges and university leaders.* San Francisco, CA: Jossey-Bass Publishers.

Bates, A. (2007) Strategic planning for e-learning in a polytechnic. In M. Bullen & D. Janes (Eds.), *Making the transition into E-Learning: Strategies and Issues.* Hershey, PA: Information Science Publishing.

Bauerline, M. (2008). *The dumbest generation: How the digital age stupefies young Americans and jeopardizes our future.* New York: Tarcher/Penguin.

Baumgartner, P., Häfele, H., & Maier-Häfele, K. (2005). *Evaluation von Lernplattformen: Verfahren, Ergebnisse und Empfelhungen (Version 1.3).* Retrieved January 5, 2009 from http://www.bildung.at/filedatabase/downloader.php?file_code=6d0873c599c24c0a7f302fba323d8065&filedb_dir=/bmbwk/dateidb/bildung2

Beare, H. (2001). *Creating the future school (Student Outcomes and the Reform of Education)*. London: Routledge Falmer.

Beasley, R., & Vila, J. (1992). The identification of navigation patterns in a multimedia environment: A Case Study. *Journal of Educational Multimedia and Hypermedia*, *1*, 209–222.

Beasley, R., & Waugh, M. (1997). Predominant initial and review patterns of navigation in a fully constrained hypermedia hierarchy. *Journal of Educational Multimedia and Hypermedia*.

Beck, J. C., & Wade, M. (2004). *Got game: How the gamer generation is reshaping business forever*. Boston, MA: Harvard Business School Press.

Beck, K. (2002). *Test-driven development: By example*: Addison-Wesley.

Beck, K. (2006). *Computervermittelte Kommunikation im Internet*. München, Germany: Oldenbourg.

Becker, B. (2004). Zwischen Allmacht und Ohnmacht: Spielräume des "Ich" im Cyberspace. In U. Thiedeke (Ed.), *Soziologie des Cyberspace. Medien, Strukturen undSemantiken* (pp. 170-192). Wiesbaden, Deutschland: VS.

Becta. (2008). *Harnessing technology: next generation learning*. Retrieved Augusat http://publications.becta.org.uk/display.cfm?resID=37348&page=1835, last accessed 8/2/09.

Bedau, M. A. (2003). Artificial life: organization, adaptation and complexity from the bottom up. *Trends in Cognitive Sciences*, *7*(11), 505–512. doi:10.1016/j.tics.2003.09.012

Beder, H., & Carrea, N. (1988). The effects of andragogical teacher training on adult students' attendance and evaluation of their teachers. *Adult Education Quarterly*, *38*(2), 75–87. doi:10.1177/0001848188038002002

Beedle, J. B. (2004). *What educators can learn from multiplayer computer gaming: A study of who is playing and their perceptions of learning*. Dissertations Abstracts International, AAT 3155858.

Beetham, H., & Sharpe, R. (Eds.). (2007). *Rethinking pedagogy for a digital age: designing and delivering e-learning*. Oxford, UK: Routledge.

Bell, D. (1973). *The coming of post-industrial society: a venture in social forecasting*. New York: Basic Books.

Bell, W. (1996). What do we mean by future studies? In R. A. Slaughter (Ed.), *New Thinking for a New Millennium* (pp. 3-25). London: Routledge.

Bendel, O. (2006). Wikipedia als Methode und Gegenstand der Lehre. In K. Hildebrand (Ed.), *Social Software* (pp. 82–88). Heidelberg: dpunkt.verlag.

Benjamin, W. (1978). On the mimetic faculty. In P. Demetz (Ed.), *Reflections: essays, aphorisms, autobiographical writings* (pp. 333–36). (E. Jephcott, Trans.). New York: Random House.

Bennett, G., & Green, F. P. (2001). Student Learning in the Online Environment: No significant Difference? *Quest*, *53*(1), 1–13.

Bennett, S., Maton, K., & Kervin, L. (2008). The 'digital natives' debate: A critical review of the evidence. *British Journal of Educational Technology*, *39*(5), 775–786. doi:10.1111/j.1467-8535.2007.00793.x

Bennett, S., Maton, K., & Kervin, L. (2008). The 'digital natives' debate: A critical review of the evidence. *British Journal of Educational Technology*, *39*(5), 775–786. doi:10.1111/j.1467-8535.2007.00793.x

Bensley, L., & Eenwyk, J. (2001). Video games and real-life aggression: Review of the literature. *The Journal of Adolescent Health*, *29*, 244–257. doi:10.1016/S1054-139X(01)00239-7

Berendt, B., & Brenstein, E. (2001). Visualizing individual differences in Web navigation: STRATDYN, a tool for analyzing navigation patterns. *Behavior Research Methods, Instruments, & Computers*, *33*(2), 243–257.

Biggs, J. B. (1999). *Teaching for quality learning at university*. Buckingham, UK: Open University Press.

Bildungsbericht2006: Bildung in Deutschland, 2. nationaler Bildungsbericht. (n.d.). Retrieved October

23, 2008, from http://www.bildungsbericht.de/zeigen.html?seite=6129

Bildungsstandards Chemie. (2005). Retrieved October 25, 2009, from http://www.kmk.org/fileadmin/veroeffentlichungen_beschluesse/2004/2004_12_16-Bildungsstandards-Chemie.pdf

Billinghurst, M., Kato, H., & Poupyrev, I. (2001). The MagicBook: A transitional AR interface. *Computers & Graphics, Elsevier*, *25*(5), 745–753. doi:10.1016/S0097-8493(01)00117-0

Bimber, O., Fröhlich, B., Schmalstieg, D., & Encarnação, L. M. (2001). The Virtual Showcase. *IEEE Computer Graphics and Applications*, *21*(6), 48–55. doi:10.1109/38.963460

Bingle, R. G., & Hatcher, J. A. (2002). Campus-community partnerships: The terms of engagement. *The Journal of Social Issues*, *58*(3).

BinSubaih A. Maddock S., Romano D.M. (2006). An architecture for portable serious games. In *Doctoral Symposium hosted at the 20th European Conference on Object-Oriented Programming ECOOP 2006*, Nantes, France.

BITKOM - Bundesverband Informationswirtschaft. Telekommunikation und neue Medien e.V. (2007). *Fast jeder fünfte Mensch ist online*. Retrieved October 20, 2008, from http://www.bitkom.org/46074.aspx

Bleeker, H., & Mulderij, K. J. (2002). The experience of motor disability. *Phenomenology + Pedagogy*. Retrieved from http://www.phenomenologyonline.com/articles/bleeker.html

Bloom, B. S. (1956). *Taxonomy of educational objectives: The classification of educational goals*. Chicago, IL: Susan Fauer Company, Inc.

Bloom, B. S. (Ed.). Engelhart, M. D., Furst, E. J., Hill, W. H., & Krathwohl, D. R. (1956). *Taxonomy of educational objectives: The classification of educational goals. Handbook I: Cognitive domain*. New York: David McKay.

Bloom, H. (1995). *The Lucifer principle: A scientific expedition into the forces of history*. St. Leonards, NSW, Australia: Allen and Unwin.

Bois, J. R. (2002). *Decisions within complex systems: an experimental approach using the STRATEGEM-2 computer game*. Unpublished Doctoral thesis, State University of New York, Albany.

Boon, M. J., Rusman, E., & van der Klink, M. R. (2005). Developing a critical view on e-learning reports: Trend watching or trend setting? [from http://www.qou.edu/homePage/arabic/researchProgram/eLearningResearchs/developingACritical.pdf]. *International Journal of Training and Development*, *9*(3), 1–27. Retrieved December 25, 2008. doi:10.1111/j.1468-2419.2005.00229.x

Bopp, M. (2005). Immersive Didaktik. Verdeckte Lernhilfen und Framingprozesse in Computerspielen. In B. Neitzel & R.F. Nohr (Ed.), *Das Spiel mit dem Medium. Partizipation - Immersion – Interaktion* (pp. 170-186). Marburg, Deutschland: Schüren.

Borkenhagen, F., Igel, C., Mester, J., Olivier, N., Platen, P., Wiemeyer, J., & Zschorlich, V. (2006). Strategiepapier: Zum Einsatz der neuen Medien in der Sportwissenschaft. Hochschulpolitische Empfehlungen und fachwissenschaftliche Programmatik. *Leipziger Sportwissenschaftliche Beiträge*, *47*(2), 126–146.

Bossomaier, T., & Green, D. (1998). *Patterns in the sand: Computers, complexity and life*. St. Leonards, NSW, Australia: Allen and Unwin.

Bostrom, N. (2003). *The transhumanist FAQ: a general introduction*. Retrieved from http://www.transhumanism.org/resources/FAQv21.pdf

Böttger, I. (2001). *Methodenlexikon - Open Space*. Retrieved February 6, 2009, from http://www.sowi-online.de/methoden/lexikon/open-space-boettger.htm

Boyle, T. (2003). Design principles for authoring dynamic, reusable learning objects. *Australian Journal of Educational Technology*, 19(1), 46-58. *Breadcrumbs image*. (n.d.). Retrieved from http://wiki.openstreetmap.org/images/1/19/Weekend_traces_cropped.png

Brady, L., Segal, G., Bamford, A., & Deer, C. (1998). *Student perceptions of the theory/practice nexus in teacher education: a longitudinal study.* A paper presented at the Australian Association for Research in Education (AARE), Adelaide, Australia.

Brandt-Pook, H. (2007 June). Geschlossene Wikis als aktivierendes Element in der Hochschullehre. *HMD – Praxis der Wirtschaftsinformatik*, 255.

Bransford, J. D., Brown, A. L., & Cocking, R. R. (2003). *How people learn: Brain, mind, experience, and school. Expanded edition.* Washington DC: National Academy Press.

Bransford, J. D., Vye, N., Kinzer, C., & Risko, V. (1990). Teaching thinking and content knowledge: Toward an integrated approach. In B.F. Jones & L. Idol (Eds.), *Dimensions of thinking and cognitive instruction* (pp. 381-413). Hillsdale, NJ: Lawrence Erlbaum Associates.

Brasher, A., Conole, G., Cross, S., Clark, P., Brasher, A., & Weller, M. (2008). CompendiumLD – a tool for effective, efficient and creative learning design. In *Proceedings of LAMS conference*, Cadiz, Spain.

Bredel, F. J. (2003). *Schwimmen. Bausteine für einen sicheren und attraktiven Unterricht.* Münster, Germany: Gemeindeunfallversicherungsverband Westfalen-Lippe.

Bredel, F. J., Fischer, U., & Thienes, G. (2005). Beispiele zum Einsatz digitaler Medien in der fachpraktischen Universitätsausbildung und im Sportunterricht. *Sportunterricht*, *54*(1), 17–21.

Breivik, P. S. (2005, March/April). 21st century learning and information literacy. *Change*, *37*(2), 20–27. doi:10.3200/CHNG.37.2.21-27

Breuer, K., & Kummer, R. (1990). Cognitive effects from process learning with computer-based simulations. *Computers in Human Behavior*, *6*, 69–81. doi:10.1016/0747-5632(90)90031-B

Briggs, L. (2008). The power of wikis in higher education. *Campus Technology*. Retrieved February 9, 2009, from http://campustechnology.com/Articles/2008/08/The-Power-of-Wikis-in-Higher-Ed.aspx

Brohn, D. (1983). Academic priorities in structural engineering - the importance of a visual schema. *The Structural Engineer, 61 A*(1), 13-16.

Brophy, J. (Ed.). (2004). *Using video in teacher education*: Elsevier.

Brown, A., & Thompson, H. (1997). Course design for the WWW - Keeping online students onside. In *Proceedings of the 14th Annual ASCILITE conference* (pp 74 – 81). Perth, Western Australia: Academic Computing Services, Curtin University of Technology.

Brown, J. S. (2002). Growing up digital: How the Web changes work, education, and the ways people learn. *United States Distance Learning Association*. Retrieved January 2008, from http://www.usdla.org/html/journal/FEB02_Issue/article01.html

Brown, J. S., & Duguid, P. (2000). *The social life of information*. Cambridge, MA: Harvard Business School Press.

Brown, J. S., Collins, A., & Duguid, P. (1989). Situated cognition and the culture of learning. *Educational Researcher*, *18*(1), 32–42.

Brown, L. R. (2006). Teaching technical and professional skills using a laboratory exercise: A comparison of two methods of plasmid preparation. *Biochemistry and Molecular Biology Education*, *34*(3), 194–198. doi:10.1002/bmb.2006.49403403194

Bruns, A., & Humphreys, S. (2005). Wikis in teaching and assessment. In *The M/Cyclopedia Project, WikiSym 2005.* New York: ACM Press.

Brusilovsky, P., & Rizzo, R. (2005). Using Maps and Landmarks for Navigation between Closed and Open Corpus Hyperspace in Web-based Education. *Computers & Education*, *44*(4), 441–457. doi:10.1016/j.compedu.2004.04.007

Buchanan, I. (2005). Space in the age of non-place. In I. Buchanan & G. Lambert (Eds.), *Deleuze and Space*. Edinburgh, Scotland: Edinburgh University Press.

Buchanan, M. (2002). *Small world: Uncovering nature's hidden networks*. London: Weidenfeld & Nicolson.

Buckingham, D. (2003). *Media education: Literacy, learning and contemporary culture*. Cambridge, UK: Polity Press.

Büffel, S. (2007). *Dokumentation zum Skypecast*. Retrieved February 4, 2009, from http://www.media-ocean.de/2007/06/21/dokumentation-zum-skypecast-vorlesung-20-online/

Bundeministerium für Bildung und Forschung. (2007). Neue Medien in der beruflichen Bildung. In *Digitale Medien eröffnen der beruflichen Aus- und Weiterbildung neue Chancen,* Bonn, Germany (pp. 6-7).

Buntine, M. A., Read, J. R., Barrie, S. C., Bucat, R. B., Crisp, G. T., & George, A. V. (2007). Advancing chemistry by enhancing learning in the laboratory (acell): A model for providing professional and personal development and facilitating improved student laboratory learning outcomes. *Chemistry Education Research and Practice*, *8*(2), 232–254.

Burbules, N., & Callister, T. A. (1996). Knowledge at the crossroads: Some alternative futures of hypertext learning environments. *Educational Theory.*

Burkle, M. (2003). *The impact of Information and Communication Technologies on Higher Education Systems*. Unpublished doctoral dissertation, University of Sussex, England.

Burkle, M., Miller, N., Soderquist, L., & Radke, D. (2008, May). *Using video iPods to support teaching and learning.* Paper presented at the Canadian Network of Innovation in Education Conference, Banff, AB, Canada.

Busstra, M. C., Hartog, R., Kersten, S., & Műller, M. (2007, March). Design guidelines for the development of digital nutrigenomics learning material for heterogeneous target groups. *Advances in Physiology Education*, *31*, 67–75. doi:10.1152/advan.00090.2006

Butler, L. L. (2004). Chalk, what chalk? [JOPERD]. *Journal of Physical Education, Recreation & Dance*, *75*(9), 12.

Bybee, R. (2004). Scientific inquiry and science teaching. In *Scientific inquiry and nature of science* (pp. 1-14).

Bybee, R. (Ed.). (2002). *Learning science and the science of learning*. Arlington, VA: NSTA Press.

Byra, M. (2006). Teaching styles and inclusive pedagogies. In D. Kirk, D. Macdonald & M. O'Sullivan (Eds.), *The Handbook of Physical Education* (pp. 449-466). London: Sage.

Cadez, I., Heckerman, D., Meek, C., Smyth, P., & White, S. (2003). Visualization of navigation patterns on a web site using model based clustering. *Journal of Data Mining and Knowledge Discovery*, *7*(4), 399–424. doi:10.1023/A:1024992613384

Cagle, B. (2004). Stepping up with pedometers. *Strategies: A Journal for Physical and Sport Educators, 17*(3), 27-28.

Calcaterra, A., Antonietti, A., & Underwood, J. (2005). Cognitive style, hypermedia navigation and learning. *Computers & Education*, *44*(4), 441–457. doi:10.1016/j.compedu.2004.04.007

California Department of Education. (2009). *Key elements of service learning*. Retrieved March 28, 2009, from http://www.cde.ca.gov/ci/cr/sl/keyelements.asp

Caligiuri, P. M., Jacobs, R. R., & Farr, J. L. (2000). The Attitudinal and Behavioural Openness Scale: Scale development and construct validation. *International Journal of Intercultural Relations*, *24*, 27–46. doi:10.1016/S0147-1767(99)00021-8

Callaghan, M. J., Harkin, J., McGinnity, T. M., & Woods, D. N. (2006, November 8-10). Evaluation of technology supported pedagogy. In *Proceedings of APRU Distance Learning and the Internet Conference,* University of Tokyo, Japan.

Campbell, G. (2005, November). There's something in the Air. Podcasting in Education. *EDUCAUSE Review*. Retrieved January 10, 2008, from http://net.educause.edu/ir/library/pdf/erm0561.pdf

Campos, M. (2004, April). A constructivist method for the analysis of networked cognitive communication and the assessment of collaborative learning and knowledge-building. *Journal of Asynchronous Learning Networks*, *8*(2).

Candy, P. (2004 August). *Linking thinking: Self-directed learning in the digital age*. Report funded under the Research Fellowship Scheme of the Department of Education, Science and Training.

Canter, D., Powell, J., Wishart, J., & Roderick, C. (1986). User navigation in complex database systems. *Behaviour & Information Technology*, *5*(3), 249–257. doi:10.1080/01449298608914518

Canter, D., Rivers, R., & Storrs, G. (1985). Characterising user navigation through complex data structures. *Behaviour & Information Technology*, *4*(2), 93–102. doi:10.1080/01449298508901791

Carmean, C., & Haefner, J. (2002, November/December). Mind over matter: Transforming course management systems into effective learning environments. *EDUCAUSE Review*, ▪▪▪, 5.

Carroll, J. M., & Mack, R. L. (1999). Metaphor, computing systems, and active learning. *International Journal of Human-Computer Studies*, *51*(2), 385–403. doi:10.1006/ijhc.1984.0316

Cartier, J. (2007). *Chemical reactors and fermentors: Simulation and modeling*. Lausanne, Switzerland: Ecole Polytechnique Federale de Lausanne.

Cassell, J., & Jenkins, H. (1998). *From Barbie to Mortal Kombat: Gender and computer games*. Cambridge, MA: MIT Press.

Castells, M. (1998). *The rise of the network society*. Cambridge, MA: Blackwell.

Casti, J. L. (1994). *Complexification: Explaining a paradoxical world through the science of surprise*. New York: HarperCollins.

CEO Forum on Education and Technology. (2001). *Student achievement in the 21st Century. Assessment, alignment, accountability, access, analysis.* Retrieved February 12, 2009, http://www.ceoforum.org/

Chabra, T., & Figueiredo, J. (2001). *How to design and deploy handheld learning*. Retrieved September, 2005, from http://www.empoweringtechnologies.net/eLearning/eLearning_expov5.htm

Chamberlin, B., & Gallagher, R. (2008). *Exergames. Using video games to promote physical activity*. Paper presented at the Children, Youth and Families At Risk (CYFAR) Conference, San Antonio, TX. Retrieved April 10, 2009, from http://www.cyfernet.org/cyfar08/research/chamberlin/chamberlin-research1.pdf

Chandler, P., & Sweller, J. (1991). Cognitive load theory and the format of instruction. *Cognition and Instruction*, *8*, 293–332.

Chao, C. (2005). Evaluating teacher's attitudes towards the use of wireless-mobile technologies in supporting learning: an instrument development study. In *IEEE International Workshop, Wireless and Mobile technologies in Education, 2005.* Retrieved March 27, 2008, from http://ieeexplore.ieee.org/xpl/freeabs_all.jsp?tp=&arnumber=1579245&isnumber=33360

Chapman, D., & Wiessner, C. (2008). *Exploring engaged learning as a tool for evaluating Web conferencing.* Paper presented at the E-Learn 2008, World Conference on E-Learning in Corporate, Government, Healthcare, & Higher Education of the Association for the Advancement of Computing in Education, Las Vegas, NV, USA.

Cheal, C. (2007). Second Life: Hype or hyperlearning. *Horizon*, *15*(4), 204–210. doi:10.1108/10748120710836228

Chen, C., & Rada, R. (1996). Interacting With Hypertext: A Meta-Analysis of Experimental Studies. *Human-Computer Interaction*, *11*, 125–156. doi:10.1207/s15327051hci1102_2

Chen, N. S., & Lin, K. M., & Kinshuk. (2008). Analysing users' satisfaction with e-learning using a negative critical incidents approach. *Innovations in Education and Teaching International*, *45*(2), 115–126. doi:10.1080/14703290801950286

Chen, S. Y., & Macredie, R. D. (2002). Cognitive Styles and Hypermedia Navigation: Development of a Learning Model. *Journal of the American Society for Information Science and Technology*, *53*(1), 3–15. doi:10.1002/asi.10023

Chen, S. Y., & Macredie, R. D. (2004). Cognitive Modelling of Student Learning in Web-Based Instructional

Programs. *International Journal of Human-Computer Interaction*, *17*(3), 375–402. doi:10.1207/s15327590ijhc1703_5

Chen, S. Y., Fan, J. P., & Macredie, R. D. (2006). Navigation in Hypermedia Learning Systems: Experts vs. Novices. *Computers in Human Behavior*, *22*(2), 251–266. doi:10.1016/j.chb.2004.06.004

Chen, W., & Frotjord, L. (2006). Scaffolding the comprehension of complex systems with explanation. In Kinshuk, R. Koper, P. Kommers, P. Kirschner, D. Sampson & W. Didderen (Eds.), *The Sixth IEEE Int. Conf. on Advanced Learning Technologies* (pp. 869-871). Kerkrade, The Netherlands: IEEE Computer Society.

Cheok, A. D., Fong, S. W., et al. (2003). Human Pacman: a sensing-based mobile entertainment system with ubiquitous computing and tangible interaction. In *Proc. of the 2nd Workshop on Network and System Support for Games*, California (pp. 106-117). New York: ACM Press.

Child, M. L. (2007, February 26). Professors split on wiki debate. *Thecrimson.com*. Retrieved January 15, 2009, from http://www.thecrimson.com/article.aspx?ref=517305

Chincholle, D. (2003). *Wireless service usability and design, tutorial 19*. Retrieved May, 2008, from http://www.chi2003.org/docs/t19.pdf

Christensen, C., Johnson, C. W., & Horn, M. B. (2008). *Disrupting class – how disruptive innovation will change the way the world learns*. New York: McGraw Hill.

Christian, W. (2008). Physlets®. Retrieved January 15, 2009, from http://webphysics.davidson.edu/Applets/Applets.html

Chung, Q. B. (2004). *The sage on the stage in the digital age: In support of digital lecture higher e-learning.* Paper presented at the Proceedings of the 3rd European Conference on E-Learning, Paris, France.

CIBER. (2007). An evaluation of BL Learning: a website for younger scholars. *University College London, School of Library, Archive and Information Studies: Information Behaviour of the Researcher of the Future*. Retrieved from http://www.ucl.ac.uk/slais/research/ciber/

Clark, D. R. (1999). Learning *domains or Bloom's taxonomy: The three types of learning*. Retrieved January 7, 2009, from http://www.nwlink.com/~donclark/hrd/bloom.html

Clough, M. P. (2002). Using the laboratory to enhance student learning. In R. W. Bybee (Ed.), *Learning science and the science of learning: Science educators' essay collection* (pp. 85 - 96). Arlington VA: NSTA Press.

Coburn, P. (2004). The change function. *Always on: The Insider's Network*. Retrieved April 19, 2006, from http://www.alwaysonnetwork.com/comments.php

Cognition and Technology Group at Vanderbilt. (1990). Anchored instruction and its relationship to situated cognition. *Educational Researcher*, *19*(6), 2–10.

Cohen, N. (2007, February 21). A history department bans citing Wikipedia as a research source. *The New York Times*. Retrieved January 15, 2009, from http://www.nytimes.com/2007/02/21/education/21wikipedia.html?ex=1329714000&en=156f770bd93c4fa0&ei=5088&partner=rssnyt&emc=rss

Colby, A., Kohlberg, L., Speicher, B., Hewer, A., Candee, D., Gibbs, J., & Power, C. (1987). *The measurement of moral judgment (Vol. 2), standard issue scoring manual.* Cambridge, UK: Cambridge University Press.

Cole, A. L., & Knowles, J. G. (2000). *Researching Teaching: Exploring Teacher Develoment Through Reflective Inquiry*. Boston: Allyn and Bacon.

Collis, B., & Moonen, J. (2001). *Flexible learning in a digital world*. London: Kogan Page.

Colwill, B. (2006, January 10). *Wikipedia and the feminist production of knowledge.* Retrieved January 15, 2009, from http://pict.sdsu.edu/Jan06/collwill/wikipedia%20presentation1.ppt.

Committee on Science. Engineering, and Public Policy. (2006). *Rising above the gathering storm: Energizing and employing America for a brighter economic future*. Washington, DC: National Academies Press. Retrieved June 8, 2006, from http://www.nap.edu/books/0309100399/html

Common Sense Media. (2008). Media + Child and Adolescent Health: A Systematic Review. *Common Sense Media.*

CompactCampus. (2001). Retrieved July 30, 2008, from

Conklin, J. (1987). Hypertext: An introduction and survey. *IEEE Computer, 20*(9), 17–41.

Conole and Culver. (forthcoming). Cloudworks: social networking for learning design, Australian Journal of Educational Technology Cross, S. & Conole, G. (2009). *Learn about learning design (OU Learn About Series).* Milton Keynes, UK . *The Open University.*

Conole, G. (2006). What impact are technologies having and how are they changing practice? In I. McNay (Ed.), *Beyond Mass Higher Education: Building on Experience* (pp. 81-95). New York: McGraw-Hill Education.

Conole, G. (2008). New schemas for mapping pedagogies and technologies. *Ariadne.* Retrieved from http://www.ariadne.ac.uk/

Conole, G. (in press). Stepping over the edge: the implications of new technologies for education. In M. Lee & C. McLoughin, *Web 2.0-based e-learning: applying social informatics for tertiary teaching.* Hersey, PA: IGI Global.

Conole, G. and Culver, J. (2009), The design of Cloudworks: applying social networking practice to foster the exchange of learning and teaching ideas and designs, Computers and Education, doi: 1-.1016/j.compedu.2009.09.013

Conole, G., & Mulholland, P. (2007). *Using the concepts of design and narrative. PI working paper No. 2.* Milton Keynes, UK: The Open University.

Conole, G., Brasher, A., Cross, S., Weller, M., Clark, P., & White, J. (2008). Visualising learning design to foster and support good practice and creativity. *Educational Media International.*

Conole, G., Culver, J., Well, M., Williams, P., Cross, S., Clark, P., & Brasher, A. (n.d). *Cloudworks: social networking for learning design.* Melbourne, Australia: Ascilite Conference.

Council of Europe. (2002). *Compass. A manual on human rights education with young people.* Strasbourg, France: Council of Europe Publishing.

Crang, M. (2003). The hair in the gate: Visuality and geographical knowledge. *Antipode, 35,* 238–243. doi:10.1111/1467-8330.00321

Crawford, C. (1984). *The art of computer game design.* Berkeley, CA: McGraw-Hill.

Crawford, K. (1996). Vygotskian approaches to human development in the information era. *Educational Studies in Mathematics,* (31): 43–62. doi:10.1007/BF00143926

Creanor, L., et al. (2006 August). *LEX: The learner experience of e-learning.* Final report presented at Glasgow Caledonian University, Scotland. Retrieved January 10, 2008, from http://www.jisc.ac.uk/uploaded_documents/LEX%20Final%20Report_August06.pdf

Cross, J. (2006). *Informal Learning: Rediscovering the natural pathways that inspire innovation and performance.* San Francisco: Pfeiffer.

Cross, S., Conole, G., Clark, P., Brasher, A., & Weller, M. (2008). Mapping a landscape of learning design: Identifying key trends in current practice at the Open University. In *LAMS Conference*, Cadiz, Spain.

Csikszentmihalyi, M. (1992). *Flow - the psychology of optimal experience.* Stuttgart, Germany: Klett-Cotta.

Csikszentmihalyi, M. (2000). *Das Flow-Erlebnis. Jenseits von Angst und Langeweile: im Tun aufgehen.* Stuttgart, Deutschland: Klett.

CUBoulder. (2008). PhET. Retrieved January 15, 2009, from http://phet.colorado.edu/

Dalsgaard, C. (2009). Social software: E-learning beyond learning management systems. *European Journal of Open, Distance and E-Learning.* Retrieved February, 2009, from http://www.eurodl.org/materials/contrib/2006/Christian_Dalsgaard.htm

Daniel, J. S. (1996). *Mega-universities and knowledge media: Technology strategies for higher education.* London: Kogan Page.

Daniels, J. S. (1998). *Mega universities and knowledge Media: Technology strategies for higher education.* London: Routledge.

Danisch, M. (2008). *Das Web 2.0 in der Sportwissenschaft.* Invited paper presented at a meeting of the Multimedia Initiative Hessen, Wiesbaden.

Danisch, M., & Friedrich, G. (2007). Neue Medien im Sportunterricht. In H. Lange & S. Sinning (Eds.), *Handbuch Sportdidaktik* (pp. 319-329). Balingen, Germany: Spitta.

Danisch, M., Müller, L., & Schwier, J. (2006). eLearning in der Sportspielvermittlung. Entwicklung von multimedialer Lernsoftware für die Optimierung von Sportspiel-Techniken und Aufbau eines sportwissenschaftlichen Webportals "Sportspiele." *Spectrum der Sportwissenschaften, 18*(1), 23–39.

Dansereau, D. F. (1983). *Cooperative learning: Impact on acquisition of knowledge and skills (Report No.341).* Abilene, TX: U.S. Army Research Institute for the Behavioral and Social Sciences.

Darling-Hammond, L. (1999). *Reshaping teaching policy, preparation, and practice: Influences of the National Board for Professional Teaching Standards.* Washington, DC: American Association of Colleges for Teacher Education.

David, B., Bouthier, D., Marsenach, J., & Durey, A. (1999). French research into the didactics and technology of physical activities and sports: An expanding new field. *Instructional Science, 27,* 147–163.

David, T., Patel, L., Burdett, K., & Rangachari, P. (2009). *Problem- based learning in medicine: A practical guide for students & teachers.* London:Royal Society of Medicine Press.

Davis, F. D. (1989). Perceived usefulness, perceived ease of use and user acceptance of information technology. *MIS Quarterly, 13*(3), 318–340. doi:10.2307/249008

Davis, F. D., Bagozzi, R., & Warshaw, P. (1989). User acceptance of computer technology: A comparison of two theoretical models. *Management Science, 35*(8), 982–1003. doi:10.1287/mnsc.35.8.982

De Bra, P. M. E. (2008). Adaptive hypermedia. In H. H. Adelsberger, Kinshuk, J. M. Pawlowski, & D. Sampson, (Eds.), *Handbook on Information Technologies for Education and Training* (pp. 29-46). Berlin, Germany: Springer.

de Freitas, S. (2006). *Learning in immersive worlds. A review of game-based learning.* Retrieved August 28, 2007 from http://www.jisc.ac.uk/media/documents/programmes/elearning_innovation/gaming%20report_v3.3.pdf

De Freitas, S. (2008). *Serious Virtual Worlds. A scoping study.* SGI.

de Freitas, S., & Jarvis, S. (2007). Serious games – Engaging training solutions: A research and development project for supporting training needs. *British Journal of Educational Technology, 38*(3), 523–525. doi:10.1111/j.1467-8535.2007.00716.x

de Freitas, S., & Jarvis, S. (2008). Towards a development approach for serious games. In T.M. Connolly, M. Stansfield, & E. Boyle (Ed.), *Games-based learning advancements for multi-sensory human-computer interfaces: Techniques and effective practices.* Hershey, PA: IGI Global.

de Freitas, S., & Neumann, T. (2008). The use of 'exploratory learning' for supporting immersive learning in virtual environments. *Computers and Education.*

de Freitas, S., & Oliver, M. (2006). How can exploratory learning with games and simulations within the curriculum be most effectively evaluated? *Computers & Education, 46,* 249–264. doi:10.1016/j.compedu.2005.11.007

de Jong, T., & van Joolingen, W. R. (1998). Scientific discovery learning with computer simulations of conceptual domains. *Review of Educational Research, 68,* 179–201.

de Jong, T., Beishuizen, J., Hulshof, C., Prins, F., van Rijn, H., & van Somersen, M. (2005). Determinants of discovery learning in a complex simulation learning environment. In P. Gardenfors & P. Johansson (Eds.), *Cognition, education, and communication technology* (pp. 257-283). Mahwah, NJ: Lawrence Erlbaum Associates, Inc.

de Lisi, R., & Wolford, J. L. (2002). Improving children's mental rotation accuracy with computer game playing. *The Journal of Genetic Psychology, 163*(3), 172–182.

de Witt, C. (2008, Januar 1). Vom Mängelwesen zum Superhirn? – Wissenserwerb und Kompetenzentwicklung durch Partizipation im Web 2.0. In *Vortrag auf der Learntec 2008*, Karlsruhe.

de Witt, C., & Czerwionka, T. (2007). *Mediendidaktik. Studientexte für Erwachsenenbildung.* Bielefeld, Deutschland: Bertelsmann.

Deal, A. (2007). Podcasting. A Teaching with Technology white paper. *Office of Technology for Education & Eberly Center for Teaching Excellence, Carnegie Mellon University.* Retrieved December 12, 2008, from http://connect.educause.edu/files/CMU_Podcasting_Jun07.pdf

Debray, R. (2004). Für eine Mediologie. In *Kursbuch Medienkultur. Die maßgeblichen Theorien von Brecht bis Baudrillard* (pp. 76-75). Stuttgart, Germany: DVA.

Deci, E. L., & Ryan, R. M. (1985). *Intrinsic motivation and self-determination in human behavior.* New York: Plenum.

Deci, E., & Ryan, R. (Eds.). (2002). *Handbook of self-determination research.* Rochester, NY: University of Rochester Press.

Dede, C. (2009). Immersive interfaces for engagement and learning. *Science, 323*(5910), 66–69. doi:10.1126/science.1167311

Dee, F., Donnelly, A., Radio, S., Leaven, T., Zaleski, M., & Kreiter, C. (2007). Utility of 2D and 3D virtual microscopy in cervical cytology education and testing. *Acta Cytologica, 51*(4), 523–529.

Deleuze, G., & Guattari, F. (1987). *A thousand plateaus: Capitalism and schizophrenia.* (B. Massumi, Trans.). Minneapolis: University of Minnesota Press.

Desharnais, R. A., & Limson, M. (2007). Designing and implementing virtual courseware to promote inquiry-based learning. *MERLOT Journal of Online Learning and Teaching, 3*, 30–39.

Desire2learn. (2005). CLOE: Cooperative learning object exchange. Retrieved January 15, 2009, from http://cloe.desire2learn.com/

Dewey, J. (1938). *Experience and education.* New York: Macmillian.

Diaper, D. (2004). Understanding task analysis for human-computer interaction. In N. Stanton (Ed.), *The Handbook of Task Analysis for Human-Computer Interaction* (pp. 5-48). Mahwah, NJ: Erlbaum.

Dickey, M. D. (2006). Game design narrative for learning: Appropriating adventure game design narrative devices and techniques for the design of interactive learning environments. *Educational Technology Research and Development, 54*(3), 245–263. doi:10.1007/s11423-006-8806-y

didaktik/texte/aufgabenorientierte_didaktik_des_eLearning.pdf

Diederen, J., Gruppen, H., Hartog, R., & Voragen, A. G. J. (2006). Design and evaluation of digital assignments on research experiments within food chemistry. *Journal of Science Education and Technology, 15*(3,4), 227 - 246.

Dillenbourg, P. (1999). What do you mean by collaborative learning? In P. Dillenbourg (Ed.), *Collaborative-learning: Cognitive and Computational Approaches* (pp.1-19). Oxford, UK: Elsevier.

Dillenbourg, P., & Hong, F. (2008). The mechanics of CSCL macro scripts in computer-supported collaborative learning. *International Journal of Computer-Supported Collaborative Learning, 3*(1). doi:10.1007/s11412-007-9033-1

Dillenbourg, P., Baker, M., Blaye, A., & O'Malley, C. (1996). The evolution of research on collaborative learning. In E. Spada & P. Reiman (Eds.), *Learning in humans and machine: Towards an interdisciplinary learning science* (pp. 189–211). Oxford, UK: Elsevier.

Döbeli Honegger, B. (2007). Wiki und die starken Potenziale: Unterrichten mit Wikis als virtuellen Wandtafeln. In *Web 2.0 - Internet Interaktiv (Journal Computer und Unterricht)* (pp. 39-41). Retrieved May 1, 2009, from http://beat.doebe.li/publications/2007-doebeli-honegger-wiki-und-die-starken-potenziale.pdf

Dober, R. (2003). Sportpädagogik und Sportpraxis im Internet. www.sportunterricht.de – Ein Mitmachprojekt für alle, die sich für Lehren und Lernen im Sport interessieren. *SportPraxis, 44*(5), 33-35.

Dober, R. (2004). Neue Medien im Sportunterricht. Ideen und Anregungen zum Computereinsatz beim Lehren und Lernen im Sport. In E. Christmann, E. Emrich & J. Flatau (Eds.), *Schule und Sport* (pp. 281-288). Schorndorf, Germany: Hofmann.

Dober, R. (2006). Mit dem Notebook in die Turnhalle. *L.A. Multimedia, 3*(1), 18–19.

Dohmen, G. (2001). Das informelle Lernen, Die internationale Erschließung einer bisher vernachlässigten Grundform menschlichen Lernens für das lebenslange Lernen aller. In *Bundesministerium für Bildung und Forschung, Das informelle Lernen*, Bonn, Deutschland (pp. 18-49).

Doignon, J.-P., & Falmagne, J.-C. (1985). Spaces for the assessment of knowledge. *International Journal of Man-Machine Studies, 23*, 175–196. doi:10.1016/S0020-7373(85)80031-6

Domin, D. S. (1999a). A content analysis of general chemistry laboratory manuals for evidence of higher-order cognitive tasks. *Journal of Chemical Education, 76*(1), 109–111.

Domin, D. S. (1999b). A review of laboratory instruction styles. *Journal of Chemical Education, 76*(4), 543–547.

Döring, N. (2003). Sozialpsychologie des Internet. In Göttingen et al., *Die Bedeutung des Internet für Kommunikationsprozesse, Identitäten, soziale Beziehungen und Gruppen (2nd ed.)*. Göttingen, Germany: Hogrefe.

Döring, N. (2005). Pädagogische Aspekte der Mobilkommunikation. In J. R. Höflich & J. Gebhardt (Hrsg.), *Mobile Kommunikation – Perspektiven und Forschungsfelder* (pp. 89-100). Frankfurt am Main, Deutschland: Peter Lang.

Döring, N. (2008). *M-Learning*. Retrieved May, 2008, from http://www4.tu-ilmenau.de/m-learning/index.html

Döring, N., & Dietmar, C. (2005). Medienproduktion für die Mobilkommunikation. In H. Krömker & P. Klimsa (Hrsg.), *Handbuch der Medienproduktion. Produktion von Film, Fernsehen, Hörfunk, Print, Internet, Mobilfunk und Musik* (pp. 545-577). Wiesbaden, Deutschland: VS Verlag für Sozialwissenschaften.

Downes, S. (2005). E-learning 2.0. *eLearn magazine*. Retrieved February 7, 2009, from http://elearnmag.org/subpage.cfm?section=articles&article=29-1

Downes, S. (2006). E-learning 2.0. *eLearning magazine: education and technology in perspective*. Retrieved April 20, 2007 from http://elearnmag.org/subpage.cfm?section=articlesandarticle=29-1

Dreher, H. (2006). *Interactive On-line Formative Evaluation of Student Assignments*. Paper presented at InSITE 2006, June 25-28, Greater Manchester, England. Retrieved October 2007, from http://2006.informing-science.org/

Dreher, H., & Williams, R. (2006). Assisted query formulation using normalised word vector and dynamic ontological filtering: Flexible query answering systems. In *Proceedings of 7th International Conference, FQAS 2006*, Milan, Italy (pp. 282 –294).

Dresel, M., & Ziegler, A. (2006). Langfristige Förderung von Fähigkeitsselbstkonzept und impliziter Fähigkeitstheorie durch computerbasiertes attributionales Feedback. *Zeitschrift fur Padagogische Psychologie, 20*(1-2), 49–63. doi:10.1024/1010-0652.20.12.49

Dreyfus, H. (1991). *Being-in-the-world: A commentary on Heidegger's Being and Time, div. I*. Cambridge, MA: MIT Press.

Duchastel, P. (1997). A web-based model for university instruction. *Journal of Educational Technology Systems, 25*, 221–228. doi:10.2190/UFF9-KB1X-NGG4-UHKL

Dunn, L., & Tannehill, D. (2005). Using pedometers to promote physical activity in secondary physical education. *Strategies: A Journal for Physical and Sport Educators, 19*(1), 19-25.

Dye, A. K'Odingo, J., & Solstad, B.-E. (2003). Mobile Education – A glance at a future. *Bekkestua*. Retrieved May, 2008, from http://nettskolen.nki.no/forskning/mobile_education.pdf

Ebner, E. (2007). Wikipedia. Hype oder Zukunftshoffnung für die Hochschullehre. In *E-Learning: Strategische Implementierungen und Studiengang. Tagungsband zur 13. FNMA-Tagung* (pp. 139–146). Köln, Germany: Verlag Forum Neue Medien.

Ebner, M. (2008). *Has the net-generation arrived at the university? - oder der Student von Heute, ein digital native?* Retrieved October 25, 2009, from http://lamp.tu-graz.ac.at/~i203/ebner/publication/08_gmw.pdf

Ebner, M., & Walder, U. (2007). *e-Learning in Civil Engineering - Six years of experience at Graz University of Technology*. Paper presented at the 24th W78 Conference.

Ebner, M., & Walder, U. (2008). *E-Education in civil engineering - A promise for the future?* Paper presented at the 6th AECEF Symposium Education in Changing Europe.

Ebner, M., Kickmeier-Rust, M. D., & Holzinger, A. (2008). Utilizing Wiki-Systems in higher education classes: a chance for universal access? In *Universal Access in the Information Society*. New York: Springer.

Ebner, M., Scerbakov, N., & Maurer, H. (2006). New Features for eLearning in higher education for civil engineering. *Journal of Universal Computer Science, 0*(0), 93–106.

Ebner, M., Zechner, J., & Holzinger, A. (2006). *Why is Wikipedia so successful? Experiences in establishing the principles in higher education*. Paper presented at the 6th International Conference on Knowledge Management (I-Know'06).

Education.au. (2008). *Edna: Australia's free online network for educators*. Retrieved April 9, 2009, from http://www.edna.edu.au/edna/go

Educational Training Committee. (2005). *Report on the inquiry into the suitability of pre-service teacher training in Victoria*. Presented in Melbourne, Parliament of Victoria.

Educational Uses of Second Life. (2007). Retrieved June 26, 2007, from http://sleducation.wikispaces.com/educationaluses?f=print

Edutech. (2005). *Course platform evaluation report*. Retrieved January 5, 2009 from http://www.edutech.ch/lms/ev3/index.php

Edwards, D., Hardman, L., & McAleese, R. (1989). Lost in hyperspace: cognitive mapping and navigation in a hypertext environment. In *Hypertext: Theory into Practice* (pp. 90-105). London: Intellect Books.

Eilks, I., Krilla, B., Flintjer, B., Möllencamp, H., & Wagner, W. (2004). *Computer und Multimedia im Chemieunterricht heute - Eine Einordnung aus didaktischer und lerntheoretischer Sicht*. Retrieved October 25, 2009, from http://www.uni-muenster.de/imperia/md/content/didaktik_der_chemie/computerkurs/fachgruppe_chemieunterricht___stellungnahme.pdf

E-Learning 2.0-Blog. (2007). *Online round table: E-Learning 2.0*. Retrieved January 8, 2009, from http://www.elearning2null.de/online-round-table-e-learning-20/

Electronics, J. an Information Technology Industries Association. (2002). *Exchangable image file format for digital still cameras: Exif version 2.2*. Retrieved from http://www.exif.org/Exif2-2.PDF

Elliott, S., Stanec, A. S., McCollum, S., & Stanley, M. A. (2007). Uses of the Internet by health and physical education teachers. *Strategies: A Journal for Physical and Sport Educators, 20*(5), 19-27.

El-Sayed, S., Aziz, S. K., & Chassapis, C. (2009). Content-rich interactive online laboratory systems. *Computer Applications in Engineering Education*, *17*(1), 61–79. doi:10.1002/cae.20210

Engel, C. E. (1991). Not just a method but a way of learning. In D. Boud & G. Feletti (Eds.), *The Challenge of Problem Based Learning*. London: Kogan Page.

Engel, C. E. (1992). Problem-based learning. *British Journal of Hospital Medicine*, *48*, 325–329.

Engeström, J. (2005, April 13). Why some social network services work and others don't — Or: the case for object-centered sociality. Retrieved August 8, 2008, from http://www.zengestrom.com/blog/2005/04/why_some_social.html

Erpenbeck, J., & Sauter, W. (2007). *Kompetenzentwicklung im Netz. New Blended Learning mit Web 2.0.* Köln, Deutschland: Wolters Kluwer.

e-teaching.org. (2006). Didaktische Modelle. *Redaktionsteam PELe.* Retrieved May, 2008, from http://www.e-teaching.org/didaktik/theorie/didaktik_allg/Didaktische%20Modelle_19_07_06_bg.pdf

Euler, D., Hasanbegovic, J., & Kerres, M. Seufert, S. (2006). *Handbuch der Kompetenzentwicklung für E-Learning Innovationen*. Bern, Switzerland: Huber.

Evans, J. (2007). Tomorrow's students: Are we ready for the new 21st-century learners? Video Podcast. *Educause Conference 2007.* Retrieved from http://hosted.mediasite.com/hosted4/Viewer/Viewers/Viewer320TL.aspx?mode=Default&peid=ce8f0201-7d54-4abb-b1b0-4f8a0479f481&pid=06155cca-0a78-4cd5-880f-d4c5ce23ba9c&playerType=WM64Lite

Evans, T., & Nation, D. (2000). *Changing university teaching. Reflection on creating educational technologies*. London: Routledge.

Eyler, J., & Giles, D. E. (1999). *Where's the learning in service learning?* San Francisco, CA: Jossey-Bass.

Eyler, J., Giles, D., Stenson, C., & Gray, C. (2001). At a glance: What we know about the effects of service-learning on college students, faculty, institutions and communities, 1993-2000 (3rd ed.). *Learn and Serve America National Service-Learning Clearinghouse.*

Fast, K., & Sedig, K. (2005). The INVENT framework: Examining the role of information visualisation in the reconceptualization of digital libraries. *Journal of Digital Information*, *6*(3).

Feeney, L. (2007). Digital denizens. In *Instructional technology resources: In the spotlight*. Retrieved May 16, 2007, from http://loki.stockton.edu/~intech/spotlight-digital-denizens.htm

Feisel, L. D., & Rosa, A. J. (2005). The role of the laboratory in undergraduate engineering education. *Journal of Engineering Education*, *94*(1), 121–130.

Feltovich, P. J., Coulson, R. L., & Spiro, R. J. (2001). Learners' (mis)understanding of important and difficult concepts. In K. D. Forbus & P. J. Feltovich (Eds.), *Smart machines in education: The coming revolution in educational technology* (pp. 349-375). Menlo Park: CA: AAAI/MIT Press.

Fendt, W. (2008). *Java applets on physics*. Retrieved April 9 2009, from http://www.walter-fendt.de/ph14e/

Fenley, S. (1997). Educational objectives and the promotion of learning in the construction of multimedia packages. In *Proceedings of Euro AI-ED*, Lisbon

Fenley, S. (1998). Navigational issues in interactive multimedia. In *Proceedings of ICCE 1998 Conference, International Conference on Computers in Education*, Beijing, China.

Fenley, S. (2006). *Navigational patterns in interactive multimedia*. PhD thesis, Open University.

Ferry, B., Kervin, L., Cambourne, B., Turbill, J., Hedberg, J., & Jonassen, D. (2005). Incorporating real experience into the development of a classroom-based simulation. *Journal of Learning Design*, *1*(1), 22–32.

Feuer, D., & Gerber, B. (1988). Uh-oh: Second thoughts about adult learning theory. *Training (New York, N.Y.)*, *25*(12), 31–39.

Ficher, U. (2005). *Volleyball. Bausteine für einen sicheren und attraktiven Unterricht*. Münster, Germany: Gemeindeunfallversicherungsverband Westfalen-Lippe.

Fiedler, D. (2003). Soziale Kompetenz - Ein unvollständiger Begriff. *Verhaltenstherapie & Psychosoziale Praxis, 35*, 87–95.

Fiorentino, L. H., & Castelli, D. (2005). Creating a virtual gymnasium. [JOPERD]. *Journal of Physical Education, Recreation & Dance, 76*(4), 16.

Fischer, U., Thienes, G., & Bredel, F. J. (2005). CD-ROMs für den Sportunterricht und die Sportlehrerausbildung - ausgewählte Evaluationsergebnisse. *Sportunterricht, 54*(1), 11–16.

Flick, L. B., & Lederman, N. G. (2006). *Scientific inquiry and nature of science: Implications for teaching, learning, and teacher education*. New York: Springer.

Flowers, N. (2000). *The human rights education handbook. Effective practices for learning, action, and change*. Minneapolis, MN: Human Rights Resource Center, University of Minnesota. Retrieved February 3, 2007, from http://www1.umn.edu/humanrts/edumat/hreduseries/hrhandbook/toc.html

Fodor, J. (1997). Connectionism and the problem of systematicity: Why Smolensky's solution still doesn't work. *Cognition, 62*, 109–119. doi:10.1016/S0010-0277(96)00780-9

Fodor, J., & McLaughlin, B. (1990). Connectionism and the problem of systematicity: Why Smolensky's solution doesn't work. *Cognition, 35*, 183–204. doi:10.1016/0010-0277(90)90014-B

Fodor, J., & Pylyshyn, Z. (1988). Connectionism and cognitive architecture: A critical analysis. *Cognition, 28*, 3–71. doi:10.1016/0010-0277(88)90031-5

Foertsch, J., Moses, G., Strikwerda, J., & Litzkow, M. (2002). Reversing the lecture/homework paradigm using eTEACH web-based streaming video software. *Journal of Engineering Education, 91*, 267–275.

Ford, N., & Chen, S. (2000). Individual Differences, Hypermedia Navigation, and Learning: An Empirical Study. *Journal of Educational Multimedia and Hypermedia, 9*(4), 441–457.

Forte, A., & Bruckman, A. (2006). From Wikipedia to the classroom: exploring online publication and learning. In *Proceedings of the International Conference of the Learning Sciences, 1*, 182–188.

Forterra Systems Inc. (2008). OLIVE - Purpose driven virtual worlds for everyone. Retrieved September 18, 2008, from http://www.forterrainc.com/images/stories/pdf/OLIVE_Dec07_Final_Rev.pdf

Foucault, M. (1969). *Archäologie des Wissens*. Frankfurt, Germany: Suhrkamp.

Frand, J. L. (2000). The information-age mindset. Changes in students and implications for higher education. *EDUCAUSE Review*, 35(5), 15-24. Retrieved from http://www.educause.edu/ir/library/pdf/ERM0051.pdf

Frand, J. L. (2000, September/October). Information-Age mindset: The changes in students and implications for higher education. *EDUCAUSE Review, (Sept/Oct)*, 17–24.

Friedman, T. (2008). *Hot, flat, and crowded: Why we need a green revolution--and how it can renew America*. New York: Farrar, Straus and Giroux.

Friedman, T. L. (2005). *The world is flat: A brief history of the globalized world in the twenty-first century*. New York: Farrar, Straus and Giroux.

Friedrich, G. (2004). *Fußball. Bausteine für einen sicheren und attraktiven Unterricht*. Münster, Germany: Gemeindeunfallversicherungsverband Westfalen-Lippe.

Fritzsche, K. P. (2004). *Menschenrechte. Eine Einführung mit Dokumenten*. Paderborn, Germany: Schönigh.

Fromme, J., & Sesink, W. (2008). *Pädagogische Medientheorie*. Wiesbaden, Germany: VS Verlag für Sozialwissenschaften.

Frydenberg, M. (2006). Principles and pedagogy: The two P's of podcasting in the information technology classroom. In *Proceedings of Information Systems Education Conference (ISECON)* (Vol. 23). Retrieved on December

10, 2008, from http://www.isedj.org/isecon/2006/3354/ISECON.2006.Frydenberg.pdf

Fucks-Kittowski, F., Köhler, A., & Fuhr, D. (2004). *Roughing up processes the wiki way - Knowlede communities in the context of work and learning processes.* Paper presented at the I-Know 2004.

Fulk, J., & Collins-Jarvis, L. (2001). Wired meetings: Technological mediation of organizational gatherings. In L.L. Putnam & F.M. Jablins (Eds.), *New handbook of organizational communication (2nd ed.)* (pp. 624-703). Newbury Park, CA: Sage.

Gadamer, H. G. (1976). *Philosophical hermeneutics.* (D. E. Linge, Trans.). Berkeley, CA: University of California Press.

Gallus, W. A. Jr, Cervato, C., Cruz-Neira, C., & Faidley, G. (2006). A virtual tornadic thunderstorm enabling students to construct knowledge about storm dynamics through data collection and analysis. *Advances in Geosciences*, *8*, 27–32.

Gandsas, A., McIntire, K., Palli, G., & Park, A. (2002). Live streaming video for medical education: a laboratory model. *Journal of Laparoendoscopic & Advanced Surgical Techniques. Part A.*, *12*, 377 382. doi:10.1089/109264202320884135

Gapski, H. (2001). *Medienkompetenz: Eine Bestandsaufnahme und Vorüberlegungen zu einem systemtheoretischen Rahmenkonzept.* Wiesbaden, Germany: Westdeutscher. Verl.

Garris, R., Ahlers, R., & Driskell, J. E. (2002). Games, motivation, and learning: A research and practice model. *Simulation & Gaming*, *33*(4), 441–467. doi:10.1177/1046878102238607

Gassner, O. (2006). *Happy campers.* Retrieved February 5, 2009, from http://www.heise.de/tp/r4/artikel/24/24251/1.html

Gatto, D. (1993). The use of interactive computer simulations in training. *Australian Journal of Educational Technology*, *9*(2), 144–156.

Gediga, G., & Hamborg, K.-C. (1999). IsoMetrics: Ein Verfahren zur Evaluation von Software nach ISO 9241/10 [IsoMetrics: A Technique for Evaluation of Software in accordance to ISO 9241/10]. In H. Holling & G. Gediga (Eds.), *Evaluationsforschung [Evaluation Research]* (pp. 195-234). Göttingen, Germany: Hogrefe.

Gee, J. P. (2003). *What video games have to teach us about learning and literacy.* New York: Palgrave Macmillan.

Gentile, D. A., & Anderson, C. A. (2003). Violent video games: The newest media violence hazard. In D. A. Gentile (Ed.), *Media violence and children* (pp. 131-152). Westport, CT: Praeger Publishing.

Gentner, D. (2002). Mental models, Psychology of. In N. J. Smelser & P. B. Bates (Eds.), *International encyclopedia of the social and behavioral sciences* (pp. 9683-9687). Amsterdam: Elsevier Science.

Georgiev, T., Georgieva, E., & Smrikarov, A. (2004). M-Learning – a new stage of e-learning. In *Proceedings of the 5th international conference on Computer Systems and Technologies (CompSysTech '04)*, Rousse, Bulgaria.

Geser, G. (2007). *Open educational practices and resources - OLCOS roadmap 2012.* Retrieved December 30, 2008, from http://edumedia.salzburgresearch.at/images/stories/EduMedia/Inhalte/Publications/olcos_roadmap.pdf

Gibson, J. J. (1979). *The Ecological Approach to Visual Perception.* Boston: Houghton Mifflin.

Gibson, T., Koontz, D., & Van Den Hende, M. (2008, April 1-4) The digital generation: Teaching to a population that speaks an entirely new language. *Paper presented at the Chair Academy,* Denver, CO. Retrieved on January 12, 2009, from http://david.koontz.name/digital/Presentation_files/THE_DIGITAL_GENERATION.pdf

Gibson's Theory of Direct perception – Optic Flow. (n.d.). Retrieved from http://www.users.totalise.co.uk/~kbroom/Lectures/gibson.htm

Gierke, C., & Müller, R. (2008). *Unternehmen in Second Life. Wie Sie Virtuelle Welten für Ihr reales Geschäft nutzen können.* Offenbach, Deutschland: GABAL.

Gilb, T. (1997). Towards the engineering of requirements. *Requirements Engineering, 2*(3), 165–169. doi:10.1007/BF02802774

Gilbert, S. (2000, February 14). A new vision worth working toward - connected education and collaborative change. Retrieved January 2008, from http://www.tltgroup.org/gilbert/NewVwwt2000--2-14-00.htm

Gilbert, S. (2003, March 4). Why Bother? *Teaching Learning and Technology group*. Retrieved January 2008, from http://www.tltgroup.org/gilbert/WhyBotherArticle.pdf

Gillard, S., Bailey, D., & Nolan, E. (2008). Ten reasons for IT educators to be early adopters of IT innovations. *Journal of Information Technology Education, 7*, 21–33.

Gipson, S. (1996). *Feral, Facsimile of Facilitated? Technology Serving Teaching and Learning*. Tridos School Village, Chiang Mai, Thailand: Learning and Teaching: Implications for Gifted and Talented Students.

Glatz-Krieger, K., Spornitz, U., Spatz, A., Mihatsch, M., & Glatz, D. (2006). Factors to keep in mind when introducing virtual microscopy. *Virchows Archiv, 448*(3), 248–255. doi:10.1007/s00428-005-0112-2

Gleick, J. (1987). *Chaos*. London: William Heinemann Ltd.

GLOBE. (2008). *Global learning objects brokered exchange*. Retrieved June 24, 2008, from http://www.globe-info.org/

Göbel, S., Iurgel, I., Rössler, M., Hülsken, F., & Eckes, C. (2006). Design and narrative structure for the Virtual Human scenarios. *International Journal of Virtual Reality, 5*(3), 1–10.

Goguen, J. A. (1996). *Formality and informality in requirements engineering*. Paper presented at the Proceedings of the 2nd International Conference on Requirements Engineering (ICRE '96), Colorado Springs, CO, USA.

Gollwitzer, M., Kranz, D., & Vogel, E. (2006). Die Validität studentischer Lehrveranstaltungsevaluationen und ihre Nützlichkeit für die Verbesserung der Hochschullehre: Neuere Befunde zu den Gütekriterien des 'Trierer Inventars zur Lehrevaluation' (TRIL) [The validity of students' course evaluation and its benefit for the improvement of academic teaching: New results on quality factors of the 'Trierer Inventory for the Evaluation of Teaching' (TRIL)]. In G. Krampen & H. Zayer (Eds.), *Didaktik und Evaluation in der Psychologie [Didactics and Evaluation in Psychology]* (pp. 90-104). Göttingen, Germany: Hogrefe.

Gomez, J., Cachero, C., & Pastor, O. (2001). On Conceptual Modeling of Device-Independent Web Applications: Towards a Web Engineering Approach. *IEEE MultiMedia, 8*(2), 26–39. doi:10.1109/93.917969

Gonzalez-Cruz, J., Rodriguez-Sotres, R., & Rodriguez-Penagos, M. (2003). On the convenience of using a computer simulation to teach enzyme kinetics to undergraduate students with biological chemistry-related curricula. *Biochemistry and Molecular Biology Education, 31*(2), 93–101. doi:10.1002/bmb.2003.494031020193

Gordon, R. (1998). Balancing real-world problems with real-world results. *Phi Delta Kappan, 79*, 390–393.

Götzenbrucker, G. (2001). *Soziale Netzwerke und Internet-Spielewelten*. Wiesbaden, Deutschland: Westdeutscher Verlag.

Götzl, X., Pfeiffer, A., & Primus, T. (2008). *MMORPGs 360 Grad. Virtuelle Welten & moderne Mediennutzung wissenschaftlich betrachtet*. Neckenmarkt, Deutschland: Edition Nove.

Grabe, M., & Grabe, C. (2007). *Integrating technology for meaningful learning (5th ed.)*. Boston, MA: Houghton Mifflin Comp.

Graf, S., Lin, T., & Kinshuk, J. (2008). The relationship between learning styles and cognitive traits - Getting additional information for improving student modelling. *Computers in Human Behavior, 24*(2), 122–137. doi:10.1016/j.chb.2007.01.004

Graham, C. R., & Misanchuk, M. (2004). Computer-mediated learning groups: Benefits and challenges to using groupwork in online learning environments. In T.S. Roberts (Ed.), *Online collaborative learning:*

Theory and practice (pp. 181-202). Hershey, PA: Idea Group Inc (IGI).

Graham, G. M. Holt/ Hale, S. A., & Parker, M. A. (2007). *Children moving. a reflective approach to teaching physical education (8th ed.)*. New York, NY: McGraw-Hill.

Gräsel, C., & Mandl, H. (1999). Problemorientiertes Lernen: Anwendbares Wissen fördern. In *Personalführung* (Vol. 6, pp. 54-62). Düsseldorf, Deutschland: Deutsche Gesellschaft für Personalführung.

Gray, M. J., Ondaatje, E. H., Fricker, R. D., & Geschwind, S. A. (2000). Assessing service-learning: Results from a survey of 'Learn and serve America, higher education.' . *Change*, *32*, 30–39.

Greater Expectations National Panel. (2002). Greater expectations: A new vision for learning as a nation goes to college. *The Association of American Colleges and Universities*. Retrieved June 2007, from http://www.greaterexpectations.org/

Gredler, M. E. (2004). Games and simulations and their relationships to learning. In D. H. Jonassen (Ed.), *Handbook of research on educational communications and technology* (2nd ed., pp. 571-581). Mahwah, NJ: Lawrence Erlbaum.

Green, P. E., Krieger, A. M., & Wind, Y. (2003). Marketing research and modeling: Progress and prospects. In Y. Wind & P. E. Green (Eds.), *Marketing Research and Modeling: Progress and Prospects: A Tribute to Paul E. Green (1st ed.)* (pp. 117-140). Berlin, Germany: Springer US.

Green, R. D., MacDorman, K. F., Ho, C.-C., & Vasudevan, S. (2008). Sensitivity to the proportions of faces that vary in human likeness. *Computers in Human Behavior*, *24*(5), 2456–2474. doi:10.1016/j.chb.2008.02.019

Green, S., Voegeli, D., Harrison, M., Phillips, J., Knowles, J., & Weaver, M. (2003). Evaluating the use of streaming video to support student learning in a first-year life sciences course for student nurses. *Nurse Education Today*, *23*, 255–261. doi:10.1016/S0260-6917(03)00014-5

Green, T., & Brown, A. (2002). *Multimedia projects in the classroom: A guide to development and evaluation.* Thousand Oaks, CA: Corwin Press, Inc.

Greenfield, P. M., & Cocking, R. R. (1996). *Interacting with video.* Norwood, NJ: Ablex.

Gregg, D., Kulkarni, U., & Vinze, A. (2001). Understanding the philosophical underpinnings of software engineering research in information systems. *Information Systems Frontiers*, *3*(1), 169–183. doi:10.1023/A:1011491322406

Gregory, R. (1974). Distortion of visual space as inappropriate constancy scaling. In R. Gregory (Ed.), *Concepts and mechanisms of perception* (pp. 342-349). New York: Charles Scribner's Sons.

Gremmler, T. (2008). *CyberBionic. Design und Evaluation digitaler Welten.* Heidelberg, Deutschland: Spektrum.

Griffiths, M. D., Davies, M. N. O., & Chappell, D. (2003). Breaking the stereotype: The case of online gaming. *Cyberpsychology & Behavior*, *6*, 81–91. doi:10.1089/109493103321167992

Grotjahn, H. (2007). *Qualitätsmessungen an der Wikipedia: Konstruktion von Qualität - eine Metaanalyse.* Saarbrücken, Germany: VDN Verlag Dr. Müller.

Grunwald, A. (2002). *Technikfolgenabschätzung: Eine Einführung.* Berlin, Germany: Edition Sigma.

Gubacs, K. (2004). Project-based learning: A student centered approach to integrating technology into physical education teacher education. [JOPERD]. *Journal of Physical Education, Recreation & Dance*, *75*(7), 33.

Günther, T. M. F., da Silva, F. C. M., & Günther, A. R. (2003). Titrant standardizations: A research-oriented laboratory practice. *Biochemistry and Molecular Biology Education*, *31*(2), 123–126. doi:10.1002/bmb.2003.494031020201

Güntheroth, H., Schönert, U., & Rodtmann, E. (2007). Juni 12). Wikipedia. Wissen für alle. *Stern*, *50*, 30–44.

Guernsey, L. (1998). Colleges debate the wisdom of having on-campus students enroll in online-line classes.

The Chronicle of Higher Education. Retrieved January 10, 2009, from http://chronicle.com/che-data/articles.dir/art-44.dir/issue-29.dir/29a02901.htm

Guile, D. (2003). From 'Credentialism' to the 'Practice of Learning': reconceptualising learning for the knowledge economy. *Policy Futures in Education, 1*(1), 83–105. doi:10.2304/pfie.2003.1.1.10

Guzdial, M. (1999). *Teacher and student authoring on the Web for shifting agency.* Retrieved May 01, 2009, from http://guzdial.cc.gatech.edu/papers/aera99/default.html

Guzdial, M., & Rick, J. (2006). Situating CoWeb. *International Journal of Computer-Supported Collaborative Learning, 1*(1).

Guzdial, M., Kehoe, C., Realff, M., & Morley, T. (2000). *A catalog of CoWeb uses.* Retrieved May 1, 2009, from http://guzdial.cc.gatech.edu/squeakers/coweb-catalog.pdf

Guzdial, M., Rick, J., & Kehoe, C. (2001). Beyond adoption to invention. *Journal of the Learning Sciences, 10*(3). doi:10.1207/S15327809JLS1003_2

Gyambrah, M. K. (2007). *E-learning technologies and its application in higher education: A descriptive comparison of Germany, United Kingdom and United States.* Dissertation, LMU München, Fakultät für Psychologie und Pädagogik. Retrieved December 30, 2008, from http://edoc.ub.uni-muenchen.de/7358

Haber, P. (2007). Weltbibliothek oder Diderots Erben? Traditionslinien von Wikipedia. In R. Koschke, O. Herzog, K. H. Rödiger et al. (Eds.), *Informatik 2007 - Informatik trifft Logistik. Bd. 2. Beiträge der 37. Jahrestagung der Gesellschaft für Informatik e.V. (GI)* (pp. 497–502). Bonn, Germany: Köllen.

Habermas, J. (1981). *The Theory of Communicative Action.* London: Beacon Press.

Habgood, M. P. J., Ainsworth, S. E., & Benford, S. (2005). Endogenous fantasy and learning in digital games. *Simulation & Gaming, 36*(4), 483–498. doi:10.1177/1046878105282276

Haefner, K. (1982). *Die neue Bildungskrise.* Basel, Switzerland: Birkhäuser.

Hall, R., Balestra, J., & Davis, M. (2000). *A Navigational Analysis of Linear and Non-Linear Hypermedia Interfaces.* American Educational Research Association, New Orleans, LA.

Hamburg, I., Busse, T., & Marin, M. (2005). Using e-learning scenarios for making decisions in organisations. In *6th European Conferene E-COMM-LINE 2005,* Bucharest. Retrieved December 26, 2008, from http://www.iatge.de/aktuell/veroeff/2005/hamburg01.pdf

Hamilton, B. (2007). *It's elementary! Integrating technology in the primary grades.* Washington, DC: International Society for Technology in Education (ISTE).

Hamlin, B. (2005). Motor competency and video analysis. *Teaching Elementary Physical Education, 16*(5), 8–13.

Hansen, J., Sato, M., Ruedy, R., Kharecha, P., Lacis, A., & Miller, R. (2007). Climate simulations for 1880-2003 with GISS modelE. *Climate Dynamics, 29,* 661–696. doi:10.1007/s00382-007-0255-8

Hansen, M. (2000). *Embodying technesis: technology beyond writing.* Ann Arbor, MI: University of Michigan Press.

Hansen, M. (2006). Media theory. *Theory, Culture & Society, 23*(2-3), 297–306. doi:10.1177/0263276406062300256

Harasim, L. (1990). *Online Education: Perspectives on a new environment.* New York: Praeger Publishers.

Harris, D. (2000). Knowledge and networks. In T. Evans & D. Nation (Eds.), *Changing University Teaching: Reflections on Creating Educational Technologies* (pp. 36 – 7). London: Kogan Page.

Harrow, A. J. (1972). *A taxonomy of the psychomotor domain: A guide for developing behavioral objectives.* New York: David McKay.

Hart, S. (2006). Breaking literacy boundaries through critical service-learning: Education for the silenced and marginalized. *Mentoring & Tutoring, 14*(1). doi:10.1080/13611260500432236

Harter, S. (1982). The perceived competence scale for children. *Child Development*, *53*, 87–97. doi:10.2307/1129640

Hartnell-Young, E. (2003). From facilitator to knowledge-builder: A new role for the teacher of the future. In C. Dowling & K.-W. Lai (Eds), *Information and Communication Technology and the Teacher of the Future* (pp. 159-164). Boston, MA: Kluwer Academic Publishers.

Hartog, R., Schaaf, H. V. D., & Verver, J. (2003). Elearning. *Agro Informatica*, *16*(4), 9–11.

Hashmi, M., & Guvenli, T. (2001). Multimedia content on the web: problems and prospects. *Managerial Finance*, *27*, 34–41. doi:10.1108/03074350110767277

Hassenzahl, M. (2001). The effect of perceived hedonic quality on product appealingness. *International Journal of Human-Computer Interaction*, *13*(4), 481–499. doi:10.1207/S15327590IJHC1304_07

Hassenzahl, M. (2004). Mit dem AttrakDiff die Attraktivität interaktiver Produkte messen [Measuring the Attractiveness of Interactive Products with AttrakDiff]. In M. Hassenzahl & M. Peissner (Eds.), *Usability Professionals 2004* (pp. 96-100). Stuttgart, Germany: German Chapter of the Usability Professionals Association.

Hassenzahl, M., & Hofvenschiöld, E. (2003). 'If it doesn't feel right, who cares if it works?' oder: Muss Software mehr als nur gebrauchstauglich sein? ['If it doesn't feel right, who cares if it works?' or: Does Software have to be more than Useful?] In M. Peissner (Ed.), *Usability Professionals 2003* (pp. 135-139). Stuttgart, Germany: German Chapter of the Usability Professionals Association.

Hassenzahl, M., Burmester, M., & Koller, F. (2003). AttrakDiff: Ein Fragebogen zur Messung wahrgenommener hedonischer und pragmatischer Qualität [AttrakDiff: A Questionnaire for the Measurement of Perceived Hedonic and Pragmatic Quality]. In G. Szwillus & J. Ziegler (Eds.), *Mensch & Computer 2003: Interaktion in Bewegung [Human & Computer 2003: Interaction on the Move]* (pp. 187-196). Stuttgart, Germany: Teubner.

Hastie, P. A., & Sinelnikov, O. A. (2007). The use of web-based portfolios in college physical education activity courses. *Physical Educator*, *64*(1), 21–28.

Hauser, J. R., & Rao, V. R. (2003). Conjoint analysis, related modeling, and applications. In Y. Wind & P. E. Green (Eds.), *Marketing Research and Modeling: Progress and Prospects: A Tribute to Paul E. Green (1st ed.)* (pp. 141-168). Berlin, Germany: Springer US.

Hawkes, S. J. (2004). Chemistry is not a laboratory science. *Journal of Chemical Education*, *81*(9), 1257.

Hayles, N. K. (1999). *How we became posthuman: virtual bodies in cybernetics, literature, and informatics.* Chicago: University of Chicago Press.

Healy, J. M. (1991). Endangered minds. In D. Dickinson (Ed.), *Creating the Future: Perspectives on Educational Change* (pp. 52 – 8). Aston Clinton, UK: Accelerated Learning Systems Limited.

Hebbel-Seeger, A. (2007). Blended Learning in Theorie-Praxis-Veranstaltungen: Beispiele für den Einsatz von computergestützen Lehr- und Lernanwendungen. In V. Scheid (Ed.), *Sport und Bewegung vermitteln* (Schriften der Deutschen Vereinigung für Sportwissenschaft, No. 165, pp. 185-187). Hamburg: Czwalina.

Hebbel-Seeger, A. (2008a). Hochschuldidaktik im Zeitalter digitaler Medien: Erfolg und Nachhaltigkeit setzen auf den "shift from technology to use". *Ze-phir*, *14*(2), 19–22.

Hebbel-Seeger, A. (2008b). Videospiel und Sportpraxis – (K)ein Widerspruch. *Zeitschrift für e-learning, 4*(3), 9-20.

Heckhausen, J., & Heckhausen, H. (2006). Motivation und Handeln: Einführung und Überblick. In J. Heckhausen & H. Heckhausen (Eds.), *Motivation und Handeln* (p. 1-8). Heidelberg, Germany: Springer Verlag.

Hehl, W. (2008). *Trends in der Informationstechnologie. Von der Nanotechnologie zu virtuellen Welten.* Zürich, Deutschland: VDF.

Heidegger, M. (1962). *Being and Time.* (J. Macquarrie & E. Robinson, Trans.). New York: Harper & Row.

Heidegger, M. (1971). *Poetry, language, and thought.* (A. Hofstadter, Trans). New York: Harper Colophon Books.

Heidegger, M. (1972). *What is called thinking* (F. D. Wieck & J. Grey, Trans.). New York: Harper and Row.

Heidegger, M. (1977). *The question concerning technology.* (W. Lovitt, Trans.). New York: Harper and Row.

Heinrich, E., & Maurer, H. (2000). Active documents: Concept, implementation and applications. *Journal of Universal Computer Science*, *6*(12), 1197–1202.

Henderson, L. (1993). Interactive multimedia computer courseware and culturally appropriate ways of learning. In C. Latchem, J. Williamson & L. Henderson-Lancett (Eds.), *Interactive multimedia: Practice and promise* (pp. 189-203). London: Kogan Page.

Henrysson, A., Billinghurst, M., & Ollila, M. (2006). AR tennis. In *International Conference on Computer Graphics and Interactive Techniques archive ACM SIGGRAPH 2006 Sketches.* New York: ACM Press.

Hentig, H. V. (2002). *Der technischen Zivilisation gewachsen bleiben*. Weinheim, Germany: Beltz.

Hernández-Morales, B., Reyes-González, A., Barrera-Godínez, J. A., & Ingalls-Cruz, A. (2005). *A virtual laboratory for teaching transport phenomena.* Paper presented at the World Conference on Educational Multimedia, Hypermedia and Telecommunications 2005, Montreal, Canada.

Herring, S. C. (2008). Questioning the generational divide: Technological exoticism and adult constructions of online youth identity. In D. Buckingham (Ed.), *Youth, Identity, and Digital Media* (pp. 71-92). Cambridge, MA: MIT Press.

Herrington, J., & Herrington, A. (1998). Authentic assessment and multimedia: How university students respond to a model of authentic assessment. *Higher Education Research & Development*, *17*(3), 305–322. doi:10.1080/0729436980170304

Herrington, J., & Oliver, R. (2000). An instructional design framework for authentic learning environments. *Educational Technology Research and Development*, *48*(3), 23–48. doi:10.1007/BF02319856

Herrington, J., Reeves, T. C., & Oliver, R. (2006). A model of authentic activities for online learning. In C. Juwah (Ed.), *Interactions in online learning: Implications for theory and practice* (pp. 91-103). New York: Routledge.

Herrington, J., Reeves, T. C., & Oliver, R. (2007). Immersive learning technologies: Realism and online authentic learning. *Journal of Computing in Higher Education*, *19*(1), 65–84. doi:10.1007/BF03033421

Herrington, J., Reeves, T. C., Oliver, R., & Woo, Y. (2004). Designing authentic activities in web-based courses. *Journal of Computing in Higher Education*, *16*(1), 3–29. doi:10.1007/BF02960280

Hersh, R. H., & Merrow, J. (Eds.). (2005). *Declining by degrees: Higher education at risk*. New York: Palgrave Macmillan.

Hevner, A. R., March, S. T., Park, J., & Ram, S. (2004). Design science in information systems research. *MIS Quarterly*, *28*(1), 75–105.

Hill, J. R., & Hannafin, M. J. (2001). Teaching and learning in digital environments: The resurgence of resource-based learning. *Educational Technology Research and Development*, *49*(3). doi:10.1007/BF02504914

Hiltz, S. R. (1990). Evaluating the virtual classroom. In L. Harasim (Ed.), *Online education: Perspectives on a new environment*. New York: Praeger Publishers.

Hiltz, S. R. (1995). *The virtual classroom: Learning without limits via computer networks*. New York: Ablex Publishing Corp.

Hiltz, S. R., & Goldman, R. (2005). What are asynchronous learning networks? In Hiltz, S. R., & Goldman, R. (Eds.), *Learning together online: Research on asynchronous learning networks* (pp. 3–18).

Hmelo, C., & Day, R. (1999). Contextualized questioning to scaffold learning from simulations. *Computers & Education*, *32*(2), 151–164. doi:10.1016/S0360-1315(98)00062-1

Hmelo-Silver, C. E., Duncan, R. G., & Chinn, C. A. (2006). Scaffolding and achievement in problem-based and inquiry learning: A response to Kirschner, Sweller, and Clark. *Educational Psychologist, 42*(2), 99–107.

Hmelo-Silver, C., & Azevedo, R. (2006). Understanding complex systems: Some core challenges. *Journal of the Learning Sciences, 15*(1), 53–62. doi:10.1207/s15327809jls1501_7

Hodel, J., & Haber, P. (2007). Das kollaborative Schreiben von Geschichte als Lernprozess. Eigenheiten und Potential von Wiki-Systemen und Wikipedia. In M. Merkt, K. Mayrberger, R. Schulmeister et al. (Ed.), *Studieren neu erfinden – Hochschule neu denken* (pp. 43–53). Hamburg, Germany: Waxmann.

Hoffmann, N. (2004). Problemorientiertes Lernen. In J. Haake, G. Schwabe, & M. Wessner (Hrsg.), *CSCL-Kompendium. Lehr und Handbuch zum computerunterstützten kooperativen Lernen*. München, Deutschland: Oldenbourg.

Holley, D., & Haynes, R. (2003). 'The INCOTERMS challenge': using multimedia to engage learners. *Education and Training, 45*(7), 392–401. doi:10.1108/00400910310499965

Hollingworth, H. (2006). Learning about teaching – using video. *Professional Educator, 5*(2), 30–34.

Holzinger, A. (1997). Computer-aided Mathematics Instruction with Mathematica 3.0. *Mathematica in Education and Research, 6*(4), 37–40.

Holzinger, A. (2000). *Basiswissen Multimedia. Band 2: Lernen. Kognitive Grundlagen multimedialer Informationssysteme*. Würzburg, Germany: Vogel Buchverlag.

Holzinger, A. (2002). *Multimedia Basics, Vol. 2: Learning. Cognitive Fundamentals of multimedia Information Systems*. New Delhi, India: Laxmi.

Holzinger, A., Emberger, W., Wassertheurer, S., & Neal, L. (2008). Design, development and evaluation of online interactive simulation software for learning human genetics. *Elektrotechnik und Informationstechnik, 125*(5), 190–196. doi:10.1007/s00502-008-0537-9

Holzinger, A., Kickmeier-Rust, M., & Albert, D. (2008). Dynamic media in computer science education; content complexity and learning performance: Is less more? *Educational Technology & Society, 11*(1), 279–290.

Holzinger, A., Kickmeier-Rust, M., Wassertheurer, S., & Hessinger, M. (2009). Learning performance with interactive simulations in medical education: Lessons learned from results of learning complex physiological models with the HAEMOdynamics SIMulator. *Computers & Education, 52*(1), 292–301. doi:10.1016/j.compedu.2008.08.008

Holzinger, A., Nischelwitzer, A., & Meisenberger, M. (2005, March 8-12). *Mobile phones as a challenge for m-learning: Examples of mobile interactive learning objects (MILOs).* Paper presented at the Third Annual IEEE International Conference on Pervasive Computing and Communications, Kauai Island, HI.

Holzrichter, D. (2001). Gymnasium makeovers. *Athletic Business, 25*(1), 59-60, 62-65.

Hoppe, H. U., Ogata, H., & Soller, H. (Eds.). (2007). *The role of technology in CSCL: studies in technology enhanced collaborative learning.* New York: Springer.

Horney, M. A. (1993). Case Studies of Navigational Patterns in Constructive Hypertext. *Computers & Education,* 20(3), 257-270. Hutchings, G., Hall, W., & Colbourn, C. (1992). *The Effect of Navigation Tool Presentation on Hypermedia Navigation Strategies and User Disorientation.*Technical Report, University of Southampton. Retrieved from http://eprints.ecs.soton.ac.uk/4410/

Horx, M. (2006). *Wie wir leben werden. Unsere Zukunft beginnt jetzt* (3rd rev. ed.). Frankfurt/ Main: Campus.

Howe, N., & Strauss, W. (2000). *Millennials rising: The next great generation.* New York: Vintage Books.

Howells, K. (2007). PowerPoint: friend or foe? In J. Sigafoos & V. Green (Eds.), *Technology and Teaching* (pp. 137-146). New York: Nova Science Publishers.

Howie, E., Sy, S., Ford, L., & Vicente, K. J. (2000). Human - computer interface design can reduce misperceptions of feedback. *System Dynamics Review, 16*(3), 151–171. doi:10.1002/1099-1727(200023)16:3<151::AID-SDR191>3.0.CO;2-0

Huang, C. (2008). Virtual labs interactive media Stanford University. Retrieved January 17, 2009, from http://virtuallabs.stanford.edu

Huang, C., & Huang, H. K. (2003). Interactive instruction of cellular physiology for remote learning. *Cellular and Molecular Biology, 49*(8), 1377–1384.

Hughes, C. E. (2005). Mixed reality in education, entertainment, and training. *IEEE Computer Graphics and Applications*, 24–30. doi:10.1109/MCG.2005.139

Huizinga, J. (1947). *Homo ludens. Proeve eener bepaling van het spelelement der cultuur.* (R.F.C. Hull, Trans.). New York: Roy Publishers. (Original work published in 1938).

Huynh, M. Q. (1999). *A critical study of computer-supported collaborative learning.* Unpublished PhD, SUNY Binghamton, New York.

Ihde, D. (1990). *Technology and the lifeworld: From garden to earth.* Bloomington, IN: Indiana University Press.

Iiyoshi, T., & Kumar, M. S. V. (Eds.). (2008). *Opening up education – the collective advancement of education through open technology, open content and open knowledge.* Cambridge, MA: MIT Press.

Iiyoshi, T., Kumar, M. S. V., & Seely Brown, J. (2008). *Opening up education: the collective advancement of education through open technology.* Cambridge, MA: MIT Press.

Illich, I. (1970). *Deschooling society.* New York: Harper and Row.

Illich, I. (1997). Philosophy... artifacts... friendship—and the history of the gaze. In T.-A. Druart (Ed.), *Philosophy of Technology: Proceedings of the American Catholic Philosophical Association, 70* (pp. 61-82). Washington, DC: Catholic University of America.

IMS. (2005). *Question and test interoperability.* Retrieved April 9, 2009, 2006, from http://www.imsglobal.org/question/index.html#version2.0

Ince, M. L., Goodway, J. D., Ward, P., & Lee, M.-A. (2006). The effects of professional development on technological competency and the attitudes urban physical education teachers have toward using technology. *Journal of Teaching in Physical Education, 25*(4), 428–440.

Institut für Demoskopie Allensbach. (2008). Allensbacher Computer- und Technik-Analyse. *Allensbach am Bodensee.*

International Journal of Teaching and Learning in Higher Education. Volume 19 (1), 84-92. Retreived on Jan 16, 2008, from: http://www.isetl.org/ijtlhe/pdf/IJTLHE152.pdf

International Society for Technology in Education. (2008). *NETS for teachers.* Retrieved March 28, 2009, from http://www.iste.org/AM/Template.cfm?Section=NETS

Internet World Stats. (2008). *Internet usage statistics. The Internet big picture. World Internet users and population stats.* Retrieved October 20, 2008, from http://www.internetworldstats.com/stats.htm

Introna, L. (2007). Maintaining the reversibility of foldings: Making the ethics (politics) of information technology visible. *Ethics and Information Technology, 9*, 11–25. doi:10.1007/s10676-006-9133-z

Jacobson, M., & Wilensky, U. (2006). Complex systems in education: Scientific and educational importance and implications for the learning sciences. *Journal of the Learning Sciences, 15*(1), 11–34. doi:10.1207/s15327809jls1501_4

Jacoby, B. (1996). *Service-learning in higher education: Concepts and practices.* San Francisco: Jossey-Bass.

Jacoby, B. (2006). Public work and the academy: An academic administrator's guide to civic engagement and service-learning. *The Journal of Higher Education, 77*(3). doi:10.1353/jhe.2006.0022

Jadin, T., & Batinic, B. (2006, May 23-24). Social Skills durch Social Software. In *Interdisziplinäre Fachtagung zu Bildungs- und Arbeitstechnologien im Semantic Web*, Salzburg. Retrieved May 1, 2009, from http://www.hotel-virgil.at/fileadmin/user_upload/downloads/jadintrack_1-3.pdf

James, R., Mcinnis, C., & Devlin, M. (2002). Assessing learning in Australian universities: Ideas, strategies and resources for quality in student assessment. *Centre for the Study for Higher Education for the Australian Universities Teaching Committee.* Retrieved January 2008, from http://www.cshe.unimelb.edu.au/assessinglearning/docs/Online.pdf

Jarvis, P. (1992). *Paradoxes of learning: On becoming an individual in society.* San Francisco: Jossey Bass.

Jaschniok, M. (2007). *Wikipedia und ihre Nutzer: Zum Bildungswert der Online-Enzyklopädie*. Marburg, Germany: Tectum.

Jeffreys, A., Falconer, I., Conole, G., & Littlejohn, A. (2006). *LADIE project final repost – Learning Activity Design in Education – reference model project.* Retrieved February 5, 2009, from http://www.jisc.ac.uk/media/documents/programmes/elearningframework/ladie_finalreport.pdf

Jenkins, J. (1999). *Teaching for tomorrow: The changing role of teachers in the connected classroom.* Retrieved October 25, 2009, from http://www.eden-online.org/papers/jenkins.pdf

Jensen, E., & Brehmer, B. (2003). Understanding and control of a simple dynamic system. *System Dynamics Review, 19*(2), 119–138. doi:10.1002/sdr.267

JHU. (2000). *Virtual laboratories.* Retrieved January 17, 2009, from http://www.jhu.edu/virtlab/virtual laboratory/

Jih, H., & Reeves, T. (1992). Mental Models: A Research Focus for Interactive Learning Systems. *ETR&D, 40*(3), 39–53. doi:10.1007/BF02296841

Johnson, D. W., Johnson, R. T., & Holubec, E. J. (1990). *Circles of learning: Cooperation in the classroom.* Edina, MN: Interaction Book Co.

Johnson, L., Levine, A., & Smith, R. (2009). *The 2009 horizon report.* Austin, TX: The New Media Consortium. Retrieved February 16, 2009, from http://wp.nmc.org/horizon2009

Johnstone, A. H., & Al-Shuaili, A. (2001). Learning in the laboratory; some thoughts from the literature. *University Chemistry Education, 5*, 42–50.

Jonassen, D. (2000). Toward a design theory of problem solving. *Educational Technology Research and Development, 48*(4), 63–85. doi:10.1007/BF02300500

Jonassen, D., & Cho, Y. H. (2008). Externalizing mental models with mindtools. In *Understanding models for learning and instruction* (pp. 145-159).

Jong, T. d. (2006). Computer simulations: Technological advances in inquiry learning. *Science, 312*(5773), 532–533. doi:10.1126/science.1127750

Joosten-Brinke, D., Bruggen, J. v., Hermans, H., Burgers, J., Giesbers, B., Koper, R., et al. (2005). Modeling assessment for re-use of traditional and new types of assessment. *Computers in Human Behavior.*

Jörissen, B., & Marotzki, W. (2008). Neue Bildungskulturen im "Web 2.0": Artikulation, Partizipation, Syndikation. In F. von Gross, W. Marotzki & U. Sander (Eds.), *Internet – Bildung – Gemeinschaft* (pp. 203-225). Wiesbaden, Germany: VS Verlag für Sozialwissenschaft.

Joseph, B. (2007, August). Best practices in using virtual worlds for education. In *Second Life Education Workshop, Part of the Second Life Community Convention,* Chicago.

Jukes, I., & Dosaj, A. (2004). Understanding digital kids: Teaching and learning in the new digital landscape. *The InfoSavvy Group.* Retrieved January 15, 2009, from http://web.mac.com/iajukes/thecommittedsardine/Articles_files/ndl.pdf

Jukes, I., & Dosaj, A. (2006). *Understanding digital children (DKS): Teaching and Learning in the new digital landscape.* Retrieved April 1, 2009, from http://www.ibo.org/ibap/conference/documents/IanJukes-UnderstandingDigitalKids.pdf

Jung, M.-L., Loria, K., Mostaghel, R., & Saha, P. (2008). E-Learning: Investigating university student's acceptance of technology. *European Journal of Open, Distance and E-Learning.* Retrieved January 10, 2009, from http://www.eurodl.org/materials/contrib/2008/Jung_Loria_Mostaghel_Saha.htm

Juniu, S. (2002). *Implementing Handheld computing technology in Education*. The Journal of Physical Education, Recreation and Dance, Vol. 73.

Kalyuga, S., Chandler, P., & Sweller, J. (1999). Managing split-attention and redundancy in multimedia instruction. *Applied Cognitive Psychology, 13*, 351–371. doi:10.1002/(SICI)1099-0720(199908)13:4<351::AID-ACP589>3.0.CO;2-6

Kammerl, R. (2001). Computerunterstütztes Lernen – Eine Einführung. In: R. Kammerl (Ed.), *Computergestütztes Lernen* (pp. 7-22). München, Germany: Oldenbourg.

Karpinski, A. C., & Duberstein, A. (2009, April). *A description of Facebook use and academic performance among undergraduate and graduate students*. Paper presented at the Annual Meeting of the American Educational Research Association, San Diego, CA. Retrieved April 18, 2009, from http://www.aera.net/

Kay, A., & Goldberg, A. (1977). Personal dynamic media. *Computer, 10*(3), 31–41. doi:10.1109/C-M.1977.217672

Kaye, C. B. (2004). *The complete guide to service learning*. Minneapolis, MN: Free Spirit Publishing Inc.

Kearsley, G. (1994). Social learning theory. Retrieved May 1, 2009, from http://www.gwu.edu/~tip/bandura.html

Keller, I. (2008). Blended Learning in der methodisch-didaktischen SportlehrerInnenausbildung am Beispiel Leichtathletik. *Zeitschrift für e-learning, 4*(3), 33-44.

Keller, J. M. (1987). Development and use of the ARCS model of motivational design. *Journal of Instructional Development, 10*(3), 2–10. doi:10.1007/BF02905780

Keller, J. M. (2008). First principles of motivation to learn and e3-learning. *Distance Education, 29*(2), 175–185. doi:10.1080/01587910802154970

Kennedy, G. E., Judd, T. S., Churchward, A., Gray, K., & Krause, K. (2008). First year students' experience with technology: Are they really digital natives? *Australian Journal of Educational Technology, 24*(1), 108–122.

Kennedy, G., Judd, T., Churchward, A., Gray, K., & Krause, K. (2008). First year students' experiences with technology: Are they really digital natives? *Australasian Journal of Educational Technology, 24*(1), 108–122.

Kerawalla, L., Luckin, R., Seljeflot, S., & Woolard, A. (2006). Making it real: exploring the potential of augmented reality for teaching primary school science. *Virtual Reality (Waltham Cross), 10*(3), 163–174. doi:10.1007/s10055-006-0036-4

Kerawalla, L., Minocha, S., Kirkup, G., & Conole, G. (2009). A framework for blogging in Higher Education. *Journal of Computer Assisted Learning, special issue on Web 2.0 technologies*. Retrieved from http://www.blackwell-synergy.com/doi/abs/10.1111/j.1365-2729.2008.00286.x

Kerres, M. (2001). *Multimediale und telemediale Lernumgebungen. Konzeption und Entwicklung*. München, Deutschland: Oldenbourg.

Kerres, M., & de Witt, C. (2003). A didactical framework for the design of blended learning arrangements. *Journal of Educational Media, 28*, 101–114. doi:10.1080/1358165032000165653

Kerres, M., & de Witt, C. (2004). Pragmatismus als theoretische Grundlage für die Konzeption von E-Learning. In H. O. Mayer & D. Treichel (Hrsg.), *Handlungsorientiertes Lernen und eLearning* (pp. 77-99). München, Deutschland: Oldenbourg.

Kervin, L., & Turbill, J. (2003). Teaching as a craft: Making links between pre-service training and classroom practice. *English Teaching: Practice and Critique, 2*(3), 22–34.

Kervin, L., & Vardy, J. (2006). A partnership for iPod pedagogy: Using technology of millennial learners across educational contexts. Proceedings of the 23rd Annual Ascilite conference. Sydney, Australia. Retrieved Dec 12, 2008, from: http://www.ascilite.org.au/conferences/sydney06/proceeding/pdf_papers/p111.pdf

Kezar, A. (2002). Assessing community service learning. *About Campus, 7*(2).

Kickmeier-Rust, M. D., & Albert, D. (2008). The ELEKTRA ontology model: A learner-centred approach to resource description. In *Advances in Web Based Learning – ICWL 2007* (LNCS 4823, pp. 78-89). Berlin, Germany: Springer.

Kickmeier-Rust, M. D., Göbel, S., & Albert, D. (2008). 80Days: Melding adaptive educational technology and adaptive and interactive storytelling in digital educational games. In R. Klamma, N. Sharda, B. Fernández-Manjòn, H. Kosch, & M. Spaniol (Eds.), *Proceedings of the First International Workshop on Story-Telling and Educational Games (STEG '08) - The power of narration and imagination in technology enhanced learning*, Maastricht, The Netherlands.

Kickmeier-Rust, M. D., Hockemeyer, C., Albert, D., & Augustin, T. (2008). Micro adaptive, non-invasive assessment in educational games. In M. Eisenberg, Kinshuk, M. Chang, & R. McGreal (Eds.), *Proceedings of the second IEEE International Conference on Digital Game and Intelligent Toy Enhanced Learning*, Banff, Canada (pp. 135-138).

Kickmeier-Rust, M. D., Marte, B., Linek, S. B., Lalonde, T., & Albert, D. (2008). Learning with computer games: Micro level feedback and interventions. In M. E. Auer (Ed.), *Proceedings of the International Conference on Interactive Computer Aided Learning (ICL)*, Villach, Austria. Kassel, Germany: Kassel University Press.

Kickmeier-Rust, M. D., Marte, B., Linek, S. B., Lalonde, T., & Albert, D. (2008). The effects of individualized feedback in digital educational games. In T. Conolly & M. Stansfield (Eds.), *Proceedings of the 2nd European Conference on Games Based Learning*, Barcelona, Spain (pp. 227-236). Reading, UK: Academic Publishing Limited.

Kickmeier-Rust, M. D., Peirce, N., Conlan, O., Schwarz, D., Verpoorten, D., & Albert, D. (2007). Immersive digital games: The interfaces for next-generation e-learning? In C. Stephanidis (Ed.), *Universal Access in Human-Computer Interaction. Applications and Services* (LNCS, 4556, pp. 647-656). Berlin, Germany: Springer.

Kiili, K. (2005). Digital game-based learning: Towards an experiential gaming model. *The Internet and Higher Education, 8*, 13–24. doi:10.1016/j.iheduc.2004.12.001

Kinshuk, D., & Sampson, G. (2004). Special issue on cognition and exploratory learning in the digital age. *Innovations in Education and Teaching International, 43*(2), 105–108.

Kirakowski, J. (1996). The software usability measurement inventory: Background and usage. In P. W. Jordan (Ed.), *Usability evaluation in industry* (pp. 169-177). London: Taylor & Francis.

Kirk, D., & McPhail, A. (2002). Teaching games for understanding and situated learning: Rethinking the Bunker-Thorpe model. *Journal of Teaching in Physical Education, 21*, 177–192.

Kirk, D., Macdonald, D., & O'Sullivan, M. (Eds.). (2006). *The handbook of physical education*. London: SAGE.

Kirriemuir, J. (2002). A survey of the use of computer and video games in classrooms. *Internal report for Becta (British Educational Communications and Technology Agency)*. Retrieved August, 12, 2008 from http://www.slideshare.net/silversprite/use-of-computer-and-video-games in the classroom

Kirschner, P. A., & Huisman, W. (1998). Dry laboratories in science education. *International Journal of Science Education, 20*(6), 655–682. doi:10.1080/0950069980200605

Kirschner, P. A., & Meester, M. A. M. (1988). The laboratory in higher science education: Problems, premises and objectives. *Higher Education, 17*, 81–98. doi:10.1007/BF00130901

Kirschner, P. A., Sweller, J., & Clark, R. E. (2006). Why minimal guidance during instruction does not work: An analysis of the failure of constructivist, discovery, problem-based, experiential, and inquiry-based teaching. *Educational Psychologist, 41*(2), 75–86. doi:10.1207/s15326985ep4102_1

Kirstein, J., & Nordmeier, V. (2007). Multimedia representation of experiments in physics. *European Journal of Physics*, *28*(3), 115–126. doi:10.1088/0143-0807/28/3/S11

Kittler, F. A. (1986). *Grammophon, Film, Typewriter*. Berlin, Germany: Brinkmann & Bose.

Klafki, W. (2000). Kritisch-konstruktive Pädagogik. Herkunft und Zukunft. In *Eierdanz, Jürgen / Kremer, Armin (Hrsg.): Weder erwartet noch gewollt - Kritische Erziehungswissenschaft und Pädagogik in der Bundesrepublik Deutschland zur Zeit des kalten Krieges*, Baltmannsweiler, Germany (pp. 152-178).

Klamma, R., Chatti, M. A., Duval, E., Hummel, H., Hvannberg, E. T., & Kravcik, M. (2007). Social software for life-long learning. *Educational Technology & Society*, *10*(3), 72–83.

Klebl, M. (2007). Die Verflechtung von Technik und Bildung -Technikforschung in der Bildungsforschung. *bildungsforschung,* 4(2). Retrieved December 30, 2008, from http://www.bildungsforschung.org/Archiv/2007-02/technik/

Klebl, M. (2008). Explicating the shaping of educational technology: Social construction of technology in the field of ICT and education. In *Reading in Education and Technology: Proceeding of ICICTE 2008*, 278-289.

Kleimann, B., Özkilic, M., & Göcks, M. (2008). *HISBUS-Kurzinformation Nr. 21. Studieren im Web 2.0. Studienbezogene Web- und E-Learning-Dienste*. Hannover, Germany: HIS-Projektbericht. Retrieved January 15, 2009, from https://hisbus.his.de/hisbus/docs/hisbus21.pdf

Kleimann, B., Özkilic, M., & Göcks, M. (2008). Studieren im Web 2.0. Studienbezogene Web und E-Learning-Dienste. *HISBUS Kurzinformation, 21.*

Klippert, H. (2007). *Lehrerentlastung: Strategien zur wirksamen Arbeitserleichterung in Schule und Unterricht.* Weinheim, Germany: Beltz Verl.

KMK. (2004). *Standards für die Lehrerbildung: Bildungswissenschaften.* Retrieved October 25, 2009 from http://download.bildung.hessen.de/lakk/stsem_gym/fulda/modul/standards_lehrerbildung.pdf

Knowles, M. (1970). *The modern practice of adult education: Andragogy versus pedagogy.* New York: Association Press.

Knowles, M. (1980). *The modern practice of adult education: From andragogy to pedagogy.* Englewood Cliffs, NJ: Cambridge Adult Education.

Knowles, M. (1984). *Andragogy in action: Applying modern principles of adult education.* San Francisco: Jossey-Bass.

Knowles, M., Holton, E., III, & Swanson, R. (1998). *The adult learner.* Houston, TX: Gulf Publishing.

Koehler, T. (1999). Sozialwissenschaftliche Theorien und Befunde zur computervermittelten Kommunication. In W. Frindte & T. Koehler (Eds.), *Kommunikation im Internet* (pp. 137-182). Frankfurt, Germany: Peter Lang.

Koestler, A. (1978). *Janus – A summing up.* Tiptree, UK: The Anchor Press Ltd.

Kohlert, C., Schlickum, S., & Brübach, M. (2008). Die Entmystifizierung eines Phänomens — Die Generation Y?! Recruiting the Next Generation (rng-Studie). *DEGW Deutschland.* Retrieved from http://www.recruitingthenextgeneration.de/index.php?article_id=62&clang=1

Koistinen, K. (2002). Towards virtual academy – teacher's changing role. In *FIG XXII International Congress, TS2.4, Virtual Academy and New Teaching and Learning Methods.* Retrieved October 25, 2009, from http://www.fig.net/pub/fig_2002/Ts2-4/TS2_4_koistinen.pdf

Kolb, D. (1975). *David A. Kolb on experiential learning.* Retrieved March 28, 2009, from http://www.infed.org/biblio/b-explrn.htm

Kolbe, K. (1990). *The conative connection: Acting on instinct.* Reading, MA: Addison-Wesley.

Konieczny, P. (2007). Wikis and Wikipedia as a teaching tool. *International Journal of Instructional Technology and Distance Learning, 1*, 15–34.

Korossy, K. (1997). Extending the theory of knowledge spaces: A competence-performance-approach. *Zeitschrift fur Psychologie mit Zeitschrift fur Angewandte Psychologie*, *205*, 53–82.

Korris, J. (2004). Full spectrum warrior: How the Institute for Creative Technologies built a cognitive training tool for the Xbox. In *24th Army Science Conference*, Orlando, Florida.

Kosko, B. (1994). *Fuzzy Thinking - A New Science of Fuzzy Logic*. Hammersmith, London, UK: Harper Collins.

Kosow, H., & Gaßner, R. (2008). Methoden der Zukunfts-und Szenarioanalyse Überblick, Bewertung und Auswahlkriterien. *WerkstattBericht Nr. 103. Berlin: Institute for Futures Studies and Technology Assessment*. Retrieved December 20, 2008, from http://www.izt.de/fileadmin/downloads/pdf/IZT_WB103.pdf

Krathwohl, D. R., Bloom, B. S., & Masia, B. B. (1964). *Taxonomy of educational objectives: The classification of educational goals, handbook II: The affective domain*. New York: David McKay.

Kravcik, M., Specht, M., Kaibel, A., & Terrenghi, L. (2003). *Collecting data on field trips - RAFT approach*. Paper presented at the The 3rd IEEE International Conference on Advanced Learning Technologies.

Kretschmann, R. (2008). Development of Competencies by Playing Digital Sports-Games?! In T. Conolly & M. Stansfield (Eds.), *Proceedings of the 2nd European Conference on Games-Based Learning* (pp. 243-250). Reading, MA: Academic Publishing Limited.

Kretschmann, R. (2008). *Einsatzmöglichkeiten und Entwicklungsszenarien digitaler Medien im Schulsport*. Paper presented at the Annual Conference of the Sektion Sportpädagogik (eng. Division Sport Pedagogy) of the Deutsche Vereinigung für Sportwissenschaft (engl. German Association of Sport Science), German Sport University, Cologne.

Krippendorf, B. B., & Lough, J. (2005). Complete and rapid switch from light microscopy to virtual microscopy for teaching medical histology. *Anatomical Record. Part B, New Anatomist*, *285B*(1), 19–25. doi:10.1002/ar.b.20066

Krueger, C. (2006 January). Shared futures: Two universities' global learning initiatives. *Academic Leader, (1)*.

Kuh, G. D. (2003). What we're learning about student engagement from NSSE. *Change*, *35*(2), 24–32.

Kuh, G. D., Laird, T. N., & Umbach, P. (2004). Aligning faculty activities and student behavior: Realizing the promise of greater expectations. *Liberal Education*, *90*(4), 24–31.

Kukulska-Hulme, A., & Traxler, J. (2005). *Mobile Learning. A handbook for educators and trainers*. New York: Taylor & Francis.

Kvavik, R. (2005). Convenience, communications, and control: How students use technology. In D.G. Oblinger & J.L. Oblinger (Eds.), *Educating the Net Generation*. Boulder, CO: Educause.

Kvavik, R. B., & Caruso, J. B. (2005). *ECAR study of students and information technology 2005: Convenience, connection, and control, Vol. 6*. Retrieved from http://www.educause.edu/ecar

Kvavik, R. B., Caruso, J. B., & Morgan, G. (2004). *ECAR study of students and information technology 2004: Convenience, connection, and control, Vol. 5*. Retrieved from http://www.educause.edu/ecar

Ladda, S., Keating, T., Adams, D., & Toscano, L. (2004). Including technology in instructional programs. [JOPERD]. *Journal of Physical Education, Recreation & Dance*, *75*(4), 12.

Lai, Y. C., & Wong, T. W. (2006). The cluster model for conducting Learning Study for minor subjects in schools. In P. L. Jeffrey (Ed.), *Proceedings of the Australian Association for Research in Education (AARE) Annual Conference 2006*. Adelaide, Australia: AARE.

Lamb, B. (2004). Wide open spaces: Wikis, ready or not. *Educause Review*, *39*(5), 36–48. Retrieved January 12, 2007, from http://www.educause.edu/pub/er/erm04/erm0452.asp

Lambourne, R. (2007). Laboratory-based teaching and the physics innovations centre for excellence in teaching and learning. *European Journal of Physics*, *28*(3), 29–36. doi:10.1088/0143-0807/28/3/S03

Landry, B. J. L., Rodger, G., & Hartman, S. (2006). Measuring student perceptions of blackboard using the technology acceptance model. *Decision Sciences Journal of Innovative Education, 4*(1), 87–99.

Lane, A. (2006). *From pillar to post: Exploring the issues involved in re-purposing distance learning materials for use as Open Educational Resources.* Retrieved fromhttp://kn.open.ac.uk/public/document.cfm?docid=9724

Lange, H., & Sinning, S. (Eds.). (2007). *Handbuch Sportdidaktik*. Balingen, Germany: Spitta.

Langton, C. (Ed.). (1995). *Artificial life*. Cambridge, MA: MIT.

Lanier, J. E., & Little, J. W. (1986). Research on teacher education. In M.C. Wittrock (Ed.), *Handbook of Research on Teaching* (pp. 527-569). New York: Macmillan.

Latour, B. (1992). Where are the missing masses? A sociology of a few mundane artefacts. In W. E. Bijker & J. Law (Ed.), *Shaping Technology/Building Society: Studies in sociotechnical change* (pp. 225-258). Cambridge, MA: MIT Press.

Latour, B. (2007). *Eine neue Soziologie für eine neue Gesellschaft.* Frankfurt, Germany: Suhrkamp.

Laurillard, D. (2002) *Rethinking University Teaching.* London: Routledge.

Lawler, C. (2006). Wikipedia as a learning community: content, conflict and the 'common good'. In B. Lutterbeck, M. Bärwolff, & R. A. Gehring (Eds.), *Open Source Jahrbuch 2006 - Zwischen Softwareentwicklung und Gesellschaftsmodell.* Berlin, Germany: Lehmanns Media. Retrieved May 1, 2009, from http://www.opensourcejahrbuch.de/portal/articles/pdfs/osjb2006-06-04-en-lawler.pdf

Lawless, K. A., & Kulikowich, J. M. (1996). Understanding hypertext navigation through cluster analysis. *Journal of Educational Computing Research, 14*(4), 385–399.

Leal, D. (2008). *EduCamp Colombia.* Retrieved February 4, 2009, from http://www.diegoleal.org/social/blog/blogs/dotedu-dotco/index.php/2008/11/16/educamp-colombia-1

Leal, D. (2008). *EduCamp Colombia 2007: Bogotá.* Retrieved February 4, 2009, from http://www.diegoleal.org/social/blog/blogs/dotedu-dotco/index.php/2008/11/16/educamp-colombia-2007-bogota-1

Learn and Serve, America's National Service-Learning Clearinghouse. (2008). *Standards and indicators for effective service-learning practice.* Retrieved March 28, 2009, from http://www.servicelearning.org/instant_info/fact_sheets/k-12_facts/standards/index.php

Lebow, D., & Wager, W. W. (1994). Authentic activity as a model for appropriate learning activity: Implications for emerging instructional technologies. *Canadian Journal of Educational Communication, 23*(3), 231–144.

Lee, J. (1999). Effectiveness of computer-based instructional simulation: A meta analysis. *International Journal of Instructional Media, 26*(1), 71–85.

Lee, S. (2005). Virtual microscopy:Applications to hematology. *Laboratory Hematology, 11*(1), 38–45. doi:10.1532/LH96.04059

Leidner, D. E., & Jarvenpaa, S. L. (1995, September). The use of information technology to enhance management school education: A theoretical view. *MIS Quarterly, 19*(3), 265–292. doi:10.2307/249596

Lepper, M. R., & Malone, T. W. (1987). Intrinsic motivation and instructional effectiveness in computer-based education. In R. E. Farr (Ed.), *Aptitude, learning and instruction* (pp. 255-287). Hillsdale, NJ: Lawrence Erlbaum.

Leser, R., Uhlig, M., & Uhlig, J. (2008). T-A-P – Eine E-Learning-Anwendung aus der Fußballpraxis. *Zeitschrift für e-learning, 4*(3), 21-32.

Leuf, B., & Cunningham, W. (2001). *The wiki way.* Reading, MA: Addison Wesley.

Lewin, R. (2001). *Complexity: Life at the edge of chaos.* Guernsey, Channel Islands: The Guernsey Press.

Lewis, B. A. (1995). *The kid's guide to service projects.* Minneapolis, MN: Free Spirit Publishing Inc.

Lewis, B. A. (1998). *The kid's guide to social action.* Minneapolis, MN: Free Spirit Publishing Inc.

Liarokapis, F. (2006). An exploration from virtual to augmented reality gaming. *Simulation and Gaming, Symposium: Virtual Reality Simulation, 37*(4), 507-533.

Liarokapis, F. (2007). An augmented reality interface for visualising and interacting with virtual content. *Virtual Reality (Waltham Cross), 11*(1), 23–43. doi:10.1007/s10055-006-0055-1

Liarokapis, F., Greatbatch, I., et al. (2005). Mobile augmented reality techniques for geovisualisation. In *Proc. of the 9th Int'l Conference on Information Visualisation*, London (pp. 745-751).

Liaw, S.-S. (2007). An activity-theoretical approach to investigate learners' factors toward e-learning systems. *Computers in Human Behavior, 23*, 1909–1920.

Liber, O. (2004). Cybernetics. e-Learning and the Education System. *International Journal of Learning Technology, 1*(1), 127–140. doi:10.1504/IJLT.2004.003686

Limniou, M., Papadopoulos, N., Giannakoudakis, A., Roberts, D., & Otto, O. (2007). The integration of a viscosity simulator in a chemistry laboratory. *Chemistry Education Research and Practice, 8*(2), 220–231.

Limniou, M., Roberts, D., & Papadopoulos, N. (2008). Full immersive virtual environment CAVE™ in chemistry education. *Computers & Education, 51*(2), 584–593. doi:10.1016/j.compedu.2007.06.014

Linde, A. R., & Garcia-Vazquez, E. (2006). A simple assay to quantify metallothionein helps to learn about bioindicators and environmental health. *Biochemistry and Molecular Biology Education, 34*(5), 360–363. doi:10.1002/bmb.2006.494034052653

Linden Research. (2008). *Second Life*. Retrieved September 18, 2008 from http://www.secondlife.com

LindenLab. (2005). *Second life*. Retrieved January 16, 2009, from http://secondlife.com

Lingis, A. (2004). *Trust*. Minneapolis, MI: University of Minnesota.

Linn, M. C., Davis, E. A., & Bell, P. (2004). Inquiry and technology. In M. C. Linn, E. A. Davis & P. Bell (Eds.), *Internet environments for science education* (pp. 3 - 27). Mahwah, NJ: L. Erlbaum Associates.

Linn, M. C., Lee, H.-S., Tinker, R., Husic, F., & Chiu, J. L. (2006). Inquiry learning: Teaching and assessing knowledge integration in science. *Science, 313*(5790), 1049–1050. doi:10.1126/science.1131408

Lipman, M. (1988). Critical thinking: What can it be? *Resource Publication,* 1(1).

Liu, D., Amagai, S., & Cordon, A. (2001). Development and evaluation of virtual labs and other interactive learning tools. *Biochemistry and Molecular Biology Education, 29*, 163–164.

Locke, E. A., & Latham, G. P. (1990). *A theory of goal setting and task performance.* Englewood Cliffs, NJ: Prentice Hall.

Lockyer, L., Bennett, S., Agostinho, S., & Harper, B. (2008). *Handbook of research on learning design and learning objects*. New York: Information Science Reference.

Lokken, F., & Womer, L. (2007). *Trends in e Learning: Tracking the Impact of e-learning in Higher Education.* Washington, DC: Instructional Technology Council.

Lorenz, M. (2006). Wikipedia. Zum Verhältnis von Struktur und Wirkungsmacht eines heimlichen Leitmediums. *WerkstattGeschichte, 43*, 84–95.

LORNET. (2007). *LORNET.* Retrieved February 5, 2009, from http://www.lornet.org/

Lovett, M., Meyer, O., & Thille, C. (2008). The Open Learning Initiative: the effectiveness of the OLI statistics course in accelerating student learning. *Journal of Interactive Media in Education,* (14). Retrieved from http://jime.open.ac.uk/2008/14/jime-2008-14.pdf

Lumpkin, A. (2007). *Introduction to physical education, exercise science, and sport studies* (7th ed.). New York: McGraw-Hill.

Lunetta, V. N., Hofstein, A., & Clough, M. P. (2007). Learning and teaching in the school science laboratory: An analysis of research, theory, and practice. In *Handbook of research on science education* (pp. 393-441).

Lyotard, J. (1989). *The postmodern condition: A report on knowledge*. Manchester, UK: University Press.

Ma, J., & Nickerson, J. V. (2006). Hands-on, simulated, and remote laboratories: A comparative literature review. [CSUR]. *ACM Computing Surveys*, *38*(3). doi:10.1145/1132960.1132961

MacDonald, D., & Isaacs, G. (2001). Developing a professional identity through problem-based learning. *Teaching Education*, *12*, 315–333. doi:10.1080/10476210120096579

MacDorman, K. F. (2005, December). *Mortality salience and the uncanny valley*. Paper presented at the IEEE-RAS International Conference on Humanoid Robots, Tsukuba, Japan.

Magerkurth, C., Engelke, T., & Memisoglu, M. (2004). Augmenting the virtual domain with physical and social elements: towards a paradigm shift in computer entertainment technology. *Computers in Entertainment*, *2*(4), 12. doi:10.1145/1037851.1037870

Malone, T. W. (1981). Towards a theory of intrinsically motivating instruction. *Cognitive Science*, *3*(4), 333–369.

Mandl, H., Gruber, H., & Renkl, A. (2002). Situiertes Lernen in multimedialen Lernumgebungen. In Issing, L.J. & Klimsa, P. (Hrsg.), *Information und Lernen mit Multimedia und Internet. Lehrbuch für Studium und Praxis, 3, vollständig überarbeitete Auflage*. Weinheim, Deutschland: BeltzPVU.

Marginson, S. (2000, May). Rethinking academic work in the global era. *Journal of Higher Education Policy and Management*, *22*(1), 23–35. doi:10.1080/713678133

Markus, M. (2006): *Bild-Medien und Welt-Bild. Versuch einer geistesgeschichtlichen Kontextualisierung der Geschichtsmächtigkeit der Bild-Medien.* PhD thesis, University of Salzburg, Austria.

Marsh, H. W. (1990). The structure of academic self-concept: The Marsh/Shavelson model. *Journal of Educational Psychology*, *82*(4), 623–636. doi:10.1037/0022-0663.82.4.623

Marshall, S. J., Biddle, S. J. H., Gorely, T., Cameron, N., & Murdey, I. (2004). Relationships between media use, body fatness and physical activity in children and youth: a meta-analysis. *International Journal of Obesity*, *28*, 1238–1246. doi:10.1038/sj.ijo.0802706

Martin, J.-P. (2006). Gemeinsam Wissen konstruieren: am Beispiel der Wikipedia. In M. Klebl & M. Köck (Ed.), *Projekte und Perspektiven im Studium Digitale, Medienpädagogik*, (Vol. 3, pp. 157–164). Berlin, Germany: LIT.

Martin, J.-P. (2008). *LdL (Lernen durch Lehren) goes global: Paradigmenwechsel in der Fremdsprachendidaktik unter Beruecksichtigung kulturspezifischer Lerntraditionen.* Retrieved February 7, 2009, from http://de.wikiversity.org/wiki/Benutzer:Jeanpol/guido

Martin, M. (2005). Seeing is believing: the role of videoconferencing in distance learning. *British Journal of Educational Technology*, *36*(3), 397–405. doi:10.1111/j.1467-8535.2005.00471.x

Marzano, R., Pickering, D., & Pollock, J. (2001). *Classroom instruction that works:* Research-based strategies for increasing student achievement. Alexandria, VA: Association for Supervision and Curriculum Development (ASCD).

Mask, T. (2002). *Are millennials smarter?* Retrieved November 2008, from http://www.citeulike.org/user/smbrower/author/Mask:T

Mason, R. (1998). *Using Communications Media in Open and Flexible learning.* London: Kogan Page.

Mateas, M., & Stern, A. (1997). *Façade, an artificial intelligence-based art/research experiment in electronic narrative*. Retrieved February 5, 2007 from http://www.interactivestory.net/

Mat-Hassan, M., & Levene, M. (2003). *Understanding Web Searching & Navigation Patterns*. Retrieved from http://www2003.org/cdrom/papers/poster/p061/p61-mathassan.html

Maurer, H. (2003). Important aspect of knowledge management. In *Important aspect of knowledge management* (pp. 245 - 254).

Mayer, R. E. (1997). Multimedia learning: Are we asking the right questions? *Educational Psychologist, 32*(1), 1–19. doi:10.1207/s15326985ep3201_1

Mayer, R. E. (2001). *Multimedia learning.* New York: Cambridge University Press.

Mayer, R. E., & Moreno, R. (2003). Nine ways to reduce cognitive load in multimedia learning. *Educational Psychologist, 38*(1), 43–52. doi:10.1207/S15326985EP3801_6

Mayes, J., Draper, S., McGregor, A., & Oatley, K. (1988). Information flow in a user interface: the effect of experience and context on the recall of Macwrite screens. In D. Jones & R. Winder (Eds.), *People and Computers IV.* Cambridge, UK: Cambridge University Press.

Mayo, M. J. (2009). Video games: A route to large-scale stem education? *Science, 323*(5910), 79–82. doi:10.1126/science.1166900

McAndrew, P. (2006). Motivations for OpenLearn: the Open University's Open Content Initiative, OpenLearning workshop paper, the OECD experts meeting on Open Educational Resources 26-27 October 2006 in Barcelona, Open University: Milton Keynes, http://kn.open.ac.uk/public/document.cfm?docid=8816

McAndrew, P. (2008). *OLnet network to support sharing methodologies and evidence on the effectiveness of OER.* Milton Keynes, UK: The Open University.

McAndrew, P., & Santos, A. I. (Eds.). (2009). *Learning from OpenLearn: Research Report 2006-2008.* Milton Keynes, UK: The Open University.

McAndrew, P., Conole, G., Clow, D., Buckingham Shum, S., & Wilson, T. (in press). *Sharing designs for Open Learning: applying learning design to support open participation.* Paper submitted for special issue.

McCaughtry, N., & Dillon, S. R. (2008). Learning to Use PDAs to enhance teaching: The perspectives of preservice physical educators. *Journal of Technology and Teacher Education, 16*(4), 483–508.

McCune, S. D. (1991). Restructuring education. In D. Dickinson (Ed.), *Creating the future: Perspectives on educational change* (pp. 162-182). Aston Clinton, UK: Accelerated Learning Systems Limited.

McGrath, D. (1992). Hypertext, CAI, paper, or program control: Do learners benefit from choices? *Journal of Research on Computing in Education, 24*, 513–532.

McGuffin, M. J., & Schraefel, M. C. (2004) A Comparison of Hyperstructures: Zzstructures, mSpaces, and Polyarchies. In: *ACM Conference on Hypertext and Hypermedia, 2004*, Santa Cruz, California, USA, 153-162

McKnight, C., Dillon, A. P., & Richardson, J. H. (Eds.). (1993). *Hypertext: A Psychological Perspective.* Chichester, UK: Ellis Horwood.

McLuhan, M. (1964). *Understanding media: the extensions of man.* New York: McGraw-Hill.

Mediawiki. (2008). *Help:Templates.* Retrieved March 24, 2009, from http://www.mediawiki.org/w/index.php?title=Help:Templates&oldid=163132

Mediawiki. (2008). *Manual:Special pages.* Retrieved March 24, 2009, from http://www.mediawiki.org/w/index.php?title=Manual:Special_pages&oldid=171875

Megarry, J. (1989). Hypertext and compact discs: The challenge of multimedia learning. In C. Bell, J. Davies & R. Winders (Eds.), *Promoting Learning: Aspects of Educational and Training Technology XXII* (pp. 50). London, UK: Kogan Page.

Mengel, S. (2009). *Beispielanwendungen und -szenarien für mobiles Lernen.* Unpublished paper, Hagen, Deutschland.

Merleau-Ponty, M. (2002). *Phenomenology of perception.* (C. Smith, Trans.). New York: Routledge. (Original work published in 1962).

MERLOT. (2007). *Multimedia educational resource for learning and online teaching.* Retrieved April 9, 2009, from http://www.merlot.org/merlot/index.htm

Merriam, S. B., & Brockett, R. (1997). *The profession and practice of adult education: An introduction.* San Francisco: Jossey-Bass Publishers.

Merriam, S. B., & Caffarella, R. S. (1991). *Learning in adulthood: A comprehensive guide.* San Francisco: Jossey-Bass Publishers.

Merriam, S. B., & Caffarella, R. S. (1999). *Learning in adulthood: A comprehensive guide.* San Francisco: Jossey Bass.

Merrill, D., Kalanithi, J., & Maes, P. (2007). Siftables: Towards sensor network user interfaces. In *Proceedings of the First International Conference on Tangible and Embedded Interaction (TEI'07)*, Baton Rouge, Louisiana. Retrieved from http://web.media.mit.edu/~dmerrill/siftables.html

Meyer, T. (2008). Zwischen Kanal und Lebens-Mittel: pädagogisches Medium und mediologisches Milieu. In J. Fromme & W. Sesink (Eds.), *Pädagogische Medientheorie* (pp. 71-94). Wiesbaden, Germany: VS Verlag für Sozialwissenschaften.

Meyer-Lucht, R. (2008, October 16). So nutzen die Deutschen Internet, Zeitung und Fernsehen. *spiegel.de.* Retrieved January 15, 2009, from http://www.spiegel.de/netzwelt/web/0,1518,584572,00.html

Michel, L. (2008). Digitale Schule – wie Lehrer Angebote im Internet nutzen: Eine Bestandsaufnahme im Auftrag des Bundesministeriums für Bildung und Forschung (BMBF). *MMB-Institut für Medien- und Kompetenzforschung, Essen.* Retrieved October 25, 2009, from http://www.dlr.de/pt/Portaldata/45/Resources/dokumente/bildungsforschung/MMB_Veroeffentlichung_Lehrer_Online_20080505_final.pdf

Microsoft, & MTV. (2007). *Circuits of Cool - Germany.* Retrieved October 25, 2009, from http://www.viacombrandsolutions.de/de/research/studien/national/index.html

Mifsud, L. (2002). *Alternative learning arenas - Pedagogical challenges to mobile learning technology in education.* Paper presented at the IEEE International Workshop on Wireless and Mobile Technologies in Education (WMTE'02), Växjö, Sweden.

Miller, R., Shapiro, H., & Hilding-Hamann, K. E. (2008). School's over: Learning spaces in Europe in 2020: An imagining exercise on the future of learning. *JRC Scientific and Technical Reports.* Retrieved December 26, 2008, from http://ftp.jrc.es/EURdoc/JRC47412.pdf

Misanchuk, E. R., & Schwier, R. A. (1992). Representing Interactive Multimedia and Hypermedia Audit Trails. *Journal of Educational Multimedia and Hypermedia, 1*, 355–372.

Mistry, P., Maes, P., & Chang, L. (2009). WUW - Wear Ur World - A wearable gestural interface. In *CHI '09 extended abstracts on Human factors in computing systems*, Boston, MA. Retrieved from http://www.pranavmistry.com/projects/sixthsense/

Mitchell, A., & Savill-Smith, C. (2004). *The use of computer and video games for learning: A review of the literature.* London: Learning and Skills Development Agency.

Mitchell, M. S. (2001). Using technology in elementary physical education. *Strategies: A Journal for Physical and Sport Educators, 14*(6), 28-31.

Mitchell, M., & McKethan, R. (2003). *Integrating technology and pedagogy in physical education teacher education.* Cerritos, CA: Bonnie's Fitware Inc.

Mitchell, S. (2006). Unpacking the standards. [JOPERD]. *Journal of Physical Education, Recreation & Dance, 77*(2), 20–24.

Mohan, J. (1995). Thinking local: Service-learning, education for citizenship and geography. Journal of Geography in Higher Education, July, 19(2).

Mohnsen, B. (1999). *The new leadership paradigm for physical education. What we really need to lead.* Reston, VA: NASPE Publications.

Mohnsen, B. (2005). Addressing technology standards: What is the role of the physical educator? [JOPERD]. *Journal of Physical Education, Recreation & Dance, 76*(7), 48.

Mohnsen, B. (2005). Integrating the NETSS into physical education. *Learning and Leading with Technology, 32*(6), 20–21.

Mohnsen, B. (2005). Notebooks, handhelds, and software in physical education (Grades 5-8). *Teaching Elementary Physical Education, 16*(5), 18–21.

Mohnsen, B. (2008). *Using technology in physical education (6th ed.).* Cerritos, CA: Bonnie's Fitware Inc.

Möller, E. (2006). *Die heimliche Medienrevolution - Wie Weblogs, Wikis und freie Software die Welt verändern.* Hannover, Germany: Heinz Heise.

Moller, L. (1998). Designing Communities of Learners for Asynchronous Distance Education. *Educational Technology Research and Development, 46*(1), 115–122. doi:10.1007/BF02299678

Moodle. (2008). *Philosophy.* Retrieved January 24, 2009, from http://docs.moodle.org/en/Philosophy

Moore, G. (1965). Cramming more components onto integrated circuits. *Electronics, 38*(8).

Mor, E., & Minguillón, J. (2004). E-learning Personalization based on Itineraries and Long-term Navigational Behavior. In *Proceedings of the 13th International, World Wide Web (Bussum), 2004*, 264–265.

Moravec, H. (1988). *Mind children: The future of robot and human intelligence.* Harvard University Press: Cambridge, MA.

Moreno, R., & Mayer, R. E. (1999). Cognitive principles of multimedia learning: The role of modality and contiguity. *Journal of Educational Psychology, 91*, 358–368. doi:10.1037/0022-0663.91.2.358

Moreno, R., & Mayer, R. E. (2007). Interactive multimodal learning environments - special issue on interactive learning environments: Contemporary issues and trends. *Educational Psychology Review, 19*, 309–326. doi:10.1007/s10648-007-9047-2

Morgan, C. F., Beighle, A., & Pangrazi, R. P. (2007). What are the contributory and compensatory relationships between physical education and physical activity in children? *Research Quarterly for Exercise and Sport, 78*(5), 407–412.

Morrison, G., & Lowther, D. (2005). *Integrating computer technology into the classroom (3rd ed.).* Upper Saddle River, NJ: Prentice Hall.

Moser, H. (2006). Standards für die Medienbildung . *Computer & Unterricht, 16-18*(63), 49–55.

Mössle, T. Kleimann; M., & Rehbein, F. (2007). *Bildschirmmedien im Alltag von Kindern und Jugendlichen: Problematische Mediennutzungsmuster und ihr Zusammenhang mit Schulleistungen und Aggressivität* (Interdisziplinäre Beiträge zur kriminologischen Forschung, 33). Baden-Baden, Germany: Nomos.

Mott, J. D., & Granata, G. (2006). The value of teaching and learning technology: Beyond ROI. *EDUCAUSE Quarterly, 29*(2), 48–54.

Müller, A., & Leidl, M. (2007). *Virtuelle (Lern-)Welten. Second Life in der Lehre.* Retrieved January 23, 2009, from http://www.e-teaching.org/didaktik/gestaltung/vr/SL_lehre_langtext_071207_end.pdf

Mullis, I. V. S., Martin, M. O., Gonzales, E. J., & Chrostowski, S. J. (2004). *TIMSS 2003. International Science Report Findings From IEA's Trends in International Mathematics and Science Study at the Fourth and Eighth Grades.* Chestnut Hill, MA: Boston College.

Mullis, I. V. S., Martin, M. O., Kennedy, A. M., & Foy, P. (2007). *PIRLS 2006. International Report: IEA's Progress in International Reading Literacy Study in Primary School on 40 countries.* Chestnut Hill, MA: Boston College.

Mzoughi, T., Herring, S. D., Foley, J. T., Morris, M. J., & Gilbert, P. J. (2007). Webtop: A 3D interactive system for teaching and learning optics. *Computers & Education, 49*(1), 110–129. doi:10.1016/j.compedu.2005.06.008

Naismith, L., Lonsdale, P., Giasemi, V., & Sharples, M. (2004). Literature Review in Mobile Technologies and Learning. Future Lab series. Retrieved online on March 31st, from: http://www.futurelab.org.uk/resources/documents/lit_reviews/Mobile_Review.pdf

Narayanan, N. H., & Hegarty, M. (1998). On designing comprehensible interactive hypermedia manuals. *International Journal of Human-Computer Studies*, *48*, 267–301. doi:10.1006/ijhc.1997.0169

Narciss, S., & Huth, K. (2004). How to design informative tutoring feedback for multi-media learning. In H. M. Niegemann, D. Leutner, & R. Brunken (Eds.), *Instructional design for multimedia learning* (pp.181-195). Munster, NY: Waxmann.

National Association for Sport and Physical Education (NASPE). (2004). *Moving into the future. National standards for physical education (2nd ed.).* Reston, VA: McGraw-Hill.

National Center for Education Statistics. (1999 September). *Service-learning and community service in K-12 public schools, report number 1999043.* Retrieved March 28, 2009 from http://nces.ed.gov/surveys/frss/publications/1999043/

National Educational Technology Standards. (2008). *NETS for teachers.* Retrieved March 28, 2009, from http://www.iste.org/AM/Template.cfm?Section=NETS

National Service Learning Cooperative. (1999). *Essential elements of service-learning for effective practice, organizational support.* Retrieved March 28, 2009 from http://servicelearning.org/filemanager/download/203_Essential_Elements_of_Service-Learning,Revised.pdf

Negroponte, N. (1995). *Being digital.* New York: Alfred A. Knopf.

Neisser, U. (1976). *Cognition and Reality.* San Francisco: W.H. Freeman.

Neuenhausen, B. (2004). *Bildung in der Digitale. Zur Bildungsrelevanz virtueller Welten.* Frankfurt am Main, Deutschland: Peter Lang.

Neumann, K., & Welzel, M. (2007). A new labwork course for physics students: Devices, methods and research projects. *European Journal of Physics*, *28*(3), 61–69. doi:10.1088/0143-0807/28/3/S06

Nichols, A. J., & Levy, Y. (2009). Empirical assessment of college student-athletes' persistence in e-learning courses: A case study of a U.S. National Association of Intercollegiate Athletics (NAIA) institution. *The Internet and Higher Education*, *12*(1), 14–25. doi:10.1016/j.iheduc.2008.10.003

Niederhauser, D., Reynolds, R., Salmen, D., & Skolmoski, P. (2000). The Influence of Cognitive Load on Learning from Hypertext. *Journal of Educational Computing Research*, *23*(3), 237–255. doi:10.2190/81BG-RPDJ-9FA0-Q7PA

Nielsen, J. (1997). *Community is dead; long live mega-collaboration.* Retrieved December 2, 2008, from http://www.useit.com/alertbox/9708b.html

NIME. (2008). *National institute for multimedia education.* Retrieved February 5, 2009, from http://www.nime.ac.jp/en/

Nintendo. (2008). *Wii.* Retrieved April 9, 2009, from http://www.nintendo.com/wii

Nischelwitzer, A., Lenz, F.-J., Searle, G., & Holzinger, A. (2007). Some aspects of the development of low-cost augmented reality learning environments as examples for future interfaces in technology enhanced learning. In *Universal Access to Applications and Services (LNCS 4556)* (pp. 728-737). New York: Springer.

Nixon, J. E., & Locke, L. (1973). Research in teaching in physical education. In R. M. W. Travers (Ed.), *Second handbook of research on teaching* (pp. 1210-1242). Chicago, IL: Rand McNally.

Norris, C., & Soloway, E. (2004). Envisioning the handheld-centric classroom. *Journal of Educational Computing Research*, *30*(4), 281–294. doi:10.2190/MBPJ-L35D-C4K6-AQB8

Nösekabel, H. (2005). *Mobile education.* Berlin, Germany: Gito.

Notari, M. P., & Minder, S. (2008). Electronic messaging in collaborative e-learning environments. A method to assess two key factors of communication quality: HCI and language. In *Proceeding of World Conference on Educational Media, Hypermedia and Telecommunications (ED-Media)* (pp. 1098-1103).

Novak, J. D., & Gowin, D. B. (1985). *Learning how to learn*. Cambridge, UK: Cambridge University Press.

NSDL. (2005). *Ilumina educational resources for science and mathematics*. Retrieved April 9, 2009, from http://www.ilumina-dlib.org/

NSDL. (2008). *The BEN portal*. Retrieved April 9, 2009, from http://www.biosciednet.org/portal/

NSF. (2008). *Fostering learning in the networked world: learning opportunity and challenge. A 21st Century agenda for the National Science Foundation*. Retrieved August 2, 200, from http://www.nsf.gov/publications/pub_summ.jsp?ods_key=nsf08204

O'Malley, C., Vavoulea, G., Glew, J. P., et al. (2005). *Mobilearn, WP 4 – Pedagogical methodologies and paradigms. Guidlines for learning/teaching/tutoring in a mobile environment (Report)*. Retrieved February, 2009, from http://www.mobilearn.org/download/results/guidelines.pdf

O'Reilly, T. (2004). *The architecture of participation*. Retrieved November 12, 2008, from http://www.oreillynet.com/pub/a/oreilly/tim/articles/architecture_of_participation.html

O'Reilly, T. (2005). *What is Web 2.0? Design patterns and business models for the next generation of software*. Retrieved April 10, 2009, from http://www.oreillynet.com/pub/a/oreilly/tim/news/2005/09/30/what-is-web-20.html

Oblinger, D. (2003). Boomers, Gen-Xers & Millennials. Understanding the new students. *EDUCAUSE Review*, 38(4), 37-47. Retrieved from http://www.educause.edu/ir/library/pdf/ERM0342.pdf

Oblinger, D. (2005). Educating the Net generation. EDUCAUSE: Retreived on Jan 15, 2009, from: www.educause.edu/educatingthenetgen/

Oblinger, D. (2006 May). *Simulations, games, and learning*. ELI White Paper. Retrieved August 28, 2007 from http://www.educause.edu/ir/library/pdf/ELI3004.pdf

Oblinger, D. G., & Oblinger, J. L. (2005). Is it age or IT: First steps toward understanding the net generation. In D.G. Oblinger & J.L. Oblinger (Eds.), *Educating the Net Generation*. Boulder, CO: Educause.

Oblinger, D., & Oblinger, J. (Eds.). (2005). *Educating the Net generation*. Washington, DC: EDUCAUSE.

OCWconsortium. (2007). *Open courseware consortium*. Retrieved April 9, 2009, from http://www.ocwconsortium.org/

OECD. (2007). Giving knowledge for free – the emergence of open educational resources, report for OECD. *Centre for Educational Research and Innovation*. Retrieved May 2, 2009, from http://www.oecd.org/dataoecd/35/7/38654317.pdf

OECD. (2007). Participative Web and user-created content: Web 2.0, wikis and social networking. *Organisation for Economic Co-Operation and Development*. Retrieved January 30, 2009, from http://213.253.134.43/oecd/pdfs/browseit/9307031E.PDF

Oehmichen, E., & Ridder, C.-M. (2003). Die MedienNutzerTypologie. Ein neuer Ansatz der Publikumsanalyse. *Media Perspektiven, 17*.

Oehmichen, E., & Schröter, C. (2007). Zur typologischen Struktur medienübergreifender Nutzungsmuster. *Media Perspektiven*, *8*, 406–421.

Oliver, B., & Goerke, V. (2007). Australian undergraduates' use and ownership of emerging technologies: Implications and opportunities for creating engaging learning experiences for the Net Generation. Australian Journal of Educational Technology 23 (2), 171 – 186. Retrieved on Jan 15, 2009, from: http://www.ascilite.org.au/ajet/ajet23/oliver.html

Ong, W. (1982). *Orality and literacy: The technologizing of the word*. New York: Routledge.

Opaschowski, H. W. (1999). *Generation @: die Medienrevolution entläßt ihre Kinder: Leben im Informationszeitalter*. Hamburg, Germany: BAT.

Orey, M. A., & Nelson, W. A. (1994). *Visualizing Techniques for Examining Learner Interactions with Hypermedia Environments*. ERIC Document Reproduction Service . *No. ED, 373*, 747.

Orlich, D., Harder, R., Callahan, R., Trevisan, M., & Brown, A. (2007). *Teaching Strategies: A guide to effective instruction (8th ed.)*. Boston, MA: Houghton Mifflin Company.

Osborne, R. E., Hammerich, S., & Hensley, C. (1998). Student effects of service-learning: Tracking change across a semester. *Michigan Journal of Community Service Learning, 5*, 5–13.

Owen, M. (2004). *The myth of the digital native*. Retrieved February 10, 2009, from http://www.futurelab.org.uk/resources/publications-reports-articles/web-articles/Web-Article561

Özmen, H. (2008). The influence of computer-assisted instruction on students' conceptual understanding of chemical bonding and attitude toward chemistry: A case for Turkey. *Computers & Education, 51*, 423–438. doi:10.1016/j.compedu.2007.06.002

Paas, F., Renkl, A., & Sweller, J. (2003). Cognitive load theory and instructional design: Recent developments. *Educational Psychologist, 38*(1), 1–4. doi:10.1207/S15326985EP3801_1

Paechter, M., Fritz, B., Maier, B., & Manhal, S. (2007). *eSTUDY - eLearning im Studium: Wie beurteilen und nutzen Studierende eLearning?* Retrieved from http://www.e-science.at/dokumente/eSTUDY_Endbericht.pdf

Paivio, A. (1990). *Mental representations: A dual coding approach*. New York: Oxford University Press.

Palloff, R. M., & Pratt, K. (2003). *Virtual student: A profile an guide to working with online learners*. San Francisco, CA: Jossey-Bass.

Palloff, R., & Pratt, K. (2001). Lessons from the Cyberspace Classroom. San Francisco: Jossey-Bass

Panke, S., & Thillosen, A. (2008). Unterwegs auf dem Wiki-Way. Wikis in Lehr- und Lernsettings. *e-teaching.org*. Retrieved January 15, 2009, from http://www.e-teaching.org/didaktik/kommunikation/wikis/08-09-12_Wiki_Panke-Thillosen.pdf.

Park, J., & Kim, J. (2000). Contextual Navigation Aids for Two World Wide Web Systems. *International Journal of Human-Computer Interaction, 12*(2), 193–217. doi:10.1207/S15327590IJHC1202_3

Park, N. (2008). *User acceptance of e-learning in higher education: An application of technology acceptance model*. Paper presented at the annual meeting of the International Communication Association, Sheraton New York, New York City, NY. Retrieved January 10, 2009, from http://www.allacademic.com/meta/p14794_index.html

Parker, K. R., & Chao, J. T. (2007). Wiki as a teaching tool. *Interdisciplinary Journal of Knowledge and Learning Objects, 3*, 57–72.

Pasnik, S. (2007). iPod in Education: the Potential for Teaching and Learning. Series of iPod in Education white papers. Retreived Dec 12, 2008, from: http://edcommunity.apple.com/ali/galleryfiles/15300/ipod_in_educ_whitepaper.pdf

Patzig, F. (2007). *Was ist eigentlich BarCamp?* Retrieved January 8, 2009, from http://www.franztoo.de/?p=113

Patzig, F. (2007). Swarm (Picture). Retrieved January 8, 2009, from http://www.flickr.com/photos/franzlife/390044262/(permission granted)

Pedró, F. (2006). The new millennium learners: Challenging our views on ICT and learning. *OECD-CERI*. Retrieved from http://www.oecd.org/dataoecd/1/1/38358359.pdf

Pehkonen, M. & Turunen, H. (2004 Juli). A case study on the futures mobile work-based learning. *MLearn*, 5-6.

Pennington, T., & Graham, G. (2002). Exploring the influence of a physical education listserv on K-12 physical educators. *Journal of Technology and Teacher Education, 10*(3), 383–405.

Pennington, T., Wilkinson, C., & Vance, J. (2004). Physical educators online: What is on the minds of teachers in the trenches? *Physical Educator, 61*(1), 45–56.

Pentzold, C. (2007). *Wikipedia: Diskussionsraum und Informationsspeicher im neuen Netz.* München, Germany: R. Fischer.

Perreault, E. J., Litt, M., & Saterbak, A. (2006). Educational methods and best practices in BME laboratories. *Annals of Biomedical Engineering, 34*(2), 209–216. doi:10.1007/s10439-005-9030-3

Perry, D. (2003). Hand-held computers (PDAs) in Schools. Coventry, UK: Becta.

Piaget, J. (1926). *The language and thought of a child.* London: Routledge & Kegan Paul.

Piaget, J. (1937). *La construction du réel chez l'enfant.* Neuchatel, Switzerland: Delacheaux.

Pietzner, V., & Lutz, B. (2005). Themenheft Lernen mit dem Computer, *Naturwissenschaften im Unterricht – Chemie*, 16 (90).

Pietzner, V., & Schmidkunz, H. (2006). *Computer im Chemieunterricht: Eine praxisorientierte Einführung.* Köln, Germany: Aulis-Verl. Deubner.

Pinch, J. T., & Bijker, W. E. (1987). The social construction of facts and artefacts: or how the sociology of science and the sociology of technology might benefit each other. In W. E. Bijker, T. P. Hughes & J. T. Pinch (Eds.), *The Social Construction of Technological Systems: New Directions in the Sociology and History of Technology* (pp. 17-50). Cambridge, MA: MIT Press.

Pituch, K. A., & Lee, Y. K. (2006). The influence of system characteristics on e-learning use. *Computers & Education, 47*, 222–244. doi:10.1016/j.compedu.2004.10.007

Pivec, M., & Dziabenko, O. (2004). Game-based learning in universities and lifelong learning - UniGame: Social Skills and Knowledge Training, Game Concept 1. *Journal of Universal Computer Science, 10*(1).

Pivec, M., Koubek, A., & Dondi, C. (Eds.). (2004). *Guidelines for game-based learning.* Lengerich, Germany: Pabst.

Postman, N. (2003). Questioning media. In M. S. Pittinsky (Ed.), *The wired tower: Perspectives on the impact of the internet on higher education* (pp.181-200). Upper Saddle River, NJ: Prentice Hall.

Pratt, D. D. (1998). Andragogy as a relational construct. *Adult Education Quarterly, 32*(3), 160–181.

Prensky, M. (2001) Digital Natives, Digital Immigrants. *On the Horizon* (MCB University Press, Vol. 9 (5) October. Retreived on Jan 15, 2009, from: http://helpdesk.muscatine.k12.ia.us/external/MPrensky.pdf

Prensky, M. (2001). *Digital game-based learning.* London: McGraw Hill.

Prensky, M. (2001). *Digital game-based learning.* New York: McGraw-Hill.

Prensky, M. (2001). Digital natives, digital immigrants. *On the Horizon, 9*(5). Retrieved from http://www.marcprensky.com/writing/Prensky%20-%20Digital%20Natives,%20Digital%20Immigrants%20-%20Part1.pdf

Prensky, M. (2001). Digital natives, digital immigrants, part II: Do they really think differently? *On the Horizon, 9*(6). Retrieved from http://www.marcprensky.com/writing/Prensky%20-%20Digital%20Natives,%20Digital%20Immigrants%20-%20Part2.pdf

Prensky, M. (2003). Digital game-based learning Computers in Entertainment (CIE). Retrieved from http://portal.acm.org Qui, L. (1994). Frequency Distribution of Hypertext Path Patterns: A Pragmatic Approach. *Information Processing & Management,* 30, 131–40.

Prensky, M. (2005). *Listen to the natives Educational Leadership.* Retrieved from http://centre4.core-ed.net

Prensky, M. (2006). *Don't bother me, mom – I'm learning: How computer and video games are preparing your kids for twenty-first century success.* St. Paul, MN: Paragon House.

Prensky, M. (2007). How to teach with technology: keeping both teachers and students comfortable in an era of exponential change. *Emerging Technologies for Learning, Vol. 2.* British Educational Communications and Technology Agency (BECTA) (2007). http://partners.

becta.org.uk/page_documents/research/emerging_technologies07_chapter4.pdf

Prensky, M. (2008a). *Digital natives, digital immigrants, part 1*. Retrieved October 25, 2009, from http://www.marcprensky.com/writing/Prensky%20-%20Digital%20Natives,%20Digital%20Immigrants%20-%20Part1.pdf

Prensky, M. (2008c). *The role of technology in teaching and the classroom: They got gameplay*. Retrieved October 25, 2009, from http://www.marcprensky.com/writing/Prensky-The_Role_of_Technology-ET-11-12-08.pdf

Prensky, M. (2009). H. sapiens digital: From digital immigrants and digital natives to digital wisdom. *Innovate: Journal of Online Education, 5*(3). Retrieved February 12, 2009, from http://www.innovateonline.info

Priedhorsky, R., Jordan, B., & Terveen, L. (2007). *How a personalized geowiki can help bicyclists share information more effectively*. Paper presented at the 2007 International Symposium in Wikis (WikiSym).

Prümper, J. (1997). Der Benutzungsfragebogen ISONORM 9241/10: Ergebnisse zur Reliabilität und Validität [The usability questionnaire ISONORM 9241/10: Results on reliability and validity]. In R. Liskowsky (Ed.), *Usability Engineering. Integration von Mensch-Computer-Interaktion und Software-Entwicklung [Usability Engineering. Integration of Human-Computer Interaction and Software Engineering]* (pp. 253-262). Stuttgart, Germany: Teubner.

Pütz, M. (2006). *E-Learning 2.0 - Buzzword oder ernstzunehmende Entwicklung?* Retrieved December 2, 2008, from http://www.fortbildung-bw.de/wb/09_bildungsanbieter/05_e-learning/zwei_null.php

Puustinen, M., & Pulkkinen, L. (2001). Models of self-regulated learning: A review. *Scandinavian Journal of Educational Research, 45*, 269–286. doi:10.1080/00313830120074206

Rachal, J. R. (2002). Andragogy's detectives: A critique of the present and a proposal for the future. *Adult Education Quarterly, 53*(3), 210–227. doi:10.1177/0741713602052003004

Raineri, D. (2001). Virtual laboratories enhance traditional undergraduate biology laboratories. *Biochemistry and Molecular Biology Education, 29*, 160–162.

Ramasundaram, V., Grunwald, S., Mangeot, A., Comerford, N. B., & Bliss, C. M. (2005). Development of an environmental virtual field laboratory. *Computers & Education, 45*(1), 21–34. doi:10.1016/j.compedu.2004.03.002

Raschke, M. (2007). *‚Im Computerspiel bin ich der Held.□ Wie virtuelle Welten die Identitätsentwicklung von Jugendlichen beeinflussen*. Hamburg, Deutschland: Diplomica.

Reader, K. (1995). *Régis Debray: a critical introduction*. London: Pluto Press.

Reardon, K. M. (1998). Participatory action research as service learning. *New Directions for Teaching and Learning*, 73.

Recker, M. M. (1994). *A Methodology for Analysing Students' Interactions within Educational Hypertext*. ERIC Document Reproduction Service . *No. ED, 388*, 288.

Reed, S. *(1988)*. James J. Gibson and the Psychology of Perception. *New Haven, CT: Yale University Press.*

Reeves, T. C. (2006). How do you know they are learning?: The importance of alignment in higher education. *International Journal of Learning Technology, 2*(4), 294–309. doi:10.1504/IJLT.2006.011336

Reeves, T. C., & Oh, E. J. (2007). Generation differences and educational technology research. In J. M. Spector, M. D. Merrill, J. J. G. van Merriënboer, & M. Driscoll. (Eds.) *Handbook of research on educational communications and technology* (pp. 295-303). Mahwah, NJ: Lawrence Erlbaum Associates.

Reigeluth, C. M., & Schwartz, E. (1989). An instructional theory in the design of computer-based simulations. *Journal of Computer-Based Instruction, 16*(1), 1–10.

Reinmann, G. (2005). *Blended Learning in der Lehrerbildung. Grundlagen für die Konzeption innovativer Lernumgebungen*. Lengerich, Germany: Pabst.

Reinmann-Rothmeier, G., & Mandl, H. (1998). Lernen in Unternehmen. Von einer gemeinsamen Vision zu einer effektiven Förderung des Lernens. In P. Dehnbostel, H.-H. Erbe, & H. Novak (Hrsg.), *Berufliche Bildung im lernenden Unternehmen: Zum Zusammenhang von betrieblicher Reorganisation, neuen Lernkonzepten und Persönlichkeitsentwicklung.* Berlin, Deutschland: Edition Sigma.

Reiser, B. J., Smith, B. K., Tabak, I., Steinmuller, F., Sandoval, W. A., & Leone, A. J. (2001). Bguile: Strategic and conceptual scaffolds for scientific inquiry in biology classrooms. In *Cognition and instruction: Twenty-five years of progress* (pp. 263 - 305). Mahwah, NJ: L. Erlbaum Associates.

Reitz, S. (2004). Menschenrechtsbildung als E-Learning. In C. Mahler & A. Mihr (Eds.). *Menschenrechtsbildung. Bilanz und Perspektiven* (pp. 265-278). Wiesbaden, Germany: VS Verlag für Sozialwissenschaften.

Reitz, S. (2009). *Improving social competence via e-learning: The example of human rights education.* Unpublished Doctoral Dissertation, Otto-von-Guericke University, Magdeburg.

Renevier, P., Nigay, L., Bouchet, J., & Pasqualetti, L. (2004). Generic interaction techniques for mobile collaborative mixed systems. In *Proc. of the International Conference on Computer-Aided Design of User Interfaces (CADUI'2004)*, Funchal, Portugal (pp. 314-327).

Rezaei, M., Mohammadi, H. M., Asadi, A., & Kalantary, K. (2008). Predicting e-learning application in agricultural higher education using technology acceptance model. *Turkish Online Journal of Distance Education*, 9(1), 85-95. Retrieved February 2, 2009, from http://tojde.anadolu.edu.tr/tojde29/pdf/Volume9Number1.pdf

Rheinberg, F. (1989). *Zweck und Tätigkeit.* Göttingen, Germany: Hogrefe.

Rheinberg, F. (2006). *Motivation.* Stuttgart, Germany: Verlag W. Kohlhammer.

Rheinberg, F., Vollmeyer, R., & Burns, B. D. (2000). Motivation and self-regulated learning. In J. Heckhausen (Ed.), *Motivational Psychology of human development: Developing motivation and motivating development* (pp. 81-108). Amsterdam: Elsevier Science Publisher.

Ribando, R. J., Richards, L. G., & O'Leary, G. W. (2004). A 'hands-on' approach to teaching undergraduate heat transfer. In *Symposium on Mechanical Engineering Education (ASME IMECE '04)*, Anaheim, CA.

Rice, R. E., & Gattiker, U. E. (2001). New media and organizational structuring. In F.M. Jablin & L.L. Putnam (Eds.), *The new handbook of organizational communication* (pp. 544-581). Thousand Oaks, CA: Sage.

Richardson, G. P. (1996). Problems for the Future of System Dynamics. *System Dynamics Review*, *12*(2). doi:10.1002/(SICI)1099-1727(199622)12:2<141::AID-SDR101>3.0.CO;2-O

Richardson, W. (2006). *Blogs, wikis, podcasts, and other powerful web tools for classrooms.* Thousand Oaks, CA: Corwin Press.

Richter, T. (2007). *Basketball Elements* [Computer Software]. Schorndorf, Germany: Hofmann.

Rieber, L. P. (1996). Seriously considering play: Designing interactive learning environments based on the blending of microworlds, simulations, and games. *Educational Technology Research and Development*, *44*(2), 43–58. doi:10.1007/BF02300540

Risko, V. (1991). Videodisc-based case methodology: A design for enhancing preservice teachers' problem-solving abilities. In B. Hayes & K. Camperell (Eds.), *Developing lifelong readers: Policies, procedures, and programs* (Vol. 11, pp. 121-136). Utah State University: American Reading Forum.

Rittmann, T. (2008). *MMORPGs als virtuelle Welten. Immersion und Repräsentation.* Boizenburg, Deutschland: Werner Hülsbusch.

Robert, C. P., Paul, D. C., & Mark, S. (2007). *Geotagging for imprecise regions of different sizes.* Paper presented at the Proceedings of the 4th ACM workshop on Geographical information retrieval.

Roberts, P. (2002). *Kids taking action: Community service learning projects, K-8.* Turner Falls, MA: Northeast Foundation for Children.

Roberts, T., & Brown, L. (2008). Learn more in less time: fundamental aquatic skill acquisition via video technology. *Strategies: A Journal for Physical and Sport Educators, 21*(4), 29-31.

Robin, S., Reardon, R., & Strand, B. (2001). A video streaming pilot project: applications in social work training and education. *Journal of Technology in Human Services, 18*, 133–143. doi:10.1300/J017v18n03_09

Rolf, B. (2001). *Eine kleine Sammlung von Dilemmata.* Retrieved January 29, 2009, from http://www.learn-line.nrw.de/angebote/praktphilo/didaktik/dilemma_slg.pdf

Röll, F. J. (2005). Hinweise zur Notwendigkeit einer neuen Lernkultur. *Seelsorge - Ergebnisse aus Sozialwissenschaft und Theologie*, (2), 2–6.

Rosen, L. D., & Weil, M. M. (1995). Computer availability, computer experience and technophobia among public school teachers. *Computers in Human Behavior, 11*(1), 9–31. doi:10.1016/0747-5632(94)00018-D

Rosenberg, M. (1965). *Society and the adolescent self-image*. Princeton, NJ: Princeton University Press.

Ross, S. (2006). *User: Ragesoss/Assignments.* Retrieved January 15, 2009, from http://en.wikipedia.org/wiki/User:Ragesoss/Assignments

Rossi, G., Schwabe, D., & Lyardet, F. (2000). User interface patterns for hypermedia applications AVI. In *Proceedings of the working conference on Advanced visual interfaces,* Palermo, Italy, 136 - 142.

Rucker, R. (1988). *Mind tools: The mathematics of information.* London: Penguin Books.

Rus, C. (2008). Intercultural and citizenship education through the use of information technologies. In V. B. Georgi (Ed.), *The Making of Citizens in Europe: New Perspectives on Citizenship Education* (pp. 148-152). Bonn, Germany: Bundeszentrale für politische Bildung.

Rychen, D. S., & Salganik, L. H. (2001). *Defining and Selection Key Competencies.* Toronto, Canada: Hogrefe & Huber Publishing.

Sabelli, N. (2006). Complexity, technology, science, and education. *Journal of the Learning Sciences, 15*(1), 5–9. doi:10.1207/s15327809jls1501_3

Salaway., et al. (2008). The ECAR (Educause Center for Applied Research) Study of Undergraduate Students and Information Technology. Internet download Dec 10, 2008: http://net.educause.edu/ir/library/pdf/ers0808/rs/ers0808w.pdf

Salmi, J. (2000 June). Tertiary education in the twenty-first century: Challenges and opportunities. *World Bank's Tertiary Education Thematic Group.* Retrieved March 2008, from http://wbln0018.worldbank.org/LAC/lacinfoclient.nsf/0/2d9645fd1eaab499852569ed005ccbc3/$FILE/62.pdf

Salmon, G. (2001). E-Moderating: The key to teaching and learning online. London: Routlege/Falmer

Salmon, G. (2002). *E-tivities. The key to active online learning.* London and New York: Routledge.

Salonius-Pasternak, D. E., & Gelfond, H. S. (2005). The next level of research on electronic play: Potential benefits and contextual influences for children and adolescents. *Human Technology, 1*(1), 5–22.

Salpeter, J. (2003). 21st century skills: Will our students be prepared? *Technology & Learning, 24*(3), 17–26.

Samson, T., Igel, C., & Meiers, R. (2006). An empirical analysis of the utilization of new media in sports science. *International Journal of Computer Science in Sports, 2*(5), 86–89.

Sancho, P., Gómez-Martín, P. P., & Fernández-Manjón, B. (2008). Multiplayer role games applied to problem based learning. In *DIMEA '08: Proceedings of the 3rd international conference on Digital Interactive Media in Entertainment and Arts* (pp. 69-76). New York: ACM.

Sax, L. J., & Astin, A. W. (1997). The benefits of service: Evidence from undergraduates. *The Educational Record, 78*, 25–32.

Schaaf, H. d., Vermue, M., & Tramper, J. (2003). *Downstream process design.* Retrieved April 9, 2009, from http://pkedu.fbt.wur.nl/demos/design.html

Schaaf, H. d., Vermue, M., Tramper, J., & Hartog, R. (2003). A design environment for downstream processes for bioprocess-engineering students. *European Journal of Engineering Education*, *28*(4), 507–521. doi:10.1080/0304379032000101863

Schaffert, S. (2004). Einsatz von Online-Prüfungen in der beruflichen Weiterbildung: Gegenwart und Zukunft. *Deutsches Institut für Erwachsenenbildung*. Retrieved February 2, 2009, from http://www.die-bonn.de/esprid/dokumente/doc-2000/schaffert00_01.pdf

Schaffert, S., Bischof, D., Bürger, T., Gruber, A., Hilzensauer, W., & Schaffert, S. (2006 June 11-14). Learning with Semantic Wikis. In *3rd Annual European Semantic Web Conference (ESWC), First Workshop SemWiki2006 - From Wiki to Semantics,* Budva, Montenegro.

Schell, L. A. (2004). Teaching learning styles with technology. [JOPERD]. *Journal of Physical Education, Recreation & Dance*, *75*(1), 14.

Schiefele, U., & Rheinberg, F. (1997). Motivation and knowledge acquisition: Searching for mediating processes. In M. L. Maehr & P. P. Pintrich (Eds.), *Advances in motivation and achievement* (Vol. 10, pp. 251-301). Greenwich, CT: JAI Press.

Schiller, J. (2003). *Mobilkommunikation*. München, Deutschland: Pearson Studium.

Schmidt, F. A. (2006). *Parallel Realitäten*. Sulgen, Deutschland: Niggli.

Schmidt, R. A. (1980). Past and future issues in motor programming. *Research Quarterly*, *51*(1), 122–140.

Schmoll, L. (2007). *Lernen an Stationen im Sportunterricht. Sechs Lernen an Stationen mit Kopiervorlagen für den Sportunterricht in der Sekundarstufe I und II.* Baltmannsweiler, Germany: Schneider Hohengehren.

Schoenfeld, R. M. (2003). *Service-learning – Student's guide & journal.* Seattle, WA: Guide and Journal Publications.

Schorb, B. (2007). *Mit eLearning zu Medienkompetenz: Modelle für Curriculumgestaltung, Didaktik und Kooperation* (Vol. 2). München, Germany: Kopaed Verl.

Schulmeister, R. (2001). *Virtuelle Universität - virtuelles Lernen*. München, Deutschland: Oldenbourg.

Schulmeister, R. (2003). *Lernplattformen für das virtuelle Lernen. Evaluation und Didaktik*. München, Germany: Oldenbourg.

Schulmeister, R. (2008). *Gibt es eine Net Generation? Version 2.0.* Retrieved Oktober, 25, 2009, from http://www.zhw.uni-hamburg.de/uploads/schulmeister-net-generation_v2.pdf

Schulmeister, R. (2008a). *Gibt es eine Net Generation?* Retrieved from http://www.zhw.uni-hamburg.de/uploads/schulmeister-net-generation_v2.pdf

Schulmeister, R. (2008b). Gibt es eine Net Generation? Widerlegung einer Mystifizierung. In S. Seehusen, U. Lucke & S. Fischer (Eds.), *DeLFI 2008: Die 6. E-Learning Fachtagung Informatik der Gesellschaft für Informatik* (Vol. 7-10, pp. 15-28). Bonn, Germany: GI.

Schulmeister, R. (2008c). Is There a Net Generation in the House? Dispelling a Mystification (Trans.). *eLeed*. Retrieved from http://eleed.campussource.de/

Schuur, K. (2003). *A holistic vision of the future of eLearning*. Paper presented to a seminar series on Exploring Models and Partnerships for eLearning in SMEs. Retrieved March 2006, from http://www.theknownet.com/ict_smes_seminars/papers/Schuur.html

Schwalbe, C., & Meyer, T. (2009). Umbauten im und am Bildungsraum – Zum medieninduzierten Wandel der Kommunikationsstrukturen in der Hochschulbildung. In W. Marotzki & J. Fromme (Eds.), *Neue Kultur- und Bildungsräume*.

Schwartz, L., et al. (2004, April). Educational Wikis – features and selection criteria. *International Review of Research in Open and Distance Learning*. Retrieved May 6, 2009, from http://www.irrodl.org/index.php/irrodl/article/view/163/692

Schwartz, R. S., Lederman, N. G., & Crawford, B. A. (2004). Developing views of nature of science in an authentic context: An explicit approach to bridging the gap between nature of science and scientific inquiry. *Science Education*, *88*(4), 610–645. doi:10.1002/sce.10128

Schweiger, W. (2004). Mythen der Internet-Nutzung — Ursachen und Folgen. In U. Hasebrink, L. Mikos & E. Prommer (Eds.), *Mediennutzung in konvergierenden Medienumgebungen* (pp. 89-113). München, Germany: Verlag Reinhard Fischer.

Scott, P., Castañeda, L., Quick, K., & Linney, J. (2008). Synchronous symmetrical support: A naturalistic study of live online peer-to-peer learning via software videoconferencing. *Interactive Learning Environments, 16*(1), 1–16. doi:10.1080/10494820701772645

Scrimshaw, P. (1997). Computers and the teacher's role. In B. Somekh & N. Davis (Eds.), *Using Information Technology Effectively in Teaching and Learning. Studies in pre-service and in-service teacher education* (pp. 99-112). London: Routledge.

Seamon, D. (2002). *Phenomenology, place, environment, and architecture: a review of the literature.* Retrieved from http://www.phenomenologyonline.com/articles/seamon1.html

Secretary's Commission on Achieving Necessary Skills. (1991). *What work requires of schools: A SCANS report for America 2000.* Washington, DC: Government Printing Office. Retrieved January 11, 2009, from http://wdr.doleta.gov/SCANS/

Sefton-Green, J. (2004). Literature review in informal learning with technology outside school. *VAC Performing Arts and Media College, Futurelab Series, Report 7.* Retrieved April 26, 2009, from http://hal.archives-ouvertes.fr/docs/00/19/02/22/PDF/Sefton-Green_2004.pdf

Sesink, W. (2008). Bildungstheorie und Medienpädagogik. Versuch eines Brückenschlags. n: J. Fromme & W. Sesink (eds.), *Pädagogische Medientheorie*. Wiesbaden: VS Verlag für Sozialwissenschaften, 13-35.

Sessink, O. (2005). *Cell growth experiments.* Retrieved April 9, 2009, from http://pkedu.fbt.wur.nl/demos/growth.html

Sessink, O., Beeftink, R., Tramper, J., & Hartog, R. (2006). Virtual parameter-estimation experiments in bioprocess-engineering education. *Bioprocess and Biosystems Engineering, 28*, 379–386. doi:10.1007/s00449-005-0042-z

Sfard, A. (1998). 'On two metaphors for learning and the dangers of choosing just one'. *Educational Researcher, 27*(2), 4–13.

Shapiro, A., & Niederhauser, D. (2004). *Handbook of research on educational communications.*

Sharon, S. (Ed.). (1990) *Cooperative learning: Theory and research.* New York: Praege.

Sharples, M. (2000). The design of personal mobile technologies for lifelong learning. *Computers & Education, 34*, 177–193. doi:10.1016/S0360-1315(99)00044-5

Sharples, M. (2002). Disruptive devices: mobile technology for conversational learning. *International Journal of Continuing Engineering Education and Lifelong Learning, 12*(506), 504–520. doi:10.1504/IJCEELL.2002.002148

Sharples, M., Corlett, D., & Westmancott, O. (2002). The design and implementation of a mobile learning resource. *Personal and Ubiquitous Computing, 6*(3), 220–234. doi:10.1007/s007790200021

Shavelson, R. G., Hubner, J. J., & Stanton, G. C. (1976). Validation of construct interpretations. *Review of Educational Research, 46*, 407–441.

Sheldrake, R. (1988). *The presence of the past.* London, UK: William Collins Sons and Co.

Sherry, J. L. (2001). The effects of violent video games on aggression: A meta-analysis. *Human Communication Research, 27*, 409–431.

Shin, D., Yoon, E. S., Lee, K. Y., & Lee, E. S. (2002). A web-based, interactive virtual laboratory system for unit operations and process systems engineering education: Issues, design and implementation. *Computers & Chemical Engineering, 26*(2), 319–330. doi:10.1016/S0098-1354(01)00749-9

Shulman, L. (1987). Knowledge and teaching: Foundations of the new reform. *Harvard Educational Review, 57*, 1–22.

Shum, S. (1990). Real and Virtual Spaces: Mapping from Spatial Cognition to Hypertext. *Hypermedia, 2*(2), 133–158.

Shute, V. J. (2008). Focus on formative feedback. *Review of Educational Research, 78*(1), 153–189. doi:10.3102/0034654307313795

Siedentop, D. (2008). *Introduction to Physical Education, Fitness, and Sport* (7th ed.). Boston, MA: McGraw-Hill.

Siedentop, D., Hastie, P. A., & van der Mars, H. (2004). *Complete Guide to Sport Education*. Champaign, IL: Human Kinetics.

Siemens, G. (2004). *Connectivism: A learning theory for the digital age*. Retrieved February 2008, from http://www.elearnspace.org/Articles/connectivism.htm

Siemens, G (2006). *Learning in Sync with life: New Models, new processes. Google 2006 Training Summit white paper. Retrieved online on March 22, 2009 from:*http://www.elearnspace.org/Articles/google_whitepaper.pdf

Siemens, G. (2006). Connectivism: Learning and knowledge today. In *Education.au Global summit 2006: Technology connected futures*. Retrieved February 2008, from http://www.educationau.edu.au/jahia/webdav/site/myjahiasite/shared/globalsummit/gs2006_siemens.pdf

Silcox, H., & Leek, T. E. (1997). International service learning. *Phi Delta Kappan, 78*(8).

Silver, J. (Producer), Wachowski, A., & Wachowski, L. (Directors). (1999). *The Matrix* [Motion picture]. Hollywood: Warner Bros. Pictures.

Sime, J.-A., & Kemp, B. (2008). A 3D multi-user virtual laboratory: Is successful implementation enough? In *Proceedings of world conference on educational multimedia, hypermedia and telecommunications* (pp. 3539-3547). Chesapeake, VA: AACE.

Simon, B. (2001). *E-Learning an Hochschulen. Gestaltungsräume und Erfolgsfaktoren von Wissensmedien [E-Learning in Academics. Design Scope and Success Factors of Knowledge Media]*. Köln, Germany: Josef Eul Verlag.

Simpson, A., & McKnight, C. (1990). Navigation in hypertext: structural cues and mental maps. In R. McAleese & C. Green (Eds.), *Hypertext: State of the Art*, 73-83. Oxford, UK: Intellect.

Sinclair, G., McClaren, M., & Griffin, M. (2006). *E-Learning and beyond: A discussion paper prepared as part of the Campus 2020 process for the British Columbia Ministry of Advanced Education*. Retrieved February 2, 2009, from http://www.aved.gov.bc.ca/campus2020/documents/e-learning.pdf

Siozos, D., & Palaigeorgiou, G. (2008). Educational technologies and the emergence of e-learning 2.0. In D. Politis (Ed.), *E-Learning Methodologies and Computer Applications in Archaeology* (pp. 1-17). Hershey, PA: IGI Global.

Skartveit, H.-L. (2008). *Representing the real: Documentary, simulation and play.* Unpublished PhD Dissertation, University of Bergen, Bergen.

Skartveit, H.-L., Goodnow, K., & Viste, M. (2003, June). *Visualized system dynamics models as information and planning tools.* Paper presented at the Informing Science + Information Technology Education Joint Conference, Pori, Finland.

Slator, B. M., & Associates. (2006). *Electric worlds in the classroom: Teaching and learning with role-based computer games.* New York: Teachers College Press.

Slavin, R. E. (1987). *Cooperative learning: Student teams*. Washington, DC: National Educational Association.

Slavin, R. E. (1996). Research on cooperative learning and achievement: What we know, what we need to know. *Contemporary Educational Psychology, 21*, 43–69. doi:10.1006/ceps.1996.0004

Sleeman, D. H., & Brown, J. S. (Eds.). (1982). *Intelligent tutoring systems*. New York: Academic Press.

Sloman, M. (2001). *The e-learning revolution*. London: Chartered Institute of Personnel and Development

Slotta, J. D. (2004). The web-based inquiry science environment (wise): Scaffolding knowledge integration in the science classroom. In M. C. Linn, E. A. Davis & P. Bell

(Eds.), *Internet environments for science education* (pp. 203 - 231). Mahwah NJ: L. Erlbaum Associates.

Smed, J., & Hakonen, H. (2003). *Towards a definition of a computer game. Technical Report 553.* Turku, Finland: Turku Centre for Computer Science.

SMETE-Open-Federation. (2003). *SMETE digital library.* Retrieved January 15, 2009, from http://www.smete.org

Smith, P. E. (1987). Simulating the classroom with media and computers. *Simulation & Games, 18*(3), 395–413. doi:10.1177/104687818701800306

Smith, P., & Ragan, T. (1999). *Instructional Design (2nd ed.).* Upper Saddle River, NJ: Prentice-Hall, Inc.

Smith, S. (1991). Experiential learning. In S. Pendelton & A. Myles (Eds.), *Curriculum planning in nursing education.* London: Edward Arnold.

Smith-Stoner, M., & Willer, A. (2003). Video streaming in nursing education: bringing life to online education. *Nurse Educator, 28*, 66–70. doi:10.1097/00006223-200303000-00007

Snow, R. E., Corno, L., & Jackson, D. (1996). Individual differences in affective and conative functions. In D. C. Berliner & R. C. Calfee (Eds.), *Handbook of educational psychology* (pp. 243-310). New York: Macmillan.

Sommerville, I. (2007). *Software engineering* (8th ed.): Pearson Education.

Song, S. H., & Keller, J. M. (2001). Effectiveness of motivationally adaptive computer-assisted instruction on the dynamic aspects of motivation. *Educational Technology Research and Development, 49*(2), 5–22. doi:10.1007/BF02504925

Sørensen, B. H., & Meyer, B. (2007). Serious games in language learning and teaching – a theoretical perspective. In *Proc. of the 3rd International Conference of the Digital Games Research Association*, Tokyo, Japan (pp. 559-566).

Sorin, R. (2004). Webfolio: An online learning community to help link university studies and classroom practice in preservice teacher education. *Australasian Journal of Educational Technology, 20*(1), 101–113.

Spannagel, C. (2008). *Der öffentliche Wissenschaftler.* Retrieved February 7, 2009, from http://cspannagel.wordpress.com/2008/05/18/der-offentliche-wissenschaftler/

Specht, M., Kaibel, A., & Apelt, S. (2005). *Extending LCMS for remote accessible field trips in RAFT.* Paper presented at the Third IEEE International Conference on Pervasive Computing and Communications Workshops.

Spiliopoulou, M., Faulstich, L. C., & Winkler, K. (1999). A Data Miner analyzing the Navigational Behaviour of Web Users. In *Proc. of the Workshop on Machine Learning in User Modelling of the ACAI'99*, Greece.

Squire, K., & Jenkins, H. (2004). Harnessing the power of games in education. *Insight (American Society of Ophthalmic Registered Nurses), 3*(1), 5–33.

SREB. (2006). SCORE sharable content object repositories for education. Retrieved juli 31 2007

Srivastava, J., Cooley, R., Deshpande, M., & Tan, P. N. (2000). Web usage mining: discovery and applications of usage patterns from Web data. *ACM SIGKDD Explorations Newsletter, 1*(2), 12–23. doi:10.1145/846183.846188

Stanford University Metaphysics Research Lab. (1997). *The Stanford encyclopedia of philosophy: Connectionism.* Retrieved October 2007, from http://plato.stanford.edu/entries/connectionism/#3

Stanton, T. K., Giles, D. E., & Cruz, N. I. (1999). *Service learning: A movement's pioneers reflect on its origins, practice, and future.* San Francisco, CA: Jossey-Bass.

Stapleton, C. B., Hughes, C. E., & Moshell, J. M. (2003). Mixed fantasy: Exhibition of entertainment research for mixed reality. In *Proc. of the 2nd International Symposium on Mixed and Augmented Reality (ISMAR 2003)*, Tokyo, Japan (pp. 354-355).

Steffes, J. (2004). Creative powerful learning environments beyond the classroom. *Change, 36*(3).

Steinkuehler, C. A. (2008). Cognition and literacy in massively multiplayer online games. In J. Coiro, M. Knobel, C. Lankshear, & D. Leu (Eds.), *Handbook of Research on New Literacies* (pp. 611-634). Mahwah NJ: Erlbaum.

Steinmüller, K. (2002). *Workshop Zukunftsforschung. Teil 2 Szenarien: Grundlagen und Anwendungen*. Essen: Z_punkt GmbH.

Sterman, J. (1994). Learning in and about complex systems. *System Dynamics Review*, *10*(2-3), 291–330. doi:10.1002/sdr.4260100214

Sterman, J. (2000). *Business dynamics: Systems thinking and modelling for a complex world*. New York: Irwin/McGraw-Hill.

Stewart, C. (2006). Coach education online: The Montana model. [JOPERD]. *Journal of Physical Education, Recreation & Dance*, *77*(4), 34–36.

Stewart, J., Bevans-Wilkins, K., Bhattacharya, A., Ye, C., Miyazaki, K., & Kurtycz, D. F. I. (2008). Virtual microscopy: An educator's tool for the enhancement of cytotechnology students' locator skills. *Diagnostic Cytopathology*, *36*(6), 363–368. doi:10.1002/dc.20821

Stickel, S., Ebner, M., & Holzinger, A. (2008). Useful oblivion versus information overload in e-learning examples in the context of wiki systems. *Journal of Computing and Information Technology*, *16*(4), 271–277.

Stone, D. C. (2007). Teaching chromatography using virtual laboratory exercises. *Journal of Chemical Education*, *84*(9), 1488–1496.

Sturm, R. (2008). Offene Lernressourcen in Sport und Sportwissenschaft – Hochschulübergreifende E-Learning-Angebote am Beispiel des Bildungsnetzwerkes ‚Bewegung und Training'. *Zeitschrift für e-learning*, *4*(3), 45-55

Suarez, D., & Ramirez, F. (2004). *Human rights and citizenship: the emergence of human rights education. center on democracy, development and the rule of law*. Stanford, CA: Stanford Institute for International Studies. Retrieved November 22, 2006, from http://iis-db.stanford.edu/pubs/20682/ramirez_suarez_6.25.2004.pdf

Suchman, L. A. (2007). *Human-machine reconfigurations: plans and situated actions (2nd ed.)*. New York, NY: Cambridge University Press.

Sun, P.-C. (2008). What drives a successful e-Learning? An empirical investigation of the critical factors influencing learner satisfaction. *Computers & Education*, *50*, 1183–1202. doi:10.1016/j.compedu.2006.11.007

Surowiecki, J. (2004). *The wisdom of crowds: Why the many are smarter than the few and how collective wisdom shapes business, economies, societies and nations*. New York: Doubleday.

Surowiecki, J. (2004, May). *The wisdom of crowds*. New York: Bantam Books

Susi, T., Johannesson, M., & Backlund, P. (2007). Serious games - an overview. *Technical Report HS-IKI-TR-07-001*. Retrieved October 10, 2008, from http://www.his.se/upload/19354/HS-%20IKI%20-TR-07-001.pdf

Suthers, D. D. (2006). Technology affordances for intersubjective meaning making: A research agenda for CSCL. *International Journal of Computer-Supported Collaborative Learning*, *3*(1), 315–337. doi:10.1007/s11412-006-9660-y

Swaak, J., & de Jong, T. (2001). Discovery simulations and the assessment of intuitive knowledge. *Journal of Computer Assisted Learning*, *17*, 284–294. doi:10.1046/j.0266-4909.2001.00183.x

Swaak, J., & de Jong, T. (2001). Learner vs. system control in using online support for simulation-based discovery learning. *Learning Environments Research*, *4*, 217–241. doi:10.1023/A:1014434804876

Swanson, E. B. (1988). *Information system implementation: Bridging the gap between design and utilization*. Homewood, IL: Irwin.

Swartz, A. (2006). *Who writes Wikipedia?* Retrieved December 3, 2008, from http://www.aaronsw.com/weblog/whowriteswikipedia

Sweller, J., van Marrienboer, J. J. G., & Paas, F. W. C. (1998). Cognitive architecture and instructional design. *Educational Psychology Review*, *10*, 251–296. doi:10.1023/A:1022193728205

System Data mining and Analysis. (n.d.). Retrieved from http://www.nec-labs.com/research/robust/robust_ASM-website/main/projects.php

Tan, P. N., & Kumar, V. (2002). Discovery of web robot sessions based on their navigational patterns. *Data Mining and Knowledge Discovery*, *6*(1), 9–35. doi:10.1023/A:1013228602957

Tapscott, D. (1998). *Growing Up Digital. The Rise of the Net Generation*. New York: McGraw-Hill.

Tapscott, D. (2008). *Grown up digital: How the net generation is changing your world*. New York: McGraw-Hill.

Tapscott, D., & Williams, A. D. (2007). *Wikinomics: How mass collaboration changes everything*. New York: Portfolio Hardcover.

Tatar, D., Roschelle, J., Vahey, P., & Penuel, W. R. (2003). Handhelds go to school: Lessons learned. *Computer*, *36*(9), 30–37. doi:10.1109/MC.2003.1231192

Tauscher, L., & Greenberg, S. (1996). *Revisitation Patterns in World Wide Web Navigation.* Technical Report Research report 96-587-07, University of Calgary, Calgary, USA.

Taylor, J. C. (2001 June). Fifth Generation Distance Education. Higher Education Series Report No. 40. *DETYA, Higher Education Division.*

Taylor, J. C. (2002). *Automating e-Learning: The Higher Education Revolution*. Paper submitted to the Australian Government Department of Education, Employment and Workplace Relations report 'Our Universities Backing Australia's Future Higher Education Review Process.' Retrieved February 2008 from http://www.backingaustraliasfuture.gov.au/submissions/issues_sub/pdf/i43_3.pdf

Tearle, P., & Golder, G. (2008). The use of ICT in the teaching and learning of physical education in compulsory education: how do we prepare the workforce of the future? *European Journal of Teacher Education*, *31*(1), 55–72. doi:10.1080/02619760701845016

Terdiman, D. (2005, December 16). Study: Wikipedia as accurate as Britannica. *CNET News.* Retrieved January 15, 2009, from http://news.cnet.co.uk/software/0,39029694,39195096,00.htm

Tergan, S.-O. (2002). Hypertext und Hypermedia: Konzeption, Lernmöglichkeiten, Lernprobleme und Perspektiven. In Issing, L.J. & Klimsa, P. (Hrsg.), *Information und Lernen mit Multimedia und Internet. Lehrbuch für Studium und Praxis* (pp. 99-112). Weinheim, Deutschland: BeltzPVU.

Thackara, J. (2005). *In the bubble: Designing in a complex world.* Cambridge, MA: MIT Press.

The Horizon Report. (2007). *The new media consortium*. Retrieved January 23, 2009, from http://www.nmc.org/pdf/2007_Horizon_Report.pdf

The INTENTS Project. (2007). Dublin, Ireland: University of Dublin.

The Tulip project. (n.d.). Retrieved from http://www.linuxsoft.cz/screenshot_img/4150-a.jpg

Thiedeke, U. (2003). Einleitung. In U. Thiedeke (Ed.), *Virtuelle Gruppen. Charakteristika und Problemdimensionen (2nd. Ed.)* (pp. 7-19). Wiesbaden, Germany: Westdeutscher Verlag.

Thiedeke, U. (2003). Virtuelle Gruppen: Begriff und Charakteristik. In U. Thiedeke (Ed.), *Virtuelle Gruppen. Charakteristika und Problemdimensionen (2nd. Ed.)* (pp.23-67). Wiesbaden, Germany: Westdeutscher Verlag.

Thiedeke, U. (2004). Wir Kosmopoliten: Einführung in eine Soziologie des Cyberspace. In U. Thiedeke (Ed.), *Soziologie des Cyberspace. Medien, Strukturen und Semantiken* (pp. 15-50). Wiesbaden, Deutschland: VS.

Thiedeke, U. (2004). Cyberspace: Die Matrix der Erwartungen. In U. Thiedeke (Ed.), *Soziologie des Cyberspace. Medien, Strukturen und Semantiken* (pp. 122-143). Wiesbaden, Deutschland: VS.

Thienes, G., Fischer, U., & Bredel, F. J. (2005). Digitale Medien im und für den Sportunterricht. *Sportunterricht, 54*(1), 6–10.

Thillosen, A. (2005). Arbeits- und Lernaufgaben in der betrieblichen Ausbildung. *Literaturbericht*. Retrieved May, 2008, from www.ausbildernetz.de/media.php/2886/5738/Literaturbericht_ALA.pdf

Thomas, A., & Stratton, G. (2006). What we are really doing with ICT in physical education: A national audit of equipment, use, teacher attitudes, support, and training. *The British Journal of Educational Psychology, 37*(4), 617–632.

Thomas, K. (2006). Augmented reality: a new approach to learning. *FutureLab*. Retrieved January 8, 2008, from http://www.futurelab.org.uk/resources/publications_reports_articles/web_articles/Web_Article496

Thon, J.-N. (2007). Schauplätze und Ereignisse: Über Erzähltechniken im Computerspiel des 21. Jahrhunderts. In C. Müller, & I. Scheidgen (Eds.), *Mediale Ordnungen: Erzählen, Archivieren, Beschreiben* (pp. 40-55). Marburg, Deutschland: Schüren.

Thrift, N. (2005). Beyond mediation: three new material registers and their consequences. In D. Miller (Ed.), *Materiality* (pp. 231–56). Durham, NC: Duke University Press.

Tiffin, J., & Rajasingham, L. (1995). *In search of the virtual class - Education in an Information Society*. London, UK: Routledge.

Titlebaum, P., Williamson, G., Daprano, C., Baer, J., & Brahler, J. (2004). *Annotated History of Service Learning 1862-2002*. Retrieved March 28, 2009 from http://www.servicelearning.org/page/index.php?detailed=311

Toledo, C. (2007) Digital Culture: Immigrants and Tourists. Responding to the Natives' Drumbeat

Treadwell, M. (2001). *1001 Best Internet Sites for Educators* (2nd ed.). Arlington Heights, IL: SkyLight Professional Development.

Tretiakov, A., & Kinshuk. (2008). Towards designing m-learning systems for maximal likelihood of acceptance. *International Journal of Engineering Education, 24*(1), 79–83.

Treumann, K. P., Meister, D. M., Sander, U., et al. (2007). *Medienhandeln Jugendlicher. Mediennutzung und Medienkompetenz. Bielefelder Medienkompetenzmodell*. Wiesbaden, Germany: VS Verlag für Sozialwissenschaften.

Trindade, J., Fiolhais, C., & Almeida, L. (2002). Science learning in virtual environments: A descriptive study. *British Journal of Educational Technology, 33*(4), 471–488. doi:10.1111/1467-8535.00283

Trout, J., & Zamora, K. (2005). Using Dance Dance Revolution in Physical Education. *Teaching Elementary Physical Education, 16*(5), 22–25.

Tsai, F. H., Yu, K. C., & Hsiao, H. S. (2007). Designing constructivist learning environment in online game. In *Proceedings of the First IEEE International Workshop On Digital Game And Intelligent Toy Enhanced Learning*, Jhongli, Taiwan.

Tulodziecki, G. (2007): Entwicklung eines Kompetenzmodells für die Medienbildung - Grundlagen für die Formulierung von Bildungsstandards. *Computer & Unterricht*,(65), 50-54.

Turkle, S. (2004). The fellowship of the microchip: global technologies as evocative objects. In M. M. Suárez-Orozco & D. B. Qin-Hilliard (Eds.), *Globalization: Culture and Education in the New Millennium* (pp. 97–113). Berkeley, CA: University of California Press.

Twenge, J. M. (2006). *Generation me: Why today's young Americans are more confident, assertive, entitled -- and more miserable than ever before*. New York: Free Press.

Tyler-Smith, K. (2006). Early attrition among first time e-learners: A review of factors that contribute to drop-out, withdrawal and non-completion rates of adult learners undertaking e-learning programmes. *Journal of Online Learning and Teaching, 2(2)*. Retrieved October 20, 2008, from http://jolt.merlot.org/Vol2_No2_TylerSmith.htm

United Nations Decade for Human Rights Education No. 4. (2003). *ABC: Teaching human rights. Practical activities for primary and secondary schools*. New York: United Nations Publications. Retrieved Jan 20, 2009, from http://www.unhchr.ch/html/menu6/2/abc.htm

Unz, D., & Hesse, F. (1999). The use of hypertext for learning. *Journal of Educational Computing Research*, *20*(3), 279–295.

van Eck, R. (2006, March). Digital game-based learning: It's not just the digital natives who are restless. *EDUCAUSE Review*, 16–30.

Van Manen, M. (1997). *Researching lived experience: human science for an action sensitive pedagogy (2nd ed.)*. London, Ontario: The Althouse Press.

Van Manen, M. (2007). The phenomenology of practice. *Phenomenology & Practice*, *1*, 11–30.

Van Oudenhoven, J. P., Van der Zee, K. I., & Van Kooten, M. (2001). Successful adaptation strategies according expatriates. *International Journal of Intercultural Relations*, *25*, 467–482. doi:10.1016/S0147-1767(01)00018-9

VanDeventer, S. S., & White, J. A. (2002). Expert behavior in children's video game play. *Simulation & Gaming*, *33*(1), 28–28. doi:10.1177/1046878102033001002

VanSlyke, T. (2003, May/June). Digital natives, digital immigrants: Some thoughts from the generation gap. *The Technology Source*. Retrieved February 12, 2009, from http://technologysource.org/?view=article&id=77

Vavoula, G., & Sharples, M. (2002). KLeOS: A personal, mobile, knowledge and learning organisation system. In Milrad, M., Hoppe, U. & Kinshuk (Hrsg.), *Proceedings of the IEEE International Workshop on Mobile and Wireless Technologies in Education* (pp. 152-156). Växjö, Sweden: IEEE Computer Society Press.

Veenman, M. V. J., Prins, F. J., & Elshout, J. J. (2002). Initial inductive learning in a complex computer simulated environment: The role of metacognitive skills and intellectual ability. *Computers in Human Behavior*, *18*(3), 327–341. doi:10.1016/S0747-5632(01)00038-3

Veermans, K., & van Joolingen, W. R. (1998). Using induction to generate feedback in simulation based discovery learning environments. In B. P. Goettl, H. M. Halff, C. L. Redfield & V. J. Shute (Eds.), *Lecture Notes in Computer Science, Proceedings of the 4th International Conference on Intelligent Tutoring Systems*. (Vol. 1452, pp. 196-205). London: Springer-Verlag.

Venezky, R., & Davis, C. (2002). Quo vademus? The transformation of schooling in a networked world. *OECD/CERI*. Retrieved February 2, 2009, from http://www.oecd.org/ dataoecd/48/20/2073054.pdf

Venkatesh, V. (2000). Determinants of perceived ease of use: Integrating perceived behavioral control, computer anxiety and enjoyment into the technology acceptance model. *Information Systems Research*, *11*, 342–365. doi:10.1287/isre.11.4.342.11872

Venkatesh, V., & Davis, F. D. (2000). A theoretical extension of the technology acceptance model: Four longitudinal field studies. *Management Science*, *46*(2), 186–204. doi:10.1287/mnsc.46.2.186.11926

Vertinsky, P., McKay, S., & Petrina, S. (2004). In P. Vertinsky & S. McKay (Eds.), *Disciplining Bodies in the Gymnasium. Memory, Monument, Modernism*. London: Routledge.

Verver, J., & Bisseling, T. (1997). *Simple cloning lab*. Retrieved January 15, 2009, from http://fbt.wur.nl/bmtl/

Vickers, J. N. (1990). *Instructional Design for Teaching Physical Activities: A Knowledge Structures Approach*. Champaign, IL: Human Kinetics Publishers.

Viégas, F. B., Wattenberg, M., & Dave, K. (2004). Studying cooperation and conflict between authors with history flow visualizations. In *Proceedings of SIGCHI*, Vienna, Austria (pp. 575-582). New York: ACM Press.

Visser, K. (2007). *Digital immigrants abroad: Learning the language of e-learning*. Retrieved May 16, 2007, from http://web.archive.org/web/20050616154156/http://ilp.anu.edu.au/Digital_natives.htm

Vlahakis, V., & Ioannidis, N. (2002). Archeoguide: An augmented reality guide for archaeological sites. *IEEE Computer Graphics and Applications*, *22*(5), 52–60. doi:10.1109/MCG.2002.1028726

Vrasidas, C., & Glass, G. V. (2000). *Distance education and distributed learning*. Charlotte, NC: Information Age Publishing.

Vygotsky, L. S. (1978). *Mind in society: The development of higher psychological processes*. Cambridge, MA: Harvard University Press.

Wade, R. C. (2001). Social action in the social studies: From the ideal to the real. *Theory into Practice*, *40*(1). doi:10.1207/s15430421tip4001_4

Wagner, H., & Weibel, S. (2005). The Dublin Core Metadata Registry: Requirements, Implementation and Experience. *Journal of Digital Information*, *6*(2).

Wagner, M. (2006). On the scientific relevance of eSports. In H. R. Arabnia (Ed.), *Proceedings of the 2006 International Conference on Internet Computing and Conference on Computer Game Development* (pp. 437-440). Las Vegas, NV: CSREA Press.

Wales, J. (2008, December 11). Die Bildung wird revolutioniert. *DIE ZEIT, 51*. Retrieved January 15, 2009, from http://images.zeit.de/text/2008/51/Traum-51/

Wallace, F. L., & Wallace, S. R. (2001). Electronic office hours. A component of distance learning. *Computers & Education*, *37*(3-4), 195–209. doi:10.1016/S0360-1315(01)00046-X

Waller, J. C., & Foster, N. (2000). Training via the web: A virtual instrument. *Computers & Education*, *35*, 161–167. doi:10.1016/S0360-1315(00)00023-3

Wandke, H. (2004). Usability-Testing. In R. Mangold, P. Vorderer & G. Bente (Eds.), *Lehrbuch der Medienpsychologie [Textbook of Media Psychology]* (pp. 325-354). Göttingen: Hogrefe.

Ward, D. (2000, January/February). Catching the waves of change in American higher education. *Educause Review*. Retrieved January 2008, from http://www.educause.edu/pub/er/erm00/pp022031.pdf

Warwick, K. (2002). *I, Cyborg*. London: Century.

Wegis, H., & van der Mars, H. (2006). Integrating assessment and instruction: Easing the process with PDAs. [JOPERD]. *Journal of Physical Education, Recreation & Dance*, *77*(1), 27–34.

Weiner, B. (1974). *Achievement motivation and attribution theory*. Morristown, NJ: General Learning Press.

Weinert, F. E. (2001). Leistungsmessung in Schulen – Eine umstrittene Selbstverständlichkeit. In *Leistungsmessung in Schulen*. Weinheim, Deutschland: Beltz.

Weinstein, R. S., Descour, M. R., Liang, C., Richter, L., Russum, W. C., Goodall, J. F., et al. (2005). Reinvention of light microscopy: Array microscopy and ultrarapidly scanned virtual slides for diagnostic pathology and medical education. In J. Gu & R. W. Ogilvie (Eds.), *Virtual microscopy and virtual slides in teaching: Diagnosis and research* (pp. 9–35). Philadelphia, PA: CRC Press.

Weiser, M. (1991). The Computer for the 21st Century. *Scientific American*, *65*(3), 94–104.

Weiß, S. (n.d.). *Blended-Learning Kurse in der Chemielehrerfortbildung zur Erhöhung der Medienkompetenz*. Unpublished doctoral dissertation, University of Frankfurt, Germany.

Weiß, S., & Bader, H. J. (2008). Mehr Medienkompetenz für Chemielehrer: Das Drei-Fliegen-Konzept. In D. Höttecke (Ed.), *Kompetenzen, Kompetenzmodelle, Kompetenzentwicklung: Jahrestagung in Essen* (Vol. 28). Münster, Germany: LIT-Verl.

Weiß, S., & Bader, H. J. (in press). Wodurch erwerben Lehrkräfte Medienkompetenz? Auf der Suche nach geeigneten Fortbildungsmodellen. *Jahrbuch Medienpädagogik, 8*, Germany . *VS Verl.*

Weiß, S., & Bader, H.J.(2007). Wie kommen WebQuests in den Chemieunterricht? Erfolgreiche Ansätze in der Lehrerfortbildung. *Computer & Unterricht*, (67), 52-53.

Wen, J. R., & Shih, W. L. (2008). Exploring the information literacy competence standards for elementary and high school teachers. *Computers & Education*, *50*(3), 787–806. doi:10.1016/j.compedu.2006.08.011

Wenger, E. (1998). *Communities ofpractice*. Cambridge, UK: Cambridge University Press.

Wenger, E. (2005). *Learning for a Small Planet – A Research Agenda, Version 2.0 (revised September 2006).* Retrieved November 2007, from http://ewenger.com/research/LSPfoundingdoc.doc

Wesch, M. (2007). A vision of students today. YouTube video. Retrieved Dec 10, 2008, from: http://www.youtube.com/watch?v=dGCJ46vyR9o

Wesch, M. (2007). The Machine is Us/ing us. YouTube video. Retrieved Dec 10, 2008, from: http://www.youtube.com/watch?v=6gmP4nk0EOE&feature=channel_page

Wesch, M. (2008 June 17). *A portal to media literacy.* Presentation at University of Manitoba. Retrieved February 10, 2009, from http://mediatedcultures.net/ksudigg/?p=174

West, J. J., & Dowlatabadi, H. (1999). On assessing the economic impacts of sea-level rise on developed coasts. In T. E. Downing, A. A. Olsthoorn & R. S. J. Tol (Eds.), *Climate changes and risk* (pp. 205-220). New York: Routledge.

Wieman, C. E., & Perkins, K. K. (2006). A powerful tool for teaching science. *Nature Physics*, *2*(may).

Wieman, C. E., Adams, W. K., & Perkins, K. K. (2008). PhET: Simulations that enhance learning. *Science*, *322*, 682–683. doi:10.1126/science.1161948

Wiemeyer, J. (2003). Learning with multimedia - more promise than practice? *International Journal of Computer Science in Sport*, *2*(1), 102–116.

Wikibooks. (2009). *Wikibooks: Guidelines for class projects.* Retrieved January 15, 2009, from http://en.wikibooks.org/wiki/Wikibooks:Guidelines_for_class_projects

WikimediaFoundation. (2008). *Wikimedia.* Retrieved April 9, 2009.

Wikipedia. (2008). *WikiProject Geographical coordinates.* Retrieved from http://en.wikipedia.org/w/index.php?title=Wikipedia:WikiProject_Geographical_coordinates&oldid=174960235

Wikipedia. (2009). *School and university projects.* Retrieved January 15, 2009, from http://en.wikipedia.org/wiki/Schools_and_universities_project

Wikipedia. (2009). *BarCamp.* Retrieved January 8, 2009, from http://de.wikipedia.org/wiki/BarCamp

Wikipedia. (2009). *Wikipedia: Statistics.* Retrieved January 15, 2009, from http://en.wikipedia.org/wiki/Wikipedia:Statistics

Wikipedia. (2009). Open Space Technology. Retrieved February 4, 2009, from http://en.wikipedia.org/w/index.php?title=Open_Space_Technology&oldid=266025253

Wikipedia. (2009). *Wikipedia: Verifiability.* Retrieved January 15, 2009, from http://en.wikipedia.org/wiki/Wikipedia:Verifiability

Wikipedia. (2009). *Wikipedia: Community portal.* Retrieved January 15, 2009, from http://en.wikipedia.org/wiki/Wikipedia:Community_portal#help_out

Wikipedia. (2009). *Wikipedia: School and university projects/Past projects. Truman State University (Fall 2007).* Retrieved January 15, 2009, from http://en.wikipedia.org/wiki/Wikipedia:School_and_university_projects/Past_projects#Truman_State_University_.28Fall_2007.29

Wikipedia. (2009). *Featured content from schools and universities.* Retrieved January 15, 2009, from http://en.wikipedia.org/wiki/Wikipedia:Wikipedia_Signpost/2008-05-09/Dispatches

Wikipedia. (2009). *Wikipedia: School and university projects/Past projects. University of Hong Kong (Spring 2007).* Retrieved January 15, 2009 from http://en.wikipedia.org/wiki/Wikipedia:School_and_university_projects/Past_projects#University_of_Hong_Kong_.28Spring_2007.29

Wikipedia. (2009). *Category: Wikipedia_articles_as_assignments.* Retrieved January 15, 2009, from http://en.wikipedia.org/wiki/Category:Wikipedia_articles_as_assignments

Wikiversity. (2009). *Wikiversity: School and university projects.* Retrieved January 15, 2009, from http://

en.wikiversity.org/wiki/Wikiversity:School_and_university_projects

Wilensky, U., & Resnick, M. (1999). Thinking in levels: A dynamic system approach to making sense of the world. *Journal of Science Education and Technology*, *8*, 3–19. doi:10.1023/A:1009421303064

Wills, E. (2006). Let's get virtual. *Teacher Magazine*, *17*(6), 9–10.

Wilmsen, T., Bisseling, T., & Hartog, R. (2002). Web based learning support for experimental design in molecular biology. In P. Barker & S. Rebelsky (Eds.), *Proceedings of Ed-media 2002,* Denver (pp. 2063-2068).

Wissick, C. A., Gardner, J. E., & Langone, J. (1999). Video-based simulations: Considerations for teaching students with developmental disabilities. *Career Development for Exceptional Individuals*, *22*(2), 233–249. doi:10.1177/088572889902200206

Wissick, C. A., Lloyd, J. W., & Kinzie, M. B. (1992). The effects of community training using a videodisc-based simulation. *Journal of Special Education Technology*, *11*, 207–222.

Wittgenstein, L. (1953). *Philosophical investigations*. (G. E. Anscombe & R. Rhees, Eds., G. E. Anscombe, Trans.). Oxford, UK: Blackwell.

Wolf, A. (2007). Wikipedia: Kollaboratives Arbeiten im Internet. In T. Hengartner & J. Moser (Ed.), *Grenzen und Differenzen. Zur Macht sozialer und kultureller Grenzziehungen* (pp. 639–650). Leipzig, Germany: Leipziger Universitätsverlag.

Wolf, M. J. P., & Perron, B. (Eds.). (2003). *The video game theory reader*. New York: Routledge.

Wongwiwatthananukit, S., & Popovich, N. G. (2000). Applying the ARCS model of motivational design to pharmaceutical education. *American Journal of Pharmaceutical Education*, *64*, 188–196.

Woods, M. L., Karp, G. G., Shimon, J. M., & Jensen, K. (2004). Using Webquests to create online learning opportunities in physical education. [JOPERD]. *Journal of Physical Education, Recreation & Dance*, *75*(8), 41.

Wright, P. (1991). Designing and evaluating documentation for IT users. In B. Shackel & S. J. Richardson (Eds.), *Human factors for informatics usability*. Cambridge, UK: Cambridge University Press.

Wright, P., & Lickorish, A. (1994). Menus and memory load: Navigation strategies in interactive search tasks. *International Journal of Human-Computer Studies*, *40*, 968–1008. doi:10.1006/ijhc.1994.1045

Yaman, C. (2008). The abilities of physical education teachers in educational technologies and multimedia. *The Turkish Online Journal of Educational Technology*, 7(2), 20-31. Retrieved April 10, 2009, from http://www.tojet.net/results.asp?volume=7&issue=2&year=2008

Yaman, M. (2007). The competence of physical education teachers in computer use. *The Turkish Online Journal of Educational Technology, 6*(4), 46-55. Retrieved April 10, 2009, from http://www.tojet.net/results.asp?volume=6&issue=4&year=2007

Yaman, M. (2009). Perceptions of students on the applications of distance education in physical education lessons. *The Turkish Online Journal of Educational Technology, 8*(1), 65-72. Retrieved April 10, 2009, from http://www.tojet.net/results.asp?volume=8&issue=1&year=2009

Yamazaki, Y., & Kayes, D. (2004). An experiential approach to cross-cultural learning: A review and integration of competencies for successful expatriate adaptation. *Academy of Management Learning & Education*, *3*, 362–379.

Young, J. R. (2006, June 12). Wikipedia founder discourages academic use of his creation. *Chronicle.com.* Retrieved January 15, 2009, from http://chronicle.com/wiredcampus/article/1328/wikipedia-founder-discourages-academic-use-of-his-creation

Young, M. (1998). *The Curriculum of the Future. From the 'new sociology of education' to a critical theory of learning.* London: Falmer Press.

Young, M. F. (1993). Instructional design for situated learning. *Educational Technology Research and Development*, *41*(1), 43–58. doi:10.1007/BF02297091 *yWorks*. (n.d.). Retrieved from http://www.yworks.com/

Zacharia, Z. C., Olympiou, G., & Papaevripidou, M. (2008). Effects of experimenting with physical and virtual manipulatives on students' conceptual understanding in heat and temperature. *Journal of Research in Science Teaching*, *45*(9), 1021–1035. doi:10.1002/tea.20260

Zachte, E. (2008). Wikimedia page view stats I. *infodisiac.com*. Retrieved January 15, 2009 from http://infodisiac.com/blog/2008/10/wikimedia-page-view-stats-i/

Zaiane, O. R. (2002). Building a recommender agent for e-learning systems, In . *Proceedings of the International Conference on Computers in Education*, *1*, 55–59. doi:10.1109/CIE.2002.1185862

Zheng, R., Perez, J., & Williamson, J, &; Flygare, J. (2008). WebQuests as perceived by teachers: Implications for online teaching and learning. *Journal of Computer Assisted Learning*, *24*(4), 295–304. doi:10.1111/j.1365-2729.2007.00261.x

Zimmer, G. (2003 April). Aufgabenorientierte Didaktik des E-Learning. In *Handbuch E-Learning*. Retrieved May, 2008, from http://www.weiterbildungsportal.ch/mas/ndkele/

Zimmerman, B. J. (2002). Becoming a self-regulated learner: An overview. *Theory into Practice*, *41*, 64–70. doi:10.1207/s15430421tip4102_2

Zyda, M. (2005). From visual simulation to virtual reality to games. *Computer*, *38*(9), 25–32. doi:10.1109/MC.2005.297

About the Contributors

Martin Ebner is currently head of the Department for Social Learning of Computer and Information Services at Graz University of Technology. He is responsible for all e-Learning activities of the University. His research focuses strongly on the use of Web 2.0 for teaching and learning purposes. Martin has delivered a number of lectures and seminars around the topic of e-Learning and the use of computers in educational settings. He studied civil engineering from 1995–2000 and got his M.Sc. from the Institute of Structural Concrete. Afterwards Martin worked as scientific assistant at the Institute of Structural Concrete and wrote his Ph.D. thesis about e-Learning in structural engineering. Since 2005 he holds a Ph.D. in technical sciences from Graz University of Technology. From 2005 to 2006 he worked at the Institute for Building Informatics as Assistant Professor. Since September 2006 Martin is head of the Department for Social Learning at the Computing and Information Services. He wrote not only an amount of international publications and gave a number of presentations about e-Learning, he is also member of various national and international research groups and scientific boards. Martin is one of the biggest EduBlogger in the German speaking area and conducts the e-Learning Blog (http://elearningblog.tugraz.at).

Mandy Schiefner is vice head at the center for university teaching and learning at University of Zurich. She studied educational science, information science and art history at Saarland University in Germany. After assistant activities at the chair of educational science at Saarland University, she worked at University of Applied Sciences Northwestern Switzerland. In different projects she implement e-learning in further education in companies. From 2006 she worked at the E-Learning Center at University of Zurich and supported university lecturers in implementing e-learning technologies. Since 2007 she works at the University teaching and learning center. Mandy publicates primarly in media education and teacher education. She's also a PhD candidate in the Faculty of Media Education, University of Augsburg. Her research interests include teaching and learning in higher education and teacher education, especially with digital media."

* * *

Catherine Adams is an Assistant Professor in the Department of Secondary Education at the University of Alberta, Canada. Dr. Adams' primary research interests concern the pervasive integration of digital technologies in education. Her main approach to inquiry is phenomenology, which she sometimes augments with complementary qualitative research methods such as human environmental aesthetics, media ecology, and Actor-Network-Theory. There are strong historical links between phenomenology, philosophy of technology, and media scholarship, and these convergences of understandings and insights form the basis of her approach to a pedagogy of technology. Dr. Adams' other research interests extend into the following areas: ethical, pedagogical, and curricular issues provoked by information and communication technology (ICT) integration in schools; philosophy of technology, critical media studies, and media ecology; Human-Computer Interaction (HCI) studies; aesthetics of human environments, particularly educational software architectures; and computer science teacher education.

Dietrich Albert is professor of psychology at University of Graz, senior scientist at Graz University of Technology, Knowledge Management Institute and key researcher at the Know-Center Graz. Since 1993 Dietrich is the head of the Cognitive Science Section at the University of Graz, the Department of Psychology's largest working group. In the preceding years he was with the Universities of Göttingen, Marburg, Heidelberg, and Hiroshima. His research topics cover several areas, including learning and memory, psychometrics, anxiety and performance, psychological decision theory, computer based tutorial systems, values and behaviour. Dietrich's actual focus is on knowledge and competence structures, their applications, and empirical research. By working with psychologists, computer scientists, and mathematicians several academic disciplines are represented within his research team. Beside national activities, his expertise in European research and development projects is documented by several successful European projects.

Thomas Bernhardt is research assistant and PhD student at the University of Bremen / Germany in the Faculty of Pedagogy and Educational Sciences. His main focus lies in Web 2.0 especial the effects of social software on education. In this connection he designs implementations of social media for classroom and university teachings (E-Learning 2.0). Furthermore he is interested in the developement of personal learning enviroments (PLE) by learners for their lerning management. He is one of the co-founders and organisators of the German EduCamps.

Adriaan (Adrie) J. M. Beulens graduated in mathematics and informatics at the Technical University Eindhoven (TUE), NL in 1972. Presently he is full professor of Information Systems at Social Sciences Group of Wageningen University (WU) and chair of the Information Technology Group. He is member of a wide range of councils and boards in organizations that rely on ICT and information management. With respect to ICT the following positions are relevant. He is Dutch representative in the IFIP - TC7 council and member of the TC7.6 task group. He is member of the advisory council of the Professional University INHOLLAND, Delft, NL and member of the board of EDICT, a foundation aimed to support education with information and communication technology. He is member of the advisory board of the Maastricht School of Management. He is (co-) author of a large number of papers of which most in peer-reviewed scientific journals.

Martha Burkle is the CISCO Research Chair in e-Learning at SAIT Polytechnic. A pioneer in the research field of the use of technologies for development, her research examines the role of technologies in the knowledge society, and the impact of e-Learning within the Knowledge economy. After completing her PhD on Technology Policies and Higher Education at the University of Sussex, Dr. Burkle moved to Mexico where she was Associate Professor at the Doctoral Program in Humanities at the Monterrey Institute of Technologies University. In 2006 she moved to Calgary and assumed the CISCO Research Chair position at SAIT, where she has been doing research on the impact of information technologies in teaching and learning. Her research interests include the impact of mobile technologies in just in time training, the use of Second Life to facilitate hands on learning, and students' e-readiness in Canada. She is a Board Member for a number of higher education institutions, an author of numerous research papers, case studies and research reports, and has presented her work at a number of conferences around the world.

Lisa Carrington is a PhD candidate in the Faculty of Education, University of Wollongong. Lisa's PhD utilises a comparative case study approach focusing on the experiences of first and final year pre-service teachers enrolled in an undergraduate education degree who engaged with a virtual learning environment provided by an online classroom simulation (ClassSim). Lisa Carrington expects to submit her PhD thesis late 2009. Lisa is currently teaching in the area of ICT education and research methods and is completing a Graduate Certificate in Research Commercialisation at the University of Wollongong.

Weiqin Chen is an Associate Professor in the Department of Information Science and Media Studies, University of Bergen. She received her Ph.D in Computer Science (AI) from the Chinese Academy of Sciences. Before moving to Bergen she worked first as a researcher at Osaka University in Japan, then as researcher and project leader at an Internet start-up company in Tokyo. She has participated in several national and international projects in technology-enhanced learning including DOCTA-NSS (Design and use of Collaborative Telelearning Artefacts –Natural Science Studio) and EU Network of Excellence, Kaleidoscope. She is currently leading UiB's participation in EU 7th framework project SCY (Science Created by You). Her current research focuses on intelligent support for learning, emerging learning objects, and multimedia learning. Her work has been published in major conferences, books and journals dealing with advanced research in learning and intelligent systems for education.

Grainne Conole is Professor of E Learning in the Institute of Educational Technology at the Open University in the UK. Her research interests include the use, integration and evaluation of Information and Communication Technologies and e-learning and the impact of technologies on organisational change. Two of her current areas of interest are how learning design can help in creating more engaging learning activities and on Open Educational Resources research. She has published and presented over 300 conference proceedings, workshops and articles, including over 100 publications on a range of topics, including the use and evaluation of learning technologies. She is co-editor of the the RoutledgeFalmer book ëContemporary perspectives on e-learning research.

Thomas Czerwionka, born 1969, has a university degree in educational science and is specialized in media pedagogy, adult education and evaluation. After his studies he worked in different research projects at the University of Hamburg and at the FernUniversität in Hagen/University of Hagen. The main focus of all projects was on the use of new digital media in higher education, e.g. web-based learning environments and communication tools. In the mentioned projects Thomas Czerwionka particularly contributed to all stages of the accompanying evaluation (conceptualization, realization, data analysis). Since 2008 he has been working at the Hamburg University of Technology in the research project "studIPort 2.0", which has as one focal point the use of electronic portfolios in academic engineering education.

Nils M. Djupvik is a System Architect and Lead Developer at MindLab AS, a Norwegian company that specializes in creating distributed simulation-based training systems which provide training on strategic and operational levels. He received his Master's Degree in Information Science at the University of Bergen in 2006. His Master's project focused on using visualizations in simulations to facilitate the understanding of complex dynamic behaviors.

Sue Fenley is the research facilitator in the Research technologies service in OUCS. Her role involves both running specific research services and in co-ordinating research activity within OUCS and across the university. Her previous work at King's College London involved liaising with different departments across Computer Science and Medicine and then being seconded as Project Director to a large Invest to Save project in Harrow for the NHS with a budget of Â£2.1 million, which was completed on time and within budget. Moving to the University of Reading in 2002 she worked as Director of Research in a Health Research Centre and then moved to the Informatics Research Centre where she was Director of Teaching and Learning and taught on master's courses. She has extensive experience of project direction and management over many research projects.

Brian Ferry is a Professor in the Faculty of Education, University of Wollongong. His research interests focus on pre-service teacher education and the use simulations and games as authentic learning environments. He teaches science and ICT education and currently supervises nine PhD students. Outside of university he is interested in travel and golf.

Sara de Freitas is director of Research at the Serious Games Institute at Coventry University where she leads an applied research team working closely with industry. Sara publishes in the areas of: pedagogy and e-learning; change management and strategy development for implementing e-learning systems and educational games and electronic simulations for supporting post-16 training and learning. Voted the 'Most Influential Woman in Technology 2009' by US Fast Company, Sara chaired the IEEE Serious Games and Virtual Worlds conference in 2009, and is a regular speaker at international conferences. Sara currently holds funding from the Advantage West Midlands, Erasmus Scheme, European Regional Development Fund, European Union, Higher Education Funding Council for England and the UK Technology Strategy Board. Her current lines of research are examining multimodal interfaces, experience design and perceptual modelling in games and virtual worlds.

Rob Johannes Maria Hartog (1948) graduated in experimental (solid state) physics at the University of Amsterdam, NL in 1974. From 1979 till 1986 he taught physics and physics education at a teacher training centre. Since 1986 he is employed by Wageningen University (WU). He has been program manager instruction technology and managed a range of eLearning projects. Currently he is directing the Wageningen Multi Media Research Centre (WMMRC). WMMRC is a small business unit within the Social Science Group of WU that supports university professors in the design, realization, implementation, use and evaluation of interactive digital learning materials and computer-based assessment. He is (co-) author of over 70 papers of which over 30 in peer-reviewed scientific journals.

Jan Herrington is a Professor in Education at Murdoch University in Perth, Western Australia. Her current research focuses on the design of effective web-based learning environments for higher education and the use of authentic contexts and problem-based scenarios as a central focus for web-based course delivery. She also investigates other ICT–related areas such as: computer games in early childhood, authentic learning in museums, design-based research and mobile learning. She has published over

130 refereed journal articles, conference papers and chapters, and several books including a co-edited book (with Anthony Herrington) entitled *Authentic Learning in Higher Education*. She has won many awards for her research including the Association for Educational Communication and Technology (AECT) Young Researcher of the Year Award, and several Outstanding Paper awards at international conferences. More information can be found at: http://murdoch.academia.edu/JanHerrington

Janet Holland completed a Ph.D. in Teaching and Leadership, Instructional Design and Technology, with a minor in Communications from the University of Kansas. Dr. Holland currently serves as an Assistant Professor at Emporia State University, teaching pre-service teachers and master degree students of Instructional Design and Technology. Research interests include improving curriculum pedagogy issues including, service learning, affective learning communities, peer mentoring, and the globalization of instruction. As an instructional designer, new technologies are continually examined in an effort to inspire innovative teaching and learning practices. Dr. Holland's goal is to create authentic, relevant, meaningful, engaging learning experiences.

Andreas Holzinger is head of the Research Unit HCI4MED, Medical University Graz, Associate Professor of Information Processing at Graz University of Technology and chair of the workgroup Human–Computer Interaction and Usability Engineering (HCI&UE) of the Austrian Computer Society. He was Visiting Lecturer at the Nations Health Career Center, Berlin (Germany) 2002/03, Visiting Professor at Innsbruck University, Institute for Organization & Learning 2004/05, Visiting Professor at Vienna University of Technology, Institute for Software Technology & Interactive Systems 2005/06, Visiting Professor at Vienna University of Economics, Health Care Management 2006/07 and Visiting Professor at Middlesex University London, School of Computing Science 2007. His research areas include Technology Enhanced Life Long Learning. He has served as consultant for several European ministries, industry and as national e-Learning expert in the European Commission. He is member of the ACM, IEEE, BCS, German Society of Psychology and board member of the Austrian Computer Society (OCG).

Frank Kappe completed his study of technical mathematics at Graz University of Technology, Austria, in 1988. As part of his PhD dissertation, completed in 1991, he developed the design and a prototype of an Internet-based hypermedia system, "Hyper-G", and then headed its further development until 1996. As a Web pioneer, he developed the first Austrian Web server in 1991, at a time when there were only 12 Web servers in the world, and as an inventor of a content management system, he has published some 60 scientific articles and given numerous talks on hypermedia systems. He commercialized his ideas and cofounded a company, Hyperwave, in 1997. After 10 years as CTO of this company, he is now a professor for innovative media technologies at Graz University of Technology. With his background in academia and industry, he not only looks at technological aspects but also at business models and their impact on society. His current research focus is on virtual worlds and potential applications in academic and commercial environments.

Michael Kerres is Professor of Education (Chair of Educational Media and Knowledge Management, University Duisburg-Essen, Germany) and member of the board of the center for higher education and quality development at University Duisburg-Essen. From 1998 - 2001 he has been Professor for educational psychology, Bochum University, and from 1990-1998 Professor for media didactics and media psychology at Furtwangen University of Applied Sciences. Michael Kerres' present research interests include learning innovations in higher education, instructional design of learning environments, usability research in e-learning.

Lisa Kervin is a lecturer in the Faculty of Education, University of Wollongong. She has taught across the primary grades and has been employed in consultancy roles within New South Wales education systems. She graduated in July 2004 with her PhD and her thesis was focused on the professional development of teachers in literacy. Lisa Kervin's current research interests are related to the literacy development of children, the use of technology to support student learning and teacher professional development.

Michael D. Kickmeier-Rust is a psychologist and software programmer. Since 2001 he is with the Department of Psychology at the University of Graz, Austria. His research and development activities are concentrating primarily on intelligent, adaptive educational systems. In particular, Michael is working on the evolution of psycho-pedagogical frameworks and models of adaptivity on the macro and micro levels. This work includes individualized navigation within learning environments, individualized presentation of educational material, as well as non-invasive assessment and interventions. Since 2006 his very focus is on the psychological aspects of learning with immersive digital computer games and the integration of intelligent educational technology in game-based learning. Since 2008 Michael is coordinating the FP7 ICT project 80Days that is dealing with game-based learning. Related fields of interest are human-computer interaction and specific fields of aviation psychology, dealing with education and training.

Marcel Kirchner is a PhD student at the Technical University of Ilmenau in Thuringia / Germany and research assistant at the department of communication science. He is engaged in the implementation of Social Software in educational context, especially in school and university teachings (E-Learning 2.0). Foremost he is interested in competent presenting in the internet and supporting learning activities by using E-Portfolios to establish contacts, network and finally apply succesfully. He is one of the main organisators of the first EduCamps in Germany.

In January 2006, **Michael Klebl** was appointed assistant professor for Computer Supported Collaborative Learning (CSCL) at the Institute for Educational Science and Media Research of the FernUniversität in Hagen/University of Hagen. Michael Klebl, born 1967, changed from the Catholic University Eichstätt-Ingolstadt to Hagen. In Eichstätt he was working for four years as a research assistant at the Department for Ergonomics and Industrial Pedagogy, where attained his doctorate with his thesis on the multiple use of digital educational media. During his studies and in full-time after his graduation he worked as a designer, project manager and information architect in different areas of further education, vocational training and instructional design. Insights culled from various areas of activity serve as the point of origin for his systematic approach in research and teaching.

Rolf Kretschmann studies Sport Science and Philosophy at the University of Dortmund in Germany. He also majored Certification Studies in Media Pedagogy at the Technical University of Dortmund in Germany, and Health Pedagogy at the University of Freiburg and the University of Applied Sciences in Germany. He currently holds the position of an Assistant Professor for Sport Pedagogy at the Department of Sport and Exercise Science at the Chair for Sport and Health Sciences at the University of Stuttgart in Germany. His research interests are in Sport Pedagogy and Didactics, Sport Philosophy and Ethics, Media Pedagogy and Didactics, and Health Pedagogy.

Maciej Kuszpa studied business and social sciences at the University of Dortmund and the University of Memphis. As a long time Mobile 2.0 Entrepreneur and Scientist he has two areas of expertise; on the one hand in the field of 'Mobile Social Networks', based on his work in the mobile industry since 2000 as founder and CEO of Peperoni Mobile & Internet Software GmbH which develops software solutions around user generated content and social media. On the other hand Maciej is familiar with the field of 'Mobile Learning'. Back in 2000 he started as a research associate at the University of Hagen, Department of Business Administration and Economics and there in 2002 he founded the Mobile Education Center of Excellence which is an international research project on Mobile Learning. In 2008 Maciej also joined the mobile learning research group at the Institute of Educational Science and Media Research, University of Hagen

Fotis Liarokapis is the director of Interactive Worlds Applied Research Group (iWARG) and a research fellow at the Serious Games Institute, Coventry University. He holds a DPhil in Computer Engineering at the University of Sussex, an MSc in Computer Graphics and Virtual Environments at the University of Hull and a BEng in Computer Systems Engineering at the University of Sussex. He is also a visiting lecturer at the Centre for VLSI and Computer Graphics, University of Sussex and a visiting research fellow at the giCentre, City University. Fotis is a member of IEEE, IET, ACM and BCS, has contributed to more than 45 refereed publications and has more than 115 citations. Finally, he is on the editorial advisory board of The Open Virtual Reality Journal published by Bentham, he has co-organised the VS-GAMES 2009 conference and the STARS session of the VAST 2009 conference.

Elke Mattheiss is a psychologist working at the Department of Psychology at the University of Graz since 2008. Her research work focused hitherto mainly on the integration of motivational aspects and concepts in educational games. Currently she is concerned with approaches of adaptivity - on a macro and micro level - in the field of game-based learning, aiming for the non-invasive and individualized presentation of motivational interventions. Her research experience also implies the scientific evaluation of usability issues and learning effectiveness within the FP7 ICT project 80Days. Related fields of interests are cognitive psychology of learning and memory, and human-computer interaction, especially interaction design

Patrick McAndrew is Senior Lecturer in The Open University's Institute of Educational Technology. He has led a range of research projects addressing how materials and environments can support learning through the use of learning design and the provision of tools for learners. Patrick has a degree in Mathematics from the University of Oxford and a PhD in Computer Science from Heriot-Watt University in Edinburgh. He is currently leading OLnet, a collaborative initiative to research the use open content for free education. OLnet is supported by The William and Flora Hewlett Foundation.

Sandro Mengel studied media education and human resource development at the University of Dortmund. He is an expert in media didactics and practical application of e-learning scenarios and tools in educational institutions. Since 2005 he is a scientific staff member at the Institute of Educational Science and Media Research at the University of Hagen. His activities contain didactical conceptions, consulting and research for innovative e-learning and mobile learning applications as well as the management of such projects. Further activities are the e-moderation of online based trainings and live online collaboration courses in virtual classrooms. Since 2008 he is member of the mobile learning research group at the Institute of Educational Science and Media Research, University of Hagen. His field of activities in this group includes the consulting and the development of didactical conceptions for mobile learning scenarios in the context of learning on the job and their evaluation.

Michele Notari acquired a master degree in Biology and Informatics at the University of Bern (Switzerland) and a master in Educational Technologies at the University of Geneva (TECFA). After his regular study he achieved a diploma of High School Teaching. He has been teaching for over 10 years Biology and lead adult education courses. At the present he is lecturer at the School of Teacher Education, University of Applied Sciences in Bern. He has been working and researching on didactical methods for computer supported collaborative hypertext creation and visualisation concepts for learning scenarios. His actual research focus is on computer supported written communication in collaborative project based learning settings.

Nadine Ojstersek is Research Assistant (Chair of Educational Media and Knowledge Management, University Duisburg-Essen, Germany). From 2000 - 2001 she has been Scientific Assistant at the chair of Paedagogical Pychology II, Prof. Dr. M. Kerres, Institute of Education at the Ruhr-University Bochum. Her research interests are: instructional design of learning environments, virtual worlds, learner support in distance and e-learning.

Stephen Quinton works as a senior researcher with the Digital Ecosystems and Business Intelligence Institute (DEBII) at Curtin University (Perth, Western Australia). His main interest is in Advanced Learning Systems that advantage the growing sophistication of computer and information technologies. His research vision is to establish learning environments that assist students to identify concepts and form cognitive associations to synthesise information and create knowledge. At present, Dr Quinton is exploring a range of learning environment design and pedagogical strategies that increase learner motivation to produce more than just rote answers and assist to organise, analyse and reflect on information and ideas. The goal is to devise learning solutions that cultivate abstract thinking and enhance conceptual understanding supported by 'intelligent' feedback systems and interactive human interface (HCI) systems that accommodate the varying cognitive schemas individuals draw on in their search for understanding.

Thomas C. Reeves is a Professor of Learning, Design, and Technology in the Department of Educational Psychology and Instructional Technology in the College of Education at The University of Georgia. After completing his Ph.D. at Syracuse University in 1979, he spent a year as a Fulbright lecturer in Peru, and he has worked in 30 other countries. His research interests include evaluation of educational technology, socially responsible educational research, mental models and cognitive tools, authentic learning tasks, and educational technology applications in developing countries. In 2003, he was the first person to receive the AACE Fellowship Award from the Association for the Advancement of Computing in Education. He has published a book titled Interactive Learning Systems Evaluation book (with John Hedberg) as well as nearly 200 other publications. More information can be found at: http://it.coe.uga.edu/~treeves/

Sandra Reitz works as a Research Associate ("Wissenschaftliche Mitarbeiterin") at the Goethe-University of Frankfurt. Her main research and teaching areas are educational politics and human rights education. Since 1993, she has been a volunteer at Amnesty International (AI), focusing on Human Rights Education. In 1998, she became the speaker of the German Human Rights Education Coordinating Group of AI, and in 2005, she was elected European Representative in the Global Coordinating Committee for Human Rights Education, AI. Having finished her studies at the University of Münster in 2000, Sandra Reitz worked for eight years as an IT Project Manager and IT Training Program Manager, while at the same time planning and writing her dissertation "Can Social Competencies be improved via E-Learning? The Example of Human Rights Education" at the Otto-von-Guericke University, Magdeburg. Her mentor is K.-Peter Fritzsche, UNESCO Chair for Human Rights Education.

Christian Safran is a scientific assistant and doctoral candidate at the Institute for Information Systems and Computer Media at the Graz University of Technology. He received his diploma in Telematics in 2006 and is working on a PhD thesis on collaborative tools for online learning communities. He is lecturer for "Introduction to Structured Programming" and "Software Development Practical Exercises". His research interests include social software, online communities of practise, and the influence of social media on learning. His current research focus is on the development of mobile social applications for technology enhanced learning.

Hylke van der Schaaf (1976) graduated in Bioprocess Technology at Wageningen University (WU), NL in 1999. From 1999 till 2007 he worked within the bioprocess engineering group of Wageningen University on design and development of digital learning materials and learning environments for bioprocess engineering. In addition, he acted as a consultant and software engineer in learning technology for several other research groups in life sciences. In 2007 he completed his PhD research on design and development of digital learning material for Bioprocess Technology. Since 2008 he works within Wageningen Multi Media Research Centre (WMMRC) designing and developing digital learning materials for various knowledge domains, ranging from molecular biology and fluorescence microscopy to logistics and process design.

Sandra Schaffert coordinates the application area "Education and Media" at Salzburg Research in Austria. Born 1976, she studied educational science, psychology and computer science at the University in Munich (master and PhD degree). The research group "Education and Media" deals with Web-based educational innovations. Sandra's research interest lies in open educational practices and resources, the concept and realization of personal learning environment and other new technological and didactical solutions to support individual learners, communities and teachers. As a researcher and project manager Sandra Schaffert is involved in national and international research projects and publications. Regularly, she posts about her work on her Weblog sandra.schaffert.ws.

Claudia Schrader, born 1980, is a PhD on educational games at the Department of Instructional Technology & Media of the FernUniversität in Hagen/University of Hagen. She studied communication science and psychology at the Friedrich Schiller University of Jena. In her doctorate she investigates in research on computer-based educational games, their immersive character and how this influences learners' presence and learning.

Frank Schulenburg is the Wikimedia Foundation's Head of Public Outreach. He first contributed to Wikipedia in 2005, and quickly grew involved with the other Wikimedia projects as well. In 2006, he founded Wikipedia Academy, an event aimed at increasing quality in the encyclopedia by encouraging contributions from targeted groups, primarily in academia. In 2006, he organized an exhibition documenting Wikipedia‚Äôs first five years, and created the media literacy project, ÄúWikipedia in the classroom, Äù. He created the Zedler medal for distinguished encyclopedic contributions, awarded since 2007 by Wikimedia Deutschland and the Mainz Academy of Sciences and Literature. He had been a board member of Wikimedia Deutschland from 2006 to 2008, and had served, from 2007 to 2008, as its vice chair.

Rolf Schulmeister has founded the Interdisciplinary Center for Higher Education at the University of Hamburg in 1970. He was appointed as professor for Higher Education, Learning Methods and Technology in 1976. His main interest in higher education since 25 years are multimedia learning systems and eLearning. In 1987 he co-founded the Institute for German Sign Language and Communication of the Deaf within the department of Linguistics. After years of research into the psychology of cognitive learning, the author has developed learning programs for learning statistics and sign language. Some recent books are: *Grundlagen hypermedialer Lernsysteme (Hypermedia Learning Systems).* Addison Wesley: Bonn, Paris u.a. 1996; 4th ed. Oldenbourg: München 2007. *Virtuelle Universitäten – Virtuelles Lernen (Virtual Universities – Virtual Learning).* Oldenbourg: München 2001, 2n ed. 2003. *Lernplattformen für das virtuelle Lernen (Learning Management Systems for Virtual Learning).* Oldenbourg: München 2003. *eLearning: Einsichten und Aussichten (eLearning: Insights and Prospects).* Oldenbourg: München 2006. His homepage is: http://www.zhw.uni-hamburg.de/zhw/?page_id=148

Christina Schwalbe, born 1978, works as a research assistant at the MultiMedia-Studio at the University of Hamburg, Faculty of Education, Psychology and Human Movement. She studied Media Technology at the University of Applied Sciences in Hamburg (Dipl. Ing, FH) and Educational Science and ePedagogy Design at the University of Hamburg and the University of Art and Design in Helsinki (M.A.). Her focus of research is the connection of media history and cultural history with focus on the development of educational concepts and institutions of education. Further interests of research are knowledge formation, education in digitally-networked structures and mediology. Further information about her work and interest can be found at http://mms.uni-hamburg.de/schwalbe

Christina M. Steiner completed her Diploma (MS) in Psychology at the University of Graz. She is currently a researcher at the Cognitive Science Section, Department of Psychology of the University of Graz. Her work within several European R&D projects on e-learning focuses on the representation, modelling, and assessment of knowledge and competence. She is doing research on psycho-pedagogically founded design and adaptation of digital educational games. Furthermore, her work includes the evaluation of the effectiveness of learning technologies based on sound psychological methods and techniques. Further interests lie in the use of concept maps as a means to build prerequisite structures among learning objects and competences, on the validation of concept maps, and their application as a learning and teaching strategy.

Johannes Tramper has academic degrees from the Technical University Delft, NL (Ir. Chemical Engineering 1973), Purdue University, USA (M.Sc. Biochemical Engineering 1974), Wageningen University (WU), NL (Ph.D. Agricultural Sciences 1979) and an honorary degree from the Technical University of Lodz, PL (Doctor Honoris Causa 2000). Since 1987 he is full professor Bioprocess Technology at WU, the last years with special focus on education development. He is one of the founders of the WU study Bio(process)technology in 1990. From 1996 to 1999 he was director of the WU educational institute Technology & Food and initiated then the development of digital learning modules. He is (co-)author of ample 500 papers with over 300 in peer-reviewed scientific journals. Since March 2007 he is on the ISI list of highly cited authors in the category Microbiology. Presently he is coordinator of the educational program within the Dutch research program on industrial biotechnology.

Klaus Wannemacher studied at the universities of Göttingen, San Diego and Heidelberg. He received his doctorate at the University of Heidelberg. Since 2002 he is an IT management and e-learning consultant for the higher education sector at the Hochschul-Informations-System (HIS) in Germany. Working for HIS' university management division, he has focused on various topics such as the development of academic e-learning strategies, new teaching forms based on social software as well as the implications of IT-supported university management processes. Wannemacher has done research on the academic programme development and evaluations concerning the e-learning implementation at universities. He is a panel moderator for university IT at the German portal wissenschaftsmanagement-online.de. He has published monographs and articles on e-learning strategies, the introduction of Web 2.0 applications into teaching, the benefits of IT service management for universities or on new examination management procedures.

Silke Weiß was born on 10. December 1970. She is married since 1993 and has two daughters (12 and 15 years old). She studied at the University of Heidelberg and is now a secondary school teacher with the subjects Chemistry, Biology, Spanish and German. She worked for 6 years in a secondary school (Gymnasium) in Bensheim, where she taught mainly chemistry lessons. Since 2006 she is working in the institute of chemistry didactics, researching and making a dissertation about teachers' in-service trainings as blended-learning courses to improve media literacy. In her work, she develops offers for students, for teacher trainees (or student teachers) and teachers in school to improve media literacy in all phases of the teachers' education which is the aim of the "Projekt Lehr@mt", a cooperative project between the University of Frankfurt and the "Amt für Lehrerausbildung" (department of teachers education) in Frankfurt where she participates.

Claudia de Witt is Professor of Educational Science and Media Education at the University of Hagen, Institute of Educational Science and Media Research. She is chair of the Mobile Learning group in this department. Her scientific activities are in eLearning and Mobile Learning, she is also expert in theories of media education and media didactics. She researchs internet based knowledge communication and online communities of inquiry, didactical design of internet based scenarios of communication and collaboration with synchronous and asynchronous tools, their implementation and evaluation in different contexts. She published several chapters about new media (eLearning) and pragmatism and is co-editor of the online journal MedienPaedagogik.org.

Index

D

E

J

K

L

M

R

S

T

U

V

W

Y

Z